GW00771924

The Great Book of

FRENCH

CUISINE

REVISED EDITION

HENRI-PAUL PELLAPRAT

Originally edited by Avanelle Day and David White

with a new Introduction and revision by

JEREMIAH TOWER

VENDOME

Revised edition published in the United States of America in 2003 by
The Vendome Press
1334 York Avenue
New York, NY 10021

Originally published under the title *L'Art culinaire moderne.*

Copyright © 1966 René Kramer, Publisher Castagnola/Lugano, Switerzerland
Copyright © 1994 R.C.S. Libri and Grandi Opere S.p.A. Milano
English translation copyright © 1982 The Vendome Press
Introduction copyright © 2003 Jeremiah Tower

All rights reserved. No part of the contents of this book may be reproduced
without written permission of the publisher.

ISBN: 0-86565-231-7

Library of Congress Cataloging-in-Publication Data

Pellaprat, Henri-Paul.
    [Art culinaire moderne. English]
    The great book of French cuisine / Henri-Paul Pellaprat ;
        edited and introduced by Jeremiah Tower. — Rev. ed.
        p. cm.
    ISBN 0-86565-231-7
    1. Cookery, French. I. Tower, Jeremiah. II. Title.

TX719.P3813 2003
641.5944—dc21   2003053752

Designed by Susi Oberhelman

PRINTED IN THE UNITED STATES

CONTENTS

INTRODUCTION

ONE COULD BE TEMPTED TO SUBTITLE THIS BOOK "A Paradise of Gastronomy," and I would, but Maurice-Edmund Saillant, the "Prince-Elect of Gastronomes," who wrote with the *nom de plume* of Curnonsky, already did so in his preface to the 1950 English edition of Pellaprat's great book, then titled *Modern Culinary Art*. Pellaprat, died a year before Curnonsky, himself almost an octogenarian at the time, wrote the introduction.

Henri-Paul Pellaprat was born in 1869 and, following the culinary profession tradition of the times, apprenticed as a pastry cook and then as a confectioner at the age of thirteen. His first job was at the famous Belle Epoque restaurant and institution, the Café de la Paix, where he trained classically with Père Lépey before going on to more training at La Maison Dorée with the great chef Casimir Moisson. After military service at Verdun, he entered the Cordon Bleu cooking school as a professor. War intervened as Pellaprat was called up in 1914 only to be discharged in 1915 because, at 46, he had 7 children to support. The school was closed temporarily by the war, with Pellaprat working at Lucas Carton and the Terminus Demain, but when the Cordon Bleu reopened, Pellaprat rejoined it, staying there as head chef until 1932, when he retired from active participation in his profession. But he could not sit still. His first book, *La Cuisine au Vin,* appeared in 1934, and was followed by a book on sandwiches, another on puff pastry, and finally, in 1935, his masterpiece *L'Art culinaire moderne* with its 3,500 recipes and 700 pages, which Curnonsky, in his preface to the book, calls a "real Encyclopedia of the Table and Culinary Art."

This great book, Curnonsky tells us, summarizes not only the four types of French cookery, but, in the belief that the book should be of universal interest, includes many recipes for his choice of the best foreign dishes. These four types of French cookery are:

La haute cuisine. The most elaborate and sophisticated cooking, one of the greatest achievements of France.

La cuisine bourgeoise. Middle-class cooking, the triumph of both Cordon Bleu holders and housewives. Pellaprat was a fervent feminist who had rendered homage to the finesse, the grace, and the simplicity that the precious rivalry of these women has brought to French cooking.

La cuisine regionale. The provincial cooking of France, unique in the world because of the diversity, richness, and originality of its countless local dishes and specialties.

La cuisine impromptue: Impromptu cooking which, using whatever is at hand, is the simplest and the quickest type of cooking.

Curnonsky lavishly calls *Modern Culinary Art* the work of a great cook, an impeccable master of technique, and a perfect artist in love with his work. Pellaprat proudly announces that the book is about menus, wine service, floral decoration, beverages, and table duties as well as cooking, because he wants to be the same kind of teacher (after fifty-three years in kitchens) to households as he was to thousands of students. Like the great Fernand Point (of La Pyramide, the most famous and influential restaurant in France at the time), Pellaprat believed that it was the duty of a good *cuisinier* to transmit to the generations who would replace him everything he had learned and experienced.

In that spirit, this new edition is revised from the first American edition, entitled *The Great Book of French Cuisine,* taken from René Kramer's 1966 and 1971 translation called *Modern French Culinary Art.* The introduction to those editions is by the late and great Michael Field, who had a legendary cooking school in New York, and was consulting editor for the Time-Life series *Foods of the World* (one volume was *The Cooking of Provincial France* by M.F.K. Fisher with Julia Child serving as a consultant). Field was obviously very impressed with Pellaprat's book—which had been translated into five languages and had sold 750,000 copies throughout the world—and felt that the appearance of the American edition was in the nick of time. America needed Pellaprat: in the grips of the religion of convenience and synthetic foods, the country was in danger of forgetting what the aroma, taste, and even appearance of good, honest food can be. But Pellaprat would give us heart. The new American edition, translated in practical American terms, reaffirmed "lucidly, persuasively, and precisely" the dignity of our relation to the food we eat.

But it was not just for the food that Michael Field thought Pellaprat had arrived in the United States at just the right moment. It is no mistake on Henri-Paul's part that "The Art of Entertaining and Serving" sets the mood and tone of his culture before we get to cook its food. In this revised edition I have left this section on manners, since its message seems even more relevant or necessary (some of it now tongue in a very well-bred cheek) today, as then. As Margaret Visser reminds us in her superb recent book *The Rituals of Dinner,* "words to do with etiquette tend to derive from French." She and Pellaprat both make the point that an enlightened, polite or polished person knows that polite behavior is a ritual performed for the sake of other people. If you are aiming at having a successful lunch or dinner party at home, pleasantly astonishing your guests as they first enter the door and having them leave with a radiant warmth is what entertaining is all about. And even the most individualistic host must know that there are time-tried rules that work. The wit of Pellaprat's contemporary, Cole Porter, tells us all:

Don't hit the person across from you with bits of toast,

And don't, when dinner is nearly through, say "Who's the host?"

It isn't done.

The best sense of etiquette comes from experience of successful hospitality. James Beard's first cookbook (1940), *Hors d'Oeuvre and Canapés,* grew out of entertaining and his catering business. In a 2003 article on Jim and his book by another hospitality maven, Nina Griscom, she worries that giving a party today using Beard's guidelines would cause her guests to think she was giving "an anthropological theme party!" She wonders about the tongue, stuffed eggs, and melon balls ("anything in ball shapes is deader than raspberry vinaigrette"), just as I did when reading the recipes for them in Pellaprat. But then I reminded myself that in one of the first French cookbooks, *Le Cuisiner francais* by La Varenne, there is berry vinaigrette; that stuffed eggs are back in style and never really left; and that melon balls did give me a start, but when Pellaprat steeps them in Madeira, I could forget the currently time-worn shapes and love the flavors. Griscom does finally admit that the fundamentals of giving a great party have not changed in the last sixty-five years. The point is that Pellaprat's recipes and their style should not be lost to time.

So that is why the word *moderne* in the original title of Pellaprat's cookbook is most important: for despite the heavy (and for me delightful) dose of classicism, the book has not aged and is as convenient to use now as it was in the 1930s. As Michael Field points out, French cooking for Pellaprat was a dynamic process, and his procedures and recipes kept constant pace with its movement, without committing the egregious error of letting the recipes lose their specific profiles and the individuality of the cuisine. Therefore the recipes "have surprising quality of contemporaneity and are never needlessly complex or contrived, whether they depart from tradition or not." The foreign dishes (Italian, Spanish, Indian, and American) that Pellaprat tasted in his travels are reproduced with culinary intelligence and fidelity. So don't be surprised to see included amongst the French dishes, non-French ones like Chicken Sukiyaki, Cockaleekie Soup, and Schtchi Russki.

The preface to the Kramer English edition points out that the scope of the book is such that every aspect of cooking is dealt with, even (and especially) the most simple, and it is here that the work may prove of the greatest value to the cook with enthusiasm. In the truest French tradition, the simple, everyday dish is no less a triumph than the more elaborate "works of art" with which the book also deals. And just as most of the cooking in this book is built on the foundations of its stocks, sauces, and basic preparations (and therefore conveniently appear first in the book), so many of the recipes refer to each other. When a recipe or its presentation requires a preparation for which the recipe is given elsewhere, the title of the recipe referred to is capitalized (Béchamel Sauce, Basic Crêpe Batter, or Plain White Stock, for example) in the recipe list of ingredients and can be found in the index by its specific name as well as under its category (Sauce, etc.). Most or all of the ingredients called for are available to the household cook, and when they are not, alternatives are suggested. It is important also to feel free to improvise with the final garnishes of herb sprigs, olives, cut tomato shapes, and truffles.

The menus presented in the section devoted to entertaining and serving have been retained in this revised edition for their teaching ability and historical interest.

The other menu section in the original book, simply called "Menus," I have dropped, even though many might enjoy reading them. They are not, simply, as eloquent to us now as they were for Pellaprat's time. I would not mind (if only for a one-stop lesson in grand French cooking) enjoying a grand buffet of:

HORS D'OEUVRE BARQUETTES

CANAPES

EGGS CARMEN

FILETS OF SOLE FLORALIES

SALMON MOSCOW STYLE

COLD STEAMED WHOLE SALMON

GLAZED TROUT VLADIMIR

ROCK LOBSTER BOUQUETIERE

GLAZED FILLET OF BEEF

COLD SADDLE OF VEAL

STUFFED DUCK CHARLES VAUCHER

SCALLOPS OF FOIE GRAS LUCULLUS

SALAD BELLE HELENE

CHARLOTTE ROYALE

MACEDOINE OF FRUIT IN CHAMPAGNE

NEOPOLITAN CASSATA

MEXICAN CAKE

DOBOS TORTA

GLACEED FRUITS

SPUN-SUGAR BASKET WITH FROSTED PETITS-FOURS

But I would not be enthusiastic about being served most of the "Menus" in the deleted section, such as the following example:

TURKISH CHEESE ROLLS

CHICKEN PILAF ORIENTAL STYLE

APPLE CHARLOTTE

Though I would like each of the dishes separately.

I would, however, browse the menu section and put together one of my own, following the rules set down in "The Art of Entertaining," keeping in mind its firm instruction to improvise. One possibility might be:

BOTVINIA

DEVILED SPRING CHICKEN

SOUFFLE POTATOES

SALADE MIMOSA

SNOW EGGS

Would any lover of French cooking *not* want to join me?

Then, after dinner, I would remember the final words in the preface of Pellaprat himself: "Let the ministering angels of the home be assured that we have done all possible to be of service to them and to give a wider knowledge of the art which is so dear to our heart —the best 'French Cookery.'"

AMEN.

THE ART OF ENTERTAINING AND SERVING

THE ART OF ENTERTAINING AND OF SERVING is a little like the art of creating a theatrical production, in which the text, the actors, the decor, and the music are the major elements that must be coordinated by the producer. He brings out their various qualities and above all sees that they are in harmony with one another. The host or hostess must play a similar part. The quality of the dishes, the harmonious sequence of the menu, and the choice of wines require as much care, as much subtlety, as the table decorations and the attention that surrounds each guest. Entertaining means giving. And the way in which we give, in our own sphere, is as important as what we give.

Entertaining means honoring one's guests; the same consideration must be shown to friends as to celebrities, to affection as to power. For family and friends, customs are modified, made more flexible and personal. But everyone who entertains should nevertheless be familiar with the fundamental rules that govern the preparation of a dinner, a luncheon, or a traditional tea. In spite of the exigencies of modern life, the universal tendency toward simplification, and the very difficult problem of service, there are still occasions on which the basic requirements—which are unchanged—must be observed, or at least approached as closely as possible. And even on the most intimate and informal occasions, it does no harm—quite the contrary—to observe the rules that have proved their value. Moreover, if a party, whatever its nature, is carefully planned and arranged beforehand, the hosts will be able to relax and to devote themselves more completely to their guests.

THE DECOR

IN A PREVIOUS EDITION OF *L'Art culinaire moderne*, Stephane Faniel pertinently analyzed the reasons why the decor is important, a fact that is frequently not recognized. "For many it is an aesthetic and social manifestation, often full of consequences, and one on which the guests will certainly form a judgment."

The atmosphere of a meal consists of a thousand imponderable elements, all aimed at the essential purpose of putting everyone at ease. Here a host's great gift comes into play—to put him or herself in the position of others, to think in advance of what they would enjoy, to remember their dislikes—in fact, to take charge, for however short a time, of their pleasure. Some will feel happier in rather formal surroundings, at a very sophisticated table, equipped with all that is best in china, linen, crystal, and silver. Others will attach more importance to the dazzling freshness of flowers, the smiling grace and informality of a more imaginative table. But all guests will appreciate the personal note, the attentions that discreetly remind them that everything has been done for *their* pleasure, *their* comfort, and *their* relaxation.

Unfortunately one cannot always know the precise tastes of all of one's guests, but at least one knows their age, their occupation or profession, their native region or nationality. Anything that will, in one form or another, evoke, recall, or underline the personality of the guests of honor is welcome.

In the best productions the audience does not see the wheels go around, just as true elegance consists in not drawing attention to oneself. Nevertheless, the fact that the wheels are invisible does not mean that they are missing; this is only a warning against an excessive show of the means being used or the belongings that one has.

The extreme case is a grand ceremonial dinner where the loveliest silver, the most dazzling crystal, the most delicate china, and the finest linen are laid out; but in order to use all these, one must also have the necessary staff. This staff may quite well be engaged only for one evening. Equally, if one has a staff, the objects used must be up to the level of the service. If necessary, equipment can be hired from specialized firms. The constant aim, here as elsewhere, must be to achieve harmony—harmony between the hosts and the arrangement of the meal and of the table, between the staff and the equipment, between the general decoration of the room and that of the table. One does not engage two menservants in tailcoats and white gloves to place plates of peasant pottery, however charming, on placemats, any more than a hostess alone, or with the assistance of a single servant, can pull out all the stops of ceremonial service.

There must be harmony, too, between the size of the room and the number of guests, whether it is a large room and a numerous party or a small room and a family gathering. A formal dinner or a party can succeed only if the guests have enough space, for themselves, between one another, and for those around them. The most trying kind of embarrassment is to feel that one is embarrassing others. The staff must be able to move freely. The table must be big enough for the glasses, plates, covers, and various accessories not to be cramped. It is better to have two fewer guests than to "squash" either objects or people. Attention must also be paid to ventilation and temperature. Many delightful occasions are spoiled by a room so hot that people are made uncomfortable!

Tradition has it that the style of the silver should determine that of the plates and glasses and that all should, as far as possible, be of the same style and period. Obviously, one avoids all risks by setting a table in a single style, especially a good one. But the development of modern taste (or dare we say of taste as such?) makes it permissible to deviate from this golden rule. There need be nothing discordant in using beautiful old plates with contemporary cutlery, the quality of which may be superb. We must be quite clear about this: Principles have an undeniable value, and rules are useful; the matter is one of codifying the language of good breeding. But, quite apart from the fact that languages evolve, rules and a thorough knowledge of them must never be allowed to paralyze initiative. Such initiative should be taken only if one is sure of oneself, but then one should not hesitate.

The important factors are taste, discernment, and an infinite amount of tact. The producer knows quite well that a harmony, more difficult but by no means less subtle, may be achieved by contrast as well as by the use of similar elements.

A discreet progression should be observed in the utilization of the various elements—silver, china, glass. It would be unfortunate if for lack of knowledge of how to graduate the choice of plates or glasses the meal were to finish less elegantly than it began. Even if there is no progression, there should be no regression. The same principles apply here as to the progression of wines.

In the past, centerpieces were large, ornate pieces of plate, complicated in design and often allegorical in theme. These may still be used for very traditional receptions, but nowadays flowers, possibly reflected in a discreet mirror base, are preferred; they are an inexhaustible source of decoration, from the simplest to the most sumptuous. The decorative theme may, according to individual taste, spread some way beyond the center of the table, but the flowers must not engulf the place settings; a table turned into a greenhouse or a florist's display window is distinctly out of place. Nor should the flowers be too strongly scented, otherwise they may overpower or form dubious alliances with the subtle odors of well-cooked food and well-made wines

The lighting gives the finishing touch to the table, to the whole of the decor. Wherever possible, the gentle, warm, and living light of candles should be used in the evening. Candelabra and chandeliers give a table a sparkle, a shimmer, for which there is no substitute. But their use does not exclude a source of indirect or filtered electric light.

Obviously the decor will vary with the time of day and with the nature of the meal or party. In the following paragraphs we analyze possible preparations for various meals, from breakfast to a formal dinner. Naturally the suggestions we make can always be changed to suit the house, the equipment, and the staff available. From the first ray of morning sunshine to the last glimmer of the last candle, it is the warmth of the welcome that counts.

BREAKFAST

The tea or coffee service may be placed in front of the hostess, who pours the tea or coffee and passes the cups around, with cream and sugar following on a small tray for the guests to serve themselves. Butter, marmalade or jam, and honey are served in separate dishes, each with its own serving piece, placed on the table within easy reach of the guests. There should also be salt and pepper cellars for dishes that require additional seasoning. Toast may be placed on a toast rack or, better, toasted in an electric toaster that is on a tea cart or side table. If rolls are served, arrange them attractively in a dish or basket and place it on the table.

Naturally the service can be less formal, without being any the less attentive. Especially in the country, it is permissible to be fanciful, as long as attentiveness prevails. Guests from other countries will be very grateful if they are allowed to follow their national customs in the matter of breakfast.

LUNCH

The lunch table may be laid with either a tablecloth or placemats. An informal elegance is entirely suitable. Lacking more original ideas, one may use a bowl of fruit or flowers as a centerpiece; either makes a pleasant and gracious decoration.

The place settings are the same as for dinner but simplified in accordance with the menu and the wines served. Two glasses per guest are enough. The luncheon knife is always placed to the right of the plate, with the cutting edge turned toward it. Next to it place the oyster or melon fork, if required. The luncheon fork goes at the left of the plate. The dessert fork and cheese knife may be placed behind the plate at the foot of the glasses or brought in on dessert plates, as the fruit knife is.

TEA

The hostess herself serves the guests, passing to them the filled cups, the sugar bowl, cream pitcher, and plates of toast or sandwiches and cakes.

There are two customary ways of serving. One is to use a large table around which the guests are invited to sit. At each place there is a tea plate, a fork (if one is needed), and a tea-size napkin. The tea service stands on a tray, and cups and saucers are placed in stacks of two near the hostess's place. She, while seated, pours the beverage and passes it to the guests. Cream, lemon, and sugar are passed on a tray for the guests to serve themselves. Toast, sandwiches, and cakes are passed around the table on separate plates.

The alternate method is to place the tea service on a small table, along with the cups, saucers, and small plates. The hostess will hand each guest his cup and plate. This method is less formal and is preferable if the guests come and go at various times. It also gives the hostess more opportunity to mingle with her guests.

The cups should be emptied into a waste basin, a part of the tea service, before they are refilled.

BRIDGE TEAS

At a bridge tea, the serving is done from a tea cart. The space on the trays is limited, and all the hostess's ingenuity is needed to find room for the necessary objects—cups, saucers, glasses, cake plates, and so on. The assistance of a waiter who will carry the teapot and sugar bowl, pour out, and remove cups to be refilled, will simplify the serving problem. If possible, use small side tables, to avoid putting food and drink on the card tables.

Canapés, sandwiches, pastries, and petits fours may be served, and, in addition to tea, the drinks may include fruit juice, port, whisky, and so on. Passionate bridge players may remain indifferent to these delights, but most guests will do them justice.

Bridge is no longer the only game that can be made the occasion for such a tea; any game that is fashionable will do.

COCKTAILS

In today's homes, a corner of a room, or a piece of furniture, is often reserved for the purpose of a "house bar" and for the preparation of cocktails. Either its purpose is announced by suitable decorations or the equipment is concealed. A popular custom is to adapt for this purpose a marquetry cabinet with doors which, when opened, reveal the contents, perhaps multiplied by a mirror lining. Many pieces of furniture, from bureaus to all kinds of cabinets, lend themselves to transformation into a drawing room bar.

Cocktails are easily prepared in a beaker or shaker

Be sure to have fresh fruit juice and water on hand, and remember that canapés are always appreciated with cocktails. These should be small and require no plates or cutlery.

DINNER

Even if the number of guests is small, dinner always involves some formality. Our suggestions on table decorations and service may be helpful here. The general considerations involved in giving a well-regulated dinner have already been discussed. Here we present the details of the table setting.

The glasses are placed in a row at a forty-five degree angle to the left from the top right hand of the plate, starting with the champagne glass, then dry white wine(s), red wine(s), dessert wine(s) and finally the water glass. Some people prefer the water glass first in the line up of glasses.

The napkins are folded simply, without any attempt at elaboration, and put on the plates, unless the soup is brought in before the guests come to the table; in that case, the napkins, like the bread, are put to the left of the plate. When there are many guests, place cards may be put behind the plate, next to the glasses. For a large dinner, it is customary for the hostess to provide handwritten menus, which are also put behind the plate or on top of the napkin.

The dessert plates and appropriate cutlery, together with the finger bowls, may be laid out on a side table in advance. The coffee service and cups, as well as the liqueurs, will be carried into the drawing room when the guests leave the table.

The place setting for a dinner is as follows:

- A flat plate on which the napkin is laid. (The soup plate is handed, ready filled, when the guests are seated, unless it has been set in place beforehand.)
- Table knife, cutting edge turned toward the plate.
- Fish knife.
- Soup spoon. In France, the convex side is laid uppermost. In Great Britain and the United States, the hollow side is turned up. The same applies to forks.
- Oyster fork or melon fork, if required.
- Table fork. This is changed with each course, together with the plate.
- Fish fork.
- Dessert knife and fork or spoon. In Great Britain, these are sometimes placed behind the plate. In France, they are more frequently brought in on the dessert plate. In the United States, they may be brought in on the dessert plate at the time the dessert is served, or fork or spoon may be placed on the table at the time the cover is laid, with the fork on the left of the plate and the spoon on the right.

If finger bowls are to be used, fill them one-third full with warm water and place each, with a small doily under it, on a dessert plate, which is placed before the guest.

Then the guests will move the finger bowls and doilies to a position just behind the dessert plate and a little to the left. If fruit is to be served after the dessert course, do not put finger bowls on the dessert plates. Instead, arrange dessert silver at each place, unless it has been previously laid, and then serve the dessert. When the dessert is finished, replace each dessert plate with a fruit plate that has on it a finger bowl and doily in the center, the fruit knife to the left of the bowl, and the spoon to the right. The guest places the finger bowl and doily on the table at the top of the plate, and the silver on the table, the fork on the left of the bowl and the spoon on the right. The fruit bowl is passed.

HOLIDAY PARTIES

Dinners or suppers on Christmas Eve or New Year's Eve, whether celebrated intimately in a small group or by a large number of friends, must have a domestic solemnity. Christmas Eve is traditionally more of a family affair, quieter; in France, the party usually follows the celebration of midnight Mass. New Year's Eve, a purely secular occasion, is more animated, not to say exuberant. Decorations on these occasions are a matter of personal taste, a time for new and gay ideas. There is always room for a Christmas tree, small or large. Candles are more than ever indicated.

For these occasions, nothing is too beautiful. Once a year, one can indulge in an accumulation of crystal, silver, china, an abundance of light and reflections. But as always, good taste will keep the display within bounds.

As to the menu, it remains traditional: oysters or cold consommé, chicken (or turkey, at Christmas) in aspic, foie gras, Christmas chocolate log. That is only the basis; regional specialties will evoke more or less distant provinces.

One must experiment with innovations while carefully preserving the atmosphere of tradition. A successful Christmas Eve or New Year's Eve party can be an enchanted memory for a whole year.

SERVICE FOR A FORMAL DINNER

UNDOUBTEDLY THE NUMBER OF PRIVATE HOUSES where service on the grand scale is still practiced has decreased in recent years. In any case, the information and suggestions we offer concerning service at receptions and formal dinners are valuable even for occasions on a reduced scale.

Present-day usage demands quick service. For this reason the dishes leave the kitchen already carved, with joints, birds, and game reformed in their original shape. In first-class and distinguished restaurants the dishes are first presented to the customer and then carved at a side table placed in front of or next to the customer's table.

In houses of great tradition and at ceremonial meals, a head waiter will present the dish on the guest's left, starting with the lady sitting on the host's right and finishing with the hostess. A second waiter starts with the gentleman seated on the right of the hostess and finishes with the host. If the dish is accompanied by a sauce, it is best to have another service person offer the sauce immediately. Usually, however, the same waiter who presents the dish holds the sauceboat in his right hand and the dish in his left, and turns slightly to present the sauceboat as soon as the guest has served herself or himself to the dish.

As soon as the guests have finished, the plates, knives, and forks are removed and replaced by warmed plates (except for cold dishes, of course) and new cutlery. After entrées and dishes in a sauce have been served, the roast usually follows, accompanied by salad. However, if the menu includes a cold dish, the salad will be served with the latter.

We recommend that both food and serving dishes be very hot. When hot dishes have been carved and prepared, they must be put back into the oven for a moment. The underside of a dish must be wiped when it is removed from the oven, to avoid soiling the staff's white gloves. If the dining room is rather far away from the kitchen the dishes should be covered to keep the food hot. The cover is removed outside the dining room door. If the serving dish does not have a cover, a warmed deep plate may be used instead.

After the roast and salad comes the cheese course. It is usual to offer at least two kinds of cheese, one soft and one hard—for the guests to choose from. For the cheese course, each guest is handed a small plate with the cheese knife lying on it.

After the cheese course, the staff will remove the cutlery and salt cellars, brush off the crumbs, working from the right-hand side of each guest, and then set finger bowls filled with lukewarm, perfumed water.

Ices or desserts are usually served by the waiter, using an ice-cream ladle or a spoon for the dessert. On ceremonial occasions the plates of petits fours and dessert will be handled by the manservant, but on more informal ones they are placed on the table and the guests serve themselves when invited to do so by the hostess.

The dinner is now concluded, and the host and hostess rise to indicate that the time has come to go into the drawing room. At large dinners the staff quickly draws back the chairs so that the guests can leave the dining room without noise or obstacle. When the dinner is a ceremonial one, each gentleman will offer his arm to his dinner partner to lead her out of the room. Coffee and liqueurs are served in the drawing room.

On formal or ceremonial occasions, the party will break up not later than 11 P.M. It is only on more intimate occasions that the evening is prolonged, and it is then the duty of the host and hostess to circulate refreshments—lemonade, orangeade, iced coffee, for example.

When the guests start to leave, someone must be in the cloakroom in order to hand over the coats and help the guests into them, and must stay until the last guest has gone.

As we suggested earlier, it is possible to hold very charming and very brilliant receptions without the help of a large staff. The whole art is to prepare everything in advance so that the host and hostess are not constantly forced to leave their guests. It is better to have a cold buffet, where everyone can serve himself and the host and hostess can really devote themselves to their guests, than one of those ghastly dinners at which every time the hostess gets up, everyone feels he must offer to help, only to let her do it alone in the end after all.

In conclusion, no guest must ever be allowed to feel for a second that he is causing trouble. Let us repeat what we said at the beginning: The secret of successful entertainment is to put everyone at ease. Entertaining successfully also means making friends, and what in the world is of greater value?

MENUS

THE GREAT TRADITIONAL MENUS OF TEN TO TWELVE COURSES belong to the past. Even a menu of six to seven courses has become exceptional. Though these elaborate menus have vanished as the result of changing customs, social necessity, and even the demands of health and beauty, our present menus are worthy successors.

The composition of a grand traditional menu was roughly as follows:
1. Soup—clear or thickened.
2. Hot hors d'oeuvre.
3. Cold hors d'oeuvre.
4. Fish.
5. A remove of meat, poultry, or game—usually a piece of roasted or braised meat with a garnish. (A remove—French relevé—is a dish that follows another; it usually precede the entrée.)
6. Entrée. Many dishes could be served as an entrée, but it was usually a dish in a sauce.
7. Roast—usually poultry or game. The roast was accompanied by a green salad, but this could also be served separately.
8. Sherbet or ice (sorbet). It used to be compulsory to serve an ice after the roast, to cleanse the palate for the next courses.
9. Cold entrée. This could be a foie gras pâté or parfait, an artistic presentation of lobster or rock lobster, a cold chicken, or other cold dish.
10. Side dishes (entremets). These included not only desserts and ices but also vegetables and cheeses.
11. Dessert and fruit.

A menu for what is described as a "simple dinner" at the beginning of the nineteenth century is given in Antonin Carême's book *Le Maitre d'Hôtel Français*. It consisted of two soups, two hors d'oeuvre, two removes, two removes of soup, twenty entrées, four different roasts, two large, two medium-sized and sixteen smaller side dishes of eggs, vegetables, and desserts.

Toward the middle of the nineteenth century, radical deletions began to be made, as this menu for a dinner at the court of Napoleon III shows.

Dinner at the Tuileries on February 1, 1858

Potage printanier • Rice in consommé

Turbot with lobster and Hollandaise sauce

Fillet of beef jardinière • Small chicken, fricasseed

Pheasant Perigord style
Chaud-froid of partridge • Rice casseroles Toulouse style
Strasbourg pâté de foie gras

Venison • Woodcock • Rouen duck

Asparagus • French beans

Puff pastry gâteau Pompadour
Orange and tangerine jelly • Timbale Châteaubriand
Basket of apricots with rice

At the beginning of the twentieth century, the number of dishes was again reduced. The menu, even at a banquet, was something like this: one soup, thick or clear; one fish dish; one remove or entrée; one roast, usually accompanied by a salad; one vegetable dish; one side dish, hot or cold, followed by an ice; dessert. At very elegant dinners, a cold hors d'oeuvre—caviar, melon, oysters—was served, contrary to general usage. The chief simplification consisted in serving only one dish for each course.

The remarkable simplification of menus in the second half of the twentieth century should be noted. Even on the occasion of the marriage of King Baudouin of the Belgians to Doña Fabiola de Mora y Aragon on December 13, 1960, only the following simple meal was served.

*Wedding of King Baudouin to
Doña Fabiola de Mora y Aragon, December 13, 1960*

Clear soup Diane
Lobster with herbs • Saddle of boar Nesseirode with chestnut puree
Strasbourg foie gras in sherry jelly • Royal parfait

Some other recent menus for important occasions follow.

Luncheon of the
Disciples of Antonin Carême, 1959

Foie gras parfait
Sole soufflé Abel Luquet • Saddle of lamb Antonin Carême
Cointreau sherbet • Cold sliced Nantes duck with orange
Selection of cheeses
Omelette Duc de Praslin

Luncheon at the
Jean-Drouant Hotel School, Paris

Terrine Lucullus with toast, or
Russian-style pink salmon with mayonnaise

Royal chicken with morels, or
grilled entrecote Maître d'Hôtel

Selection of spring vegetables • Salad • Selection of cheeses
Choice of desserts

Dinner Given by the
French Culinary Academy in Honor of
Monsieur Eugène Lacroix at
Lucas Carton, Paris

Salmon trout, Hermitage sauce
Timbale of sweetbreads with peas • Roast beef, Macaire potatoes
Terrine Brillat-Savarin, lettuce hearts
Delices de France
Peaches Madeleine • Rock of vanilla ice • Petits fours

Pouilly-Fuissé 1956 • Château Montrose 1937 • Irroy Champagne 1950

All these menus show that while the number of dishes offered has decreased considerably and some changes have been made in the composition of the dishes, the basic construction of the menu has not changed.

However, there have been major changes of detail. Before going into these it is necessary to explain what an entrée was in a traditional menu. It never meant, as one might expect, the first dish on a menu. In a traditional menu, without any exception whatsoever, the entrée followed the dish known as a remove, which was served after the fish if fish appeared on the menu. In principle, an entrée should be a hot dish in a white or brown sauce, though at a formal dinner a cold dish may be served instead. Although this principle is inviolable for formal dinners, ordinary usage must be taken into account. Thus in certain restaurant menus there is a choice of several courses, and the first is described as the "entrée" or "first course."

The most important changes that have taken place in menus are the result of the present-day way of life. Nobody wants to spend a long time at the table. Nor does anyone wish to put on weight, so people tend to be active after meals. A large roast is no longer as popular as it used to be, especially for a luncheon. Small, easily digested dishes are preferred—quickly sautéed meats or poultry, or grills. Ragoûts have become much less popular. People want a light, appetizing meal, with plenty of vegetables, salad, and fruit—in fact, a meal that does not overload the digestion and after which work can be resumed without any difficulty. There are no absolute rules, but in practice a present-day luncheon might be something like this:

1. A cold hors d'oeuvre, an egg dish, or fish. (Some people like soup at lunch time.)
2. A hot entrée or a grilled meat, garnished. In summer, cold meat may be served, accompanied by salad.
3. Cheese.
4. A small dessert: ice, stewed fruit, pastry, or fresh fruit.

The evening meal may be more substantial, since time is not so limited. Nevertheless, dinners also are far less rich than they used to be. A dinner consists of:

1. Clear or thick soup, or a small cold hors d'oeuvre.
2. Fish, a hot entrée, or a dish of garnished vegetables.
3. A roast garnished with vegetables. (If the entrée is substantial, a small cold dish with salad may be served instead.)
4. A hot or cold dessert or an ice, if possible with fruit.

All this still makes for a rather plentiful evening meal, which will be reduced to three courses on everyday occasions. Banquets and formal dinners are, of course, arranged differently. Before we come to these, certain rules that are compulsory both for the daily menu and more important occasions must be explained.

A correct menu, gastronomically speaking, is much more difficult to select than one might think. In planning menus for a restaurant or a household, some fundamental principles must be borne in mind, of which these are the most important:

1. The same meat or poultry must never appear twice on one menu, even if prepared in different ways.
2. Colors must be alternated—that is, one must not serve two white or two brown sauces in succession. If there is fish in a white sauce, it must not be followed by chicken in a white sauce.
3. Garnishes must be varied. If one serves mushrooms, tomatoes, or artichoke bottoms as garnish for a fish dish, these cannot be served with another course. It is, however, permissible to use truffles to garnish a cold dish, even if they have already accompanied a previous dish.
4. Cooking methods must be varied. A boiled or poached fish cannot be followed by boiled chicken, for example. An exception may be made only if the menu is a very full one, and even then only if other dishes have been served between the two similar ones.
5. A thick and nourishing soup is served only in cold weather. The same applies to fat or filling dishes, which are served only in winter.
6. Menus should be written in clear and comprehensible language. Technical hotel expressions are usually Greek to the layman. They should be correct, without a single error. A menu that is handwritten or typewritten is always more pleasant than a mimeographed one.

These rules apply to daily meals and even more to formal occasions. It is not easy to compose menus of this kind. The chef must bear in mind not only the customer's wishes, the cost, and the time of year, but a lot of other things as well. A wedding breakfast will be quite different from the closing banquet of a scientific congress. A hunting breakfast has quite a different character from a diplomatic dinner. But even on the most formal occasions, it is unusual to go beyond the following courses:

1. A small, first-class thick soup or clear soup served in cups. At a large official dinner a cold hors d'oeuvre—caviar, oysters, foie gras parfait—may be served before the soup.
2. Fish or shellfish.
3. An entrée or a roast garnished with vegetables.
4. A cold dish with a salad or a fine vegetable—or even a roast, if a very light entrée is served.
5. Cheese.
6. A hot or cold dessert or an ice.
7. Fruit.

Salad or vegetables, and fruit, must be included in all meals. The question of cheese at large dinners is a controversial one; many connoisseurs maintain that it is out of place at an elaborate dinner. In France, cheese is served before the dessert, but in some countries it is eaten at the end of the meal.

Here is a selection of menus, some simple, some more elaborate, for various seasons and special circumstances.

Spring

LUNCHEON
Avocados with seafood
Lamb noisettes Salvatore
Cheese
Fruit Salad

DINNER
Chicken broth
Cheese straws
Asparagus with three sauces
German-style saddle of venison
Endive salad
Charlotte Russe

Summer

LUNCHEON
Hors d'oeuvre platter
Venison steak Madame Lacroix
Hearts of lettuce
Cheese
Strawberries with Chantilly cream

DINNER
Cream soup Ilona
Crayfish tails au gratin
Chicken in Riesling wine
Noodles Alsatian style
Beatrice salad
Iced soufflé with strawberries

Winter

LUNCHEON
Artichokes à la Grecque
Sweetbread fillets Jèrome
Cheese
Profiteroles with chocolate sauce

DINNER
Lobster cocktail
Soup à la Reine
Saddle of hare a la bergère
Simone salad
Ice pudding Diane

Autumn

LUNCHEON
Poached eggs Massena
Brisket of beef Flemish style
Cheese
Cream à la Vigneron

DINNER
Consommé Madrilène
Pike quenelles Lyonnaise
Pheasant Vallée d'Auge
Mercedes salad
Pears Cardinal

Wedding Breakfast

Rich hors d'oeuvre
Cream Duquinha
Salmon trout Doria
Breasts of guinea fowl with
lychee nuts
Hearts of palm Milanese
Soufflé with almonds;
zabaglione with port

Closing Dinner for a Congress or Convention

Melon cocktail
Consommé à la diable
Red mullet Niçoise
Spit-roasted chicken
Green peas French style
Cress and beet salad
Kirsch parfait
Friandises

Diplomatic Dinner	*Christmas Eve*
Clear turtle soup with sherry	Lobster medallions Windsor style
Fillets of sole Atelier	Consommé
Saddle of lamb Richelieu	Fillets of sole Nabuchu
Lettuce hearts with celery	Turkey breasts Tamburlaine
Sliced duck in aspic with oranges	Apples Marie-Louise
Savarin Othello	Chicory and tomato salad
	Biscuit glacé with small cakes

COLD BUFFETS

AN INVITATION TO A COLD BUFFET not only indicates the eclectic taste of the hosts but is also most likely to promise a successful party. It provides the opportunity for a real spectacle of culinary art and color, ranging from the simplest to the most splendid, depending on the brilliance and importance you wish to give to the occasion, and on the standing and taste of your guests. Whether it is a simple buffet for friends or a ceremonial occasion, aesthetic beauty and culinary skill are bound to triumph.

According to their wishes and facilities, the hosts may prepare their own buffet or have it done by a catering firm that will send the food to their home. Or they will hold a reception at a hotel that specializes in that kind of service.

For a cold buffet at home, hosts with a limited number of rooms at their disposal will choose one—for instance, the dining room—in which the cold buffet will be set out. If possible this should not be the same room as that in which they receive their guests. The buffet, laid out on a long and preferably narrow table covered with a cloth reaching to the floor, will be the center of attention. The table should be neither too high nor too large, in order to make service easier. A second smaller table will be set aside for drinks, which the staff will hand around to the guests. Lacking a serving staff, you may serve drinks on a chest, desk, or any other convenient place, in addition to the table. Do not forget to provide enough plates, cutlery, and napkins. The size of the plates must be suitable for the dishes provided. If the guests are to serve themselves, put these accessories in a place where they will not interfere with the guests' freedom of movement.

The table decorations are of the utmost importance. If there is no serving staff, the floral decorations, tastefully arranged and harmonizing with the colors of the food, may be high and sumptuous; otherwise they should not be too bulky, in order not to hamper the staff. In the evening, candelabra, chandeliers, and candlesticks will give a festive air to your buffet table, and the soft light of the candles will create an exquisite atmosphere.

COCKTAIL BUFFET

Platters or trays should not be so large that the staff cannot pass them easily without inconveniencing the guests.

Some suggestions for buffets for various occasions are:

- Small choux-paste puffs filled with anchovies, cheese, caraway seeds, ham. Smoked eel or fish canapés with pickled cucumber; canapés of dried beef with stuffed olives; raw ham canapés with gherkins; cheese cubes sprinkled with caraway seeds and garnished with grated white of hard-cooked egg.
- Puff-pastry boats filled with truffled chicken salad; canapés of white bread with Gervais cheese; canapés of rye bread with slices of tomato and Emmentaler cheese sprinkled with paprika; slices of apple cooked slowly in butter and wrapped in slices of lean grilled bacon.
- Canapés of shrimp and fresh butter; comets of dried beef filled with cream cheese; canapés of hard-cooked eggs and caviar.
- Whole grapefruit into which small slices of salami, round slices of gherkins and pickled cucumbers, small cocktail onions pickled in vinegar, pieces of pimiento, and cheese cubes dusted with paprika are stuck with toothpicks. Surround with small pieces of puff pastry cut in fancy shapes. Or grapefruit stuck with black olives, radishes, slices of pickled cucumber, and cheese cubes dusted with paprika.
- Whole head of red cabbage, stuck with crayfish tails, black olives, stuffed olives, small radishes, and small celery hearts. Surround with small sausages and pieces of puff pastry cut in fancy shapes.
- Slices of fresh cucumber spread with salmon; small canapés of rye bread spread with cream cheese with a slice of tomato on top; canapés of Swedish bread spread with salmon mousse and cream cheese.
- Puff-pastry boats filled with truffled lobster salad. Gorgonzola and creamed Gruyère cheese mixed with diced rye bread and served in paper cups.
- Canapés of whole wheat bread, buttered and spread with cheese and garnished with pimientos.
- Thin slices of buttered white bread with a slice of tomato topped with a small artichoke bottom on each; slices of cheese garnished with sweet peppers.
- Salted almonds.
- Drinks: All cocktails, apéritifs, white wine, red wine, champagne, fresh fruit juices, tomato juice.

DANISH BUFFET

It is the ideal formula for a summer party in the country. The dishes may be selected from among the following:

- Sliced roast pork garnished with pickled cucumbers, lettuce hearts, thinly sliced tomatoes.

- Sliced pickled tongue with lettuce hearts.
- Cold sliced roast beef garnished with fresh cucumbers.
- Sliced boiled ham garnished with fresh cucumbers.
- Danish caviar, chopped onions, parsley, and radishes.
- Hard-cooked eggs in mayonnaise, garnished with tomatoes, asparagus, and lettuce leaves.
- Shrimp in cocktail sauce, surrounded with lettuce leaves.
- Julienne of pickled tongue and beets mixed with mayonnaise, garnished with cucumbers, tomatoes, and sliced sweet peppers.
- Salad of asparagus tips in Chantilly mayonnaise.
- Seafood salad with Chantilly mayonnaise seasoned with ketchup.
- Quartered hard-cooked eggs and sliced tomatoes, garnished with parsley.
- Asparagus tips.
- Comets of smoked salmon with asparagus tips and parsley.
- Small steaks tartare on lettuce leaves, egg yolks and salt served separately.
- Sliced whole wheat, white, and rye bread arranged on a breadboard, with fresh butter.
- Small pickled onions, black olives, radishes, gherkins, and pickles.
- Small fillets of cold pork garnished with orange sections.
- Danish pâté de foie gras in jelly, garnished with lettuce leaves and slices of grilled bacon.
- Gripsholm-style herring salad (pickled herring, diced apple and cucumber, mayonnaise, sour cream, and horseradish).
- Sardines marinated in ketcup.
- Canned smoked herring.
- Salad of herring, cucumbers, and macédoine of vegetables, with sweet and sour dressing.
- Matjes herring garnished with onion rings.
- Smoked mussels with mayonnaise.
- Pickled herring garnished with gherkins and cucumber.
- Drinks: For a reception in the country, first serve an apéritif and in summer Bellini cocktails; with the buffet serve white and rosé wine, local wine, Danish beer, fruit juice, carbonated beverages.

FORMAL BUFFET

At home. Many recipes and suggestions for simple dishes will be found in chapter 4, "Cold Hors d'Oeuvres, Canapés, and Sandwiches" Skill, taste, and culinary experience will enable you to prepare fine cold dishes ranging from fish to game, which will give great pleasure to your guests. Fruit salads, cold zabaglione in coupes, charlottes, savarins, parfaits, and iced coupes will be the favorite desserts, with plates of petits fours and cakes.

If you have more than ten guests, prepare two plates of each dish.

Choose the drinks to suit the dishes and the time of day; in the late morning and at lunchtime serve vermouth, sherry, Bellini cocktails, white and rosé wine, champagne; in the evening, all apéritifs, cocktails, wines, fruit juice, and carbonated beverages.

In a hotel. A formal buffet in a first-class hotel is always an occasion of great brilliance.

To avoid confusion, the chef and some of his assistants, or the waiters, will stand behind the buffet tables to serve the guests. The number of servers will depend on the number of guests. The guests themselves will choose the dishes they want. To avoid gastronomic and culinary incompatibility, the serving staff will not place fish and poultry, shellfish and game, and so forth, on the same plate. Soup is optional; it will be hot or cold according to the time of year. If only one dessert is provided—for example, Oranges Riviera, it will be served to the guests in portions.

The drinks will be served in the appropriate glasses, placed on silver trays handed around by waiters. If the guests sit down to eat, the waiters will go around pouring wine for each place setting, as requested by the guests. It is not usual to serve beer at a formal buffet unless a guest asks for it especially.

Dishes for formal and ceremonial buffets. A selection of dishes may be made from the list that follows. An asterisk indicates that the recipe is included in this section. Recipes for the other dishes listed can be found in the relevant chapters by consulting the index. When the ingredients of a recipe include elements to be prepared in advance, the title is capitalized (Chantilly Sauce, Truffles Surprise) and the recipe can be located from the index.

HORS D'OEUVRE COCKTAILS

SHELLFISH
- cold lobster and rock lobster dishes

FISH
- Cold Cod Russian Style
- Salmon in an artistic presentation
- Salmon Steaks Louis XVI*
- Salmon Moscow Style
- Comets of Smoked Salmon Russian Style
- Any other cold salmon dishes
- Fillets of Sole Floralies
- Trout: any cold trout dishes that are sufficiently showy

BEEF
- Glazed Fillet of Beef
- Fillet of Beef Rothschild
- Russian-Style Fillet of Beef
- Pickled Tongue Karachi Style
- Tongue Princesse

VEAL
- Jellied Veal Pot Roast
- Cold Saddle of Veal

HAM
- Ham Roulade*
- Ham Glazed with Aspic
- Ham Villandry
- Ham Mousse
- Any other of the more elegant cold ham dishes

Salmon Steaks Louis XVI

2 fillets of salmon (¾ pounds without bones and skins)
50 jumbo shrimp tails
Hot fish stock (court bouillon) to cover fish
Mayonnaise
1¼ cups jellied clear stock
1 cup each cooked julienne carrots, green beans, and peas
1 cup raw julienne celery strips
24 small poached mushroom caps
8 ounces red caviar
12 ripe olives
3 tangerine sections
Chives
4 hen's eggs, or 12 quail or gull eggs, hard-cooked
1 cup melted jellied stock
23 cherry tomatoes
Salt
Ground black pepper
1 (7-ounce) can pimento
Honeydew balls from 1 large honeydew melon
Chantilly Sauce or Green Mayonnaise

Wrap salmon in buttered paper or cheesecloth and place in a deep baking dish. Add enough fish stock (court bouillon) to cover. Cook in a preheated moderate oven (350°F) 15 minutes, or until the fish is flaky but still holds its shape. Chill with a plate placed on top of it to give a small amount of pressure until ready to serve.

Cook shrimp; peel, devein, and set aside. Combine 1 cup mayonnaise and ¾ cup of the jellied stock, having it about half set. Fold in the carrots, green beans, peas, and celery. Turn the mixture into a lightly oiled 1½-quart round shallow mold. Just before serving, unmold onto a very large plate or tray. Frost top and sides completely with mayonnaise. Decorate top as desired with 2 of the poached mushroom caps, a little of the caviar, 2 of the olives, the tangerine sections, chives, and wedges of the hard-cooked eggs. Brush melted jellied stock over decorations, saving remaining melted stock for later use. Place shrimp around the mold. Cut the chilled salmon into 22 uniform slices and arrange them around the shrimp, with the rounded ends pointed inward. Stuff the remaining mushrooms with the rest of the caviar and place one on each pointed end of salmon slices. Brush both shrimp and salmon with melted jellied stock. Remove and discard centers of tomatoes, sprinkle the cavities with salt and black pepper, and drain well. Drain and discard oil from pimientos. Push pimientos through a sieve, and mix with ½ cup jellied stock. Spoon into cavities of tomatoes. Top each with ¼ slice hard-cooked hen's egg or ½ slice quail or gull egg, and ½ pitted ripe olive. Place the tomatoes between the pointed outer ends of salmon slices. Arrange a row of honeydew balls around the salmon. Brush both tomatoes and honeydew balls with melted jellied stock. Serve with Chantilly Sauce or Green Mayonnaise. Serves 20 to 22.

Ham Roulade

8 large eggs
¾ teaspoon salt
2 cups sifted cake flour
7 tablespoons butter
1½ cups finely ground cooked ham

1½ teaspoons paprika
Brandy to taste
1 cup half-set jellied chicken stock
⅔ cup heavy cream

Break eggs into a large bowl; add salt. Place over warm water and beat until the mixture is very thick and lemon-colored. Gently fold in flour. Melt butter, cool, and add it, in a thin stream, to the mixture, and stir lightly to prevent batter from becoming heavy. Pour batter into two buttered, lightly floured pans, 10 by 15 by 1 inch (jelly-roll pans). Spread batter uniformly over the bottom of the pans. Bake in a preheated hot oven (425° F) for 8 to 10 minutes. Remove from baking pans immediately, roll up as for jelly roll in a slightly moistened cloth, and let stand until cold. Mix ham with paprika, brandy, and the half-set stock. Whip the cream and fold into ham mixture. Unroll the baked sponge layers. Spread with the ham mixture. Roll up, wrap in foil or towel, and chill. Cut into slices ⅓ inch thick. Serves 50 to 60.

Assortment of Cold Poultry and Pâtés

1 (5-pound) cold roast duck
1 (5-pound) cold roast chicken
1 pound 5 ounces Foie Gras Mousse
12 peeled, seeded, and
    quartered tomatoes
3 hard-cooked egg whites
1½ cups clear meat jelly
10 small slices cold chicken
1 quart Waldorf Salad
10 small mushrooms
1 (2-ounce) can pimento
1 (2-pound) cold cooked pheasant

2 pounds chilled firm butter
1 cold Pâté of Chicken
10 small Green Peppers à la Grecque
2 cups diced cold cooked chicken
2 cups diced raw mushrooms
¾ cup Vinaigrette Sauce
¾ cup crushed, peeled, and
    seeded tomato
¾ cup diced gherkins
1 tablespoon ketchup
5 to 7 Truffles Surprise
1 large bunch grapes

Remove breast and breast bones from duck and chicken. Discard the breast bones and save the meat of the breasts to use later. Fill the duck carcass with most of the Foie Gras Mousse. Completely cover it with some of the tomato slices. Cut hard-cooked egg whites in crosswise slices and place in a row down the center of the duck. Glaze with melted clear jelly. Chill. Slice duck breast diagonally and place the slices on the 10 slices of cold cooked chicken, which have been spread thinly with the remaining Foie Gras Mousse. Glaze with melted clear jelly. Chill.

Fill chicken carcass with most of the Waldorf Salad, having it piled high in the shape of a dome. Cover with slices of chicken breast. Poach mushroom caps in boiling water 2 to 3 minutes and place in a line down the center of the stuffed chicken, top side up. Garnish with a straight line of pimiento strips. Glaze with clear meat jelly. Chill.

Glaze pheasant with melted clear jelly and chill.

Sculpture butter in the shape of a fowl and place it on one end of a large platter or tray. Arrange stuffed duck, chicken, and pheasant in front of it. Cut slices cold Pâté of Chicken and place them in a lengthwise row on one side of the tray. Cut green peppers in half and fill with mushroom salad made with the next six ingredients. Place them in a row next to the slices of Pâté of Chicken. Garnish the chilled slices of duck breast with tomato slices and a bit of hard-cooked egg white. Put them in a row next to the stuffed peppers. Arrange a row of quartered Truffles Surprise and a row of the remaining tomatoes, quartered and filled with the remaining Waldorf Salad. Glaze with melted clear jelly. Garnish tray with a bunch of grapes placed between the butter sculpture and the duck. Serves 20 to 30.

Turkey Breasts Champs Elysées

15 to 20 slices cooked celeriac (celery root)	2½ cups Waldorf Salad
	¾ cups jellied stock
5 large raw green peppers, cut in julienne strips	10 artichoke bottoms
	9 to 10 pounds roast turkey breast
1 cup olive oil or salad oil	30 slices poultry galantine
¼ cup wine vinegar	30 tangerine sections
Salt	15 pistachio nuts, halved
Freshly ground black pepper	Truffles Surprise
15 to 20 (2-inch) tomatoes, peeled and centers removed	1 baked 4-inch tart shell
	About 55 radish roses

Marinate celeriac and green pepper in separate bowls, in the oil, vinegar, 1 teaspoon salt, and ¼ teaspoon black pepper, 2 hours. Set aside. Sprinkle inside of tomatoes with salt and pepper; invert to drain well. Fill cavities with some of the Waldorf Salad and place each on a slice of marinated, well-drained celeriac. Glaze with jellied stock. Chill. Fill artichoke bottoms with well-drained green pepper. Glaze and chill. Slice turkey breasts and place one piece on each slice of poultry galantine. Garnish each slice with a tangerine section and ½ pistachio nut. Glaze with jellied stock and chill. Glaze Truffles Surprise and chill.

To serve, fill the tart shell with remaining Waldorf Salad and place it in the center of a large round tray. Around this arrange, in order given, Truffles Surprise, artichoke bottoms with green peppers, stuffed tomatoes on celeriac slices, slices of poultry galantine and turkey breast, and radish roses. Serves 20 to 30.

Saddle of Venison Grand Duchy Style

1 saddle of venison, about 6½ pounds	2 large raw green peppers, cut into julienne strips and marinated 2 hours in French Dressing
4 slices pineapple	
8 truffles	
3½ cups jellied stock	8 baked 2-inch tart shells
24 round slices poached apples	3 cups Waldorf Salad
12 maraschino cherries	10 slices bread
32 fluted and marinated mushrooms	Butter
20 cooked artichoke bottoms	Cumberland Sauce

The venison should be cooked very quickly, 6 to 7 minutes per pound, in a preheated hot oven (450°F). Cool. Remove meat from the bones and cut it into thin diagonal slices. Replace the slices on the bones so that they overlap. Cut each pineapple slice into 8 wedges and arrange them close together down the center of the sliced meat to simulate the vertebrae. Garnish each wedge with a bit of truffle. Glaze the whole saddle with melted jellied stock. Chill. Garnish each apple slice with ½ cherry and a bit of truffle. Glaze and chill. At the same time, glaze 6 of the truffles and the mushrooms and chill. Fill artichoke bottoms with marinated green peppers, glaze, and chill. Fill tart shells with Waldorf Salad. Cut bread into 20 rounds, using a 2-inch cookie cutter. Brown on both sides in butter to make croutons. Cool. Top with chopped jellied stock. Coat the bottom of a large rectangular tray with a thin layer of melted jellied stock. When stock is set, place the saddle of venison in the center. Place apple slices down each side, and a truffle flanked with two mushrooms at each end. Place artichoke bottoms filled with green pepper strips on one side of the tray and the jelly-topped croutons on the other. Place salad-filled tarts at each end. Arrange a truffle surrounded by 7 fluted mushrooms in each corner. Serve with Cumberland Sauce, if desired. Serves 18 to 20.

Saddle of Venison Renoir

Lardoons (thick strips dry, white, firm pork fat)	¼ cup olive oil or salad oil
1 cup brandy	2 fillets of venison
6 each coriander seeds, whole black peppercorns, and crushed juniper berries (if available)	Salt
	Freshly ground black pepper
	½ pound bacon, thinly sliced
1 whole clove	1½ pounds mousseline forcemeat made with venison trimmings
½ bay leaf	Melted meat jelly
1 tablespoon chopped parsley	Waldorf Salad
1 small clove garlic	

Marinate the lardoons 2 hours in brandy, seasonings, and oil. Lard the venison fillets with the lardoons. Rub the outside of the venison lightly with salt and ground black pepper. Set aside. Butter a long mold with a rounded bottom and line it with bacon slices. Cover the bottom and sides of the mold with a thick layer of forcemeat, over which place venison and cover with remaining forcemeat. Tap the bottom of the mold several times to spread and settle the forcemeat. Cover with lightly buttered parchment paper or foil. Place mold in a pan of hot water. Cook in a preheated oven (350°F) 35 to 40 minutes. The meat should be undercooked. Cool. Chill at least 6 hours before slicing. Cut into slices, allowing 5 to 6 ounces per serving. Glaze with melted meat jelly. Serve with Waldorf Salad.

COCKTAIL MIXING AND SERVING

COCKTAILS AND DRINKS ARE SO MUCH A PART OF entertaining that this chapter would be incomplete without some suggestions for their preparation and service. The recipes included are for the cocktails most frequently served the world over. You may wish to experiment with the recipes that follow, but whatever formula you use, be sure to measure the ingredients accurately. Have glasses chilled or frozen. Shake or stir drinks with ice just long enough to chill them thoroughly; otherwise the melting ice will dilute the drink.

Fashions in drinks are constantly changing. New cocktails are invented, others forgotten. Nothing changes more quickly than whether a drink should be served "up" or "on the rocks," with ice cubes in the glass. This applies to Martinis, Manhattans, and various other cocktails that are classically poured from the beaker or shaker with the ice strained out. Drinks "on the rocks" are usually served in a 4-ounce Old-Fashioned glass instead of a small cocktail glass. Long drinks usually have ice in the glass.

The basic ingredients for cocktails are whisky (Scotch, rye, bourbon), gin, vodka, brandy, liqueurs, vermouths, and fruit juices. A well-stocked bar will also provide Angostura bitters, orange bitters, Worcestershire sauce, Tabasco sauce, cocktail onions, small green olives, lemons, limes, oranges, and maraschino cherries. Cocktails are mixed either in a shaker or in a mixing beaker with a glass rod for stirring and a strainer. Other necessary equipment includes jiggers, measuring cups, droppers, drinking straws (long and short), lemon squeezer, and a small sharp knife or zester for cutting the rind (never the pith) of lemons or oranges. The glasses most often used are cocktail glasses, 2-ounce and 4-ounce; Old-Fashioned glasses, 4- to 6-ounce; highball glasses, 8-ounce and 10-ounce; Collins glasses, 10-, 12-, and 14-ounce.

 ## Alaska

IN THE SHAKER:
⅓ yellow Chartreuse
⅔ gin
Ice

Stir, strain, and serve in a cocktail glass.

 ## Americano

IN AN 8-OUNCE HIGHBALL GLASS:
1 ounce bitter Campari
2 ounces sweet vermouth
Ice

Fill with carbonated water; stir slightly. Squeeze a twist of lemon peel over the drink and add the peel.

 ## Alexander

IN THE SHAKER:
1 teaspoon fresh cream
½ crème de cacao
⅔ brandy
Ice

Shake and strain into a 4-ounce cocktail glass.

 ## Barbotage

IN THE SHAKER:
1 teaspoon grenadine
1 ounce lemon juice
1 ounce orange juice
Ice

Shake, strain into a 4-ounce cocktail glass, and fill with champagne.

Bellini

IN A 6-OUNCE GLASS:
1 ounce chilled peach juice
   (see below)
Chilled dry champagne or
   prosecco to fill

To make the peach juice, take
8 ripe peaches, remove the stones,
and press the peaches through
a sieve until only the skin
remains. Add the strained juice
of 2 lemons, bottle, and keep in the
refrigerator. Will keep 2 days.

Black Velvet

½ ice-cold dark stout
½ chilled champagne

Gently pour both stout and
champagne simultaneously into a
14-ounce glass.

Bloody Mary

IN AN 8-OUNCE GLASS:
Dash of lemon juice
2 dashes Worcestershire sauce
1½ ounces vodka
3 ounces tomato juice
Ice

Stir well and serve on the
rocks or strain into chilled
wine glasses.

Bourbon Collins

See Tom Collins.

Brandy Egg Nog

IN THE SHAKER:
1 teaspoon sugar
1 egg yolk
1½ ounces brandy
½ cup milk ice

Shake, strain into a 10-ounce
highball glass, and dust the top
with grated nutmeg.

Brandy Flip

IN THE SHAKER:
½ teaspoon sugar
1 egg yolk
1½ ounces brandy
Ice

Shake and serve in a 4-ounce
cocktail glass. Dust top with
grated nutmeg.

Bronx

IN THE SHAKER:
2 dashes orange juice
⅙ dry vermouth
⅙ sweet vermouth
⅔ gin ice

Shake, strain, and serve in a cocktail
glass.

❧ Cardinal

IN THE SHAKER:
⅙ bitter Campari
⅓ dry vermouth
½ gin ice

Shake, strain into a 4-ounce cocktail
glass, and add a twist of lemon peel.

❧ Champagne Cocktail

IN A CHAMPAGNE GLASS:
¼ lump of sugar
Dash Angostura bitters
Dash brandy

Fill with champagne and add a twist
of orange peel.

❧ Cuba Libre

IN A 10-OUNCE GLASS FILLED WITH ICE:
1½ ounces Bacardi rum

Fill up with Coca-Cola and decorate
with a slice of lemon.

❧ Daiquiri

IN THE SHAKER:
½ teaspoon simple syrup
Juice of ½ lemon
1½ ounces white rum
Finely shaved ice

Shake well, strain, and serve in a cocktail glass.

❧ Frozen Daiquiri

IN THE SHAKER:
1½ ounces light rum
Juice of ½ lime
1 teaspoon sugar
Finely crushed ice

Shake vigorously, or mix in an electric
blender. Serve unstrained in a saucer-
shaped champagne glass or 4-ounce
cocktail glass, with a short straw.

❧ Dubonnet Cocktail

IN THE MIXING BEAKER:
⅔ Dubonnet
⅓ gin
Ice

Stir, strain, and serve in a cocktail glass.

❧ Gimlet

IN THE MIXING BEAKER:
¾ dry gin
¼ Rose's sweetened lime juice
Ice

Stir, strain, and serve in a cocktail glass.

❧ Gin Daisy

IN THE SHAKER:
Dash grenadine
Juice of ½ lemon
1½ ounces gin

Shake and pour without straining into
an 8-ounce highball glass filled with
finely crushed ice.

Gin Fizz

IN THE SHAKER:

1 teaspoon sugar
Juice of ½ lemon
1½ ounces gin
Ice

Shake, pour into an 8-ounce highball glass, and fill with carbonated water. Fizzes may also be made with brandy or rum.

Golden Fizz

IN THE SHAKER:

1 egg yolk
1 teaspoon sugar
Juice of ½ lemon
1½ ounces gin
Ice

Shake, pour into an 8-ounce highball glass, and fill with carbonated water.

Silver or Ramos Fizz

IN THE SHAKER:

1 egg white
1 teaspoon sugar
Juice of ½ lemon
1½ ounces gin
Ice

Shake, pour into an 8-ounce highball glass, and fill with carbonated water.

Honeymoon

IN THE SHAKER:

Juice of 1 ½ lemons
½ teaspoon honey
1½ ounces rum
½ egg white
Ice

Shake, strain, and serve in a 4-ounce cocktail glass.

Manhattan

IN THE MIXING BEAKER:

1 or 2 dashes Angostura bitters
⅕ sweet vermouth
⅘ bourbon, rye, or blended whisky

Stir, strain, and serve in a cocktail glass. Add a maraschino cherry if desired. For a Dry Manhattan, use dry vermouth and omit the cherry.

Dry Martini

IN THE MIXING BEAKER:

⅕ dry vermouth
⅘ gin
Ice

Stir, strain, and serve in a cocktail glass. Add a twist of lemon peel or an olive if desired. A Martini served with 2 or 3 small pearl onions is called a Gibson. Vodka may be used instead of gin in Martinis.

Negroni

IN THE MIXING BEAKER:
⅓ bitter Campari
⅓ gin
⅓ sweet vermouth
½ slice orange
Ice

Stir, strain into an 8-ounce highball glass, and add the zest of a lemon.

Old-Fashioned

In an Old-Fashioned glass, put a small lump of sugar. Shake 2 or 3 dashes of Angostura bitters and a little carbonated water over the sugar and muddle until sugar dissolves. Fill glass with ice. Decorate with twist of lemon peel, maraschino cherry, and ½ slice orange (if desired). Add 1½ ounces of bourbon or rye.

Orange Blossom

IN THE SHAKER:
Juice of ½ orange
1½ ounces gin
Ice

Shake, strain, and serve in a 4-ounce cocktail glass.

Paradise

IN THE SHAKER:
½ teaspoon orange juice
⅓ apricot brandy
⅔ gin
Ice

Chill and serve in a cocktail glass.

Pink Lady

IN THE SHAKER:
Dash grenadine
Juice of ½ lemon
1½ ounces gin
Ice

Shake, strain, and serve in a 4-ounce cocktail glass.

Planter's Punch

IN THE SHAKER:
2 dashes Angostura bitters
Juice of ½ lemon or lime
3 ounces rum
Ice

Shake vigorously, pour into a 10-ounce Collins glass, and decorate with ½ slice of pineapple. Fill with carbonated water.

Port or Sherry Flip

IN THE SHAKER:
½ teaspoon sugar
1 egg yolk
1½ ounces port or sherry
A few drops brandy
Ice

Shake vigorously and serve in a 4-ounce glass. Dust with grated nutmeg.

 Rob Roy

IN THE MIXING BEAKER:
1 or 2 dashes Angostura bitters
⅔ Scotch
⅓ sweet or dry vermouth

Fill beaker with cracked ice, stir, strain, and serve in a cocktail glass.

 Sidecar

IN THE SHAKER:
½ teaspoon lemon juice
⅓ Cointreau
⅔ brandy
Ice

Shake, strain, and serve in a cocktail glass.

Singapore Sling

IN THE SHAKER:
Juice of ½ lemon
½ gin
½ cherry brandy
Ice

Shake, strain into an 8-ounce highball glass, and fill with carbonated water.

Tom Collins

IN A 10-OUNCE COLLINS GLASS:
Ice
½ teaspoon sugar or simple syrup
Juice of ½ lemon
1½ ounces gin

Add carbonated water and stir. A Collins may also be made with bourbon.

Whisky Sour

IN THE SHAKER:
1 ounce fresh sweet & sour
1½ ounces bourbon or rye whisky
Ice

Shake vigorously and strain into a 4-ounce cocktail glass that contains a slice of orange and a maraschino cherry.

White Lady

IN THE SHAKER:
½ teaspoon lemon juice
⅓ Cointreau
⅔ gin
Ice

Shake, strain, and serve in a cocktail glass.

ADVICE ON SERVING WINE

ACCORDING TO ONE'S TASTES AND CERTAIN RULES, one will seek out the wine that will be the best accompaniment to a certain dish, or choose a dish that will best consort with the chosen wine. This is not to say that there may not be some charm in certain discords, as in music. But dissonance is a form of art which must not be confused with a false note, a squawk.

GLASSES

Just as sound needs a room built in accordance with the best rules of acoustics in order to spread, vibrate better, and captivate us, so the aroma of a wine must be able to benefit by that olfactory sounding box, the glass. Pouring a great wine into a small glass is like putting a full symphony orchestra on the stage of an intimate theater. A wine glass must be capacious; it must never be filled up. The finer and thinner the crystal, the more intimate will be the contact between lips and liquid.

There are various types of glasses.

A cabernet sauvignon glass should not be too full-bellied; its curve should have a harmonious line, with the top of the bowl slightly narrowed for red wine in order to hold the bouquet captive for a moment. A pinot noir glass, on the other hand, should have long sides (but without being too much like a tankard). This difference is explained by the fact that the aroma of that varietal, more vegetable in character, gives the impression of rising in a sheaf, while that of pinot noir, more animal in nature, seems to spread in the round.

For Champagne, a coupe (saucer-shaped glass) should never be used, in spite of the elegance of the shape. It stupidly lets the subtle scent of the wine escape. A flute glass is better, but the ideal is a large tulip glass

White wines also have their traditional glasses, in general smaller than those for red wines. A chardonnay or sauvignon blanc glass resembles a cabernet glass except in size. Rieslings used to be served in a small goblet with a long stem. Now a small white wine glass is used. But it is perfectly correct also to select an all-purpose wine glass whose shape most nearly resembles that of the cabernet glass.

THE TEMPERATURE OF WINES

How many sins are committed in this area, the worst being to ruin white wine by too much and too long refrigeration, and to serve lukewarm red wine.

Where lies the happy medium between these two equally annoying extremes?

It would be bold indeed—not to say arbitrary—to lay down a precise temperature for every wine. The laws of relativity must be applied. A wine at 70°F. will seem almost lukewarm if served in a room where the temperature is 65°F, and almost cold if served in a room at 80°.

One can therefore say that a dry white wine should give an impression of pleasant coolness, but not of cold, not to mention being iced. It should be served at cellar temperature, which is usually 50° to 55°F. Champagne can be served colder, at about 45°F. The great rich white wines are best at lightly higher temperatures—that is, 55–60°F

Important note: The wine cooler should not be stuffed full of ice but filled with very cold water, or water made cold with pieces of ice. When the wine is cool enough, remove it from the cooler.

Light red wines of the type drunk young, are served cool. Though cellar temperature may seem to be rather cold, remember that at the table their temperature will quickly rise to about 60°F.

It is generally said that red wines should be served *chambré*—that is, at room temperature. True enough, but this does not mean the temperature of the dining room (which is usually about 70°F). It means that the wine should be brought up from the cellar early enough to let it take on the temperature of the coolest room in the house.

As a general rule, red wines, especially old ones, must be brought up in advance so that they can rest and any sediment can settle on the bottom of the bottle. If the bottle has to be fetched at the last moment, a wine cradle should be used. This is frequently used without rhyme or reason, especially in restaurants wishing to impress. Its only purpose is to keep the bottle in the horizontal position it has had in its rack, so that the sediment will remain undisturbed on the lower side. A bottle that has been standing upright, therefore, must not be placed in a cradle; this would mix the sediment with the wine, which is precisely what one is trying to avoid. The bottle must be slid gently from the rack into the cradle without turning it and carried carefully upstairs.

The problem of sediment is discussed further in the section on decanting. As regards temperature, pinot noir should be brought to the table at about 60°F; they develop their full bouquet at about 65°F.

Cabernet sauvignon, zinfandels and Rhone varieties are served at 65°F; it reaches its full aroma at about 70°F, but it must never be served at this temperature.

DECANTING

This is the operation of separating the wine from the sediment or lees. Decanting has its supporters and its opponents. The opponents say that wine is too sensitive, that it suffers trauma, that it is best to pour it from its bottle at table carefully, until the sediment becomes apparent.

On the side of the supporters, there are two cases when decanting should be practiced: for separating old wine from the sediment and for oxidizing certain young wines. The older the wine, the more necessary it is usually to avoid the aeration brought about by decanting and to postpone this operation to the last moment before the wine is to be drunk. With young wines that one wants to mature artificially by oxidization (and also with wines that have remained "hard" or "aggressive," which do not mellow), decanting should be done in advance, sometimes several hours before serving.

Hold the bottle in the right hand by the bottom—not the neck; hold the decanter in the left hand in front of a bright light and pour the wine from the bottle into the decanter as gently as possible, without letting it gurgle. Stop pouring as soon as the first threads of sediment are seen floating toward the bottle neck.

Allowing Wine to Settle

Wine is a living thing; traveling tires it. Let it rest in the cellar for several days—several weeks for venerable bottles—before drinking it. In the same way, if you buy good wine from the grocer, it is best to let it settle for a few days. After the bottle has been in your cellar, it should be brought up in the morning for dinner, and the night before for next day's lunch.

The Order of Wines During a Meal

In principle, the first wine served with a meal is a dry white wine. This is followed by red, from the youngest to the oldest, from the lightest to the most full-bodied. Sweet white wine is served with dessert. But exceptions are possible. In Bordeaux, for example, Sauternes is served with foie gras at the beginning of the meal. In this case the Sauternes must be followed by a dry white wine with sufficient body, then by a generous red wine.

There are also exceptions to the rule of an order of increasing age. One must not serve a wine of a light year after one of a full-bodied one, simply because it is older.

In conclusion, let us point out that the drinking of wine, while it is a matter of knowledge and even more of experience, is also a matter of taste, in both senses of the word.

THE
PRINCIPLES
AND
BASIC
MATERIALS OF
COOKERY

THE TWO MOST IMPORTANT FACTORS IN GOOD COOKING are the quality of the materials and the skill used in their preparation. Every cook can benefit from a knowledge of the nature, sources, food values, and uses of basic materials, both for purchasing, handling, and preparing them, and in planning dishes and menus. In this chapter we first discuss herbs and spices. Methods of cooking are then described in detail. The final section presents, with recipes, the doughs, stocks, and mixtures that form the foundation of the great French cuisine and lists the classic garnishes that embellish it. The user of this book will find this chapter an important preparation for the recipes in the chapters that follow.

HERBS AND SPICES

THE DISTINCTION BETWEEN HERBS AND SPICES is often misunderstood, but generally speaking, herbs are defined as leaves of certain edible plants, and spices as various other parts of plants such as the seeds, roots, fruit, flowers, bark, and so on. However, some of the leaves of some of these can be used as herbs; anise and mustard are examples. In the onion family, the leaves of chives, the leaves and bulbs of spring onions, and the bulbs of garlic and shallots are the parts used in cooking and flavoring. The leaves of herbs can be used fresh or dried; spices are dried (rarely fresh), and many can be used either whole or in a freshly powdered form. In the following lists, the most common culinary use is the criterion for classifying as herb or spice in doubtful cases. The French names, where they differ from the English, are given in parentheses.

AROMATIC PLANTS AND HERBS (PLANTES AROMATIQUES)
(Unless otherwise noted, the fresh leaves are the part used.)

NAME AND DESCRIPTION	CULINARY USES
BASIL *(basilic)*. Sweet, fragrant.	Soups, sauces, sausages, pâtés, salads.
BAY LEAVES *(laurier)*. Strong, pungent; use with discretion.	Dried meat, poultry, fish, stews.
BORAGE *(bourrache)*. Fragrant, pronounced cucumber flavor. Leaves and flowers.	Salads and summer drinks.
BURNET, PIMPERNEL *(pimprenelle)*. Odoriferous, pungent.	Soups, sauces; young leaves as salad.
CHERVIL *(cerfeuil)*. Mild, aromatic, pleasing shape. Leaves and stalks.	Soups, sauces, salads, decoration of cold dishes.

CHIVES *(ciboulettes)*. Very mild onion flavor; slender tubular leaves.	Soup, hot or cold, cold sauces, salads meat, fish, mixed with butter or cream cheese.
DILL *(aneth)*. Fragrant, permeating flavor. Leaves and seeds.	Soups, sauces, crayfish, salads, pickles (seed).
FENNEL *(fenouil)*. Mild, fragrant, penetrating, resembles anise.	Leaves: sauces, decoration of cold dishes; seeds: liqueurs, cakes, candies. Stalks and root: as vegetable, in salads.
GARLIC *(ail)*. Strong, pungent, penetrating; to be used with discretion.	Sections of bulb, whole, chopped, or crushed. Meats, fish, poultry, vegetables, salad dressing.
HORSERADISH *(raifort)*. Strong, hot, pungent.	Grated root. Sauces, meat dishes, marinades, pickles.
JUNIPER BERRIES *(baies de genièvre)*. Pleasantly pungent. Partially dried.	Sauerkraut, game, pork, charcuterie, sauces.
LEMON BALM *(citronelle)*. Fragrant, lemon smell.	Salads, summer drinks, punch.
LOVAGE. Celery flavor.	Soups, seafood, meats, salads.
MARJORAM *(marjolaine)*. Odoriferous, fragrant. Related to oregano. Fresh and dried.	Soups, sauces, fish, meat preparations.
MINT *(menthe)*. Mild, fragrant.	Soups, sauces, potatoes, other vegetables, lamb, jelly, vinegars.
OREGANO *(origan)*. Related to marjoram, but stronger and more pungent; use with discretion. Fresh and dried.	Indispensable in Italian cooking, especially pizza; bouquet garni, soups, sauces, fish, meat, potatoes, other vegetables.
ROSEMARY *(romarin)*. Strong and pungent. Fresh and dried.	Pork, lamb, mutton, duck, goose, infusions, vinegars, fish soups, sauces, risottos, sausages.
SAGE *(sauge)*. Medicinal, aromatic, astringent; bitter if used to excess. Fresh and dried.	Sausages, fish, pork, goose, duck, brines and marinades.

SAVORY *(sarriette)*. Rather peppery and piquant. Summer savory is known in some countries as the bean herb. Winter savory is similar but has a stronger aroma. Fresh and dried.	Green beans, peas, mushrooms, soups, sauces, meats.
SHALLOTS *(echalotes)*. Member of the onion family, but with very delicate flavor.	Bulbs. Many culinary uses, especially fish, meat dishes, poultry, sauces.
SPRING ONIONS *(ciboules)*. *Also* called green onions or scallions. Odoriferous, mildly pungent.	Bulbs and leaves. Peas, salads, egg dishes.
TARRAGON *(estragon)*. Fragrant, taste and smell resembling anise.	Soups, sauces, eggs, fish, meat and poultry dishes; mustard, preserves, vinegar; mixed with butter; decoration of cold dishes.
THYME *(thym)*. Fragrant, pungent. Fresh and dried.	Most culinary preparations; salads, marinades, vinegar.

SPICES (EPICES)

NAME AND DESCRIPTION	CULINARY USES
ALLSPICE *(toute-épice)*. Berry with combined flavors of cinnamon, clove, and nutmeg (not a blend of spices).	Whole or ground: meats, gravies, pickles, curry powder, sausages. Ground: cakes, meatloaf, soups, salads.
ANISE *(anis)*. Mediterranean origin; grows in temperate or hot climates. Delicate, sweet fragrance, medicinal.	Seeds, whole or ground: soups, meats, pastries, breads, cheese, fruits. Leaves: salads, sauces, shellfish.
CARAWAY *(carvi, cumin des prés)*. Origin Asia Minor; grows in temperate climates. Aromatic, distinctive flavor.	Seeds: Austrian specialties, breads, cakes, cheese.

CARDAMOM *(cardamome)*. Pleasantly aromatic. Fruits containing 8 to 16 seeds are harvested before they have ripened, then dried in the sun and sometimes bleached.	Seed, whole or ground: curries, syrups, sausages, pastries.
CAYENNE PEPPER *(poivre rouge)*. Made from the dried ground pods (with seeds) of small very hot capsicums; not related to black or white pepper. To be used with discretion.	Barbecued or curried meats and poultry, cheese dishes, sauces.
CINNAMON *(cannells)* . Made from the bark of a tree of the laurel family, peeled, dried, and trimmed into quills. Both quills (sticks) and ground cinnamon are used. Delicate, sweet, aromatic.	Beverages, pastries, breads, fruits, preserves.
CLOVES *(clous de girofle)*. Flower buds, picked just before opening and dried in the sun. Used whole or ground. Strong, aromatic, high oil content, medicinal.	Meats, vegetables, fruit, sauces, mannades and brines, pickles, preserves.
GINGER *(gingembre)*. Root *(rhizome)* is used; the young shoots crystallized, preserved; the older roots dried or ground into powder. Very fragrant, pungent, medicinal.	Gingerbread, cakes, pastries, sausages, pickles, curries, Japanese food.
MACE *(macis)*. The dried outer shell of the kernel of the fruit of the nutmeg tree, flattened and dried or ground into powder. Fragrant; flavor between nutmeg and cinnamon but stronger.	Sweet baked goods, preserves, cheese, fruit, soups, sauces, meats, fish, shellfish, potatoes, other vegetables.
MUSTARD *(moutarde)*. Two varieties, black (dark-brown seeds) and white (yellow seeds) are both used in preparing dry mustard (powder or mustard flour). The powder must be mixed with liquid to bring out its pungent flavor. Prepared mustards in paste form are widely available commercially; the formula varies with the manufacturer.	Young leaves: salad, or cooked greens. Powder: vinegar, sauces, salad dressings, meats, eggs, pickles. Prepared mustard is used with meats or in sauces.

NUTMEG *(muscade)*. Seed or nut found inside the kernel of the fruit of the nutmeg tree (see mace), dried. Sold whole and grated at home; also available in powdered form. Delicate, pungent.	Cakes, fruit pies, fruits, vegetables, meats, sauces, soups, milk drinks.
PAPRIKA. Red powder made from the ripe dried pods of the larger and sweeter varieties of capsicum;the color, flavor, and pungency varywith the exact variety used. Hungarian paprika has a distinctive sweet aroma. Spanish paprika is usually more pungent than American or Hungarian.	Hungarian dishes; as seasoning and decoration for hors d'oeuvre, fish, shellfish, meat, poultry, salads, vegetables.
PEPPER *(poivre)*. Dried berry of a tropical vine, available whole (peppercorns) or ground. Black peppercorns are the whole berries; white peppercorns are berries fromwhich the outer husks have been removed.	All foods except sweet pastries or desserts. To secure best flavor, either black or white peppercorns should be freshly ground in a pepper mill just before using. Commercially ground pepper loses flavor and is often adulterated. Whole peppercorns are used in soups, stews, sausages.
POPPY SEED *(pavot)*. Dried seed of the poppy plant, white to deep blue. Aromatic, flavor resembles walnut.	Breads, cakes, pastries, canapes, vegetables, sauces.
SAFFRON *(safran)*. The dried stamens of a variety of crocus, whole or powdered. Difficulty of harvesting makes saffron the most expensive of spices. Aromatic, pungent, to be used sparingly.	Soups, sauces, risottos, bouillabaise, curries, pastries, preserves.
TURMERIC *(circuma)*. Powder made from the dried root of a plant of the ginger family. Color varies from light yellow to orange. Sweet, tangy flavor.	A main ingredient of curry powder; Asian dishes, fish, shellfish, meats, pickles, sauces.
VANILLA *(vanille)*. Pod (bean) of a climbing orchid. Used whole, powdered, or as an extract.	Pastries, confectionery, ice cream, and some savory dishes

Various Methods of Cooking and Their Technology

METHODS

IN GENERAL, METHODS OF COOKING ARE DIVIDED into five classes according to the cooking medium: water, steam, air (dry heat), fat, and a combination of two or more of these methods.

COOKING IN WATER

The terms used to designate the water method of cooking are *boiling, parboiling, simmering, poaching,* and *stewing.*

Boiling. Cooking in boiling water (bubbles of steam rise to the surface and break). Pure water boils under standard atmospheric pressure at 212°F. However, it boils at lower temperatures at high altitudes, and mixtures such as sugar syrup boil at higher temperatures. This method is used for the following purposes:

- ❧ To make stock from bones where no meat is present; boiling is necessary to extract the flavor from the bones.
- ❧ To reduce or concentrate meat stock or fish stock by evaporating part of the water. These robust-flavored reduced stocks are used in soups and sauces having meat or fish flavor, in braising, and in glazing.
- ❧ To cook cereals, pastas, and boiled dumplings, making them more digestible and palatable by softening their cellulose, swelling their starch grains, and developing their flavor.
- ❧ To make sugar syrup, cooked candies and frostings, and meatless sauces and dessert sauces containing starch.

Parboiling. Partial cooking by boiling in water. It is used when another method is employed to complete the process or when strong flavors or water-soluble elements are to be removed and fresh water added to finish cooking.

Simmering. Cooking in very hot water below boiling point (180° to 210°F). At simmering point tiny bubbles form slowly and break before they reach the surface. This is a slow method, used for making stocks from meats, chicken, or fish, which require long, slow cooking, for cooking tough cuts of meat, tongue, country-cured ham, dried beans and peas, and certain milk and egg dishes requiring slow cooking.

Poaching. Cooking in water or other liquid just below boiling point, either basting the food with the hot liquid or covering with a lid so the steam will perform a self-basting action. Foods which may be cooked by this method are eggs, fish, vegetables, and some raw fruits.

Stewing. Cooking below boiling point in just enough liquid to produce steam. If rapid boiling were to take place, the small quantity of water would evaporate. Foods cooked by this method require long, slow cooking in a saucepan or kettle covered with a tight-fitting lid. This method is used for tough cuts of meat (cut into small pieces), poultry, certain vegetables, and fresh and dried fruits.

COOKING WITH STEAM

Steaming is cooking in moist heat without having the food in direct contact with water. The advantage of steam cooking is that the minerals, vitamins, and flavor of the foods are not destroyed to the extent that they are by boiling in water. There are three commonly used methods.

Steaming by use of a steamer. Place the food in the perforated inset pan. Place the inset pan in the saucepan containing water. Cover and bring to the boiling point. The steam from the boiling water will pass through the perforations and cook the food. This process is recommended for cooking vegetables, but not meats. Steamer pans are available in various sizes and may contain one to three inset pans for cooking more than one food at one time.

Waterless cooking. Steam is generated by the water that is in the food. No water is added. This method of cooking should be done over very low heat in a heavy-bottomed saucepan with a tight-fitting lid. This is an excellent method of cooking soft fruits such as plums, berries, and cherries.

Pressure cooker. This method cooks food in a shorter time than does any other method, because the cooking is done in an atmosphere of steam at a temperature higher than the normal 212°F boiling point. The small amount of water used conserves nutrients and flavor. Foods suitable for cooking at such high pressure are tough meats and poultry, tongue, potatoes, and mature beets that require long cooking. Pressure-cooking is not recommended for quick-cooking vegetables, since it is easy to overcook them.

COOKING WITH DRY HEAT

Dry-heat cooking is cooking with air as the medium of heat transfer. The cooking terms used to designate this method are *broiling, roasting,* and *baking.*

Broiling. Cooking by dry heat on a grill over an open fire, under the heat unit (broiler) of an electric or gas range, or in a skillet on top of the range (pan-broiling).

Broiling is suited to tender, small cuts of meat, such as steaks, chops, cutlets, and ham slices, as well as sausage and other meat patties.

To use a broiler, place the meat on the rack in the broiler pan without water. Place the broiler two to five inches from the source of heat, the distance from the heat depending on the thickness of the cut of the meat. Cook meat on one side, then turn and cook on the other side to the desired degree of doneness. Serve at once.

To pan-broil, put the meat in a skillet and cook on top of the stove, uncovered, without fat or liquid. Cook slowly, turning occasionally, and pouring off fat as it accumulates. Cook to the desired degree of doneness.

In both methods of broiling, slash the fat around the edges of the meat to prevent curling.

Roasting. Originally, roasting meant cooking meat on a spit over a hot fire, turning the meat frequently or constantly. This method went out of style with the development of ovens, and roasting by dry heat became the vogue. Now with the increased interest in outdoor cooking and the availability of motor-driven spits, this method of meat cookery has been revived. It is a simple, delicious way of cooking meat and is also a good method to use for cooking large pieces such as leg of lamb and large chunky roasts, as well as small and large fowl. The size of the spit determines the size and weight of the meat it will accommodate. Consult the directions that come with the equipment to avoid over-loading and to obtain best results.

Oven-roasting is still the most generally used method of roasting. It is done in two ways: at constant low temperature (300° to 350°F); and by searing, which is coagulating the surface of the meat by high heat. The low, constant heat achieves meat with less shrinkage. This method has two disadvantages: the cooking time is increased and browning is insufficient. The latter objection may be overcome by increasing the temperature at the end of the roasting period for browning purposes.

Some prefer the flavor, aroma, and color of roasts cooked by the searing method of roasting. The meat is first seared in a pan over high heat on top of the stove, or placed in a very hot oven (450° to 500°F) for the first few minutes of the cooking period in order to coagulate the surface protein and for browning. The roasting is then continued at a lower temperature.

Baking. The method used in baking is essentially the same as in roasting, both using dry heat. However, when we speak of roasting, we generally refer to meats (or chestnuts), and when we speak of baking we usually think of breads, cakes, cookies, pies, rolls, and to some extent vegetables and fruits.

When food is baked, a crust forms on the parts that are directly exposed to the hot air and on the bottoms and sides where the heat is so intense that it penetrates the pans.

Baking is done at various temperatures, each suited to the particular food being cooked. Therefore, it is important to have well-insulated, thermostatically controlled ovens. This is particularly important with products made from batters and doughs, and with pastries, souffles, and other dishes containing eggs or cheese, where the cooking temperature means the difference between success and failure.

Fresh vegetables and fruits containing enough moisture to prevent drying, such as potatoes, onions, carrots, beets, apples, bananas, and pears, may be baked whole in their skins by direct oven heat, or they may be pared, sliced, and baked in a covered casserole. The casserole serves much the same purpose as the skins in holding in the steam. To prevent baked starchy vegetables from becoming soggy, prick the skins when baking is finished to allow the steam to escape.

COOKING IN FAT

There are three methods of cooking in fat, or frying: deep frying, pan-frying, and sautéing.

Deep frying. Cooking foods in hot fat deep enough to allow the food to be completely submerged. Foods suitable for deep frying are small units, such as doughnuts, croquettes, fritters, oysters, fish, soft-shell crabs, and some sliced vegetables, such as potatoes, onions, eggplant, and parsnips. The chief advantage of this method over pan-frying is that because of the high temperature the foods will absorb a minimum of fat during cooking.

Fats for deep frying include cottonseed, corn, canola, peanut, soybean oils, vegetable shortenings, or high-grade lard.

In the average home, the best utensil for deep frying is a deep kettle made of heavy aluminum or iron, equipped with a frying basket. The surest method of determining the temperature of the fat is to have a deep-fat thermometer clipped to the side of the pan or kettle. If observed closely, it protects against underheating or overheating the fat. If a thermometer is not available, rough tests may be made with a 1-inch cube of bread dropped into the fat. If the cube browns in 40 seconds, the fat is suitable for precooked foods, and if it browns in 60 seconds the fat is hot enough for uncooked foods.

All foods to be fried in deep fat should be at room temperature, and all excess moisture should be removed to prevent cooling and spattering the fat. Dry raw vegetables, such as potatoes for chips or french fries, thoroughly between clean towels. The food may be first rolled in fine dry cracker crumbs or breadcrumbs, then dipped in egg beaten with milk, using 1 to 2 tablespoons of milk for each egg, and then rolled in crumbs again. Another method is to dip each piece of food in a thin batter, using as little batter as possible in order to give a crisp, delicate crust.

To eliminate the excess fat, it is important to drain the food on paper towels as soon as it is removed from the hot fat, placing it on the towels in a single layer—never piling pieces of food one on top of another.

Pan-frying. Cooking in a small amount of fat in an uncovered skillet over heat. This differs from pan-broiling in that the fat is permitted to accumulate in the pan and that meat and vegetables may first be floured or breaded to give a brown, crisp crust.

Sautéing. The French word *sauté* literally means "jumped." This is cooking in a skillet lightly greased to make it possible to "flip" or turn the food without its sticking to the pan. The food is fried lightly and quickly and is turned several times in the process.

COMBINATION METHODS OF COOKING

Methods of cooking that consist of combinations of two of the methods already described include braising, pot-roasting, *à la poele*, au gratin, and glazing.

Braising (fricasséeing). These terms represent a method that consists of first sautéing and then cooking in a small amount of liquid in a covered saucepan or Dutch oven.

Pot-roasting. A form of braising, this is the term applied to cooking large pieces of meat. The meat is first browned and may then either be cooked slowly in a covered pan on top of the range or in the oven. Vegetables are sometimes added near the end of the cooking period, in time for them to be done when the meat has become tender.

A la poele. A term in French cookery applied to a method of pot-roasting meat or poultry that is a combination of pan-frying and steaming. The procedure is as follows: Brown meat in hot fat over moderately high heat, using the same casserole in which the meat is to be cooked. Remove meat and set aside. Add 2 or 3 sliced carrots and onions and a sliced rib of celery to the casserole. Cover and cook over low heat about 5 minutes without browning. Return meat to casserole. Sprinkle with salt and black pepper and pour melted butter over the top. Cover and cook in a low oven until meat is done, basting two or three times with pan juices. Remove meat to a warmed platter. Skim from the pan juices all but about 2 tablespoons fat. Scrape the bottom of the casserole and mash the vegetables into the remaining juice. Heat, season to taste, and strain the sauce into a gravy boat.

Au gratin. This French term designates a dish in which the food is mixed with a sauce, covered with buttered breadcrumbs, and cooked in the oven until the food is done and a brown crust has formed over the top. The sauce should be sufficient to cover the food but not enough to become thin when it combines with the juices released from the other ingredients. This type of dish may be made with either raw or precooked foods. In the latter, the dish may be browned under the broiler instead of in the oven. This is the authentic method of preparing au gratin dishes.

Another method, which is erroneously called au gratin or gratinéed, specifies the use of cheese. It is used mainly for potatoes, vegetables, and various kinds of seafoods and meats, with the addition of cheese. The method of preparation and cooking is the same as that for the authentic au gratin dish, except that the top is sprinkled with grated cheese and the dish may be made either with or without breadcrumbs.

Glazing. This operation is the application of a coating that gives food a smooth, glossy surface, thereby improving its appearance and flavor. It is applied to both hot and cold dishes.

Materials used for glazing include butter, thick sauces such as Béchamel or Mornay, grated cheese, reduced meat juices acquired in cooking, reduced meat stock, gelatin, jelly, honey, corn syrup, simple sugar syrups, sugar (granulated, brown, and confectioners), and chocolate. Some of the methods of glazing both hot and cold dishes follow.

GLAZING WITH SAUCES:

- **Butter sauce.** Cover food (such as fillet of sole) heavily with melted butter, then brown quickly in a very hot preheated broiler, having the dish in a large pan of cold water to prevent the butter from curdling.
- **Thick sauces.** Coat the food with a thick sauce, usually Béchamel or Mornay, and sprinkle with grated cheese. Brown quickly in a very hot preheated broiler.
- **Meat juices.** Baste meat or poultry (braised or roasted) with reduced juices acquired in cooking and then subject it to intense oven heat.

GLAZING WITH JELLY, HONEY, OR SYRUP:

- **Meat.** Mix equal parts jelly, honey, or syrup, and prepared mustard. Spread over meat (usually ham), and bake in a preheated oven (325° to 350°F) until glazed and browned. If mustard is not desired, replace it with water, using 1 tablespoon to each ½ cup jelly.
- **Cold desserts.** Make glaze with water instead of mustard, heat, and use to glaze cold desserts, such as pies and tarts.

GLAZING WITH SUGAR

- **Vegetables.** Sprinkle granulated white or brown sugar over vegetables and place in a hot oven to glaze and brown.
- **Cake.** Sprinkle white granulated sugar over cake. Bake in a hot preheated broiler, leaving door open and watching closely, until sugar melts and forms a brown glaze.
- **Crème Brulée.** Sift sugar over baked custard made with light cream and caramelize thesugar under the broiler. Bake in a very low preheated broiler (250°F), leaving door open, until sugar melts and forms a smooth caramel topping.

Other glazes are described in various recipes throughout the book.

GENERAL RULES FOR COOKING VEGETABLES AND FRUITS

FRESH VEGETABLES

Fresh vegetables should be cooked immediately before serving in a large amount of water and for the shortest amount of time possible. Use several quarts of water depending on the amount of vegetables being cooked. Before vegetables are put in, add salt to the boiling water. Then put in the vegetable, and quickly bring to the boiling point again. Cook only until vegetables are crisp-tender.

Red vegetables, such as beets and red cabbage, take on a bluish tone when cooked in alkaline water. To prevent this, add 1 teaspoon lemon juice or vinegar to the cooking water.

Vegetables of the cabbage family, onions, and turnips develop a strong flavor and odor if overcooked. Cook such vegetables by any of these methods:

- Cut vegetables into small pieces so that the vegetables cook so quickly that no objectionable flavor develops. It is important that the pieces are all the same size so that they cook at the same rate.
- Whole vegetables cut in large pieces, produce a milder flavor, but more of the nutrients are lost.

Panned or skillet vegetables. French and Chinese chefs are famous for this simple method, which produces crisp-tender vegetables with delicious flavor. Vegetables lending themselves to this method are cabbage, celery, carrots, green beans, potatoes, and spinach and other greens. Shred, slice, or dice vegetables and place in a heavy saucepan or skillet with 1 or 2 tablespoons of melted butter or margarine. Mix lightly. Cook, covered, until vegetables sizzle, then reduce heat. Cook only until crisp-tender, stirring once or twice. The French rinse a couple of lettuce leaves in cold water and place them, dripping wet, over the vegetables. Steam is produced by moisture given off by the lettuce.

Baked vegetables. Baking is an excellent method of cooking vegetables to retain minerals and vitamins, especially for those vegetables containing enough water to prevent drying out. When they are cooked whole, the skins hold in the steam, so they remain moist.

To cook in the skin, just wash vegetables and bake until tender. Rubbing skins of potatoes with fat prevents crustiness. Overbaking starchy vegetables, or failure to open skins as soon as vegetables are done, results in sogginess.

Another method is to bake sliced, diced, or shredded vegetables, with seasonings and a very small amount of liquid, in a covered casserole. The cover holds in the steam, which prevents the vegetables from becoming too dry.

DRIED VEGETABLES

The first step in cooking dried vegetables, such as beans, is to wash them thoroughly, changing the water until it is clear. Then rehydrate them by one of these methods:

- ❧ Soak vegetables 5 or 6 hours or overnight in enough cold water to cover generously.
- ❧ Cover vegetable generously with boiling water and boil 2 minutes, then allow to stand for 1 hour before cooking. Drain off that water and cook the beans in fresh water.

Many process-dried vegetables, such as onions and potatoes, rehydrate adequately during cooking. Follow the cooking directions on the package for best results.

FRESH FRUITS

Although fruit is delicious eaten raw, there are many good reasons for cooking it: to give variety to the menu, to increase keeping qualities, to develop palatability in some fruits, to soften the cellulose, and to cook the starch. The method of cooking fruits is determined by the product desired. For making purées, sauces, and other products that do not require a definite shape, the fruit is first stewed quickly in a small amount of water to soften it and the sugar is added last. If the fruit must hold its shape after cooking—cooked whole apples or fruits for compotes, for example—cook, without stirring, in sugar syrup. In general, cook fruits a short time in a deep, covered saucepan for retention of flavor and nutrition, using a minimum amount of sugar.

FROZEN FRUITS

Fruits may be frozen whole, sliced, or crushed, with or without sugar. Generally, they are thawed before using. Frozen berries such as strawberries and raspberries can be served while still slightly frozen unless they are to be cooked. Use frozen fruits as sauces, in frozen desserts, over ice cream, and for making pies, preserves, and jams.

DRIED FRUITS

Tenderized packaged dried fruits are ready for cooking and do not need soaking. However, dried fruits that are not tenderized should be washed and soaked 30 minutes to several hours in two to four times as much water as fruit. Cook slowly until tender, in the water in which fruit was soaked. Add sugar last.

THE BASES OF
FINE FRENCH COOKERY

The rich variety of the French cuisine is based on a number of different preparations that are used in a great many ways. These preparations include doughs and batters; stocks made with meat, poultry, or fish, and the essences, glazes, and jellies made from stock; the court bouillons used in poaching fish and vegetables; roux for thickening sauces; marinades and brines; forcemeats *(farces)* and quenelles; and *appareils* (mixtures that go into the making of dishes).

When one knows how to make all these, the preparation of the dishes in the following chapters is greatly simplified. For convenience, the recipes are grouped here. Finally, a number of the garnishes that in France traditionally accompany certain dishes are listed and described.

DOUGHS AND BATTERS

THE TWO BASIC INGREDIENTS OF all doughs and batters are flour and liquid. When the proportion of liquid to flour results in a mixture thin enough to be stirred with a spoon and either poured or dropped from a spoon, it is a batter. Batters are used for making pancakes, waffles, fritters, cakes, and muffins. Mixtures that are thick enough to roll or knead (too stiff to stir with a spoon or pour) are doughs. Doughs are used for yeast breads, rolls, biscuits, pastry, and some cookies. A dough may be soft (barely stiff enough to handle) or stiff.

With the addition of fat, eggs, salt, leavening agent, fruit, nuts, and flavoring to these two basic ingredients an endless variety of breads, cakes, cookies, pastries dumplings, and croquettes can be made.

Success in making dishes from batters and doughs requires a good recipe, high-quality ingredients, the proper size of mixing bowl, the proper size of baking pan, and an oven equipped with an accurate thermostat to control the heat. Then it is up to the cook to measure the ingredients accurately, to mix and handle them skillfully, and to bake them for the proper time at the proper temperature, checking the baking to the proper "point" (a French expression) by means of suitable tests. It is important that a beginner be taught to recognize certain characteristics of various finished products so that he or she may be able, to judge the finished dish.

To ensure accurate measurements, standard measuring cups and spoons are important. Only level measurements should be used.

The most commonly used methods of mixing batters and doughs are:

The muffin method. The dry ingredients are sifted together into a mixing bowl. Beaten eggs, liquid, and melted fat are added. The liquid ingredients are then blended with the dry ingredients with varying amounts of stirring, depending on the mixture. For batters with minimum amounts of fat and sugar, such as for muffins, stir only until ingredients are blended, about 28 strokes. Richer batters may be stirred more.

The cake method. The butter or shortening and the sugar are mixed together until fluffy, the eggs are beaten in, usually one at a time, or they may be beaten separately, the yolks being added at this stage and the beaten whites folded in as the last step. Then the dry and liquid ingredients are added alternately, beginning and ending with flour.

The pastry method. The dry ingredients are sifted together into a mixing bowl. The fat is cut into the dry mixture, the liquid is sprinkled over the top, and the whole mass is tossed very lightly only until its ingredients are blended. Care must be taken not to stir the dough after the liquid has been added since this would develop the gluten in the flour and would make a tough pastry.

Yeast breads, sponge cakes, cream puffs *(choux paste)* are mixed by special methods adapted to each. The optimum amount of manipulation varies with the type of product and with the character, proportions, and temperature of the ingredients.

Different types of batters and doughs must be mixed by special methods and to different degrees in order to obtain the texture required for the particular product. Considerable kneading is required to develop the gluten (the protein in flour that gives it the elastic property) in yeast dough. Only a very little kneading is required for biscuit dough. Pastry dough should never be kneaded; it must be handled as little as possible in order to obtain a tender, flaky product.

French Bread

1 envelope active dry yeast	½ teaspoon salt
½ teaspoon sugar	2 tablespoons softened shortening or butter
1 cup lukewarm water	About 3½ cups sifted all-purpose flour

Combine the first three ingredients and let stand 5 minutes to soften. Add salt, shortening or butter, and 2 cups of the flour. Turn dough onto a floured pastry board and gradually knead in remaining flour, adding more if needed. Knead dough until it is smooth and satiny. Cover and let it rise until doubled in size. Place dough on a lightly floured board and pound it lightly with a rolling pin to deflate it. Cover and let dough rise 30 minutes in a warm place (80° to 85°F). Divide the dough in half and shape each half into a roll about 1½ inches in diameter. Place on lightly greased baking sheets, put in a warm place, and let rise until doubled in size. Brush with water and make diagonal slashes in the top with a sharp knife. Place in a preheated oven (400°F) with a shallow pan of hot water in the bottom of the oven. Bake 45 minutes, or until the bread is crusty and brown. Makes 2 loaves.

Croissants

2 envelopes (2 scant tablespoons) active dry yeast	1½ cups lukewarm milk
¼ cup lukewarm water	1 teaspoon salt
1½ tablespoons sugar	¾ pound (3 sticks) butter
4 cups sifted all-purpose flour	1 egg yolk beaten with 1 tablespoon milk

Soften yeast in lukewarm water with 1 teaspoon of the sugar. Stir in 1 cup of the flour. Shape into a ball, cut a cross (+) in the top, place it in a bowl, cover, and keep in a warm place (80° to 85°F) to rise until doubled in bulk. Add the remaining sugar, flour, milk, and salt. Mix well and knead until dough is smooth and elastic. Place dough in a greased bowl, grease the top of the dough, cover, and let rise in a warm place until it has doubled in bulk. Roll the dough into a rectangle ½ inch thick. Wash the butter in cold water, working it well and pressing it in a clean cloth to remove excess water. Spread the butter over the dough and fold the dough into thirds, making three layers. Roll dough out again and fold it into thirds. Wrap it in waxed paper and chill well, preferably overnight. When ready to use, roll the dough out and fold the ends to the center. Roll out and fold again twice more. Chill thoroughly, about 1 hour. Divide dough in half and roll each half into a circle ⅛ inch thick. Cut each circle into 18 triangles or wedges. Starting at the wide end, roll the wedges of dough to the tip end, pressing to seal the end. Shape into crescents and place on greased baking sheets. Brush the egg yolk mixture over the tops of the crescents. Cover them with waxed paper and let them rise in a warm place until doubled in bulk. Bake in a preheated oven (400°F) 5 minutes. Reduce heat to 350°F and bake 15 minutes, or until crescents are golden brown. Makes 3 dozen.

 Brioches

2 envelopes active dry yeast	1 teaspoon salt
⅓ cup warm water (110° to 115°F)	¾ cup (1½ sticks) butter
2 tablespoons sugar	2 large eggs
3½ cups sifted all-purpose flour	

Soften yeast in warm water in a small bowl along with 1 teaspoon of the sugar. Stir in ¾ cup of the flour. Cover and let rise in a warm place (80° to 85°F) for 1 hour or until the mixture has doubled in bulk. In a 1arge mixing bowl, mix together the remaining flour, sugar, and salt. Add the butter, cutting it in until the particles are the size of peas. Blend in the eggs.

Add yeast-flour mixture and mix well. Knead on a well-floured board until dough is smooth and satiny, about 8 minutes. Cover and let rise in a warm place until doubled in bulk, about 1 hour. Shape three-fourths of the dough into 24 two-inch balls. Place in greased small tart pans or muffin pans. Shape remaining dough into 24 one-inch balls. Make a depression in the top of each large ball, and place the small ball in it. (This forms the topknot.) Cover and let rise in a warm place until doubled in size. With scissors, make four light slits in the dough of the larger ball around the topknot. Bake in a preheated hot oven (400°F) 10 to 12 minutes or until golden brown. Makes 3½ dozen rolls.

Cream Puff Pastry or Choux Paste

2 cups water
1 cup (2 sticks) butter
¼ teaspoon salt

2 cups sifted all-purpose flour
8 large eggs

Mix the first 3 ingredients together in a 1½-quart saucepan. Bring to the boiling point. Remove from heat and stir in all the flour at one time, using a wooden spoon. Beat vigorously. Return to heat and cook until the mixture leaves the sides of the pan and forms a very stiff ball. Remove from heat and beat in eggs one at a time, beating each until it is completely absorbed before adding another. Do not overheat, as this reduces the volume and the consistency for piping purposes. Squeeze paste from a pastry bag or drop from a tablespoon 2 inches apart onto ungreased baking sheets. Bake in a preheated oven (425°F) 30 to 35 minutes, or until golden brown. Do not underbake. Turn off oven heat. Prick puffs with a knife to allow steam to escape, and leave in oven 20 minutes to allow centers to dry out. Cool. Split and fill with creamed mixtures for entrées or with cream fillings for desserts. Makes 24 large puffs.

To make small hors d'oeuvre puffs, drop the dough from a teaspoon and bake 20 to 25 minutes. This recipe will make 48 small puffs.

Choux Paste for Quenelles, Gnocchi, & Dumplings

2 cups milk
½ cup (1 stick) butter
2½ cups sifted all-purpose flour

6 large eggs
¾ cup grated Parmesan cheese
1 cup grated Gruyère cheese

Use the milk, butter, flour, and eggs to make a choux paste (see previous recipe), then beat the cheeses into the warm dough. Let the mixture stand about 10 minutes. Then shape into 1-inch balls. Drop these in boiling stock or boiling salted water (½ teaspoon salt to 1 quart water). Cook until dumplings double in size and rise to the top. Serve hot with Mornay Sauce. Sprinkle with additional grated cheese. Makes 6 servings.

Cheese Puffs

Beat 1 cup grated Parmesan or Swiss cheese into 2 cups warm Choux Paste. Drop the dough from a teaspoon onto ungreased baking sheets and bake 20 to 25 minutes. Serve hot or cold, with or without filling, as hors d'oeuvre or cocktail accompaniments.

Gnocchi Baked with Cheese

Drain cooked Gnocchi Choux Paste and arrange in a buttered baking dish. Sprinkle with ½ cup grated Parmesan cheese and dot with 2 tablespoons butter. Bake in a pre-heated moderate oven (350°F) 20 minutes. Serve at once.

Noodle Dough

3 cups sifted all-purpose flour
¼ teaspoon salt
4 large eggs

Place flour and salt in a large mixing bowl. Add eggs and mix with your hands until the dough is stiff enough to be gathered into a ball. Knead on a pastry board until all the crumbly particles have been incorporated. This dough should be very stiff; if necessary, knead in a little more flour. Divide the dough into thirds. Roll one portion at a time into a very thin sheet with a lightly floured rolling pin. Cover with a clean towel and let stand 30 minutes, then roll each sheet up as for a jelly roll and cut into wide or narrow strips as desired. Lay out on baking sheets to dry well. Cover. Store in covered containers and use as needed. Makes about 1 pound.

Puff Pastry or Pâte Feuilletée

This dough is also called puff paste.

1½ cups (3 sticks) butter
3 cups sifted all-purpose flour,
**   plus 2 tablespoons**

¾ teaspoon salt
2 teaspoons lemon juice
⅔ cup ice water

Cut each stick of butter lengthwise into three strips. Sprinkle waxed paper with 2 tablespoons flour, and arrange the butter strips over the flour. Wrap up the butter and refrigerate until ready to use. Mix flour and salt together in a mixing bowl. Combine lemon juice and ice water and stir into the flour, using a circular motion. The dough should be firm yet slightly sticky. Knead dough 20 minutes. It should be smooth and satiny. Cover dough and let it rest 20 minutes.

Roll dough ¼ inch thick into a 2-by-8-inch rectangle on a well-floured board. Place chilled butter strips side by side on half the dough to within ½ inch of the edges. Fold the remaining half of the dough over the butter. Press edges together firmly with fingertips. Wrap in waxed paper or foil and refrigerate 30 minutes.

Tap dough lightly several times with rolling pin to flatten the butter. Quickly roll out dough on a well-floured pastry board to a 12-by-8-inch rectangle about ¼ inch thick. Be careful not to roll over the edges of the dough until it is 12 inches long; then roll over the edges very gently. Fold both ends of the dough to the center of the rectangle, making sure edges and corners are even. Press edges together firmly. Fold dough in half to make 4 layers. Wrap in waxed paper or foil and refrigerate 30 minutes.

Roll dough again into a rectangle, fold as before, and chill 30 minutes. Repeat the rolling, folding, and chilling 3 more times. The last chilling period should be for 3 hours.

Use Puff Pastry for making Patty Shells, vol-au-vents, pastry horns for cream filling, croissants, palm leaves, and pie crust, according to directions in individual recipes.

Patty Shells *or* Bouchées *or* Vol-au-Vents

Make the recipe for Puff Pastry and divide into thirds. Roll one portion at a time, keeping the others refrigerated until ready to use. Roll paste to ⅛ inch thick on a well-floured board. For each patty shell, cut three 3-inch pastry circles, using a sharp 3-inch fluted cookie cutter. (For 12 patty shells, 36 circles.) Place 12 of the pastry circles on an ungreased baking sheet. Brush surface of each with 1 egg yolk beaten with 1½ teaspoons cold water. Do not let egg drip on the sides. Using a 2-inch cutter, cut out centers of 12 pastry circles, making a ring as for doughnuts. Place one ring on each of the pastry circles on the baking sheet. Brush with egg yolk. Press a 1½-inch cookie cutter into the centers of remaining 12 pastry circles, but do not cut through it. Place these on top of the first ring. Brush with egg yolk. Bake in a preheated oven (450°F) for 10 minutes. Reduce oven temperature to 350°F and bake 20 minutes, or until shells are golden. Remove the indented centers of the top layer with a pointed knife. Return the shells to the oven and bake 10 minutes longer to dry out centers. Fill the shells with mixtures such as creamed chicken, shrimp, or vegetables. Replace the tops. Makes 12 patty shells.

Cream Cornets *or* Horns

Roll out Puff Pastry on a lightly floured pastry board to ⅛ inch thick and about 30 inches long. Cut into strips about ½ inch wide (for metal horn tubes 5½ inches long). If smaller tubes are desired, use shorter strips of pastry. Beginning at the small end of a metal horn tube, start wrapping the pastry strips around it, overlapping the edges slightly. Do not pull or stretch pastry. Repeat with remaining strips. Chill. Brush tops and sides with beaten egg. Sprinkle with granulated sugar, preferably coarse sugar if available. Place horns 1 inch apart on paper-lined baking sheets. Bake in a preheated oven (425°F) for 10 minutes. Reduce oven temperature to 350°F and bake until pastry is golden brown. Remove tubes from pastry horns immediately by twisting the tubes to free them from the pastry. Cool. Fill with pastry cream or sweetened whipped cream. Makes 18.

Plain Pastry Dough or Pâte Brisée

FOR A 9-INCH PASTRY SHELL:

1 cup sifted all-purpose flour
¼ teaspoon salt
¼ cup (½ stick) butter

1½ tablespoons vegetable shortening
About 3 tablespoons cold water

Sift flour and salt into a mixing bowl. Add butter and shortening and cut them in until the mixture resembles coarse meal. Add water and blend it in quickly, using a tossing motion. Press the dampened particles together into a ball. Roll into a circle ⅛ inch thick and 2 inches larger than the diameter of the pie plate. Carefully fold the dough into quarters and place it in the pie plate. Unfold and fit it loosely in the plate without stretching or pulling the pastry. Trim the edge of the pastry ½ inch larger than the outside rim of the plate. Flute or crimp edge with your fingers or a fork. If the filling is to be baked in the shell, bake as directed in the individual recipe. If the crust is to be filled after it has been baked, prebake the shell: Prick the bottom and sides of the pastry with a fork, then fit a smaller pan or bean bag into the pie crust. Bake in a preheated oven (425°F) 12 to 15 minutes, removing the smaller pan or bean bag after the pastry has baked 10 minutes. Bake until golden brown. Makes one 9-inch pie crust. For a two-crust 9-inch pie, double the ingredients, except use only about 5 tablespoons cold water.

Sweet Pie Pastry

1½ cups sifted all-purpose flour
⅓ cup sifted confectioners' sugar
⅛ teaspoon salt

½ cup (1 stick) butter
3 tablespoons milk or cold water

Sift the first 3 ingredients together into a mixing bowl. Add butter and cut it in with a pastry blender until the mixture resembles coarse meal. Add milk or water. Mix lightly to form a dough.

For individual tart shells, divide dough into 8 equal parts. Roll each to 1/16 to ⅛ inch thick. Fit into tart pans measuring 3½ inches across the top and 2 inches across the bottom. Prick the bottom and sides of pastry with a fork to prevent blistering. Bake in a preheated oven (350°F) 15 to 20 minutes. Cool thoroughly, then remove tart shells from pans. Fill with pastry cream or fruit fillings. Makes 8 tart shells.

For a 9-inch or 10-inch pie, roll pastry to ⅛ inch thick and fit it into a 9-inch or 10-inch pie plate. Trim dough and turn under and flute edge. Prick bottom and sides with a fork. Bake as for tart shells.

Fritter Batter

1 cup sifted all-purpose flour
½ teaspoon salt
1 large egg, slightly beaten

¾ cup milk
1 tablespoon butter, melted

Sift together flour and salt. Combine egg, milk, and butter, and stir into dry ingredients. Dip vegetables such as sliced onions, sliced zucchini, cauliflower, spinach leaves, and okra; shrimp or other shellfish; or Cheddar cheese cubes in the batter. Fry in deep hot fat preheated to 370°F 3 to 4 minutes. Drain on absorbent paper. Makes about 6 servings.

Sweet Fritter Batter

To the flour in Fritter Batter add 2 tablespoons sugar and 1 teaspoon doubleacting baking powder. Use to make fruit fritters.

Basic Crêpe Batter

1 cup sifted all-purpose flour
½ teaspoon salt
3 large eggs, beaten

2 cups milk
2 tablespoons butter, melted

Sift together the flour and salt and set aside. Combine eggs and milk and stir into the flour mixture. Blend in melted butter. Pour 2 tablespoons batter for each crêpe into a hot, lightly greased 6-inch skillet. Tilt to coat bottom. Cook until browned on the bottom. (When crêpes are ready to turn, bubbles will form over the top.) Turn bottom and brown the other side. Stack crêpes in an ovenware plate and place in the oven to keep warm. Makes about 20 crêpes.

STOCKS

THE STOCKPOT IS THE GREATEST TREASURE of the French chef, for in it lies the secret of French sauces, soups, aspics, and glazes.

Stocks are made by simmering (not boiling) meat, poultry, or fish, and vegetables, fresh herbs, and spices in water for several hours. They are used for braising meats and vegetables and as the liquid for making meat-, poultry-, and fish-flavored sauces, soups, and stews. If stock of stronger flavor is desired, it may be concentrated (reduced) by cooking down to a smaller volume after the bones, meat, and vegetables are removed and the stock strained and degreased. In French cooking this essence is used as a base for sauces, for making aspics, and for glazing.

The stocks are made from cracked beef and veal bones; meats such as beef, veal, and poultry; soup vegetables such as onions, leeks, carrots, celery, and mushroom stems; plus spices and fresh herbs. Starchy vegetables cloud stock and should never be used, nor should strong-flavored vegetables.

All solid particles should be removed by straining the stock through a very fine sieve or through two layers of cheesecloth wrung out in cold water. All fat should be removed, either while the stock is still hot or by refrigerating the stock and then lifting off the solidified fat. The clear stock may then be made into soups, sauces, and so on.

Plain White Stock

3 pounds shoulder of veal	2 medium-sized carrots
4 pounds knuckle of veal	2 medium-large onions
4 pounds chicken giblets or backs, necks, and wings	4 ribs celery
3 tablespoons salt	Large bouquet garni
About 6 quarts of cold water	4 leeks

Bone meat and tie it up with a string. Crack bones, wash chicken parts, and place all in a 12-quart stockpot. Add salt. Add water to cover the ingredients by 1 inch. Bring to the simmering point. Skim off and discard any scum that rises to the surface. Peel carrots and onions and add them along with celery and bouquet garni, to stockpot. Wash leeks thoroughly and add to stockpot. Bring to the simmering point again. Reduce heat and simmer 4 hours or more, never allowing the water to boil. Add more boiling water if water evaporates to the level of the ingredients. Remove meat and bones and let stock cool. Strain through two layers of rinsed cheesecloth. Refrigerate stock, uncovered, until fat has hardened on the surface, then lift off and discard fat. (If desired, the fat can be removed while the stock is hot.) Use for making White Sauce, Velouté Sauce, gravies, aspics, and soups. Makes about 4 quarts.

White Chicken Stock

Proceed as for Plain White Stock, but add a whole 3-pound chicken, or 3 pounds chicken giblets, backs, necks, or wings.

Beef and Veal Brown Stock

5 pounds lean beef soup meat
1 pound rind of salt pork
6 pounds knuckle of veal
2 pounds each beef and
    veal bones
2 medium-large onions

3 tablespoons vegetable oil
2 large carrots
About 7 quarts cold water
3 tablespoons salt
Large bouquet garni
1 large clove garlic

Cut meat and pork rind into large pieces. Crack bones. Peel and slice onions. Brown all, including bones and carrots, in the oil. Add 2 quarts of the water and the salt. Simmer 1 hour, partially covered. Add remaining water, or enough to cover ingredients by 1 inch. Add bouquet garni and garlic. Simmer 5 or more hours, removing scum from surface from time to time. Remove meat and bones from the stock, strain stock nd skim off fat as described for Plain White Stock. Use in making brown sauces, braising, stews, and in meat jellies. Makes about 4 quarts.

Quick Beef and Veal Brown Stock

3 pounds beef soup meat
3 pounds cracked beef bones
3 pounds cracked veal bones
1 cup sliced carrots
1 cup sliced onion

8½ quarts cold water
3 ribs celery
3 sprigs parsley
1 bay leaf
1 tablespoon salt

Cut meat into small pieces and place in a roasting pan with beef bones and veal bones, carrots, and onion. Cook in a preheated oven (450°F) 40 to 50 minutes, or until meat and vegetables are browned, turning 2 to 3 times to brown uniformly. Remove pan from oven and drain off and discard fat. Transfer meat, bones, and vegetables to a stockpot. Pour 1 cup of the water into the roasting pan and heat about 30 seconds, scraping all the browned particles from the bottom of the pan. Pour into the stockpot. Rinse the pan with another cup of water and pour into the stockpot. Add remaining water and salt. Bring to the boiling point and simmer 2-3 hours. Remove bones and meat from the stock. Strain. Either remove fat while hot or refrigerate and remove solidified fat from the surface. Makes about 4 quarts.

Brown Veal Stock

6 pounds shoulder of veal
½ cup vegetable oil
5 pounds knuckle of veal
2 pounds veal bones
2 large carrots

2 medium-large onions
Large bouquet garni
7 quarts White Stock
2 teaspoons salt or to taste

Brown the meat with the vegetable oil on all sides in a skillet on top of the stove. Crush the bones, peel and slice carrots and onions, and put all in the bottom of a 10-quart stockpot, along with the bouquet garni. Top with the browned meat. Cover and let stand 15 minutes. Add 2 quarts of the stock and the salt. Simmer 1 hour. Add remaining stock. Bring to the boiling point, and skim off scum from the surface. Reduce heat and simmer 5 hours. Remove meat and bones from the stock, strain, and skim off fat as for Plain White Stock. Use for making thin veal gravy or brown sauces, for braising vegetables and red meats, and for making consommé. Makes about 5 quarts.

Thickened Veal Stock

Cook 2 quarts Brown Veal Stock until it has reduced by three-quarters. Thicken with 1½ tablespoons cornstarch mixed with 3 tablespoons cold Clear Brown Stock. Strain through two layers of rinsed cheesecloth. Keep hot. Serve as gravy for roasts. Makes about 2 cups.

Tomato-Flavored Veal Stock

Combine 2½ quarts Brown Veal Stock and 1 cup tomato puree. Simmer until the mixture has reduced to 5 cups. Strain through two layers of cheesecloth. Makes 1¼ quarts.

Game Stock

2 pounds each venison and rabbit	4½ quarts water
4 pounds venison bones, cracked	1 cup sliced mushroom stems
¼ cup vegetable oil	1 tablespoon salt
4 medium-sized carrots	6 juniper berries (if available)
1 medium-large onion	1 whole clove
4 leeks	1 small bay leaf

Brown meat and bones in the vegetable oil. Peel and slice carrots and onion and add to the meat. Wash leeks thoroughly and slice. Add leeks to meat, along with remaining ingredients. Simmer 3 hours. Remove meat, bones, and fat and strain as for Plain White Stock. Use in making game sauces and to serve with small pieces of game cooked in butter. If the stock is reduced to three-quarters it may be used to flavor game dishes. Makes about 2½ quarts.

🐟 Fish Stock

6 pounds non-oily white fleshed fish heads, bones, tails, and fins (pike, haddock, sole, whiting, halibut, etc.)	1 tablespoon chopped fresh thyme or 1 teaspoon dried thyme
1 medium-large onion	1 bay leaf
1½ cups sliced mushroom stems	1½ teaspoons salt
½ cup chopped parsley	2½ quarts cold water
	2 cups dry white or red wine

Wash fish trimmings and place them in an 8-quart stockpot. Peel and slice onion, and add to the pot, along with remaining ingredients except the white wine. Bring to the boiling point. Reduce heat and skim off any scum from the surface. Simmer 20 minutes. Add the white wine and cook another 15 minutes. Cool. Strain through two layers of rinsed cheesecloth. Refrigerate. Use for poaching or braising fish, for fish stews, and for fish sauces. Makes about 2 quarts.

ESSENCES AND GLAZES

Essences are obtained by boiling down stocks until they are reduced by half their volume. Essences are used for poaching fish and for flavoring sauces.

Glazes are progressive and very intensive reductions of clear meat stocks or game stocks. Reduce very slowly over low heat. A glaze is ready when it coats the spoon without running off. Glazes are used for coating certain dishes (such as Cha'ud-froid of Game, or roasts) to improve the flavor and make them look attractive. Glazes are also used, like essences, to lend body to a sauce or a preparation.

ASPICS AND JELLIES

To the French chef an aspic is the whole decorated dish of food coated with or molded in jelly. To the average American cook, however, aspic means stock or consommé that stiffens when cold, because it contains either commercial gelatin or natural gelatin obtained from the bones and meat from which it was made. The French term for this is *gelée*.

The stock for aspic or gelée should be of the same general base as the food that is to be molded or coated. It must be rich enough in gelatin and free enough of suspended solid particles for the finished product to be firm and sparkling clear.

To clarify the stock, remove all traces of fat and have all equipment free from grease. For each quart of cold stock, add 1 beaten egg white and 1 crumbled egg shell. Stir, and heat just to the simmering point and simmer 15 minutes (never, never boil). Remove the saucepan from the heat and let stock stand 30 minutes. Strain through two layers of rinsed cheesecloth. The egg white and shell attract all the cloudy particles in the stock, leaving it crystal-clear.

Quick Aspic or Gelée

1½ envelopes (4½ teaspoons) unflavored gelatin
⅓ cup cold water, stock, or dry white wine
2½ cups consommé or bouillon

Soften gelatin in ⅓ cup cold water, stock, or wine. Heat consommé or bouillon to boiling point, remove from heat, and stir in gelatin. Cool. Use as a base for aspic molds and spoon over chaud-froid coated foods. Makes about 2¾ cups.

COURT BOUILLONS

COURT BOUILLONS ARE LIQUIDS cooked only a short time with seasonings. Their composition varies with their use-from simple acidulated water (water with vinegar, lemon juice, or wine, and salt) to more highly seasoned preparations of stocks, fresh herbs, spices, and vegetables.

Court bouillons are used as; (1) the liquid for cooking and marinating vegetables used on the hors d'oeuvre tray or for garnishing; (2) the liquid for poaching fish and variety meats; (3) a hot marinade for fish; (4) a base for sauces, gravies, chowders, and aspics; or (5) bouillon.

Court Bouillon for Fish

½ cup diced carrots
¾ cup diced celery
½ cup chopped onion
2 tablespoons cooking oil or butter
3 pounds fish trimmings
   (heads, bones, tails, and fins)
    tied in a cheesecloth bag
1 cup dry white wine, or ¾ cup
   vinegar or lemon juice

½ cup chopped parsley
1 tablespoon chopped fresh thyme,
   or 1 teaspoon dried thyme
3 quarts cold water
1 bay leaf

1 tablespoon salt
8 whole peppercorns

Sauté carrots, celery, and onion in oil or butter in a 4-quart saucepan until vegetables are limp but not browned. Add all remaining ingredients except peppercorns. Cover and slowly bring to the boiling point. Reduce heat and simmer (do not boil) 30 minutes. Add peppercorns 10 minutes before cooking time is up. Cool. Remove fish trimmings and strain court bouillon through two layers of rinsed cheesecloth. Makes about 3 quarts.

Poached Whole Fish

Ask your fish supplier to gut and clean a 4-to 5-pound fish (salmon, halibut, trout, cod, or striped bass) for cooking whole. Wrap fish in cheesecloth and place it on a rack in a pan long enough to accommodate it. Add strained Court Bouillon to cover. Bring to the boiling point, reduce heat, and simmer 5-8 minutes per pound, or until fish is flaky when prodded with a fork. If fish is to be served cold, shorten the cooking time by 1 to 2 minutes per pound and cool it in the stock. If fish is to be served hot, lay it on a clean towel or napkin on a warm platter so the napkin can absorb the excess liquid. Carefully lift the top skin and cut away and discard the dark flesh. Serve hot with Hollandaise Sauce or a fish sauce, or chill and serve cold with flavored mayonnaise. Makes 6 servings.

Court Bouillon for Vegetables à la Grecque

Vegetables prepared this way are often served on the hors d'oeuvre tray or are used as a garnish for meat trays or in salads.

¾ cup olive oil
1 quart cold water
1 medium-sized clove garlic, crushed
2 celery tops
¼ cup chopped parsley
2 tablespoons chopped shallots or onion

15 coriander seeds
2 teaspoons chopped fresh thyme
¼ teaspoon fennel seeds
8 whole peppercorns
1 lemon rind

Combine all ingredients except peppercorns and lemon rind in a 3-quart saucepan. Slowly bring to the boiling point. Reduce heat and simmer 20 minutes. (Do not boil.) Add peppercorns and lemon rind. Remove from heat and allow the mixture to stand 15 minutes for seasonings to blend. Remove and discard lemon rind. Bring to the boiling point again. Add prepared vegetables (see below), the mild-flavored ones first, and bring the liquid to the boiling point. Turn off heat and let vegetables cool in the stock, then remove them to a jar or bowl. Add the rest of the vegetables. Bring to the boiling point, cook, and cool in the same manner as the first ones. Either combine the cooked vegetables or put each type of vegetable in a separate jar. Cover with the court bouillon and refrigerate until ready to use.

Vegetables that are suitable for this method of preparation are: julienned carrots, cauliflowers, artichoke bottoms, sliced cucumbers, celery ribs, fennel ribs, mushrooms, green beans, leeks, very small white onions, and eggplant. To prevent the vegetables from discoloring, toss each pound of fresh prepared vegetables with 3 tablespoons lemon juice.

ROUX

Roux is used by French cooks as a thickening agent for sauces, soufflés, and croquettes. Roux is made by cooking flour with butter or other fat; the liquid is added after the flour and butter have cooked to a certain point. The cooking process prevents the finished dish from having a pasty, raw-flour taste and whisking prevents the formation of lumps so often found in incorrectly made sauces.

There are three general types of roux: white, brown, and blond.

White roux is made by stirring and cooking the butter and flour together until it is bubbly but not browned. The liquid added to the roux may be milk or light stock (veal, chicken, or fish). This makes a basic white sauce (Béchamel or Velouté).

Brown roux is made like white roux, with the following exceptions: The butter and flour are stirred and cooked together until the mixture has turned nut-brown in color but has not burned or scorched. Half again as much flour is used, since browning reduces the thickening power of the flour by converting the starch to dextrin. Beef stock is used as the liquid added to the roux, and stronger-flavored seasonings may be added. Brown roux is used to thicken brown sauces such as Espagnole and Demi-Glace.

Blond roux is made the same way as brown roux, except that it is cooked only until its color is pale golden and it is always made with clarified butter (butter that is melted and strained, leaving the milky deposit in the strainer). It is usually used with light (white) stock (veal, chicken, or fish). It is used in delicately flavored dishes, such as eggs, fish, white meat of chicken, and so on.

Proportions for Basic White Sauces

FOR THIN SAUCE OR SOUP:
1 tablespoon butter
and flour to 1 cup liquid

FOR MEDIUM SAUCE:
(creamed or scalloped dishes)
2 tablespoons butter and
flour to 1 cup liquid

FOR THICK SAUCE:
(croquettes or soufflés)
3 to 4 tablespoons butter
and flour to 1 cup liquid
Salt and freshly ground black
pepper

Melt butter over low heat. Remove from heat and stir in flour. Return to heat and stir and cook until the butter-flour mixture is bubbly. Remove from heat and stir in liquid. Stir and cook until thickened. Add salt and pepper, using ¼ to ½ teaspoon salt for each 1 cup liquid, the amount depending upon the salt that is in the stock. Add pepper to taste. Makes about 1 cup.

Béchamel and Velouté sauces are basically the same simple white sauce, the principal difference being that Velouté Sauce is made with white stock (poultry or veal, or with fish stock when it is to be used with a fish dish), while Béchamel Sauce is made either with milk or white stock with the addition of heavy cream. See chapter 3, "Sauces," for recipes.

Brown Sauce

Make as for White Sauce, using half again as much flour and cooking the roux longer until golden. Add beef stock and seasonings.

MARINADES AND BRINES

A marinade is a seasoned liquid, cooked or uncooked, used for steeping certain foodstuffs, such as meat, fish, poultry, and vegetables. Its purpose is to flavor the food, to tenderize the less tender cuts of meat, and to increase the keeping quality of the foods. The length of time for marinating depends upon the type of food and the size of the pieces into which it is cut. Small pieces, such as meat for Shish Kebabs, require only a few hours' marinating time, while large cuts, such as thick roasts, may require 24 hours to 3 or 4 days, with the meat turned frequently to marinate it uniformly.

Uncooked Marinade for Meats

3 medium-sized carrots,
    pared and sliced
½ cup sliced onion
3 shallots, sliced
6 whole peppercorns, crushed
6 juniper berries, crushed
½ cup chopped parsley
¾ teaspoon dried thyme, or
    2 teaspoons chopped fresh thyme

1 teaspoon salt
1 bay leaf
½ cup wine vinegar
2¾ cups dry red or white wine
¼ cup vegetable oil or olive oil

Place meat in bottom of a nonreactive dish with half the carrots, onion, and shallots underneath the meat and the remaining half over the top. Combine all the other ingredients except the oil and pour over the meat. Then pour oil over meat to prevent the top from turning dark. Refrigerate roasts or other large pieces of meat 2 to 3 days, smaller pieces 12 to 24 hours, depending upon size of pieces, turning meat frequently in the marinade. Makes about 3¼ cups.

Cooked Marinade for Meats

Use the same ingredients as in Uncooked Marinade, increasing the vinegar to ⅔ cup and the wine to 3 cups to allow for evaporation during cooking. Place meat and vegetables in a suitable dish as for Uncooked Marinade. Combine all remaining ingredients except the oil in a 2-quart nonreactive saucepan, slowly bring to the boiling point, and simmer 10 minutes. Pour marinade over the meat first and then pour the oil over it. Steep large pieces of meat such as roasts or leg of lamb 24 hours, smaller pieces 4 to 5 hours, turning meat frequently in the liquid. Makes approximately 3¼ cups.

Marinade for Small Pieces of Venison

Sprinkle both sides of venison cutlets, steaks, or chops with salt and freshly ground black pepper, and rub into the meat. Place meat in a dish and pour just enough olive oil over it to cover the top (about ¼ cup for 6 servings). Marinate 1 hour, turning meat twice.

Saumure or Brine for Pickling Ox Tongue

4 quarts water	2 tablespoons chopped fresh thyme,
1½ cups salt	or 2 teaspoons dried thyme
½ cup sugar	4 bay leaves
8 whole peppercorns	⅔ cup butchers' salt
4 juniper berries	½ ounce saltpeter

Combine all ingredients in an 8-quart kettle, bring to the boiling point, then remove from the heat and let cool.

Wash a fresh beef tongue, trim, discard excess fat, and prick it with a needle. Pound it well with a spatula or large spoon to expel the air from the meat. Mix ⅔ cup butchers' salt with ½ ounce saltpeter and rub over the surface of the tongue. Add tongue to the brine solution. Cover and steep in a cool place 8 to 9 days.

Dry Pickled Tongue

Prepare uncooked fresh beef tongue as in preceding recipe and set aside. Mix ½ cup butchers' salt with ¼ cup sugar and 1¾ ounces saltpeter and rub over the surface of the tongue. Mix 1 ⅓ cups butchers' salt with 1½ ounces saltpeter and sprinkle over the bottom of a glass or earthenware dish, using all the mixture. Place tongue on this mixture and weigh it down with a heavy bowl or board. Cover. Let stand for a few days to allow enough liquid to form to cover the tongue. In 6 days, tongue will be half pickled; in 11 to 12 days, tongue will be fully pickled and ready for cooking. Before cooking, soak tongue in water 24 hours, changing water frequently.

Brine for Large Pieces of Meat

8 quarts water
1½ pounds (3 cups) butchers' salt
1 pound sugar

Combine all ingredients in a 12-quart kettle. Bring to the boiling point. Cool. Trim a 10- to 11-pound piece of beef (brisket, plate, flank, or rump), prick it deeply with a large needle or ice pick, and place it on a rack in the bottom of an earthenware or enamel brine tub or kettle. Pour in brine. Cover and let stand in a cool place 8 or 9 days. Makes about 9 quarts brine.

FORCEMEATS (FARCES)

FORCEMEATS ARE INDISPENSABLE to the fine cuisine of the French chef. They are used in a variety of ways: for making quenelles, mousse, mousselines, pâtés, loaves, molds, vol-au-vents, borders, garnishes, canapé spreads, and for stuffing breast of veal or lamb, poultry, game, fish, vegetables, and eggs.

Forcemeats are made of meat, poultry, or lean, close-grained fish (halibut, salmon, pike, cod, or swordfish), finely ground or pureed and mixed with seasonings. (In addition to those given here, recipes for forcemeats appear in other chapters in connection with the dishes in which they are used.)

The preparation of some kinds of forcemeats requires the addition of a panada, a flour mixture similar to Choux Paste. Panadas act as binding agents in forcemeat mixtures and also give them body. In the past, panadas were almost always made of bread, but now a mixture made of flour and water or milk is preferred, since quenelles made with this are lighter and more delicate.

Flour Panada

½ cup water
3 tablespoons butter

¼ teaspoon salt
1 cup sifted all-purpose flour

Mix the first 3 ingredients in a 1-quart saucepan. Bring to the boiling point. Remove from heat and beat in all the flour at one time, using a wooden spoon. Continue beating about 1 minute. Return to heat. Stir and cook slowly for 5 minutes, or until mixture forms a ball or leaves the sides of the pan. Remove from heat and spread mixture on a buttered plate. Cover with buttered paper to prevent crusting over the top. Refrigerate until thoroughly chilled. Mix with twice-ground meat, chicken, game, or fish as specified in each recipe. Makes 1 cup.

Milk Panada

In the recipe for Flour Panada, replace the water with milk.

Egg Panada

Use recipe for Milk Panada, and add 1 large whole egg, beating it in well. This panada is used a great deal with fish forcemeats and fish pastries.

Fine Forcemeat for Chicken, Veal or Fish Quenelles

1 pound raw boneless white meat of
    chicken, rump of veal, gristle and
    fat removed, or firm-textured fish
½ teaspoon salt
⅛ teaspoon freshly ground
    black pepper

⅛ teaspoon grated nutmeg
5 tablespoons softened butter
2 large egg whites
1 cup chilled Egg Panada
About 6 tablespoons chilled
    heavy cream

Put chicken meat, or fish through a food processor twice, using the finest blade. Add seasonings and beat well. Add butter and beat well. Beat in egg whites, one at a time. Beat in Egg Panada, beating vigorously after all of it has been added. Spread the mixture on a buttered plate, cover with buttered paper, and refrigerate until thoroughly chilled. Beat in cream ½ tablespoon at a time, adding only enough for mixture to hold its shape while poaching. Make a test quenelle, and it it is too dense, add more cream. If too loose, add more egg white. When the correct texture is achieved, shape into quenelles and poach in simmering stock or water. Makes approximately 18 quenelles.

Gratin Forcemeat

For stuffing game or as a spread for canapés.

½ pound fat salt pork
1 pound liver (poultry, veal, or game)
½ cup chopped onion or shallots
2 tablespoons chopped parsley

¾ teaspoon salt
1½ teaspoons chopped fresh thyme
¾ teaspoon freshly ground
    black pepper

Cut salt pork into small dice and cook over low heat until all fat has been rendered. Add liver and onion to the hot fat. Stir and cook over medium heat until lightly browned. Add remaining ingredients. Stir and cook 1 to 2 minutes. Lift out liver and onion, reserving the fat. Put liver and onion through a food chopper twice, using the finest blade Add the reserved fat and beat with a wooden spoon just until incorporated. Do not overbeat. Makes about 2 cups.

Chicken, Veal or Fish Mousseline Forcemeat

¾ pound boneless breast of chicken
   or rump of veal, gristle, skin,
   and fat removed, or filet of fish
¼ teaspoon salt

⅛ teaspoon ground white pepper
2 or 3 large egg whites
About 1 cup chilled heavy cream

Put chicken veal, or fish through a food processor twice, using the finest blade. Add salt and white pepper. Gradually beat in 2 of the egg whites. Push the mixture through a fine sieve into a bowl. Place bowl on a bed of ice and beat the mixture with a wooden spoon until it is thoroughly chilled. Beat in cream, a little at a time. Chill about 2 hours. Test a small portion in simmering water for correct consistency. If the mixture is too soft, add another egg white. If too dense, add more cream. Use for stuffing poultry or game.

The mixture may be shaped with a spoon into the shape of large olives. Place these mousselines in a buttered pan. Cover with simmering stock or water. Poach, uncovered, 10 to 15 minutes, or until firm, never allowing the water to boil. Transfer with a slotted spoon to a clean towel or cloth to drain. Use to garnish meat or vegetable dishes. Makes about 1 cup.

Mousseline Forcemeat may also be made into quenelles or mousse.

Mousse

Pack the Mousseline Forcemeat mixture into buttered individual molds. Place molds in a pan of very hot water. Bake in a preheated oven (350°F) until mousse is puffed, firm, and begins to pull away from the sides of the molds, 40 to 50 minutes

Quenelle Forcemeat with Panada

1 pound (2 cups ground) boneless,
   raw white meat of poultry, veal,
   gristle and fat removed, or
   firm-textured white fleshed fish,
½ teaspoon salt
⅛ teaspoon freshly ground black pepper

⅛ teaspoon grated nutmeg
1 cup cold Flour Panada
½ cup (1 stick) softened butter
2 large whole eggs
2 to 4 large egg yolks
Heavy cream

Put poultry, veal, or fish through a meat grinder twice, using the finest blade Add salt, pepper, and nutmeg and beat well. Add Flour Panada and beat it into the meat with a wooden spoon. Beat in butter. Beat in whole eggs and 2 of the egg yolks, one at a time. Push the forcemeat through a sieve. Test the consistency by shaping a spoonful of the mixture into a small ball or cylinder and poaching it in simmering water. If it disintegrates, beat in 1 or 2 more egg yolks; if the mixture is too dry, beat in a little cream, 1 tablespoon at a time. Test after each addition. Make into quenelles and poach. Makes about 3 cups.

Shrimp Forcemeat

For quenelles, mousselines, or mousses, or as a stuffing for fish.

1 pound raw shrimp	¼ teaspoon grated nutmeg
1 teaspoon salt	2 or 3 large egg whites
¼ teaspoon freshly ground black pepper	About 2 cups heavy cream

Peel and devein shrimp and put them through a food processor, using the finest blade. Place the flesh in a mortar or chopping bowl and pound to a paste. Add salt, pepper, and nutmeg and mix well. Gradually beat in 2 of the egg whites, and push the mixture through a fine sieve into a bowl. Place bowl on a bed of ice and gradually work in heavy cream, using a wooden spoon. Test the mixture for consistency by putting a 1-inch ball in a small saucepan and pouring in a little hot water. Cook about 2 minutes. If the mixture is too soft, add a little more egg white; if it is too firm, work in a little more cream. Test after each addition. Makes about 3½ cups.

Lobster Forcemeat

In the recipe for Shrimp Forcemeat, replace shrimp with 1 pound raw lobster meat, using also the lobster coral. Use in the same manner as Shrimp Forcemeat.

Fish Forcemeat

In the recipe for Shrimp Forcemeat, replace shrimp with 1 pound raw boneless fish. Use in the same manner as Shrimp Forcemeat.

PREPARATION OF QUENELLES

Quenelles, which are made of forcemeat bound with eggs and sometimes with Panada, are of different shapes and sizes and may be shaped in several ways: with spoons, by hand, in molds, or by forcing the mixture through a pastry bag. The size and shaping method depend on the way the quenelles are to be used. They are cooked uncovered in simmering water or stock; if the water is allowed to boil they are likely to split.

Spoon method. Wet a soup spoon or dessert spoon and measure out a rounded spoonful of the cold forcemeat. Smooth the top with the inverted bowl of another spoon of the same size that has been dipped in very hot water. Loosen the dumpling from the first spoon and slide it into simmering water or broth. Cook, uncovered, 5-10 minutes, depending on their size.

Shaping by hand. Measure out a rounded soup spoon or dessert spoon of forcemeat and roll it with the palms of your hands on a floured board to form 2½-inch cylinders. Simmer as for spoon-shaped dumplings.

In molds. Forcemeat for garnishes may be shaped like large olives, using the spoon method, or it may be cooked in individual flared, round, or boat-shaped molds. First butter molds generously and make a simple design on the bottom of each with bits of truffles, pimiento, or ripe olives. Fill generously with forcemeat, making sure there are no air pockets along the sides. Poach in simmering water as for spoon-shaped quenelles. The quenelles will unmold themselves and float to the surface of the liquid.

With a pastry bag. Place a round ½-inch tube in a large pastry bag and put the forcemeat into the bag. Pipe small round or 1½-inch elongated quenelles onto the bottom of a buttered saucepan or skillet. Cover with simmering water or broth and poach as for spoon-shaped quenelles. To make quenelles for soup, put forcemeat through a pastry bag fitted with a small tube, moving the bag a short distance back and forth to give the quenelles a slight curl. Cover with simmering water or stock and cook, uncovered, 12 to 15 minutes. Serve in soup.

MIXTURES OR APPAREILS

THE FRENCH CULINARY TERM *appareil* means a simple mixed preparation used in making a dish; for example, *appareil à biscuit* (sponge mixture), *appareil à crème renversée* (custard mixture), *appareil à croquette* (croquette mixture). The following mixtures are frequently used.

Rich Duxelles

Duxelles is a cooked mixture resembling hash, made of finely chopped mushrooms and shallots, cooked in butter. After cooling, it may be stored in a covered jar in the refrigerator to use as needed to add flavor to gravies and sauces.

9 or 10 medium-sized mushrooms	1 teaspoon fresh lemon juice
1 tablespoon butter	Salt and freshly ground black
1 tablespoon chopped shallots	pepper

Wash and finely chop mushrooms and squeeze them in a cloth to extract the moisture. Cook in butter, along with shallots until they begin to brown. Cook slowly at first, then when the liquid begins to appear, turn up the heat and cook 7 to 8 minutes, or until the moisture has evaporated. Add salt, pepper and lemon juice. Cool. Store in a covered jar in the refrigerator to use as needed. Makes about 1 cup.

Matignon

Matignon is a mixture of carrots, celery, onions or shallots, and fresh herbs that are cooked in butter until they are tender and then with Madeira until most of the liquid has evaporated. Thin strips of ham or crumbled crisp bacon, may be added. Matignon may be served with meat or fish dishes or it may be cooked with the meat, as for veal roast or roasted fish.

5 small carrots, pared and finely chopped	1 tablespoon chopped parsley
2 shallots, finely chopped	1 teaspoon chopped fresh thyme
1 cup thinly sliced onion or shallots	1 small bay leaf
¼ cup finely chopped celery	⅓ cup Madeira
¼ cup (½ stick) butter	¼ teaspoon salt
	¼ teaspoon freshly ground black pepper

Cook vegetables in butter until they are soft. Add remaining ingredients and cook until most of the liquid has evaporated. Serve with meat or fish dishes or cook with roasts or fish. Makes about 6 servings.

Matignon with Bacon

Replace 2 tablespoons of the butter with 2 tablespoons diced bacon in the recipe for Matignon.

Matignon with Ham

Add ½ cup finely chopped ham to the recipe for Matignon. Makes about 7 servings.

Mirepoix

Mirepoix is a mixture of cooked carrots, celery, and onion, seasoned with fresh herbs. It is used to enhance the flavor of sauces, gravies, meats, fish, and shellfish.

1 carrot, pared	1 small bay leaf
1 rib celery	1 teaspoon chopped fresh thyme
1 medium-sized onion, peeled	1/16 teaspoon minced garlic
1 tablespoon chopped parsley	Salt and freshly ground black
1 tablespoon butter	pepper

Finely dice vegetables. Cook in butter, along with the fresh herbs and garlic, 7 to 8 minutes, or until the vegetables are soft. Season with salt and pepper. Cool. Makes about 1 cup.

Mirepoix with Bacon

Add ¼ cup finely chopped ham or 2 strips minced bacon bacon to cook with the Mirepoix mixture. Makes about 1¼ cups.

Salpicon

Salpicon is a mixture made from pickled tongue, mushrooms, truffles, sometimes foie gras, Demi-Glace Sauce, and Madeira. It is used to fill tart shells, very small vol-au-vents, barquettes, and croustades, to make cromesquis, to spread on canapés, and to stuff small cuts of meat or fish filets.

2 cup julienned pickled tongue
1¼ cups julienned poached mushrooms
¾ cup thick Demi-Glace Sauce

¼ cup Madeira
Salt and freshly ground black pepper

Cook the first 4 ingredients together until the mixture is very thick. Add salt and pepper to taste. Use to fill lamb cutlets, tart shells, or very small vol-au-vents. If desired, replace Demi-Glace sauce with pureed foie gras. Makes about 1½ cups.

Duchess Potato Mixture

Duchess Potatoes are fluffy mashed potatoes into which beaten eggs have been incorporated. They may be served as a dish or put through a pastry bag while hot and formed into cases for serving creamed dishes or into borders or rosettes for decorating a casserole or planked meat or fish. For such uses the potatoes are painted with beaten egg, melted butter, or milk and browned lightly in a preheated oven (450°F) or broiler. Duchess Potatoes are also used for making croquettes.

6 medium-sized potatoes
   (about 2 pounds)
1 teaspoon salt
¼ teaspoon ground white pepper

pinch grated nutmeg
2 large whole eggs
2 large egg yolks

Peel potatoes and cut into quarters. Cook in a covered saucepan in 1 inch of boiling water with the salt until soft but still firm. Drain well. Put through a potato ricer or food mill. Beat until potatoes are smooth. Add white pepper and nutmeg. Beat whole eggs and egg yolks together until light and foamy and add to potatoes. Whip until fluffy. Put through a pastry bag as desired. Makes 6 servings.

Tomato Fondue

Tomato Fondue is made of very ripe tomatoes, peeled, seeded, quartered or chopped, and cooked in butter with onions, shallots, and crushed garlic until the pulp is firm. The mixture may be seasoned with Hungarian paprika, chopped fresh tarragon, saffron, or chopped sweet green pepper. Tomato Fondue is served as an accompaniment to eggs, fish, meat, and poultry dishes and to fill small baked tart shells.

5 medium-sized tomatoes	½ teaspoon salt
¼ cup chopped onion or shallots	⅛ teaspoon sugar
1 very small clove garlic, crushed	¹⁄₁₆ teaspoon freshly ground black pepper
2 tablespoons butter	Chopped parsley

Peel, seed, and quarter or chop tomatoes. Set aside. Cook onions and garlic in butter until soft. Add tomatoes and seasonings. Cook over low heat until most of the liquid has evaporated. Sprinkle with parsley. Makes 6 servings.

GARNISHES

A garnish, to Americans, means a simple decoration or an embellishment for a dish. The garnish may be parsley or other greens, radishes, slices of cucumber, tomato, orange, lemon, or apple, clusters of grapes or berries, slices of chopped hard-cooked eggs, mushroom caps, olives, nuts, whipped cream or mayonnaise put through a decorating tube, a sprinkling of paprika, or any other foods that enhance the appearance of the dish. To the French chef, however, garnish includes not only such items as those, but everything that is served with the principal dish in every course of the meal-from pastas and vegetables in soup and stews to such accompaniments as potatoes, stuffings, rice, vegetables, gravies, sauces, butters, and relishes. The garnishes are either placed on the platter or tray with the main dish or served in separate dishes.

A garnish may derive its name from a place, from the man who originated it, from an occasion, in compliment to a person, or from various other sources. The garnish often gives its name to the dish so garnished.

GARNISH	MAIN DISH
AGNES SOREL. Mousseline Forcemeat made of chicken with slices of sautéed mushrooms, poached, in tartlet molds; round slices of pickled tongue; slices of truffle; Sauce Allemande.	Chicken breasts, poached chicken
ALBUFERA. Stuffing of forcemeat with rice plus coarsely diced truffles and balls of foie gras; puff-pastry tartlets garnished with a salpicon of truffles; mushrooms; quenelles of chicken; bound with Albuféra Sauce; decorated with round slices of pickled tongue; Albuféra Sauce served separately.	Poached chicken

ALGERIENNE. Sweet-potato croquettes; small seeded tomatoes cooked slowly in oil; light Tomato Sauce to which julienned red pepper has been added.	Roast or sautéed meat.
ALSACIENNE. Tarts filled with braised sauerkraut with a round slice of ham on top; gravy of the meat juices.	Meats.
AMERICAINE. Sliced lobster tails; Lobster Sauce.	Fish.
AMIRAL. Oysters and mussels Villeroi; fluted mushroom caps; crayfish tails; truffle slices; Sauce Normande enriched with crayfish butter.	Large fish, especially turbot and brill.
ANDALOUSE. Grilled halves of peppers à la Grecque; thick slices of peeled eggplant fried in oil and garnished with Tomato Fondue; chipolata sausages; thickened gravy (Jus Lié).	Meats, chicken.
ARGENTEUIL. White asparagus tips coated with Hollandaise Sauce.	Meats, chicken.
ARLESIENNE. Slices of eggplant fried in deep fat; peeled, sliced, and sautéed tomatoes; floured and deep fried onion rings; tomato-flavored Demi-Glace Sauce.	Tournedos (small round slices of beef tenderloin) and noisettes (similar slices of lamb or veal).
BEAUGENCY. Artichoke bottoms with Tomato Fondue, topped with slices of blanched beef marrow; Béarnaise Sauce.	Small pieces of sautéed meat.
BEAUHARNAIS. Quarters of sautéed artichoke bottoms; stuffed mushroom caps; Château Potatoes; Béarnaise Sauce.	Small pieces of sautéed or grilled meat.
BELLE HELENE. Round flat asparagus croquettes; truffle slices; thickened gravy (Jus Lié).	Tournedos.

BERRICHONNE *(Berry style)*. Balls of steamed cabbage; whole chestnuts and small glazed onions; small slices of bacon cooked with the cabbage; meat juices thickened with Demi-Glace.	Braised meats.
BONNE- FEMME. Chopped shallots, sliced mushrooms, and chopped parsley poached with the fish in white wine and fish stock; the stock is reduced and mixed with a white wine sauce enriched with butter, which is poured over the fish to glaze it.	Small fish, fillets of fish.
BOUQUETIERE. Carrots and turnips scooped out with a spoon and glazed; small green beans; peas; florets of cauliflower coated with Hollandaise Sauce; Château Potatoes, light gravy.	Roasts and smaller cuts of meat.
BOURGUIGNONNE. Diced browned bacon; quartered sautéed mushrooms; small glazed onions; the braising liquid (always made with Burgundy).	Braised beef, ham.
BRUXELLOISE. Braised endive; Brussels sprouts slowly cooked in butter; Château Potatoes; light Madeira Sauce.	Roasts and smaller cuts of meat.
CARDINAL. Sliced lobster tails and claws, truffle slices; Cardinal Sauce.	Fish.
CASTILLIANE. Small nests of Duchess Potatoes, filled with diced tomatoes sautéed in olive oil; deep fried onion rings; the meat juices, reduced and flavored with tomato.	Roasts, small cuts of meat, tournedos, noisettes, poultry.
CATALAN. Grilled tomatoes; artichoke bottoms; tomato-flavored Demi-Glace.	Tournedos, noisettes.
CHAMBORD. Quenelles of fish with truffles; truffles cut into olive shapes; fluted mushroom caps; fried roe; crayfish cooked in court bouillon; heart-shaped croutons fried in butter; sauce made with red wine.	Braised whole fish.

CHASSEUR. Mushroom caps filled with onion puree; Duchess Potatoes; sauce made of white wine, Demi-Glace, and fresh herbs.	Roasts, small pieces of sautéed meat.
CHIPOLATA. Small glazed onions and carrots; chestnuts cooked in consommé; diced fried salt pork; chipolata sausages; meat stock reduced with Demi-Glace.	Roasts, poultry.
CHOISY. Braised half lettuce; Château Potatoes; buttered meat glaze.	Tournedos, noisettes.
CHORON. Artichoke bottoms with green asparagus tips or very small peas cooked in butter; Noisette Potatoes; tomato-flavored Béarnaise Sauce.	Sautéed meats, tournedos.
CLAMART. Macaire Potato Cakes; tartlets garnished with French-style peas; thickened veal stock.	Sautéed meats.
CONDE. Puree of red beans cooked in red wine with salt pork; meat stock thickened with Demi-Glace.	Braised meats.
CONTI. Lentil puree cooked with rectangles of salt pork; the liquid used to braise the meat.	Braised meats.
DEMIDOFF. Slices of onion and half-moons of carrots and turnips cooked in butter; diced celeriac cooked with the bird in a covered casserole; add truffle half-moons last.	Poultry, game birds.
DIEPPOISE. Shelled shrimp tails; mussels cooked in white wine; White Wine Sauce made with the reduced stock in which the fish was poached.	Small fish, fillets of fish.
DORIA. Cucumber cut into olive-shaped pieces cooked slowly in butter; slices of peeled and seeded lemon.	Pan-fried fish.

DUBARRY. Cauliflower cooked and shaped into balls, coated with Mornay Sauce, sprinkled with cheese, and browned; meat juices blended with Demi-Glace.	Roasts, tournedos, noisettes.
FINANCIERE. Mushroom caps; veal forcemeat quenelles; truffle slices; blanched olives; cockscombs and cocks' kidneys; Sauce Financière.	Roasts, poultry.
FLAMANDE. Balls of cooked cabbage; duck. glazed carrots and turnips; small boiled potatoes; rectangles of salt pork cooked with the cabbage; stock of the braised meat.	Braised or boiled meats,
FORESTIERE. Morels (or mushrooms) sautéed in butter; diced fried potatoes; diced lean bacon, blanched and fried; Duxelles Sauce blended with the meat juices or with Demi-Glace and reduced.	Roasts, small cuts of meat, poultry.
GODARD. Veal forcemeat quenelles with chopped truffles and mushrooms; chicken forcemeat quenelles decorated with truffles and pickled tongue; fluted mushrooms; olive-shaped truffles; glazed lamb sweetbreads; sauce made of champagne boiled with Mirepoix, Demi-Glace, and mushroom essence.	Large roasts, poultry.
GRAND DUKE. Green asparagus tips bound with butter; truffle slices; crayfish tails; Mornay Sauce.	Fish.
HELDER. Artichoke bottoms garnished alternately with buttered asparagus tips, Noisette Potatoes, and coarsely chopped tomatoes; Béarnaise Sauce.	Tournedos, noisettes, sautéed meats.
HENRI IV. Artichoke bottoms garnished with very small Noisette Potatoes rolled in melted meat glaze; Béarnaise Sauce.	Tournedos, noisettes.

HUSSARDE. Mushroom caps filled with onion puree; Duchess Potatoes; sauce made with white wine, Demi-Glace, and fresh herbs.	Roasted or sautéed meats.
ITALIENNE. Quarters of Italian-style artichokes; triangular macaroni croquettes with a lot of cheese; Sauce Italienne.	Roasts, smaller cuts of meat, poultry.
JARDINIERE. Carrots and turnips scooped out with a spoon and glazed; peas; green beans cut into lozenges and flageolets thickened with Beurre Manié; balls of cauliflower coated with Hollandaise Sauce; light veal stock.	Large and small cuts of meat.
JOINVILLE. Coarsely chopped mushrooms, crayfish tails, and truffles bound with Joinville Sauce; truffle slices; crayfish tails; Joinville Sauce.	Fish.
LA VALLIERE. Artichoke bottoms garnished with buttered green asparagus tips; Château Potatoes; Bordelaise Sauce.	Tournedos, small pieces of sautéed meat.
LORETTE. Asparagus tips or peas thickened with Beurre Manié, very small chicken croquettes; truffle slices; veal juices, thickened (Jus Lié).	Tournedos, noisettes.
MAILLOT. Carrots and turnips scooped out with a spoon and glazed; small glazed onions; braised lettuce; peas, green beans; thickened meat stock.	Braised meats, especially ham.
MARAICHERE. Slices of salsify bound with thin Béchamel Sauce; Brussels sprouts cooked in butter; Château Potatoes; juice of the braised meat.	Braised meats.
MARECHALE. The food is dipped in melted butter, then in chopped truffles or breadcrumbs mixed with chopped truffles; the garnish consists of truffle slices, green asparagus tips, peas thickened with Beurre Manié.	Sliced veal sweetbreads, lamb chops, chicken breasts.

MARIE-LOUISE. Artichoke bottoms garnished with 3 parts mushroom puree and 1 part onion puree; Madeira Sauce or thickened gravy.	Sautéed meats and poultry.
MASCOTTE. Artichoke bottoms cooked in butter; potatoes cut into the shape of olives and sautéed in butter; truffle balls; casserole is rinsed with white wine and veal stock.	Tournedos, noisettes, poultry, cooked in a casserole and surrounded by the garnish.
MASSENA. Artichoke bottoms garnished with thick Béarnaise Sauce; slices of poached beef marrow placed on the meat; Tomato Sauce.	Tournedos, grilled meats, small pieces of sautéed meat.
MEXICAINE. Large grilled mushroom caps garnished with Tomato Fondue; small grilled peppers; well-seasoned tomato-flavored gravy.	Roasts, smaller cuts of meat, poultry.
MIRABEAU. Anchovy fillets placed on the meat; border of blanched tarragon leaves; pitted olives; Anchovy Butter.	Grilled beef or mutton.
MONTMORENCY. Macedoine of vegetables; bunches of green asparagus tips; Madeira Sauce mixed with the meat stock.	Large or small cuts of meat, poultry.
MONTREUIL. Boiled potato balls coated with Shrimp Sauce, surrounding the fish; the fish coated with White Wine Sauce.	Small fish and fillets of fish.
MURAT. The fillets of fish, cut in coarse julienne strips, are sautéed in butter and mixed with diced artichoke bottoms and diced potatoes sautéed in butter, garnished with tomato slices sautéed in butter, chopped parsley, lemon juice; a little meat glaze; Brown Butter (Beurre Noisette).	Fillets of fish.
NANTUA. Crayfish quenelles bound with Nantua Sauce; truffle slices; Nantua Sauce.	Fish.

NIÇOISE I. Tomato Fondue with chopped garlic and chopped tarragon; anchovy fillets; black olives; peeled, seeded lemon slices; Anchovy Butter.	Fish
NIÇOISE II. Tomato Fondue with a little chopped garlic and tarragon; green beans sautéed in butter; Château Potatoes; thickened gravy.	Meats, poultry.
NORMANDE. Oysters and mussels scraped clean and poached; small mushroom caps; peeled shrimp tails; truffle slices; shelled crayfish; small deep fried gudgeon or smelt; half-moons of puff pastry; Sauce Normande.	Fish.
ORIENTALE. Timbales of rice à la Grecque; halved tomatoes cooked slowly in olive oil; sweet-potato croquettes; Tomato Sauce.	Poultry.
PORTUGAISE. Small tomatoes garnished with Duxelles; Château Potatoes; Tomato Sauce.	Meats, poultry.
PRINCESSE. Asparagus tips bound with cream sauce; truffle slices; Allemande Sauce with mushroom essence.	Veal sweetbreads, poultry.
PROVENÇALE. Small cooked tomatoes; mushroom caps garnished with Duxelles with a little garlic; Sauce Provençale.	Meats, poultry.
RACHEL. Artichoke bottoms, each garnished with a large slice of beef marrow and sprinkled with chopped parsley; Bordelaise Sauce.	Tournedos and small cuts of meat.
REGENCE I. Spoon-shaped quenelles of whiting forcemeat with crayfish butter; poached oysters; mushroom caps; truffle slices; poached roe; Sauce Normande.	Fish.

REGENCE II. Spoon-shaped quenelles of chicken forcemeat; large quenelles of veal orcemeat decorated with truffles; small slices of sautéed foie gras; cockscombs; truffles cut into olive shapes; mushroom caps; Sauce Allemande with truffle essence	Poultry, veal sweetbreads.
REINE MARGOT. Stuffing of fine chicken forcemeat and pureed almonds; small chicken forcemeat quenelles finished with pistachio butter; small chicken forcemeat quenelles with crayfish butter; Sauce Suprême mixed with almond milk.	Poached poultry.
RICHE. Rock lobster medallions; truffle slices; Victoria Sauce.	Fillets of fish.
RICHELIEU. Tomatoes and mushroom caps filled with Duxelles; braised lettuce; Château Potatoes; meat juices, lightly thickened.	Roasts, especially beef tenderloin.
ROMAINE. Tartlets garnished with Roman-style Gnocchi; Spinach Loaf with chopped anchovy baked in brioche molds; Sauce Romaine.	Meats.
ROSSINI. Medallions of foie gras lightly sautéed in butter; truffle slices; Demi-Glace with truffle essence, or Madeira Sauce.	Tournedos, noisettes.
SAINT-GERMAIN. Carrot balls, glazed; small timbales of pea puree; small potato croquettes; Béarnaise Sauce; the gravy of the meat.	Meats.
SAINT-MANDE. Base of Macaire Potatoes; fine green beans; peas sautéed in butter; thickened gravy.	Meats.
SARDE. Rice croquettes with saffron; tomatoes stuffed with Duxelles; pieces of hollowed-out cucumber garnished with Duxelles and browned; light Tomato Sauce.	Meats.

TALLYRAND. Small pieces of macaroni mixed with butter and grated cheese to which diced foie gras and truffle have been added; Periqueux Sauce with truffle sticks.	Meats, poultry.
TORTUE. Salpicon of veal forcemeat quenelles, mushrooms, truffles, blanched and stuffed olives and gherkins; sliced of calves' brains; crayfish; French Fried Eggs; heart-shaped fried croutons; Sauce Tortue.	Calf's head.
TOULOUSAINE. Small chicken forcemeat quenelles; small mushroom caps; small slices of calf and lamb sweetbreads; cockscombs and cocks' kidneys; truffle slices; Allemande Sauce with mushroom essence.	Poultry, vol-au-vents.
TROUVILLAISE. Shrimp tails; poached mussels; small fluted mushroom caps; Shrimp Sauce.	Fish.
TSARINE *(Czarina)*. Cucumber balls braised in butter; fluted mushroom caps; glazed Mornay Sauce.	Fish.
TYROLIENNE. Deep fried onion rings; Tomato Fondue; thickened veal gravy with butter added.	Grilled beef or mutton.
VALOIS. Large boiled potatoes; poached roe; crayfish tails; Valois Sauce.	Fish.
VERT-PRE. Potato sticks; watercress; Maître d'Hôtel Butter.	Grilled meats or poultry.
VICTORIA. Medallions of rock lobster; truffle slices; glazed Victoria Sauce.	Fish.

SAUCES

THE WORLDWIDE REPUTATION OF FRENCH CUISINE (haute, bourgeoise, and regional) has often been that all its dishes rely on sauces to make them great; that without accompanying sauces, the food would not be so sought after and loved. That is certainly true if the person making the sauces was the only genius in the kitchen. "In the orchestra of *la grande cuisine*, the *saucier* is the soloist," said Fernand Point, at one time (from 1930 to 1955) the most famous French restaurateur in the world. But without the true equality and perfect marriage of everything on the plate, there is no good cuisine. Still what distinguishes French cooking in the world of cuisines is the vast roster of sauces. And even though the list of individual sauces seems endless, all French sauces are organized into just a few groups, each one of which has seemingly "endless" variations.

- **White sauces.** Based on a butter and flour roux cooked with milk or cream (Béchamel) or white stock or bouillon from poultry, game, fish and shellfish, or meat (Velouté).
- **Brown sauces.** Based on the great Espagnole, also thickened with roux, but the stock or bouillon is brown by drawing out the essences and juices of meats.
- **Tomato sauces.** Roux-thickened juices of tomato, herbs, ham, and aromatic vegetables (carrots, celery, and onions).
- **Hollandaise.** Egg yolk and butter liaison sauces.
- **Mayonnaises.** Egg yolk and olive oil sauces.
- **Vinaigrettes.** Sauces based on oil and vinegar (or other acids).
- **Flavored butters.** Simple or compound, either used as butter by itself or used in making hot butter sauces based on stocks and essences.

And these sauces are made from three main elements:

- **The liquids.** Water, beef bouillon, consommé of poultry or game, essence of meats, milk, cream, butter, the blood of certain animals and birds, wine, vinegar, and oil.
- **The flavors or seasonings (*Assaisonnement*).** Essences of truffles, mushrooms, ham, root vegetables, tomatoes, garlic, onions and shallots, citrus and other fruits; game, crayfish, and fish and shellfish broths; spices like pepper, nutmeg, cinnamon, vanilla, mustard; aromatics like thyme, bay, chives, fennel, leeks, parsley, chervil.
- **The liaison.** Sauces are thickened either by reducing the liquids or by using a liaison—a butter and flour roux, or potato flour or corn starch mixed first into cold bouillon, water, or milk.

BROWN SAUCES

THE BASIC BROWN SAUCES ARE THE CLASSIC *Sauce Espagnole* and Brown Sauce. *Sauce Espagnole Maigre is* the basis for brown sauces made with fish stock.

SAUCE ESPAGNOLE AND DERIVATIVES

 ### *Sauce Espagnole*

½ cup fat (lard or unsalted beef, veal,
   or pork rendered fat)
½ cup flour
8 cups (2 quarts) brown beef stock
1 tablespoon chopped fresh thyme,
   or 1 teaspoon dried thyme

½ cup thick tomato puree
1 cup Mirepoix
Salt and freshly ground
   black pepper

Melt fat in a 3-quart saucepan. Blend in flour. Stir and cook until flour has turned the color of a hazelnut, about 10 minutes. Add 6 cups of the stock, mix well, and simmer 4 hours. Strain. Add thyme, tomato puree and Mirepoix. Add remaining 2 cups stock and continue simmering 2 more hours, or until sauce has reduced to about 4 cups, stirring occasionally. Add salt and pepper to taste. Strain. Makes about 4 cups.

Quick Sauce Espagnole

¼ cup (½ stick) butter
½ cup finely chopped onion
½ cup finely chopped carrots
2 tablespoons finely chopped parsley
2 teaspoons chopped fresh thyme,
   or ½ teaspoon dried thyme
½ small bay leaf

4 tablespoons flour
1 cup dry white wine
2½ cups clear brown stock or bouillon
1 tablespoon tomato puree
⅛ teaspoon freshly ground black pepper
Salt to taste

Melt butter in a 1½-quart saucepan. Add the next 5 ingredients and stir and cook over low heat for 12 minutes, or until vegetables are soft and begin to brown. Remove from heat and blend in flour. Stir and cook over medium-low heat until the roux turns the color of a hazelnut. Stir in the wine and stock. Bring to the boiling point and simmer 30 to 40 minutes. Add tomato puree and pepper. Add salt to taste if needed. Makes 1½ cups.

Beef Marrow Sauce or Sauce Bordelaise

Ask butcher to split the marrow bone so the marrow can be easily removed.

1 tablespoon finely chopped
    shallot or onion
1 tablespoon butter
¾ cup dry red wine
1 cup Sauce Espagnole

⅓ cup diced beef marrow
½ cup brown stock or bouillon
¾ teaspoon lemon juice
¾ teaspoon chopped parsley
¹⁄₁₆ teaspoon freshly ground black pepper

Cook shallot in butter until limp. Add wine and cook until reduced to ¼ cup. Add Sauce Espagnole. Poach marrow gently in hot water 1 to 2 minutes. Remove from water and drain well. Add marrow to the sauce, along with remaining ingredients, just before serving. Serve with grilled meats (steaks, chops) or sweetbreads. Makes about 1 cup.

Rouennaise Sauce

2 cups Sauce Espagnole
4 uncooked duck livers
Dry red wine

Heat Sauce Espagnole to near the boiling point. Finely chop livers and push them through a sieve into the sauce. Heat just enough to barely cook the livers. Add wine until sauce is desired consistency. Serve with wild or domestic duck. Makes about 2⅓ cups.

Sauce Italienne

1 teaspoon chopped shallot
1 cup peeled and seeded tomatoes
¾ cup dry white wine
2 tablespoons finely chopped
    mushrooms
1 tablespoon butter

½ cup Sauce Espagnole
2 tablespoons chopped cooked lean ham
1 teaspoon chopped parsley
1 teaspoon lemon juice
Salt and freshly ground black
    pepper

Cook shallot and tomatoes in wine until the mixture has reduced by half. Stew the mushrooms in the butter and add them to the tomato mixture, along with the Sauce Espagnole and ham. Cook 5 minutes, stirring constantly. Strain. Add parsley and lemon juice. Season to taste with salt and pepper. Use with meats, poultry, fish, leftover meats, and vegetables, especially artichokes. Makes about 1 cup.

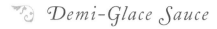

Demi-Glace Sauce

2 cups Sauce Espagnole
2 cups brown meat stock
2 tablespoons sherry

Combine Sauce Espagnole and meat stock in a 1½-quart saucepan. Simmer until the mixture has reduced to 2 cups. Remove from heat and stir in sherry. Makes 2 cups.

Venison Sauce

1 cup dry red wine
2 teaspoons caramelized sugar
¼ cup chopped onion
2 cups Demi-Glace Sauce

2 tablespoons butter
1⁄16 teaspoon freshly ground black pepper
Dash cayenne

Combine the first 3 ingredients in a 1-quart saucepan. Bring to the boiling point and simmer until reduced by half. Add Demi-Glace and cook until reduced to 2 cups. Strain. Add remaining ingredients. Use with marinated meats and game. Makes 2 cups.

Sauce Diable

2 shallots, finely chopped
1 cup dry white wine
2 cups Demi-Glace Sauce

Dash cayenne
Chopped fresh chervil

Cook shallots in wine until reduced by half. Stir in Demi-Glace and simmer until the liquid is reduced to 2 cups. Strain. Add cayenne and parsley. Use with broiled chicken or other broiled meats. Makes 2 cups.

Tarragon Brown Sauce

2 teaspoons chopped fresh tarragon,
    or ½ teaspoon dried tarragon
1 cup dry white wine

2 cups Demi-Glace Sauce
1 teaspoon chopped fresh tarragon

Simmer 2 teaspoons fresh or ½ teaspoon dried tarragon in wine for 15 minutes. Strain into Demi-Glace and cook until reduced to 2 cups. Add 1 teaspoon fresh tarragon or parsley. Use with chicken, fish, or lamb dishes. Makes about 2 cups.

BASIC BROWN SAUCE AND DERIVATIVES

Basic Brown Sauce

¼ cup (½ stick) butter or ¼ cup cooking oil
6 tablespoons flour
4 cups brown stock
Salt and freshly ground black pepper

Melt butter or heat oil in a 1-quart saucepan. If onion flavor is desired, cook 1 table-spoon finely chopped onion with the butter or oil. Remove from heat and blend in flour. Stir and cook over medium-low heat until the roux has browned, being careful not to burn it. Remove from heat and add stock. Stir and cook 2 to 3 minutes, or until sauce has thickened. Simmer for 2 hours, skimming occasionally to get rid of the fat and any scum from the surface of the sauce while it cooks and reduces. Strain, cool, and refrigerate until needed. Season with salt and pepper. Makes about 1¾ cups.

Madeira Sauce

Cook 2 cups Brown Sauce until reduced to 1 cup. Add ½ cup Madeira or sherry. Heat only to the boiling point. Do not boil. Serve with beef, veal, ham, or poultry. Makes 1¾ cups.

Mushroom Sauce

Cook ½ cup thinly sliced mushrooms in 1 tablespoon butter until tender. Drain well and add to 1 cup Brown Sauce. Cook only until hot. Stir in 1 additional table-spoon butter. Use with chicken, fish, eggs, or roast meats, or in casseroles. Makes about 1 cup.

Sauce Tortue

Add 1 teaspoon mixed dried herbs basil, marjoram, rosemary, and sage) to ⅓ cup boil-ing Madeira or sherry. Cover and steep 5 minutes. Strain into 2 cups of hot Brown Sauce. Heat 30 seconds. Add freshly ground black pepper to taste. Use with turtle meat, calf's head, or veal. Makes 2¼ cups.

Sauce Chasseur

1 cup sliced mushroom stems
2 shallots or 1 small white onion,
   finely chopped
¼ cup (½ stick) butter
½ cup dry white wine
1 cup Brown Sauce

¾ teaspoon chopped fresh tarragon
2 tablespoons thick tomato puree
½ teaspoon salt
½ teaspoon each chopped parsley
   and tarragon
Freshly ground black pepper

Cook mushrooms and shallots in the butter until they are tender and the butter has browned. Add wine and cook until reduced by half. Stir in Brown Sauce, tarragon, tomato puree, and salt. Simmer 5 minutes. Add parsley and pepper. Makes 1½ cups.

Sauce Lyonnaise

⅓ cup finely chopped onion
2 tablespoons butter
½ cup dry white wine

1 cup Brown Sauce
1 teaspoon chopped parsley
Salt and freshly ground black pepper

Cook onion in butter until golden brown. Add wine and cook until reduced by half. Add Brown Sauce. Stir and cook 10 to 15 minutes. Remove from heat and add parsley. Season to taste with salt and pepper. Use with meats and vegetables. Makes about 1 cup.

Sauce Robert

⅓ cup finely chopped onion
1 tablespoon butter
½ cup dry white wine
1 tablespoon vinegar
1 cup Brown Sauce

2 tablespoons Tomato Sauce
1 tablespoon prepared mustard
1 tablespoon chopped parsley
1 tablespoon chopped sour pickle
Salt and freshly ground black pepper

Cook onion in butter until golden brown. Add wine and vinegar and cook until reduced by one-fourth. Add Brown Sauce and Tomato Sauce. Simmer 10 minutes. Add mustard, parsley, and pickle. Season with salt and pepper. Use with meats. Makes about 1¼ cups.

Sauce Romaine

2 tablespoons sugar
½ cup vinegar
1 cup Brown Sauce

¼ cup dry white wine
2 tablespoons currants
1 tablespoon pine nuts

Stir and cook sugar in a heavy saucepan until it has melted and is golden in color. Add vinegar and cook until the liquid has reduced to a thick syrup. Stir in Brown Sauce and wine. Heat to the boiling point and simmer 15 minutes. Ten minutes before serving, combine raisins, and currants and cook 1 minute, or until fruits are plump. Add pine nuts. Use with beef, ham, tongue, or venison. Makes about 1 scant cup.

Red Wine Sauce Bourguignonne

2 tablespoons minced shallot or onion
2 cups red Burgundy
2 sprigs parsley
1 teaspoon chopped fresh thyme
½ small bay leaf
¼ cup sliced mushroom stems
2 tablespoons flour
2 tablespoons butter

Combine the first 6 ingredients in a 1-quart saucepan. Bring to the boiling point, reduce heat, and simmer until the liquid has reduced to 1 cup. Strain. Knead flour with butter and add to the sauce. Cook only long enough to cook the flour and thicken the sauce, 1 to 2 minutes. Use with meat, egg, or snail dishes. Makes 1 scant cup.

Sauce Duxelles

¼ cup chopped mushroom stems
1 tablespoon finely chopped onion
1 shallot, chopped
¼ cup chopped lean cooked ham
1 tablespoon butter
2 tablespoons flour
1 cup brown stock
1 tablespoon chopped parsley
2 tablespoons dry red wine
2 tablespoons tomato puree
Salt and freshly ground black
    pepper

Cook the first 4 ingredients in the butter until golden brown. Blend in flour and stir and cook until browned. Add stock, parsley, wine, and tomato puree. Stir and cook until thickened. Strain. Season to taste with salt and pepper. Use with roasts, poultry, or game. Makes about 1 cup.

Salmis Sauce

2 shallots, finely chopped
1 tablespoon olive oil or cooking oil
½ small bay leaf
½ teaspoon chopped fresh thyme
1 tablespoon finely chopped
    mushroom stems
½ cup dry white or red wine
1 cup game stock, (made from the
    carcass of cooked game bird)
1/16 teaspoon grated nutmeg
Dash cayenne
Salt and freshly ground black
    pepper
2 teaspoons currant jelly

Brown shallots in oil. Add the next 4 ingredients and cook slowly 5 to 6 minutes. Add stock and simmer 15 minutes. Strain. Add seasonings. Stir in jelly just before serving. Use with game birds. Makes about ¾ cup.

BROWN SAUCES
MADE WITH FISH STOCK

Sauce Espagnole Maigre

⅔ cup (1⅓ sticks) plus
   2 tablespoons butter
1 cup sifted all-purpose flour
8 cups (2 quarts) fish stock

¼ cup chopped onion
½ cup chopped mushroom stems
½ cup dry white wine

Melt the ⅔ cup butter in a 3-quart saucepan. Heat it until it begins to turn golden. Remove from heat and blend in flour. Stir and cook until the mixture is the color of a hazelnut. Remove from heat and add stock. Mix well. Cook 5 minutes, stirring constantly. In a sauté pan, cook onion and mushrooms in the remaining 2 tablespoons butter until they are tender. Add the wine to the onion mixture, then stir into the sauce. Simmer until sauce is semi-translucent, 1 to 2 hours, stirring and skimming frequently. The long cooking time makes a better-flavored sauce. Use with fish and egg dishes. Makes about 1 quart.

Sauce Bordelaise for Fish and Shellfish

Cook 2 tablespoons finely chopped shallot and ¼ cup finely chopped mushrooms in 2 tablespoons butter. Drain off liquid and reserve for later use. Add ½ cup dry white wine to shallot and mushrooms. Cook until the liquid is reduced by one-fourth. Add reserved liquid and 2 cups Sauce Espagnole Maigre. Simmer until mixture is reduced to 2 cups. Add an additional 2 tablespoons butter and 1 teaspoon chopped parsley. Makes about 2 cups.

Sauce Bourguignonne for Fish and Shellfish

Cook 2 tablespoons chopped onion in 1 tablespoon butter until limp. Add 1 sprig fresh thyme or ¼ teaspoon dried thyme, 1 small bay leaf, ½ cup diced mushrooms, and 1 cup dry red wine. Cook until reduced by half. Stir in 2 cups Sauce Espagnole Maigre and 2 tablespoons butter. Heat and strain. Makes about 2 cups.

Sauce Duxelles for Fish and Shellfish

Cook 2 tablespoons chopped shallot in 2 tablespoons each of butter and olive oil (or cooking oil) about 2 minutes. Add ½ cup each dry white wine and fish stock. Cook until reduced by half. Add ½ cup Sauce Duxelles, 1½ cups Sauce Espagnole Maigre, and ½ cup Tomato Sauce. Stir and bring to the boiling point. Reduce heat and simmer 20 minutes. Add 1 tablespoon chopped parsley. Makes about 2¼ cups.

Sauce Italienne for Fish and Shellfish

Cook ¼ cup each finely chopped onion and shallots in 2 tablespoons each of olive oil and butter until limp. Add 1 cup finely chopped mushrooms. Stir and cook 5 minutes. Add ½ cup dry white wine. Simmer until the liquid is reduced by half. Add 1½ cups Sauce Espagnole Maigre and ½ cup Tomato Sauce. Simmer 20 minutes. Stir in 1 teaspoon chopped fresh tarragon or ¼ teaspoon dried tarragon. Use with fish, cheese, egg dishes. Makes about 2¼ cups.

Red Wine Matelote Sauce

Cook ½ cup red wine marinade until reduced by half. Add 2 cups Sauce Espagnole Maigre and cook slowly until the liquid has reduced to 2 cups. Remove from heat and blend in 2 tablespoons butter, 2 teaspoons lemon juice, and a dash of cayenne. Serve with fish dishes. Makes about 2 cups.

Sauce Genévoise

½ cup chopped onion	2 pounds haddock, halibut, and
½ cup finely diced carrots	codfish bones
6 tablespoons butter	3 cups dry red wine, plus more as needed
1 bay leaf	Fish stock
1 sprig parsley	4 quarts Sauce Espagnole Maigre
1 small sprig fresh thyme	1 anchovy, mashed
2 pounds salmon heads, fins, and tails	¼ cup brandy

Cook onion and carrots in 2 tablespoons of the butter 10 to 12 minutes, or until lightly colored. Add herbs, salmon trimmings, and fish bones. Cover and let stand 30 minutes. Add the 3 cups wine and enough fish stock to cover the bones. Cover and simmer 20 minutes. Strain and let stock stand 20 minutes. Bring to the boiling point, add Sauce Espagnole Maigre, and cook until reduced to 1 quart. Strain. Blend in remaining 4 tablespoons butter, the anchovy, and brandy. If sauce is too thick, thin with additional red wine. Makes about 1 quart.

WHITE SAUCES

In spite of the wide diversity that characterizes and confuses the classification of French sauces, Béchamel and Velouté are always conceded to be basic white sauces. All the other white sauces included here have therefore been treated as variations or derivatives of one or the other.

BECHAMEL SAUCE AND DERIVATIVES

Basic Béchamel Sauce

4 tablespoons (½ stick) butter
4 tablespoons flour
1½ cups milk
½ cup heavy cream

1 teaspoon salt, or to taste
¹⁄₁₆ teaspoon freshly ground
    white pepper, or to taste

Melt butter in a 1-quart saucepan. Remove from heat and stir in flour. Stir and cook over medium-low heat about 1 minute. Remove from heat and add milk. Stir and bring to the boiling point. Add cream, salt and white pepper. Cook 30 seconds. If desired, use as a base for other sauces. Makes about 2 cups.

Ecossaise Béchamel Sauce

Cook 2 tablespoons each finely chopped onion, celery, carrot, and string beans in 3 tablespoons butter until vegetables are tender. Mix with 2 cups Béchamel Sauce. Makes about 2¼ cups.

Béchamel Mornay Sauce

Blend 1 cup light stock (veal, poultry, or fish) with 2 cups Béchamel Sauce. Bring to the boiling point and stir and cook 3 to 4 minutes. Remove from heat and add 3 tablespoons butter and ½ cup each grated Gruyère and Parmesan cheeses. Do not boil after adding cheeses. Makes about 3 cups.

Egg and Cream Mornay Sauce II

Blend 1 egg yolk with ¼ cup heavy cream and add to 2 cups hot Béchamel Sauce. Stir and cook 30 seconds. Add ½ cup grated Gruyère or Parmesan cheese. Cook only until cheese has melted. Do not boil. Makes about 2½ cups.

Rock Lobster Béchamel Sauce

Blend ¼ cup minced cooked rock lobster with ¼ cup (½ stick) butter. Add 2 cups hot Béchamel Sauce. Stir and cook 2 to 3 minutes. Season to taste with salt and cayenne. Use with shellfish dishes. Makes about 2⅓ cups.

Nantua Sauce

Grind the shells of crayfish with an equal amount of fish stock. Simmer together for 15 minutes. Add 2 cups Béchamel Sauce and simmer, while stirring another 10 minutes. Strain.

Sauce Cardinal

Use the same method as for Nantua Sauce, but substitute cooked lobster shells. Then add 1 tablespoon finely chopped truffle and ¼ cup heavy cream. Use with seafood or egg dishes. Makes about 2 ⅓ cups.

Shrimp Cardinal Sauce

In Sauce Cardinal, replace lobster shells with shrimp shells. Use with seafood or egg dishes.

Sauce Française

Cook ½ cup diced mushrooms in ½ cup water and 1 cup fish stock until liquid has reduced by half. Strain liquid into 2 cups Béchamel Sauce. Add ⅟₁₆ teaspoon each ground mace and minced garlic. Bring to the boiling point, stirring constantly. Blend 1 mashed anchovy with 2 tablespoons butter and stir into the sauce. Season with freshly ground white pepper to taste. Use with egg, cheese, fish dishes. Makes 2½ cups.

Onion Sauce Soubise

2 cups finely diced onions
1 cup water
2 tablespoons butter
2 cups Béchamel Sauce

½ cup heavy cream
½ teaspoon lemon juice
Salt and freshly ground white pepper

Cook onions in water until three-fourths done. Drain; discard water. Cook onions in butter until they are soft. Add Béchamel Sauce. Stir and cook 2 to 3 minutes. Push through a sieve into a saucepan. Bring to the boiling point. Add cream and lemon juice. Season to taste with salt and white pepper. Use with egg, lamb, sweetbreads, or beef dishes. Makes 2 cups.

VELOUTE SAUCE AND DERIVATIVES

Basic Velouté Sauce

4 tablespoons (½ stick) butter
4 tablespoons flour
2 cups white stock (veal, poultry, or fish)
Salt and freshly ground white pepper

Melt butter in a 1-quart saucepan. Remove from heat and stir in flour. Stir and cook over medium-low heat 1 minute, but do not brown. Remove from heat and add stock. Mix until well blended. Stir and cook until sauce thickens. Simmer over low heat for 30 minutes. Add salt and white pepper. Makes about 2 cups.

Fish Velouté Aurora Sauce

1½ cups fish Velouté Sauce
½ cup Tomato Sauce
¼ cup (½ stick) butter

Mix Velouté and Tomato Sauces in a 1-quart saucepan. Bring to the boiling point. Remove from heat and add butter. Makes about 2 cups.

Bretonne Sauce

½ cup julienned celery
½ cup julienned mushrooms
½ cup sliced white portions of leeks
3 tablespoons butter
½ cup fish stock
2 cups fish Velouté Sauce
Salt and freshly ground
  white pepper

Cook vegetables in 2 tablespoons of the butter 3 to 4 minutes over medium heat. Add stock and cook until vegetables are tender. Add to Velouté Sauce, along with remaining butter. Season with salt and white pepper. Makes about 3½ cups.

Fish Velouté Caper Sauce

2 cups fish Velouté Sauce
2 tablespoons capers
¼ cup (½ stick) butter
Salt and freshly ground white pepper

Heat Velouté Sauce. Remove from heat and blend in capers and butter. Add salt and white pepper. Use with fish, egg, or vegetable dishes. Makes about 2 cups.

White Wine Herb Sauce Chivry

2 tablespoons each chopped fresh
    parsley chives, chervil, tarragon
½ cup dry white wine
2 cups Velouté Sauce
¼ cup heavy cream
2 tablespoons chopped watercress
1 tablespoon chopped fresh tarragon
¼ cup (½ stick) butter

Combine herbs, wine and Velouté Sauce in a 1½-pint saucepan. Cook until the wine is reduced by half. Add cream. Blend watercress and tarragon with butter and add to the sauce. Season to taste with salt and white pepper. Makes about 2½ cups.

Curry or Indian Sauce

¼ cup finely chopped onion
1 tablespoon butter
1 tablespoon curry powder
¼ cup fish or chicken stock
1½ cups fish or chicken Velouté Sauce
½ teaspoon dried thyme
$\frac{1}{16}$ teaspoon ground mace
½ cup heavy cream
Salt and freshly ground black
    pepper to taste

Cook onion in butter until limp but not browned. Add curry powder and stir and cook 2 minutes. Add stock (fish stock if used with fish dishes; chicken stock if used with chicken dishes). Bring to the boiling point and stir in Velouté Sauce, thyme, and mace. Bring to the boiling point again and simmer for 30 minutes, stirring constantly. Add cream and season to taste with salt and pepper. Use with eggs, crab, prawns or chicken dishes. Makes about 2 cups.

Sauce Dieppoise

6 cooked, peeled, and deveined shrimp
2 tablespoons butter
1½ cups fish Velouté Sauce
2 tablespoons mussel stock
¾ cup shelled small mussels
    (cooked in dry white wine)
Salt and freshly ground white
    pepper

Mince and mash shrimp. Mix with butter and add to Velouté Sauce. Beat in the stock. Stir and cook only until hot. Add mussels and heat through. Season with salt and white pepper. Use with fish dishes. Makes about 2 ⅓ cups.

Sauce Victoria

Add ½ cup diced mushrooms cooked in 1 tablespoon butter to Sauce Homard. Serve over cheese puddings, fish puddings, or souffles.

⁓ Sauce Fines Herbes

1 tablespoon chopped shallot
1 tablespoon butter
2 cups fish Velouté Sauce
½ cup heavy cream
1 tablespoon chopped parsley

1 tablespoon chopped chives
1 teaspoon chopped fresh chervil
1 teaspoon chopped fresh tarragon
Salt and freshly ground
   white pepper

Cook shallots in butter until they are limp. Add to Velouté Sauce and cream. Heat to the boiling point. Strain, then add herbs. Season with salt and white pepper. Use with fish or egg dishes. Makes 2 cups.

⁓ Sauce Homard

2 cups fish Velouté Sauce
½ cup heavy cream
1 teaspoon paprika
2 tablespoons uncooked lobster coral,
   pounded and minced

¼ cup (½ stick) butter
½ cup diced cooked lobster
Salt and freshly ground white
   pepper

Combine Velouté Sauce, cream, and paprika. Stir and cook over low heat 2 to 3 minutes. Mix lobster coral with butter and whisk into the sauce, along with the diced lobster. Season with salt and white pepper. Serve over fish puddings or seafood soufflés. Makes about 2¼ cups.

⁓ Tarragon Velouté Sauce

The Velouté Sauce should be made with fish stock or chicken stock, according to the use for which the Tarragon Sauce is intended.

2 tablespoons plus 1 teaspoon
   chopped fresh tarragon
½ cup white wine

2 cups fish or chicken Velouté Sauce
¼ cup heavy cream
Salt and freshly ground white pepper

Parboil 2 tablespoons of the fresh tarragon in wine. Cool, strain, and mash with ¼ cup of the Velouté Sauce. Push through a fine sieve, then blend with the cream and the remaining Velouté Sauce. Stir and cook only until hot, add 1 teaspoon fresh tarragon and salt and white pepper to taste. Use with fish, chicken, or egg dishes.

Parsley Sauce

6 tablespoons coarsely chopped parsley
½ cup hot water
2 cups Velouté Sauce

¼ cup heavy cream
Salt and freshly ground white pepper

Blanch 5 tablespoons of the parsley in the hot water. Cover and steep 5 minutes. Cool, strain, and pat dry in a clean towel. Add the remaining 1 tablespoon parsley to the Velouté Sauce. Bring to the boiling point and simmer 3 to 4 minutes. Add blanched parsley and the cream. Heat 30 seconds. Season with salt and white pepper. Use with fish, egg, poultry, or vegetable dishes. Makes 2 cups.

Sauce Ravigote

½ cup dry white wine
¼ cup wine vinegar
2 cups Velouté Sauce
1 tablespoon minced shallot
2 tablespoons butter

1 tablespoon chopped chives
¼ teaspoon each fresh chervil
   and tarragon
Salt and freshly ground white pepper

Combine wine and vinegar and cook until reduced by half. Add to Velouté Sauce. Bring to the boiling point. Remove from heat and add shallot, butter, and herbs. Season to taste with salt and white pepper. Heat 30 seconds. Use with egg, fish, or lamb dishes. Makes 2 cups.

Venetian Sauce

½ cup tarragon vinegar
2 tablespoons chopped shallot
2 teaspoon each chopped fresh
   chervil and tarragon

2 cups fish Velouté Sauce
1 tablespoon each finely chopped
   parsley and watercress
¼ cup (½ stick) butter

Cook together vinegar, shallot, chervil, and tarragon until the liquid has reduced to ¼ cup. Strain into Velouté Sauce. Stir and cook 2 to 3 minutes. Blend parsley and watercress with butter and add to the sauce. Heat 30 seconds. Use with fish or egg dishes. Makes 2 cups.

SAUCE SUPRÊME AND VARIATIONS

Sauce Suprême is made by adding heavy cream to thick Velouté Sauce, using only enough cream to thin the sauce to the correct consistency. It may be made in a small amount for immediate use, or in a larger quantity and stored in a covered jar in the refrigerator and used as a base for making variations. Use for eggs, fish, poultry, vegetables, and for dishes that are to be gratinéed.

Sauce Suprême

FOR ABOUT 2 1/2 CUPS:

2 cups Velouté Sauce
About 1½ cups heavy cream

Salt and freshly ground white pepper
Lemon juice

Heat Velouté sauce to the simmering point. Beat in cream, 1 tablespoon at a time, until sauce is of desired consistency. Season to taste with salt, white pepper, and lemon juice.

Sauce Ambassadrice

Whip ⅓ cup heavy cream and fold it into 1 cup Sauce Suprême along with ⅔ cup finely chopped white meat of chicken. Use for egg, poultry, or vegetable dishes.

Sauce Albuféra

Add 2 tablespoons concentrated chicken or veal stock to 2 cups Sauce Suprême. Heat to the simmering point and stir in 1 tablespoon pimento puree and a dash of cayenne. Use for sweetbreads and poached or braised poultry. Makes a generous 2 cups.

Sauce Alexandra

Stir ¼ cup light stock and 1 teaspoon finely chopped truffles into 1 cup Sauce Suprême. Heat. Use for fish or poultry dishes. Makes 1¼ cups.

Suprême Sauce Aurora

Add 3 tablespoons thick tomato puree or well-reduced Tomato Sauce to 2 cups Sauce Suprême. Heat and stir in 1 tablespoon butter just before using. Use for eggs, fish, or poultry. Makes 2¼ cups.

Celery Sauce

Cook 1 cup finely chopped celery and a small bouquet garni in 1 cup rich chicken stock or bouillon until celery can be mashed to a pulp. Push through a sieve. Add to 2 cups Sauce Suprême. Heat to the simmering point. Do not boil. Use for broiled or braised poultry. Makes about 2⅓ cups.

Suprême Sauce Chivry

Cook 2 teaspoons each chopped fresh chervil, chives, and tarragon and 1 tablespoon chopped watercress in ½ cup rich chicken stock or dry white wine until the liquid is reduced by two-thirds. Add 1 tablespoon cooked spinach and push through a fine sieve. Stir into 2 cups Sauce Suprême. Heat only to the boiling point. Use with eggs or poultry. Makes about 2¼ cups.

Sauce Duchesse

Cook ¼ cup finely chopped mushrooms in 2 tablespoons butter for 2 minutes. Add ¼ cup chopped pickled tongue and heat 1 minute. Stir into 2 cups Sauce Suprême. Heat to the simmering point. Do not boil. Use with eggs, vegetables, or meats. Makes about 1⅓ cups.

Sauce Ivoire

To 2 cups hot Sauce Suprême, add enough chicken glaze to make an ivory-colored sauce. Use with eggs, sweetbreads, or poultry. Makes 2 cups.

Sauce à la Reine

Just before serving, heat 2 cups Sauce Suprême to the boiling point. Do not boil. Whip ⅓ cup heavy cream and fold it into the sauce, along with ¼ cup finely julienned white chicken meat. Use with eggs, poultry, or vegetables. Makes 2¾ cups.

Rich Tarragon Sauce

Cook ¼ cup chopped fresh tarragon in ½ cup rich chicken stock, dry white wine, or dry vermouth until the liquid is reduced to 3 tablespoons. Push through a sieve into 2 cups Sauce Suprême. Heat. Just before serving, stir in 1 teaspoon each chopped parsley and tarragon. Use with eggs, fish, chicken, or vegetables. Makes a scant 1¼ cups.

SAUCE ALLEMANDE AND VARIATIONS

Sauce Allemande is a variation of Sauce Suprême, which in its turn is a derivative of Velouté Sauce. Since Sauce Allemande is rich with cream and eggs, serve it only with less rich foods such as boiled chicken or poached fish and vegetables.

Sauce Allemande

FOR 2½ CUPS:

2 large egg yolks
½ cup heavy cream

2 cups Sauce Suprême
2 teaspoons lemon juice

Beat egg yolks lightly with a little of the cream and blend with Sauce Suprême. Stir and cook only to the boiling point. Gradually stir in lemon juice and remaining cream. Do not boil after egg yolks have been added, or the sauce will curdle. Serve with boiled chicken, poached fish, or vegetables, and as the base for making numerous other sauces.

Sauce Polonaise

Blend 3 tablespoons grated fresh horseradish with 2 cups Sauce Allemande. Heat only until hot. Stir in ½ teaspoon sugar, 1 tablespoon each chopped parsley, lemon juice, and butter. Thin sauce with stock or bouillon, if necessary, to desired consistency. Heat 30 seconds. Use with meat dishes. Makes about 2¼ cups.

Sauce Imperatrice

Heat 1⅓ cup Sauce Allemande. Stir in 1 tablespoon chicken glaze and 1 teaspoon finely chopped truffles. Whip ⅓ cup heavy cream and fold it into the mixture. Use with fish, chicken, or egg dishes. Makes about 2 cups.

Sauce Gasconne

Cook 1 cup chicken or veal stock until reduced to ½ cup. Add 1 teaspoon chopped chives, ¼ teaspoon each fresh chervil and tarragon, and 2 teaspoons chopped parsley. Strain and cook until the mixture is reduced nearly to a glaze. Add 2 cups Sauce Allemande and heat to the boiling point. Blend in anchovy paste to taste. Use with seafood, egg, or vegetable dishes. Makes about 2 cups.

Sauce Poulette

Cook ½ cup minced mushrooms in 1 tablespoon butter over low heat until soft but not brown. Add 2 cups Sauce Allemande and bring to the boiling point. Remove from heat and stir in 2 teaspoons lemon juice and 1 teaspoon chopped parsley. Serve with fish, brains, poached lamb's feet, eggs, or poultry. Makes about 2 cups.

Sauce Regence

Cook ½ cup finely diced mushroom stems in ¾ cup water until mushrooms are tender, about 5 minutes. Strain off the water and place it in a saucepan with ½ cup white Rhine wine. (Discard mushroom stems.) Cook until the liquid is reduced by half. Stir in 2 cups Sauce Allemande, 2 teaspoons finely chopped truffles, and a dash of cayenne. Heat only until hot. Serve with sweetbreads, oven roasts, or braised chicken. Makes about 2¼ cups.

Sicilian Sauce

Combine ¼ cup each Tomato Sauce, pimento puree, and chicken stock with 2 cups Sauce Allemande. Mix well. Stir and cook over low heat only until hot. Do not boil. Serve with fish or egg dishes. Makes about 2½ cups.

SAUCE NORMANDE AND VARIATIONS

Sauce Normande

1 tablespoon flour	2 large egg yolks
2 tablespoons butter, melted	½ cup heavy cream
1 cup fish stock, or oyster or	Dash cayenne
mussel liquor	Salt and freshly ground white
¼ cup mushroom stock	pepper

Blend flour with butter. Stir and cook 3 minutes without letting it turn color. Remove from heat and add stocks. Mix well. Bring to the boiling point and simmer 30 minutes, stirring frequently. Blend egg yolks with cream. Add to the sauce. Heat only until hot. Do not boil. Add cayenne and salt and white pepper. Strain. Use with fish and shellfish. Makes about 1¼ cups.

Anchovy Sauce

To Sauce Normande recipe, add 1 teaspoon anchovy paste or 1 finely diced anchovy fillet. Strain. Use with fish.

Sauce Diplomate

To Sauce Normande recipe, add 2 tablespoons finely chopped lobster meat and 1 teaspoon finely chopped truffles. Strain. Use with fish and shellfish.

Sauce Normande Ecossaise

Cook 1 tablespoon each finely diced carrots, celery, turnips, and leeks or onions in 2 tablespoons butter until vegetables are tender. Blend with Sauce Normande, along with 1 teaspoon finely chopped truffles. Strain. Use with fish.

Sauce Normande with Oysters

Poach 1 dozen small oysters in their own liquor only until edges curl. Remove oysters and finely chop them. Strain liquor and cook until reduced by half. Add to Sauce Normande, along with the oysters. Add salt and freshly ground white pepper to taste. Strain. Use with fish and oysters. Makes about 1¾ to 2 cups.

Sauce Joinville

Add 1 tablespoon each finely chopped cooked shrimp and crayfish tails and 1 teaspoon finely chopped truffles to Sauce Normande. Strain. Use with shellfish.

Sauce Laquipière

Add 2 tablespoons sherry and 1 teaspoon finely chopped truffles to Sauce Normande. Strain. Use with fish.

WHITE WINE SAUCES
WITH A FISH VELOUTE BASE

White Wine Fish Velouté Sauce

4 cups fish Velouté Sauce
2 cups fish stock
1 cup (2 sticks) butter, plus
    additional for keeping

Juice of half a lemon
Dry white wine

Add fish stock and the white wine to the Velouté Sauce. Cook over high heat until reduced to 1 quart. Remove from heat; blend in the 1 cup butter and the lemon juice. Strain. If you plan to hold the sauce, butter the surface. Makes about 5 cups.

Glazed White Wine Sauce

4 cups fish stock
2 cups heavy cream
¼ cup (½ stick) butter

Juice of half a lemon
Dash cayenne
Dry white wine

Cook the stock until reduced to a glaze, add cream, and cook until reduced to the consistency of sauce. Remove from heat and allow to cool a little (this is important). Beat in the butter. Stir in lemon juice and cayenne. Add wine until sauce is of desired consistency. Makes about 2 cups.

Glazed Fish Velouté White Wine Sauce

1¾ cups fish Velouté Sauce
⅓ cup plus 1 tablespoon fish stock
½ cup dry white wine
1 shallot, chopped

2 large egg yolks
¼ cup (½ stick) butter
Salt and freshly ground white
    pepper

Combine the Velouté Sauce, ⅓ cup fish stock, the wine, and shallot in a 1½-quart saucepan. Boil down to half the original amount. Mix egg yolks with the 1 tablespoon fish stock and gradually add to the sauce. Stir and cook over low heat 30 seconds. Add butter and stir until melted. Season with salt and white pepper. Makes about 1¼ cups.

Sauce Bercy

4 shallots, chopped
1½ tablespoons butter
1⅓ cups white wine
1⅓ cups fish stock

2⅔ cups fish Velouté Sauce
1 teaspoon lemon juice
1 tablespoon chopped parsley

Cook shallots in butter until they are limp and transparent (do not brown). Add wine and fish stock and boil down to one-third the original amount. Add Velouté Sauce and heat only to the boiling point. Remove from heat and whisk in the butter, lemon juice, and parsley. Serve with fish. Makes about 3 cups.

Sauce Marinière

½ cup mussel liquor
3 large egg yolks
2 cups Sauce Bercy

1 tablespoon butter
Salt and freshly ground white
    pepper

Cook mussel liquor until reduced by half. Blend egg yolks with Sauce Bercy and add to the mussel liquor, along with butter. Season with salt and white pepper. Use with fish dishes. Makes about 2¼ cups.

Sauce Comtesse

2 cups fish Velouté Sauce
½ cup dry white wine
¼ cup heavy cream
1 anchovy filet

2 tablespoons butter
1 teaspoon lemon juice
Salt and freshly ground black
    pepper

Mix Velouté Sauce with wine in a 1-quart saucepan. Cook until reduced by one-third. Add cream. Heat only to the boiling point. Mash anchovy to a paste, blend with butter, and add to the sauce, along with lemon juice. Season with salt and pepper. Use with fish or egg dishes. Makes about 1¾ cups.

Sauce Grandville

¾ cup diced mushrooms
4 tablespoons (½ stick) butter
2 cups fish Velouté Sauce
½ cup dry white wine
1 tablespoon finely chopped truffles

⅓ cup cooked shrimp,
    peeled and deveined
Salt and freshly ground white
    pepper

Cook mushrooms in 2 tablespoons of the butter and strain the liquid into Velouté Sauce, reserving mushrooms. Add wine, mix well, and cook sauce until it has reduced to 2 cups. Add remaining butter, reserved mushrooms, the truffles, and shrimp. Season with salt and white pepper. Use with fish puddings, souffles, or other fish dishes. Makes about 2¼ cups.

Fish Velouté Hungarian Sauce

½ cup chopped onion
3 tablespoons butter
½ cup dry white wine
2 cups fish Velouté Sauce

2 tablespoons paprika
Small bouquet garni
Salt and freshly ground white
    pepper

Cook onion in 1 tablespoon of the butter until limp but not browned. Add wine and cook until reduced by half. Stir in the next 3 ingredients. Simmer 5 minutes. Remove from heat and add remaining butter and salt and white pepper to taste. Use with fish or egg dishes. Makes about 2 cups.

White Matelote Sauce

½ cup sliced mushroom stems
½ cup dry white wine
2 cups fish Velouté Sauce

¼ cup (½ stick) butter
Salt and freshly ground white
    pepper

Cook mushrooms in wine until they are tender and the liquid has been reduced by half. Strain into Velouté Sauce. Stir and cook 2 to 3 minutes. Add butter. Season with salt and white pepper. Use with fish or egg dishes. Makes about 2 cups.

Sauce Orleannaise

¼ cup chopped mushroom stems
½ cup fish stock
¼ cup dry white wine
2 cups fish Velouté Sauce

¼ cup cooked, minced, mashed crayfish tails
2 tablespoons butter
Salt and freshly ground white
    pepper

Cook mushroom stems in stock and wineuntil stock has reduced by half. Strain into the Velouté Sauce. Stir and cook 3 minutes. Stir in crayfish and butter. Season with salt and white pepper. Use with seafood dishes or eggs. Makes 2¼ cups.

Sauce Pompadour

½ cup fish stock
½ cup dry white wine
2 cups fish Velouté Sauce
1 tablespoon truffles, julienned

¼ cup cooked, minced, mashed crayfish
2 tablespoons butter
Salt and freshly ground white
    pepper

Cook stock and wine together until the liquid is reduced by half. Add to Velouté Sauce. Bring to the boiling point. Add the next 3 ingredients. Season with salt and white pepper. Use with fish dishes. Makes 2½ cups.

Shrimp and Lobster Sauce

2 cups fish Velouté Sauce
½ cup fish stock
¼ cup heavy cream
¼ cup cooked, peeled, deveined,
    and minced shrimp

2 tablespoons minced cooked lobster
¼ cup (½ stick) butter
Salt and freshly ground white
    pepper
Whole cooked shrimp, peeled and deveined

Combine the first 3 ingredients in a 1½-quart saucepan. Cook over medium heat until reduced to 2 cups. Remove from heat and stir in minced shrimp, lobster, and butter. Heat only until hot. Season with salt and white pepper. Garnish with whole cooked shrimp. Use over seafood dishes. Makes about 2½ cups.

OTHER TYPES
OF FRENCH SAUCES

CERTAIN TYPES OF SAUCES, though equally characteristic of French cookery, have features that distinguish them from the brown sauces and white sauces already described. These include chaud-froid sauces—jellied sauces that can be based on Béchamel, Velouté, or Brown Sauce; tomato sauces; Hollandaise and related cooked emulsion sauces; mayonnaises and other cold emulsion sauces; and various simple and compound butters and butter sauces.

CHAUD-FROID SAUCES

A CLASSIC CHAUD-FROID SAUCE is actually a jellied white sauce. It is used to coat shapely and elegant cooked cold dishes—fish, chicken, ham, roasts, and other dishes for cold buffets.

The authentic French method of making chaud-froid is by cooking Velouté or Béchamel Sauce, white stock, heavy cream, and jellied veal, chicken, or fish stock (see "Jellies") together until the liquid is reduced to the desired consistency and will coat a spoon, the cream and jelly being added to the other ingredients a little at a time (see Chaud-Froid Sauce). The kind of stock and jelly used is determined by the food to be coated. If jelly is not available, a very good and easily made coating sauce can be made by softening 1 envelope unflavored gelatin in ¼ cup dry white wine or dry vermouth (or stock or water) and stirring it into 2 cups hot Velouté or Béchamel Sauce. The sauce is then strained and cooled but no refrigerated.

Another method is to simmer stock or consommé and heavy cream with herbs and aromatics (such as parsley, tarragon, thyme, onion) for about 10 minutes, then stir softened unflavored gelatin into the hot liquid (see Cream Chaud-Froid Sauce).

Chaud-froid may also be made with Brown Sauce. This is especially appropriate for some meat and chicken dishes, and some cooks prefer it because of its appetizing brown color.

To apply a chaud-froid sauce, first thoroughly chill the food, then coat it with the sauce and refrigerate until the coating is almost set (about 2 hours). If the first coat is not thick enough, apply another one and refrigerate again. Decorations are then applied to the food; they may be as simple or as elaborate as desired. Finally, coat the whole with a thin layer of clear liquid aspic.

The decorations may be strips of pimento, eggplant peel, and green bell pepper, lemon and orange rinds, thinly sliced ham and tongue, slice hard-cooked eggs and cucumbers, green olives or ripe olives, thin carrot slices, cooked green peas, truffles, mushrooms, chives, and the stems and leaves of herbs. Dip decorations in clear aspic before placing them on the coated food. To make stems and leaves of herbs more pliable for decorative purposes, dip them in boiling water for about 30 seconds and pat them dry.

Always test the chaud-froid sauce before you start to work with it. Pour a little into a small chilled dish and refrigerate it. If it does not set in 10 to 15 minutes, add a little melted softened gelatin and test again.

Chaud-Froid Sauce

4 tablespoons flour	2 cups chicken, veal, or fish jelly
4 tablespoons (½ stick) butter, melted	¾ cup heavy cream
2 cups chicken, veal, or fish stock	Salt and freshly ground white pepper

Blend flour with butter. Stir and cook over low heat 1 minute. Remove from heat and stir in stock (the kind depends upon the food to be coated). Mix well. Stir and cook slowly 30 minutes removing the scum occasionally. Add jelly and cream, a little of each at a time, and cook until the sauce is reduced to desired consistency and will coat a metal spoon. Add salt and white pepper. Strain. Cool the sauce while stirring (to prevent a skin forming) until it is quite cold. Do not refrigerate until it has been spooned over the food. Makes about 2½ cups.

Cream Chaud-Froid Sauce

In the preceding recipe, omit the jelly and reduce the amount of cream to ¼ cup. Soften 1 envelope unflavored gelatin in ¼ cup dry white wine or vermouth (or stock or water) and add to the hot sauce. Strain and cool. Makes about 2 cups.

Brown Chaud-Froid Sauce

Use either of the two preceding recipes for Chaud-Froid Sauce, making the following changes: Cook flour with butter until the mixture has browned but not burned. Replace light stock with brown stock.

Aromatic Chaud-Froid Sauce

½ cups rich chicken, veal, or fish stock, or canned chicken broth or consommé	¼ teaspoon dried thyme or tarragon, Salt and freshly ground white pepper
1 cup heavy cream	1 envelope unflavored gelatin
1 small onion, sliced	¼ cup dry white wine, vermouth,
¼ cup diced carrot	stock, or water

Place the first 5 ingredients in a 1½-quart saucepan and bring to the boiling point. Reduce heat and simmer until the liquid has reduced to 2 cups. Add salt and white pepper to taste. Soften gelatin in wine and add to the sauce. Strain and cool. Makes about 2¼ cups.

Green Chaud-Froid Sauce

Add 2 tablespoons cooked, pureed green herbs (parsley, chervil, tarragon, or thyme) to 2 cups of any of the preceding chaud-froid sauces. Strain and cool.

Chaud-Froid à l'Indienne

Cook 2 tablespoons chopped onion and 1 teaspoon curry powder in 1 tablespoon butter until onion is limp. Add to 2 cups of any of the preceding chaud-froid sauces. Strain through two layers of cheesecloth or a very fine sieve.

Chaud-Froid Madeira

Add Madeira to taste to the basic chaud-froid recipes. Strain and cool.

Chaud-froid Nantua

Add 2 tablespoons crayfish puree to 1 cup of the basic chaud-froid sauce. Strain and cool.

Paprika Chaud-Froid

Add 1 teaspoon paprika to 1 cup of the basic chaud-froid sauce and stir in a dash of cayenne.

Chaud-Froid Rosé

Add ¼ cup thick tomato puree to 2 cups of the basic chaud-froid sauce. Mix well, strain, and cool.

Chaud-Froid Royale

Add 2 tablespoons truffle puree to 2 cups of the basic chaud-froid sauce. Mix well, strain, and cool.

Saffron Chaud-Froid Sibérienne

Steep ⅛ teaspoon crumbed saffron strands in 1 tablespoon boiling stock or water for 10 minutes. Strain into 2 cups of the basic chaud-froid sauce.

TOMATO SAUCES

Tomato Sauce

½ cup finely diced carrots	1½ cups brown stock
¼ cup finely diced celery	½ bay leaf
¼ cup finely diced onion	1 teaspoon each fresh thyme and oregano
1 small clove garlic, cut in half	¼ teaspoon freshly ground black pepper
3 tablespoons butter or olive oil	2 teaspoons salt
2½ cups diced fresh	

Cook the first 4 ingredients in butter until onion is tender but not browned. Add remaining ingredients. Bring to the boiling point and boil gently 20 minutes, or until sauce has thickened, stirring frequently. Push sauce through a sieve. Heat again. Use with fish, shellfish, meat, or vegetables. Makes about 2½ cups.

Sauce Creole

Cook 1 tablespoon chopped shallot in 1 tablespoon butter until shallot is tender but not brown. Add ½ cup dry white wine and cook until reduced by one-third. Add to recipe for Tomato Sauce. Cook ½ cup diced green or red bell pepper in 2 tablespoons butter or olive oil until peppers are tender. Add to sauce mixture and cook 10 minutes. Strain through a sieve. Use with fish, shellfish, chicken, or vegetables. Makes about 2¾ cups.

Sauce Portugaise

½ cup finely chopped onion	½ cup thick tomato puree
1 small clove garlic	2 teaspoons chopped fresh basil
3 tablespoons butter or olive oil	2 teaspoons chopped fresh thyme
4 medium-sized tomatoes, diced	Salt and freshly ground black
1 cup fish stock	pepper
½ bay leaf	2 tablespoons chopped parsley

Cook onion and garlic in 2 tablespoons of the butter until onion is soft. Remove and discard garlic. Add the tomatoes, stock, and bay leaf and cook gently 30 minutes, or until sauce has thickened. Add tomato puree, herbs, and salt and pepper. Stir and cook 5 minutes. Push through a sieve. Add parsley and remaining butter or oil. Use with fish. Makes about 2¼ cups.

 Sauce Provençale

3 shallots, chopped
1 small clove garlic
⅓ cup olive oil
3 pounds (12 small or 9 medium-sized) tomatoes, diced

1 cup veal stock
½ cup chopped parsley
1 teaspoon sugar
Salt and freshly ground black pepper

Cook shallots and garlic in oil until shallots are soft. Add the next 4 ingredients. Cook gently 40 to 50 minutes, or until sauce has thickened. Season with salt and pepper. Push through a sieve. Use with eggs, fish, chicken, meat, or vegetables. Makes about 3 cups.

HOLLANDAISE AND RELATED SAUCES

Hollandaise Sauce

¾ cup (1½ sticks) butter
3 large egg yolks, well beaten
4 teaspoons lemon juice

Dash salt
Dash cayenne

Break butter into 3 pieces. Put 1 piece in the top of a double boiler. Add egg yolks and lemon juice. Beat with a wire whisk constantly while cooking over hot water (not boiling) until butter is melted. Add the second piece of butter, and continue beating and cooking until the mixture thickens, never allowing the water to boil. Add the last piece of butter. Stir and cook until sauce has thickened. Remove from heat and stir in salt and cayenne. Serve with fish, shellfish, or vegetables, or, if desired, use as the base for one of the following variations.

Should the Hollandaise mixture curdle, add 1½ tablespoons boiling water, beating constantly, to rebuild the emulsion. Makes ¾ cup.

Anchovy Hollandaise Arlesienne

To ¾ cup Hollandaise Sauce, stir in ½ teaspoon anchovy paste or to taste. Serve over fish, eggs, or vegetables. Makes ¾ cup.

Caviar Hollandaise Marquis

To ¾ cup Hollandaise Sauce, add 1 ounce black caviar. Serve over fish, eggs, or asparagus. Makes ¾ cup.

Cucumber Hollandaise

To ¾ cup Hollandaise Sauce, add 1½ cups well-drained, finely chopped peeled cucumbers. Serve with fish and shellfish. Makes about 2 cups.

Curry Hollandaise

To ¾ cup Hollandaise Sauce, add 1 teaspoon curry paste. Serve on fish, shellfish, or eggs. Makes ¾ cup.

Tomato Hollandaise Figaro

To ¾ cup Hollandaise Sauce, add 3 tablespoons Tomato Sauce, 1 teaspoon finely chopped parsley, and a dash each of salt and cayenne. Serve with fish. Makes 1 scant cup.

Citrus Hollandaise

To ¾ cup Hollandaise Sauce, add ¼ teaspoon grated lemon, orange, lime or other citrus zest. Serve over vegetables or fish. Makes ¾ cup.

Mustard Hollandaise

Replace lemon juice in recipe for Hollandaise Sauce with 1½ tablespoons tarragon vinegar. Mix 1½ teaspoons dry mustard with 1 tablespoon water and let stand 5 minutes for flavor to develop. Stir into the sauce. Serve with fish, shellfish, chicken, or eggs. Makes ¾ cup.

Orange Hollandaise Maltaise

To ¾ cup Hollandaise Sauce, add 2 tablespoons blood orange juice and ½ teaspoon grated blood orange zest. Serve on asparagus or whole string beans. Makes 1 scant cup.

Sauce Mousseline

Into ¾ cup Hollandaise Sauce, fold ⅓ cup heavy cream, whipped, after the last piece of butter is added. Serve on vegetables or fish. Makes 1 generous cup.

Sauce Paloise

To ¾ cup Hollandaise Sauce, add 1 tablespoon mint infusion at the time the last piece of butter is added. Just before serving, fold in 1 teaspoon chopped fresh mint. Serve with lamb or veal. Makes ¾ cup.

Béarnaise Sauce

3 tablespoons white wine vinegar	¾ cup unsalted butter
1 chopped shallot	1 tablespoon each chopped fresh
1 teaspoon each chopped chervil and	chervil and tarragon leaves
tarragon stems	salt and pepper
3 large egg yolks	

Reduce in a small pan the vinegar, shallot and herb stems over low heat until 1 table-spoon of liquid is left. Strain and put in a double boiler with the egg yolks. Whisk and heat while adding and whisking in the butter a piece at a time. Add the chopped chervil and tarragon at he last moment. Season with salt and pepper.

Sauce Valois or Foyot

To ¾ cup Béarnaise Sauce, add ¾ teaspoon melted beef essence or glaze. Serve with eggs or broiled chicken. Makes ¾ cup.

Sauce Choron

To ¾ cup Béarnaise Sauce, add 1 to 1½ teaspoons tomato puree, and omit herbs. Serve with fish, vegetables, or chicken. Makes ¾ cup.

MAYONNAISE AND OTHER
COLD EMULSION SAUCES

Mayonnaise

2 large raw egg yolks or
   1 large whole egg
½ teaspoon salt or to taste
¼ teaspoon paprika

¹⁄₁₆ teaspoon freshly ground white pepper
Dash cayenne
2 tablespoons lemon juice
1 cup olive or pure vegetable oil

Put eggs, salt, paprika, white pepper, and cayenne in a 1-quart bowl. Beat well. Beat in 1 tablespoon of the lemon juice. Gradually beat in oil, ½ teaspoon at a time, until ¼ cup has been added. Beat in 1 to 2 tablespoons oil at a time, beating well after each addition. Add remaining lemon juice after ½ cup oil has been added. Beat in remaining oil. Use for salads, sandwiches, and sauces. Makes about 1¼ cups.

If mayonnaise curdles when making, beat in another egg yolk and continue as directed above.

Coating Mayonnaise

Soften 1½ teaspoons unflavored gelatin in cold water. Melt in a pan of hot (not boiling) water and stir into 1 cup mayonnaise. Use immediately to coat cold dishes where regular mayonnaise may have a tendency to slip off. This mayonnaise may also be forced through a decorating tube to make designs on salads and mousses. Makes 1 cup.

Sauce Berlinoise

To cup 1 mayonnaise, add 2 tablespoons red currant jelly and 1 teaspoon grated lemon zest. Beat with a fork. Use with fruit salads. Makes 1 generous cup.

Sauce Dijonnaise

Add prepared Dijon mustard to taste to mayonnaise. Use for egg, meat, poultry, fish, or shellfish salads.

Mayonnaise Espagnole

To 1 cup mayonnaise, add ⅓ cup finely chopped cooked lean ham, 1 tablespoon paprika, and ¹⁄₁₆ teaspoon minced garlic. Use for meat or egg salad. Makes 1⅓ cups.

Green Mayonnaise or Sauce Verte

To 1 cup mayonnaise, add 1 tablespoon each finely chopped parsley, watercress, chervil, and tarragon. Add ½ tablespoon chopped cooked, squeezed spinach. Adjust seasonings with a little lemon juice, salt, and freshly ground black pepper to taste. Use with vegetables, eggs, fish, or shellfish. Makes 1 generous cup.

Horseradish Mayonnaise

Blend 1 cup mayonnaise with 1 tablespoon each well-drained horseradish sauce, black caviar, and chopped fresh parsley. Use for egg or seafood salad. Makes 1 generous cup.

Roquefort Mayonnaise

To 1 cup mayonnaise, add ½ cup finely crumbled Roquefort. Add a dash of cayenne. Use with apple, fruit, celery, cabbage, or potato salads. Makes 2 cups.

Lobster Mayonnaise Americaine

To 1 cup mayonnaise, add ½ cup pureed cooked lobster, 1 tablespoon each paprika and chopped parsley, and 1 teaspoon dry mustard soaked in 1 tablespoon water. Use with fish, shellfish, eggs, or vegetables. Makes 1½ cups.

Sauce Antiboise

To 1 cup mayonnaise, add 1 teaspoon anchovy paste (or to taste), ¼ teaspoon dried tarragon or ¾ teaspoon chopped fresh tarragon, and 2 tablespoons thick tomato sauce. Use with vegetables, fish, or shellfish. Makes 1 generous cup.

Cypriote Sauce

Push 3 large hard-cooked egg yolks through a sieve and mix with 1 mashed anchovy and ¼ cup thick Tomato Sauce. Mix with 1 cup mayonnaise and ¹⁄₁₆ to ⅛ teaspoon ground fennel seeds. Use with fish, egg, or vegetable salads. Makes about 1½ cups.

Grimod Sauce

Cut enough truffles into short julienne strips to make 2 tablespoons. Simmer until almost dry in ⅓ cup sherry. When cool, add to 1 cup mayonnaise. Use with chicken or ham salads. Makes 1 generous cup.

Ravigote Mayonnaise

To 1 cup mayonnaise, add 1 mashed anchovy filet, 1 finely chopped hard-cooked egg white, and 1 tablespoon lemon juice. Cook 2 tablespoons each chopped parsley, chervil, capers, onion, and shallot in ¼ cup dry white wine until all but 1 tablespoon of liquid is evaporated. Cool. Add to mayonnaise mixture. Chill. Use with eggs, fish, or shellfish. Makes a scant 1¼ cups.

Rémoulade Sauce

1 cup mayonnaise
2 tablespoons prepared Dijon or
   Creole mustard
1 tablespoon each finely chopped
   parsley, celery, capers, and
   gherkin pickle

1 teaspoon each chopped fresh
   tarragon and chervil
1 anchovy, mashed

Combine all ingredients. Use for fish, shellfish, or egg salads, or for fried or broiled fish. Makes about 1 ⅓ cups.

Rémoulade à l'Indienne

Cook 2 tablespoons minced onion and 2 teaspoons curry powder in 1 tablespoon pure vegetable oil 2 to 3 minutes and push through a sieve. Blend with 1 cup mayonnaise, along with 1 tablespoon chopped capers, 1 tablespoon chopped chives, ¼ teaspoon fresh tarragon, ⅛ teaspoon fennel seeds, and 1 mashed anchovy filet. Use for fish, shellfish, or eggs. Makes 1 generous cup.

Tartar Sauce I

To 1 cup mayonnaise, add 1 tablespoon each finely chopped parsley, gherkin pickle, green olives, and capers, and ½ teaspoon paprika. Use for fried or broiled fish, fried oysters, frogs' legs, or scallops. Makes about 1¼ cups.

Tartar Sauce II

To 1 cup mayonnaise, add 1 large hard-cooked egg (pushed through a sieve) and 1 teaspoon each chopped parsley and chives. Adjust seasonings to taste with salt and freshly ground black pepper. Serve with grilled or broiled fish and shellfish. Makes 1¼ cups.

Garlic Mayonnaise or Aioli Sauce

1 hot medium-sized cooked potato	3 large raw egg yolks
1 small clove garlic	2 cups salad oil
2 large hard-cooked egg yolks	Salt and freshly ground white pepper

Mash potato until smooth. Mash the garlic and add to potato. Push cooked egg yolks through a sieve and add. Mix well. Beat in raw egg yolks. Gradually beat in oil. Add salt and white pepper. Use for potato, egg, fish, shellfish, vegetable, or meat salads. Makes about 3 cups.

BUTTERS AND BUTTER SAUCES

Brown Butter or Beurre Noisette

Melt butter over very low heat until it is the color of a hazelnut. Serve over fish or vegetables. (It is important that this butter be browned over very low heat for best flavor.) To serve over grilled fish, allow 2 teaspoons browned butter per serving. For 6 servings of cooked vegetables, make ¼ cup browned butter.

Black Butter or Beurre Noir

Melt ½ cup (1 stick) butter and cook over medium-low heat until dark brown, being careful not to burn the butter. Remove from heat. Add 2 tablespoons chopped parsley and lemon juice to taste. Use with calves' brains or vegetables. Makes ½ cup.

Clarified Butter

Melt butter over hot water. Pour off the butter and discard the milky sediment left in the bottom of the saucepan or cup.

Thickening Butter or Beurre Manié

Blend ¾ cup sifted flour with 1 cup (2 sticks) butter. Use for sauces and gravies. Makes about 1½ cups.

Anchovy Butter

1 tablespoon anchovy paste, or 2 anchovies, mashed
½ cup (1 stick) butter, softened
Lemon juice

Blend anchovies with butter until well mixed. Add lemon juice to taste.
Use on broiled or poached fish. Makes ½ cup.

Caper Butter

Melt ½ cup (1 stick) butter over low heat. Skim off and discard foam. Stir in 1 tablespoon lemon juice, 3 tablespoons capers, and salt and freshly ground white pepper to
taste. Serve with calves' brains, vegetables, eggs, or fish. Makes ½ cup.

Garlic Butter

2 large cloves garlic
½ cup (1 stick) butter, softened
2 tablespoons chopped fresh parsley

Boil unpeeled garlic cloves in water covered for 5 to 6 seconds. Drain off water, peel
garlic, and rinse in cold water. Bring to the boiling point again in water covered and
boil 30 seconds. Remove from water and rinse. Push through a garlic press or pound
to a smooth paste in a mortar. Add to butter, along with parsley. Season with salt, pepper, and herbs, if desired. Use on steaks. Makes ½ cup.

Horseradish Butter

Push 2 tablespoons grated fresh horseradish through a sieve and blend with ½ cup (1
stick) softened butter. Use for meats. Makes ½ cup.

Maître d'Hôtel Butter

Blend 2 tablespoons chopped parsley and 1 tablespoon lemon juice into ½ cup (1
stick) softened butter. Season to taste with salt and freshly ground white pepper. Use
with chicken and fish dishes. Makes ½ cup.

Herb Butter

Blend ¼ cup softened butter with any of the following herbs or combinations:

1 teaspoon chopped fresh rosemary
2 teaspoons chopped fresh thyme
2 teaspoons chopped fresh tarragon
2 tablespoons chopped watercress and 1 teaspoon chopped fresh parsley
1 tablespoon chopped parsley and 2 tablespoons chopped chives

Makes about ¼ cup.

Lobster Butter

Break up and pound shells from 2 cooked lobsters, plus any of the creamy parts that may cling to inside of shells. Place in the top part of a double boiler along with 1 cup (2 sticks) butter. Melt slowly over hot water. Strain through 2 layers of cheesecloth. Cool. Store in a covered jar in the refrigerator for up to three days to use for adding flavor to fish sauces. Makes 1 cup.

Mustard Butter

Mix 2 tablespoons mustard with ½ cup (1 stick) softened butter. Use with fish, ham, or beef and as butter for canapés.

Nut Butter

½ cup toasted hazelnuts or almonds
½ cup (1 stick) butter

Put half the nuts at a time in an electric blender. Turn on blender and run 4 to 6 seconds, or until nuts are very fine. Mix with butter. Use in cream sauces. Makes ¾ cup.

Paprika Butter

1 shallot, finely chopped
2 tablespoons butter plus ¼ cup (½ stick) butter, softened
1 teaspoon paprika

Cook shallot in the 2 tablespoons butter until golden. Stir in paprika. Cool. Blend with the remaining ¼ cup butter. Serve with broiled poultry or fish. Makes a generous ¼ cup.

Smoked Salmon Butter

Mince smoked salmon and push through a sieve to make ¼ cup. Then blend with ½ cup (1 stick) softened butter. Stir in ½ teaspoon paprika and a few drops of lemon juice. Use as butter for canapés and in fish sauces. Makes ¾ cup.

Tomato Butter

Cook 1 small tomato and 1 finely chopped shallot in 2 tablespoons butter until the mixture is almost dry. Push through a sieve, then cool. Blend with ½ cup (1 stick) softened butter. Use with fish and white meat of poultry. Makes a generous ½ cup.

COMPOUND FLAVORED BUTTERS

Bercy Butter

4 shallots, finely chopped
½ cup dry white wine
½ cup (1 stick) butter, softened

Lemon juice to taste
Salt and freshly ground black
    pepper

Cook shallots in wine until almost all the liquid has evaporated. Cool. Beat in butter. Season with lemon juice, salt, and pepper. Serve on broiled steaks and chops. Makes a generous ½ cup.

Shallot Butter

3 shallots, finely chopped
½ cup dry white wine
½ cup (1 stick) butter, softened

Cook shallots in wine until half the liquid has evaporated. Strain. Cook liquid until almost all the liquid has evaporated. Cool. Beat in butter. Use to spread on sandwiches, corn on the cob, fish, or steaks. Makes ½ cup.

Chivry Butter

4 shallots, chopped
2 tablespoons chopped parsley
1 teaspoon chopped tarragon

2 teaspoons chopped chervil
½ cup (1 stick) butter

Blanch herbs and shallots for 5 minutes in hot water to cover contents. Drain and pat dry thoroughly with a towel. Push through a sieve. Cool and blend with butter. Serve with fish. Makes ½ cup.

Fermière Butter

5 large hard-cooked egg yolks	Dash cayenne
1 cup (2 sticks) sweet butter, softened	3 tablespoons dry white wine
Salt and freshly ground black pepper	Lemon juice to taste
	1 teaspoon prepared mustard

Push egg yolks through a sieve and blend with butter. Add salt and pepper, cayenne, wine, lemon juice, and mustard. Mix well. Use with fish or vegetable dishes. Makes 1⅓ cups.

Butter à l'Indienne

Cook 2 tablespoons chopped shallot in 2 tablespoons butter until tender but not browned. Add 1 teaspoon curry powder. Stir and cook 1 minute. Blend in 1 tablespoon Allemande or Béchamel Sauce. Heat 30 seconds. Cool, beat in ½ cup (1 stick) softened butter. Use with fish, shellfish, poultry, or egg dishes. Makes ½ cup.

SAUCES FROM OTHER COUNTRIES

A number of sauces developed by cooks outside France are worthy additions to the sauce repertoire. For the convenience of the cook, they are divided here into sauces made with stock or wine, those made with oil, and fruit and herb sauces to be served with meat.

SAUCES MADE WITH STOCK OR WINE

English Fried Bread Sauce

1 shallot, chopped	⅓ cup finely diced cooked ham
1 cup soft breadcrumbs	Salt and freshly ground white pepper
½ cup (1 stick) butter	Lemon juice to taste
1½ cups chicken stock	1 tablespoon chopped parsley

Cook shallot and breadcrumbs in butter until bread and butter are golden. Add stock and simmer 10 minutes, stirring frequently. Stir in remaining ingredients. Serve with roast game birds or poultry. Makes approximately 1¾ cups.

English Caper Sauce

2 tablespoons flour
2 tablespoons butter, melted
2 cups lamb or mutton stock

1 tablespoon capers or to taste
Salt and freshly ground black pepper

Blend flour with butter. Stir and cook 1 minute. Remove from heat and add stock. Bring to the boiling point and simmer 5 minutes, stirring constantly. Add remaining ingredients. Use on boiled lamb or mutton. Makes about 1½ cups.

English Egg Sauce

2 cups Béchamel Sauce
Salt and freshly ground white
   pepper

6 hard-cooked eggs, diced
About ¼ cup heavy cream

Heat the Béchamel Sauce, add the eggs, season, and thin to desired consistency with cream. Heat 30 seconds. Serve with fish, shellfish, or vegetables. Makes about 2½ cups.

English Game Sauce

½ teaspoon whole peppercorns,
   crushed
2 whole cloves
½ teaspoon dried thyme
1 small bay leaf

½ cup vinegar
2 cups veal stock
1 cup water
½ cup red currant jelly
⅓ cup each currants and raisins

Place the first 5 ingredients in a 1-quart saucepan. Cook until the liquid is reduced by half. Add stock and cook to reduce by half. Strain. Cook 1 minute, or until thickened. Stir in jelly. Bring currants and raisins to the boiling point with 1 cup water. Drain and pat dry on paper towels. Add to the sauce. Serve with game. Makes about 2½ cups.

English Brown Oyster Sauce

2 tablespoons flour
2 tablespoons butter, melted
½ cup oyster liquor
1 cup brown stock

12 oysters, chopped
Dash cayenne
Salt and ground white pepper

Blend flour with butter. Stir and cook until the mixture is light brown. Remove from heat and add oyster liquor and stock. Mix well. Bring to the boiling point, stirring constantly. Stir and simmer 30 minutes. Add oysters. Cook 2 minutes. Add cayenne and salt and white pepper to taste. Do not boil after adding oysters. Use for meat puddings, codfish, or grilled meats. Makes about 1½ cups.

Russian Smitane Sauce

½ cup chopped onion
2 tablespoons butter
Dash salt

1 cup dry white wine
1 cup sour cream
Lemon juice

Cook onion in butter until limp. Add salt and wine and cook until wine is reduced to ¼ cup. Add sour cream. Heat but do not boil. Add lemon juice to taste. Use with meats or vegetables. Makes about 1¼ cups.

SAUCES MADE WITH OIL

English Cambridge Sauce

4 hard-cooked egg yolks
2 anchovies
1 tablespoon capers, chopped
1 tablespoon chopped chives
¼ teaspoon chervil

¼ teaspoon tarragon
1½ cups pure vegetable oil
2 tablespoons vinegar
1 tablespoon chopped parsley

Push egg yolks through a sieve. Mash anchovies and capers together with herbs and add to the egg yolks. Mix to a smooth paste. Gradually beat in oil and vinegar as for Mayonnaise. Add parsley. Serve with game, fish, or eggs. Makes about 2¼ cups.

Russian Sauce

½ cup cooked lobster
1 tablespoon black caviar
2 cups mayonnaise

Mash lobster and caviar to a pulp. Fold into mayonnaise. Serve with cold fish. Makes 2½ cups.

Turkish Sauce

1 cup fresh breadcrumbs
3 large egg yolks
1 small clove garlic

1½ cups olive oil
1 tablespoon lemon juice or to taste
Salt and freshly ground black pepper

Mix breadcrumbs with egg yolks. Push garlic through a press and add to bread crumb mixture. Gradually blend in the oil and lemon juice. Add salt and pepper. Use with eggs or fish. Makes about 1⅔ cups.

Hungarian Ziska Sauce

2 teaspoons dry mustard
1½ tablespoons water
2 tablespoons chopped gherkin pickle
2 teaspoons sugar

Salt and freshly ground black
 pepper to taste
1½ cups olive oil
½ cup vinegar

Mix mustard with water and let stand 10 minutes. Then whisk with remaining ingredients. Serve with cold meat. Makes about 2 cups.

FRUIT AND HERB SAUCES

Austrian Apfelkern

3 medium-sized apples, grated
¼ cup sugar
1 tablespoon prepared horseradish

2 teaspoons paprika
Dry white wine

Combine apples, sugar, horseradish, and paprika. Stir in wine until sauce is of desired consistency. Use with pork, duck, and goose. Makes about 1½ cups.

English Applesauce

4 pounds (12 medium-sized) tart
 cooking apples
About 1 cup boiling water
1½ -inch stick cinnamon

¾ to 1 cup sugar
Dash salt
¼ teaspoon grated nutmeg (optional)

Peel, core, and slice apples. Cook in a covered saucepan with boiling water and cinnamon until apples are tender, stirring occasionally. Remove from heat, mash, and push through a sieve, if desired. Stir in sugar, salt, and nutmeg, if desired. Serve with meats, poultry, or as a topping for gingerbread and cake. Makes about 6 cups.

American Sanford Sauce

2 cups cooked Applesauce
1 tablespoon prepared horseradish
½ cup heavy cream, whipped

Combine applesauce and horseradish. Fold in whipped cream. Serve with duck, goose, or pork. Makes about 2¾ cups.

Danish Applesauce

4 cups cooked, sieved tart apples
¼ cup sugar or to taste
¼ cup orange juice
1 tablespoon lemon juice

1 tablespoon grated orange zest
1 teaspoon grated lemon zest
Sherry

Combine apples, sugar, orange and lemon juices, and orange and lemon zests. Add sherry until the sauce reaches the desired consistency, stirring sherry in well. Use with game birds, duck, goose, or pork. Makes about 4½ cups.

Swedish Applesauce

1 pound (3 medium-sized) tart apples
½ cup dry white wine

½ cup mayonnaise
Grated fresh horseradish to taste

Peel, core, and slice apples. Cook in wine in a covered saucepan until apples are tender and sauce is thick. Remove from heat and cool. Fold in Mayonnaise and horseradish. Use with pork, duck, or goose. Makes about 2 cups.

American Cranberry Relish

1 pound raw cranberries
1 medium-sized navel orange
2 cups sugar

Wash cranberries and set aside to drain. Grate the zest of the orange. Set aside. Peel off and discard the white portion of the orange rind. Put peeled orange through a food chopper, along with cranberries, using the medium blade. Add orange zest and sugar. Mix well. This relish will keep several weeks in a covered jar in the refrigerator. Use with poultry and meats. Makes about 4 cups.

English Cumberland Sauce

¼ teaspoon each salt, ground ginger
½ cup seedless raisins
1½ cups port
¼ cup currant jelly
¼ cup orange juice

2 tablespoons lemon juice
2 teaspoons grated orange zest
1 teaspoon grated lemon zest
1 teaspoon mustard
pinch cayenne

Put salt, ginger, and raisins in a saucepan with the port and simmer 8 to 10 minutes Add remaining ingredients. Cook 1 minute. Use with venison or other furred game. Makes about 1¾ cups.

English Fennel Sauce

⅓ cup finely chopped fresh fennel bulb
½ cup boiling water
½ cup (1 stick) butter, melted

Cook fennel in boiling water for 30 seconds. Drain and pat dry with paper towels. Add to butter. Stir and cook 1 to 2 minutes, or until butter begins to turn color. Do not brown. Serve with poached mackerel or other poached fish. Makes about ½ cup.

English Gooseberry Sauce

4 pounds fresh gooseberries
2 cups sugar
½ cup vinegar
¼ teaspoon salt

1 small stick cinnamon
¼ teaspoon whole allspice
¼ teaspoon whole cloves

Combine the first 5 ingredients in a 3-quart saucepan. Tie allspice and cloves in a cheesecloth bag and add. Cook 30 to 40 minutes, stirring frequently. Remove and discard spices. Cool sauce. Store in a covered jar in the refrigerator. Serve with poultry, meats, or game. Makes about 4 cups.

English Mint Sauce

¼ cup water
½ cup vinegar

⅓ cup finely chopped mint
1 tablespoon sugar or to taste

Combine all ingredients in a saucepan and heat. Do not boil. Let stand about 30 minutes before serving. Serve with lamb. Makes 1 generous cup.

English Orange Sauce

1 cup red currant jelly
¼ cup port
¼ cup orange juice

1 tablespoon lemon juice
1 tablespoon grated orange zest
½ teaspoon grated lemon zest

Break up jelly by beating with a fork. Add port and orange juice and heat only until jelly is melted. Stir in remaining ingredients. Serve with game, chicken, lamb, or veal. Makes about 1½ cups.

COLD
HORS D'OEUVRES,
CANAPES,
AND
SANDWICHES

THE 1950 ENGLISH EDITION OF THIS BOOK, called *Modern Culinary Art*, states about hors d'oeuvres that "from these thousand nothings, with a little taste of science, the most delightful things may be made." Of course they are not "nothings," because in the same breath, Pellaprat says that there is nothing like the presentation of a well-arranged tray of hors d'oeuvres to awaken the appetite.

How they look on the tray is half the secret to their success, and these little "nothings," which are as much a part of "impromptu" cooking with leftovers as they are made from the most sumptuous ingredients, can often steal the show if made properly and freshly. But whatever they are made of, there are a few guidelines to follow:

- If they precede a meal they should never ruin the appetite, only stimulate it.
- They should always be one-bite-sized so that they are easily, and without a mess, eaten.
- Never use raw onion or garlic if the occasion is a reception or cocktail party.
- When using toast or crackers, make sure the toast is not too brittle or it will shatter and the food will go flying.

Other suggestions for hors d'oeuvres are found elsewhere in the book, particularly in the chapters dealing with eggs, shellfish, and foie gras.

CAVIAR

THE ROE OR EGGS OF VARIOUS SPECIES of the sturgeon family is called caviar. Salmon roe is called red caviar. The roe is removed as soon as the fish is caught and prepared by removing the membrane and cellular tissue and salting the roe slightly (malossol) or more.

Either black or red caviar is served alone as an hors d'oeuvre, or mixed with sour cream and served with blinis or as an ingredient in sauces and salads.

With caviar, white wine, champagne, or iced vodka should be served.

FISH AND SHELLFISH HORS D'OEUVRES

Anchovies with Potato Salad Toulon

1 quart potato salad
3 hard-cooked eggs

9 large rolled anchovies
9 green olives, pitted

Mound potato salad in the center of an hors d'oeuvre dish. Slice the hardcooked eggs into thick rounds, remove the yolks, and place the egg-white rings around the salad. (Reserve the yolks and end slices for other use.) Put an anchovy in the center of each egg-white ring and an olive in the center of each anchovy. Makes 9 servings.

Anchovies Nîmes Style

Cut anchovies in half lengthwise and arrange them in lattice fashion in the center of an hors d'oeuvre dish. Sprinkle with oil from the can and with chopped hard-cooked egg yolk. Garnish with slices of small pickled beets. Allow 3 anchovies per serving.

Mixed Fish Hors d'Oeuvre

Place shredded lettuce in the bottom of an hors d'oeuvre dish. Cut various kinds of poached fish into large dice and coat with mayonnaise seasoned with dry mustard, cayenne, and lemon juice to taste. Garnish with sliced tomatoes, sliced hard-cooked eggs, and chopped parsley or onions.

Russian Herring

3 medium-sized crisp apples
1 tablespoon lemon juice
¼ cup finely chopped onion
3 to 4 pickled raw herring

Freshly ground black pepper
¼ cup dry white wine
2 tablespoons olive oil

Peel, core, and finely dice apples. Add lemon juice and onion. Mix well and mound in the center of an hors d'oeuvre dish. Trim all bones from herring and cut each lengthwise into 3 pieces. Arrange in lattice fashion on the apples. Mix remaining ingredients and sprinkle over apples and fish. Makes 6 servings.

Marinated Fresh Herring

¾ cup dry white wine
¾ cup wine vinegar
3 tablespoons chopped onion
⅓ cup thinly sliced carrots
2 shallots, sliced
6 whole peppercorns

1 small bay leaf
¼ teaspoon fresh thyme
2 tablespoons chopped parsley
Salt to taste
6 fresh herring, cleaned and dressed,
    heads removed

Place all ingredients except herring in a small saucepan. Cover and boil slowly 5 minutes. Place the herring in a larger saucepan and pour the marinade over them. Cook 5 minutes, or until herring is flaky, never allowing the sauce to boil. Cool and serve in the marinade. Makes 6 servings.

Fresh mackerel can be marinated in the same way.

Rollmops

In the recipe for Marinated Fresh Herring, replace whole fresh herring with fresh herring fillets. Roll the marinated fillets around gherkins and marinated onions, holding them in place with toothpicks or cocktail picks. Serve in the marinade.

Fillet of Smoked Herring Russian Style

4 smoked herring fillets
2 ripe firm apples
1 small onion, finely chopped

¼ cup dry white wine
2 to 3 tablespoons olive oil

Remove skins of the herrings. Cut fillets lengthwise into strips. Set aside. Core the apples but do not peel them. Dice the apples and mix with the onion. Mound in the center of an oval-shaped hors d'oeuvre dish. Garnish with herring strips in lattice fashion. Mix wine and oil and sprinkle over all. Makes 6 servings.

Red Mullet Oriental Style

10 (4-ounce) red mullet,
    cleaned and dressed
Salt and freshly ground black
    pepper to taste
¼ cup olive oil
4 medium-sized tomatoes, peeled,
    seeded, and diced

1 clove garlic, crushed
1 teaspoon chopped parsley
⅓ cup dry white wine
2 threads saffron
Sliced tomatoes

Roll mullet in flour seasoned with salt and pepper. Brown on both sides in hot oil. Remove fish to an ovenproof dish. Add diced tomatoes and the garlic to the hot oil; stir and cook 5 minutes. Blend in parsley, wine, and saffron; stir and cook slowly 5 minutes. Pour the sauce over the fish. Cook 10 minutes in a preheated oven (350°F). Chill. Garnish with sliced tomatoes. Makes 10 servings.

Norwegian Cured Salmon

Cut a dressed fresh salmon lengthwise into 2 halves. Rub each side with salt, then rub very generously with olive oil or salad oil. Sprinkle with chopped dill, chopped thyme, and 2 small crumbled bay leaves. Place fish in a shallow baking dish and cover with plastic wrap or cheesecloth. Refrigerate for 3 days, turning the salmon every day and keeping the dish covered. Remove fish from the dish and wipe dry. Rub very lightly with oil. Smoke 48 hours at a temperature between 64° and 68° F.

To serve the salmon, slice it very thinly and garnish with curly parsley. Serve with horseradish, whipped cream, lemon, and buttered toast. Or the slices may be shaped into cornets and filled with horseradish mixed with sour cream. Arrange radially on a round dish. Garnish the center with parsley.

Rock Lobster Parisienne

Cover the bottom of an hors d'oeuvre dish with shredded lettuce. Make a lobster form out of the pieces down the center line of the lettuce with the slices of the lobster. Then coat the lobster pieces with a highly seasoned mayonnaise (mustard, lemon juice, and tomato puree) and garnish with quartered hard-cooked eggs or lettuce hearts. If desired, replace rock lobster with cold poached fish. Makes 6 servings.

Sardines in Oil

Arrange sardines on one side of a round hors d'oeuvre dish in a fan shape. On the other side of the dish, put chopped hard-cooked egg yolks and chopped hard-cooked egg whites, chopped onion, and chopped parsley. Serve toast and butter on the side. Place slices of lemon around the edge of the dish. Allow 3 sardines per serving.

Sardines Rovigo

12 canned sardines
½ cup cold Tomato Sauce
Ground dried or chopped fresh sage

Green bell pepper, finely julienned
Chopped hard-cooked egg whites

Drain sardines and place on an hors d'oeuvre dish. Combine Tomato Sauce and sage and spread over sardines. Sprinkle with green-pepper strips and egg white. Makes 6 servings.

Marinated Smelts

18 smelts, cleaned and dressed
Flour
Salt and freshly ground black
    pepper to taste
¼ cup olive oil

⅓ cup dry white wine
2 tablespoons wine vinegar
3 shallots, chopped
1 tablespoon chopped parsley
½ teaspoon mustard

Roll smelts in flour seasoned with salt and pepper. Brown quickly on both sides in hot oil and remove to a warm platter. In a saucepan, combine remaining ingredients except for the mustard. Cover and cook just below the boiling point for 5 minutes. Then mix in the mustard. Bring to boiling point. Quickly remove from heat, chill the sauce, and pour over the smelts. Makes 6 to 9 servings.

Creamed Tuna Fish Mirabeau

1 (7-ounce) can tuna
¼ cup olive oil
½ cup (1 stick) softened butter
¼ cup mayonnaise

Lemon juice
Salt and freshly ground black pepper
18 pitted green olives
4 medium-sized tomatoes

Mash tuna with the olive oil. Mix with butter and mayonnaise until smooth. Add lemon juice, salt, and pepper to taste. Mound in the center of an oval dish and smooth the surface. Decorate the top with olives and make a border of tomatoes cut into eighths. Serve chilled. Makes 8 servings.

COLD PASTRY BOATS, TARTLETS, AND CANNELONI

VARIOUS HORS D'OEUVRE MIXTURES ARE SERVED in small pastry shells, either oval (boats or barquettes) or round (tartlets), or in puff pastry patties or horns. For cold mixtures, the shells are usually baked in advance; for hot hors d'oeuvres, they may be baked with the filling. They are always small, and served immediately after they are assembled.

Chicken Barquettes

2 cups finely diced cooked chicken
½ cup thick mayonnaise
1 teaspoon chopped fresh tarragon
¼ teaspoon lemon juice
Salt and freshly ground black
ƒ pepper

Aspic
Truffles
Tarragon or parsley leaves
36 baked boat-shaped tart shells, cooled

Combine chicken, mayonnaise, dried or chopped tarragon, lemon juice, salt and pepper. Spoon into tart shells or pipe the mixture into the shells with a pastry bag, using a round or star tube. Glaze the tops with aspic. Garnish with slices of truffle and tarragon or parsley leaves. Makes 3 dozen.

Goose-Liver Barquettes Strasbourgeoises

1 cup foie gras puree
6 tablespoons softened butter
18 small baked puff pastry boats, cooled

Aspic
1 truffle

Blend foie gras with butter until smooth and creamy. Spoon or pipe into pastry boats. Glaze with aspic. Garnish with a small slice of truffle. Makes 18.

Fish Barquettes Beauharnais

1½ cups diced cooked fillet of sole
½ cup diced cooked mussels
½ cup plus white fish
    Chaud-Froid Sauce
Salt and freshly ground black
    pepper

Cooked crayfish tails or very small
    cooked shrimp
Truffles
36 baked boat-shaped tart shells, cooled

Combine sole, mussels, ½ cup Chaud-Froid Sauce, salt and pepper. Spoon or pipe the mixture into baked tart shells. Coat with additional Chaud-Froid Sauce. Garnish each with a crayfish tail or a shrimp and a bit of truffle. Makes 3 dozen.

Roquefort Cheese Boats or Barquettes

6 tablespoons butter
4 ounces Roquefort cheese
½ teaspoon paprika
About 3 tablespoons port

2 tablespoons unsweetened whipped cream
12 small baked puff pastry boats, cooled
½ cup port wine jelly, melted

Beat butter until creamy. Add cheese and paprika and enough port to make a smooth creamy consistency. Fold in whipped cream. Spoon the mixture into pastry boats, or pipe it in with a pastry bag, using the star tube. Allow filling to set. Glaze with melted wine jelly. Makes 12.

Shrimp Barquettes

2 cups finely diced cooked shrimp
½ cup mayonnaise
½ teaspoon lemon juice
Salt and freshly ground black
    pepper

36 baked boat-shaped tart shells, cooled
Aspic
Hard-cooked egg
Chervil or parsley leaves

Combine shrimp, mayonnaise, lemon juice, salt and pepper. Spoon into tart shells. Glaze with aspic. Garnish with hard-cooked egg slices cut into halves and chervil or parsley leaves. Makes 3 dozen.

Tuna Boats

1 (7-ounce) can white-meat tuna in oil
Lemon juice
Salt and freshly ground black pepper

12 small baked puff pastry boats, cooled
Anchovies
Aspic

Flake undrained tuna and mix it well with the oil in which it was canned. Add lemon juice, salt, and pepper to taste. Spoon into pastry boats. Garnish each with an anchovy. Glaze with aspic. Makes 12.

Cornets with Camembert

Roll puff pastry ⅛ inch thick and cut into strips ½ inch wide. Roll strips around small wooden or tin cones or funnels. Brush with mixture of beaten egg yolk and milk, using 1 teaspoon milk to each egg yolk. Sprinkle with grated Cheddar cheese. Bake in a preheated oven (425° F) about 12 minutes, or until browned. Remove cones while cornets are still hot. Cool. Fold enough whipped cream into soft Camembert cheese to make it fluffy, then fill cornets with Camembert mixture.

COLD MOLDED MOUSSES

A mousse to be served as a cold appetizer or luncheon dish is a rich, velvety-textured molded aspic made of poultry, ham, liver, fish, or shellfish forcemeat, enriched with whipped cream and sometimes with softened butter.

The mixture may be molded in one large mold or in individual molds. The molds are lined with rich aspic and decorated with truffles, hard-cooked eggs, herb leaves, sometimes olives, and strips of lean cooked ham or tongue.

A mousse is very impressive as an hors d'oeuvre or luncheon main dish, or on a cold buffet.

Chicken Mousse

About 3 cups clear chicken aspic	1 cup chicken Velouté Sauce
Truffles or black olives	1 cup heavy cream, whipped
Hard-cooked egg whites	Salt and freshly ground white pepper
2 slices pickled tongue	Lemon juice
2 cups finely ground poached breast of chicken	1 cup puree or mousse of foie gras
	Jellied aspic

Coat a 1½-quart mold or 6 to 8 individual molds with some of the aspic and chill until aspic is set. (If aspic does not jell, soften 1 envelope unflavored gelatin in ¼ cup water, melt over hot water, and add to the aspic.) Decorate mold as desired with bits of truffle or olives and egg whites and pickled tongue cut into fancy shapes. Affix each decoration with a few drops of aspic. Chill until aspic is set. Coat the mold again with another layer of aspic. Chill until aspic is set.

Combine chicken and Velouté Sauce and push the mixture through a sieve. Gradually add 2 cups of the aspic. Chill until the mixture just begins to set. Fold in whipped cream. Season to taste with salt, white pepper, and lemon juice. Spoon half of the mousse mixture into the prepared mold or molds until half-filled. Cover with a layer of sliced, chilled pâté. Finish filling with remaining mousse mixture. Chill until mousse is firm and ready to serve. Unmold onto a chilled serving plate and garnish with cubes of jellied aspic. Makes 6 to 8 servings.

Foie Gras Mousse

About 3 cups clear, well-seasoned
   chicken aspic
Truffles
Hard-cooked egg whites
1½ envelopes unflavored gelatin
¾ cup water
2 cups finely ground cooked goose
   or duck foie gras

¼ cup heavy cream, whipped
Salt and freshly ground white pepper
Lemon juice
Jellied aspic
Watercress

Coat a 1-quart mold or 6 individual molds with some of the aspic. Chill until aspic is set. Decorate with truffles and egg whites cut into fancy shapes. Affix each decoration to the mold with a few drops of aspic. Chill until aspic is set. Coat the mold again with aspic and chill until set.

    Soften gelatin in water. Melt over hot water. Remove from heat and cool to room temperature. Push foie gras through a fine sieve. Stir in melted gelatin. Fold in cream. Season to taste with salt, white pepper, and lemon juice. Turn the mixture into the mold or molds, filling a large mold to within ½ inch of the top, smaller molds to within ¼ inch of the tops. Finish filling with remaining aspic. Chill until set and ready to serve. Unmold onto a chilled serving plate. Garnish with cubes of jellied aspic and watercress. Makes 6 servings.

Ham Mousse

1 cup beef or veal aspic
Truffles
Hard-cooked eggs, sliced
4 cups very finely ground cooked ham
3 tablespoons dry sherry
2 tablespoons tomato puree
2 teaspoons prepared mustard

2 envelopes unflavored gelatin
⅓ cup cold water
1 cup very hot beef or veal stock
Salt
¼ teaspoon freshly ground black pepper
1 cup heavy cream, whipped

Coat a 1½-quart mold with some of the aspic and chill until set. Decorate the bottom of the mold with truffles and eggs. Affix each decoration with a few drops of aspic. Chill until aspic is set. Coat with another layer of aspic and chill again until set. Combine ham, sherry, tomato puree, and mustard. Mix until well blended. Soften gelatin in cold water. Add hot stock and stir until gelatin is dissolved. Add to the ham mixture, along with salt and pepper. Chill until mixture just begins to set. Fold in whipped cream. Turn into the prepared mold. Unmold onto a chilled plate. If desired, garnish with small deep baked tart shells filled with vegetable salad and diced jellied aspic. This mousse may also be molded in 6 or 8 individual molds. Makes 6 to 8 servings.

Salmon Mousse

1½ cups cooled fish aspic
Pimento
Hard-cooked egg whites
1 small round truffle
1½ firmly packed cups flaked
    poached salmon
1 envelope unflavored gelatin
½ cup cold water

¼ cup mayonnaise
¼ cup heavy cream
Lemon juice
Salt and freshly ground white pepper
Cayenne
Cubed jellied aspic
Watercress

Coat the bottom and sides of a fish-shaped mold with a thin layer of aspic. Chill until aspic is set. Outline the mouth, tail, and fins with thin strips of pimento, and the scales down the back with thin crescents of egg whites. Make the eye with a round piece of truffle. Affix these garnishes with a few drops of aspic. Chill until aspic is set. Pour in enough aspic to make a layer ½ inch thick. Chill until set.

Push salmon through a sieve. Soften gelatin in cold water and set in pan of hot water to melt. Blend with mayonnaise and cream and add to salmon. Mix well. Season to taste with lemon juice, salt, white pepper, and cayenne and spoon into mold. Chill until set. Unmold onto a chilled silver or glass platter. Surround fish with jellied aspic cubes. Garnish with watercress. Makes 6 servings.

HORS D'OEUVRE COCKTAILS

"COCKTAILS" AS HORS D'OEUVRES INCLUDE seafood, fruit, melon, and other food served cold with appropriate sauces in glasses or coupes. Like alcoholic cocktails, they are an American invention.

Avocado Cocktail

2 avocados
1½ tablespoons salad oil or olive oil
1½ tablespoons wine vinegar
¼ teaspoon salt
¼ teaspoon freshly ground
    white pepper
½ cup tomato ketchup

1 teaspoon each chopped parsley,
    chopped chives, and
    grated fresh horseradish
½ teaspoon finely chopped shallot
½ teaspoon prepared mustard
Dash Tabasco sauce
6 slices hard-cooked egg

Peel avocados, cut in half lengthwise and remove stones. Cut into slices ¼ inch thick. Combine oil, vinegar, salt, and white pepper, pour over avocado, and marinate at least 30 minutes in the refrigerator. Drain the marinade from the avocados and blend it with all remaining ingredients except the eggs. Add to avocados, mix gently, and chill. Serve in chilled coupes or cocktail glasses. Garnish each with a slice of egg. Makes 6 servings.

Crayfish Cocktail

½ cup mayonnaise
1 tablespoon tomato paste
2 tablespoons chile sauce
1½ teaspoons each chopped chives
   and chopped parsley
½ teaspoon onion juice

½ teaspoon Worcestershire sauce
Salt and freshly ground black
   pepper to taste
24 to 28 chilled cooked crayfish tails
2 diced chilled tomatoes
Cold hard-cooked egg whites

Combine all ingredients except the last 3. Add crayfish, mix gently, and chill. Just before serving, add tomatoes. Spoon into chilled coupes or cocktail glasses. Cut egg white into julienne and scatter over the top. Makes 4 servings.

The crayfish may be replaced with 1 cup chilled diced lobster, or with 24 chilled medium-sized whole shrimp.

Lobster Cocktail

½ cup thick mayonnaise
2 teaspoons grated fresh horseradish
3 tablespoons tomato ketchup
½ teaspoon paprika
½ teaspoon prepared mustard
¾ teaspoon each chopped fresh
   chervil and tarragon

1 teaspoon each brandy and dry sherry
Few drops Tabasco sauce
1 cup chilled cooked lobster in
   medium-sized chunks, plus
   4 large chunks cooked lobster
¼ head lettuce
8 chilled cooked asparagus tips

Combine all ingredients except lobster, lettuce, and asparagus tips. Add medium-sized lobster chunks to half the sauce and chill. Just before serving, shred the lettuce and place in 4 coupes or cocktail glasses. Divide the lobster mixture equally among the glasses. Garnish each with a large lobster chunk and 2 asparagus tips. Coat with the remaining sauce. Makes 4 servings.

Oyster Cocktail

⅓ cup mayonnaise
2 teaspoons grated fresh horseradish
2 tablespoons tomato ketchup
Lemon juice
Worcestershire sauce

Salt
Few drops Tabasco sauce
20 large raw oysters
Chopped parsley

Combine all ingredients except oysters and parsley. Add 16 of the oysters to the sauce. Chill. Serve in 4 coupes or cocktail glasses. Top each with a whole raw oyster. Garnish with chopped parsley. Makes 4 servings.

MELON COCKTAILS AND HORS D'OEUVRESS

Melon-Ball Cocktail

Cut a well-chilled honeydew, cantaloupe, or similar melon in half and remove seeds. Cut melon into small balls with a melon ball cutter. Pour red or white port over the balls, to partially cover them. Chill thoroughly. Serve in chilled coupe or cocktail glasses If desired, replace port with sherry, Marsala, or Madeira, or with rum or gin, with sugar and lemon juice to taste. Makes 6 servings. The melon balls can also be served in the halved melon shells, surrounded with cracked ice, on glass plates.

Melon Cocktail with Wine

Cut a slice from the stem end of a ripe cantaloupe, honeydew, or similar melon. Insert a tablespoon in the hole and remove the seeds. Pour in ½ cup red or white port, Madeira, sherry, Marsala, or Tokay. Replace the slice that was cut off. Chill at least 2 hours. Serve the melon in halves placed in crushed ice. Makes 6 servings.

Sliced Melon as Hors d'Oeuvre

Some ways of serving melons as an hors d'oeuvre are:
- Slice melon (cantaloupe, honeydew, Spanish) and serve with a slice of lemon or lime.
- Slice melon and sprinkle with sherry, Marsala, Tokay, Madeira, Kirsch, or Triple Sec.
- Slice melon and sprinkle with freshly ground black pepper or chopped fresh ginger.

Melon and Parma Ham

1 large cantaloupe or honeydew melon
Sherry
6 thin slices Parma ham

Cut a slice from the stem end of the melon. Scoop out the seeds with a spoon and drain well. Using a melon baller, cut balls from the flesh, leaving the rind intact. Replace the balls. Sprinkle with sherry. Chill 2 hours. To serve, spoon the balls onto silver or glass dishes, surrounded with (but not under) very thin slices of cooked ham. Makes 6 servings.

Melon with Prosciutto

1 large honeydew melon
6 slices prosciutto
1 lemon or lime

Cut melon in half. Scoop out seeds and drain well. Cut each half into 3 wedges and place each on a serving plate. Surround with very thin slices of prosciutto. Garnish each serving with a wedge of lemon or lime. Makes 6 servings.

Fresh figs are also often served with prosciutto as an hors d'oeuvre.

OLIVES

OLIVES, NATIVE TO THE EASTERN MEDITERRANEAN AREA, are grown throughout the Mediterranean countries, as well as in California, Mexico, and southern Australia. They are marketed in two forms: green olives, harvested before they are fully ripe, specially treated to remove the bitter taste, and then pickled in brine; and ripe olives, harvested after they have ripened, washed several times in water, put into boiling brine, dried, and pickled in oil.

The French cultivate a special variety of olive for the table. Known as *picholines*, they are large, elongated, and reddish black in color and are preserved in the finest olive oil. As an hors d'oeuvre they are served with a little of their marinade.

Either, green or black olives may be stuffed. Choose large olives, hold them upright on a folded towel, and remove stones with a cherry pitter or skewer.

Joinville Olives

6 large peeled, deveined, cooked shrimp
2 tablespoons softened salted butter
24 large pitted green or black olives

Pound or finely grind the shrimp, or puree them in a food processor. Mix with the butter and use the mixture to fill the olives. Serve as an hors d'oeuvre or use as a garnish for cold fish dishes.

Olives Sicilian Style

½ cup pureed fresh tomatoes
¼ cup pureed red or green bell pepper
Salt and ground white pepper

1½ teaspoons unflavored gelatin
2 tablespoons cold water
1 (9-ounce) jar large green olives, pitted

Combine tomato and pepper purees. Season to taste with salt and white pepper. Soften gelatin in cold water in a ramekin; set in a pan of hot water until gelatin melts. Add to the puree. Chill until the mixture just begins to set. Fill a decorating tube fitted with a small nozzle with the mixture and pipe into the olive cavities. Chill until the filling is set. Serve on an hors d'oeuvre tray or use to garnish salads or cold meat dishes.

VEGETABLES A LA GRECQUE

VEGETABLES À LA GRECQUE ARE COOKED IN WATER or court bouillon with olive oil, lemon juice, wine, and various herbs and spices. They are usually served slightly chilled as hors d'oeuvre, with some of the cooking liquor used as a sauce.

Artichokes à la Grecque

8 very small artichokes
1 teaspoon salt
¾ cup boiling water or bouillon
¾ cup dry white wine
¼ cup olive oil
1 sliced onion

1 tablespoon lemon juice
1 bay leaf
6 whole peppercorns
1 sprig parsley
¼ teaspoon each chervil and tarragon

Trim artichokes, cut off the tips of the leaves, wash, and drain well. Place artichokes with all the remaining ingredients, cover, and cook 30 minutes, or until artichokes are crisp-tender. Cool in the liquor. Makes 8 servings.

Celery à la Grecque

18 celery hearts
½ teaspoon salt
Boiling water
¾ cup boiling water or bouillon
¾ cup dry white wine
¼ cup olive oil

2 tablespoons lemon juice
1 small bay leaf
6 whole peppercorns
1 sprig parsley
¼ teaspoon each chervil and tarragon

Place celery in a saucepan with salt and enough boiling water to cover it. Cover and boil 3 minutes. Drain off and discard water. Add remaining ingredients. Cover and cook only until celery is crisp-tender, 5 to 10 minutes. Cool in liquor. Makes 6 servings.

Leeks à la Grecque

In the Celery à la Grecque recipe, replace celery with the white part of leeks cut into 2- to 3-inch pieces. Proceed as for celery. Makes 6 servings.

Fennel à la Grecque

In the preceding recipe, replace the celery with ribs of fennel, the large ribs cut in half lengthwise. Leave a few fennel leaves attached to the ribs. Blanch fennel in salted boiling water 10 minutes. Drain off and discard the water. Finish cooking as in directions for the celery. Makes 6 to 8 servings.

Mushrooms à la Grecque

1¼ pounds large white mushrooms
1 cup boiling water
¾ cup dry white wine
½ cup olive oil
3 tablespoons lemon juice

1 small bay leaf
6 whole peppercorns
¼ teaspoon salt
2 sprigs parsley

Wash mushrooms. Remove stems and save them for soups or sauces. Cut mushroom caps into quarters. Place all other ingredients in a saucepan, cover, and cook over low heat 5 minutes. Add mushrooms and cook 6 to 8 minutes over low heat. Cool in liquor. Makes 8 servings.

Onions à la Grecque

1½ pounds small white onions
1 teaspoon plus ¼ teaspoon salt
Boiling water
¾ cup dry white wine

½ cup olive oil
3 tablespoons lemon juice
1 small bay leaf
6 whole peppercorns

Peel onions and place in a saucepan with the 1 teaspoon salt and boiling water to cover. Cover and cook over low heat 10 minutes. Drain off and discard water. Put ¼ teaspoon salt, 1 cup boiling water, and remaining ingredients in a saucepan, cover, and cook over low heat 5 minutes. Add onions and cook over medium heat until onions are tender, 12 to 15 minutes. Cool in liquor. Makes 10 to 12 servings.

STUFFED VEGETABLES

Stuffed Artichoke Bottoms

12 cooked artichoke bottoms
French dressing
1 cup finely diced cooked
    crayfish tails or shrimp
⅓ cup finely diced celery

Salt and freshly ground blackpepper
½ teaspoon curry powder
½ teaspoon lemon juice
¼ cup thick mayonnaise
3 large tomatoes
3 black olives

Marinate artichoke bottoms 2 hours in enough dressing to cover them. Combine crayfish, celery, and salt and pepper. Mix curry powder and lemon juice with mayonnaise and combine with the crayfish or shrimp mixture. Drain artichoke bottoms and fill with the mixture. Peel tomatoes and cut the peels into 36 strips, 1¼ inches long and ¼ inch wide, and arrange 3 strips over each artichoke. (Save the tomatoes to use in another dish.) Garnish the top of each artichoke with a small piece of olive. Makes 12 hors d'oeuvres.

Avocados With Seafood

2 avocados	1 tablespoon dry sherry
Lemon juice	2 teaspoons tomato puree
½ cup diced cooked lobster	2 teaspoons grated fresh horseradish
½ cup diced cooked shrimp	½ teaspoon dry mustard
⅓ cup diced mushrooms	1½ tablespoons unsweetened
2 tablespoons olive oil or salad oil	whipped cream
Salt and freshly ground black	20 peeled, deveined, cooked whole shrimp
pepper	20 balls yellow cheese
⅓ cup mayonnaise	Black olives

Cut avocados in half lengthwise and remove stones. Scoop out the meat, leaving ¼ inch clinging to the shells. (Reserve the scooped-out portion.) Brush insides of shells with lemon juice to prevent discoloration. Dice the reserved avocado meat and combine with the lobster, shrimp, mushrooms, 2 teaspoons lemon juice, the oil, and salt and pepper. Cover and refrigerate 1 hour. Combine mayonnaise, sherry, ketchup, horseradish, mustard, and whipped cream. Combine with the lobster and shrimp mixture. Spoon into the avocado halves. Garnish each with 5 whole shrimp and 5 cheese balls, each topped with a bit of black olive. Makes 4 servings.

Cucumbers with Salmon and Herring

2 medium-sized cucumbers	Salt and freshly ground white pepper
French dressing	¾ cup poached herring
1 cup flaked poached salmon	1 hard-cooked egg, diced
2 tablespoons softened butter	½ teaspoon wine vinegar
1 tablespoon heavy cream	Grated fresh horseradish

Prepare cucumbers as in the preceding recipe and marinate 1 hour in the dressing. Drain. Mash salmon with butter and cream and push the mixture through a coarse sieve. Add salt and white pepper to taste. Marinate herring in French dressing, drain well, finely dice, and add to salmon mixture, along with egg and vinegar. Mix well and spoon into cucumber cups. Sprinkle with horseradish. Makes 6 to 8 servings.

Cucumber and Ham Hors d'Oeuvre

2 medium-sized cucumbers	Heavy cream
French dressing	Salt and freshly ground black pepper
2 cups diced cooked ham	Grated fresh horseradish

Peel cucumbers, cut them into 1-inch lengths, and scoop out the centers, leaving a bottom in each piece. Marinate 1 hour in dressing. Remove from dressing, invert on a plate, and drain well. Combine ham with enough cream to make a medium-thick mixture. Season with salt and pepper to taste. Spoon into cucumber cups. Sprinkle with horseradish. Makes 6 to 8 servings.

Cucumber Stuffed with Vegetable Salad

2 medium-sized cucumbers	1 tablespoon chopped onion
French dressing	Salt and freshly ground black pepper
¼ cup each cooked green peas, diced carrots, diced new potato, and green beans	¼ cup mayonnaise
	Few drops Tabasco
	½ teaspoon paprika
⅓ cup diced celery	Parsley sprigs

Prepare the cucumbers as in the two preceding recipes and marinate 1 hour in the dressing. Drain. Season vegetables with salt and pepper to taste. Mix mayonnaise with Tabasco sauce and paprika and add to vegetables. Mix gently. Spoon into cucumber cups. Garnish with parsley. Makes 6 servings.

Stuffed Tomatoes Andalusian

4 medium-sized tomatoes	1 cup cold cooked rice
Salt and freshly ground black pepper	Mayonnaise
3 tablespoons chopped red onion	Thin green bell pepper strips and rounds
⅓ cup chopped green bell pepper	Lettuce
2 tablespoons olive oil or salad oil	

Cut a slice from the stem ends of tomatoes and scoop out the centers, leaving the shells intact. Sprinkle the cavities with salt and pepper and let stand 30 minutes. Invert on a plate to drain. Sauté onion and chopped pepper in oil until vegetables are limp but not browned. Add to rice. Add enough mayonnaise to moisten the mixture. Season to taste with salt and pepper. Chill. Spoon rice mixture into cavities of tomatoes. Garnish tops with pepper strips and rounds. Serve on a bed of parsley. Makes 4 servings.

Tomatoes Stuffed with Baltic Herring

3 medium-sized tomatoes
Salt and freshly ground black pepper
Wine vinegar
2 small potatoes, cooked and diced
½ cup pickled herring fillets

¼ cup diced unpeeled apple
1 small cucumber pickle
2 tablespoons mayonnaise
1 gherkin

Cut tomatoes in half lengthwise, scoop out the centers, and season the shells to taste with salt, pepper, and vinegar. Let stand 30 minutes. Invert on a plate to drain. Combine potatoes, herring, and apple. Dice half of the cucumber pickle and add to the potato mixture along with mayonnaise. Add salt and pepper to taste and mix gently. Spoon the salad into tomato cavities. Cut remaining cucumber pickle into thin crosswise slices and arrange a few of these on the top of each salad, having them overlapping. Place a round slice of gherkin in the center. Makes 3 servings.

Tomatoes Stuffed with Tuna Beaulieu

3 medium-sized tomatoes
Salt and freshly ground black pepper
½ (7-ounce) can of tuna in oil
2 tablespoons softened butter
2 tablespoons mayonnaise

Lemon juice
1 hard-cooked egg
3 pitted black olives
Lettuce

Prepare tomatoes as in the preceding recipe, seasoning with salt and pepper. Let stand 30 minutes, then drain. Mash tuna with the oil in which it was canned, the butter, and mayonnaise. Season to taste with lemon juice, salt, and pepper. Spoon into cavities of tomatoes. Chop egg white and egg yolk separately. Sprinkle egg white on one half of each tomato and egg yolk on the other half. Cut olives in half and place one piece in the center of each salad. Serve on lettuce. Makes 3 servings.

Tomatoes Stuffed with Chicken

8 small tomatoes
½ cup sliced mushrooms
1 cup diced cooked chicken
Lemon juice

Salt and freshly ground black pepper
¼ cup mayonnaise
¼ sweet green bell pepper
Lettuce or parsley

Prepare whole tomatoes for stuffing as in preceding recipes. Combine mushrooms, chicken, lemon juice, salt, pepper, and mayonnaise. Spoon into tomato cavities, rounding the tops slightly. Cut pepper into short juliennes and arrange over tops. Serve on lettuce or parsley. Makes 4 to 8 servings.

Tomatoes Stuffed with Crayfish

6 medium-sized tomatoes
Salt and freshly ground black pepper
Mayonnaise

1½ cups cooked crayfish tails
Aspic
6 green pistachios

Cut off a slice from the stem end of the tomatoes. Scoop out the centers. Sprinkle cavities with salt and pepper. Let stand 30 minutes. Drain well. Put a layer of mayonnaise on the bottom of each tomato and fill with crayfish tails. Glaze with aspic. Sprinkle with pistachios just before serving. Makes 6 servings.

Tomatoes Stuffed with Potatoes and Gruyère Fribourg

6 medium-small tomatoes
Salt and freshly ground black pepper
Chopped chives
¾ cup diced boiled potatoes

¾ cup diced Gruyère cheese
1 tablespoon chopped onion
Mayonnaise

Cut tomatoes in half and scoop out centers. Drain. Sprinkle cavities with salt, pepper, and chives. Combine remaining ingredients and spoon into tomato cavities. Garnish with more chopped chives.

Russian Tomatoes

6 medium-sized tomatoes
2 cups Salad Mimosa I
3 to 4 tablespoons mayonnaise

1 hard-cooked egg, sliced
Parsley

Prepare whole tomatoes for stuffing as in preceding recipes. Mix Russian salad with mayonnaise and spoon into tomato cavities. Top each with a slice of egg. Serve on a bed of parsley. Makes 6 servings

Tomatoes Stuffed with Shrimp or Lobster

In the recipe for Tomatoes Stuffed with Crayfish, replace crayfish with cooked shrimp or diced cooked lobster. Garnish with cucumber balls. Serve on lettuce. Makes 6 servings.

HORS D'OEUVRE SALADS

Salads served as hors d'oeuvres may be made from vegetables, fruit, leftover meat, poultry, fish, and shellfish. The types and varieties to serve are limited only by the imagination of the person preparing them. There are three rules to follow:

1. The salads should be freshly made and designed to stimulate the appetite.
2. No food that appears in the salad hors d'oeuvre should appear in any dish in the main part of the meal. For example, if there are tomatoes in the salad, tomato must not be used in a sauce or in another dish.
3. The salad must be small to prevent dulling the appetite for the rest of the meal.

Beef Salad

Marinate thin slices of leftover beef for 2 hours in a dressing of oil and vinegar, a little chopped onion, and parsley. Serve on lettuce. Garnish with gherkins and sliced hard-cooked egg.

Beet Salad

Marinate thinly sliced cooked beets in a dressing of oil and vinegar. Sprinkle with chopped hard-cooked egg whites and chopped parsley. Serve on lettuce.

Red Cabbage Salad

Cut out and discard the thick ribs of the tender inside leaves of red cabbage. Finely shred enough of the leaves to make 4 cups. Dice 3 strips lean bacon and cook until crisp. Add cabbage and ¼ cup dry white wine. Stir and cook until half done. Season to taste with salt, freshly ground black pepper, ½ teaspoon sugar, 2 tablespoons olive oil, and 1 tablespoon wine vinegar. If desired, add 2 tablespoons finely chopped onion. Serve cold. Makes 6 servings.

White Cabbage Salad

Finely shred enough of the heart of tender white cabbage to make 3 cups. Combine 2 tablespoons salad oil or olive oil, 1 tablespoon cider vinegar, ½ teaspoon sugar, ⅛ teaspoon salt or to taste, ¹⁄₁₆ teaspoon freshly ground black pepper, and 2 tablespoons finely chopped onion. Pour over cabbage and marinate 1 hour. Serve on lettuce. Garnish with chopped parsley. Or, if desired, fry 2 strips bacon until crisp, add the marinade, heat, and pour over cabbage. Serve cold. Makes 4 to 6 servings.

Cauliflower Salad

Cut cauliflower into florets and cook in boiling water only until crisp-tender. Marinate 1 hour in a dressing of oil and vinegar. Arrange on an hors d'oeuvre dish, sprinkle with chopped hard-cooked egg yolks, and surround with small tomato slices or marinated cooked French green beans (*haricots verts*).

Celery Salad

Remove the leaves from the center ribs of celery stalks. Cut the ribs into strips 1½ inches long and very thinly slice them lengthwise. Combine ½ cup mayonnaise, 1 tablespoon each capers, finely chopped gherkins, and chopped parsley, and ½ teaspoon Dijon mustard (or to taste). Mix with celery and marinate 1 to 2 hours. Serve on lettuce.

Cucumber Salad

Peel cucumbers and cut into thin slices. Arrange on hors d'oeuvre dishes, with the slices overlapping. Chill. Just before serving, dust lightly with salt and freshly ground black pepper, and sprinkle with oil, vinegar, and chopped parsley.

Egg Salad

Cut hard-cooked eggs into slices ¼ inch thick. Arrange them in an hors d'oeuvre dish. Pour Vinaigrette Sauce lightly over them, or cover them with a thin coating of mayonnaise mixed with dry mustard, using ½ teaspoon mustard to each ½ cup mayonnaise. Arrange long anchovy fillets over the top in lattice fashion.

Egg and Tomato Salad

Arrange alternate slices of hard-cooked eggs and tomatoes in an hors d'oeuvre dish. Sprinkle Vinaigrette Sauce over the top. Sprinkle with chopped parsley.

Mushroom Salad

Slice enough well-cleaned white mushrooms to make 2 cups. Immediately marinate 1 hour in dressing made with 3 tablespoons salad oil, 1 tablespoon lemon juice, salt and cayenne to taste, and ¼ teaspoon sugar. Divide into 6 portions, place each on a lettuce leaf, and surround with sliced tomatoes, each topped with a slice of gherkin and a pickled onion. Makes 6 servings.

Potato Salad

1 quart hot ¼-inch-thick potato slices
Salt and freshly ground black
    pepper to taste
¼ cup chopped onion
⅓ cup hot beef stock or dry white wine

¼ cup Vinaigrette Sauce
Mayonnaise
Chopped parsley
Lettuce

Combine potatoes, salt and pepper, onion, stock, and Vinaigrette. Mix gently. Marinate several hours or overnight. Before serving, add thin mayonnaise and chopped parsley. Mix gently to avoid breaking potatoes. Serve on lettuce. Makes 6 to 8 servings.

Poultry Salad

Remove skin from cooked chicken or turkey and cut meat into thin slices. Arrange in a salad bowl on shredded lettuce. Coat with mayonnaise and garnish with anchovy fillets, quartered hard-cooked eggs, and quartered hearts of lettuce.

Fish Salad

In the recipe for Poultry Salad, replace chicken or turkey with cooked, skinned, and sliced fish.

Rich Poultry Salad

Arrange thin slices of skinned cooked poultry on a bed of shredded lettuce. Coat with thick mayonnaise seasoned to taste with grated fresh horseradish and ketchup and thinned to the desired consistency with orange juice and a little brandy. Garnish with quartered hard-cooked eggs, and half slices of small tomatoes.

Madrid Spinach Salad

Remove most of the stems from spinach leaves and cut the leaves into coarse julienne. Blanch quickly in hot water, drain, cool, and squeeze out moisture. Season to taste with salt, ground black pepper, and a mixture of 3 parts oil to 1 part wine vinegar. Serve garnished with hard-cooked eggs.

Tomato Salad

Peel medium-sized, firm, ripe tomatoes and cut into slices ¼ inch thick. Arrange on hors d'oeuvre dishes so the slices overlap. Dust with salt and freshly ground black pepper and sprinkle with French dressing of oil and vinegar. Arrange thin onion rings over the top. Sprinkle with chopped parsley.

Fish Salad

Combine diced cold fillet of sole, turbot, or halibut, diced tomatoes, sliced white onions, and bits of truffle or black olives. Mix with Vinaigrette.

Venison Salad

Combine small slices of cold cooked fillet of venison and sliced mushrooms with mayonnaise.

Veal Salad

Combine diced cold cooked veal and diced celery with mayonnaise mixed with a little tomato puree. Garnish with paprika.

Chicken and Asparagus Salad

Combine diced cold cooked chicken with diced cold cooked asparagus and sliced poached mushrooms and mix with mayonnaise. Garnish each serving with cold cooked asparagus tips.

Roast Beef Salad Diable

Mix diced cold roast beef with diced celery, a little *piccalilli*, and mayonnaise.

Chicken and Peach Salad

Marinate diced cold cooked chicken in Vinaigrette and combine with sliced fresh peaches and mayonnaise.

Roast Beef and Vegetable Salad

Mix diced cold roast beef with mixed vegetable salad.

Alsatian Salad

Combine diced Cheddar or Gruyère cheese, sliced sausages, and sliced radishes with mayonnaise.

Asparagus Salad

Marinate cold cooked asparagus 1 hour in oil and vinegar. Combine with julienned ham and pickled tongue. Serve with a little mayonnaise.

Lobster Salad

Cut cold cooked lobster meat into chunks and combine with diced celery and mayonnaise.

Artichoke and Smoked Salmon Salad

Marinate cooked artichoke bottoms in oil and vinegar 1 hour. Fill with julienned smoked salmon.

Shrimp Salad

Arrange cold cooked shrimp, lightly salted sliced cucumbers, sliced hard-cooked eggs, and sliced tomatoes on lettuce. Sprinkle with Vinaigrette.

Mussel Salad

Arrange cooked mussels, lightly salted sliced cucumbers, and sliced tomatoes in an hors d'oeuvre dish. Sprinkle with oil and vinegar.

Crayfish and Artichoke Salad

Place cooked crayfish tails on cooked artichoke bottoms marinated in Vinaigrette and top with slices of hard-cooked egg.

SANDWICHES

SANDWICHES FOR HORS D'OEUVRES, TEA, RECEPTIONS, and cocktail affairs may be simple or elaborate. In any case, they should be small, colorful, and in a variety of shapes. The best bread for preparing sandwiches is firm-textured and a day or two old. The butter should be soft and creamy for easy spreading and the fillings varied.

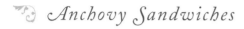 *Anchovy Sandwiches*

6 tablespoons softened butter
2 tablespoons mashed anchovies
4 thin slices white or dark bread,
    crusts removed

2 hard-cooked eggs
Finely chopped parsley

Combine butter and anchovies. Mix well. Spread on slices of bread. Finely chop eggs and sprinkle over the top. Cut the sandwiches into triangles and garnish the edges with parsley. Makes 16 sandwiches.

Camembert and Apple Sandwiches

Softened butter
Thinly sliced bread
Ripe Camembert cheese

Thinly sliced apples
Watercress

Butter one side of each slice of bread and spread with soft Camembert cheese. Place apple slices on half the bread slices and top with remaining bread. Cut into triangles. Garnish the top of each with a leaf of watercress. Allow 3 or 4 little sandwiches per person.

Caviar Sandwiches

Lightly salted butter
Thinly sliced white sandwich bread,
    crusts removed

Black caviar
Lemon juice
Finely chopped parsley

Soften butter and spread over one side of slices of bread. Spread lightly with caviar. Sprinkle with a few drops lemon juice. Cover with the remaining bread. Cut each slice into 4 squares. Garnish the edges with parsley. Allow 3 or 4 little sandwiches per person.

Cheshire and Gruyère Cheese Sandwiches

Thinly sliced bread, crusts removed
Prepared Dijon mustard
Softened butter

Sliced Cheshire cheese
Sliced Gruyère cheese

Spread bread slices with butter. Then spread one side of half the pieces with mustard butter made by blending 1½ teaspoons mustard with ¼ cup (½ stick) butter. Cut the cheese slices to fit the bread and place a piece of each kind on half the slices. Cover with remaining bread. Cut each sandwich into 4 triangles or into 3 or 4 strips. Decorate the center of each sandwich with a tiny piece of Cheshire cheese cut in the shape of the sandwich. Allow 3 or 4 little sandwiches per person.

Cucumber Sandwiches

Parsley
Watercress
Softened butter

Thinly sliced bread
Thinly sliced unpeeled cucumbers
Salt and freshly ground black pepper

Finely chop parsley and watercress and mix 1 tablespoon parsley and 2 tablespoons of watercress with each ½ cup (1 stick) butter. Cut the bread into rounds the same size as the cucumber slices. Spread one side of each round with the herb butter and top with a slice of cucumber. Sprinkle very lightly with salt and pepper. Cover with the remaining bread rounds. Place a watercress leaf in the center of each sandwich. Allow 3 sandwiches per person.

Open-Faced Cucumber Sandwiches

Top each round of buttered bread with a thin slice of cucumber. Sprinkle very lightly with salt and freshly ground black pepper. Decorate half the slices with a leaf of watercress and the remainder with a dash of paprika. Allow 3 sandwiches per person.

Egg and Anchovy Sandwiches

4 hard-cooked eggs
1½ tablespoons minced celery
¼ teaspoon paprika
⅛ teaspoon freshly ground
    black pepper
Mayonnaise

1/16 teaspoon freshly ground
    white pepper
Thinly sliced bread, crusts removed
Softened butter
1 jar anchovy fillets in oil

Remove yolks from hard-cooked eggs and mash them. Reserve whites. Add the next 3 ingredients and enough mayonnaise to moisten. Set aside. Mince egg whites and mix with white pepper and enough mayonnaise to moisten them. Spread bread slices with butter. Cut each slice into 4 squares. Spread half of each square with egg yolk mixture and the other half with the egg white mixture. Top each square with an anchovy. Makes about 16 sandwiches.

⁊ Foie Gras Sandwiches

Cooked foie gras
Softened butter

Ground hazelnuts, almonds, or pistachio nuts
Thinly sliced bread, crusts removed

Combine foie gras with butter, using 3 parts pâté to 1 part butter. Add 3 tablespoons ground nuts to each 1 cup of the mixture. Spread half the bread slices with the foie gras mixture. Spread remaining slices with butter and put on top. Cut each sandwich into 4 squares or triangles. Allow 3 sandwiches per person.

⁊ Ham or Tongue Sandwiches

Thinly sliced bread, crusts removed
Softened butter
Prepared Dijon mustard

Sliced cooked lean ham or cooked tongue
Watercress

Spread one side of each bread slice with mustard butter using 1½ teaspoons mustard to ¼ cup (½ stick) butter. Cut ham or tongue to fit the bread and place a slice on half the bread slices. Cover with remaining bread and cut into triangles, squares, or strips. Allow 3 sandwiches per person.

⁊ Lettuce Sandwiches

1 tablespoon chopped tarragon
Thinly sliced bread, crusts removed
Softened butter
Finely shredded lettuce

Salt
Freshly ground black pepper
Prepared Dijon mustard

Mix the tarragon with the butter. Spread one side of bread slices with butter. Top each with shredded lettuce and sprinkle lightly with salt and pepper. Cover with remaining slices of bread spread with mustard butter, using 1½ teaspoons mustard to ½ cup (1 stick) butter. Cut diagonally. Allow 2 sandwiches per person.

Poultry Sandwiches

Thinly sliced bread
Grated fresh horseradish,
   or horseradish sauce
Softened butter

Sliced cold cooked chicken, turkey,
   duck, goose, or game bird
Salt
Freshly ground black pepper
Grapes, cut in half

Cut bread into rounds and spread one side of each with butter mixed with horseradish, using 4 teaspoons horseradish to ½ cup (1 stick) butter. Top with a slice of poultry cut to fit the bread. Sprinkle lightly with salt and pepper. Garnish each with a grape half. Allow 3 sandwiches per person.

Radish Sandwiches

2 tablespoons finely chopped
Toasted walnuts
Softened butter

Thinly sliced bread
Thinly sliced radishes
Salt
Parsley

Combine the walnuts and the butter. Cut bread into rounds or ovals. Spread one side of each piece with softened walnut butter and on top arrange slightly overlapping slices of radishes. Sprinkle lightly with salt. Decorate the center of each with a leaf of parsley. Allow 3 sandwiches per person.

Open-Faced Tomato Sandwiches

Thinly sliced bread
Softened butter
Grated fresh horseradish,
   or horseradish sauce
Tomatoes, sliced

Salt
Freshly ground black pepper
Hard-cooked egg yolks
Parsley or sliced ripe or
   pimento-stuffed olives

Cut bread into rounds and spread with horseradish butter, using 4 teaspoons horseradish to ½ cup (1 stick) butter. Top each with a slice of tomato. Sprinkle with salt and pepper. Decorate the top with a little sieved hard-cooked egg yolk and a bit of parsley or a slice of ripe or pimento-stuffed olive. Allow 2 sandwiches per person.

Sausage Sandwiches

Chopped parsley
Crumbled dried rosemary
Softened butter
Thinly sliced bread, crusts removed

Links of cooked pork sausage,
   1 inch in diameter
Watercress

Combine herbs with butter, using 2 tablespoons parsley and ½ teaspoon rosemary to ½ cup (1 stick) butter. Spread one side of each bread slice with herb butter. Cut sausage into slices ⅛ inch thick and arrange over half the bread slices. Cover with the remaining bread. Cut into triangles or squares. Decorate the top of each with a leaf of watercress. Allow 2 or 3 sandwiches per person.

Open-Faced Pickled Tongue Sandwiches

Thinly sliced bread, crusts removed	Watercress
Softened butter	Sliced pickled tongue

Spread one side of each bread slice with watercress butter, blending 2 tablespoons finely chopped watercress to ½ cup (1 stick) butter. Cover with slices of pickled tongue. Cut into triangles, squares, or strips. Decorate the centers with watercress leaves. Allow 2 to 3 sandwiches per person.

Veal Sandwiches

Thinly sliced bread, crusts removed	Softened butter
Horseradish sauce	Sliced cold cooked veal

Spread bread slices with horseradish butter, blending 4 teaspoons horseradish sauce with ½ cup (1 stick) butter. Top half the slices with sliced veal cut to fit the bread. Cover with remaining bread. Cut into triangles, squares, or strips. Allow 2 to 3 sandwiches per person.

Smoked Salmon Sandwiches

Thinly sliced bread, crusts removed	Smoked salmon, thinly sliced
Softened sweet butter	Gherkin pickle

Spread bread slices with butter. Cover with smoked salmon cut to fit the bread. Cut into triangles, squares, or strips. Allow 3 sandwiches per person.

Make Smoked Salmon Sandwiches with any of the following additions:

- *Curry Powder.* Mix 1 teaspoon curry powder with each ½ cup (1 stick) butter.
- *Horseradish.* Mix 4 teaspoons grated fresh horseradish or horseradish sauce with each ½ cup (1 stick) butter.
- *Herbs.* Mix 2 tablespoons finely chopped parsley and ½ teaspoon ground dried thyme with each ½ cup (stick) butter.

CANAPES

CANAPES ARE TIDBITS SERVED AS AN HORS D'OEUVRE or as tea or cocktail accompaniments. The base is made from firm-textured day-old white or whole wheat bread, sliced ¼ to ⅛ inch thick. These slices are cut into squares, triangles, or finger-length strips, or cut with cookie cutters into rounds or other shapes small enough to be eaten gracefully with the fingers. They are either deep fried, sautéed in butter, or toasted in the oven, and then buttered. Shortly before serving, they are spread with various seasoned mixtures or covered with thinly sliced fish, meat, poultry, or cheese cut to fit the bread. Canapés may be garnished with parsley, watercress, truffles, green or black olives, pimentos, mushrooms, hard-cooked eggs, anchovies, and so on. They may be served hot or cold. Allow 2 to 3 of any one kind per serving.

Anchovy Canapés

Crustless white bread cut into
   ½-by-1½-inch pieces
Butter or oil
Anchovy paste

Softened butter
Hard-cooked eggs
Anchovies
Aspic

Fry bread in butter or oil. Cool. Spread with anchovy paste mixed with butter, using 1 tablespoon anchovy paste for each ½ cup (1 stick) butter. Garnish one end of each canapé with finely chopped egg white and the other end with sieved egg yolk. Arrange 2 anchovy fillets in crossed fashion in center of each. Glaze with aspic.

Chicken Liver Canapés

1 pound chicken livers
Chicken stock
2 large hard-cooked eggs
¼ cup finely chopped onion
2 tablespoons rendered chicken fat,
   or butter

Salt and freshly ground black
   pepper
Softened butter
Toast strips
Chopped parsley

Cook livers in hot stock to cover until they have lost their pink color. Remove livers from stock, drain, and put them through a food chopper, along with the eggs, using the medium blade. Cook onion in chicken fat, stirring until soft. Add to the livers. Season to taste with salt and pepper. Mix well. (Makes 2 cups.) Spread on buttered toast strips. Sprinkle parsley around the edges.

This mixture may also be piled in mounds on lettuce leaves, sprinkled with diced hard-cooked egg and diced onion, and served with toast rounds or crackers.

Caviar Canapés

Spread 1½-inch rounds of toasted white or whole wheat bread with lightly salted softened butter. Cover with a thin layer of chilled black or red caviar. Cut thin slices of lemon into quarters, remove seeds, and place 1 in the center of each canapé. Allow 3 per serving.

Cheese Canapés

Add enough Béchamel Sauce to grated Gruyère cheese to make a smooth spreadable mixture. Season to taste with freshly ground white pepper and paprika. Spread on rectangles of buttered white bread. Brown quickly in a preheat oven (425° F) or under the broiler. Serve hot or cold.

Chicken and Paprika-Butter Canapés

Mix softened butter with enough paprika to give it a delicate pink color. Spread over oval slices of white bread. Mix finely chopped cooked chicken with enough mayonnaise to make a spreadable mixture. Season to taste with salt and black pepper. Spread over the buttered bread. Garnish with very short, fine julienne of red and green bell pepper.

Curried-Egg Canapés

Push hard-cooked eggs through a sieve. Mix with enough heavy cream to make the mixture smooth and spreadable. Season to taste with salt, freshly ground black pepper, curry powder, and lemon juice. Butter toasted 2-inch rounds of white bread and spread with the egg mixture. Top each with a 2-inch slice of tomato and sprinkle with salt and pepper. Garnish with finely chopped gherkins.

Ham and Chicken or Egg Canapés

Blend 2 tablespoons prepared mustard with 6 tablespoons softened butter. Spread on rectangles of sautéed white or whole wheat bread. Sprinkle ground cold cooked ham on one half of each rectangle and ground cold cooked chicken or finely chopped hard-cooked egg on the other half.

Hard-Cooked Egg Canapés

Spread rectangular pieces of cold toast with mayonnaise. Cover with overlapping slices of hard-cooked eggs. Garnish the yolks with finely diced gherkins.

Goose Foie Gras Canapés

Cut ovals of white bread ¼ to ⅜ inch thick. Fry in butter, or toast in the oven and then spread with softened butter. Cover with oval slices of chilled goose foie gras cut to fit the bread. Garnish with a bit of truffle or with sieved hard-cooked egg yolk and chopped parsley. Glaze with aspic. Allow 3 canapés per serving.

Canapé Niçoise

Spread rounds of toast or bread fried in butter with Anchovy Butter. Arrange finely chopped tomato in the centers and top each with half a black olive.

Oyster Canapés

Cook small soup oysters in oyster liquor over very low heat or over hot water only until the edges curl. Remove from liquor, drain, and chill. Coat with mayonnaise mixed with prepared mustard to taste. Chill. Season softened butter with prepared mustard to taste. Spread over 2-inch squares of white bread, top each with an oyster, and encircle with sieved hard-cooked egg yolks.

Roast Beef and Egg Canapés

Mix equal parts of finely chopped leftover roast beef and finely chopped hard-cooked eggs with enough mayonnaise to make the mixture smooth and spreadable. Season to taste with salt, freshly ground black pepper, and finely chopped gherkins. Spread on 2-inch squares of sautéed bread. Garnish each with a slice of cherry tomato.

Smoked Salmon Canapés

Spread softened butter on fried, sautéed, or toasted bread. Cover with thin slices of smoked salmon cut to fit the bread. Garnish with sieved hard-cooked egg yolks. Top each with half a black olive.

Shrimp Canapés

6 medium-sized cooked shrimp	1 large hard-cooked egg yolk
6 rounds of bread, 2 inches in diameter, sautéed in butter	Lemon juice
	36 tiny cooked shrimp
2 tablespoons butter	6 butter curls
Salt	

Mash or pound the 6 medium-sized shrimp and blend with the butter. Season to taste with salt and a few drops of lemon juice. Spread over rounds of bread sautéed in butter and roll edges of bread in egg yolk. Place 6 tiny shrimp in a circle on each and garnish center with a butter curl. Makes 6 servings.

Sardine Canapés

Blend 1 tablespoon lemon juice with 6 tablespoons softened butter and spread over rectangle-shaped toasts. Garnish edges with chopped parsley and place a boned sardine down the center of each. Sprinkle with paprika.

Watercress and Egg Canapés

Sauté squares or rounds of white bread in butter and spread with mayonnaise. Sprinkle with chopped watercress and top with sieved hard-cooked egg yolks. Allow 2 or 3 per serving.

Chive Butter and Ham

Mix softened butter with finely chopped chives to taste. Spread over fried, sautéed, or toasted bread. Cover with thin slices of cooked ham cut to fit the bread. Garnish with cold cooked asparagus tips. Glaze with aspic.

Steak Tartare and Anchovy

Mix 1 pound ground raw sirloin or tenderloin steak with ½ cup finely chopped onion and salt and freshly ground black pepper to taste. Spread thickly on fried, sautéed, or toasted 2½-inch squares of bread. Make an indentation in the center of each, into which place the yolk of a raw egg, and top with a rolled anchovy. Garnish with capers, small pickled white onions, and chopped parsley.

Mustard Butter and Boiled Ham

Spread mustard butter on fried, sautéed, or toasted bread, using 2 tablespoons prepared mustard to 6 tablespoons softened butter. Cover with thin slices of boiled ham cut to fit the bread. Glaze with aspic.

Smoked Trout

Cover toasts with slices of smoked trout cut to fit the bread. Garnish each with ½ teaspoon Tomato Fondue.

HOT
HORS D'OEUVRES
AND
SMALL FIRST
COURSES

MUCH OF THE TIME THE ONLY DIFFERENCE BETWEEN a hot hors d'oeuvre and a small first course is the size of the portion. The same variety of mixtures (meat, fish, shellfish, poultry, cheese, vegetables, and so on) that might be served as a first course can also be served in tart and tartlet shells, barquettes, puff pastry cases of various shapes and sizes, or in small ovenproof dishes as hors d'oeuvre. Croquettes and cromesquis, croustades, small timbales, cassolettes, fritters, mousses, soufflés, quiches, and savories make up the rest.

HOT PASTRY BOATS AND TARTLETS

BOATS (*BARQUETTES*) AND TARTLETS, usually made with pastry dough, are filled with various mixtures and served as hors d'oeuvre, small entrées, or as desserts. Unbaked shells are always filled with uncooked mixtures and baked in a preheated oven (425°F). Shells may be baked in advance and filled with cooked mixtures; these usually need no further cooking except to melt a cheese topping. Prebaked shells may also be filled with cold mixtures.

Shrimp Barquettes Mornay

2 cups diced cooked shrimp
1½ cups Mornay Sauce
Salt and freshly ground black
   pepper

12 small baked boat-shaped tart shells
Grated Parmesan cheese
12 small whole cooked shrimp,
   peeled and deveined

Combine diced shrimp with 1 cup of the Mornay Sauce. Season with salt and pepper and spoon mixture into tart shells. Coat with remaining Mornay Sauce, sprinkle with cheese, and garnish each with a whole shrimp. Bake in a preheated oven (425°F) or under the broiler until cheese is melted. Serve hot as an hors d'oeuvre. Makes 12 servings.

Lobster Barquettes

1½ cups medium-thick cream sauce
½ cup grated Gruyère cheese
¾ cup finely diced cooked lobster
¼ teaspoon mustard
1 teaspoon water
Dash Worcestershire sauce

Salt to taste
1⁄16 teaspoon freshly ground
   white pepper
18 baked boat-shaped tart shells
Truffles, black olives, or hard-cooked
   egg yolks

Combine the first 3 ingredients. Soak add the mustard to the mixture, along with remaining seasonings. Stir and cook only until hot. Divide the mixture equally among the tart shells. Garnish with bits of truffles, olives, or sieved egg yolks. Serve hot. Makes 18.

Crabmeat Barquettes

Replace lobster in recipe for Lobster Barquettes with the same amount of cooked, flaked crabmeat, and add a few drops lemon juice.

Cadogan Boats

1 cup ground cooked ham
2 tablespoons chopped gherkins
½ tablespoon butter
18 small baked boat-shaped tart shells

1 cup Mornay Sauce
⅓ cup grated Gruyère cheese
Chopped parsley

Heat ham and gherkin in butter. Put an equal amount in each of the tart shells. Cover with Mornay Sauce. Sprinkle with grated cheese. Bake in a preheated oven (450°F) only until cheese melts. Serve hot, garnished with parsley. Makes 18.

Chicken and Mushroom Tartlets Marion Delorme

Plain Pastry Dough (Pâte Brisée)
1½ cups finely ground cooked
    skinless chicken
1 cup finely ground raw mushrooms
¾ cup Béchamel Sauce

Salt, freshly ground black pepper,
    and lemon juice
2 tablespoons butter
3 large egg yolks, beaten

Line small tartlet molds with thinly rolled pastry and set aside. Combine chicken, mushrooms, Béchamel Sauce, seasonings, and butter. Stir and cook 2 to 3 minutes. Remove from heat, add a little of the hot mixture to the beaten egg yolks, and then add them to the remaining hot mixture. Mix well. Spoon into the tart shells. Place the shells on a baking sheet. Bake in a preheated oven (425°F) 10 to 12 minutes, or until pastry has browned. Serve as a hot hors d'oeuvre, or make larger tarts and serve as a small entrée. Makes 12 tartlets or 6 large tarts.

Milanese Tartlets

Plain Pastry Dough (Pâte Brisée)
½ cup well-drained, finely chopped
    cooked macaroni
½ cup grated Gruyère cheese
½ cup ground cooked lean ham

½ cup ground pickled tongue
¼ cup finely chopped mushrooms
Highly seasoned thick tomato sauce
Salt and freshly ground black pepper

Line small tartlet molds with thinly rolled pastry. Prick the pastry all over with a fork to prevent it from puffing. Bake in a preheated oven (425°F) 10 minutes, or until browned. Cool. Combine macaroni, cheese, ham, tongue, and mushrooms. Stir in enough tomato sauce to make a spreadable mixture. Add salt and pepper to taste. Stir and cook until hot. Spoon into baked tartlets. Serve very hot as an hors d'oeuvre, or make the tarts larger and serve as an entrée. Makes 12 to 18 tartlets or 6 large tarts.

Curried Shrimp Tartlets Rajah

1 teaspoon curry powder	Few drops lemon juice
1 teaspoon finely chopped onion	Salt
1 tablespoon butter	12 baked 1½-inch tart shells
1 cup Béchamel Sauce	12 small whole mushrooms,
¾ cup diced cooked shrimp	sautéed in butter

Stir and cook curry powder and onion in butter 2 to 3 minutes. Add to Béchamel Sauce, along with shrimp and lemon juice. Add salt to taste. Heat. Spoon into tart shells. Top each with a mushroom cooked in butter. Serve hot. Makes 12 small tarts.

Romanian Cheese Tarts

Plain Pastry Dough (Pâte Brisée)	2 cups thick Béchamel Sauce
½ recipe Choux Paste	3 large egg yolks
1⅓ cups grated Gruyère cheese	

Line six 3-inch tart pans with thinly rolled pastry dough and set aside. Mix warm Choux Paste with ⅓ cup of the cheese, and put the Choux Paste mixture into a pastry bag fitted with a small round nozzle. Pipe 3 rings of the mixture on top of one another in each unbaked tart shell.

Combine Béchamel Sauce and the remaining 1 cup cheese. Beat in egg yolks. Stir and cook over low heat only until hot. Fill the center of the tarts with this mixture. Bake in a preheated oven (400°F) 20 to 25 minutes, or until the pastry has browned. Serve hot as an entrée. Makes 6 tarts.

Swiss Cheese Tartlets

Plain Pastry Dough (Pâte Brisée)	⅛ teaspoon freshly ground white pepper
2 cups Béchamel Sauce	Dash cayenne
½ teaspoon salt	2 large eggs, lightly beaten
¼ teaspoon dry mustard	1 cup grated Gruyère or Emmentaler cheese

Line small tartlet molds with thinly rolled pastry. Set aside. Heat the Béchamel Sauce and add salt, mustard, white pepper, and cayenne. Blend a little of the hot mixture into the eggs and add to the remaining hot mixture. Add cheese and mix well. Spoon into the unbaked tartlet shells. Place tarts on a baking sheet and bake in a preheated oven (425°F) 15 to 20 minutes, or until crust has browned. Cool to 10 minutes. Serve as a hot hors d'oeuvre, or make the tart shells larger and serve as an entrée. Makes about 16 tartlets.

PUFF PASTRY PATTIES AND HORNS

PATTY SHELLS (*BOUCHEES*), HORNS (*CORNETS*), rolls, and similar preparations are made of puff pastry or choux paste and filled. They are sometimes baked in advance and sometimes baked with the filling.

Chicken Bouchées à la Reine

3 cups diced cooked chicken
½ cup sautéed mushrooms
1 small truffle, finely diced (optional)

1¾ cups Sauce Suprême
Salt and freshly ground white pepper
8 baked puff pastry patty shells

Combine chicken, mushrooms, truffle (if using), and Sauce Suprême. Season with salt and pepper. Heat. Fill patty shells and top with the caps removed from the centers of the baked patty shells.) Makes 4 to 8 servings.

Mixed Vegetable Patties

Replace the chicken in the preceding recipe with 3 cups diced mixed vegetables. Omit the truffle. Mix with 1¼ cups sauce Suprême Sauce and heat. Serve in puff pastry patty shells, as directed for Chicken Patties.

Shrimp and Mussel Patties

Replace chicken in recipe for Chicken Patties with 2 cups diced cooked shrimp and ½ cup diced poached mussels, and mix with 1¼ cups White Wine Sauce. Heat and serve in 8 baked puff pastry patty shells, as directed for Chicken Patties.

Lobster Patties

Replace chicken in recipe for Chicken Patties with 3 cups diced cooked lobster meat. Mix with 1¼ cups Velouté, or Supreme Sauce. Add 2 tablespoons dry sherry. Heat and scrve in 8 baked puff pastry patty shells, as directed for Chicken Patties.

Fish and Shellfish Patties

Replace chicken in recipe for Chicken Patties with 1 cup diced cooked fish, ½ cup each diced cooked shrimp and mussels, and ½ cup diced mushrooms sautéed in butter. Mix with 1¼ cups Supreme Sauce. Adjust seasonings. Heat and serve in 8 baked puff pastry patty shells, as directed for Chicken Patties.

Cornets with Hard-Cooked Eggs

Puff Pastry	6 diced hard-cooked eggs
1 egg yolk	½ cup Béchamel Sauce
2 tablespoons milk	Salt and freshly ground black pepper

Roll puff pastry dough ¼ inch thick and cut into strips ¼ inch wide and 6 inches long. Wrap the pieces around 6 small metal or wooden horn-shaped molds. Brush surface with egg yolk beaten together with milk. Place molds 1 inch apart on paper-lined cookie sheets. Bake 10 minutes in a preheated oven (450°F). Reduce heat to 350° and bake until pastry is golden. Remove the molds from the pastry immediately by twisting them free. Cool. Fill with diced hard-cooked eggs mixed with Béchamel Sauce and seasoned with salt and pepper to taste. Makes 6 servings.

Baked Cheese Puffs or Gougères

½ recipe for Choux Paste
⅔ cup very finely diced Gruyère cheese
Small thin slices Gruyère cheese

Mix warm Choux Paste with the diced cheese. Using a pastry bag and a large round nozzle, pipe a ring on a slightly buttered baking sheet, using all the mixture. Cover evenly with slices of cheese. Bake in a preheated oven (425°F) 20 to 25 minutes. Serve at once. Makes 6 servings.

Cheese Rolls

2 cups grated Cheshire, Cheddar, or other firm cheese	2 large egg yolks
	Salt and freshly ground black pepper
⅔ cup cold thick Béchamel Sauce	Puff pastry dough

Mix cheese with Béchamel Sauce and egg yolks. Add seasonings. Set filling aside. Roll puff pastry ¼ inch thick. Cut into strips 3 inches wide, and then cut strips into 2-inch lengths, making the pastry for each roll 3- by 2-inches. Spread the filling over each piece of dough to within ¼ inch of the edges. Roll up jelly-roll fashion and press down the ends to prevent the cheese from seeping out while baking. Place on baking sheet, seam side down. Bake in a preheated oven (425°F) 12 minutes, or until browned. Serve as a hot hors d'oeuvre or small entrée. Makes 6 servings.

Turkish Cheese Rolls or Beurrecks

1½ cup Béchamel Sauce
2 (3-ounce) packages cream cheese
Salt and freshly ground black
    pepper to taste

Noodle dough
1 large egg beaten with 1 tablespoon water
Fine white breadcrumbs
Tomato Sauce (optional)

Warm the Béchamel Sauce and add cream cheese, salt and pepper. If the mixture is too soft to shape, chill until it is manageable. Shape into 1-inch balls and form them into rolls 1½ inches long on a lightly floured board. Roll noodle dough ¹⁄₁₆ inch thick. Cut into 3-by-2-inch pieces. Moisten the dough very lightly and place one cheese roll on each piece. Roll up and pinch the dough together at each end to seal the rolls. Dip in egg mixture and then into breadcrumbs. Fry in deep preheated to 375°F. Drain on paper towels. Serve as a hot hors d'oeuvre, or serve as an entrée with Tomato Sauce. Makes about 1 dozen.

CROUSTADES

CROUSTADES ARE SMALL CASES made from puff pastry, rich pie pastry, or from Duchess Potatoes, to hold various fillings.

Lobster Croustades

In the recipe for Shrimp Croustades, replace shrimp with 2 cups diced, cooked lobster meat.

Hard-Cooked Egg Croustades

8 hard-cooked eggs, peeled and diced
1½ cups hot Béchamel Sauce
Dash cayenne
Salt and freshly ground white pepper

12 baked 2½-inch puff pastry
    or rich pastry shells
Chopped parsley

Combine eggs with Béchamel Sauce and cayenne. Season to taste with salt and white pepper. Spoon into pastry shells. Sprinkle with parsley. Serve as a hot entrée. Makes 6 servings.

Shrimp Croustades

Cook 1 pound shrimp in court bouillon 5 minutes, or until the shrimp develop a red color. Remove from heat, peel, and devein. Add to 1 cup hot, thick Béchamel Sauce. Season to taste with salt, freshly ground white pepper, and lemon juice. Spoon into 18 small baked pastry shells. Serve as a hot hors d'oeuvre. Makes 18 tarts.

Mushroom Croustades

3 cups sliced mushrooms	Salt and freshly ground black pepper
2 tablespoons butter	12 baked 2½-inch puff pastry
1 cup hot Demi-Glace Sauce	or rich pastry shells
2 tablespoons chopped parsley	2 strips crisp bacon, broken into pieces
1 teaspoon chopped fresh thyme	Onion strips, fried in batter

Cook mushrooms in butter 5 minutes, or until they are tender. Add to Demi-Glace Sauce. Blend in herbs, salt, and pepper. Stir and cook 2 to 3 minutes. Spoon into pastry shells. Garnish with bacon and fried onion. Makes 6 servings.

SMALL TIMBALES

A TIMBALE WAS ORIGINALLY A MOLD in which food was cooked. They are of various sizes and shapes, from ovals to baba molds, and either metal, porcelain, or made out of pastry. For hors d'oeuvre, small entrées, or garnishes, small timbale cases are usually filled with forcemeat, chicken, fish, shellfish, sweetbreads, or mushrooms, bound with a cream sauce.

Chicken Timbales Courtisane

12 thin pancakes	3 large egg yolks
3 cups finely ground cooked chicken	Salt and freshly ground black pepper
1¼ cups Béchamel Sauce	Soubise Sauce

Butter six 6-ounce custard cups. Cut out circular pieces from pancakes to fit the bottom of the molds and line the bottom of the molds with them. Cut the remaining pancakes into strips long enough and wide enough to line the sides. Mix the chicken with the Béchamel Sauce, and pound and beat well with a wooden spoon. Push mixture through a sieve. Beat in egg yolks, one at a time, and add salt and pepper. Spoon into the prepared custard cups. Place cups in a pan of hot water. Bake in a preheated oven (350°F) 30 to 40 minutes. Unmold onto a warm serving plate. Serve with Soubise Sauce . Makes 6 servings.

❦ Timbales Regina

In the preceding recipe, replace 3 cups chicken with cup finely ground raw pike, halibut, or haddock, 1 cup ground raw shrimp, and ½ cup ground raw mussels. Serve with Shrimp Sauce.

❦ Chicken Forcemeat Timbales

1 small truffle (optional)
8 round slices cooked tongue
¾ pound chicken breasts
¼ teaspoon salt
¹⁄₁₆ teaspoon freshly ground
    black pepper

1 large egg white
1 cup heavy cream
1½ cups diced cooked tongue or ham
¾ cup chicken Velouté Sauce
Mushroom Sauce

Butter eight 6-ounce custard cups. Place a slice of truffle in the bottom of each and cover with a larger round of tongue. Set aside. Cut chicken into small pieces and put it through a food chopper twice, using the finest blade. Add salt and pepper, and gradually stir and beat in the egg white. Push mixture through a sieve. Put the pan on a bed of cracked ice and work the mixture with a wooden spoon until it is well chilled. Beat in the cream, a little at a time, working it in well after each addition. Line the molds with some of the forcemeat. Set aside. Mix diced tongue with Velouté Sauce and spoon into the molds. Cover the top with forcemeat. Place cups in a pan of hot water. Bake in preheated oven (350°F) 30 to 40 minutes, or until a pointed knife inserted in the center comes out clean. Serve with Mushroom Sauce. Makes 8 servings.

❦ Veal Forcemeat Timbales

In the preceding recipe, replace the chicken breasts with the same amount of raw veal and the chicken Velouté Sauce with veal Velouté Sauce.

❦ Chicken Liver Timbales

¾ cup chicken Velouté Sauce
½ cup heavy cream
2 large eggs, separated
2 tablespoons butter
1 pound chicken livers

1 small onion
¾ teaspoon salt or to taste
¼ teaspoon freshly ground black pepper
3 tablespoons Madeira
Mushroom Sauce

Beat cream and egg yolks into cool Velouté Sauce. Sauté liver in the butter and put it through a food chopper twice, along with onion, using the finest blade. Add sauce, salt, pepper, and 2 tablespoons of the Madeira. Beat egg whites until they hold soft stiff peaks (not too dry) and fold them into the liver mixture. Turn the mixture into 6 well-buttered 6-ounce custard cups. Place cups in a pan of hot water. Cover pan loosely with foil. Bake in a preheated oven (325°F) 40 to 50 minutes, or until a knife inserted in the center comes out clean. Cool a few minutes. Turn onto a warm serving dish. Serve with Mushroom Sauce flavored with the remaining Madeira. Makes 6 servings.

The liver may be replaced with 2 cups ground cooked veal, chicken, ham, fish (haddock, halibut, sole, or pike), crabmeat, lobster, or shrimp.

Milanese Timbales

Plain Pastry Dough (Pâte Brisée), made with 4 cups flour	½ cup sautéed mushrooms
Milk or beaten egg	1 cup diced cooked ham
1 cup medium-sized macaroni, broken into small pieces	1 cup diced cooked tongue
2 tablespoons butter	½ cup grated Parmesan cheese
	1½ cups thick well-seasoned Tomato Sauce

Roll one-third of the pastry at a time ⅛ inch thick. Cut it into circles large enough to line 6-ounce custard cups, pressing the pastry down well against the sides, bottoms, and edges of the cups. Cut off the dough that hangs over the edges and reserve the pieces to use later. Prick the bottom and sides of the pastry all over to prevent it from puffing up. Fit waxed paper into the pastry-lined cups and fill them with dried beans or rice to hold the pastry in shape. Bake in a preheated oven (425°F) 10 to 15 minutes, or until the pastry has set and partially baked. Remove the beans or rice and the paper and discard. Continue baking until the pastry has delicately browned. Remove from oven. Roll remaining pastry and trimmings ⅛ inch thick. Using the top of a custard cup, or a large cookie cutter, cut out pastry circles to use as the top crust for the timbales. Cut pastry leaves from remaining pastry, and place 2 on each unbaked crust. Place on ungreased baking sheet, brush with milk or beaten egg, and bake 10 to 12 minutes, or until golden brown.

Cook macaroni in boiling salted water as directed on the package. Drain well and toss with butter. Add mushrooms, ham, tongue, cheese, and Tomato Sauce. Heat and spoon into pastry cases. Top with the pastry lids and serve very hot. Makes 6 servings.

Salmon and Mushroom Timbales Beckendorf

1 cup medium-sized macaroni broken into small pieces	1 cup diced mushrooms
1½ cups thick Tomato Sauce, plus additional for serving	2 tablespoons butter
3 large egg yolks, lightly beaten	½ pound smoked salmon, cut into small pieces
	Fine dry white breadcrumbs

Cook macaroni in salted boiling water as directed on the package. Drain, mix with 1½ cups Tomato Sauce, and heat. Blend a little of the hot mixture with the beaten egg yolks and add to the remaining hot mixture. Cook mushrooms in butter 5 minutes, then add to macaroni, along with salmon. Mix well. Butter six 6-ounce custard cups and coat them with breadcrumbs. Fill with the macaroni mixture. Place cups in a pan of hot water. Bake in a preheated oven (350°F) 30 to 40 minutes. Umnold onto a warm serving dish. Serve with Tomato Sauce. Makes 6 servings.

CASSOLETTES

CASSOLETTES TAKE THEIR NAME FROM the small individual fireproof dishes or casseroles in which the food is cooked and served.

Mixed Vegetable Cassolettes

4 cups cooked mixed vegetables	2 cups Duchess Potatoes
1 cup heavy cream	Milk
Salt and freshly ground black pepper	18 cooked asparagus tips

Heat the vegetables in the cream. Season with salt and pepper. Spoon an equal amount into each of 6 cassolette dishes (individual casseroles). Make a border of Duchess Potatoes around the edges. Brush potatoes with a little milk. Cook in a preheated oven (375°F) until potato is well flecked with brown. Garnish each with 3 asparagus tips. Serve hot as an entrée. Makes 6 servings.

Spinach Cassolettes Florentine

2 cups drained, chopped, cooked spinach	¾ cup chicken Velouté Sauce
1 tablespoon butter	2 cups Duchess Potatoes
Salt and freshly ground black pepper	Milk
2 cups diced cooked chicken	

Heat spinach in butter and season with salt and pepper to taste. Divide spinach equally among 6 buttered cassolette dishes, spreading it uniformly over the bottom of the dishes. Combine chicken and Velouté Sauce and spoon into each of the dishes, covering the spinach. Make a border around the edges of the dishes with Duchess Potatoes. Brush potatoes with a little milk. Cook in a preheated oven (375°F) until potato is well flecked and brown. Serve hot as an entrée. Makes 6 servings.

Lamb Cassolettes Deauville

2 pounds diced cooked lamb
2 cups Demi-Glace Sauce

1 cup Tomato Fondue
3 hard-cooked eggs

Combine lamb and Demi-Glace Sauce. Heat and spoon into 6 buttered cassolette dishes. Cover with Tomato Fondue. Garnish each with ½ slice of hard-cooked egg. Serve as an entrée. Makes 6 servings.

Mushroom and Ham Cassolettes

2 cups mushrooms, julienned
1 cup cooked ham, julienned
2 tablespoons butter
1 cup Demi-Glace Sauce
2 teaspoons soy sauce

1 tablespoon sake or dry sherry
¾ teaspoon ground ginger
24 hard-cooked quail eggs,
    or 6 hard-cooked hens eggs

Cook mushrooms and ham in butter until mushrooms are tender. Add Demi-Glace Sauce and cook 2 to 3 minutes, stirring. Season with soy sauce, sake, and ginger. Spoon into 6 cassolette dishes. Peel quail eggs, cut each in half, and arrange 8 halves over each dish, or peel and quarter hens eggs and arrange 4 quarters over each serving. Serve as a hot entrée. Makes 6 servings.

Game and Ham Cassolettes Milord

2 cups diced cooked game
1 cup diced cooked ham
¾ cup Salmis Sauce

1 cup fresh white breadcrumbs
3 tablespoons butter

Combine game, ham, and Salmis Sauce. Heat and spoon into 6 cassolette dishes. Brown breadcrumbs in butter and sprinkle over the top of each cassolette. Serve as a hot entrée. Makes 6 servings.

Chicken Cassolettes Regency

3 cups diced cooked chicken
1 truffle, diced (optional)
1½ cups chicken Velouté Sauce
Salt and freshly ground black pepper

2 cups Duchess Potatoes
Milk
18 cooked asparagus tips

Combine chicken, truffles, if using, and Velouté Sauce. Add salt and pepper to taste. Spoon into 6 buttered cassolette dishes. Pipe a border of Duchess Potatoes around the edge of the cassolettes. Brush potatoes with a little milk. Cook in a preheated oven (375°F) until potatoes are well flecked with brown. Garnish each with 3 cooked asparagus tips. Serve as a hot entrée. Makes 6 servings.

Game and Chestnut Cassolettes Sultan

3 cups diced cooked game
½ cup Chestnut Puree
1 cup Salmis Sauce

1 truffle
Chopped pistachio nuts

Combine game, Chestnut Puree, and ½ cup of the sauce. Adjust seasonings. Heat and keep warm in a pan of hot water. Spoon the mixture into small heatproof cocotte dishes, or individual baked unsweetened pastry shells. Coat each with a little of the remaining sauce. Place a slice of truffle on each, and sprinkle with chopped pistachio nuts. Serve as a hot entrée. Makes 6 servings.

 ## Cassolettes Suzanne

2 cups cooked spinach
2 tablespoons butter
Salt and freshly ground black pepper
3 cups diced cooked chicken

½ cup sautéed sliced mushrooms
1⅓ cups Béchamel Sauce
6 truffle slices (optional)

Put spinach in a sieve and press out excess liquid. Cook spinach in butter 1 to 2 minutes. Season to taste with salt and pepper. Divide the spinach equally among 6 cassolette dishes. Combine chicken, mushrooms, and 1 cup of the Béchamel Sauce. Season to taste with salt and pepper. Spoon an equal amount into each of the cassolettes. Coat lightly with remaining Béchamel Sauce. Heat in a preheated oven (375°F) 15 minutes. Garnish if desired with a slice of truffle. Serve as a hot entrée. Makes 6 servings.

COQUILLES

WHEN COQUILLES, EITHER NATURAL SCALLOP SHELLS or fireproof dishes in the shape of shells, are served with hot food, the shells are first heated and buttered. Then a border of Duchess Potatoes is piped around the edge of each shell, the filling is put in, and the shells are baked.

 ## Coquilles of Calves' Brains Mornay

3 calves' brains
1 teaspoon salt
1 tablespoon lemon juice or vinegar
1 cup Mornay Sauce
3 cups Duchess Potatoes

1 cup fresh white breadcrumbs
3 tablespoons butter, melted
½ cup grated Parmesan cheese
6 sautéed mushroom caps

Wash the brains, remove membranes, and soak brains ½ hour in cold water. Rinse. Cover with fresh cold water, add salt and lemon juice, cover, and simmer 20 minutes. Drain and cool. Cut brains into small pieces and mix with Mornay Sauce. Butter 6 coquilles. Pipe a border of Duchess Potatoes around the edge of each. Fill with the brain mixture. Mix the breadcrumbs with the butter and cheese and sprinkle over the mixture. Bake in a preheated oven (350°F) 20 minutes, or until crumbs are browned. Garnish each with a sautéed mushroom cap. Makes 6 servings.

Coquilles of Chicken Mornay

3 cups Duchess Potatoes	Salt and freshly ground black pepper
3 cups diced cooked chicken	6 tablespoons grated cheese
2 cups Mornay Sauce	3 tablespoons butter, melted

Pipe a border of Duchess Potatoes around the edges of buttered coquilles. Set aside. Combine chicken with Mornay Sauce, salt, and pepper. Heat. Spoon the mixture into the prepared coquilles. Sprinkle with cheese and butter. Cook in a preheated oven (350°F) until the top is browned. Makes 6 servings.

Deviled Scallops or Coquilles Saint-Jacques à la Diable

3 cups Duchess Potatoes	½ teaspoon mustard
2 pounds (about 1 quart) scallops	1 tablespoon water
5 tablespoons butter	Salt and freshly ground black pepper
About 2 cups dry white wine	Dash cayenne
2 shallots, chopped	1 cup soft white breadcrumbs
2 cups Béchamel Sauce	

Pipe a border of Duchess Potatoes around the edges of 6 buttered coquilles. Set aside. Place scallops, 2 tablespoons of the butter, the wine, and shallots in a saucepan. Bring to the boiling point, reduce heat, and simmer 8 to 10 minutes. Remove the scallops. Strain the liquid and simmer it until reduced by three-fourths. Add 1½ cups of the Béchamel Sauce and strain the mixture through a fine sieve. Add the mustard to the sauce, along with the rest of the seasonings. Slice scallops and add to the mixture. Spoon into the prepared coquilles. Coat with remaining Béchamel Sauce. Melt the remaining 3 tablespoons butter and mix with the breadcrumbs. Sprinkle over the tops of the prepared shells and bake in a preheated oven (350°F) 15 to 20 minutes, or until crumbs are browned. Makes 6 servings.

Coquilles of Shrimp

In the preceding recipe, replace the scallops with 3 cups cooked shrimp.

Coquilles of Game Duchesse

The meat may be rabbit, squirrel, or small game birds.

3 cups Duchess Potatoes
2½ cups diced cooked game
1 cup diced cooked ham
1 small truffle, chopped

1½ cups Game Sauce
Salt and freshly ground black pepper
1 cup soft breadcrumbs
3 tablespoons butter, melted

Pipe a border of Duchess Potatoes around the edges of 6 buttered coquilles. Combine game, ham, truffle, and Game Sauce. Season with salt and pepper to taste. Heat. Spoon the mixture into the prepared coquilles. Mix breadcrumbs with butter. Sprinkle over the tops. Bake in a preheated oven (350°F) 20 minutes, or until the top is browned. Makes 6 servings.

Lobster Thermidor in Coquilles

3 cups Duchess Potatoes
1 cup Soubise Sauce
1 cup light cream
2 tablespoons dry sherry

1 tablespoon brandy
3½ cups cubed cooked lobster meat
⅓ cup grated Gruyère cheese

Pipe a border of Duchess Potatoes around the edges of 6 buttered coquilles. Set aside. Heat the Soubise and add the cream, sherry and brandy. Cook until the sauce has thickened stirring constantly. Add the lobster. Spoon into the prepared shells. Sprinkle the tops with cheese. Brown lightly under the broiler. Makes 6 servings.

CROMESQUIS AND CROQUETTES

CROMESQUIS AND CROQUETTES ARE PREPARED exactly the same way, except that croquettes are dipped in egg and breadcrumbs before frying, while cromesquis are either wrapped in small thin pancakes or rolled in a slice of uncooked bacon, dipped into frying batter, and then deep-fat fried. They are served as hot hors d'oeuvre or small hot entrées.

Spinach Cromesquis Florentine

2 cups cooked, drained spinach
1 teaspoon finely chopped onion
1 tablespoon butter
1 cup grated Parmesan cheese
½ cup very thick Béchamel Sauce

Salt and freshly ground black pepper
6 thin 4-inch round pancakes
Fritter Batter
Oil for frying

Cook spinach and onion in butter 1 to 2 minutes. Add cheese and Béchamel Sauce. Season with salt and pepper to taste. Mix well. Spread over pancakes, and roll up jelly-roll fashion. Cut each in half. Dip in Fritter Batter. Fry until brown in deep fat preheated to 375° F. Drain on paper towels. Serve as a hot hors d'oeuvre. Makes 12.

Beef and Mushroom Cromesquis Bonne Femme

2 cups finely diced mushrooms
2 tablespoons finely chopped onion
2 tablespoons butter
3 cups finely diced cooked beef
1½ cups thick Velouté Sauce

3 large egg yolks
Salt and freshly ground black pepper
Fritter Batter
Oil for frying

Stir and cook mushrooms and onion in butter 5 minutes. Add beef and Velouté Sauce. Stir and cook until the mixture leaves the sides of the pan. Remove from heat. Mix a little of the hot mixture with the egg yolks, and add to the hot mixture. Season with salt and pepper to taste. Spread on a buttered baking sheet. Cover lightly and chill. Shape into round croquettes 2 inches long and ¾ inch in diameter. Dip in Fritter Batter. Fry in deep fat preheated to 375°F. Drain on paper towels. Serve as a hot hors d'oeuvre or as a small entrée. Makes 18.

Sole and Crayfish Cromesquis Vladimir

1 pound fillet of sole, poached
12 shelled cooked crayfish tails,
    or 12 small cooked shrimp, diced
1 truffle, chopped
1 cup Velouté Sauce
Salt and freshly ground black pepper

Lemon juice
12 thin 3-inch pancakes
2 cups Duchess Potatoes
Fritter Batter
Oil for frying
Sauce Normande

Finely dice sole and mix with the crayfish, truffle, and Velouté Sauce. Stir and cook until the mixture leaves the sides of the pan. Season to taste with salt, pepper, and lemon juice. Spread the mixture ¾ inch thick on a buttered baking sheet and chill. Shape into croquettes 2 inches long and ¾ inch in diameter. Spread pancakes with Duchess Potatoes. Place a croquette in the center of each. Roll up, pressing the edges together. Dip in fritter batter and fry in deep fat preheated to 375°F. Drain on paper towels. Serve as a small entrée with Sauce Normande. Makes 6 servings.

Mixed Vegetable Cromesquis

3 cups mixed diced vegetables
1 cup thick Béchamel Sauce
1 cup grated Parmesan cheese

Salt and freshly ground black pepper
8 thin 4-inch pancakes
Fritter Batter

Combine vegetables and Béchamel Sauce. Stir and cook until the mixture leaves the sides of the pan. Add cheese and season to taste with salt and pepper. Spread over pancakes and roll up jelly-roll fashion. Trim the ends square, and cut each in half. Dip in Fritter Batter. Fry in deep fat preheated to 375°F. Drain on paper towels. Serve as a hot hors d'oeuvre. Makes 16.

Beef and Mushroom Croquettes

1½ cups finely chopped mushrooms	2 egg yolks
1 tablespoon butter	Salt and freshly ground black pepper
3 cups ground boiled beef	Fine dry white breadcrumbs
¼ cup dry sherry	1 large egg, beaten
1 cup thick Béchamel Sauce	Oil for frying

Stir and cook mushrooms in butter 5 minutes. Stir in beef and sherry. Cook until the liquid has evaporated, stirring constantly. Add Béchamel Sauce, mix well, and cook, stirring, until the mixture leaves the sides of the pan.

Beat in egg yolks, one at a time. Season with salt and pepper to taste. Spread on a buttered baking sheet. Cover loosely and chill. Shape into croquettes 2 inches long and ¾ inch in diameter. Roll in breadcrumbs, then dip in beaten egg, and roll in crumbs again. Let stand 20 minutes to allow crumbs to set.

Fry in deep fat preheated to 375° F. Drain on paper towels. Serve as a hot hors d'oeuvre or as a small entrée. Makes 18.

Cheese Croquettes

1 cup thick Béchamel Sauce	1⁄16 teaspoon ground mace
2 large whole eggs	⅛ teaspoon freshly ground white pepper
2 large egg yolks	Fine dry white breadcrumbs
2 cups grated cheese	1 large egg, beaten
(Gruyère or Parmesan)	Oil for frying

Cook Béchamel Sauce over low heat until very thick. Beat in the 2 whole eggs and 2 egg yolks, one at a time. Stir and cook over low heat until very thick. Remove from heat; blend in cheese, mace, and white pepper. Mix well. Spread on a buttered baking pan. Cover lightly and chill. Shape into croquettes 2 inches long and ¾ inch in diameter. Roll in breadcrumbs, then dip in beaten egg, and roll again in crumbs. Set croquettes aside for 20 minutes to allow crumbs to set. Brown in deep fat preheated to 375°F. Drain on paper towels. Serve as a hot hors d'oeuvre or small entrée. Makes 12.

Lobster Croquettes

In the recipe for Beef and Mushroom Croquettes, replace beef with the same amount of finely diced cooked lobster meat. Season with a dash of cayenne.

Rock Lobster Croquettes

In the recipe for Beef and Mushroom Croquettes, replace beef with the same amount of finely diced cooked rock lobster meat.

Game Croquettes

1 cup finely chopped mushrooms
1 tablespoon butter
¾ cup well-reduced Demi-Glace Sauce
3 cups ground cooked lean game
1 tablespoon brandy

Salt and freshly ground black pepper
Fine dry white breadcrumbs
1 large egg, beaten
Oil fir frying
Venison Sauce (optional)

Stir and cook mushrooms in butter 5 minutes. Blend in Demi-Glace Sauce and cook 2 to 3 minutes. Add game and brandy. Season to taste with salt and pepper. Mix well. Spread the mixture on a baking sheet and chill. Shape into croquettes 2 inches long and ¾-inch in diameter. Roll in breadcrumbs, dip in egg, and roll again in crumbs. Set aside 20 minutes to allow crumbs to set. Brown in deep fat preheated to 375° F. Drain on paper towels. Serve as a hot hors d'oeuvre, or as a small entrée with Venison Sauce. Makes 12.

Oyster Croquettes

3 cups small soup oysters with liquor
1½ cups finely chopped mushrooms
1 tablespoon butter
1 cup thick Béchamel Sauce
2 large egg yolks
Dash cayenne

Salt to taste
Fine dry white breadcrumbs
1 large egg, beaten
Oil for frying
Sauce Normande (optional)

Cook oysters in their liquor over low heat, only until edges curl. Remove from liquor. Finely chop and set aside. Stir and cook mushrooms in butter 5 minutes. Add Béchamel Sauce. Stir and cook until very thick. Add a little of the hot mixture to the egg yolks, mix well, and stir egg yolks into remaining hot mixture. Add oysters, cayenne, and salt. Stir and cook over low heat 2 minutes. Spread on a buttered tray.

Cover lightly and chill. Shape into croquettes 2-inches long and ¾-inch in diameter, or into small balls. Roll in breadcrumbs, dip in beaten egg, and roll again in crumbs. Set aside 20 minutes to allow crumbs to set. Brown in deep fat preheated to 375°F. Drain on paper towels. Serve as a hot hors d'oeuvre, or as a small entrée with Sauce Normande. Makes 6 servings.

English Fish Balls

2 cups flaked cooked fish (cod, haddock, tuna, salmon, or turbot)
2 cups mashed potatoes
1 teaspoon grated onion
1 teaspoon finelychopped fresh thyme
2 tablespoons finely chopped parsley
3 large eggs

Salt and freshly ground black pepper
1 teaspoon lemon juice
Fine dry white breadcrumbs
Oil for frying
Fried Parsley
Lemon wedges
Tomato Sauce

Combine fish, potatoes, onions, herbs, 2 of the eggs, beaten lightly, salt, pepper, and lemon juice. Mix well. Shape into 2-inch balls. Beat the remaining egg together with tablespoon water and dip fish balls into it and then roll them in breadcrumbs. Fry until brown in deep fat preheated to 375°F. Drain on paper towels. Serve as an entrée with fried parsley, lemon wedges, and Tomato Sauce. Makes 6 servings.

The mixture may also be made into 1-inch balls, fried in the same way, and served as a hot hors d'oeuvre. Makes about 3 dozen small balls.

FRITTERS

Ham and Almond Fritters

2 cups Choux Paste
4 large eggs
½ cup grated Gruyère cheese
½ cup cooked lean ham cut into short julienne

¼ cup slivered toasted blanched almonds
Oil for frying
Tartar Sauce (optional)

Beat the eggs into the warm Choux Paste, one at a time, beating vigorously after each addition. Stir in cheese, ham, and almonds. Let the dough stand 10 minutes. Drop the mixture, about ½ rounded teaspoonful at a time, into deep fat preheated to 385°F. Cook until fritters are golden brown. Drain on paper towels. Serve hot as a hot hors d'oeuvre or serve the fritters as an first course with Tartar Sauce. Makes 18 hors d'oeuvre fritters or 6 entrée servings.

Pignatelli Fritters

In the recipe for Almond Fritters, toss the ham with melted butter before adding it to the mixture.

Camembert Fritters

1 cup Béchamel Sauce	Salt and freshly ground black pepper
4 ounces Camembert cheese	Fine dry white breadcrumbs
(without crust)	1 large egg, beaten with 1 tablespoon water

Add cheese, salt, and pepper to the warm Béchamel Sauce, and allow cheese to melt. Mix well. Spread the mixture ¾-inch thick on a buttered baking sheet. Chill. Cut into rounds with a 1½-inch biscuit cutter. Roll in breadcrumbs, dip in egg, and roll again in crumbs. Set aside for 20 minutes to allow crumbs to set. Brown in deep fat preheated to 375°F. Drain on paper towels. Serve as a hot hors d'oeuvre. Makes 12 fritters.

Fish Fritters

Cut poached or braised firm fish fillets into medium-sized pieces. Marinate ½ hour in 3 parts salad oil or olive oil to 1 part lemon juice, with salt and freshly ground black pepper to taste, and chopped parsley. Drain fish well, and dip each piece in Fritter Batter. Fry in deep fat preheated to 375° F. Drain on paper towels. Serve as a hot entrée, or cut into small pieces and serve as a hot hors d'oeuvre. Allow 1½ to 2 pounds fish for 6 entrée servings.

Oyster Fritters

2 cups sifted all-purpose flour	1 tablespoon finely chopped onion
2 teaspoons double-acting	2 large eggs, lightly beaten
baking powder	½ cup milk
1 teaspoon salt	½ cup oyster liquor
½ teaspoon grated nutmeg	1 cup drained fresh oysters
⅛ teaspoon freshly ground	Oil for frying
black pepper	Celery salt
1/16 teaspoon cayenne	

Sift the first 6 ingredients together into a mixing bowl. In a separate bowl, combine the next 4 ingredients and stir into the dry mixture. Chop oysters coarsely and blend with the batter. Drop 1 teaspoon of the batter at a time into deep fat preheated to 375°F. Fry 3 minutes, or until browned. Drain on paper towels. Sprinkle with celery salt. Makes about 50 fritters.

SAVORIES

SAVORIES, IN ENGLISH COOKERY, are small, highly seasoned dishes usually served after the dessert. Many of these, including the ones given here, are equally suitable for serving as hot hors d'oeuvre or small first courses.

Fried Camembert

Beat eggs together with water, using 1 tablespoon water for each egg. Into this dip wedges of Camembert cheese, then roll in fine dry white breadcrumbs and in again eggs and roll again in breadcrumbs. Fry in deep fat preheated to 375°F until browned, 1 to 2 minutes. Drain on paper towels. Serve on toast. Allow 2 per person.

Cheese Balls

1 cup grated Cheddar cheese	Dash cayenne
⅓ cup soft white breadcrumbs	Salt to taste
1 large egg, separated	Dry white breadcrumbs
½ teaspoon prepared mustard	Oil for frying

Combine cheese, soft breadcrumbs, egg yolk, and seasonings. Beat egg white until soft stiff (not dry) peaks form. Fold into the cheese mixture. Shape into 1-inch balls. Roll in dry breadcrumbs. Fry in deep fat preheated to 375°F. Drain on paper towels. Serve as a hot hors d'oeuvre. Makes about 12.

Stilton Cheese Balls

1½ cups grated Stilton cheese	About ¾ cup red or white port
½ cup fine dry white breadcrumbs	White breadcrumbs
2 tablespoons chopped parsley	1 large egg
1 teaspoon finely chopped	1 tablespoon water
chives or onion	Oil for frying

Combine the first 4 ingredients. Add port until the mixture can be shaped into balls. Shape into 1-inch balls. Roll in breadcrumbs. Dip in egg beaten together with the water and roll again in crumbs. Fry until golden in deep fat preheated to 375°F. Drain on paper towels. Serve hot. Makes about 24.

Friar's Toast

6 thin slices lean bacon	Worcestershire sauce
1 cup plus 6 tablespoons	6 slices toast
grated Cheddar cheese	18 pickled onion rings

Broil bacon until crisp. Crumble and mix with 1 cup of the cheese and a little Worcestershire sauce. Spread thickly on toast. Top each with 3 onion rings, having them overlapping. Sprinkle with remaining cheese. Place under broiler until cheese is melted. Serve hot. Makes 6 servings.

Tartines Marquise

1 cup grated Gruyère cheese	White bread, cut into slices ½ inch thick
¾ cup thick Béchamel Sauce	Oil for frying
2 egg yolks	

Combine cheese, Béchamel Sauce, and egg yolks. Mix well. Cut bread into circles with a 2-inch cookie cutter. Spread one side of each piece thickly with the cheese mixture. Smooth the surface. Drop, cheese side down, into deep fat preheated to 375°F. Fry until very brown. Remove from fat and drain on paper towels. Serve as a hot hors d'oeuvre. Makes about 18.

Welsh Rabbit or Welsh Rarebit

½ teaspoon dry mustard	½ cup ale or beer
½ teaspoon paprika	¾ pound shredded Cheshire or
Dash cayenne	Cheddar cheese
1½ teaspoons Worcestershire sauce	6 slices toast, crusts removed

Mix spices and Worcestershire sauce in a saucepan. Add ale and keep over very low heat until beer is hot. Add cheese. Stir and cook over low heat until cheese is melted. Serve on hot toast. Makes 6 servings.

Chicken Liver and Mushroom Toast Diana

8 chicken livers	3 tablespoons dry sherry or dry vermouth
¾ teaspoon salt	1 cup thick Brown Sauce
$\frac{1}{16}$ teaspoon freshly ground	6 slices buttered toast
black pepper	6 small mushrooms, sautéed
1 tablespoon butter	

Cut livers into small pieces and sprinkle with salt and pepper. Stir and cook in butter until the livers have lost their red color. Blend the sherry with the sauce. Add livers. Heat only until hot. Serve on toast as a small entrée, topping each serving with a mushroom. Makes 6 servings.

Chicken Livers with Bacon

Chicken livers
Salt and freshly ground black pepper

Thinly sliced lean bacon
Rounds buttered toast

For each person, allow 1 liver cut into 3 pieces. Season livers lightly with salt and freshly ground black pepper. Wrap each piece in a half slice bacon. Secure with toothpicks. Brown under the broiler, turning once to crisp the bacon and cook the liver uniformly. Serve on rounds of buttered toast.

Dutch Toast

½ pound smoked fillet of haddock
2 tablespoons butter
¾ cup hot Béchamel Sauce

12 (3-inch) rounds of toast
Sliced hard-cooked eggs

Dice haddock and sauté in butter until it is flaky. Add Béchamel Sauce. Pile in a dome shape on toast rounds. Garnish with eggs. Makes 12 servings.

Hot Ham and Cheese Sandwiches or Croques-Monsieur

12 thin slices bread, crusts removed
6 thin slices Gruyère cheese
6 thin slices cooked ham

Clarified butter
Parsley

Place on each of 6 bread slices 1 slice of cheese and 1 slice of ham. Top with remaining bread. Brown lightly on both sides in clarified butter. Serve hot, cut into squares or whole. Garnish with parsley. Makes 6 large sandwiches or 24 small sandwiches.

Ham and Walnut Toasts Derby

Walnut halves
1 cup ground cooked ham
½ cup Béchamel Sauce

Cayenne to taste
12 (2-inch) rounds or squares toast

Heat walnuts in a preheated oven (400°F) only until hot. Combine the next 3 ingredients. Heat. Pile in a dome on toasts. Top each with a toasted walnut half. Makes 12 servings.

Fried Oysters

2½ dozen large oysters
½ teaspoon salt
¼ teaspoon freshly ground black pepper

2 large eggs
Fine dry white breadcrumbs
Oil for frying

Drain oysters and pat dry with paper towels. Add salt and pepper to eggs and beat them lightly. Dip oysters in egg mixture, then roll in breadcrumbs. Let stand about 30 minutes for crumbs to set. Deep fry 2 to 3 minutes, or until brown, in fat preheated to 375°F. Drain on paper towels. Serve hot. Makes 6 servings.

Oyster and Mushroom Brochettes

18 oysters with liquor
9 slices bacon
18 small mushroom caps
1 large egg, beaten with
    tablespoon water
Fine dry white breadcrumbs

Oil for frying
Salt
Dash cayenne
½ cup butter, melted
1 teaspoon lemon juice
Chopped parsley

Cook oysters in their liquor over very low heat, or in the top of a double boiler over hot water, only until their edges curl. Remove oysters from the liquor and drain them well. Cut bacon slices in half and wrap one piece around each oyster. Use skewers 5 to 6 inches long, and thread 3 oysters, alternating with 3 mushrooms caps, onto each skewer. Roll in egg and then in breadcrumbs. Deep fry in fat preheated to 375°F. Drain on paper towels. Sprinkle lightly with salt that has been mixed with a dash of cayenne. Combine butter, lemon juice, and parsley and serve with oysters. Makes 6 servings.

Breaded Fried Shrimp

30 raw jumbo shrimp
½ teaspoon salt
1/16 teaspoon freshly ground
    black pepper
Dash cayenne
2 tablespoons water

2 large eggs
Fine dry white breadcrumbs
Oil for frying
Parsley fried in deep fat
Lemon wedges

Peel and devein shrimp. Set aside. Beat together salt, pepper, cayenne, water, and eggs. Dip shrimp into the mixture, roll in breadcrumbs, and deep fry until browned in fat preheated to 375°F. Serve with fried parsley and lemon wedges. Makes 6 servings.

Angels on Horseback

Sprinkle fresh raw oysters with salt, freshly ground black pepper, and paprika. Wrap each oyster in a half slice of uncooked lean bacon. Secure them with toothpicks. Place in a shallow baking pan and brown slowly in a preheated oven (350°F) until bacon is crisp. Or brown under the broiler, turning once to crisp the bacon on both sides. Serve hot on rounds of buttered toast or serve on toothpicks. Allow 3 oysters per serving.

Scotch Woodcock

6 large eggs	1 tablespoon butter
¼ cup milk or light cream	6 slices buttered toast
Salt to taste	Anchovies
⅛ teaspoon freshly ground black pepper	Capers

Beat eggs lightly together with milk, salt, and pepper. Heat butter in a skillet. Add egg mixture. Stir and cook over low heat until eggs are soft-firm. Pile on buttered toast. Top with anchovies fillets in lattice pattern and place a caper in each square. Reheat in a preheated oven (350°F). Serve hot. Makes 6 servings.

MOUSSES

Baked Chicken Mousse with Sauce Suprême

3 cups diced cooked chicken	½ teaspoon salt
1 cup Sauce Suprême	¼ teaspoon freshly ground white pepper
2 tablespoons dry sherry	1 cup heavy cream, whipped
3 large eggs, separated	Watercress

Put chicken through a food chopper twice, using the finest blade. Mix with ½ cup of the Sauce Suprême, the sherry, beaten egg yolks, salt, and white pepper. Beat egg whites together with a dash of salt until they stand in soft stiff peaks, being careful not to overbeat them. (The tips of the peaks should droop slightly when the egg beater is lifted from the whites.) Fold whites into the chicken mixture alternately with the whipped cream. Turn into 8 buttered 6-ounce custard cups and place them in a pan of hot water. Bake in a preheated oven (350°F) 20 to 30 minutes, or until a pointed knife inserted in the center comes out clean. Unmold onto a warm serving dish. Coat with remaining hot Sauce Suprême. Garnish with watercress. Serve as a hot entrée. Makes 8 servings.

Chicken Mousse Florentine

1 (¾-pound) chicken breast
¼ teaspoon salt
⅛ teaspoon freshly ground white pepper
1 large egg white
1 cup heavy cream
2 cups hot chicken stock

2 pounds cooked fresh spinach
¼ teaspoon grated nutmeg
Salt and freshly ground black pepper
2 tablespoons butter
1 cup Mornay Sauce
½ cup grated cheese

Remove skin, gristle, and bones from chicken breast, and save them for making stock. Dice the chicken breast and put the meat through a food chopper, using the finest blade. Add salt, white pepper, and egg white. Pound and beat the mixture thoroughly with a wooden spoon, and then push it through a fine sieve into a bowl. Set the bowl in a pan of ice water, and stir the mixture with a wooden spoon until it is thoroughly chilled. Work in the cream, a little at a time, using a wooden spoon. Shape the mixture into 1½-inch balls or ovals on a floured board. Place them in a buttered saucepan. Pour in stock. Bring just to the boiling point and poach *very gently* over low heat 15 minutes, or until mousseline quenelles are firm. Meanwhile, drain and press out all excess water in the spinach. Heat spinach with nutmeg, salt, pepper, and butter. Spread on the bottom of a baking dish. Arrange the mousselines over it and cover with Mornay Sauce. Sprinkle with cheese and brown in a preheated oven (400°F). Serve as an entrée. Makes 6 servings.

Chicken Mousselines With Noodles

Mix and poach chicken mousseline quenelles as directed in the preceding recipe. Add ½ pound cooked medium-wide noodles and mix lightly.

Spread over the bottom of a baking dish. Arrange mousselines over the noodles and cover with 1 cup Mornay Sauce. Sprinkle with ½ cup grated cheese. Brown in a preheated oven (400°F). Serve as an entrée. Makes 6 servings.

SAVORY CUSTARD DISHES

Quiche Lorraine

Plain Pastry Dough (Pâté Brisée)
   for 9-inch pie plate
1 tablespoon bacon drippings
1 cup thinly sliced onion
1½ cups cubed Gruyère or
   Emmentaler cheese
4 slices crisp bacon

4 large eggs, lightly beaten
1 cup each heavy cream and milk,
   or 2 cups light cream
½ teaspoon salt
¼ teaspoon grated nutmeg
¼ teaspoon freshly ground white pepper

Line a 9-inch pie plate with pastry and bake 5 minutes. Cook onion in bacon drippings until transparent. Cover bottom of pastry with cheese, onion, and crumbled bacon. Combine remaining ingredients and pour over the onion and cheese. Bake in a preheated (450°F) 10 minutes, then lower oven temperature to (350°F) and bake 15 to 20 minutes, or until a knife inserted in the center comes out clean. Serve as a hot hors d'oeuvre or as an entrée. Makes one 9-inch quiche.

Onion Quiche

Plain Pastry Dough (Pâté Brisée)
   for 2 9-inch pie plate
1 cup sliced onion
2 tablespoons bacon drippings
4 large eggs
½ teaspoon salt
¼ teaspoon dry mustard

¼ teaspoon grated nutmeg
Dash cayenne
2 cups light cream
2 teaspoons butter, melted
2 slices crisp bacon

Line a 9-inch plate with pastry dough and set aside. Cook onion in bacon drippings until transparent. Set aside. Beat eggs lightly. Combine salt, mustard, nutmeg, and cayenne, and add to eggs. Beat only enough to blend. Stir in cream and butter. Spread onion over the bottom of pastry. Pour in egg mixture. Bake in preheated oven (375°F) 40 minutes, or until custard is set. Serve as an entrée. Garnish each serving with ⅓ slice bacon. Makes 6 servings.

Leek Quiche

In the recipe for Onion Quiche, replace onion with the same amount of sliced white part of leeks.

Cheddar Cheese Custard Tarts

1½ cups finely diced Cheddar cheese
24 unbaked 1½-inch tart shells
4 large eggs
½ teaspoon salt
½ teaspoon dry mustard

1/16 teaspoon ground mace
Dash cayenne
1 cup milk
   1 cup light cream
1 tablespoon butter, melted

Divide cheese equally among the tart shells. Set aside. Beat together the next 5 ingredients, then stir in milk, cream, and butter. Strain the mixture and divide equally among the tart shells. Bake in a preheated oven (375°F) 30 minutes, or until custard is set. Serve hot. Makes 24 tarts.

 *English Cheese Pudding*

6 slices bread, crusts removed
½ pound Gruyère or Cheddar cheese,
    thinly sliced
3 large eggs

½ teaspoon salt
½ teaspoon dry mustard
Dash cayenne
2½ cups milk

Cut bread slices in half. Arrange them in the bottom of a 10-by-6-by-2-inch baking dish. Cover with cheese slices. Beat eggs until frothy. Add salt, spices, and ½ cup of the milk. Heat remaining milk and blend with egg mixture. Pour over bread and cheese. Bake in a preheated oven (325°F) 1 hour, or until custard is set. Makes 6 servings.

SOUFFLES

Cheese Soufflé

1½ cups Béchamel Sauce
1 cup (¼ pound) Gruyère or
    Cheddar cheese, grated

4 large eggs, separated
Dash cayenne
¼ teaspoon cream of tartar

Stir the cheese into hot Béchamel Sauce. Beat egg yolks until they are thick and lemon-colored. Add a little of the hot sauce to the egg yolks and then stir the yolks into the remaining hot mixture. Add cayenne. Beat egg whites until foamy. Add cream of tartar and beat until the whites stand in soft stiff peaks. Gently fold into the egg yolk mixture. Butter the bottom (not the sides) of a 1½-quart soufflé dish and pour in the mixture. Place the dish in a pan of hot water. Bake in a preheated oven (350°F) 45 minutes hours, or until soufflé is well puffed and browned. Serve immediately. Makes 6 servings.

Chicken Soufflé

1 cup creamed chicken Velouté Sauce
4 large eggs, separated
½ teaspoon salt
⅛ teaspoon freshly ground white pepper

2 cups finely chopped cooked chicken
1 teaspoon lemon juice
¼ teaspoon cream of tartar

Beat egg yolks until thick and lemon-colored, mix with a little of the Veloute Sauce, and add to the remaining sauce, along with salt, white pepper, chicken, and lemon juice. Beat egg whites until foamy. Add cream of tartar and continue beating until the whites stand in soft stiff peaks. Carefully fold into the egg yolk mixture.

Butter a 1½-quart soufflé dish and pour in the mixture. Place the dish in a pan of hot water. Bake in a preheated 350°F oven 40-50 minutes, or until the soufflé is well puffed and browned. Serve immediately. Makes 6 servings.

Ham Soufflé

In the preceding recipe, replace chicken with 2 cups ground cooked lean smoked ham. Add ½ teaspoon dry mustard at the time salt and pepper are added. Proceed as directed.

Lobster Soufflé

1 cup Béchamel Sauce	½ teaspoon dry mustard
4 eggs, separated	2 cups finely chopped lobster meat
¾ teaspoon salt	1 teaspoon lemon juice
⅛ teaspoon freshly ground white pepper	¼ teaspoon cream of tartar

Heat the Béchamel Sauce. Beat egg yolks until thick and lemon-colored. Add a little of the hot sauce to the egg yolks, then stir the yolks into the remaining hot mixture. Blend in salt and spices. Finely chop the lobster meat or put it through a food mill. Add to the remaining sauce. Beat egg whites until the whites stand in soft stiff peaks. Carefully fold into the egg yolk mixture. Butter a 1½-quart soufflé dish and pour in the mixture. Place the dish in a pan of hot water. Bake in a preheated oven (350°F) 40-50 minutes, or until the soufflé is well puffed and browned. Serve immediately. Makes 6 servings.

Shrimp or Crabmeat Soufflé

In the preceding recipe, replace the lobster with 2 cups finely diced cooked shrimp or finely flaked cooked crabmeat. Proceed as directed.

Potato Soufflé

½ cup light cream	2 cups thick mashed potatoes
1 teaspoon salt	3 tablespoons grated Parmesan cheese
¼ teaspoon freshly ground black pepper	4 eggs, separated
⅛ teaspoon grated nutmeg	¼ teaspoon cream of tartar

Add cream, salt, pepper, and nutmeg to potatoes. Stir and cook over low heat until the mixture is hot. Remove from heat and blend in cheese. Beat in egg yolks, one at a time, beating well after each addition. Cool. Beat egg whites until they stand in soft stiff peaks. Carefully fold into the potato mixture.

Butter a 1-quart soufflé dish, and pour in the mixture. Place the dish in a pan of hot water and bake in a preheated oven (350°F) 1 hour, or until the soufflé is well puffed and lightly browned. Serve at once. Makes 6 servings.

Spinach Soufflé

1½ cups Béchamel Sauce	1 cup grated Gruyère cheese
½ teaspoon salt	1 cup finely chopped, well-drained,
1/16 teaspoon freshly ground black pepper	cooked spinach
1/8 teaspoon grated nutmeg	4 large eggs, separated
2 teaspoons lemon juice	¾ teaspoon cream of tartar

Heat the Béchamel Sauce. Add salt, pepper, nutmeg, lemon juice, cheese, and spinach. Mix well. Beat egg yolks until thick and lemon-colored, then blend a little of the hot mixture with the eggs and add to the remaining hot mixture. Beat egg whites until soft stiff peaks form. Fold into hot mixture and pour into a buttered 1½-quart soufflé dish. Place the dish in a pan of hot water and bake in a preheated oven 350°F for 50-60 minutes or until the soufflé is well puffed and lightly browned. Serve at once. Makes 6 servings.

PASTA
AND
RICE DISHES

PASTA

TWO IMPORTANT ISSUES TO CONTEMPLATE WITH PASTA are whether it should be fresh or dried, and what shape or kind of pasta goes with what sauce, even when that sauce is as simple as garlic, olive oil, and chopped fresh parsley.

For the kinds of pasta like spaghetti (and all its family of various thickness, hollow or not) and macaroni, the superb brands of dried pasta now on the market are perfectly fine for any recipe. Making it fresh is not necessary. For noodles like fettuccine or filled pasta like cannelloni, fresh pasta makes a big difference in the texture and taste of the final dish.

As for saucing, the rule to follow is that cream and smooth puree sauces are suitable for noodles (or capellini), and that robust sauces that are either based on olive oil or have pieces of meat, fish, and vegetables in them are suitable only for dried pasta like the spaghetti and linguine family. Garlic, white wine, fresh parsley, olive oil, and clam sauce would be meaningless on delicate, freshly made, fettuccine, just as a sauce of cream, egg yolks, and perfect Parmesan would be on spaghetti.

RICE

THERE ARE THREE BASIC KINDS OF RICE PREPARATION—pilafs, risottos, and steamed or boiled rice. Whatever the cooking method, one should never bother with precooked or converted rice products, since rice is not difficult to cook properly, and making a wonderful risotto, for example, from scratch and with the correct variety of rice gives one great satisfaction. All one has to do is avoid overcooking and to deal with the farinaceous character of rice that wants to become glue is wash off the excess starch or cook the rice in butter or oil.

The long-grained rice like Carolina and basmati are for pilaf and boiled rice; short, fat-grained varieties like Arborio and Carnaroli are for risotto. Whichever kind you use, a rule of thumb is that 1 cup of raw rice makes about 3 cups cooked rice, or a recipe for 4 to 6 people.

MACARONI

Ham and Tongue Macaroni Milanese

½ pound macaroni
1 cup sliced mushrooms
2 tablespoons butter
1 cup well-seasoned tomato sauce
1 cup Demi-Glace Sauce

½ cup each cooked lean ham and
  tongue cut into julienne
Salt and freshly ground black
  pepper
1 cup grated Parmesan cheese

Cook macaroni as directed on the package. Drain and set aside. Stir and cook mushrooms in butter for 5 minutes, or until soft. Add tomato sauce, Demi-Glace Sauce, ham, and tongue. Heat. Add macaroni, salt, and pepper. Bring to the boiling point. Remove from heat and carefully mix in cheese. Serve hot. A depression is made in the center and filled with the sauce. Makes 6 servings.

Beef and Cheese Macaroni

½ pound macaroni	2 teaspoons each of the chopped
3 tablespoons olive oil	fresh herbs
⅓ cup finely chopped onion	1 tablespoon chopped parsley
2 cups diced cooked lean beef	Salt and freshly ground black pepper
1½ cups tomato sauce	1 cup grated Parmesan cheese

Cook macaroni as directed on the package. Drain well, toss lightly with 2 tablespoons of the butter, and set aside. Cook onion in the remaining 1 tablespoon butter until transparent. Add beef, tomato sauce, and herbs. Simmer 5 minutes. Add salt and pepper. In a well-buttered 10-by-6-by-2-inch baking dish, put layers of the ingredients in this order: sauce, macaroni, cheese. Repeat until all ingredients are used. Bake in a preheated oven (350°F) 30 minutes, or until browned. Makes 6 servings.

Eggplant and Cheese Macaroni

½ pound macaroni	About 1 cup olive oil
3 tablespoons olive oil	½ cup chopped onion
12 slices eggplant 2½ inches in	2 cups tomato sauce
diameter, or 8 slices 4 inches in	1 tablespoon chopped parsley
diameter, peeled and cut	1 teaspoon chopped fresh basil
½ inch thick	1 cup grated Parmesan cheese
Salt and freshly ground black pepper	12 thin 1-inch squares mozzarella cheese
Flour	3 tablespoons butter, melted

Cook macaroni as directed on the package. Drain well. Toss lightly with 2 tablespoons of the butter and set aside. Sprinkle eggplant slices lightly with salt and pepper, roll in flour, and brown in hot oil (eggplant absorbs a great deal of oil when frying). Drain on paper towels. Cook onion in 1 tablespoon butter or oil until transparent. Add tomato sauce, parsley, and basil. Heat; stir in salt and pepper to taste. Reserve ½ cup of the sauce to use later. Add macaroni to remaining sauce and mix lightly. In a well-buttered 9-by-9-by-2-inch baking dish, layer the ingredients in this order: macaroni, fried eggplant, Parmesan cheese. Repeat, using remaining macaroni, eggplant, and Parmesan cheese. Cover with the ½ cup reserved sauce. Top with mozzarella cheese squares and sprinkle with melted butter. Bake in a preheated oven (350°F) 30 minutes, or until cheese has melted and browned. Serve hot as an entrée. Makes 6 to 8 servings.

NOODLES

Green Noodles or Fettucine

4 cups sifted all-purpose flour
1 teaspoon salt

¾ cup well-drained spinach puree
2 large eggs, well beaten

Sift flour and salt together into a mixing bowl. Make a well in the center, into which put spinach and eggs. Mix well to form a stiff dough, adding a little water if mixture is too dry. Divide the dough into 3 equal parts and roll one part at a time. Roll out very thin into a rectangle on a lightly floured board. Roll the sheet of thin dough tightly, jelly-roll fashion, and cut into ½-inch widestrips. Arrange on a board or pan and dry until very brittle. Use as needed.

To cook Green Noodles: Cook in a large quantity of rapidly boiling water until tender, 4 to 5 minutes. Drain well. Toss over low heat with 1 cup (2 sticks) melted butter, 1 cup grated Parmesan cheese, and ⅛ teaspoon ground white pepper. Makes 6 servings.

Green Noodles or Tagliatelli with Meat Sauce

½ cup finely chopped onion
1 small clove of garlic, finely chopped
2 tablespoons butter
½ pound ground lean beef
1 cup chopped mushrooms
1 (16-ounce) can (3 cups)
    Italian plum tomatoes

2 tablespoons tomato puree
½ teaspoon thyme
Salt and freshly ground black
    pepper
½-pound cooked Green Noodles
    cut ⅛-inch wide

Cook onion and garlic in hot oil until onion is transparent. Add beef and cook until lightly browned. Add mushrooms and cook 3 minutes. Stir in tomatoes, tomato paste, and seasonings. Bring to the boiling point, reduce heat, and simmer 45 minutes, stirring frequently. Drain noodles and toss lightly with butter, then mix lightly with the sauce. Makes 6 servings.

Sausage and Mushroom Ligurian Lasagne

½ cup finely chopped onion
1 small clove garlic, minced
2 tablespoons olive oil
1 cup diced mushrooms
1 pound sausage meat
1 cup tomato sauce
1 cup Italian plum tomatoes

½ cups Béchamel Sauce
⅓ cup dry white wine
1 tablespoon chopped fresh basil
2 tablespoons chopped parsley
Salt and freshly ground black pepper to taste
1 pound lasagne noodles
1½ cups grated Parmesan cheese

Cook onion and garlic in hot oil 3 to 4 minutes, or until onion is transparent. Add mushrooms and sausage meat and brown very lightly. Add tomato sauce and tomatoes. Simmer 20 minutes, or until the sauce has thickened. Stir in Béchamel Sauce, wine, basil, parsley, salt, and pepper. Simmer 10 minutes. Cook noodles according to package directions; or, if desired, make your own noodles, using the Noodle Dough recipe in this book. Drain noodles well. In a 17-by-8-by-7-inch baking dish, put layers of the ingredients in this order: sauce, cooked noodles, cheese. Repeat until all ingredients are used. Bake in a preheated oven (350°F) 30 minutes, or until browned. Makes 10 servings.

Lasagne Casalinga

½ cup chopped onion
1 clove garlic, minced
4 tablespoons olive oil
¼ cup grated carrot
¼ cup finely chopped celery
½ pound ground chuck
1 cup chopped raw mushrooms
1 cup water or beef stock
2 tablespoons tomato puree

¼ cup Marsala
½ teaspoon sugar
Salt and freshly ground black pepper
2 cups cream sauce
2 tablespoons chopped parsley
½ pound lasagne noodles
1½ cups grated Parmesan cheese
6 tablespoons butter, melted

Cook onion and garlic in oil until onion is transparent. Add carrot and celery and cook 2 to 3 minutes. Add meat and mushrooms and cook over medium heat until meat begins to brown. Stir in water and the tomato puree. Cover and cook 30 minutes. Add the Marsala. Stir and cook 1 to 2 minutes, or until sauce has thickened. Stir in sugar, salt, pepper, cream sauce, and parsley. Set aside. Cook noodles as directed on package. Drain well. In a 10-by-6-by-2-inch baking dish, put layers of the ingredients in this order: meat sauce, noodles, cheese, and butter. Repeat until all ingredients are used. Bake in a preheated oven (350°F) 30 minutes, or until lasagne is hot and the top has browned. Serve as a hot entrée. Makes 6 servings. For a variation of this, use green lasagne noodles.

NOODLE DOUGH WITH FILLINGS

Canneloni

Canneloni are made by poaching squares or rectangles of thinly rolled noodle dough and rolling them around a filling, then dotting the rolls with butter, sprinkling with grated cheese, adding a sauce if desired, and browning in the oven. Fillings for canneloni are made of various cheeses, meat, poultry, fish, shellfish, or vegetables. They should be fresh, delicately seasoned, and blended with a sauce compatible with the main ingredient. The same fillings can be used for Ravioli.

Make the recipe for Noodle Dough (page 59). Divide dough into 3 equal parts. Roll one part at a time into paper-thin strips 4 inches wide. Straighten the edges by trimming them with scissors or a sharp knife. Cut the strips into pieces 6 inches long by 4 inches wide. Drop 4 pieces at a time into rapidly boiling water, reduce heat, and simmer 8 to 10 minutes. Remove from water with a perforated spoon or skimmer. Drain well. Spread the cooked strips of dough between two moist towels and let stand while preparing the filling.

Prepare any of the following fillings according to directions and spread in the center of each cooked strip of dough. Roll the long way, pinch at ends to hold filling in, and place side by side, seam side down, in a buttered baking dish. Cover with desired sauce and sprinkle with ½ cup grated Parmesan cheese. Dot with butter. Bake in a preheated oven (375°F) 20 minutes or place under broiler to brown. Serve hot as an entrée. Makes 6 servings.

FILLINGS FOR CANNELONI

 ## Cheese

2 cups ricotta	1 large egg, beaten
1¾ cups grated Parmesan cheese	Salt and freshly ground black pepper
¾ cup finely diced mozzarella cheese	1 cup well-seasoned tomato sauce
⅓ cup cream sauce	4 tablespoons (¼ stick) butter

Combine ricotta with 1¼ cups of the Parmesan cheese, the mozzarella cheese, cream sauce, egg, salt, and pepper and mix well. Shape the filling into 12 rolls 5 inches long. Place one roll in the center of each of 12 strips of noodle dough cooked as in Canneloni recipe, roll, and place in buttered baking dish. Cover with tomato sauce, sprinkle with remaining ¼ cup Parmesan cheese, and dot with butter. Bake as in directions for Canneloni. Makes 6 servings.

Chicken and Chicken Livers

7 chicken livers	Salt and freshly ground black pepper
¼ cup chopped onion	2 large eggs, beaten
7 tablespoons butter	2 cups Béchamel Sauce
3 cups diced cooked chicken	¼ cup grated Parmesan cheese
½ teaspoon chopped thyme leaves	Mushroom Sauce (optional)

Sauté chicken livers with onion in 3 tablespoons of the butter. Put the mixture through a food chopper, along with the chicken. Season with thyme, salt, and pepper. Add eggs and 1 cup of the Béchamel Sauce and mix. Spread on centers of pieces of noodle dough cooked as in Canneloni recipe, roll, and place in baking dish. Cover with remaining 1 cup Béchamel Sauce, sprinkle with cheese, and dot with remaining 4 tablespoons butter. Bake as in directions for Canneloni. Serve with Mushroom Sauce if desired.

 Veal and Chicken Livers

In the recipe for Chicken and Chicken Livers, replace chicken with 3 cups cooked diced lean veal.

Ham and Spinach

2 large eggs, beaten
1 cup minced ham
1 cup well-drained, finely chopped
    cooked spinach
½ cup fresh white breadcrumbs
¼ cup heavy cream

1 cup grated Parmesan cheese
1 tablespoon chopped parsley
2 tablespoons minced onion
Salt and freshly ground black pepper
About 1 cup Béchamel Sauce
4 tablespoons (½ stick) butter

Combine eggs, ham, spinach, breadcrumbs, cream, ½ cup of the cheese, the parsley, onion, salt, and pepper. Mix well. Spread on strips of noodle dough cooked as in Canneloni recipe, roll, and place in a buttered baking dish. Cover with Béchamel Sauce, sprinkle with remaining ½ cup cheese, and dot with butter. Brown as directed for Canneloni. Makes 6 servings.

Crêpes Stuffed with Ham and Cheese

2 large eggs, beaten
1 cup finely diced mozzarella cheese
1½ cups grated Parmesan cheese
2 cups ground cooked lean ham
½ teaspoon mustard

Salt and freshly ground black pepper
1½ cups Béchamel Sauce
12 very thin crêpes, 4 inches in diameter,
    made with Basic Crêpe Batter
4 tablespoons (½ stick) butter

Combine eggs, mozzarella cheese, 1 cup of the Parmesan cheese, the ham, seasonings, and ¼ cup of the Béchamel Sauce. Mix well. Put 2 tablespoons of this mixture on the center of each crêpe. Roll up. Cover the bottom of a baking dish with the remaining Béchamel Sauce, over which arrange the stuffed crêpe. Sprinkle with remaining Parmesan cheese and dot with butter. Bake in a preheated oven (375°F) 20 minutes, or until browned. Serve hot as an entrée. Makes 6 servings.

Ravioli

1 recipe Noodle Dough
Filling
Broth or water

Melted butter
Grated Parmesan cheese

Divide dough in half and roll each half on a lightly floured board to the same size and shape as the board, as thin as possible without breaking the dough. Prepare one of the following fillings (or one of the Canneloni fillings). Drop the filling from a teaspoon, in small mounds, 2 inches apart, on one sheet of dough. Cover with the second sheet, and with your index finger press dough firmly around each mound. Cut the dough between the mounds with a pastry cutter or a sharp-pointed knife. Boil the squares in hot broth or water about 12 minutes, or until the dough is thoroughly cooked but not mushy. Serve with melted butter and grated Parmesan cheese. Makes 6 servings.

FILLINGS FOR RAVIOLI

Veal and Spinach

1 cup finely ground cooked veal
1 cup sieved, chopped cooked spinach
½ cup cracker crumbs
¼ cup grated Parmesan cheese
¼ cup cream sauce or heavy cream

½ teaspoon chopped fresh marjoram
1 tablespoon chopped parsley
1 teaspoon minced onion
Salt and freshly ground black pepper

Combine all ingredients and mix well. This filling can also be used for Canneloni.

Chicken and Spinach

In the preceding recipe replace, the veal with the same amount of ground cooked chicken, and the marjoram with ½ teaspoon grated nutmeg.

Tortellini with Ricotta

2 cups ground cooked chicken breast
1½ cups ricotta
¼ cup grated Parmesan cheese,
    plus additional for serving
4 large egg yolks
2 large egg whites

¼ teaspoon grated nutmeg
½ teaspoon grated lemon zest
Salt and freshly ground pepper
1 recipe Noodle Dough
2 quarts chicken broth
Brown Butter

Combine the chicken, ricotta, ¼ cup of the Parmesan cheese, the egg yolks and whites, nutmeg, lemon zest, and salt and pepper, mix well, and set filling aside. Roll Noodle Dough on a lightly floured board into thin sheets. Cut into 2-inch squares. Put 1 teaspoon filling on each square of dough. Fold the square in half and press edges firmly together. Cook the tortellini in broth 15 to 18 minutes, or until the dough is thoroughly cooked but not mushy. Drain well and sprinkle with additional Parmesan cheese and Brown Butter. Makes 8 to 10 servings.

PIZZA

Traditional Pizza Dough

1 envelope active dry yeast
1 cup lukewarm water
½ teaspoon sugar

½ teaspoon salt
About 3¼ cups sifted all-purpose flour

Combine yeast, water, and sugar and let stand 5 minutes. Add salt and 2 cups of the flour. Turn the dough onto a floured board and gradually knead in the remaining flour. Knead until the dough is smooth and satiny. Cover and let the dough rise until it has doubled in size. Place dough on a lightly floured board and pound lightly with a rolling pin to deflate it. Cover and let dough rise 30 minutes. Roll and stretch the dough to ¼ inch thick and fit it into a 12-inch lightly oiled pizza pan. (There will be a small piece of dough left, which may be made into rolls or a smaller pizza.) Chill until ready to spread with topping.

Rich Pizza Dough

1 envelope active dry yeast
½ cup lukewarm water
¼ cup plus 1 teaspoon sugar
¾ cup hot water

½ cup shortening
1 teaspoon salt
1 large egg
About 5 cups sifted all-purpose flour

Combine yeast, lukewarm water, and 1 teaspoon sugar and let stand 5 minutes. Mix hot water, shortening, ¼ cup sugar, and salt in a large bowl. Stir to melt shortening and to dissolve sugar. Cool to lukewarm. Blend in yeast mixture and egg. Gradually add enough flour to make a soft dough. Knead until dough is smooth and satiny. Place in a greased bowl, turning the dough to bring the greased side to the top. Cover and let rise in a warm place (80° to 85°F) about 1 hour, or until the dough has doubled in size. Divide the dough in 2 equal parts. Cover and let it rest 10 minutes. Place each ball of dough on a greased cookie sheet and roll into a 15-by-12-inch rectangle. Chill until ready to spread with topping.

Pizza Topping

¼ cup finely chopped onion
⅛ teaspoon finely chopped garlic
5 tablespoons olive oil
2 cups drained canned Italian
    plum tomatoes
2 tablespoons tomato puree
1½ teaspoons chopped oregano
½ teaspoon teaspoon salt

⅛ teaspoon freshly ground black pepper
½ pound mozzarella cheese, thinly sliced
1 (2-ounce) can anchovies
¼ pound Italian sausage, sliced
¼ cup sliced fresh mushrooms
    cooked in butter
½ cup grated Parmesan cheese

Cook onion and garlic in 2 tablespoons hot oil until onion is transparent. Break up tomatoes with a fork and add to onion, along with tomato paste and seasonings. Stir and cook 5 minutes. Cool. Spread over the prepared Pizza Dough. Arrange mozzarella cheese slices over the top. Place anchovies, sausage, and mushrooms over the cheese in any desired pattern. Sprinkle with ¼ cup of the Parmesan cheese. Drizzle with remaining 3 tablespoons oil. Bake in a preheated oven (400°F) 25 to 30 minutes, or until crust is brown and the edges crisp. Sprinkle with remaining Parmesan cheese and serve hot. Makes one 12-inch pie.

Individual Pizzas

Make the Pizza Dough using either of the dough recipes. Roll it in 4-inch circles ¼-inch thick on a lightly oiled baking sheet. Spread with Pizza Topping or one of your choice, and proceed as directed; or top only with sliced mozzarella cheese, grated Parmesan cheese, and sliced black olives.

SPAGHETTI

Spaghetti with Anchovy Sauce

1 tablespoon finely chopped onion	½ teaspoon paprika
1 small clove garlic	1 tablespoon chopped parsley
½ cup olive oil	½ pound spaghetti, cooked as
1 (2-ounce) can anchovies	directed on the package
⅛ teaspoon freshly ground black pepper	3 tablespoons butter

Cook onion and garlic in hot oil until onion is transparent. Remove and discard garlic. Dice anchovies and heat in the oil 5 minutes, or just long enough for the oil to absorb the flavor of the anchovies. Add seasonings and cook 30 seconds. Drain spaghetti and toss with butter. Pour anchovy sauce over spaghetti. Garnish with pimiento strips. Makes 6 servings.

Spaghetti Carbonara

¼ cup (½ stick) butter, melted	Salt and freshly ground black pepper
2 cups cooked julienned ham	½ pound spaghetti, cooked
1 cup heavy cream	as directed on the package
3 large egg yolks	

Melt butter in a saucepan. Add ham and ¾ cup of the cream. Cook over low heat for 5 minutes. Blend remaining ¼ cup cream with egg yolks and add to hot mixture. Stir and cook 30 seconds over low heat. Add salt and pepper. Pour over well-drained cooked spaghetti. Toss lightly with two forks. Serve as a hot entrée. Makes 6 servings.

Spaghetti with Artichoke Sauce

To the sauce in the preceding recipe, add 5 chopped, freshly cooked artichoke hearts along with the seasonings. Cook 3 to 4 minutes. Serve over ½ pound cooked spaghetti.

Roman Gnocchi

4 cups milk
½ teaspoon salt
⅛ teaspoon grated nutmeg
1 cup fine semolina or farina
3 large egg yolks, beaten

6 tablespoons melted butter
1 cup grated Parmesan cheese
1 cup grated Gruyère cheese
Paprika

Heat together the first 3 ingredients in the top of a double boiler. Slowly add semolina, stirring constantly from the bottom of the pan to prevent lumping. Stir and cook the mixture 15 to 20 minutes over hot water, or until it is thick and smooth. Beat a little of the hot mixture into the egg yolks and then beat the eggs into the remaining hot mixture, beating fast to prevent the eggs from setting before they are thoroughly mixed with the semolina. Spread the mixture about ½ inch thick in a well-buttered 11-by-7-by-1½-inch baking dish. Cool and chill. Cut into 2-inch squares or into fancy shapes with cookie cutters. Brush tops with butter. Sprinkle with cheeses and paprika. Bake in a preheated oven (350°F) 30 minutes, or until cheese is melted. Makes 6 to 8 servings.

Cheese Gnocchi

½ recipe Choux Paste
1½ cups grated Gruyère cheese
½ teaspoon salt

1 cup medium-thick Béchamel Sauce
¾ cup grated Gruyère cheese
2 tablespoons butter, melted

Mix warm Choux Paste with ¾ cup of the cheese. Shape into 1-inch balls and poach 10 minutes in simmering (not boiling) salted water. Remove gnocchi from water and drain well. Add to hot Béchamel Sauce and simmer 5 to 6 minutes. Remove from heat and carefully fold in ½ cup of the remaining cheese. Put mixture in a buttered baking dish, sprinkle with remaining cheese and the butter, and bake in a preheated oven (350°F) 20 minutes. Serve as an entrée. Makes 6 servings.

Croustade of Gnocchi

2 cups grated Gruyère cheese
½ recipe Choux Paste
2½ cups Béchamel Sauce

Plain Pastry Dough (Pâté Brisée)
   for 9-inch pie
2 tablespoons butter, melted

Mix 1 cup of the cheese with warm Choux Paste. Shape into 1-inch balls and poach in boiling salted water. Remove the balls from water and drain. Add to 2 cups of the Béchamel Sauce. Stir in ¾ cup of remaining cheese. Line a 9-inch pie plate with pastry and add cheese mixture. Spread with remaining ½ cup Béchamel Sauce and sprinkle with melted butter and the remaining ¼ cup cheese. Bake the pie 10 minutes in a preheated oven (450°F); reduce heat to 375°F and continue baking 30 to 40 minutes. Serve as an entrée. Makes 6 servings.

POLENTA

Polenta

4 cups water
1 teaspoon salt

1 cup polenta
Parmesan or Gruyère cheese

Mix half the water and the salt in the top part of a double boiler and bring to the boiling point over direct heat. Sift the polenta into the boiling water. Reduce heat and stir and cook until the mixture boils. Place the pan over boiling water, cover, and cook 45 to 50 minutes, stirring frequently to prevent lumping. Serve hot with butter and, if desired, with grated Parmesan or Gruyère cheese. Makes about 4 cups.

Polenta Genovese

Add 1 cup grated Parmesan, Cheddar, or Gruyère cheese to hot Polenta. Turn the mixture into a well-buttered 1-quart mold or an 8- or 9-inch square baking pan. Let stand 15 minutes in a warm place. Turn out onto a serving dish and pour ¼ cup (½ stick) melted and browned butter over the Polenta. Makes about 4 cups.

Fried Polenta

Add 1 cup grated Parmesan, Cheddar, or Gruyère cheese to the hot Polenta mixture and turn into a well-buttered 11-by-7-by-1½-inch pan. Let stand until cold. Cut into squares or diamonds and fry until golden brown in hot butter. Makes 8 to 10 servings.

RICE DISHES

 *Rice Pilaf*

1 cup long-grain rice
4 tablespoons butter, or
   2 tablespoons chicken fat and
   2 tablespoons butter
2 tablespoons chopped onion
2¼ cups boiling chicken stock

1 teaspoon salt
1 teaspoon freshly squeezed lemon juice
1 cup cooked peas
1 cup sautéed mushrooms
⅛ teaspoon freshly ground black pepper

Soak rice in water to cover 30 minutes. Drain well. Cook in 2 tablespoons butter or chicken fat, along with onion, until rice is dry and begins to stick to the bottom of the pan. Add stock, salt, and lemon juice. Cover and cook without stirring 12 to 15 minutes, or until rice is tender and has absorbed all the stock. Add peas, mushrooms, pepper, and remaining 2 tablespoons butter. Mix lightly with a fork, being careful not to mash the rice grains. Makes 6 servings.

 *Creole Rice*

1 cup long-grain rice
⅓ cup (⅔ stick) butter

½ teaspoon salt
2⅓ cups hot water

Place rice, half the butter, the salt, and hot water in a 1-quart casserole. Cover and cook in a preheated oven (350°F) 18 to 20 minutes, or until rice is tender. Remove lid. Break remaining butter into small pieces and scatter over the top. Allow to stand 5 minutes. Separate grains with a fork. Makes 6 servings.

 *Risotto*

1 cup Arborio or Canaroli short-
   grain rice
¼ cup finely chopped onion
⅓ cup butter

½ teaspoon salt
2 -3 cups chicken stock
2 tablespoons butter
¼ cup grated parmesan cheese

Cook onion in half the butter until onion is soft. Add rice and remaining butter. Stir and cook until rice is well coated with the butter and begins to stick to the bottom of the pan. Add salt and stock in batches, stirring the entire time, until each addition of stock is absorbed, and then continue to add stock until the rice is cooked and al dente. Use more stock or water if necessary to get to this point. When the rice is cooked, stir in the butter and cheese and serve immediately. Makes 6 servings.

Risotto Milanese (with Saffron)

2 tablespoons finely chopped onion
5 tablespoons butter or beef marrow
1 cup Arborio rice
¼ teaspoon crumbled saffron threads
2 cups chicken stock or beef stock

2 tablespoons butter
½ teaspoon salt
⅛ teaspoon ground white pepper
½ cup or more grated Parmesan cheese

Cook as for Risotto, adding the saffron with the first batch of stock. Serve hot. Makes 6 servings.

Curried Risotto

To the recipe for Risotto, add 2 teaspoons curry powder and cook it with the onion.

Rice Pilaf à la Grecque

¼ cup chopped onion
½ clove garlic, crushed
2 tablespoons butter
2 tablespoons olive oil
1 cup long-grain rice
½ cup sliced mushrooms
1 cup diced lean ham

½ cup diced cooked tongue
¼ cup diced red pickled pepper or pimento
1 small bay leaf
1 teaspoon salt
¼ teaspoon freshly ground black pepper
2½ cups hot bouillon or veal stock
1 cup shelled peas

Cook onion and garlic in butter until onion is transparent. Add oil, heat, and then add rice. Stir and cook until rice is dry and sticks to the bottom of the pan. Put into a 2-quart casserole dish and add all remaining ingredients except peas. Cover and cook in a preheated oven (375°F) 20 minutes. Add peas and mix by tossing the rice lightly with a fork. Cover and cook 10 minutes longer. Serve as a hot entrée. Makes 6 to 8 servings.

Rice Pilaf with Mushrooms or Cèpes

2 tablespoons chopped onion
2 tablespoons olive oil
4 tablespoons butter
1 cup long-grain rice
1 cup white button or cèpes mushrooms

2 cups hot bouillon or stock
½ cup dry white wine
1 teaspoon salt
¼ teaspoon ground white pepper
¾ cup or more grated Parmesan cheese

Cook onion in oil until transparent, stir in 2 tablespoons of the butter, and add the rice. Stir and cook until rice is dry and begins to stick to the bottom of the pan. Add mushrooms, bouillon, wine, salt, and white pepper. Cover and cook 10 minutes. Add remaining 2 tablespoons butter and the cheese and toss lightly with a fork. Cover and let stand 15 minutes. Serve hot. Makes 6 servings.

Shrimp Pilaf

1 pound shrimp	1 teaspoon salt
1 small onion, sliced	2 tablespoons finely chopped onion
2 tablespoons chopped celery	4 tablespoons (½ stick) butter
½ clove garlic	1 cup rice
2 tablespoons olive oil	¼ teaspoon freshly ground black pepper
1 cup dry white wine	⅓ cup grated Parmesan cheese
2 cups hot water	

Peel and devein shrimp. Set both the shrimp and the shells aside. Cook sliced onion, celery, and garlic in hot oil until onion is transparent. Remove and discard garlic. Add the shrimp shells and the wine. Simmer 10 minutes. Add hot water and salt. Cover and simmer 30 minutes. Strain the stock and skim. Set aside. Cook the 2 tablespoons chopped onion in 1 tablespoon of the butter until onion is transparent. Add 2 more tablespoons butter , and the rice. Stir and cook over low heat until rice is dry and begins to stick to the pan. Add 2 cups of the strained shrimp stock and the pepper. Pour mixture into a 6-cup casserole, cover, and cook in a preheated oven (350°F) 30 minutes, or until all liquid has been absorbed and the rice is tender. Mix in the shrimp and cook another 3 minutes. Sprinkle with Parmesan cheese and mix in with the remaining 1 tablespoon butter. Serve as a hot entrée. Makes 6 servings.

Portuguese Rice

1 cup long-grain rice	1 cup cooked tomatoes
¼ cup chopped onion	1½ cups boiling beef stock
1 small clove garlic, crushed	1 teaspoon salt
¼ cup (1 stick) butter	¼ teaspoon freshly ground black pepper
1 red or green bell pepper	1 small bay leaf

Soak rice in water to cover 30 minutes. Cook onion and garlic in half the butter until onions are limp and transparent. Finely chop red or green pepper and add. Stir and cook about 2 minutes. Drain rice well and add to onion and pepper, along with the rest of the butter. Stir and cook until rice is dry. Add remaining ingredients. Turn into a buttered 1½-quart casserole dish. Cover and cook in a preheated oven (350°F) 20 to 25 minutes, or until rice is barely soft and all the liquid has been absorbed. Makes 6 servings.

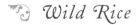 Wild Rice

1 cup wild rice	1 teaspoon salt
3 cups water	1 tablespoon butter

Wash rice. Bring 3 cups water and salt to the boiling point in a 2-quart saucepan. Add rice. Cook for 30 minutes, or until rice grains are barely tender, stirring occasionally. If rice has not absorbed all the water, drain it off and put it in a casserole, toss with the butter, and put it in a 375°F oven. Season and cook for 20 minutes, tossing it often with a fork. Makes 6 servings.

EGGS
AND
EGG DISHES

PERHAPS NO OTHER INGREDIENT IN COOKING—once it escapes the confines of breakfast recipes—is as versatile or is as kind to showing off one's culinary skills as the egg. The range of preparations, and the number of combinations of egg recipes in French cooking, is vast. And, even more than fish, egg dishes cry out for the flourish of saucing.

As a thickening agent. For custards, puddings, sauces, soufflés.

As a binding agent. To hold ingredients together in mixtures, such as meatloaf and croquettes, and also to hold a coating of breadcrumbs, flour, or cornmeal to the surface of foods for frying.

As a strengthening agent. To increase the rigidity of crusts in doughs and batters.

As a clarifying agent. As a magnet to attract and agglomerate particles that cloud broths or stocks.

As an emulsifying agent. To blend dissimilar liquids into a stable mixture, as melted butter and lemon juice in Hollandaise Sauce. Heat is not essential in forming an emulsion; for example, eggs emulsify the oil and vinegar in mayonnaise.

As a leavening agent. Air beaten into egg whites expands when heated. The whites are thus stretched and set or coagulate to form a light porous product, as in sponge cake.

As a glazing agent. Eggs beaten with a little water and brushed over the surface of bread, rolls, etc., before baking create an attractive shiny crust.

In addition, eggs improve the flavor, texture, color, and richness of such foods as cakes, puddings, and ice cream.

When eggs are used as a thickening agent, the following rules should be observed:

- Beat whole eggs only enough to blend the egg yolks with the whites. Overbeating incorporates too much air, with the result that the foam floats over the surface of the mixture that is to be thickened.
- As a safeguard against curdling when combining eggs with hot liquids or mixtures such as sauces or cream-pie and cake fillings, stir a small portion of the hot mixture, a little at a time, into the eggs. Then gradually stir the eggs into the remainder of the hot liquid.
- To prevent egg mixtures from curdling during surface cooking, use a double boiler and keep the water in the bottom part just below the boiling point. For oven cooking, set the dish in a pan of hot water and cook at 325° to 350°F. Remove egg mixture (whether surface-cooked or oven-baked) from the heat promptly when done. For soft custards, cook only until the mixture coats a metal spoon, remove from heat immediately, and replace the hot water in the

bottom of the boiler with ice water. For baked custards, cook only until a pointed knife inserted in the center comes out clean. Remove from oven and hot water and set dish on a rack to cool.

🕏 In making dishes in which flour, tapioca, potato starch, or cornstarch is used in combination with eggs, as for cream-pie filling or tapioca pudding, first combine the starchy element with sugar and liquid and cook thoroughly before adding eggs. Since starches need longer cooking than do eggs, this method guards against producing a curdled mixture.

🕏 When egg whites are used as a leavening agent, several important facts must be kept in mind:

🕏 The leavening power of egg whites depends upon the amount of air beaten into them and the amount retained while preparing the food. Egg whites at room temperature beat more easily and give a greater volume than do those at refrigerator temperature.

🕏 A small amount of salt added to the egg whites aids in producing a stiff foam. However, excessive stiffening of the walls surrounding the air cells is undesirable, because the lack of elasticity will cause the cell walls to break rather than to stretch, resulting in a loss of air, which means smaller volume.

🕏 The addition of an acid (such as cream of tartar in angel food cakes and lemon juice in sponge cakes) after egg whites have been beaten only until foamy (not stiff), results in large volume, more stable foam, and a lighter cake.

🕏 Beating a portion of the sugar into egg whites after considerable volume is obtained produces a stronger foam without decreasing the volume and also decreases the danger of overbeating.

For best results, beat eggs *only* until soft stiff peaks form—not until they are dry and stiff. They should be moist and glossy. The following tests are helpful in determining the correct stiffness of beaten egg whites:

🕏 The beaten egg whites should flow very slowly when the bowl is partially inverted.

🕏 "Tails" or peaks should form when the egg beater is withdrawn from the egg whites. For angel food cakes the peaks may curve at the tips rather than standing straight and stiff.

🕏 Air cells should be as fine and uniform in size as it is possible to obtain without beating to a dry state.

If eggs are beaten insufficiently, the foam structure will be coarse and uneven and will not be strong enough to hold other ingredients such as sugar and flour.

Combine beaten egg whites with other ingredients using a folding motion (not stirring). Mix only enough to blend the ingredients thoroughly.

The leavening power of egg whites is also affected by the cooking temperature. If the temperature is too high, the protein coagulates before the air bubbles have fully expanded, and the result is a heavy product with the outside portion overdone before the center is set.

POACHED EGGS

How to Poach Eggs

Pour into a skillet enough water to cover the eggs, and add ¼ teaspoon vinegar for each 1 cup water. Heat water to just below the boiling point. Break 1 egg at a time into a saucer and slip the egg into the water. When all are in, reheat water to the simmering point. Cover, remove from heat, and let stand 3 to 5 minutes, until eggs are of desired firmness. The eggs may be trimmed before serving They should always be trimmed before being used in hot or cold egg dishes, and if the eggs are to be reheated, cook them only until they are set and can be handled.

HOT POACHED-EGG DISHES

Firm poached eggs and eggs soft-cooked in the shell 5 to 6 minutes can be used interchangeably in the following recipes and in those for Cold Medium Soft-Cooked Egg Dishes (pages 226–227).

Poached Eggs Archduke Style

1 cup chicken Velouté Sauce	1 small truffle
¼ cup heavy cream	Salt and freshly ground black pepper
¼ teaspoon salt	Fried croutons, fried bread, or buttered toast
1 pound chicken livers	4 to 8 hot poached eggs
3 tablespoons butter or chicken fat	Chopped parsley

Heat the Velouté with the cream. Cook until sauce is of medium thickness, stirring constantly. Add salt and set aside. Sauté livers in the 3 tablespoons butter or chicken fat over moderate heat until they are tender. Sprinkle with salt and pepper. Arrange over croutons or toast. Top each serving with 1 or 2 poached eggs. Reheat sauce 30 seconds or only until hot, and spoon over eggs. Sprinkle with parsley. Makes 4 servings.

Poached Eggs Argenteuil

24 cooked large asparagus tips	1 cup Cream Sauce
4 baked tart shells	Salt and freshly ground white pepper
4 hot poached eggs	Watercress
½ cup cooked diced asparagus stalks	

Put 6 asparagus tips in each of the tart shells and place a hot poached egg on top. Mix diced asparagus with cream sauce, adjust seasonings, and spoon over eggs. Garnish with watercress. Makes 4 servings.

Poached Eggs Aurora

8 hot poached eggs
4 sandwich-sized slices bread fried
    in butter, or buttered toast
Salt and freshly ground black
    pepper

¾ cup Velouté Sauce
2 tablespoons heavy cream
2 teaspoons thick tomato puree
Hard-cooked egg yolks, sieved

Place 2 poached eggs on each of 4 slices of toast. Sprinkle with salt and pepper to taste. Combine Velouté Sauce, cream, and tomato puree, heat, and spoon over eggs. Sprinkle with egg yolks. Makes 4 servings.

Poached Eggs with Bacon

8 hot poached eggs
16 thin slices bacon, cooked until crisp
Salt and freshly ground black pepper
8 teaspoons melted bacon drippings or melted butter

Arrange 2 poached eggs on each 4 slices of bacon. Sprinkle with salt and pepper. Spoon 2 teaspoons bacon drippings or melted butter over each. Serve for breakfast. Makes 4 servings.

Poached Eggs Beaugency

8 hot poached eggs
8 large cooked artichoke bottoms
Salt and freshly ground black
    pepper

¾ cup Béarnaise Sauce
8 slices poached beef marrow

Place a poached egg on each artichoke bottom. Sprinkle with salt and pepper. Coat each with Béarnaise Sauce and top with a slice of beef marrow. Makes 4 servings.

Poached Eggs Bonvalet

8 hot poached eggs
8 thick round slices bread fried in butter
¾ cup chicken Velouté Sauce
1 teaspoon tomato puree

1 teaspoon chopped parsley
½ cup Béarnaise Sauce
8 slices truffle (optional)

Place a poached egg on each slice of fried bread. Cover with Velouté Sauce. Mix tomato puree, parsley, and Béarnaise Sauce. Spoon around each serving. Garnish with a slice of truffle, if desired. Makes 4 servings.

Poached Eggs Bayard

8 medium-sized firm tomatoes
Salt and freshly ground black
    pepper to taste
8 teaspoons butter

8 thin slices grilled bacon
8 hot poached eggs
¾ cup Tomato Sauce

Cut a slice from the stem end of each tomato and discard. Scoop out centers and invert tomatoes on a plate to drain well. Sprinkle inside of each with salt and pepper and put 1 teaspoon butter inside each. Bake in a shallow pan in a preheated oven (350°F) until tomatoes are hot, yet firm enough to retain their shape. Insert a slice of cooked bacon in each and top with a poached egg. Heat Tomato Sauce and spoon over the top. Serve as a main dish for breakfast, lunch, or supper. Makes 4 servings.

Red Wine Poached Eggs Bourguignonne

1 teaspoon chopped shallot
1 teaspoon chopped fresh thyme
2 cups dry red wine
8 fresh large eggs
1 tablespoon flour
1½ tablespoons softened butter,
    plus additional for the bread

½ cup thinly sliced mushrooms
    poached in water
Salt and freshly ground black
    pepper
4 sandwich-sized slices bread

Add shallot and thyme to wine, cover, bring to the boiling point, and boil 5 to 6 minutes. Break eggs, one at a time, into a saucer and slide into the hot wine. Bring wine to the simmering point. Cover, remove from heat, and let stand 3 to 5 minutes. Remove eggs from wine with a slotted spoon. Keep warm. Strain the wine. Blend flour with butter and add to wine. Stir and cook until the sauce is of medium thickness. Add mushrooms and salt and pepper. Fry bread in butter or toast it and spread with butter. Top each slice with 2 poached eggs. Cover with wine-mushroom sauce. Serve for lunch or supper. Makes 4 servings.

Poached Eggs Budapest Style

Cook 2 pounds fresh spinach, season to taste with salt and pepper, and put in a mound in the center of a baking dish. Poach 6 eggs in wine and make wine sauce as directed for Poached Eggs Bourguignonne, omitting the sliced mushrooms. Put each egg on a half slice of fried bread or toast and arrange around the spinach. Cover with wine sauce. Meanwhile, cook ½ pound small whole mushrooms (caps and attached stems) in 1 inch hot salted water for 5-8 minutes, or until tender. Drain, mix with ½ cup Demi-Glace Sauce, and pile on top of the spinach. Garnish with paprika. Makes 6 servings.

Poached Eggs with Lobster Cardinal

1¾ cups diced cooked lobster meat
2½ cups Béchamel Sauce
Salt and freshly ground black
    pepper to taste
½ teaspoon freshly squeezed lemon juice

6 baked 2½-inch tart shells
6 hot poached eggs
1 teaspoon minced truffle (optional)
2 tablespoons heavy cream

Combine 1½ cups of the lobster, 2 cups of the Béchamel Sauce, salt, pepper, and lemon juice. Heat. Spoon into tart shells. Top each with a poached egg and sprinkle with salt and pepper. Mince the remaining ¼ cup lobster, mix with the rest of the Béchamel Sauce, and add truffle and cream. Heat and spoon over eggs. Makes 6 servings.

Tarragon Poached Eggs Chartres

2 cups veal stock
8 hot poached eggs
8 baked 2-inch tart shells

¾ teaspoon dried tarragon, or
    1 tablespoon chopped fresh tarragon
Fresh tarragon or parsley

Cook stock until reduced by one-third. Place a poached egg in each tart shell. Add dried or chopped tarragon to stock and spoon over eggs. Garnish with fresh tarragon. Makes 4 servings.

Poached Eggs Chasseur

1 pound chicken livers
2 tablespoons butter
Salt and freshly ground black
    pepper

6 baked 2½-inch tart shells
6 hot poached eggs
¾ cup Sauce Chasseur
Chopped parsley

Sauté chicken livers in butter, add salt and pepper, and spoon an equal amount into each of 6 heated baked tart shells. Top each with a poached egg and sprinkle with salt and pepper. Coat with hot Sauce Chasseur. Garnish with parsley. Makes 6 servings.

Poached Eggs Daumont

2 cups Chicken Velouté Sauce
½ cup heavy cream
1½ cups finely diced cooked chicken
Salt and freshly ground black
    pepper

6 baked 2½-inch tart shells,
    or 6 slices toast
6 hot poached eggs
6 slices truffle, or crisp watercress

Heat the Velouté with the cream and add 1 cup sauce to 1¼ cups of the chicken. Add salt and pepper to taste. Spoon into heated tart shells or over toast. Top each with a poached egg. Very finely chop the remaining ¼ cup chicken and blend with the remaining sauce. Spoon over eggs. Garnish with a truffle slice or watercress. Makes 6 servings.

English-Style Poached Eggs

8 hot poached eggs
4 sandwich-sized slices bread fried
    in butter, or buttered toast
Salt and freshly ground black
    pepper

½ cup grated Cheshire or
    Cheddar cheese
¼ cup clarified butter
Watercress

Put 2 eggs on each slice of fried bread. Sprinkle with salt, pepper, and cheese. Heat under the broiler 1 minute. Heat clarified butter until golden brown and spoon 1 tablespoon over each serving. Garnish with watercress. Makes 4 servings.

Poached Eggs Florentine

2 pounds fresh spinach, cooked
6 tablespoons butter
6 hot poached eggs

¾ cup Mornay Sauce
¼ cup grated cheese
¼ cup fine dry white breadcrumbs

Drain cooked spinach well and sauté in 2 tablespoons of the butter. Place spinach in a shallow 1-quart baking dish. Arrange poached eggs over the top. Coat with Mornay Sauce; sprinkle with cheese and breadcrumbs. Melt remaining butter and pour over the top. Place in a preheated oven (450°F) for 5 minutes, or until well browned. Makes 6 servings.

Poached Eggs Grand Duke

8 hot poached eggs
8 slices buttered toast
Salt and freshly ground black pepper
8 cooked crayfish tails

8 slices truffle
¾ cup Mornay Sauce
1½ pounds cooked buttered asparagus

Place poached eggs on toasts and arrange them in a round ovenproof dish. Put a crayfish tail between each two eggs and a truffle slice on each egg. Coat with Mornay Sauce. Place under the broiler to glaze, watching carefully to prevent burning. Pile asparagus in the center of the dish. Makes 4 servings.

Poached Eggs with Salmon and Hollandaise Sauce

¾ pound boneless salmon
⅓ to ½ cup heavy cream
½ teaspoon freshly squeezed lemon juice
Salt and freshly ground black
    pepper

8 hot puff pastry shells or 8 baked
    2-inch tart shells or buttered toast
8 hot poached eggs
¾ cup Hollandaise Sauce

Tie salmon in cheesecloth and place in a pan of simmering water. Cover and cook just below the boiling point until salmon is flaky, 5 to 6 minutes. Remove from cloth and finely mash. Add enough cream to make the mixture a creamy consistency. Add lemon juice and salt and pepper to taste. Heat. Spoon an equal amount into each of the heated pastry shells and top with a poached egg. Coat with Hollandaise Sauce. Makes 4 servings.

Poached Eggs à l'Indienne

2 tablespoons minced onion
6 tablespoons butter
1 teaspoon curry powder
2 tablespoons flour
¾ cup chicken stock
½ cup milk or light cream

Salt and freshly ground black
    pepper
1 cup long-grain rice
2 cups boiling water
1 teaspoon salt
6 hot poached eggs

Stir and cook onion in 3 tablespoons of the butter for 3 minutes. Add curry powder. Stir and cook 3 more minutes. Remove from heat and blend in flour. Stir and cook 2 to 3 minutes. Remove from heat and add stock and milk. Cook for 30 minutes or until sauce is smooth, stirring constantly. Melt remaining 3 tablespoons butter in a 1½-quart saucepan. Add rice. Stir and cook only until rice begins to stick to the bottom of the pan. Pour in 2 cups boiling water. Add salt. Cover and cook, without stirring, 12 to 15 minutes. Arrange poached eggs in a circle on a round serving platter. Fill center with rice. Coat eggs with the curry sauce. Serve hot as a luncheon or supper dish. Makes 6 servings.

Poached Eggs Joinville

1 cup fish Velouté Sauce
¾ cup milk or light cream
Salt and freshly ground black
    pepper
½ teaspoon freshly squeezed lemon juice

½ cup finely chopped cooked shrimp
8 hot poached eggs
8 buttered toast points
8 cooked, peeled, and deveined whole shrimp
Paprika

Heat the Velouté with the cream, stirring constantly, for ten minutes. Add salt, pepper, lemon juice, and chopped shrimp. Heat. Place poached eggs on hot toast points and arrange them on a warmed platter. Coat eggs with the shrimp sauce and pour remaining sauce around them. Garnish each egg with a whole shrimp and dust with paprika. Serve hot as a luncheon or supper dish. Makes 4 servings.

Poached Eggs Mignon

1 cup cooked green peas	8 large cooked artichoke bottoms
16 cooked, peeled, and deveined shrimp	8 hot poached eggs
2 tablespoons butter	1 cup hot Shrimp Sauce
Salt and freshly ground black pepper	8 truffles, or 8 slices sautéed mushrooms

Heat together peas, shrimp, and butter only until hot. Add salt and pepper. Spoon onto artichoke bottoms, and top each with a poached egg. Cover with Shrimp Sauce. Garnish each with either a truffle or a sautéed mushroom slice. Serve for lunch or supper. Makes 4 servings.

Poached Eggs with Cod Monseigneur

½ pound poached hake or codfish	6 hot poached eggs
3 tablespoons soft butter	Salt and freshly ground black pepper
1 cup Béchamel Sauce	
6 baked 2½-inch tart shells, or 6 slices toast	Parsley

Flake fish finely and mix with the butter and ⅓ cup Béchamel Sauce. Spoon into hot tart shells or onto toast. Top each with a poached egg. Sprinkle with salt and pepper. Coat with remaining Béchamel Sauce. Garnish with parsley. Makes 6 servings.

Poached Eggs Mornay

8 poached eggs	¾ cup Béchamel Sauce
4 sandwich-sized slices fried bread or buttered toast	4 tablespoons grated cheese
	2 tablespoons fine dry breadcrumbs
Salt and freshly ground black pepper	3 tablespoons melted butter
	Watercress

Place 2 poached eggs on each slice of fried bread. Arrange on a baking sheet. Sprinkle with salt and pepper. Coat with Béchamel Sauce. Combine cheese and breadcrumbs and sprinkle over the top. Drizzle with melted butter. Place in a preheated oven (450°F) to melt cheese, 4 to 5 minutes, being careful not to overcook eggs. Garnish with watercress. Makes 4 servings.

Miss Helyett's Poached Eggs

6 large, firm, ripe tomatoes
Salt and freshly ground black
    pepper
24 cooked, peeled, and deveined
    crayfish tails
½ cup drained sautéed mushrooms
1 tablespoon heavy cream

1½ cups Nantua Sauce
6 hot poached eggs
¼ cup finely chopped crayfish tails
6 slices truffle or 6 slices
    sautéed mushrooms

Cut a slice from the stem end of each tomato. Scoop out centers and sprinkle inside with salt and pepper. Invert on a plate to drain. Heat in an oven until just warmed through. Combine crayfish tails, ½ cup mushrooms, and 1 cup of the Nantua Sauce. Adjust seasonings with salt and pepper to taste. Spoon into tomato cups and top each with a poached egg. Mix together remaining ½ cup Nantua Sauce, the chopped crayfish, and cream. Heat and spoon over eggs. Garnish each with a slice of truffle or sautéed mushroom. Makes 6 servings.

Poached Eggs Regina

½ pound poached fillet of
    sole or flounder
½ cup diced cooked shrimp
½ cup sautéed mushrooms
¾ cup Shrimp Sauce
Salt and freshly ground black
    pepper

8 baked 2-inch tart shells
8 hot poached eggs
¾ cup hot Sauce Normande
Truffles cut into julienne,
    or mushroom slices
    sautéed in butter

Flake fish and mix with shrimp, ½ cup mushrooms, and the Shrimp Sauce. Season with salt and pepper. Spoon into tart shells. Top each with a poached egg. Coat with Sauce Normande. Garnish with truffles or mushroom slices. Makes 4 servings.

Poached Eggs Polish Style

2 medium-sized tomatoes
4 tablespoons butter
Salt and freshly ground black pepper
8 puff pastry patty shells

8 hot poached eggs
¾ cup hot Sauce Suprême
3 tablespoons fine dry white breadcrumbs

Peel tomatoes, squeeze out seeds, chop, and sauté in 1 tablespoon of the butter. Add salt and pepper to taste. Spoon into patty shells. Top each with a poached egg; coat with Sauce Suprême. Fry breadcrumbs in the remaining butter. Sprinkle over eggs. Makes 4 servings.

Poached Eggs à la Reine

1 cup diced cooked chicken
2¼ cups Sauce Suprême
Salt and freshly ground black
   pepper

8 puff pastry patty shells
8 hot poached eggs
8 slices truffle, or parsley

Combine chicken and 1 cup of the sauce. Heat and add salt and pepper. Spoon into hot patty shells. Top each with a poached egg. Heat remaining sauce and spoon over eggs. Garnish with truffle slices or parsley. Makes 4 servings.

Poached Eggs Rossini

8 round 2-inch slices foie gras
2 tablespoons butter
8 round 2-inch slices toast
8 hot poached eggs

1 cup veal stock
2 tablespoons Madeira
8 slices truffle, or watercress

Cut foie gras with a round scalloped 7-inch cookie cutter. Sauté in butter. Place one slice on each round of buttered toast, and top with a poached egg. Heat stock until reduced to ½ cup and add Madeira. Spoon over eggs. Garnish with truffle slices or watercress. Makes 4 servings.

Poached Eggs Villeroi

8 cold barely cooked poached eggs
1 raw egg, beaten
Fine dry white breadcrumbs

Oil for frying
¾ cup Tomato Sauce
Fried parsley

Dip one poached egg at a time into beaten egg and roll in breadcrumbs. Let stand 30 minutes for crumbs to set. Fry in deep fat preheated to 375°F until browned, 1 to 2 minutes. Drain on paper towels. Serve hot with Tomato Sauce. Garnish with fried parsley. Makes 4 servings.

Eggs Perigord Style

8 hot poached eggs
8 round pieces fried bread, or
   8 baked 2-inch tart shells

2 cups Brown Sauce
½ cup Madeira or sherry
8 slices truffle

Place a poached egg on each piece of fried bread or in each hot tart shell. Meanwhile, cook Brown Sauce slowly until it is reduced to 1 cup. Add Madeira, mix well, heat, and spoon over eggs. Top each with a slice of truffle. Makes 4 servings.

Chilled Eggs in Aspic Colinette

6 cold poached eggs
⅔ cup Chaud-Froid Sauce
2 cups aspic
18 peeled, deveined, cooked shrimp
7 thin slices truffle
Aspic slices cut ¾ inch thick

¼ pound cooked salmon
3 to 4 tablespoons heavy cream
Salt and freshly ground white pepper
1 to 2 teaspoons freshly squeezed lemon juice
Smoked salmon, thinly sliced
Parsley

Trim edges of the poached eggs to shape them uniformly. Coat the eggs with Chaud-Froid Sauce and chill until coating is set. Coat the inside of a 9-inch ring mold with some of the aspic and chill until aspic is almost set. Decorate the bottom of mold with shrimp and truffle slices and place sauce-coated eggs on top. Finish filling the mold with aspic. Chill until aspic is firm. Just before serving, unmold the ring onto a large serving plate and surround with slices of aspic. Flake the salmon and blend with cream, salt, pepper, and lemon juice. Chill until ready to serve, then spoon into the center of the ring. Garnish with smoked salmon wedges and a truffle slice. Serve at once. Makes 6 servings.

Chilled Eggs in Aspic à la Jeannette

6 cold poached eggs
⅔ cup Chaud-Froid Sauce
1½ cups half-set aspic

⅔ cup foie gras puree
¼ cup (½ stick) softened butter
Truffle, sliced

Trim edges of the poached egg to shape eggs uniformly. Coat with Chaud-Froid Sauce. Place an egg in each of 6 custard cups and chill until coating is set. Finish filling cups with half-set aspic, but do not cover the top of the eggs. Combine foie gras puree and butter. Using a pastry bag and a fluted tube, garnish each dish with a fluted ring of the mixture. Chill until ready to serve. Garnish the top of each egg with a bit of sliced truffle. Makes 6 servings.

SOFT-COOKED OR CODDLED EGGS

How to Soft-Cook Eggs in the Shell

Place eggs in a heavy saucepan with enough water to cover them by about 2 inches. Bring to the boiling point, remove from heat, cover, and let stand 3-5 minutes. Plunge into cold water.

Serve soft-cooked eggs for breakfast or make them into hot or cold dishes.

COLD MEDIUM SOFT-COOKED EGG DISHES

In these recipes, as in those for Hot Poached-Egg Dishes (pages 216–224), medium soft-cooked eggs (5 to 6 minutes) and firm poached eggs can be used interchangeably.

Chilled Eggs in Aspic with Parma Ham

6 cold medium soft-cooked eggs
3 cups aspic
6 thin slices truffle

Tarragon or parsley
6 thin slices Parma ham

Peel eggs and set aside. Coat the insides of 6 small oval-shaped molds with aspic and chill until aspic is almost set. Decorate the bottom of the mold with truffle slices and tarragon or parsley. Wrap each egg in a slice of ham and place one in each mold. Finish filling the molds with half-set aspic. Chill until aspic is firm. There will be some aspic remaining; chill this until set. To serve, unmold eggs onto a cold serving plate, arranging them in a circle. Chop firm aspic and spoon it around the eggs. Serve for a buffet, lunch, or supper. Makes 6 servings.

Eggs in Soubise Chaud-Froid Sauce Carmen

2 cups Soubise Sauce
Salt and freshly ground black
  pepper
1 tablespoon unflavored gelatin
2 tablespoons cold water

¼ cup heavy cream
12 cold medium soft-cooked eggs
2 each green and red bell peppers
Chopped aspic
French dressing

Soften gelatin in cold water, add to the hot Soubise Sauce, and mix well. Strain sauce through a sieve, pushing as much of the onion through as possible Add cream. Peel eggs and coat with the sauce. Chill until the coating is almost firm. Decorate top of each with 3 small green and 3 small red diamond-shaped pieces bell pepper. Arrange in a cold serving dish. Surround with chopped aspic. Fill center of the dish with thin green pepper sticks marinated 30 minutes in French dressing. Makes 6 to 12 servings.

Eggs Casino

⅓ cup Coating Mayonnaise
1 tablespoon tomato puree
18 cold medium soft-cooked eggs
1 hard-cooked egg
¾ cup finely chopped cold
  cooked chicken

3 tablespoons Mayonnaise
Salt and freshly ground black pepper to taste
6 baked pastry barquettes, cooled
12 cold cooked asparagus tips
12 slices cold cooked ham
½ truffle, sliced (optional)

Combine Coating Mayonnaise and tomato puree. Peel the soft-cooked eggs. Coat 6 of them with the Coating Mayonnaise mixture. Using the white and yolk of the hard-cooked egg, make a design on the top of each to simulate a daisy. Chill until set. Mix the chicken with Mayonnaise and salt and pepper. Spoon the mixture into the barquettes. Place 2 asparagus tips and a tomato-mayonnaise-coated egg on each. Garnish the ends of the asparagus tips with a bit of Coating Mayonnaise. Arrange the barquettes in the center of a platter. Fold the ham slices into quarters and arrange 6 folded slices in a circle at each end of the platter. Decorate the remaining 12 soft-cooked eggs with a bit of truffle and place one on each slice of ham.

Eggs Frou-Frou

24 cold, cooked asparagus tips
1 cup cold cooked peas
1 cup cold cooked green beans,
    cut into 1-inch pieces

1¼ cups thick Mayonnaise
Salt and freshly ground black pepper
12 cold poached eggs
2 hard-cooked egg yolks, sieved

Combine all vegetables with ⅓ cup of the Mayonnaise. Season with salt and pepper. Pile in the center of a serving dish. Trim the edges of the poached eggs to shape eggs uniformly and coat each with Mayonnaise. Sprinkle eggs with sieved hard-cooked egg yolks and arrange them around the salad. Serve for lunch or supper. Makes 6 to 12 servings.

Eggs Tartare

4 medium-sized tomatoes
Salt and freshly ground black
    pepper to taste
2 cups mixed cooked vegetables
    (peas, diced carrots, string beans
    in 1-inch pieces), cooked

⅔ cup Mayonnaise
6 cold poached eggs
2 tablespoons chopped parsley
2 tablespoons chopped gherkin
Lettuce

Cut 3 of the tomatoes in half, scoop out and reserve the centers, and drain well. Dice the centers, drain well, and set aside. Sprinkle tomato halves with salt and pepper. Combine the cooked vegetables and the tomato centers with ¼ cup of the Mayonnaise, and salt and pepper. Trim edges of the poached egg to shape eggs uniformly. Coat the eggs with remaining Mayonnaise. Place one on each tomato half. Sprinkle with parsley and gherkin. Line a serving plate with lettuce, over which arrange salad-filled tomatoes. Garnish the center of the plate with the remaining whole tomato. Makes 6 servings.

HARD-COOKED EGGS

PROPERLY PREPARED, HARD-COOKED EGGS ARE firm enough to slice but still tender.

How to Hard-Cook Eggs in the Shell

Place eggs in a saucepan with water to cover them by about 2 inches. Bring to the boiling point, remove from heat, cover, and let stand 10 minutes. Cool eggs immediately in cold water.

Use hard-cooked eggs in hot or cold entrées and main dishes, hors d'oeuvre, sandwiches, and salads, and as garnishes.

HOT HARD-COOKED EGG DISHES

Hard-Cooked Eggs Aurora

10 hard-cooked eggs	Salt and freshly ground black pepper
2 cups Béchamel Sauce	½ cup hot Tomato Sauce

Slice 8 of the eggs and add to the Béchamel Sauce. Push the yolks of the 2 remaining eggs through a sieve and set aside. Slice the 2 remaining whites and add to the Béchamel Sauce. Season with salt and pepper. Put the mixture in a buttered 1-quart casserole and brown in a preheated oven (325°F). Sprinkle with sieved egg yolks. Serve Tomato Sauce separately. Serve as a luncheon or supper dish. Makes 6 servings.

Hard-Cooked Eggs with Béchamel Sauce

1½ cups Béchamel Sauce	Salt and freshly ground black pepper
2 tablespoons butter	6 slices toast, or 6 baked patty shells
8 hard-cooked eggs	Parsley

Combine Béchamel Sauce and butter. Heat until butter is melted. Slice eggs and add. Season with salt and pepper. Heat, without boiling, only until hot. Serve on toasts or in patty shells. Garnish with parsley. Makes 6 servings.

Hard-Cooked Eggs with Potatoes

10 hot hard-cooked eggs	Salt and freshly ground black pepper
3 hot boiled medium-sized potatoes, peeled	1¾ cups Béchamel Sauce
	Chopped parsley

Slice eggs and potatoes while they are hot. Sprinkle with salt and pepper and arrange them in a serving dish in alternate layers with Béchamel Sauce, having the potatoes as the bottom layer and the sauce as the top layer. Sprinkle with parsley. Serve at once. Makes 6 servings.

Hard-Cooked Eggs with Leeks and Mushrooms Breton

1 small onion, sliced	½ cup sautéed mushrooms
¼ cup sliced leek	1 cup Béchamel Sauce
1 tablespoon butter	Salt and freshly ground black pepper
3 tablespoons stock	10 hard-cooked eggs

Cook onion and leek in butter until they are soft. Add stock and cook 1 minute. Stir in mushrooms and combine with Béchamel Sauce. Heat without boiling. Season with salt and pepper. Pour one-third of the mixture into a serving dish. Slice eggs, saving 1 of the yolks, and arrange over the sauce. Cover with remaining sauce. Push the reserved egg yolk through a sieve and sprinkle on top. Serve as a main dish for lunch or supper. Makes 6 servings.

Hard-Cooked Eggs with Onion

1 medium-sized onion	10 hard-cooked eggs
2 tablespoons butter	Salt and freshly ground black pepper
1½ cups Béchamel Sauce	6 baked patty shells, or 6 slices toast

Peel onion and thinly slice. Sauté in butter until soft. Add to Béchamel Sauce and cook slowly 5 minutes. Slice eggs and add. Heat without boiling, 1 minute. Season with salt and pepper. Serve in patty shells or on toasts. Makes 6 servings.

Hard-Cooked Eggs in Poulette Sauce

1 cup sliced mushrooms	10 hard-cooked eggs
2 tablespoons butter	2 tablespoons chopped parsley
1 cup Poulette Sauce	Salt and freshly ground black pepper
1 tablespoon freshly squeezed lemon juice, or to taste	6 baked patty shells, or 6 slices toast Paprika

Sauté mushrooms in butter and add to the Poulette. Stir in lemon juice. Slice eggs and add, along with parsley, to the mixture. Season with salt and pepper. Serve in patty shells or on toasts. Garnish with paprika. Makes 6 servings.

Hard-Cooked Egg Tartlets

Mix finely diced hard-cooked eggs with only enough Poulette or Béchamel Sauce to bind the mixture. Season to taste with salt, freshly ground black pepper, and thyme, parsley, rosemary, or tarragon. Spoon the mixture into tiny baked hot tart shells or puff pastry patty shells or puffs. Serve hot as an hors d'oeuvre.

Egg Cromesquis

FOR THE EGGS:
10 hard-cooked eggs
2 raw eggs, lightly beaten
1¾ cups Béchamel Sauce
Salt and freshly ground
    black pepper

FOR THE BATTER:
1 cup sifted all-purpose flour
1 teaspoon double-acting baking powder
½ teaspoon salt
1 large egg, lightly beaten
¾ cup milk
1 tablespoon butter, melted

FOR FRYING:
Oil

Prepare the eggs: Finely dice hard-cooked eggs. Add raw eggs, Béchamel Sauce, salt, and pepper. Stir and cook in a saucepan until mixture is very thick. Chill. Make the batter. Sift together into a bowl the flour, baking powder, and salt. Combine egg with milk and add to dry ingredients, along with butter. Mix well. Form the chilled egg mixture into 1-inch balls. Dip them in the batter and fry until browned in deep fat preheated to 375°F. Drain on paper towels. These can be fried ahead of time and heated in a 350°F oven just before serving. Serve hot as an hors d'oeuvre, with Tomato Sauce as a dip if desired. Makes about 4 dozen.

Hard-Cooked Egg Cutlets

Make the egg and Béchamel Sauce mixture as for Egg Cromesquis. Chill. Shape into cutlets. Dip in fine dry white breadcrumbs and then into 1 egg beaten together with 1 tablespoon water, and in breadcrumbs again. Let stand 20 minutes for crumbs to set. Fry until browned in deep fat preheated to 375°F. Drain on paper towels. Press a piece of cooked macaroni into the end of each cutlet to simulate the bone. Place on a warmed serving dish with a cooked vegetable, such as asparagus, peas, or spinach. Makes 6 servings.

Hard-Cooked Egg Rissoles

Make the egg and Béchamel Sauce mixture as for Egg Cromesquis. Do not chill. Make triple quantity Plain Pastry Dough (Pâte Brisée), using 3 cups flour, and roll one-third of the dough at a time on a lightly floured board to ⅛ inch thick. Cut into circles with a 2-inch cookie cutter. Place 1 teaspoon of the egg mixture on each round. Fold the pastry over and crimp edges with a fork. Bake in a preheated oven (400°F) 5 to 8 minutes, or fry until browned in deep fat preheated to 375°F and drain on paper towels. Serve as a hot hors d'oeuvre. These may be made ahead of time and heated in the oven (350°F) just before serving. Makes about 4 dozen.

HOT STUFFED EGGS

Stuffed Eggs Aurora

9 hard-cooked eggs
4 tablespoons softened butter
⅓ cup Tomato Sauce
¾ cup Béchamel Sauce
Salt and freshly ground black pepper

Cut eggs in half lengthwise. Remove yolks and push them through a sieve. To the yolks, add 2 tablespoons of the butter, 1 tablespoon of the Tomato Sauce, and ¼ cup of the Béchamel Sauce. Season to taste with salt and pepper. Stuff into the egg whites and place in a buttered baking dish. Melt remaining 2 tablespoons butter and pour over the eggs. Bake in a preheated oven (350°F) 8 minutes. Combine remaining Tomato and Béchamel Sauces, heat, and pour over eggs. Makes 6 servings.

Stuffed Eggs Chimay

9 hard-cooked eggs
¼ cup Mornay Sauce
½ cup finely chopped mushrooms
6 tablespoons butter
Salt and freshly ground black pepper
¼ cup fine dry white breadcrumbs
¼ cup grated Parmesan cheese

Cut eggs in half lengthwise. Remove yolks and push them through a sieve. Blend yolks with Mornay sauce. Sauté mushrooms in 2 tablespoons of the butter and mix with the yolks. Season with salt and pepper. Stuff into the egg whites. Arrange in a buttered baking dish. Melt remaining butter, mix with breadcrumbs and cheese, and sprinkle over eggs. Bake in a preheated oven (350°F) until browned. Makes 6 servings.

Hungarian Stuffed Eggs

9 hard-cooked eggs
4 tablespoons finely chopped onion
4 tablespoons butter
1 teaspoon paprika
Salt and freshly ground black pepper
4 firm medium-sized tomatoes
Freshly squeezed lemon juice to taste
½ cup heavy cream

Cut eggs in half lengthwise. Remove yolks and push them through a sieve. Cook onion in butter until soft, and blend half of onion with the yolks. Set the remaining onion and butter aside. Add ½ teaspoon of the paprika to the yolk mixture and season with salt and pepper. Stuff the egg whites with the mixture and set aside. Cut tomatoes into slices ½ inch thick. Sauté them in the reserved butter and onion. Place tomato slices in the bottom of a baking dish and arrange the stuffed eggs on top. Bake in a preheated oven (350°F) 5 minutes. Add lemon juice and the remaining paprika to the cream and pour over eggs. Makes 6 servings.

COLD HARD-COOKED EGG DISHES

Cold hard-cooked eggs may be used for making hors d'oeuvre, entrées, salads, sandwiches, and garnishes.

When cold saladlike egg mixtures are served in pastry tart shells or on other pastry crusts, assembling them at the last minute prevents the pastry from becoming soggy.

Sliced Hard-Cooked Eggs with Mayonnaise

Allow 1 egg per serving. Split hard-cooked eggs in half lengthwise or cut into thick crosswise slices. Coat with Mayonnaise. Arrange on a serving dish and garnish with chopped parsley. Serve as an hors d'oeuvre or on a meat, fish, or vegetable salad plate.

Hard-Cooked Eggs Mimosa

1 cup mixed cooked green peas and
   diced carrots
½ cup finely diced celery
¾ cup finely diced cooked ham
¾ cup flaked cooked lobster meat
⅓ cup Mayonnaise, plus additional
Salt and freshly ground black
   pepper

16 baked 2-inch tart shells
8 hard-cooked whole eggs
2 hard-cooked egg yolks
Chopped parsley

Combine cooked vegetables, celery, ham, lobster, ⅓ cup Mayonnaise, salt, and pepper. Chill. Shortly before serving, fill the tart shells half full with the salad mixture. Cut eggs in half lengthwise and place one on each tart. Coat lightly with Mayonnaise. Push the 2 egg yolks through a sieve and sprinkle over eggs. Garnish with parsley. Chill a few minutes for Mayonnaise to set. Serve on a buffet table or on a meat, fish, or vegetable salad plate. Makes 16 tarts.

Herb-Stuffed Eggs

6 hard-cooked eggs
4 tablespoons softened butter
½ cup chopped, cooked,
    well-drained spinach
½ teaspoon each fresh tarragon
    and chervil

2 tablespoons finely chopped watercress
¼ cup Mayonnaise
Tarragon, watercress, or parsley
1 cup half-set aspic

Cut eggs in half lengthwise. Remove yolks and push them through a sieve. Add butter and mix well. Heat spinach with herbs 1 minute, then cool and push spinach through a sieve, and squeeze out as much of the liquid as possible. Reserve 2 tablespoons of this puree for later use. Mix remaining puree with egg yolk mixture. Stuff the egg whites with the mixture. Mix the reserved spinach puree with Mayonnaise and brush over eggs. Garnish with tarragon, watercress, or parsley. Coat with some of the half-set aspic. Spread the remaining aspic over a serving platter and chill until set, then arrange the eggs on top. Makes 6 servings.

Stuffed Eggs Roscoff

6 hard-cooked eggs
1 cup finely diced cooked lobster meat
½ cup Mayonnaise
Salt and freshly ground
    black pepper

About ¼ cup Coating Mayonnaise
1 cup cold cooked mixed vegetables
Lettuce

Cut eggs in half lengthwise and remove yolks. Set both yolks and whites aside. Combine lobster, ⅓ cup of the Mayonnaise, and salt and pepper to taste. Spoon the mixture into the cavities of the egg whites, mounding it over the tops, then coat the stuffed eggs thinly with Coating Mayonnaise. Chill until Mayonnaise is set. Combine the cooked vegetables with the remaining Mayonnaise and salt and pepper to taste. Arrange lettuce on the bottom of a serving dish. Spoon the vegetable mixture into the center and surround it with the stuffed eggs. Chop the egg yolks and sprinkle them over the eggs. Makes 6 servings.

Stuffed Eggs Toulonnaise

Spread a serving dish generously with Mayonnaise and set it aside. Cut hard-cooked eggs in half lengthwise and place them, cut side down, in the Mayonnaise-coated dish. Cut anchovies into narrow strips and arrange them over the eggs in any pattern desired. Garnish the dish with parsley. Allow 1 egg per serving.

Eggs Stuffed with Foie Gras

6 hard-cooked eggs
3½ ounces foie gras puree

Chopped truffles
2 cups aspic

Cut eggs in half lengthwise. Remove yolks and push them through a sieve. Add foie gras puree and mix well. Stuff the egg whites with the mixture. Sprinkle with truffles. Serve on a bed of chopped aspic. Makes 6 servings.

Assorted Cold Stuffed Eggs

12 hard-cooked eggs
¾ cup (1½ sticks) softened butter
½ cup Mayonnaise

Stuffings
1 cup aspic

Cut eggs in half crosswise and cut a thin slice from each end so halves will stand upright, reserving end slices to use later. Remove yolks, keeping whites intact, and push yolks through a sieve, then mix with butter and Mayonnaise. Divide this mixture into 4 equal parts and mix 1 part with each of the following four stuffings. Using a pastry bag and a large, round, smooth tube, fill 6 egg white halves with each of the stuffing mixtures. Chill all the stuffed eggs, then coat them lightly with aspic. Serve on a buffet table or to garnish a platter of meat, fish, or vegetable salad. Makes 8 to 12 servings.

Duck-Liver Stuffing

2 duck livers, sautéed
Salt and freshly ground black pepper
Chopped parsley, chervil, tarragon,
    and fresh chives

Madeira
1 small truffle

Thinly slice livers, trim slices into 6 medallions slightly smaller in diameter than the eggs, and set them aside. Puree the trimmings by pushing them through a sieve, then mix with 1 part of the egg-yolk mixture in the Assorted Cold Stuffed Eggs recipe. Season to taste with salt, pepper, herbs, and Madeira. Fill 6 egg white halves. Decorate the top of each with a liver medallion and a small slice of truffle.

Caviar Stuffing

Black or red caviar
Salt and freshly ground black pepper
Herbs as in Duck-Liver Stuffing

Mix 1 part of the egg yolk mixture with caviar, salt, pepper, and herbs to taste. Fill 6 egg white halves with the mixture and garnish each with a bit of caviar.

Crayfish Stuffing

12 cooked crayfish tails
Salt and pepper
Herbs as in Duck-Liver Stuffing

Brandy
Chile sauce

Mash 6 of the crayfish tails and mix with 1 part of the egg yolk mixture. Very finely chop remainder of truffle reserved from Duck-Liver Stuffing and add to egg yolk mixture. Stir in salt, pepper, herbs, brandy, and chile sauce to taste. Fill 6 egg white halves with mixture and garnish each with a crayfish tail.

Anchovy Stuffing

6 anchovies
Freshly ground black pepper
Herbs as in Duck-Liver Stuffing

Slices of egg white
Garnish

Mash the anchovies and blend with 1 part of the egg yolk mixture. Very finely dice the reserved slices of egg white and add to egg yolk mixture. Mix well. Add pepper and herbs to taste. (Do not add any salt.) Fill 6 egg white halves and garnish.

FRIED EGGS

FRIED EGGS ARE COOKED OVER SURFACE HEAT. Any of the following methods may be used. See also French Fried Eggs (pages 238–241). Allow 1 or 2 fried eggs per serving.

Fried Eggs

Heat butter, bacon drippings, or other fat in a skillet, using only enough to coat the bottom of the pan. Break eggs into a saucer, one at a time, and then slip them into the pan. Sprinkle with salt and freshly ground black pepper. Cover pan tightly and cook over very low heat 2 to 3 minutes, or until the egg whites are firm and the yolks are covered with a film of coagulated white.

Flipped Fried Eggs

Prepare pan and add eggs as for Fried Eggs. Cook over very low heat until eggs have cooked underneath, 1 to 2 minutes. Turn eggs over and cook on the other side about 1 minute.

Anchovy Fried Eggs

12 rolled anchovies	8 eggs
Butter	Freshly ground black pepper

Dice 4 of the anchovies and scatter them over the bottom of a hot buttered skillet. Break the eggs over the anchovies. Cover and cook only until egg whites are firm and yolks are covered with a film of coagulated white. Transfer from skillet to a warmed serving dish. Surround with remaining rolled anchovies. Sprinkle eggs with pepper. Do not add salt.

Fried Eggs with Sausages and Tomatoes Bercy

8 hot fried eggs	8 small hot cooked sausages
Salt and freshly ground black	½ cup hot Tomato Sauce
pepper	Chopped parsley

Sprinkle eggs with salt and pepper and arrange in a serving dish. Place sausages between the eggs and surround with Tomato Sauce. Sprinkle parsley over the sauce.

Fried Eggs with Black Butter

8 hot fried eggs
4 tablespoons (¼ stick) butter
Dash each salt and freshly ground black pepper
1 teaspoon vinegar

Arrange fried eggs in a serving dish. Brown the butter in a saucepan, add a dash each of salt and pepper, and pour over eggs. Pour the vinegar into the saucepan, heat, and pour over eggs.

Fried Eggs Chasseur

½ pound chicken livers	8 fried eggs
3 tablespoons butter	Salt and freshly ground black pepper
½ cup Demi-Glace Sauce	Chopped parsley

Sauté livers in butter until centers are cooked. Heat Demi-Glace Sauce, add livers, and set aside to keep warm. Arrange fried eggs on a serving dish, sprinkle with salt and pepper, and top with livers. Sprinkle with parsley.

Fried Eggs with Ham

8 slices ham
8 eggs
Salt and freshly ground black pepper

Cook ham in a skillet until it has browned underneath. Turn, top each slice with a raw egg, and sprinkle with salt and pepper. Cover and cook over low heat until whites are firm and the yolks are covered with a film of coagulated white.

Fried Eggs with Veal Kidneys and Truffles Jockey Club

4 veal kidneys
Salt and freshly ground black
   pepper
3 tablespoons butter
¼ cup Demi-Glace Sauce
¼ truffle

8 fried eggs
8 slices buttered toast
4 ounces foie gras puree
Watercress

Trim fat and membrane from kidneys. Place in a bowl with ½ teaspoon salt and enough cold water to cover. Soak 2 hours. Remove from water, dry, and cut crosswise into slices. Melt butter in a skillet, add kidneys, salt, and pepper. Stir and cook until kidneys are tender. Add Demi-Glace and truffle, heat, and set aside to keep warm. Cut fried eggs round with a large cookie cutter or trim them round with a knife. Place each egg on a slice of buttered toast spread with foie gras puree. Arrange in a ring on a serving dish. Fill center of ring with the hot kidney mixture. Garnish with watercress.

Fried Eggs Mireille

8 chicken livers
4 tablespoons butter
12 slices firm tomatoes

Salt and freshly ground black pepper
8 fried eggs
Madeira Sauce

Sauté livers in 2 tablespoons of the butter. Set aside and keep warm. Sauté tomatoes in remaining butter. Sprinkle both livers and tomatoes with salt and pepper. Arrange eggs and tomato slices alternately on a serving dish. Garnish each serving with livers. Surround with Madeira Sauce.

Fried Eggs Mistral

4 firm tomatoes
2 tablespoons butter

8 hot fried eggs
8 pitted black olives

Cut tomatoes in half and sauté them in butter. Arrange fried eggs on a serving dish. Place a tomato half between each 2 eggs. Garnish with olives.

Portuguese Fried Eggs

4 firm tomatoes, peeled, seeded
2 tablespoons butter
8 hot fried eggs

Salt and freshly ground black pepper
Chopped parsley

Chop tomatoes and sauté briefly in butter. Season. Arrange eggs on a serving dish, with tomatoes placed between eggs. Sprinkle with salt and pepper. Garnish with parsley.

Fried Eggs Victoria

1¼ cups cooked lobster meat
½ chopped truffle sautéed in butter
2 cups hot Supreme Sauce

Salt and freshly ground black pepper
8 hot fried eggs

Combine 1 cup of the lobster and the truffle with 1½ cups of the Supreme Sauce. Very finely chop the remaining ¼ cup lobster, blend it with the rest of the cream sauce, and season with salt and pepper. Arrange eggs in a ring on a serving dish and coat each with the lobster-truffle sauce. Spoon the lobster-truffle mixture in the center of the dish.

FRENCH FRIED EGGS

Eggs that are to be cooked by this method must be absolutely fresh in order to retain their shape and appetizing appearance. In addition to being served in the ways that follow, they are also often used to garnish meat or poultry dishes—Chicken Marengo, for example. Allow 1 or 2 eggs per. serving.

How to French Fry Eggs

Heat 1 cup cooking oil in a small skillet until very hot. Break one egg at a time into a saucer and salt the white lightly. Holding the pan at a slight angle, slide the egg into the hot oil. Turn it over at once with a wooden spoon to prevent the white from bubbling. Gently press the white down with the spoon, and when the under side is browned, turn the egg over to brown the other side and to aid the egg in retaining its oval shape. The white must be firm and the yolk remain soft. Remove egg from skillet, drain on a paper towel, and keep warm while cooking the rest of the eggs.

French Fried Eggs with Ham

8 French fried eggs
8 small slices grilled ham or
    Canadian bacon
Salt and freshly ground black
    pepper

Rendered bacon or ham fat,
    or melted butter
Chopped parsley
Fried bread or buttered toast

Place a French fried egg on each slice of bacon, ham, or Canadian bacon. Sprinkle with salt, pepper, bacon or ham drippings or melted butter, and parsley. Serve with fried bread or buttered toast. Makes 4 to 8 servings.

Bordeaux-Style French Fried Eggs

1 clove garlic
2 tablespoons chopped parsley
3 tablespoons olive oil
8 firm tomatoes
8 porcini or white mushroom caps

2 tablespoons butter
8 hot French fried eggs
Salt and freshly ground black pepper
Fried parsley

Split garlic and place it in an 8-inch skillet, along with chopped parsley and oil. Heat 1 to 2 minutes. Cut tomatoes in half and place them in the hot oil, cut side down, and cook 1 minute (do not overcook). Discard garlic. Sauté mushrooms in butter only until they are tender. Arrange tomatoes in a ring on a serving dish and top each with a sautéed mushroom. Place hot fried eggs in the center of the dish and sprinkle with salt and pepper. Garnish with fried parsley.

French Fried Eggs Cavour

½ cup long-grain rice
8 firm tomatoes
Salt and freshly ground black
    pepper
8 teaspoons olive oil
3 tablespoons butter

2 tablespoons chopped onion
1 cup boiling water
½ teaspoon salt
¼ cup Tomato Sauce
8 French fried eggs
Madeira Sauce or meat glaze

Soak rice 30 minutes in water to cover. Meanwhile, scoop out centers of tomatoes, sprinkle cavities with salt, pepper, and 2 teaspoons of the oil. Bake in a preheated oven

(350°F) 10 minutes, or until tomatoes are soft but still retain their shape. Drain rice well and cook in butter, along with onion, until rice is dry and begins to stick to the bottom of the pan. Add water and salt, cover, and cook 12 to 15 minutes, or until rice is almost tender. Add Tomato Sauce and let stand 5 minutes. Stuff the tomatoes with the rice mixture, and arrange them on a serving dish. Top each with a hot French fried egg. Serve accompanied with hot Madeira Sauce or meat glaze.

Provençal-Style French Fried Eggs

Salt and freshly ground black
   pepper
1 cup fine dry white breadcrumbs
8 large slices peeled eggplant
   cut ½ inch thick
1 egg beaten with 1 tablespoon water

Olive oil
8 firm tomatoes
1 tablespoon butter, melted
8 French fried eggs
Parsley

Combine 1 teaspoon salt, ¼ teaspoon pepper, and the breadcrumbs and roll eggplant slices in the mixture. Dip in egg and roll again in breadcrumbs. Let stand 20 minutes for crumbs to set. Brown eggplant slices on both sides in hot oil . Drain on paper towels. Set aside in a warm place. Cut tomatoes in half and place them on a baking sheet, cut side up. Brush with butter and sprinkle with salt and pepper. Broil 5 to 6 minutes. Arrange eggplant slices in a circle on a serving dish. Place a broiled tomato on each. Put fried eggs in the center of the dish. Sprinkle with salt and pepper. Garnish with parsley.

French Fried Eggs with Tomato Sauce

8 French fried eggs
Salt and freshly ground black pepper

Fried parsley
1 cup hot Tomato Sauce

Arrange the eggs around the edge of a serving dish and sprinkle them with salt and pepper. Pile fried parsley in the center. Serve hot Tomato Sauce in a sauceboat.

French Fried Eggs with Salt Cod Saint Benoît

1 pound dried salt cod
1 small clove garlic
½ cup heavy cream
½ cup olive oil or salad oil

½ teaspoon freshly ground white pepper
8 French fried eggs
Salt and freshly ground black pepper
French bread

Soak salt cod 4 hours in enough water to cover, changing the water 2 times. Drain off water and rinse well. Place fish in a saucepan with enough cold water to cover.

Bring water to the boiling point, reduce heat, and simmer 10 to 15 minutes, or until fish starts to fall apart. Drain well. Remove and discard skin and bones. Break meat into small pieces and mash to a pulp. Place in a saucepan. Mash garlic and add. Heat only slightly; then, over medium-low heat, blend in cream and oil, adding 1 tablespoon each at a time, as in making Mayonnaise. The mixture should be white and creamy. Add white pepper. Place fish mixture in the center of a serving dish. Surround with French fried eggs. Sprinkle eggs with salt and black pepper. Serve with French bread.

EGGS EN COCOTTE

A COCOTTE IS A SMALL ROUND OR OVAL DISH in which food is cooked and served in a ramekin or individual casserole. It may be made of fireproof china, tempered glass, earthenware, porcelain, cast iron, lined copper, or stainless steel. The food cooked and served in such dishes is usually called "en cocotte."

How to Cook Eggs en Cocotte

The dishes should be buttered before the eggs are put in. Break 1 egg into each dish and place the dishes in a shallow pan of hot water. Cook on the stovetop 2 to 3 minutes, never allowing the water to boil. Cover the dishes with foil or a baking sheet and finish cooking in a preheated oven (325°F) about 3 to 4 minutes. The whites should be firm and the yolks soft. Allow 1 egg per serving.

A tablespoon of heavy cream or of concentrated veal stock or chicken stock may first be put in each dish. Add eggs and sprinkle with salt and pepper. Cook as described above, but cook in the oven only 3 minutes.

Eggs en Cocotte with Chicken Colbert

2 cups finely ground cooked chicken	6 eggs
1 tablespoon chopped parsley	¼ cup (½ stick) butter
¼ teaspoon chopped thyme	1 tablespoon each freshly squeezed
About ¼ cup light cream	lemon juice and liquid meat glaze

Combine chicken, parsley, thyme, and enough cream to make chicken of spreading consistency. Spread over the bottoms and sides of 6 buttered cocotte dishes. Break 1 egg into each. Cook as in basic recipe 3 minutes over low heat and 5 minutes in the oven. Combine remaining ingredients, heat, and put an equal amount on each serving.

Eggs en Cocotte Florentine

1 pound spinach, cooked
2 tablespoons butter
Salt and freshly ground black
   pepper

6 eggs
6 tablespoons warmed heavy cream
6 tablespoons grated Parmesan cheese

Drain the spinach well and sauté in butter 2 to 3 minutes. Season with salt and pepper. Spread over bottoms and sides of 6 buttered cocotte dishes. Break 1 egg into each. Sprinkle with salt and pepper. Cook as in basic recipe 3 minutes over low heat. Pour 1 tablespoon cream over each egg, then sprinkle each with 1 tablespoon cheese. Cover and cook 5 minutes in a preheated oven (325°F).

Paris-Style Eggs en Cocotte

1 cup each finely ground leftover
   cooked chicken and roast beef
¼ cup finely chopped sautéed
   mushrooms
1 tablespoon chopped truffles
   (optional)

½ cup Supreme Sauce
Salt and freshly ground black pepper
6 eggs
6 tablespoons Demi-Glace Sauce

Combine chicken, beef, mushrooms, truffles (if using), and cream sauce. Season to taste with salt and pepper. Spread over bottoms and sides of 6 buttered cocotte dishes. Break 1 egg into each. Sprinkle with salt and pepper. Cook as in basic recipe 3 minutes over low heat and 5 minutes in the oven. Heat Demi-Glace Sauce and put a spoonful on each serving.

Tarragon Eggs en Cocotte

2 sprigs tarragon
1 cup concentrated veal stock
1 tablespoon tomato puree

6 eggs
Salt and freshly ground black pepper
Parsley

Simmer tarragon sprigs in stock 5 minutes. Strain. Add tomato puree to stock. Stir and cook 1 to 2 minutes, then put 2 tablespoons of the mixture into each of 6 buttered cocotte dishes. Break 1 egg into each. Sprinkle with salt and pepper. Cook as in basic recipe 3 minutes over low heat and 3 minutes in the oven. Garnish with chopped parsley.

Eggs en Cocotte with Lamb and Mushrooms

1 cup ground roast lamb
1 cup sautéed finely chopped
  mushrooms

About ½ cup Supreme Sauce
6 eggs
Salt and freshly ground black pepper

Combine lamb, mushrooms, and sauce. Spread over the bottom and sides of 6 buttered cocotte dishes. Break 1 egg into each. Sprinkle with salt and pepper. Cook as directed in basic recipe, but cook 5 minutes in the oven. (When eggs cooked en cocotte are combined with meat they must be cooked longer, because the heat penetrates more slowly.)

MOLDED EGGS

Molded Whole Eggs

Butter the insides of 6-ounce custard cups generously. Sprinkle with minced cooked ham, crumbled crisp bacon, fine dry white breadcrumbs, chopped truffles or mushrooms, or chopped herbs. Break 1 egg into each cup. Sprinkle with salt and freshly ground black pepper to taste. Place the cups in a pan of hot water that comes three-quarters of the way up the sides of the cups. Simmer over low heat 2 to 3 minutes, then cook in a preheated oven (325°F) only until whites are set enough to retain the shape of the mold when unmolded. To unmold, run a spatula or knife around the edge of the mold and turn out the egg onto a serving dish. Garnish with parsley or watercress. The whites of these eggs should be just firm enough to retain the shape of the mold; the yolks should be soft as in poached or soft-cooked eggs, never firm or hard-cooked. Allow 1 or 2 eggs per person.

Neapolitan Molded Eggs

7 large eggs
1 tablespoon butter
1¼ cups grated Parmesan cheese

Salt and freshly ground black pepper
2 tablespoons Tomato Sauce
⅔ cup Demi-Glace Sauce

Scramble 5 of the eggs very lightly in butter. Add ¾ cup of the cheese, the 2 remaining raw eggs, and salt and pepper. Mix well. Spoon into well-buttered 6-ounce custard cups. Set cups in a pan of hot water and bake in a preheated slow oven (325°F) 10 minutes, or only until eggs are set. Turn out onto a buttered ovenproof platter. Sprinkle with remaining cheese. Combine Tomato and Demi-Glace Sauces and pour over eggs. Cook in a preheated oven (450°F) until glazed. Makes 4 servings.

Molded Scrambled Eggs

Another method of preparing molded eggs is with scrambled eggs. Use an equal number of scrambled eggs and beaten raw eggs. Mix lightly, turn into a buttered 6-ounce custard cup, and cook in a preheated oven (325°F) until the outside has set but the center is still soft. Allow 2 eggs per serving.

Molded Eggs Ninette

7 large eggs
1 tablespoon butter
Salt and freshly ground black
    pepper

20 peeled, deveined, slightly cooked shrimp
3 tablespoons whipped cream
½ cup hot Hollandaise Sauce
4 slices buttered toast

Scramble 5 of the eggs very lightly in the butter. Add salt and pepper. Dice 16 of the shrimp and mix with the cooked eggs, along with the remaining 2 raw eggs, beaten lightly. Spoon into well-buttered 6-ounce custard cups. Set cups in a pan of hot water and cook in a preheated oven (325°F) only until eggs are set. Turn out onto a buttered ovenproof platter. Fold whipped cream into Hollandaise Sauce and spread over eggs. Garnish with remaining whole shrimp. Makes 4 servings.

SCRAMBLED EGGS

How to Scramble Eggs

Break eggs into a bowl. Beat the mixture only until yolks and whites are blended Season lightly with salt and freshly ground black pepper. Pour the mixture into a buttered metal bowl or the top of a double boiler. Heat slowly, stirring all the time until the eggs are set, but still moist (soft-firm)—or about 15 minutes. Finish the eggs by adding 2 tablespoons of cold butter and a tablespoon of heavy cream. Adjust the seasoning. Allow 2 eggs per person.

Scrambled Eggs with Artichoke Bottoms

3 cooked artichoke bottoms
2 tablespoons butter
8 large eggs, scrambled

½ cup light cream
Salt and freshly ground black
    pepper

Dice artichoke bottoms and sauté over low heat in the butter in an 8-inch skillet. Fill with hot scrambled eggs and garnish with chervil. Makes 4 servings.

Scrambled Eggs with Asparagus Tips

Tips from ½ pound fresh asparagus
Salt and freshly ground pepper
2 tablespoons butter

8 large eggs, scrambled
½ cup light cream

Wash asparagus and cut tips into ½-inch pieces. Place in a saucepan with ½ inch boiling water and ½ teaspoon salt. Cover and cook 5 minutes or only until crisp-tender. Remove from water, drain well, and sauté in 1 tablespoon of the butter in an 8-inch skillet. Fold into hot scrambled eggs just before they are served. Makes 4 servings.

Scrambled Eggs Chasseur

½ pound chicken livers
2 tablespoons butter
½ cup sautéed sliced mushrooms
¾ cup cream sauce

Salt and freshly ground black
  pepper
8 eggs, scrambled
Chopped parsley

Cook livers in butter until they are no longer pink. Remove from heat and dice the livers. Add the mushrooms, cream sauce, and salt and pepper. Put the mixture in the center of a warmed serving dish and spoon the scrambled eggs around it. Garnish with parsley. Makes 6 servings.

Scrambled Eggs Clamart

¾ cup tiny French peas (petits pois),
  cooked
Salt and freshly ground black
  pepper

Scrambled Eggs
1 cup cream sauce

Add the peas to the scrambled eggs just before the eggs are done. Serve with cream sauce. Makes 6 servings.

Scrambled Eggs Georgette

1 cup peeled crayfish tails
2 tablespoons butter
Scrambled Eggs
Salt and freshly ground
  black pepper

6 large baked potatoes with centers
  scooped out
Parsley

Sauté crayfish in butter in an 8-inch skillet for 2 minutes and fold into the eggs just before they are done. Heat the potato shells and fill with egg mixture. Garnish with parsley. Serve for lunch or supper. Makes 6 servings.

Scrambled Eggs with Crayfish

1 cup peeled crayfish tails	Scrambled Eggs
2 tablespoons butter	Salt and freshly ground black pepper

Cook crayfish in 2 tablespoons of the butter over medium-low heat until tender. Add to the eggs just before they are done. Serve hot. Makes 6 servings.

Scrambled Eggs with Croutons

30 white bread croutons fried in butter
Scrambled Eggs

Add hot croutons to the eggs just before they are done. Serve on a warmed platter. Makes 6 servings.

Scrambled Eggs with Kidneys

4 veal kidneys	Scrambled Eggs
Salt and freshly ground black pepper	1 cup Madeira Sauce
1 teaspoon chopped shallot or onion	
4 tablespoons butter	
¾ cup diced tomatoes	

Soak kidneys 2 hours in enough cold water to cover, adding ¾ teaspoon salt. Remove from water, pat dry, and cut into crosswise slices, removing all fat and membrane. Sauté shallot in 2 tablespoons of the butter 2 minutes, then add kidneys and cook briskly 5 to 8 minutes. Set aside; keep warm. Sauté tomatoes in 1 tablespoon of the butter. Add salt and pepper to taste. Set aside; keep warm. Scramble the eggs adding tomatoes just before eggs are set. Make a ring of scrambled eggs in a warmed serving dish. Add Madeira Sauce and remaining butter to kidney mixture, heat, and spoon into the center of the dish. Serve for special breakfasts, lunch, or supper. Makes 6 servings.

Scrambled Eggs Magda

1 teaspoon mustard	Scrambled Eggs
⅓ cup heavy cream	Salt and freshly ground black pepper
¼ cup chopped parsley	2 tablespoons butter
½ cup grated Cheddar cheese	12 cubes white bread

Add mustard, cream, parsley, cheese, salt, and pepper to the eggs. Fry bread cubes in butter and scatter over eggs. Makes 4 servings.

Scrambled Eggs with Morels

¾ cup sliced morels
1 tablespoon butter
Scrambled Eggs

Salt and freshly ground black pepper
2 slices bacon, cooked until crisp

Sauté morels in butter in an 8-inch skillet. Season. Add to the eggs halfway through the cooking. Crumble bacon and add. Makes 4 servings.

Scrambled Eggs with Mushrooms

1 cup thinly sliced mushrooms
2 tablespoons butter

Scrambled Eggs
Salt and freshly ground black pepper

Sauté mushrooms in butter until browned. Season. Add to the eggs just before they are done. Makes 6 servings.

Portuguese Scrambled Eggs

2 cups diced tomatoes
3 tablespoons butter

Scrambled Eggs
Salt and freshly ground black pepper
2 tablespoons chopped parsley

Sauté tomatoes in the butter until most of the liquid has evaporated. Season. Set aside; keep warm. Arrange scrambled eggs in a ring in a warmed serving dish. Fill center with sautéed tomatoes. Sprinkle with parsley. Makes 4 servings.

Scrambled Eggs with Shrimp

½ pound peeled, deveined, cooked shrimp
Scrambled Eggs
Salt and freshly ground black pepper

Add the shrimp to the scrambled eggs 2 minutes before they are done. Makes 6 servings.

OMELETTES

THERE ARE THREE BASIC TYPES OF OMELETTES: French (plain), American (puffy), and Italian (flat or *frittata*). The French or plain omelette is made with whole eggs beaten only enough to blend the whites with the yolks, with no additional liquid. The American or puffy omelette is made by beating the whites and yolks separately with 1 tablespoon water to each egg. The Italian frittata is made with whole eggs beaten lightly, usually mixed with meat or vegetables, and cooked in a little oil, first on one side and then on the other, pancake-style. French and American omelettes are folded.

A variety of other foods and sauces may be added to omelettes, either cooked with the eggs or used as a filling. Mixtures added to frittatas are always cooked with the eggs. Fillings may be added to French or American omelettes after the omelette is cooked but just before it is folded. (See recipes on pages 249–256.)

Plain French Omelette

4 large eggs
½ teaspoon salt

Dash freshly ground black pepper
About 1½ tablespoons butter

Beat eggs only until the whites and yolks are mixed. Add salt and pepper and stir only until ingredients are blended. Melt butter in an 8- or 9-inch skillet. Pour in egg mixture. Cook over medium-low heat. As omelette cooks, lift the edges and turn them toward the center so the uncooked mixture flows under the cooked portion. Cook only until the bottom is light brown and the top is set. Make a crease across the center with a spatula or the back of a knife. Fold half the omelet over the other half. Serve immediately on a warmed platter. Serves 2. If desired, a filling may be spread on one side of the omelette just before it is folded or a sauce served over it.

Puffy American Omelette

A puffy omelette should have fine, uniform air cells throughout and a soft, puffy, moist texture. It should have a tender, light golden-brown crust. Overcooking or cooking at too high temperature causes the bottom to become tough and heavy, and the omelette may fall and be tough and dry.

6 large eggs
¾ teaspoon salt
⅓ cup water

¼ teaspoon freshly ground black pepper
1½ tablespoons butter

Separate eggs, placing whites and yolks in separate bowls. Add salt and water to the egg whites. Beat until soft, stiff, moist (not dry) peaks form. Add pepper to the egg yolks and beat them until they are thick and lemon-colored. Fold egg yolks into beaten egg whites. Meanwhile, melt butter in an 8- or 9-inch skillet. Pour in omelette mixture. Cook over low heat 5 to 6 minutes, or until omelette is puffy and light brown on the bottom, lifting omelette at the edges with a spatula to judge the color. Bake in a preheated oven (325°F) 12 to 15 minutes, or only until a knife inserted in the center of the omelette comes out clean. Make a crease across the center with the back of a knife or with a spatula. Fold half of the omelette over the other half. Serve promptly on a warmed platter. If desired, a filling may be added just before folding. Makes 4 generous servings.

 ## *Italian Frittata Omelette*

5 large eggs	1 tablespoon chopped parsley
½ to ¾ teaspoon salt	1 cup diced cooked vegetables,
Dash freshly ground black pepper	ham, or seafood
1 teaspoon finely chopped fresh thyme	1½ tablespoons olive oil

Beat eggs with a fork only until the whites and yolks are mixed. Add seasonings, herbs, and vegetables, ham, or seafood. Heat oil in an 8- or 9-inch skillet. Pour in the mixture. Cook over medium-low heat until the bottom of the frittata is set and the top is creamy like scrambled eggs. Invert onto a plate big enough to hold the frittata and slide the omelet back into the pan. Cook 1 to 2 minutes. Serve on a warmed plate, cut into pie-shaped wedges. Eat either hot or at room temperature. The amount of salt used depends upon the amount that is in the filling. Other ingredients may be substituted for the vegetables, ham, or seafood. Makes 4 servings.

FILLINGS, ADDITIONS, AND SAUCES FOR OMELETTES

Any of the following combinations can be used with French Omelettes or Puffy Omelettes. Only those that are added before cooking the eggs are suitable for frittata. Each of the following is sufficient for 4 servings.

 ## *Agnès Sorel*

1 cup sliced mushrooms	½ cup ground or minced cooked chicken
2 tablespoons butter	Sliced cooked tongue

Sauté mushrooms in butter. Add chicken and cook only until hot. Spread on one side of cooked omelette, before folding. Garnish with sliced cooked tongue.

 ## *Archduke*

6 raw chicken livers	Salt and freshly ground black pepper
2 tablespoons butter	Sliced truffle
1 cup medium Brown Sauce	

Slice chicken livers, sauté in butter until no longer pink, then add to Brown Sauce. Add salt and pepper. Heat. Fill cooked omelette, fold, and garnish top with sliced truffle.

Asparagus

1 cup diced cooked asparagus	3 tablespoons butter, melted
12 cooked asparagus tips	Thin slices cooked ham

Fill cooked omelette with drained diced cooked asparagus. Place omelette on a warm platter and make a lengthwise incision down the center. Heat asparagus tips in butter and place them in the incision. Serve hot on a warmed platter with thin slices of cooked ham.

Arlésienne

1 clove garlic
¼ cup each diced onion and diced
    green bell pepper
2 tablespoons olive oil
1½ cups peeled, diced eggplant
2 cups diced raw tomatoes

Salt and freshly ground black pepper
½ cup hot Tomato Sauce

Sauté garlic, onion, and green pepper in oil until they are limp. Remove and discard garlic. Add eggplant and tomatoes. Stir and cook until eggplant is soft and most of the liquid has evaporated. (If necessary, thicken the mixture by adding 1 to 2 tablespoons fine dry breadcrumbs.) Season with salt and pepper. Reserve ½ cup of mixture; use the rest to fill cooked omelette. Fold omelette and garnish top with the reserved eggplant-tomato mixture. Pour Tomato Sauce around the omelette.

Chasseur

½ pound chicken livers
½ cup sliced mushrooms
3 tablespoons butter or rendered
    bacon fat

½ cup chopped onion
Salt and freshly ground black pepper
¼ cup Demi-Glace Sauce
Chopped parsley

Sauté chicken livers and mushrooms in butter over medium-low heat until livers are no longer pink. Remove from heat, cool, and chop livers medium-fine. Sauté onion 2 to 3 minutes in the same skillet. Add livers and mushrooms, salt, pepper, and Demi-Glace Sauce. Spread two-thirds of the mixture on one side of the omelette, over which fold the other half. Place omelette on a warmed platter and make a lengthwise incision down the center. Fill with the remaining liver mixture. Sprinkle with parsley.

Bohemian

¾ cup sliced mushrooms
1½ tablespoons butter
⅓ cup diced cooked ham
1 cup stewed tomatoes

1 small truffle, chopped
Salt and freshly ground black pepper
½ cup Tomato Sauce

Sauté mushrooms in butter until tender. Add all remaining ingredients except Tomato Sauce. Stir and cook over medium heat until the liquid is reduced. Reserve ½ cup of mixture, fill omelette with remainder, and fold. Pour reserved mixture over the top. Surround with a ring of Tomato Sauce.

Boulogne

2 pairs roe (shad, carp, or flounder)
1 tablespoon finely chopped
    shallot or onion
1 tablespoon chopped parsley
2 tablespoons butter

1 teaspoon freshly squeezed lemon juice
Dash grated nutmeg
Salt and freshly ground black pepper
Melted Herb Butter

Poach fresh roe 5 minutes in boiling salted water to cover. Remove from water and drain. Cook shallot and parsley in butter 1 to 2 minutes. Remove membrane from roe and discard, break up roe with a fork, and add to the butter mixture, along with lemon juice. Stir and cook over low heat 5 minutes. Add nutmeg, salt, and pepper. Fill omelette. Serve with Herb Butter.

Chevreuse

6 cooked artichoke bottoms
1 cup diced asparagus

1 tablespoon chopped truffle
6 slices truffle

Combine artichokes, asparagus, and chopped truffles with the eggs before cooking. Garnish cooked omelette with truffle slices.

Clamart

1 cup tiny French peas (petits pois), cooked
1½ tablespoons butter
Salt and freshly ground black pepper

Heat peas in butter. Add salt and pepper. Spoon two-thirds of the peas onto one side of the omelette. Fold. Place the omelette on a warmed platter and make an incision down the center. Fill with remaining peas.

Croutons

Fry 1¼ cups ½-inch bread cubes in 3 tablespoons butter. Use 1 cup as filling for omelette and ¼ cup for garnish.

Farmhouse

1 cup chopped cooked ham
1 tablespoon chopped parsley

Mix ham and parsley with eggs before cooking. Do not fold omelette, but serve flat on a warmed round platter.

Fines Herbes

2 tablespoons chopped parsley
1 tablespoon chopped chives
¼ teaspoon each chopped chervil and tarragon

Combine herbs with eggs before cooking.

Florentine

1 cup cooked spinach
2 tablespoons butter
Salt and freshly ground black pepper

Chop spinach and drain well. Sauté 1 to 2 minutes in butter. Season with salt and pepper. Add to eggs before cooking.

Lyonnaise

1 cup sliced onions
2 tablespoons butter
1 tablespoon chopped parsley

Cook onions in butter until soft. Add parsley and cook 30 seconds. Combine with eggs before cooking.

Mushroom

1 cup sliced mushrooms
2 tablespoons butter

Chopped parsley
3 small whole mushrooms sautéed in butter

Sauté sliced mushrooms in butter 3 to 5 minutes, until tender. Combine mushrooms, butter, and parsley with eggs before cooking. Garnish cooked omelette with whole mushrooms.

 Mexican

1 cup sliced mushrooms
¼ cup diced green or red bell pepper
2 tablespoons butter

Salt and freshly ground black pepper
¾ cup stewed tomatoes

Cook mushrooms and peppers in butter until tender. Season to taste with salt and pepper. Use to fill omelette. Season tomatoes with salt and pepper. Place omelette on a warmed platter and make lengthwise incision down the center of the top. Fill with tomatoes.

 Normandy

1½ dozen small (soup) oysters
Oyster liquor

1 cup Sauce Normande
Salt and freshly ground black pepper

Put oysters in enough oyster liquor to cover. Cook in a saucepan over low heat or in the top of a double boiler over hot water only until edges curl. Remove from liquor, drain, and mix with ⅓ cup of the Sauce Normande. Add salt and pepper. Fill omelette and serve on a warmed platter surrounded with remaining sauce, or serve sauce in a separate bowl.

Parmentier

2 tablespoons butter
1 cup diced cooked potatoes
Salt and freshly ground black
   pepper

8 slices bacon, cooked until crisp
Chopped parsley

Melt butter in a 10-inch skillet. Add potatoes and cook over medium heat until browned. Sprinkle with salt and pepper. Pour egg mixture for either French or Puffy Omelette over potatoes. Cook omelette, fold, and serve on a warmed platter, garnished with bacon and sprinkled with parsley.

For the Priest in Lent

2 pairs roe (shad, carp, or flounder)
½ cup canned tuna fish
1 shallot, finely chopped

4 tablespoons (½ stick) butter
Salt and freshly ground black pepper
Chopped parsley and chives

Poach roe in boiling water 5 minutes. Remove from water, cool, remove and discard membrane, and break up roe with a fork. Add tuna and shallot and cook in butter 3 to 4 minutes over medium-low heat. Season with salt and pepper. Turn out mixture into a warm platter and place the omelette on top. Sprinkle with parsley and chives.

ᵗᵌ Princess

Cooked tips from 1½ pounds fresh asparagus
½ cup Velouté Sauce
Truffle slices

Combine asparagus tips with Velouté Sauce. Fill cooked omelette and fold. Garnish with sliced truffles.

ᵗᵌ Portuguese

3 ripe tomatoes
3 tablespoons olive oil
1 tablespoon finely chopped onion

Salt and freshly ground black pepper
1 tablespoon chopped parsley
Tomato Sauce

Peel tomatoes, squeeze out seeds, and chop the pulp rather coarsely. Cook in oil, along with onion, until the mixture is of medium thickness. Add salt and pepper; add parsley. Fill cooked omelette and fold it. Surround the omelette with Tomato Sauce or serve sauce in a separate bowl.

ᵗᵌ à la Reine

1 cup finely diced cooked chicken
2 tablespoons butter

¾ cup Sauce Suprême
Watercress

Heat chicken in butter only until hot. Spread on cooked omelette just before folding. Serve omelette on a warmed platter surrounded with a ring of hot Sauce Suprême or serve sauce in a separate bowl. Garnish with watercress.

ᵗᵌ Shrimp

4 tablespoons butter
1 tablespoon flour
2 cups shrimp stock
1 cup light cream
1 pound peeled and deveined
    cooked shrimp

¾ teaspoon salt
Freshly ground black pepper and
    freshly squeezed lemon juice
1 tablespoon butter

Melt 2 tablespoons of the butter in a 1½-quart saucepan. Blend in flour. Stir and cook 1 to 2 minutes. Remove from heat and add shrimp stock and cream. Stir and cook for 30 minutes. Divide shrimp into three equal quantities. Finely chop one-third and add it to the sauce, along with one-third of the whole shrimp. Mix well and heat. Season with salt, and pepper and lemon juice to taste. Fill omelette with one-half of this mixture. Place omelette on a warmed platter and make a lengthwise incision down the center of the top. Sauté remaining one-third whole shrimp in the rest of the butter and place in the incision. Surround the omelette with the remaining shrimp sauce or serve it in a separate bowl.

 ## Rossini

½ cup cooked foie gras
1 tablespoon finely diced truffle
Truffle slices

½ cup Demi-Glace Sauce with
    chopped truffle

Add foie gras and diced truffle to eggs before cooking. Cook as for French or Puffy Omelette and fold. Garnish with truffle slices and surround with a ring of Demi-Glace Sauce.

 ## Savoy

1 cup sliced cooked potatoes
2 tablespoons butter
⅓ cup shredded Gruyère cheese

¼ cup heavy cream
Salt and freshly ground black pepper
Chopped parsley

Sauté potatoes in butter, add cheese, cream, salt, and pepper. Add to eggs before cooking. Do not fold omelette. Turn out onto a warmed round plate. Garnish with parsley.

 ## Tuna

½ cup canned tuna in oil
2 anchovies

3 tablespoons butter, melted
Watercress

Drain oil from tuna, flake tuna with a fork, and add to eggs before cooking. Cook as in previous directions, fold, and place on a warmed platter. Mince anchovies, mix with butter, and pour over omelette. Garnish with watercress.

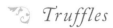 ## Truffles

2 small truffles, finely diced
Truffle slices

Mix diced truffles with eggs before cooking. Cook as in previous directions, fold, and serve on a warmed platter. Garnish the top with sliced truffles.

Victoria

½ cup finely diced cooked lobster meat
1 cup Fish Velouté Sauce
½ cup coarsely flaked lobster meat

Combine finely diced lobster and Velouté. Add ⅓ cup of the mixture to the coarsely flaked lobster. Heat and spread on the omelette, fold, and serve on a warmed platter surrounded with a ring of the remaining hot lobster sauce or serve sauce in a separate bowl.

Vosges

3 slices bacon, cooked until crisp
⅓ cup shredded Gruyère cheese
2 tablespoons heavy cream

Break bacon into bits and mix with cheese and cream. Add to eggs before cooking.

SOUPS

ALL THE DIFFERENT KINDS OF SOUP, either hot or cold, can be classified into clear soups or consommés; plain purees of meats, fish, or vegetables; those same purees creamed or buttered; vegetable soups; and compound soups, like borscht, with vegetables and chunks of meat.

Many soups that are easy and quick to make, like cream of mushroom, Potage Thourin, or leek and potato, have as profound an effect as the soups that take more time or may have more expensive ingredients, like lobster soup or cream of artichoke. But whatever the recipe, as always, the ingredients should be perfect for a perfect result.

Some other suggestions are:

- When making purees, do not use a blender. A food mill gives a much better appearance, texture, and flavor.
- The best way to reheat soup so that it retains its fresh flavors is in a microwave oven.
- Serve hot soups very hot and cold ones very cold.
- Use water instead of stock with vegetable soups for fresher and truer vegetable flavors.
- When making vegetable soups, add the vegetables to already boiling liquid, cook them at a full boil so they cook as quickly as possible, and then if you are not serving the soup immediately or making a puree, chill the soup fast in a metal bowl set in a bigger bowl of ice and water before processing.
- Serve soups in large, open soup plates to show them off and to make garnishing them easier (or use demitasse cups for small portions).

BASIC BROTHS OR BOUILLONS

Grand Marmite

2 pounds lean soup meat
2 shinbone of beef, cracked
2 pounds chicken backs and necks
2½ quarts cold water
2 teaspoons salt
2 leeks, washed well
1 cup diced turnip
1 cup sliced carrots

1 large onion studded with 2 whole cloves
1 rib celery
1 clove of garlic
½ bay leaf
6 whole peppercorns
1 tablespoon chopped fresh thyme or
    1 teaspoon dried thyme

Place meat, shinbone and chicken in a 6-quart saucepan. Add water and salt. Cover and bring to the boiling point. Skim. Add all remaining ingredients except thyme. Simmer 3½ hours. Add thyme 10 minutes before cooking time is up. Cool. Remove meat and bones. Strain broth through 2 layers of cheesecloth or through a very fine sieve. Makes about 2 quarts broth.

Pot au Feu

10 pounds beef shinbones	1 cup diced turnip
1½ pounds lean soup meat	1 cup diced celery
4½ quarts cold water	1 large onion studded with 1 whole clove
2½ teaspoons salt	1 bouquet garni
2½ cups diced carrots	1 pound chicken giblets
3 leeks, washed well	

Crack bones and put them in an 8-quart saucepan. Cut meat into 2-inch pieces and add to the bones. Add water and salt. Cover and bring to the boiling point. Skim. Add remaining ingredients. Bring to the boiling point and skim again. Simmer 3 hours. Cool. Remove meat and bones. Skim off all fat before serving. Serve hot. This is an excellent broth for preparing consommé. Makes 3 quarts of broth.

Pot au Feu with Cabbage

To hot Pot au Feu, add 3 cups cabbage chunks, cover, and cook 5 minutes. Serve with finger-length strips of bread that have been sprinkled with broth from the pot and then with grated Gruyère cheese and toasted in the oven.

Rich Clear Chicken Broth

1 pound lean ground chuck	3 pounds chicken backs and necks
1 carrot, grated	4½ cups Plain White Stock or Bouillon
1 leek (white part only), shredded	Salt and freshly ground black pepper
1 egg white	

Mix meat with vegetables and egg white. Place in a 4-quart saucepan. Cook chicken backs and necks in the oven (375°F) until they begin to brown. Drain off fat and discard. Add backs and necks to the other ingredients. Add broth. Cover and bring to the boiling point. Reduce heat and simmer 1 hour. Strain through 2 layers of cheesecloth or through a very fine sieve. Add salt and pepper to taste. Serve hot. Makes 3½ pints.

Rich Clear Fish Broth

1½ pounds pike or whiting, minced	2 egg whites
½ cup shredded white part of leeks	2 cups dry white wine
1 cup finely chopped mushroom stems	1 quart Fish Stock
¼ cup finely chopped parsley	Salt and ground white pepper

Thoroughly mix the first 6 ingredients together and put into a 4-quart saucepan. Add stock. Mix well. Cover. Slowly bring to the boiling point. Reduce heat and simmer 30 minutes. Cool. Strain through 2 layers of cheesecloth or through a very fine sieve. Serve hot, seasoned with salt and pepper. Makes 3½ pints.

 Rich Clear Game Broth

1 pound lean meat from
    furred game (deer, rabbit, etc.)
1 cup finely chopped mushroom stems
1 egg white
Whole carcasses of small game, or
    3 pounds venison bones

4½ pints game stock
1 teaspoon chopped fresh rosemary, or
    ¼ teaspoon dried rosemary
Salt and freshly ground black pepper

Put the meat through a food chopper and mix with mushroom stems and egg white. Put in a 4-quart saucepan. Brown carcasses or bones in a preheated oven (375°F) and add to the meat, along with game stock. Cover. Slowly bring to the boiling point. Reduce heat and simmer 1 hour. Add rosemary 10 minutes before cooking time is up. Cool. Remove meat and bones. Strain through 2 layers of cheesecloth or through a very fine sieve. Add salt and pepper. Serve hot. Makes 3½ pints

CONSOMMES

Consommé (Clear Soup)

1 pound ground lean beef
2 egg whites
1 leek, shredded
1 carrot, grated

2 quarts stock from Plain White Stock
1 tablespoon chopped fresh thyme
    or chervil, or 1 teaspoon dried
    thyme or chervil

Mix beef with egg white, leek, and carrot. Skim off all fat from the broth and mix with the beef and vegetables. Cover. Slowly bring to the boiling point, stirring frequently. Simmer gently for 50 minutes. Add herbs 10 minutes before cooking time is up. Cool. Remove meat; strain through 2 layers of cheesecloth or through a very fine sieve. Serve hot. Makes 3½ pints.

Consommé Aurora

3 tablespoons quick-cooking tapioca
½ cup tomato puree
2 quarts chicken Consommé

1 cup julienned strips chicken white meat
Salt and freshly ground black pepper

Combine the first 3 ingredients in a 3-quart saucepan. Cover and cook until tapioca is transparent. Add chicken and bring to the boiling point. Season with salt and pepper. Serve hot. Makes 8 servings.

Basque Consommé

2 quarts Consommé
⅓ cup julienned green bell pepper
½ cup diced, peeled, seeded tomatoes
⅓ cup cooked rice

1 teaspoon chopped fresh chervil
Salt and freshly ground black pepper
Chopped parsley

Pour Consommé into a 3-quart saucepan. Add green pepper and tomatoes. Cover and cook 5 minutes, or until pepper is crisp-tender. Add rice and chervil. Cook 2 to 3 minutes. Season with salt and pepper. Serve hot, sprinkled with parsley. Makes 8 servings.

Consommé Brunoise

Brunoise, in French cookery, means vegetables finely and evenly diced or shredded and cooked in butter.

1¼ cups shredded carrots
1½ cups shredded turnip
1 cup thinly sliced celery
2 tablespoons butter

1 cup hot Consommé
Hot Consommé for 8 to 10 servings
Salt and freshly ground black pepper

Cook vegetables in butter in a covered saucepan over low heat, stirring frequently, until vegetables are soft. Add 1 cup Consommé, cover, and cook until celery is tender. Add 1 tablespoon of the mixture to each serving of hot Consommé and season with salt and pepper. Makes enough for 8 to 10 servings.

Consommé Celestine

Cut 2 to 3 small paper-thin crêpes into julienne and put them in the bottom of soup plates. Pour in hot Consommé. Sprinkle with chopped fresh chervil or parsley. This quantity is enough for 4 to 6 servings.

Consommé with Lettuce and Sorrel Chiffonnade

If desired, add small quenelles to each serving.

¼ medium-size head lettuce, shredded
½ cup sorrel leaves
1 tablespoon butter

Dash salt
Hot Consommé for 8 servings
Chervil or parsley

Cook lettuce and sorrel in butter with salt very quickly 1 to 2 minutes. Put in the bottom of soup plates and pour in hot Consommé. Garnish with plucked leaves of chervil or parsley. Serve hot. Makes 8 servings.

Consommé with Diablotins

¾ cup Béchamel Sauce
½ cup grated Parmesan cheese
Dash cayenne

16 slices French bread
Hot Consommé for 8 servings

Combine Béchamel Sauce, cheese, and cayenne and spread over one side of each slice of bread. Toast in the oven or under the broiler and serve hot with Consommé, 2 slices to a serving.

Consommé Julienne

Cut cooked white meat of chicken, pickled tongue, poached mushrooms, and truffles into short julienne. Measure ½ cup of each and add to 1½ quarts hot Consommé. Serve hot, garnished with chopped parsley. Makes 6 servings.

Consommé Mosaic

1 cup each diced carrots and turnip
½ cup each diced green beans
   and green peas
1 small truffle (optional), diced
1 cup Bouillon

½ cup diced pickled tongue
1 hard-cooked egg white, diced
1½ quarts Consommé
Salt and freshly ground black pepper

Place vegetables, truffle, and Bouillon in a saucepan. Cover and cook until vegetables are tender, 8 to 10 minutes. Add tongue, egg white, and Consommé. Bring to the boiling point. Season with salt and pepper. Serve hot in soup plates. Makes 6 servings.

Consommé Mousseline

2 tablespoons tapioca
2 quarts boiling Consommé

3 egg yolks
½ cup heavy cream

Sprinkle tapioca into boiling Consommé. Cover and cook until tapioca is transparent. Beat egg yolks together with cream and gradually stir into the hot Consommé. Serve hot in soup plates. Makes 8 servings.

Consommé with Oxtail

2 pounds oxtail	1 cup diced carrots
1 pound knuckle of veal	½ cup diced turnip
3 quarts water	3 leeks or 1 bunch scallions
3 teaspoons salt	1 large onion studded with 1 whole clove

Cut oxtail into slices and place in an 8-quart saucepan. Add veal, water, and salt. Cover. Slowly bring to the boiling point. Skim. Add carrots, turnip, leeks, and whole onion with cloves. Cover and simmer 4 hours. Remove meat from the stock, cut the meat from the bones, and then dice it. Strain broth through 2 layers of cheesecloth or through a fine sieve. Remove all fat and scum. Add diced meat to the broth and bring to the boiling point. Serve in soup plates. Makes 6 to 8 servings.

Consommé with Vermicelli

Break ¼ pound vermicelli into 2 quarts boiling Consommé. Cover and cook 10 minutes, or until pasta is tender. Season with salt and freshly ground black pepper to taste. Serve hot in soup plates. Makes 8 servings.

Consommé with Pearl Barley

Add 2 tablespoons pearl barley to 1 cup boiling water. Cover and cook 3 minutes. Drain off water and add blanched barley to 2 quarts boiling Consommé. Cover and cook until barley is tender. Serve hot in soup plates. Garnish with chopped parsley. Makes 6 to 8 servings.

Consommé Printanier

¼ cup each diced carrot and turnip	½ quarts boiling Consommé
½ cup green beans cut into	Salt and freshly ground black pepper
⅜-inch pieces	Chopped chervil or parsley
½ cup green peas	

Cook each vegetable separately in ½ inch boiling water, 8 to 10 minutes. Drain off water and add vegetables to boiling Consommé. Bring back to the boiling point. Season with salt and pepper. Serve hot. Garnish with chervil. Makes 6 servings.

Consommé with Rice

Sprinkle ¼ cup uncooked rice into 1½ quarts boiling Consommé. Cover and cook 12 to 15 minutes, or until rice is tender. Season with salt and freshly ground black pepper to taste. Serve hot in soup plates. Garnish with finely grated carrots. Makes 6 servings.

Consommé with Profiteroles

Profiteroles are little puffs or éclairs of Choux Paste piped through a pastry bag and baked. Besides being served with Consommé, they may be filled after baking with various savory mixtures like foie gras, vegetable, meat, or fish and shellfish purees and mousses, and served as a garnish. For this recipe, cheese is mixed with the Choux Paste.

1 cup grated Parmesan cheese
2 cups warm Choux Paste
Hot Consommé

Mix the cheese with the Choux Paste and with a pastry bag with a small round tube pipe the mixture into tiny balls onto lightly buttered baking sheets. Bake in a preheated oven (425°F) 15 to 20 minutes, or until puffs are golden. Turn off oven, prick puffs with a knife to allow the steam to escape, and leave them in the oven 20 minutes to dry the centers. Put 2 or 3 profiteroles in each soup plate, pour Consommé over them, and serve at once. Makes about 24 profiteroles.

Consommé Royale

Royale is custard made from the following ingredients and then flavored with vegetable, meat, fish and shellfish, foie gras or herb purees, then used to garnish clear soups.

4 large eggs
½ cup cold beef or veal stock
3 cups hot Consommé

Salt and ground white pepper
Chopped parsley
Hot Consommé

Beat eggs lightly and blend in cold stock. Add 3 cups hot Consommé. Season to taste with salt and white pepper. Pour into a lightly buttered 8- or 9-inch square pan. Place pan in a large pan of hot water and bake in a preheated slow oven (325°F) 30 to 40 minutes, or until a knife inserted in the center comes out clean. Cool completely. Cut into cubes or small fancy shapes. Carefully place in soup plates. Pour in hot Consommé. Sprinkle with parsley. Makes enough Royale for 6 to 8 servings.

Consommé Mimosa

1 tablespoon tapioca
½ cup green beans cut into
    short julienne strips
1½ quarts boiling Consommé

Salt and freshly ground black pepper
1 cup diced Royale
1 hard-cooked egg white
1 hard-cooked egg yolk

Sprinkle tapioca and beans into boiling Consommé, cover, and cook until tapioca is transparent. Season with salt and pepper. Carefully put Royale in soup plates, along with egg white cut into strips. Pour in hot Consommé mixture. Push egg yolk through a sieve and sprinkle over each serving. Serve at once. Makes 6 servings.

Consommé Xavier

¾ cup milk
2 large eggs
½ teaspoon salt
½ cup sifted all-purpose flour

½ teaspoon chopped fresh chervil,
2 quarts boiling Consommé

Beat milk, eggs, and salt together. Gradually stir in flour and chervil. Pour this mixture through a coarse strainer into boiling Consommé. Beat well with a wire whisk. Serve at once. Makes 8 servings.

COLD JELLIED CONSOMMÉS

In the summer, or for cold buffets, Consommé is usually served cold. The consommé should be well seasoned and rich enough to jelly when chilled. If you have any doubt that it will set, add 1 envelope unflavored gelatin to each 1 quart hot Consommé. Serve very cold in chilled consommé cups.

Jellied Consommé Madrilène

1½ pounds ground chuck
1 leek (green part only),
    coarsely chopped
1 tablespoon chopped fresh chervil
2 egg whites
5 pounds cracked beef bones
2 quarts cold water

2 teaspoons salt
4 whole peppercorns
5 medium-sized tomatoes, peeled,
    seeded, and crushed
¾ cup julienned green bell pepper
1 tablespoon butter
Lemon wedges

Combine beef, leek, chervil, and egg whites. Mix well. Place in a saucepan with bones, cold water, salt, and peppercorns. Cover. Slowly bring to the boiling point. Skim. Add 4 of the tomatoes and simmer 2 hours. Cool. Remove bones. Strain. Skim off fat and scum. Add the remaining crushed tomato. Cook green pepper in butter until soft. Add to the broth. Bring to the boiling point. Adjust seasonings. Chill until broth is jellied. Break up the jelly coarsely with a fork. Serve in cold consommé cups with lemon wedges. Makes 6 servings.

Jellied Consommé with Tarragon

In the recipe for Consommé Madrilène, omit chervil and add 1 tablespoon chopped fresh tarragon 5 minutes before cooking time is up. Strain stock and skim off all fat. Chill until jellied. Break up coarsely with a fork. Serve in cold consommé cups. Garnish with chopped parsley.

Jellied Consommé with Madeira

To 10 parts Chicken Broth, add 1 part wine—Madeira, Marsala, port, or sherry—and mix well. Chill until jellied.

CREAM SOUPS

Cream of Barley Soup

4 tablespoons butter
5 tablespoons flour
5 cups beef stock
3 tablespoons pearl barley, cooked
   separately in bouillon

2 egg yolks
¾ cup milk
¼ cup heavy cream
Salt and freshly ground black pepper

Melt butter in a 2-quart saucepan. Remove from heat and blend in flour. Stir and cook until the mixture is golden. Remove from heat and add stock. Cook 30 minutes, skimming. Add cooked barley. Blend egg yolks with milk and add to the soup. Cook 5 minutes. Add cream and heat. Season to taste with salt and pepper. Serve hot. Makes 6 to 8 servings.

Cream of Rice Soup

4 tablespoons butter
3 tablespoons cream of rice
5 cups beef or veal bouillon
¾ cup milk

2 egg yolks
⅓ cup heavy cream
Salt and freshly ground black pepper

Melt butter in a 2-quart saucepan. Blend in cream of rice. Stir and cook 1 minute. Add 1 cup of the bouillon. Bring to the boiling point, stirring constantly. Add remaining bouillon. Cook gently 25 minutes. Add milk and heat. Beat egg yolks together with cream and add. Cook 1 minute. Season to taste with salt and pepper. Serve hot. Makes 6 to 8 servings.

Andalusian Cream Soup

1 medium-sized onion	1½ quarts beef or veal stock
4 tablespoons butter	Salt and ground white pepper
3 medium-sized potatoes	½ cup heavy cream
3 medium-sized tomatoes	½ cup cooked white rice
1 cup beef marrow	

Peel and slice onion and cook in butter until slices are transparent. Peel potatoes and cut in small dice and cut tomatoes into quarters, then add to onion. Stir and cook 5 minutes. Add marrow, stock, salt, and white pepper. Bring to the boiling point and simmer 5 minutes. Stir in cream and white rice. Cook 1 minute. Serve hot in soup plates. Makes 6 to 8 servings.

Cream of Artichoke Soup

5 tablespoons butter	2 egg yolks
2 tablespoons flour	1 cup milk
3½ cups stock	½ cup heavy cream
4 raw artichoke bottoms	Salt and ground white pepper

Melt 3 tablespoons of the butter in a 2-quart saucepan. Remove from heat and blend in flour. Stir and cook 1 minute. Remove from heat and add stock. Stir and cook 20 minutes, skimming. Slice artichoke bottoms and cook them in the remaining 2 tablespoons butter until soft. Add to soup. Simmer 10 minutes. Push through a fine sieve. Beat egg yolks together with milk and add. Heat 1 minute. Add cream, salt, and white pepper. Serve hot. Makes 6 to 8 servings.

Cream of Asparagus Soup

1 pound fresh asparagus	½ cup milk
1 cup Plain White Stock	Salt and ground white pepper
4 cups Chicken Velouté	½ cup heavy cream
2 egg yolks	

Wash and trim asparagus. Cut off tips and cook them in boiling water. Cut remaining asparagus into ½-inch pieces, cook in stock until tender, and add to the Velouté. Beat egg yolks together with milk, add to soup, and bring to the boiling point. Stir in salt, white pepper, cream, and asparagus tips. Heat. Serve hot. Makes 6 to 8 servings.

Calcutta Cream Soup

4 medium-sized onions
4 tablespoons butter
2 teaspoons curry paste
4 cups Cream of Rice Soup

1 cup milk
¾ cup cooked rice
½ cup heavy cream

Peel and slice onions, blanch in boiling water, drain well, and cook in butter until soft. Dust with curry, stir, and cook over low heat until browned. Add Cream of Rice Soup. Simmer 5 minutes. Add milk, rice, and cream and heat 1 minute. Serve hot. Makes 6 servings.

Cream of Carrot Soup

5 medium-sized carrots, peeled and
    thinly sliced
½ cup water
½ teaspoon salt
1 tablespoon chopped onion
¼ cup (½ stick) butter

1 cup chicken stock
2 egg yolks
1 cup milk
Salt and ground white pepper
½ cup heavy cream
Grated carrot

Place sliced carrots, water, salt, onions, and butter in a saucepan. Cover and cook slowly 10 minutes, or until carrots are soft. Add stock and cook 10 minutes over medium-low heat, stirring frequently. Mix egg yolks with the milk and add to the soup. Heat. Push through a fine sieve. Add salt, white pepper, and cream. Cook only until soup is hot enough to serve. Serve in soup plates, garnished with a little grated carrot. Makes 6 servings.

Cream of Curried Cauliflower Soup

1 large head cauliflower
4 cups boiling chicken stock or water
⅓ cup long-grain rice
½ cup finely chopped onion

¼ to ½ teaspoon curry powder
1 tablespoon butter
Salt and ground white pepper
⅓ to ½ cup heavy cream

Break cauliflower into florets and place them in a saucepan with the boiling stock or water. (If water is used, add ½ teaspoon salt.) Cover, bring to the boiling point, and cook 12 to 15 minutes, or until cauliflower is tender. Remove cauliflower from stock (or water) and put rice in. Sauté onion and curry powder in butter until onions are soft, and add to the stock. Cover and cook slowly 15 minutes, or until rice is soft. Push the mixture through a sieve or food mill. Finely chop cauliflower and add it to the soup. Heat 1 to 2 minutes. Add salt, white pepper, and cream just before serving. Makes 6 servings.

Cream of Curried Turnip Soup

Replace cauliflower in the preceding recipe with 2¾ cups diced turnips. Garnish with fried bread cubes.

Cream of Celery Soup

2 cups chopped celery or celery root
¼ cup chopped onion
6 cups chicken stock
2 egg yolks
½ cup milk
½ cup heavy cream
Salt and ground white pepper
Chopped parsley

Cook celery and onion in stock until celery is very soft. Push through a sieve or food mill. Mix egg yolks with milk, add to the celery puree, and bring to the boiling point. Turn off heat immediately. Add cream, salt, and white pepper. Serve at once, garnished with parsley. Makes 6 servings.

Cream of Chicken Soup

4 tablespoons (½ stick) butter
4 tablespoons all-purpose flour or rice flour
5 cups chicken stock
½ cup chopped celery
1 small onion, chopped
¼ cup chopped parsley
1 cup julienned cooked chicken
2 egg yolks
½ cup milk
Salt and freshly ground black pepper
½ cup heavy cream

Melt butter in a 2½-quart saucepan. Remove from heat and blend in flour. Stir and cook 1 minute. Remove from heat, add stock, celery, onion, and parsley. Cover and bring to the boiling point. Reduce heat and simmer 30 minutes. Strain. Skim off fat, if necessary. Add chicken. Mix egg yolks with milk, add to the soup, and bring to the boiling point. Turn off heat. Add salt, pepper, and cream. Serve at once. Makes 6 servings.

Cream of Corn Soup

Fresh corn on the cob to yield 2½ cups finely cut corn kernels
1 cup boiling water
2 tablespoons finely chopped onion
3 tablespoons butter
3 tablespoons flour
1½ cups veal or chicken stock
1½ cups milk
Salt and ground white pepper
½ cup heavy cream
Chopped chives

Run a sharp knife down the center of each row of corn, splitting the kernels in half. Cut off the tips from the kernel and then cut the remainder of the kernels from the cobs. Scrape the cob well, getting out all the milk. Cook corn in the boiling water 5 to 6 minutes. Set aside. Sauté onion in butter until transparent. Remove from heat and blend in flour. Stir and cook 1 minute. Add corn, stock, and milk. Cook 5 minutes, stirring frequently. Add salt, white pepper, and cream. Heat. Serve hot, with chives sprinkled over the top. Makes 6 servings.

Cream of Lettuce Soup

1 large head Romaine or iceberg lettuce	3 tablespoons butter
¼ cup finely chopped onion	5 cups chicken stock
1 leek (white part only), finely chopped	Salt and freshly ground black pepper
1¼ cups (1¼ pounds) shelled	¼ cup heavy cream
green peas	

Finely shred lettuce, saving 1½ cups for garnish. Cook remaining lettuce slowly in a covered saucepan, without water, until lettuce has wilted. Set aside. Cook onion, leek, and peas in butter over very low heat until soft, adding a little water if necessary. Push vegetables through a sieve or food mill. Add the puree to the stock. Bring to the boiling point, reduce heat, and simmer 2 to 3 minutes. Add salt, pepper, and cream. Serve hot, garnished with the reserved shredded lettuce. Makes 6 servings.

Cream of Mushroom Soup

3 tablespoons butter	¼ cup heavy cream
3 tablespoons flour	¼ cup dry sherry
⅛ teaspoon dry mustard	6 tablespoons whipped cream
1 teaspoon salt	Paprika
Dash cayenne	Toasted slivered blanched almonds
4 cups rich chicken stock	
3 cups (about ¾ pound) chopped mushrooms	

Melt butter in a 3-quart saucepan. Remove from heat and blend in flour mixed with the mustard, salt, and cayenne. Stir and cook 1 minute. Remove from heat and add stock and mushrooms. Cover and simmer 30 minutes. Strain through 2 layers of cheesecloth or through a fine sieve. Add cream and heat. Stir in sherry. Serve hot, with each serving garnished with 1 tablespoon whipped cream, a dash of paprika, and almonds. Makes 6 servings.

Portuguese Tomato and Rice Cream Soup

2 slices bacon, cut into small pieces
1 cup diced carrots
½ cup chopped onion
4 tablespoons flour
5 cups veal stock
8 medium-sized tomatoes, quartered

2 sprigs parsley
Salt and freshly ground black pepper
¼ cup heavy cream
Cooked rice

Cook bacon with carrots and onions until bacon has browned, remove from heat, and blend in flour. Stir and cook 1 minute. Add stock, tomatoes, and parsley. Cover and cook 30 minutes over low heat. Push through a sieve, pushing as much as possible of the vegetables through. Stir in salt and pepper. Bring to the boiling point. Add cream. Put 1 tablespoon cooked rice in each soup bowl and fill with hot soup. Serve at once. Makes 8 servings.

SOUPS WITH A VEGETABLE-PUREE BASE

Vegetable Puree Soup

4 tablespoons (½ stick) butter
2 tablespoons flour
5 cups veal stock
4 medium-sized tomatoes
1½ cups diced potatoes
1 cup diced turnips

1½ cups diced carrots
2 cup green beans cut into ½-inch pieces
Salt and freshly ground black pepper
¼ teaspoon sugar
Chopped parsley

Melt 2 tablespoons of the butter in a 2½-quart saucepan. Remove from heat and blend in flour. Stir and cook 1 minute. Remove from heat, add stock, mix well, and bring to the boiling point. Add tomatoes and potatoes. Cook slowly 30 minutes. Cook turnips in a separate saucepan in enough boiling salted water to cover. Cook carrots and beans together until tender with ½ teaspoon salt and in 1 inch of boiling water. Push soup through a fine sieve, pushing as much as possible of the tomatoes and potatoes through. Add salt, pepper, and sugar. Bring to the boiling point. Stir in remaining butter. Drain vegetables and add. Serve hot, garnished with parsley. Makes 6 servings.

Dried-Bean Soup

2 cups dried beans (pea, navy,
or marrow beans)
7 cups boiling water
1 ham bone
1 carrot, quartered
1 large onion, sliced
3 sprigs parsley

1 whole clove
4 whole peppercorns
2 teaspoons salt
1 cup milk
3 tablespoons butter
¼ teaspoon freshly ground black pepper
¼ cup heavy cream

Wash beans, add 4 cups of the boiling water, and bring to the boiling point. Boil 2 minutes. Remove from heat and let soak 1 hour. Drain and add boiling water to cover by two inches and next 7 ingredients. Cover and cook slowly 2 hours, adding more water if necessary, or until beans are very soft. Remove the ham bone. Pour the soup through a sieve, pushing as much of the vegetables through as possible. Add the milk and butter. Heat. Stir in ground pepper and cream just before serving. Makes 8 servings.

Potage Paulette

Garnish each serving of Dried-Bean Soup with lettuce and a few sorrel leaves cooked in butter or bacon drippings only until lettuce is wilted. Sprinkle with chopped chervil or parsley.

Red Bean Soup Condé

Make Dried-Bean Soup with red kidney beans. Garnish each serving with crumbled crisp bacon and fried bread cubes.

Carrot Soup with Rice Crécy

½ cup diced onion
2 strips bacon, cut into squares
4 cups sliced carrots
1½ quarts bouillon
½ cup raw long-grain rice

Salt and freshly ground white pepper
2 tablespoons butter
¼ cup heavy cream
6 tablespoons cooked rice

Lightly fry onion with bacon until onion is soft. Add carrots, bouillon, and raw rice. Cover and cook 20 minutes. Push through a sieve. Bring to the boiling point and add salt, pepper, butter, and cream. Sprinkle 1 tablespoon cooked rice over each serving. Makes 6 servings.

Garbure Soup

2 medium-sized carrots
2 medium-sized turnips
3 medium-sized potatoes
4 tablespoons (½ stick) butter
1 cup hot beef Bouillon
2 cups shredded cabbage

1 cup cooked dried beans
2 cups diced fresh tomatoes
Salt and freshly ground black pepper
1 egg
1 cup grated Parmesan cheese
6 slices French bread

Peel carrots, turnips, and potatoes and thinly slice. Place in a saucepan with 2 table-spoons of the butter. Heat and toss 3 minutes. Add hot stock, or water and salt. Cover and cook until vegetables are tender, adding cabbage 5 minutes before the other vegetables are done. Heat beans with tomatoes and push them through a sieve, along with the other vegetables, pushing as much of the vegetables through as possible. Thin to desired consistency with stock. Season with salt and pepper. Add remaining butter and heat. Beat egg, mix with cheese, and spread over bread slices. Toast in a very hot oven or under the broiler. Place a piece in each soup plate, pour hot soup over it, and serve immediately. Makes 6 servings.

Leek and Potato Soup Parmentier

2 leeks (white part only)
6 tablespoons butter
5 cups veal or chicken stock
4 medium-sized potatoes

1 cup milk
Salt
¼ teaspoon freshly ground black pepper
½ cup heavy cream

Shred leeks and cook them in 2 tablespoons of the butter until limp. Add stock. Peel and slice potatoes and add to the soup pot. Bring to the boiling point, reduce heat, and cook slowly 30 minutes. Push soup through a strainer, pushing as much of the potatoes and leeks through as possible. Add milk, salt, and pepper. Bring to the boiling point. Stir in remaining butter and the cream just before serving. Serve hot. Makes 6 servings.

Lentil Soup

1½ cups (½ pound) lentils
5 cups water
4 slices bacon
½ cup sliced carrots
½ cup diced green bell peppers
1 cup sliced onion

1 cup diced fresh tomatoes
2 cups beef or ham stock
Salt to taste (1 to 2 teaspoons)
2 tablespoons wine vinegar
½ teaspoon freshly ground black pepper
Fried bread cubes

Wash lentils and put in a 2½-quart saucepan with water. Cover, bring to the boiling point, reduce heat, and cook slowly 1 hour. Cut bacon into small pieces and cook until crisp. Add all the vegetables to the bacon and drippings and sauté over low heat about 5 minutes. Add to the lentils. Add stock, salt, and vinegar. Mix well. Bring to the boiling point, stirring constantly. Reduce heat, cover, and cook about 5 minutes, stirring frequently. Add black pepper. Serve hot, with fried bread cubes. Makes 6 servings.

Fresh Green Pea Soup with Cream

1½ cups shelled green peas
½ teaspoon salt
Boiling water
3¼ cups stock

3¼ cups milk
Salt and freshly ground black pepper
½ cup heavy cream
2 strips bacon (optional), cooked until crisp

Cook peas with salt in boiling water 5 minutes, or until they are soft. Drain off water and reserve ⅓ cup of the peas to use as a garnish. Push remaining peas through a sieve or food mill. Add stock and the milk. Bring to the boiling point. Season. Stir in cream just before serving. Put 1 tablespoon of the reserved cooked peas in each soup bowl and finish filling with soup. If desired, garnish with crumbled crisp bacon. Makes 6 servings.

Split-Pea Soup Saint Germain

2 cups (1 pound) green split peas
2 quarts cold water
1 rib celery
1 carrot, peeled and quartered
1 large onion, peeled and sliced
1 small ham bone, or ¼ pound bacon rind

4 cups beef or veal stock
Salt
½ teaspoon freshly ground black pepper
2 tablespoons butter
¼ cup heavy cream

Wash peas, add water, and soak overnight in the refrigerator. Add vegetables and ham bone or bacon rind. Cover and bring to the boiling point. Simmer 2 to 3 hours, or until peas are very soft and mixture is thick. Remove ham bone or bacon rind. Push soup through a sieve. Add stock. Bring to the boiling point and cook 5 minutes. Add salt and pepper. Stir in butter and cream just before serving. Makes 6 to 8 servings.

Potage Lamballe

Thin Split-Pea Soup to the desired consistency with beef or veal stock or milk. Add 1 teaspoon quick-cooking tapioca for each 1 cup soup to be served. Cook covered, until tapioca is transparent.

Potage Fontanges

Garnish Split-Pea Soup with shredded lettuce and a few sorrel leaves cooked until wilted in a little butter.

Watercress Soup

3 leeks or scallions (white parts only)	3 cups chicken stock
1 small onion	1 cup milk
2 tablespoons butter	1 bunch watercress
3 medium-sized potatoes,	Salt and freshly ground black pepper
peeled and thinly sliced	1 cup heavy cream

Slice leeks and onion and sauté in butter until golden. Add potatoes and stock. Cover, bring to the boiling point, reduce heat, and simmer 30 minutes. Pour soup through a strainer, rubbing as much of the potatoes and onion through as possible, or a food mill. Add milk, stir, and cook 5 minutes. Reserving a few leaves for garnish, cook watercress in ½ cup boiling water in a covered saucepan until it is limp. Push it through a sieve or puree in a blender. Add to soup and heat. Add salt, pepper, and cream. Serve hot or chilled. Garnish with watercress leaves. Makes 6 servings.

FISH SOUPS

THE BEST FRENCH CHEFS PREFER fish such as cod, hake, haddock, halibut, pike, sole, and eel for making fish soups. The fish should be cooked below the boiling point (except in the case of Bouillabaisse) and only until the meat is flaky and falls from the bones. These soups have a Fish Velouté base.

Fish Stock for Soups

3 shallots, sliced	1 sprig fresh tarragon
¾ cup sliced onion	2 teaspoons salt
4 sprigs parsley	3 pounds fish heads, bones, and
1 cup mushroom stems	trimmings (sole, turbot, hake,
2 ribs celery	whiting, cod, pike, etc.)
1 small bay leaf	2 quarts cold water
1 sprig fresh thyme	1½ cups dry white wine

Place the first 9 ingredients in a 4-quart saucepan. Add fish trimmings, water, and wine. Cover, slowly bring to the boiling point, reduce heat, and simmer 30 minutes. Remove and discard bones. Skim. Strain stock through 2 layers of cheesecloth or through a fine sieve. Makes about 2 quarts.

Fish Velouté Base for Fish Soups

¼ cup (½ stick) butter
¾ cup sifted rice flour or all-purpose flour
5 cups Fish Stock

Melt butter and gradually stir in rice flour. Cook, stirring, without browning. Add stock and mix well. Stir and cook until the stock is smooth and has thickened slightly. Simmer (do not boil) 45 minutes. Skim. Strain through a fine sieve. Makes about 4½ cups.

Clear Fish Soup or Consommé

1¼ pounds chopped fish
   (pike, halibut, or whiting)
2 egg whites
¼ cup finely chopped parsley
½ cup finely chopped mushroom stems
6 cups Fish Stock
1½ cups dry white wine

Combine fish, egg whites, parsley, and mushrooms. Add stock and wine. Mix well. Bring to the boiling point, reduce heat and simmer gently 10 minutes. Strain and skim off all fat and scum. Serve hot. Makes 6 servings.

Potage Jacqueline

7 cups Fish Velouté
2 egg yolks
½ cup heavy cream
½ cup cooked diced carrots
½ cup cooked peas
1½ cups cooked rice

Heat Velouté only to the boiling point. Mix egg yolks with cream and add. Mix well. Stir in vegetables and rice. Heat gently 1 minute. Makes 8 servings.

Lobster Soup Cardinal

3 cups Fish Velouté
½ cup tomato puree
⅓ cup cooked lobster meat and coral
½ cup softened butter
Salt and ground white pepper
Chunks cooked lobster

Combine Velouté and tomato puree in a 2-quart saucepan. Heat. Pound and mash lobster and coral, blend with butter, and add to the soup. Season with salt and white pepper. Serve hot, garnished with chunks of cooked lobster. Makes 6 servings.

Mussel Soup Dieppoise

5 cups Fish Velouté
1½ cups cooking liquor from the mussels
2 egg yolks
1 cup heavy cream

6 tablespoons diced cooked carrots
6 tablespoons cooked peas
6 tablespoons cooked rice
18 poached mussels

Combine Velouté and cooking liquor from the mussels. Heat, but do not boil. Combine egg yolks and cream and add to the soup. Mix well and cook only until hot. In each soup bowl place 1 tablespoon each of the carrots, peas, and rice, and 3 mussels. Pour soup over these and serve at once. Makes 6 servings.

Oyster Soup

1 cup sliced mushrooms
2 tablespoons butter
½ teaspoon lemon juice
6 cups Fish Velouté

18 small (soup) oysters in their liquor
2 egg yolks
½ cup heavy cream
Salt and freshly ground black pepper

Cook mushrooms in butter and lemon juice until tender. Add to Velouté. Stir and cook until hot. Heat oysters in their liquor only until edges curl, then add to soup. Blend egg yolks with cream and add. Cook about 30 seconds. Add salt and pepper. Serve hot. Makes 6 servings.

Regency Soup

1 pound whiting
7 cups Fish Velouté
⅔ cup heavy cream

Salt and ground white pepper
Croutons

Clean, wash, and trim the whiting. Add to Velouté. Cook until the fish falls off the bones. Remove and discard bones. Pour through a fine sieve, pushing as much of the fish through as possible. Add cream, heat, and season with salt and white pepper. Serve hot, with croutons. Makes 6 servings.

FRENCH REGIONAL SOUPS

THE RECIPES THAT FOLLOW are for soups served in the provincial towns and country regions of France.

Provençal Fish Soup

2 pounds conger eel
1½ cups coarsely chopped onions
4 tablespoons (½ stick) butter
6 cups cold water
Salt
1 leek (white part only)
1 clove garlic, crushed
2 tablespoons olive oil

3 medium-sized tomatoes
¹⁄₁₆ teaspoon crushed saffron threads
Bouquet garni
½ teaspoon grated dried orange zest
Freshly ground black pepper
Chopped parsley
French bread

Skin the eel and remove and chop all bones. Stew the bones with the onions in 2 tablespoons of the butter. Add water and 1½ teaspoons salt. Cover, bring to the boiling point, and simmer 30 minutes. Strain and set aside. Cut leek into julienne and cook, with the garlic, in the remaining 2 tablespoons butter and the oil until leek is transparent. Cut eel into 1-inch strips, add to leek, and brown lightly. Peel, seed, and dice tomatoes. Add to the strained stock along with saffron, bouquet garni, and orange zest. Cover and simmer 20 minutes. Adjust salt and pepper. Remove bouquet garni. Garnish with parsley and serve hot, with thin slices of French bread. Makes 6 servings.

Cabbage Soup

2 pounds pickled pork (such as pigs' feet)
½ pound salt pork
2 quarts cold water
4 medium-sized potatoes,
    peeled and cubed
2 medium-sized turnips,
    peeled and cubed

2 large carrots, peeled and
    sliced ¼ inch thick
1 cup sliced leeks or onions
1 small head cabbage, quartered
Salt and freshly ground black pepper

Wash the pickled pork and the salt pork. If meat is very salty, soak in cold water 1 hour. Drain off and discard water. Place the meat in a stockpot with cold water to cover generously. (Do not add salt.) Bring to the boiling point, reduce heat, and cook slowly 1 hour. Add potatoes, turnips, carrots, and leeks. Cover, bring to the boiling point, reduce heat, and simmer 30 to 40 minutes, or until vegetables are tender. Add cabbage 15 minutes before cooking time is up. Add salt and pepper. Serve as a main-dish soup with some of the meat in each serving. Makes 6 to 8 servings.

Vosges-Style Cabbage Soup

In the recipe for Cabbage Soup, replace the pickled pork with the same quantity of ham.

Soup Chevrière

2 cups green beans cut in 1-inch pieces
1 cup sliced carrots
½ cup chopped onion
6 cups boiling beef stock
1 cup milk

Salt and freshly ground black pepper
2 tablespoons butter
Croutons
Chopped chervil or parsley

Cook all the vegetables in 2 cups of the boiling beef stock until tender, then push them through a sieve. Combine remaining stock and milk and add to the vegetable puree. Heat. Add salt and pepper to taste. Add butter. Serve with croutons, as a main-dish soup, garnished with chervil. If desired, replace the green beans with 1 cup cooked dried beans. Makes 6 servings.

Farmhouse Soup

1 cup shredded carrots
1 cup shredded turnip
½ cup chopped onion
½ cup chopped leeks or scallions
2 tablespoons butter

7 cups beef, veal, or chicken stock
1 cup cooked dried beans
Salt and freshly ground black pepper
Thin slices toasted rye bread

Cook all the raw vegetables together in butter 3 to 4 minutes. Add stock and cook slowly 30 minutes, or until vegetables are tender. Add cooked beans and cook 5 minutes. Season with salt and pepper. Serve over rye toast as a main-dish soup. Makes 8 servings.

Garlic Soup Bonne Femme

2 leeks or 3 scallions, thinly sliced
3 cloves garlic, crushed
Olive oil
2 cups peeled, seeded, diced tomatoes
1½ cups diced potatoes

$\frac{1}{16}$ teaspoon crumbled saffron threads
5 cups boiling water
Salt and freshly ground black pepper
Sliced French bread
Grated Parmesan cheese

Cook leeks or scallions with garlic in hot oil until tender. Add vegetables, saffron, and water. Cover and cook slowly until vegetables are tender. Add salt and pepper. Brush bread slices with oil, sprinkle with cheese, and toast in a very hot oven until golden brown. Serve the soup as a main dish with the toasted bread. Makes 6 to 8 servings.

Soup Maraîchère

1 cup chopped onion	2 cups shredded cabbage
1 cup sliced celery	1 cup each shredded spinach and lettuce
½ cup diced turnip	½ cup shredded sorrel, if available
½ cup diced potato	1¾ cups milk
3 tablespoons butter	Salt and freshly ground black pepper
6 cups boiling stock	Chopped chives or chervil
½ cup fine noodles or spaghetti, broken into 2-inch pieces	

Cook the first 4 vegetables in butter in a covered saucepan over low heat until they are about half done. Add stock and noodles. Cover and cook until vegetables and pasta are tender. Add remaining vegetables. Cover and cook 5 minutes. Stir in milk, salt, and pepper. Heat. Serve as a main-dish soup, garnished with chives. Makes 8 servings.

Onion Soup with Cheese

4 large onions	Salt and freshly ground black pepper
3 tablespoons butter	6 to 8 thin slices French bread
1 tablespoon flour	Softened butter
2 quarts brown stock	6 to 8 thin slices Gruyère cheese

Peel and slice onions and sauté in 3 tablespoons butter until soft and golden but not browned. Add flour; stir and cook 1 minute. Add stock and simmer 10 to 15 minutes. Stir in salt and pepper to taste. Spread bread slices with softened butter and cover each with a slice of cheese. Toast under the broiler until cheese is melted. Use individual soup bowls with covers. Place 1 slice toast in each and pour the hot soup over it. Cover and let stand 5 or 6 minutes before serving. Makes 6 to 8 servings.

Onion Soup Gratinée

Make the preceding recipe. Pour the soup into an ovenproof tureen, sprinkle generously with grated Gruyère or Parmesan cheese, and place the tureen in a preheated very hot oven (450°F) until cheese melts. Sprinkle with plenty of freshly ground black pepper. Place a slice of toasted French bread with Gruyère cheese in each soup plate, pour soup over it, and serve at once. Makes 6 to 8 servings.

Pistou Soup

Pistou soup is made of various vegetables and vermicelli, with a binding agent of egg, oil, pounded garlic and herbs, and tomato puree.

1 cup diced onion
1 leek or scallion (white part only), sliced
2 tablespoons butter
1 cup green beans cut into ½-inch pieces
1 cup diced potatoes
1½ cups diced fresh tomatoes
6 cups beef Bouillon
½ cup vermicelli broken into
    1-inch pieces

Salt and freshly ground black pepper
2 cloves garlic
2 teaspoons chopped fresh basil
1 teaspoon each chopped fresh
    thyme and sage
2 egg yolks
¼ cup olive oil
2 tablespoons tomato puree
½ cup grated Parmesan cheese

Cook onion and leek in butter until they are transparent. Add vegetables and stock. Cover and bring to the boiling point. Reduce heat and cook 30 minutes, or until vegetables are soft. Add vermicelli after 15 minutes. Season with salt and pepper. Pound garlic together with herbs. Add egg yolks to garlic mixture. Gradually beat in oil as in making Mayonnaise. Add tomato puree slowly, beating constantly. Put this mixture in a soup tureen, and stir in soup gradually to prevent cooking the egg yolks. Sprinkle with cheese. Serve as a main-dish soup. Makes 6 to 8 servings.

Spiced Cream of Pumpkin Soup

1 tablespoon finely chopped onion
1 tablespoon butter
1½ cups mashed cooked pumpkin
4 cups hot chicken stock

1½ teaspoons salt
¼ teaspoon ground ginger
⅛ teaspoon ground mace
1½ cups light cream
2 large eggs, beaten
Chopped chives or parsley

Sauté onion in butter until soft, about 2 minutes, then mix with pumpkin in the top of a double boiler or in a saucepan. Add the stock and salt. Blend spices with ⅓ cup of the cream until smooth. Stir into the pumpkin mixture. Combine remaining cream with the eggs and add to the pumpkin mixture. Cook, stirring frequently, over hot water or low heat 5 to 10 minutes, or until hot. Serve hot, garnished with chives. Makes 6 servings.

Potage Thourin

Thourin soup is served in all parts of France but is especially favored in the Perigord part of the country where the onions are cooked in rendered duck or goose fat. Often fresh chopped tomatoes are added instead of the milk.

3 cups finely chopped onions
3 tablespoons butter
4 cups milk
4 large egg yolks

1 cup heavy cream
Salt and freshly ground black pepper
French bread

Cook onions in butter, stirring until they are soft and golden, but not browned. Add milk. Mix well and simmer 15 minutes, stirring frequently, never allowing the milk to boil. Blend egg yolks with ¼ cup of the cream and add to the soup. Stir and simmer 5 minutes. Add remaining cream, salt, and pepper. Heat. Serve with thinly sliced French bread toasted in the oven. Makes 6 servings.

SOUPS FROM OTHER COUNTRIES

Ukrainian Borscht

2 medium-sized carrots	½ pound lean salt pork
6 medium-sized beets	6 whole peppercorns
1 rib celery	1 bay leaf
1 parsley root, washed well	2 teaspoons salt
2 leeks (white parts only)	2 cups shredded cabbage
3 tablespoons fat skimmed from bouillon, or 3 tablespoons butter	1 teaspoon vinegar
	Chopped fresh dill
2 quarts cold water	Thick sour cream
1½ pounds beef brisket	

Peel carrots and beets and cut carrots and 4 of the beets into julienne. Thinly slice celery, parsley root, and leeks. Heat the vegetables in fat. Mix well. Add water, beef, salt pork, peppercorns, bay leaf, and salt. Cover, bring to the boiling point, reduce heat, and simmer 1½ to 2 hours, or until meat is tender. Remove meat, slice, and put into a soup tureen. Add cabbage to the soup and cook 10 to 12 minutes. Grate the 2 remaining beets and press in cheesecloth to squeeze out all the juice. Add vinegar to beet juice and mix with the soup. Pour soup into the tureen over the meat. Sprinkle with dill. Serve with sour cream in a sauceboat. A browned duck is sometimes cooked with this soup. Borsch may also be served cold. Makes 8 servings.

Russian Chilled Botvinia

1 cup chopped sorrel	½ teaspoon sugar
3 cups each finely shredded spinach and young tender beet tops	Freshly ground black pepper
	1 cup julienned peeled cucumber
Salt	Chopped parsley
5 cups light beer, kvass, or dry white wine	

Cook sorrel, spinach, and beet tops with ¼ teaspoon salt, and with only the water that clings to the leaves, in a covered saucepan until greens are wilted and soft. Push through a sieve, pushing as much of the solids through as possible. Add beer and season with sugar, salt, and pepper. Chill. Place a large chunk of ice and the cucumber in each of 6 serving bowls, and pour chilled soup over. Sprinkle with parsley. This soup is usually accompanied by a small piece of salmon or sturgeon, without skin or bone, served in a separate dish with a little grated horseradish mixed with vinegar. Makes 6 servings.

English Chicken Broth

1 (4-pound) chicken	2 cups diced carrots
6 cups cold water	1 cup diced turnip
Salt	4 whole peppercorns
1 rib celery, sliced	¼ cup long-grain rice
2 leeks (white parts only), sliced	Freshly ground black pepper

Place chicken, water, and 2 teaspoons salt in a 6-quart stockpot. Cover. Slowly bring to the boiling point and simmer 1½ hours, or until chicken is tender, adding vegetables, peppercorns, and rice after 1 hour. Lift chicken from the stockpot, remove skin, cut meat into pieces, and put into soup bowls. Adjust seasonings in the soup, and pour into the bowls. Serve hot. Makes 6 servings.

English Chicken Giblet Soup

4 each chicken necks and gizzards	1 small carrot, diced
8 chicken wings	½ cup chopped onion
4 tablespoons butter	1 rib celery, sliced
¼ cup flour	1 cup cooked rice
6 cups rich chicken stock	Salt and freshly ground black pepper

Cut chicken necks and gizzards in half and disjoint the wings. Brown the pieces lightly in butter. Remove from heat and sprinkle flour over chicken, then brown lightly. Add stock, carrot, and onion. Cover and simmer 1 hour. Cook celery separately in water. To serve, put chicken in a tureen with celery and rice. Season the soup with salt and pepper. Pour into the tureen over the chicken, celery, and rice. Makes 6 servings.

Scottish Cockaleekie

4 cups sliced leeks (white parts only)	4 whole peppercorns
2 cups boiling water	2 cups cooked white chicken meat
Salt	cut into thin strips
2 tablespoons butter or chicken fat	Freshly ground black pepper
2 cups rich chicken stock	18 dried prunes, soaked and cooked
2½ cups boiling water	in stock until tender

Cook leeks in boiling water with 1½ teaspoons salt and the butter or chicken fat for 5 minutes, or until leeks are soft. Add stock, water, and peppercorns. Cover and bring to the boiling point. Add chicken. Season with salt and pepper. Serve hot, with 3 prunes added to each serving. Makes 6 servings.

Spanish Chilled Gazpacho

4 large tomatoes
1 cucumber, sliced
1 medium-sized onion, sliced
1 medium-sized green bell pepper, sliced
2 cloves garlic
3 eggs, beaten
Dash cayenne
¼ cup vinegar

½ cup olive oil
1 cup thick fresh tomato juice
Salt and freshly ground black pepper
1 cup bread cubes
1 cup diced cucumber
¾ cup diced green bell pepper
¼ cup chopped onion
Chopped parsley

Put the tomatoes, sliced cucumber, onion, green pepper, and 1 clove of the garlic through a food mill, or puree them, a little at a time, in an electric blender. Add eggs, cayenne, vinegar, ¼ cup of the oil, the tomato juice, salt, and pepper. Mix well and chill. Crush remaining 1 clove garlic, add to remaining ¼ cup oil, and brown the bread cubes in this oil. Add to the soup, along with diced cucumber, diced green pepper, and chopped onion, just before serving. Sprinkle parsley on each serving. Makes 8 servings.

Hungarian Gulyas or Goulash Soup

1 pound lean shoulder of beef,
   cut into 1-inch pieces
1 cup sliced onion
2 tablespoons lard or other shortening
1 teaspoon salt
2 tablespoons caraway seeds, crushed
2 cups diced fresh tomatoes

2 cups diced green bell peppers
2 cups diced potatoes
5 cups water
1 teaspoon marjoram leaves
½ teaspoon freshly ground black pepper
¼ pound noodles, cooked

Cook beef and onion in lard, until meat begins to brown. Add salt and caraway seeds. Cover and cook 20 minutes. Add tomatoes and peppers, along with about ¼ cup water. Cover and cook until meat is three-quarters done, adding a little water to the pot as it is needed to prevent the mixture from cooking too dry. Add potatoes and 5 cups water. Cover and cook until potatoes and meat are done, about 30 minutes. Adjust salt. Add marjoram and black pepper. Heat 1 to 2 minutes. Add noodles and serve as a main-dish soup. Makes 6 servings.

Italian Bread Soup

4 cups fresh white breadcrumbs
1 cup grated Parmesan cheese
3 eggs, beaten

5 cups rich bouillon
Salt and freshly ground black pepper
Grated nutmeg

Combine breadcrumbs and cheese. Blend in eggs. Stir in bouillon. Beat well with a wire whisk to prevent lumping. Cook slowly 7 to 8 minutes, stirring frequently. Add salt and pepper. Sprinkle a dash of nutmeg over each serving. Makes 6 servings.

Minestrone

¼ pound lean salt pork, diced
1 quart rich beef stock
1 cup each diced potatoes, carrots,
    and turnip
¼ cup long-grain rice
1 cup sliced onion
1 cup green peas
¼ small head cabbage, shredded
¼ pound spinach, shredded
1 leek or scallion (white part only),
    shredded

½ cup diced celery
1 cup sliced zucchini
4 medium-sized fresh tomatoes, diced
2 tablespoons chopped parsley
½ teaspoon each dried sage and
    freshly ground black pepper
Salt
Grated Parmesan cheese

Cook salt pork in water to cover in a covered saucepan 30 minutes. Add stock and bring to the boiling point. Add potatoes, carrots, turnips, and rice. Cover and cook 10 minutes. Add all remaining ingredients, except cheese. Slowly bring to the boiling point and cook until soup is very thick and vegetables are tender. Serve as a main-dish soup. Sprinkle with cheese. Makes 8 servings.

Mulligatawny Soup

8 pounds chicken necks and backs
1 quart cold water
2 teaspoons salt
½ cup each sliced mushroom stems,
    celery, and carrot
2 tablespoons chopped parsley
1 small clove garlic, quartered

½ cup chopped onion
1 tablespoon curry powder
2 tablespoons butter
4 teaspoons flour
½ cup heavy cream
1 cup cooked rice

Put the chicken necks and backs, water, salt, mushrooms, celery, carrot, parsley, and garlic in a large stockpot, cover, and slowly bring to the boiling point. Reduce heat and simmer 1 hour. Remove chicken backs and necks from the stock. Strain stock in a sieve, rubbing as much of the vegetables through as possible, and set aside. Cook onion and curry powder in butter until onion is transparent. Remove from heat and stir in flour. Stir and cook 1 minute. Add stock mixture, mix well, and cook 30 minutes. Strain stock again through a fine sieve. Add cream and heat thoroughly. Pick chicken meat from bones and add a little meat to each soup bowl, along with some cooked rice. Pour soup into bowls. Serve hot. Makes 6 servings.

Spanish Stockpot or Olla-Podrida

1 cup dried chickpeas	1 cup sliced carrots
2 pounds brisket of beef	1 cup sliced leeks or scallions
1 pound shoulder of lamb or	(white parts only)
mutton stew meat	2 cups diced potatoes
¼ pound lean salt pork	2 cups shredded cabbage
2 pigs' feet	½ cup sliced onion
1 ham bone, or ½ pound raw ham	3 cloves garlic
Salt	Bouquet garni
½ pound chorizos or Spanish	Freshly ground black pepper
garlic sausage	2 cups shredded lettuce
1 (3-pound) chicken	

Wash chickpeas and soak overnight in 3 cups cold water in the refrigerator. Combine chickpeas, beef, lamb, salt pork, pigs' feet, and ham bone with 3 quarts cold water and 2 teaspoons salt. Cover and bring to the boiling point. Reduce heat and simmer 2 hours. Add sausage and chicken. Cook, covered, 30 minutes. Add all vegetables except lettuce, add bouquet garni, and cook slowly 30 minutes. Remove all meat and chicken from the pot, and keep warm in a little stock. Add pepper to the stock and adjust the salt. Add lettuce and cook 1 to 2 minutes. Do not strain. Serve soup in a tureen. Put meat and chicken on a platter and pass it to let each person serve himself. Makes 8 to 10 servings.

Russian Cabbage Soup or Schtchi

1 cup each sliced onion, carrots, and	5 cups beef stock
leeks or scallions (white parts only)	3 cups sliced cabbage
1 cup diced celery	Salt and freshly ground black pepper
1 bay leaf	1 pound boiled brisket, cut into cubes
6 whole peppercorns	Sour cream

Place onion, carrots, leeks, celery, bay leaf, peppercorns, and stock in an 8-quart stockpot. Cover, slowly bring to the boiling point, and cook gently 20 minutes. Add cabbage and cook 15 minutes. Add salt and pepper. Put some beef cubes in each soup bowl and pour the hot soup over them. Serve with sour cream in a sauceboat. Makes 6 servings.

English Oxtail Soup

2½ pounds oxtail
Beef suet
1 cup sliced onion
2 cups sliced carrots
2 tablespoons flour
2 quarts beef bouillon or stock

1 cup sliced leeks or scallions
   (white parts only)
½ teaspoon each chopped basil,
   marjoram, rosemary, and sage
8 tablespoons port

Cut oxtail into 2-inch pieces. Brown the pieces in suet, along with onion and carrots. Sprinkle with flour. Stir and cook until flour has browned. Add bouillon and leeks. Cover and simmer 2 hours. Strain the soup. (It should be gelatinous and full-bodied.) Steep all the herbs together 10 minutes in 1 cup boiling bouillon from the pot. Strain back into the soup. Put a few pieces of oxtail in each soup bowl and pour soup over them. Add 1 tablespoon port to each serving. Makes 8 servings.

Irish Scallop Soup

2 slices lean bacon
1 cup thinly sliced potato
2 tablespoons butter
6 scallops
Hot water to barely cover scallops
2½ cups fish stock
1 tablespoon each chopped parsley
   and fresh thyme

½ cup beef marrow
2 cups diced fresh tomatoes
Salt and freshly ground black pepper
½ cup cream
2 tablespoons rusk crumbs

Cook bacon until crisp. Remove from the drippings and set aside for later use. Add potatoes and butter to bacon drippings. Blanch scallops in hot water over low heat until they are flaky. Drain off the scallop stock and add it to the potatoes, along with fish stock. Add herbs. Cover and cook slowly until potatoes are tender, 15 to 20 minutes. Dice scallops and add them, along with the marrow and tomatoes. Cover and cook slowly another 5 minutes, never allowing the soup to boil. Add salt and pepper. Stir in cream and rusk crumbs just before serving. Crumble the reserved bacon and sprinkle over the top. Makes 6 servings.

Scotch Broth

1 pound lean lamb or mutton stew meat
2 quarts mutton stock
Bouquet garni
½ cup pearl barley
1 cup each diced carrots, turnip,
   celery, and onion

2 cups shredded cabbage
Salt and freshly ground black pepper
Chopped parsley

Cut meat into 1-inch cubes and place in an 8-quart stockpot with stock and bouquet garni. Cover, bring to the boiling point, and skim. Sprinkle in the barley. Simmer, covered, 1½ hours. Add carrots, turnip, celery, and onions. Cover and cook 30 minutes. Add cabbage, cover, and cook 10 to 12 minutes. Add salt and pepper. Serve hot, as a main-dish soup. Garnish with chopped parsley. Makes 8 to 10 servings.

Roman Consommé with Eggs or Stracciatella

2 large eggs, beaten
3 tablespoons fine soft breadcrumbs
3 tablespoons grated Parmesan cheese

1 teaspoon grated lemon zest
3 cups hot bouillon
Salt and freshly ground black pepper

Combine eggs, breadcrumbs, cheese, and lemon zest. Mix well. Gradually beat in hot bouillon and bring to the boiling point, stirring constantly. Reduce heat and cook slowly until soup thickens slightly. (Do not boil.) Serve hot, with salt and black pepper to taste. Makes 3 servings.

FISH

Perhaps the greatest glories of French cuisine happen when fish and shellfish (see the following chapter) meet its greatest sauces, whether hot (Américaine, Nantua, Normande, or Pompadour) or cold (Ravigote, Russian, Antiboise, and Grimod).

This chapter opens with Basic Methods of Cooking Fish and then goes on to include many various types of fish. It is important, as with all kinds of foods, that the ingredients be fresh and of perfect quality, though with fish this caveat is probably more critical than with any other type of ingredient. In choosing fish keep in mind:

- The eyes should be clear, bright, and bulging, with deep black pupils.
- The gills in a whole fish should be bright red and odorless.
- The skin and scales of a whole fish should be fresh and glistening with bright colors and should spring right back when you push the side of the fish with your finger.
- With either a fillet or a whole fish there should be no odor of anything but the cleanest ocean.
- Fillets of fish should be firm, elastic, and shining.

With fillets, one should buy about ½ a pound per person; with whole fish, 1 pound.

BASIC METHODS OF COOKING FISH

Broiled Fish

This method is suitable for fresh fish fillets, fish steaks, and small whole fish.

Cut the fish into serving-size pieces. Small fish such as whiting and butterfish should be gutted but left whole. Sprinkle both sides with salt and ground black pepper. Place fish on a preheated oiled broiler rack. Brush with melted butter, using 4 tablespoons for each 2 pounds fish. Sprinkle with lemon juice. Place in the broiler 4 inches from the heat source. Broil 5 to 8 minutes. Turn carefully, brush the other side with butter, sprinkle with lemon juice, and broil 5 to 8 minutes, or until fish is flaky. Transfer carefully to a platter, garnish, and serve immediately. Makes 6 servings.

Baked Fish Fillets

2 pounds fish fillets or steaks
1½ teaspoons salt
¼ teaspoon ground black pepper

Milk
Flour or fine dry breadcrumbs
¼ cup (½ stick) butter, melted

Cut fish into serving-size pieces. Add salt and pepper to the milk and mix well. Dip the fish into the milk and then roll it in flour or breadcrumbs. Place fish in a well-buttered baking pan. Spoon butter over the fish. Place pan on the top rack of preheated oven (500°F). Bake 10 to 12 minutes, or until the fish flakes when tested with a fork. Serve at once on a warm platter, plain or with a sauce. Makes 6 servings.

Baked Whole Fish

1 (3- to 4-pound) fish, dressed
1½ teaspoons salt
¼ teaspoon ground black pepper

¼ cup (½ stick) butter, melted
Bacon (optional)

Rub the fish inside and out with salt and pepper. Place fish in a buttered baking pan. Brush with butter and lay 1 or 2 slices bacon over the top, if desired. Bake in a preheated oven (350°F) 40 to 50 minutes, or until fish is flaky when tested with a fork. If fish seems dry while baking, baste with melted butter or pan drippings. Serve immediately, plain or with Herb Butter or Hollandaise, Béarnaise, Tartar, or Chivry Sauce. Makes 6 servings.

Pan-Fried Fish Fillets Meunière

2 pounds boned fish filets
1 tablespoon salt
¼ teaspoon ground black pepper
1 large egg, lightly beaten
⅓ cup milk

¼ cup flour
2 tablespoons each butter and
    pure vegetable oil
Freshly squeezed lemon juice

Season both sides of the filets with salt and pepper. Combine egg and milk, dip fish into the mixture, then roll it in flour. Fry in hot butter and oil over medium heat, turning carefully to brown both sides, until fish has browned and is flaky, about 10 minutes, depending on the thickness of the fish. Drain on paper towels and serve immediately, sprinkled with lemon juice. Makes 6 servings.

Deep-Fried Fish

2 pounds fish fillets, or steaks,
    or dressed fish
1 teaspoon salt
¼ teaspoon ground black pepper
1 egg, lightly beaten with
    1 tablespoon water or milk

1 cup fine white breadcrumbs or
    Batter for Frying Fish
Oil for frying

Cut fish into serving-size pieces. Sprinkle both sides with salt and pepper. Dip fish into egg and then roll in crumbs or dip in batter. Place a layer of fish in a frying basket, lower basket into deep fat preheated to 375°F, and fry 3 to 6 minutes, or until fish is golden brown. Remove fish from fat and drain on paper towels. Serve immediately. Makes 6 servings.

Batter for Frying Fish

1 large egg
½ teaspoon salt

½ cup milk
½ cup sifted flour

Beat egg, salt, and milk together. Add flour all at one time, mix, and beat until smooth. Use as a coating for fish, shellfish, chicken, or vegetables, for pan-frying or deep-fat-frying. Makes enough batter for 6 servings.

Poached Fish Fillets

2 pounds fish fillets or steaks
2 quarts fish stock, or 2 quarts boiling water with 3 tablespoons salt

Cut fish into serving-size pieces. Place in a frying basket, or place on a plate and tie plate in a piece of cheesecloth. Lower the fish into the warm stock, or salted water, and simmer (never boil) 5 to 10 minutes, or until fish is flaky when tested with a fork. Carefully remove fish to a warm platter. Garnish attractively with parsley or watercress, lemon, tomato or unpeeled cucumber slices. Serve with Herb Butter; Curry or Tarragon Sauce; or Hollandaise, Béarnaise, or Tartar Sauce. Makes 6 servings.

Steamed Whole Fish or Fish Fillets

3½ to 4 pounds dressed whole fish,
    or 2 pounds fish steaks or fillets

Salt
Ground black pepper
Water

Sprinkle fish with salt and pepper. Wrap in a piece of cheesecloth and tie the ends. Place a rack or trivet in a Dutch oven or saucepan. Pour in hot water to level of the rack. Place fish on the rack. Cover pan tightly. Steam whole fish 30 minutes, steaks or fillets 12 minutes, or until fish flakes when tested with a fork. Open cheesecloth and carefully transfer fish to a warm platter. Remove skin and bones, if desired. Serve with Egg Sauce, Herb Butter, or Chivry Sauce. Makes 6 servings.

BASS (BAR) (Salt-water)

BASS LENDS ITSELF TO NUMEROUS METHODS of preparation—poaching, broiling, frying, and baking whole, with or without a stuffing.

Poached Bass with Chivry Sauce

Allow 2 pounds boned fish, or 3½ to 4 pounds undressed fish, for 6 servings. Cut fish into serving-size pieces, or leave fish whole. Poach according to recipe for Poached Fish. Remove fish from poaching liquid, drain, and arrange on a warm platter. Garnish with parsley. Serve with Chivry Sauce and boiled potatoes.

Baked Bass

Allow 3½ to 4 pounds for 6 servings. Bake according to recipe for Baked Fish. Serve with Herb Butter or a sauce.

Whole Bass Baked in Foil or en Papillote

The parchment paper used by French cooks for this type of dish is can be replaced by aluminum foil.

½ pound mushrooms, sliced	1 (5-pound) dressed striped bass
1 teaspoon chopped shallot or onion	2 tablespoons olive oil
4 tablespoons (½ stick) butter	¼ cup dry white wine
1 cup cooked tomatoes	18 black olives
Salt and freshly ground black pepper	¾ pound ready-to-cook shellfish

Cook mushrooms and shallot in 2 tablespoons of the butter until all the liquid has evaporated. Add tomatoes, salt and pepper to taste. Cook 2 to 3 minutes, stirring constantly. Season the fish inside and out with salt and pepper. Spread the mushroom-tomato mixture over a long piece of parchment or aluminum foil about twice the length and width of the fish. Place the fish over the mixture. Spoon the mixture over the fish.Add the oil, wine, and olives. Bring long sides of the foil up over the fish and make a lengthwise drugstore fold over it. Turn up the ends, folding them 3 times to seal tightly. Place package on a baking sheet and cook in a preheated oven (400°F) 30-45 minutes, or until the fish is done Transfer the foil-wrapped fish to a platter and serve, turning the foil back at the table. Makes 6 servings.

BRILL (BARBUE)

BRILL IS A FLAT SEA FISH SIMILAR IN SHAPE TO TURBOT, but smaller and more elongated. The flesh is very delicate, light, and moist, resembling sole or turbot. It may be poached, baked, boned and stuffed, fried, or used in combination with other fish and shellfish.

Baked Whole Brill in White Wine

3½ to 4 pounds dressed brill
Salt
1 small onion, thinly sliced

Bouquet garni
½ cup dry white wine
White Wine Sauce

Rub brill inside and out with salt. Place in a well-buttered baking dish with onion and bouquet garni, and pour wine over it. Cover and bake in a preheated oven (350°F) 30 minutes, or until fish flakes when tested with a fork. Baste two or three times with the wine in the dish. Carefully transfer fish to a warm platter. Serve with White Wine Sauce, using the wine in which fish was cooked as part of the liquid for the sauce. Makes 6 servings.

Whole Brill Theodora

Cook 3½ pounds dressed brill in 1½ cups dry white wine as directed for Baked Whole Brill in White Wine. Mix together 3 tablespoons each butter and flour. Strain the wine in which fish was cooked into a saucepan. Add the roux and cook until of desired sauce consistency. Season to taste with salt and ground white pepper. Mix ⅓ cup of this sauce with 1 tablespoon tomato puree. Transfer fish to a warm platter, coat with wine sauce, and decorate in lattice pattern with the tomato sauce. Garnish with shrimp croquettes. Makes 6 servings.

Baked Fillets of Brill Chauchat

2½ pounds brill fillets
Salt
1½ cups fish stock
Ground white pepper
2 egg yolks
2 tablespoons heavy cream or
    cold fish stock

6 servings boiled potatoes
2 tablespoons grated Parmesan cheese
2 tablespoons soft breadcrumbs
2 tablespoons butter, melted

Rub both sides of fillets with salt and place in a well-buttered baking dish. Add stock. Cover and bake in a preheated oven (350°F) 20 minutes, or until fish flakes when tested with a fork. Strain stock from baking dish into a saucepan. Season with salt and white pepper. Mix egg yolks with cream and add to the sauce. Stir and cook 30 seconds over low heat. Carefully transfer fish to an ovenproof platter and arrange potatoes around it. Sprinkle fish and potatoes with cheese, coat with sauce, sprinkle with cheese, then with breadcrumbs and melted butter. Brown in the oven (450° to 500°F). Serve at once. Makes 6 servings.

CARP (CARPE)

The same cooking methods are suitable for all varieties of this freshwater fish.

Deep-Fried Whole Carp with Rémoulade Sauce

3 pounds dressed carp	White breadcrumbs
Salt	Oil for frying
Ground black pepper	Fried parsley
Flour	Lemon slices
1 large egg, beaten with	¾ cup Rémoulade Sauce
1 tablespoon water	

Split carp lengthwise and remove as many of the bones as possible. Rub fish lightly with salt and pepper. Roll in flour and dip in egg mixture and then in breadcrumbs. Fry until browned in deep fat preheated to 375°F. Drain on paper towels. Serve on a warmed platter, garnished with fried parsley and lemon slices. Pass Rémoulade Sauce in a separate dish. Makes 6 servings. Sauce Bercy may be served instead of Rémoulade Sauce.

Polish Carp Steaks

3 pounds dressed carp	1½ cups light ale or beer
Salt and freshly ground black pepper	¾ cup dry red wine
4 tablespoons butter	½ teaspoon sugar
1 cup sliced onion	1 tablespoon wine vinegar
2 sprigs parsley	3 tablespoons gingerbread or
1 bay leaf	gingersnap crumbs
1½ teaspoon chopped fresh thyme	2 tablespoons each raisins and
1 whole clove	sliced blanched almonds
¼ teaspoon coriander seeds	6 servings boiled potatoes
Carp roe	

Cut carp into 6 portions and rub lightly with salt and pepper. Set aside. Melt 2 tablespoons of the butter in a skillet. Add onion, parsley, bay leaf, thyme, cloves, and coriander seeds and lay fish and lightly salted roe on top. Add beer, wine, sugar, and vinegar. Bring to the boiling point, reduce heat, sprinkle with gingerbread or gingersnap crumbs, and cook 10 to 12 minutes, or until the fish flakes when tested with a fork. Transfer fish to a serving platter. Strain the cooking liquor. Add the remaining 2 tablespoons butter and the raisins and almonds. Bring to the boiling point. Adjust seasonings and pour the sauce over the fish. Serve with boiled potatoes. Makes 6 servings.

Whole Carp Baked in Foil or en Papillote

The carp can be cooked as in this recipe or cooked from the raw state in the foil—see also Whole Bass Baked in Foil.

1 (6-to 7-pound) whole carp	1 cup cooked tomatoes
Oil	20 olives
Butter	Lemon juice to taste
½ cup dry white wine	Salt and freshly ground black pepper
12 ounces mixed shellfish (crabmeat, lobster, shrimp)	

Make incisions in the fish along the sides of the carp. In an ovenproof skillet, fry fish lightly in 1 tablespoon each oil and butter, then cook 20 minutes in a preheated oven (350°F). Add wine and cook over low heat until the liquid has reduced by one-fourth. Add the shellfish, tomatoes, olives, lemon juice, salt, and pepper. Cook in a preheated oven (400°F) 10 minutes. Butter a large square of aluminum foil, place the shellfish in the center, and place the carp on top. Bring long sides of the foil up over the fish and make a lengthwise drugstore fold over it. Press the foil together at the ends to seal. Place the package in an oiled baking pan and bake in the oven (450°F) until the package is inflated by the interior steam. Serve at the table in this package. Makes 10 servings.

Whole Carp Baked in Beer

6 tablespoons butter	2 sprigs parsley
1 cup sliced onion	2 tablespoons gingerbread or
½ cup diced celery	gingersnap crumbs
3 pounds dressed carp	Carp roe
Salt and freshly ground black pepper	1 teaspoon lemon juice
1 cup light ale or beer	Chopped parsley

Melt 2 tablespoons of the butter in a baking dish, add onion and celery, and mix well. Rub fish lightly with salt and pepper and lay over vegetables. Add beer and parsley.

Sprinkle gingerbread or gingersnap crumbs over the top. Cover and cook in a pre-heated oven (325°F) 30 to 40 minutes, or until the fish flakes when tested with a fork. Transfer fish to a warmed platter and keep it warm. Cook the stock until reduced by half, then strain it. Meanwhile, slice carp roe, sprinkle lightly with salt, pepper, and lemon juice, and cook in 2 tablespoons of the butter over medium-low heat 5 minutes, or until done. Arrange the roe around the fish. Add remaining 2 tablespoons butter to the reduced stock, heat, adjust seasonings, and pour over the fish. Garnish with chopped parsley. Makes 6 servings.

Carp Roe Diplomat

1 pound carp roe
3 tablespoons butter
1 teaspoon lemon juice
½ teaspoon salt
6 large croustades (toasted, buttered
    bread cases) or baked puff pastry cases

1 cup Nantua Sauce
6 slices truffle, or 6 small
    sautéed mushroom caps

Soak the roe in cold water 1 hour. Melt butter in a skillet; add lemon juice and salt. Drain roe, arrange in the skillet, and cook over medium-low heat 5 to 10 minutes, or until done. Slice roe and put in croustades or baked puff pastry cases. Fill with Nantua Sauce. Garnish each with a truffle slice or a sautéed mushroom cap. Serve very hot. Makes 6 servings.

Carp Quenelles Saxony

Carp bones, skin, and heads
1 pound boned carp
½ teaspoon salt
⅛ teaspoon ground white pepper
⅛ teaspoon grated nutmeg
2 egg whites
2 cups heavy cream

¾ cup ale or beer
Fish stock
¼ cup (½ stick) butter, melted
2 tablespoons gingerbread or
    gingersnap crumbs
Chopped parsley
Cooked rice or boiled potatoes

Make stock from carp bones, skin, and heads. Set aside. Put carp through a food chopper, using the finest blade. Add seasonings. Pound and beat the fish vigorously with a wooden spoon, and beat in the egg whites. Push the mixture through a sieve into a bowl and set the bowl in a pan of cracked ice. Gradually beat and pound in cream. Beat vigorously 2 to 3 minutes, then set the quenelles mixture aside. Heat ½ cup of the beer with enough stock to barely cover the quenelles. Melt butter in a shallow skillet. Make quenelles, shaping the mixture into ovals with 2 tablespoons. Gently slide them into the buttered skillet, a few at a time. Pour in the hot beer and stock. Bring to the boiling point and simmer 5 minutes. (Do not boil.) Soften gingerbread or gingersnap crumbs in the remaining ¼ cup beer, add to the poaching liquid, and continue cooking the quenelles over low heat 5 more minutes, or until done, turning them several times to cook them uniformly. Transfer them to a serving bowl, cover with the sauce, and sprinkle with parsley. Serve with rice or potatoes. Makes 6 servings.

Cold Poached Blue Whole Carp

The term "blue" means that the carp is poached just after it is killed and the covering on its skin turns blue—so the term denotes very fresh fish as well as a method of cooking.

1 (3¼-pound) live or just killed carp, dressed	Parsley
	1 cup Béchamel Sauce
Fish stock	1 tablespoon well-drained
Aspic	prepared horseradish
Scalloped lemon halves	¼ teaspoon prepared mustard

Poach the whole fish in stock (see recipe for Poached Fish). Transfer fish to a cold platter. Brush with almost-set aspic. Chill until aspic is set. Garnish with lemon halves and parsley. Mix Béchamel Sauce with horseradish and mustard and serve with the fish. Or, if desired, serve fish with Mayonnaise. Makes 6 servings.

Cold Carp with Raisins

2 (2-pound) dressed carp	1½ cups water
⅓ cup chopped onion	Bouquet garni
2 shallots, chopped	1 teaspoon salt
4 tablespoons olive oil or pure vegetable oil	4 whole peppercorns
2 tablespoons flour	⅛ teaspoon crumbled saffron threads
1½ cups dry white wine	⅓ cup each raisins and currants

Cut carp crosswise into 2-inch-thick slices. Set aside. Cook onion and shallots in 2 tablespoons of the oil until they begin to turn golden brown. Remove from heat and blend in flour. Stir in wine and water. Add bouquet garni, salt, peppercorns, the remaining oil, and the fish. Simmer 30 minutes, or until the fish flakes when tested with a fork. Remove fish from the stock and arrange on a long platter in the shape of a carp. Cook stock until reduced by one-fourth. Add saffron, mix well, and strain over fish. Pour hot water over raisins and currants. Drain and sprinkle around fish. Chill until sauce has slightly jellied. Makes 6 servings.

COD, HADDOCK, AND HAKE
(CABILLAUD, EGLEFIN, COLIN)

THESE THREE SALTWATER FISH are members of the same family and may be used interchangeably in most recipes. They may be poached, baked, deep-fat-fried, dipped in crumbs or flour and sautéed in butter, broiled, made into croquettes, used in chowders, or served with sauces. These fish are also available in dried and salted form. In France, salt cod is called *morue*; dried hake is called *merluche*. See also Whiting.

Broiled Cod Steaks

Cut cod steaks into slices ½ to ¾ inch thick. Rub both sides with salt and freshly ground black pepper and brush with melted butter. Place on a preheated oiled broiling rack. Broil as in directions for Broiled Fish. Serve with lemon wedges and Anchovy or Maître d'Hôtel Butter. Allow 2 pounds fish for 6 servings.

Deep-Fried Cod Steaks with Tartar Sauce

Cut cod steaks ½ inch thick, or use cod fillets. Dip in egg and fine dry breadcrumbs and fry in deep fat. (See directions for Deep-Fried Fish.) Arrange fish on a warmed platter. Garnish with parsley. Serve with Tartar Sauce, separately. Allow 2 pounds fish steaks for 6 servings.

Deep-Fried Cod Fillets

Dip fish in ½ cup milk seasoned with 1 teaspoon salt and ¼ teaspoon ground black pepper. Roll in flour and fry until very crisp in deep fat preheated to 375° F. Drain on paper towels. Serve with lemon wedges and fried parsley. Allow 1½ to 2 pounds fish for 6 servings.

Poached Cod Fillets with Egg Sauce

2 pounds cod fillets
Fish stock
6 servings boiled potatoes
4 hard-cooked eggs

1½ cups thinned Béchamel Sauce
1 tablespoon chopped parsley
Salt and ground black pepper

Poach the cod fillets in fish stock following directions for Poached Fish. Drain fish well and arrange on a warmed platter, encircled with potatoes. Chop 3 of the eggs and add to the Béchamel Sauce. Stir in the parsley. Season to taste with salt and pepper. Spoon over the fish. Slice the remaining egg and arrange the slices as a garnish over the top of the fish. Makes 6 servings.

English Poached Cod Fillets

2 pounds cod fillets
Fish stock, or salted water with
    1 tablespoon vinegar
Parsley

1 lemon, sliced
6 tablespoons butter, melted
6 servings boiled potatoes

Poach cod in boiling stock or salted water to which 1 tablespoon vinegar has been added. (See recipe for Poached Fish.) Drain fish well. Carefully transfer to a warmed platter. Garnish with parsley and lemon slices. Drizzle with melted butter and serve accompanied by boiled potatoes. Makes 6 servings.

Cod Steaks Mistral

2 pounds cod steaks, cut ½ inch thick
Salt and freshly ground black
    pepper
Flour
Pure vegetable oil or butter
5 medium-sized tomatoes

1 cup sliced mushrooms
½ cup dry white wine
1 small clove garlic, crushed
½ cup fresh white breadcrumbs
3 tablespoons butter, melted

Cut fish into 6 equal portions. Rub all sides with salt and pepper. Roll in flour and fry over medium heat in oil or butter until browned on both sides. Place in a baking dish. Peel and seed tomatoes and dice coarsely. Mix with mushrooms, wine, garlic, and salt and pepper to taste. Bring to the boiling point and pour over fish. Mix breadcrumbs with butter and sprinkle over the top. Cook in a preheated oven (350°F) 30 minutes, or until crumbs are brown. Makes 6 servings.

Baked Cod Parmentier

4 medium-sized cooked potatoes
1½ pounds cold cooked cod or other fish
1 cup sliced mushrooms
4 tablespoons butter

Salt and freshly ground black pepper
2 tablespoons tomato puree
1 cup Béchamel Sauce
2 hard-cooked egg yolks, sieved

Slice potatoes and arrange them, overlapping, in a ring inside a round shallow baking dish. Flake the fish and place in the center of the dish. Cook mushrooms in 2 tablespoons of the butter and spread them thinly over the fish. Sprinkle with salt and pepper. Mix the tomato puree with the Béchamel Sauce and spread over the mushrooms. Dot with the remaining butter. Cook in a preheated oven (350°F) 25 to 30 minutes or until the top is well flecked with brown. Sprinkle the top with the egg yolk and serve hot. Makes 6 servings.

Baked Whole Cod Parisienne

1 (5-pound) whole dressed cod
Fish stock
Anchovies

1 cup fine fresh white breadcrumbs
4 tablespoons (½ stick) butter, melted
Clam or Mussel Sauce

Simmer the cod very gently in stock for 30 minutes, or until fish flakes when tested with a fork. Remove from heat and carefully transfer fish to a cold heatproof platter. Quickly remove skin from fish. Make an incision along the backbone ¼ inch deep and insert anchovies. Mix breadcrumbs with butter and sprinkle over fish. Brown in a pre-heated oven (375°F) 20 minutes. Serve with Clam or Mussel Sauce. Makes 6 servings.

Cod Fillets Florentine

1½ pounds cod fillets
Fish stock
2 pounds fresh spinach, cooked
2 tablespoons butter
½ teaspoon sugar
⅛ teaspoon grated nutmeg

Salt and freshly ground black pepper
1½ cups Mornay Sauce
3 tablespoons dry white wine
¾ cup grated Parmesan cheese
2 tablespoons butter, melted

Poach fish fillets in stock (see recipe for Poached Fish). Drain cooked spinach well and heat with butter. Add seasonings. Place spinach in the bottom of a well-buttered baking dish and arrange fish over it. Stir and cook Mornay Sauce with wine 2 to 3 minutes, then pour over fish, covering it entirely. Sprinkle with cheese and butter. Cook in a preheated hot oven (425°F) 10 to 15 minutes, or brown under broiler. Makes 6 servings.

Portuguese Cod Fillets

1½ to 2 pounds cod or other fish fillets
Salt and freshly ground black
    pepper
⅓ cup olive oil
⅓ cup chopped onion
4 medium-sized tomatoes,
    peeled, seeded, and diced

1 small clove garlic, crushed
½ cup dry white wine
½ teaspoon sugar
Chopped parsley

Toss fish fillets with 1 teaspoon salt, ¼ teaspoon pepper, and 3 tablespoons of the oil. Place in a baking dish. Stir and cook onion, tomatoes, garlic, and remaining oil in a saucepan 5 to 6 minutes or until tomatoes are soft and have thickened. Add wine and season lightly with salt, pepper, and sugar. Pour over fish. Bake in a preheated oven (350°F) 25 minutes. Serve hot as an entrée, sprinkled with parsley. Makes 6 servings.

Salt Cod Benedictine

1 pound salt cod
Boiling water
2 medium-sized hot boiled
   potatoes, drained

6 tablespoons butter
About ½ cup milk
Salt and ground white pepper
½ cup heavy cream, whipped

Soak cod in cold water 5 hours, changing the water 2 times. Drop fish into boiling water, reduce heat, and simmer 10 to 15 minutes, or until fish is tender. Remove from water, drain, flake, and mash finely together with potatoes. Mix and mash until the mixture is smooth. Heat 4 tablespoons of the butter and the milk together and add to the fish and potatoes, along with salt and white pepper. Stir and beat until the mixture is fluffy. Fold in whipped cream. Put into a well-buttered baking dish in a mound. Dot with remaining butter. Bake in a preheated oven (400°F) 20 minutes, or until browned. Serve hot. This mixture is sometimes used to fill tart shells and barquettes. Makes 6 servings.

Biscay-Style Salt Cod

1 pound salt cod
Flour
¼ cup salad oil
6 medium-sized tomatoes, peeled,
   seeded, and quartered

1 small clove garlic, crushed
Salt and freshly ground black pepper
Chopped parsley

Soak cod in cold water 5 hours, changing the water 2 times. Drain off water and pat fish dry. Roll in flour. Brown on both sides in very hot oil. Transfer fish to a warmed platter. In the same skillet and oil, cook tomatoes and garlic until tomatoes form a sauce. Add seasonings and pour the sauce over the fish. Sprinkle with parsley. Makes 6 servings.

Salt Cod Ménagère

1 pound salt cod
Fish stock or water
3 tablespoons butter
½ cup thinly sliced onion

2 tablespoons flour
1 cup milk
Salt and ground white pepper
5 medium-sized potatoes, peeled and sliced

Soak cod in cold water 5 hours, changing the water 2 times. Poach in stock or water as in recipe for Salt Cod Benedictine. Set aside to keep warm. Melt butter in a skillet, add onion, toss lightly, and sprinkle with flour. Stir and cook without letting the flour brown. Add milk, salt, and white pepper; stir and cook over low heat 10 minutes.

Arrange potatoes evenly over the bottom of a well-buttered baking dish and place well-drained poached fish on top. Cover completely with sauce. Bake in a preheated oven (350°F) 20 to 30 minutes. Makes 6 servings.

Russian Chilled Cod

2 pounds dressed cod, in 1 piece,
   with the skin
Boiling water
1 tablespoon vinegar
½ teaspoon salt
18 cooked, peeled, and deveined shrimp
18 slices truffle, or small sautéed
   mushroom caps

Aspic jelly
6 timbales of Russian or Mimosa Salad
Anchovies
Parsley
Lemon wedges

Place fish in boiling water, reduce heat, add vinegar and salt, cover, and simmer 15 minutes, or until the fish flakes when tested with a fork. Drain water from the fish and remove the skin from upper half of the sides and from the back of the fish. Chill. Place on a cold platter. Alternate shrimp and truffle slices or mushroom caps on top of fish in a row down the center. Glaze with aspic jelly. Arrange 3 salads on the platter on each side of the fish. Decorate each salad with anchovies. Garnish the platter with parsley and lemon wedges. Makes 6 servings.

Poached Haddock with Melted Butter

2 pounds fillet of haddock
2 quarts boiling water
3 tablespoons salt
6 servings boiled potatoes

¼ cup (1 stick) butter
2 tablespoons lemon juice
2 tablespoons chopped parsley
¼ teaspoon freshly ground black pepper

Cut fish into 6 serving-size pieces and poach in water and salt as directed in the recipe for Poached Fish. Arrange fish on a warmed platter with boiled potatoes. Combine remaining ingredients and serve separately as a sauce. Makes 6 servings.

English Poached Smoked Haddock

Cut a smoked haddock into half lengthwise. Cut the halves into serving-size pieces. Place in a skillet. Cover with milk or with equal amounts of milk and water. Bring to the boiling point, reduce heat, and simmer 7 to 10 minutes. Remove from the milk and serve for breakfast with melted butter. Allow ¼ pound haddock for each serving. Smoked haddock is a very popular breakfast dish in England.

❦ Smoked Haddock with Egg Sauce

2 tablespoons butter
2 tablespoons flour
2 cups milk
½ teaspoon salt
⅛ teaspoon freshly ground black pepper

½ teaspoon lemon juice
2 hard-cooked eggs, diced
Poached Smoked Haddock
Chopped parsley

Melt butter in a 3-cup saucepan. Remove from heat and blend in flour. Stir and cook 1 minute. Remove from heat and add milk. Mix well. Simmer 30 minutes. Add salt, pepper, lemon juice, and eggs. Serve on Poached Smoked Haddock. Sprinkle with parsley. Makes 4 servings.

❦ Fillets of Hake Bercy

1 shallot, chopped
2½ pounds boned hake
½ cup fish stock
½ cup dry white wine

2 tablespoons butter
½ cup heavy cream
1 tablespoon lemon juice
Chopped parsley

Butter a flameproof baking dish generously and sprinkle with shallot. Cut fish into 6 serving-size pieces and arrange in the dish. Pour in stock and wine. Dot with butter. Cover and simmer 8 minutes, or until the fish flakes when tested with a fork. Drain the cooking liquor into a saucepan. Add cream and cook until the liquid has reduced by one-fourth. Blend in lemon juice and parsley. Arrange fish on a heatproof platter and cover with the sauce. Glaze under broiler. Makes 6 servings.

❦ Fillets of Hake Bretonne

½ cup each diced carrots, leeks,
    onion, and celery
1 cup sliced mushrooms
¼ cup (½ stick) butter
Salt
2½ pounds boned hake

½ cup each dry white wine and fish stock
1 cup Fish Velouté
½ cup heavy cream
1 tablespoon or more lemon juice
Ground white pepper

Place vegetables and butter in a saucepan with ½ teaspoon salt. Cover tightly and cook slowly 10 minutes, or until vegetables are tender. Cut fish into 6 serving-size pieces, rub both sides lightly with salt, and arrange in a buttered baking dish. Add wine, stock, and vegetables. Cover and cook in preheated moderate oven (350°F) about 25 minutes, only until fish flakes when tested with a fork. Drain fish liquid into a saucepan. Add Velouté and cream. Cook to sauce consistency. Strain and add lemon juice and white pepper. Adjust the salt. Place fish on a heatproof platter, cover with the sauce, and glaze under broiler. Makes 6 servings.

EEL (ANGUILLE)

EELS ARE LONG, SNAKELIKE FISH that ascend rivers but return to the ocean to breed. Both the European and American species are important food fish.

Broiled Eel with Tartar Sauce

2 pounds eel
1 cup dry white wine
1 tablespoon chopped onion
Parsley
½ teaspoon salt
4 whole peppercorns

Boiling water
1 egg, beaten with 1 tablespoon water
Fine white breadcrumbs
¼ cup olive oil
Fried parsley
Tartar Sauce

Cut eel into pieces 2 inches long and place in a skillet. Add wine, onion, 1 sprig fresh parsley, salt, peppercorns, and enough boiling water to cover eel. Simmer 10 to 15 minutes or until eel flakes when tested with a fork. Remove from water and cool. Dip eel in egg mixture, roll in breadcrumbs, and arrange on a preheated, oiled broiler pan. Cook in the broiler, 4 inches from the heat source, until browned, turning to brown both sides. Serve with fried parsley and Tartar Sauce. Makes 6 servings.

Deviled Eel

2 pounds cooked eel, cut into 6 portions
1 egg, beaten with 1 tablespoon water
Fine white breadcrumbs
Salt and freshly ground black
    pepper

Dash cayenne
1 cup Sauce Diable
Fried parsley

Dip eel in egg mixture, roll in breadcrumbs, and fry in deep fat preheated to 375°F until browned. Drain on paper towels. Mix together salt, pepper, and cayenne and sprinkle over fish. Serve with Sauce Diable. Garnish with fried parsley. Makes 6 servings.

Belgian Green Eel

2 (1½-pound) eels
6 tablespoons butter
Sorrel (sourgrass)
Parsley
Chervil
1 sprig each savory and sage

½ cup dry white wine
½ teaspoon salt
½ teaspoon freshly ground black pepper
3 egg yolks
2 tablespoons lemon juice

Skin, clean, and wash eels and cut them into pieces. Melt butter in a skillet. Add eel. Chop herbs rather finely and scatter a medium-thick layer over the eel. Cover and cook 5 minutes over medium heat. Add wine and enough water to cover the eel and herbs. Sprinkle with salt and pepper. Cover and simmer 20 to 25 minutes. Blend egg yolks with lemon juice, then mix in a little of the eel liquor. Add to the eel and simmer (do not boil) 1 minute. Place the eel in a tureen and pour the unstrained herb sauce over it. Cool. This dish is eaten cool or lukewarm. Makes 6 servings.

Dutch Eel

2 pounds eel	½ teaspoon salt
⅓ cup sliced onion	Boiling water
Parsley	Lemon slices
1 teaspoon vinegar	¼ cup (½ stick) butter, melted
4 whole peppercorns	6 servings boiled potatoes

Cut eel into 6 portions. Place in a skillet and add onion, 2 sprigs parsley, vinegar, peppercorns, salt, and enough boiling water to cover eel. Simmer 10 to 15 minutes, or until eel flakes when tested with a fork. Transfer to a serving platter and garnish with parsley and lemon slices. Serve with butter and boiled potatoes. Makes 6 servings.

HERRING (HARENG)

HERRING ARE SOLD FRESH, salted, smoked, dried, or pickled.

Broiled Whole Herring Maître d'Hôtel

Prepare 6 small herring as in the recipe for Deviled Broiled Whole Herring, omitting the mustard, and broil as directed. Melt ½ cup (1 stick) butter, add 2 tablespoons lemon juice, 1 tablespoon chopped parsley, and salt and freshly ground black pepper to taste. Serve over broiled fish. Makes 6 servings.

Deviled Broiled Whole Herring

6 dressed herring (heads removed), ¾ to 1 pound each	Fine white breadcrumbs
Salt and freshly ground black pepper	Olive oil
Prepared mustard	Chopped parsley
	Ravigote Sauce

Rub herring lightly with salt and pepper inside and out. Brush the outside thinly with mustard. Roll in breadcrumbs. Drizzle lightly with oil. Place in the broiler 5 inches from heat source and cook until the fish flakes when tested with a fork, turning to brown both sides. (Or, if desired, fry in oil over surface heat.) Serve sprinkled with parsley, and pass Ravigote Sauce in a separate dish. Makes 6 servings.

Fried Whole Herring

6 dressed herring (heads removed), ¾ to 1 pound each	6 tablespoons butter
Salt	2 tablespoons olive oil
Freshly ground black pepper	Chopped parsley
Flour	6 lemon wedges

Rub herring lightly with salt and pepper inside and out. Roll in flour. Brown on both sides in half the butter and all the oil, adding more butter and oil as the fish cooks, if necessary. Arrange the fish on a warmed platter. Brown the remaining 3 tablespoons butter and pour over the fish. Sprinkle with parsley. Serve with lemon wedges. Makes 6 servings.

MACKEREL (MAQUEREAU)

A FATTY AND SAVORY SALTWATER FISH, mackerel is greenish blue on the back and silvery underneath. It is eaten fresh, salted, smoked, or pickled.

Fillets of Mackerel Mireille

3 pounds mackerel, dressed and filleted	1 shallot, chopped
Salt	1 tablespoon chopped onion
Freshly ground black pepper	¹⁄₁₆ teaspoon minced garlic
Flour	6 small tomatoes
Olive oil	Chopped parsley
1 cup sliced mushrooms	

Rub the fillets lightly with salt and pepper, roll in flour, and brown on both sides in hot oil. Place fish on a warmed platter and keep warm. Pour 2 tablespoons fresh oil into the skillet, heat, and add mushrooms, shallot, onion, garlic, and ¼ teaspoon salt. Stir and cook 5 minutes, or until mushrooms are tender. Pour over fish. Peel and seed tomatoes and fry in oil in the same skillet. Sprinkle with salt and pepper, and place around the fish. Garnish with chopped parsley. Makes 6 servings.

Fried Whole Mackerel

Score a mackerel across the thickest part of the flesh. Rub lightly with salt and freshly ground black pepper, roll in flour, and fry as in recipe for Pan-Fried Fish. Allow 1 dressed mackerel weighing 1 pound for each serving. Fillets of mackerel may be fried in the same way.

Venetian Fillets of Mackerel

3 pounds mackerel, dressed
    and filleted
Salt
Freshly ground black pepper
1 cup dry white wine
¼ cup tarragon vinegar

1 tablespoon tomato puree
¼ teaspoon each chopped chervil
    and tarragon
Chopped parsley
6 servings boiled potatoes

Rub the fillets lightly with salt and pepper and place them in a buttered baking dish. Pour in ½ cup of the wine. Cover and cook in a preheated oven (350°F) 25 minutes or until the fish flakes when tested with a fork. Drain the wine from the baking dish into a saucepan. Add remaining ½ cup wine and the vinegar and boil until the liquid has been reduced by half. Add tomato puree, herbs, and salt and pepper to taste. Stir and cook 2 to 3 minutes. Arrange fish on a warm platter, cover with sauce, and sprinkle with parsley. Serve with boiled potatoes. Makes 6 servings.

MULLET

THE RED MULLET, CALLED *ROUGET* IN FRANCE because of its color, is one of the most highly prized Mediterranean fish and is so delicate in flavor that it should always be prepared in the simplest way. It is sometimes called *bécasse de mer* (sea woodcock), because its insides, like those of woodcock, can be eaten. On the Côte d'Azur it is taken fresh from the water, wiped without removing the scales, floured, and grilled—a method of preparation especially esteemed by connoisseurs. The gray mullet (*muge, mulet*) belongs to a different family, of which the gray mullet and the striped mullet are the most common varieties; the American mullet, a very important food fish in the southern United States, is a striped mullet. One of the most popular ways of preparing mullet is to grill it and serve it with Maître d'Hôtel Butter.

Egyptian Whole Red Mullet with Tomatoes

6 (½- to ¾-pound) red mullet
Salt
Freshly ground black pepper
Flour
3 to 4 tablespoons olive oil
6 medium-sized tomatoes,
    peeled, seeded, and diced
½ clove garlic, crushed

Chopped parsley
½ cup fresh white breadcrumbs
2 tablespoons butter

Dress mullet, if desired. Season with salt and pepper, flour lightly, and brown quickly on both sides in hot oil in a skillet. Cook tomatoes with the garlic to a pulp. Add 1 tablespoon parsley. Season to taste with salt and pepper. Spread half of the mixture over the bottom of a baking dish. Top with fried mullet. Cover with the remaining tomatoes. Sprinkle with breadcrumbs and dot with butter. Cook in a pre-heated oven (425°F) about 10 minutes, or until breadcrumbs are browned. Garnish with parsley. Makes 6 servings.

Fried Whole Red Mullet

Allow ¾ pound to 1 pound per serving. Prepare as in recipes for fried fish.

Red Mullet Monte Carlo

6 (½- to ¾-pound) red mullet	6 tablespoons butter, melted
1 tablespoon mashed anchovy	2 tablespoons chopped parsley
6 tablespoons butter	1 tablespoon freshly squeezed lemon juice
6 slices hot toast	French fried potato sticks

Dress red mullet, if desired. Broil as in the recipe for Broiled Fish. Mix anchovy paste with 6 tablespoons butter and spread on toast. Place fish on the toast. Combine melted butter, parsley, and lemon juice and spoon over fish. Garnish with French fried potato sticks. Makes 6 servings.

Cold Red Whole Mullet Niçoise

2 (1-pound) dressed red mullet, with heads attached	Lemon slices
Salt and freshly ground black pepper	Freshly squeezed lemon juice
	Olive oil
⅓ cup sliced onion	½ lemon
2 cups dry white wine	1 black olive
Tomato slices	Parsley

Sprinkle fish lightly with salt and pepper and set aside. Place onion in a skillet and lay fish on top. Pour in wine, bring to the boiling point, reduce heat, cover, and simmer 8 to 10 minutes, or until the fish flakes when tested with a fork. Chill in the wine. Transfer the fish to a cold platter, reserving the stock to use later. Surround with alternate, overlapping slices of tomato and lemon. Cook the reserved stock until reduced by half. Season to taste with salt, pepper, lemon juice, and oil. Cool. When stock begins to set (jelly), spoon it over the fish. Chill. Notch the edge of ½ lemon, garnish with a black olive, and place between the heads of the fish. Makes 4 servings.

Gray Mullet in Aspic

Cook small mullet in water seasoned with vinegar and salt as directed for Russian Chilled Cod. Cool in the stock. Transfer fish to a cold platter. Season aspic to taste with tarragon, and when it is about half set brush it over the fish. Garnish the platter with peeled whole medium-sized tomatoes and parsley. Chill. Allow ½ pound fish for each serving.

PERCH (PERCHE)

A POPULAR FRESHWATER FISH, perch resembles trout and can be cooked in many of the same ways, although the flesh is less delicate. Small perch are usually fried in deep fat; medium-sized perch are filleted and pan-fried in butter; large ones may be stuffed and cooked like shad.

Russian Whole Perch

1 (3½- to 4-pound) dressed perch	4 whole peppercorns
1 small onion, sliced	1 tablespoon vinegar
1 sprig parsley	1½ cups grated hard-roll crumbs
1 small bay leaf	2 Hard Boiled eggs, chopped
2 teaspoons chopped fresh thyme	½ cup (1 stick) butter
1 teaspoon salt	Chopped parsley

Place perch in a large saucepan, add onion, parsley, bay leaf, thyme, salt, peppercorns, vinegar, and hot water to cover. Bring to the boiling point, reduce heat, and simmer 12 to 15 minutes, or until the fish flakes when tested with a fork. Transfer fish to a warmed platter. Fry hard-roll crumbs in half the butter, add chopped eggs, and spoon over fish. Melt remaining butter and pour over fish. Sprinkle with parsley. Makes 6 servings.

Fillets of Perch Meunière

Rub fillets lightly with salt and ground black pepper. Roll in flour and pan-fry until golden in butter or oil over medium heat, turning to brown both sides. Transfer fillets to a warm platter, sprinkle with chopped parsley, and garnish with lemon. Allow ⅓ pound per person.

Deep-Fried Perch

Soak dressed small perch 10 minutes in ½ cup milk with ½ teaspoon salt added. Drain. Roll in flour. Fry until golden in deep fat preheated to 375°F. Drain on paper towels. Garnish with parsley and lemon. Allow 3 small perch per person.

Marinated Small Perch

6 (½-pound) perch or other small
   freshwater fish
Salt
Freshly ground black pepper
Flour
Oil for frying
1 rib celery
1 small carrot, peeled

1 small onion, grated
3 tablespoons olive oil
1 cup dry white wine
¼ cup wine vinegar
1 small bay leaf
½ teaspoon slivered lemon zest

Sprinkle fish lightly with salt and pepper inside and out. Roll in flour. Fry in oil until browned on both sides. Cut celery and carrot into julienne and cook with the grated onion slowly in oil in a saucepan until tender. Add wine, vinegar, bay leaf, and lemon zest. Cover and simmer 30 minutes. Pour over the fish and cool. Makes 6 servings.

Mixed Fried Fish: Friture or Fritto Misto

Friture or *fritto misto* is a platter of assorted fried fish, usually shrimp, red mullet, and squid. The fish are dipped in flour, batter, or breadcrumbs and egg, and deep-fat-fried in very hot olive oil. The same type of dish can be made with shrimp, perch, and smelts or other small fish, such as sunfish, trout, or whiting.

18 peeled and deveined shrimp
18 smelts (or more if desired)
6 dressed small perch or other small fish
Salt and freshly ground black pepper
Flour, Fritter Batter, or fine white
   breadcrumbs and beaten eggs

Fried parsley
Lemon halves
Potato chips, Soufflé Potatoes, or
   French Fried Potatoes

Sprinkle shrimp and fish with salt and pepper. Dredge in flour; or dip in Fritter Batter; or roll in breadcrumbs; dip in beaten egg, and roll again in breadcrumbs. Fry in deep fat preheated to 370°F, until golden brown, 4 to 5 minutes. Drain on paper towels. Serve garnished with fried parsley, lemon halves, and either potato chips, Soufflé Potatoes, or French Fried Potatoes. Makes 6 servings.

PIKE (BROCHET)

PIKE IS A LARGE FRESHWATER FISH with firm white flesh of fine flavor. The best-known species in the United States are common pike, muskellunge, and pickerel.

Fried or Deep-Fried Whole Pike

6 pickerel pike, 12 inches long
1 tablespoon salt
½ teaspoon ground black pepper
1 large egg, lightly beaten with
⅓ cup milk

½ cup flour or fine white breadcrumbs
2 tablespoons butter or pure vegetable oil
Parsley

Dress pike and remove and discard heads. Rub salt and pepper over both sides of the fish. Dip fish into egg mixture, then roll in flour or breadcrumbs. Fry in hot butter or oil over medium heat until the fish have browned nicely on both sides and flake when tested with a fork, about 10 minutes. Drain on paper towels. Transfer to a warm platter and garnish with parsley. Makes 6 servings.

Pike prepared in this way may also be fried in deep fat. Place 2 fish at a time in a wire frying basket and lower into deep fat preheated to 375°F. Fry 3 to 6 minutes, or until fish is golden brown. Remove from the fat and drain on paper towels. Serve immediately. Allow 1 fish per serving.

Pike Fillets with Caper Sauce

2 pounds boned pike
2 quarts fish stock or salted water

Parsley
Caper Sauce

Cut pike into slices ½ inch thick. Place the pieces in a wire frying basket or on a plate. If a plate is used, tie plate, with the fish on it, in a piece of cheesecloth. Lower basket or plate into boiling stock or salted water. Reduce heat and simmer (never boil) 10 minutes, or until the fish flakes when tested with a fork. Carefully remove fish to a warm platter. Garnish with parsley and serve with Caper Sauce. If desired, the pike may be served with Mayonnaise or Mousseline Sauce instead of Caper Sauce. Makes 6 servings.

Whole Pike Manon

1 (4-pound) dressed pike
Fish stock
10 small cooked, peeled, and
    deveined shrimp
6 baked 2-inch pastry shells

2 cups shrimp salad
6 slices truffle
Parsley
18 cooked cold asparagus tips,
    marinated in Vinaigrette Sauce

Cook pike in simmering stock until it barely flakes. Remove from heat and cool fish in the stock. Transfer fish to a board and remove the skin from the back only, leaving head and tail attached. Place the pike on its belly on a long platter. Arrange a row of shrimp down the back of the fish, holding them in place with toothpicks. Fill pastry shells with shrimp salad. Garnish with truffle and parsley, and arrange around fish. Place asparagus tips at each end of the platter. Makes 6 servings.

Blanquette of Pike

2¼ pounds dressed, boned pike
Salt
¼ cup (½ stick) butter
2 tablespoons flour
½ cup dry white wine
½ cup hot water

½ small white onions, parboiled
½ pound small mushroom caps
2 tablespoons chopped parsley
2 egg yolks
½ cup heavy cream

Cut pike into slices ¾ inch thick and sprinkle salt over each side. Cook in butter without browning. Sprinkle fish with flour and cook 1 to 2 minutes. Add the next 5 ingredients. Cover and simmer 10 to 15 minutes or until onions are tender. Transfer fish and vegetables to a serving dish, leaving liquids in the pan. Simmer another 10 minutes. Keep warm. Blend egg yolks with cream, add to the sauce in the pan, mix well, and heat. Adjust salt and pour the sauce over the fish and vegetables. Serve hot. Makes 6 servings.

Pike Mousse with Sauce Fines Herbes

1 pound boned pike (reserve bones
    and trimmings)
1 cup thick Béchamel Sauce
Salt and freshly ground black
    pepper
1 whole egg and 4 egg yolks
½ cup heavy cream
1 small onion, sliced

1 sprig parsley
3 whole peppercorns
Water
½ cup dry white wine
1 tablespoon chopped parsley
¼ teaspoon chopped chervil
Sautéed mushroom caps (optional)
Cooked shrimp (optional)

Put pike through a food chopper 3 times, using the finest blade. Mix with Béchamel Sauce and push through a sieve. Add salt, pepper, whole egg and 2 of the egg yolks, and cream and mix well. Turn into a well-buttered 1-quart mold, set mold in a pan of hot water, and cook in a preheated oven (325°F) 1 hour, or until a knife inserted in the center of the mousse comes out clean. Meanwhile, make stock with the reserved pike bones and trimmings, onion, parsley sprig, peppercorns, 1½ cups water, and the wine. Cook 30 minutes. Strain. Cook until reduced to 1 cup. Beat remaining 2 egg yolks together with 2 tablespoons water and add to stock. Cook 30 seconds without boiling. Add chopped parsley and chervil. Unmold the mousse onto a serving plate and spoon the sauce over it. Garnish with sautéed mushroom caps and cooked shrimp, if desired. Makes 6 servings.

Glazed Chilled Pike Riga

1 (4-pound) dressed pike with
   head and tail
Fish stock
Aspic
4 small unpeeled cucumbers, sliced

3 cups shrimp salad
¼ cup finely chopped green and
   red bell peppers
Pimiento circles
Sliced truffles

Cook pike in enough stock to cover until fish is almost flaky. Remove from the heat and let cool in the stock. Transfer fish to a board and remove skin from one side of the back only. Set fish aside. Coat a long platter with aspic. Chill until aspic is set. Lay the fish on the aspic in the center of the platter. Arrange cucumber slices down the back of the fish to simulate scales. Coat with aspic. Combine shrimp salad and bell peppers and ¼ cup aspic. Mold in small (1½-inch) timbales and chill. Unmold and arrange on the platter around the fish. Garnish half of the molds with pimiento circles and the others with truffle slices. Makes 6 servings.

Pike Quenelles Lyonnaise

1 cup dry white breadcrumbs
1 cup hot milk
1 pound raw boneless pike
1 teaspoon salt
⅛ teaspoon freshly ground black pepper
1⁄16 teaspoon grated nutmeg

1 cup (2 sticks) softened butter
2 whole eggs and 2 egg yolks
Fish stock from pike bones, head, and skin
Nantua Sauce
½ pound cooked, peeled, and
   deveined shrimp

Combine breadcrumbs and hot milk and mix to form a smooth paste. If mixture is too wet, stir and cook over low heat 2 to 3 minutes. Spread the paste on a plate and chill until firm. (This is a bread panada.) Put pike through a food chopper twice, using the finest blade. Add salt, pepper, and nutmeg. Mix with butter, working it in with a wooden spoon. Add the panada and mix until smooth. Beat in the whole eggs and the egg yolks one at time. Adjust seasonings. Shape scant tablespoons of the mixture into balls on a lightly floured board. Arrange quenelles in a buttered skillet, add boiling fish stock or boiling water to cover, and cook 10 to 12 minutes over low heat, never allowing the liquid to boil, until done. Remove to a serving dish, coat with Nantua Sauce, and garnish with the shrimp. Makes 6 servings.

Cold Pike in Aspic

1 (3½- to 4-pound) dressed pike
Fish stock
Tarragon leaves
Sliced truffles on hard-cooked
   egg whites

Aspic
2 cups mixed cooked vegetable salad
6 baked 2-inch tart shells, cooled, or
   tomato cups (scooped out tomatoes)
Green Mayonnaise

Put pike in a saucepan with barely enough stock to cover it. Slowly bring to the boiling point and simmer until almost flaky when tested with a fork. Remove from the heat and let cool in the stock. Transfer fish to a board and remove all the skin except that on the head. Place the fish on a cold platter, decorate with tarragon and sliced truffles or egg whites. Glaze lightly with aspic. Spoon vegetable salad into tart shells or tomato cups. Coat lightly with aspic and arrange on the platter around the fish. Serve with Green Mayonnaise. Makes 6 servings.

Shrimp Sauce

Stir and cook 1 tablespoon finely chopped onion in 2 tablespoons butter 1 minute. Remove from heat and blend in 2 tablespoons flour. Stir and cook 1 minute. Add ¾ cup each milk and fish stock. Mix well. Stir and cook 2 to 3 minutes, or until of sauce consistency. Add 1 teaspoon chopped parsley, a dash of grated nutmeg, salt and freshly ground black pepper to taste, ¼ cup finely diced shrimp, and 1 tablespoon butter. Makes 1¼ cups sauce.

SALMON (SAUMON)

Both European and American salmon inhabit coastal seas and ascend rivers to spawn. One of the delicious food fish, salmon is characterized by its orange-pink color, which varies with the species and the season. It is a large fish, and may be prepared whole, in large pieces cut from the center of the body, or in steaks. Salmon trout (*truite salmonée*), also called sea trout, has flesh of similar color and also spawns in rivers. It is prepared in many of the same ways as salmon. Some recipes calling for either salmon or salmon trout are included here. See also "Trout" and "Whitefish."

Danish Salmon Steaks

1 shallot, finely chopped	Mashed anchovy
2 tablespoons wine vinegar	6 salmon steaks
¼ cup fish stock	Boiling fish stock
½ cup (1 stick) unsalted butter	6 servings boiled potatoes
Ground white pepper	

Cook shallot, vinegar, and stock until the liquid has reduced to 2 tablespoons. Beat in butter, a small piece at a time. Continue beating until the butter is melted and the sauce is thick and foamy. Beat in white pepper and anchovy paste to taste. Set aside. Poach salmon steaks in fish stock. Drain well. Serve with boiled potatoes and the sauce in a sauceboat. Makes 6 servings.

Broiled Salmon Steaks

6 salmon steaks
Oil
Herb or Anchovy Butter

Pat the salmon dry with a clean cloth and brush with oil. Arrange the steaks on an oiled preheated broiler rack and place them under broiler. Cook quickly on both sides. Reduce heat to medium (350°F) and cook until the backbone can be removed easily with the tip of a knife. Serve with Herb or Anchovy Butter. Makes 6 servings.

Salmon Steaks Foyot

6 salmon steaks
Salt
Freshly ground black pepper
Shortening or butter

Noisette Potatoes
½ cup Béarnaise Sauce
1 tablespoon meat glaze

Rub salmon lightly with salt and pepper. Brown on both sides in shortening or butter. Arrange on a platter and encircle with Noisette Potatoes. Make Foyot Sauce by combining Béarnaise Sauce and meat glaze. Serve over fish. Makes 6 servings.

Salmon Fillets Doria

6 (½-pound) slices salmon or
    salmon trout
Salt and freshly ground black pepper
Flour

4 tablespoons (½ stick) butter
Lemon juice
¼ cup browned butter
2 cucumbers, 6 inches long

Sprinkle salmon lightly with salt and pepper. Roll in flour and brown on both sides in some of the butter over medium heat. Transfer fish to a platter. Sprinkle with lemon juice and browned butter. Cut cucumbers in half; remove and discard seeds. Cut cucumbers into lengthwise strips and then cut the strips into 1-inch pieces. Cook 2 to 3 minutes in butter. Serve with the fish. Makes 6 servings.

Chilled Salmon Moscow

2 (1-pound) center pieces of salmon
Court bouillon
Aspic
Peeled cooked shrimp
Anchovies
24 small baked tart shells, cooled

1½ cups cooked vegetable salad (Mimosa)
Caviar
Mayonnaise
Grated fresh horseradish or
    prepared horseradish

Place salmon in a skillet with barely enough court bouillon to cover. Bring to boiling point, reduce heat, and simmer (do not boil again) 10 to 12 minutes, or until the fish flakes when tested with a fork. Do not allow the stock to boil. Cool fish in the stock. Transfer fish to a platter and glaze again with aspic. Garnish with shrimp and anchovies and glaze again with aspic. Fill 12 of the tart shells with vegetable salad. Fill the remaining tart shells with caviar. Glaze all the tarts with aspic and arrange on the platter around the fish. Season Mayonnaise to taste with horseradish and serve with the salmon. Makes 6 servings.

Salmon Fillets Maître d'Hôtel

6 (½-pound) slices salmon or
   salmon trout
Salad oil or clarified butter
½ cup butter

1 teaspoon chopped parsley
1½ tablespoons freshly squeezed
   lemon juice
Salt and freshly ground black pepper

Pat salmon dry, dip in oil or clarified butter, and place on a preheated broiler rack. Broil 3 minutes on each side. Reduce the heat and lower the rack. Cook until the fish flakes when tested with a fork. Transfer fish to a warmed platter and set aside to keep warm. Melt the ½ cup butter in a saucepan and add the remaining ingredients. Serve the butter sauce over the fish. Makes 6 servings.

Poached Whole Salmon with Mousseline Sauce

1 (3½- to 4-pound) dressed salmon
   or salmon trout
Fish stock
Parsley

Lemon wedges
6 servings cooked potatoes
Hollandaise Sauce
Whipped cream

Place fish in a flameproof baking pan and pour in enough cold stock to cover. Slowly bring the stock to the boiling point, reduce heat, and simmer until the fish flakes when tested with a fork. Remove the skin very carefully and transfer fish to a platter. Garnish with parsley and lemon wedges. Put equal parts Hollandaise Sauce and whipped cream in the top of a double boiler. Stir and cook over hot water until sauce is very hot. Serve in a sauceboat. Makes 6 servings.

Whole Poached Salmon Regency

1 (3½- to 4-pound) dressed salmon
   or salmon trout
1¾ cups court bouillon
1¾ cups Velouté Sauce
3 large egg yolks

½ cup finely chopped cooked crayfish
   tails or shrimp
¼ cup (½ stick) butter
6 small fish quenelles
1 cup sautéed mushroom caps

Place the fish in a saucepan large enough to accommodate it. Pour in court bouillon. Bring to the boiling point, reduce heat, and simmer until the fish flakes when tested with a fork. Transfer fish to a platter and set aside to keep warm. Cook the court bouillon until reduced by half and mix 1½ cups of the Velouté Sauce. Blend egg yolks with the remaining ¼ cup Velouté Sauce and add to the bouillon. Stir and cook 30 seconds. Add crayfish, butter, fish quenelles, and mushrooms. Heat and pour over fish. Makes 6 servings.

Russian Coulibiac of Salmon

1½ ounces marrow from the
    backbone of a sturgeon
1 pound salmon
¾ cup buckwheat groats
Beef broth
Brioche dough
½ teaspoon salt
⅛ teaspoon freshly ground
    black pepper

3 hard-cooked eggs, sliced
½ tablespoon chopped parsley
½ tablespoon chopped fresh dill
2 tablespoons chopped onion
6 tablespoons butter
1 raw egg, beaten
Parsley sprigs
Sour cream
Melted butter

Soak sturgeon marrow in cold water overnight. Cover and cook over low heat 5 hours, or until marrow is soft. Cool, then cut into thin slices and set aside. Poach salmon (see directions for Poached Fish), cool, remove skin and bones, and flake the salmon. Set aside. Cook buckwheat groats as directed on the package, but replace the water with beef broth. Cool. Roll out Brioche dough ¼ inch thick in a 12-by-8-inch rectangle. Spread half of the cooked groats down the center of the rectangle of dough and place half of the sturgeon marrow on top. Sprinkle the flaked salmon with salt and pepper and scatter it over the marrow, using it all. Arrange the egg slices over the salmon and sprinkle them with the parsley and dill. Sauté the onion in 1 tablespoon of the butter and scatter it over the egg slices. Cover the egg slices with the rest of the sturgeon marrow and spread the remaining buckwheat over it. Turn the two sides of the dough up, bringing it over the filling and having the edges overlap down the center. Turn up the dough at the ends and place the roll, seam side down, on a lightly buttered baking sheet. Roll the trimmings of the dough ¼ inch thick, cut it into narrow strips, ¼ to ½ inch wide, and arrange them in lattice fashion over the roll. Cut a hole in the center of the top to allow steam to escape as it bakes. Brush the surface with beaten egg. Cover the roll with a clean towel, set it in a warm place (80° to 85°F), and let the dough rise for 30 minutes. Bake in a preheated oven (400°F) 30 minutes, or until browned. Remove from oven. Melt remaining butter and pour it through a funnel into the hole in the top of the crust. Transfer to a serving platter and garnish the platter with parsley. Cut the roll into slices and serve with sour cream and melted butter. Makes 8 to 10 servings.

Cold Steamed Whole Salmon with Artichokes and Asparagus

1 (5- to 6-pound) whole salmon
Salt
Freshly ground black pepper
1 small bay leaf
1 small onion, quartered
¼ cup sliced celery
¼ cup sliced carrot
½ sprig parsley

3 cups aspic
Thick mayonnaise
34 cooked artichoke bottoms
68 cooked asparagus tips, 1½ inches long
Vinaigrette
2 truffles (optional)
34 Deviled Hard-Cooked Egg halves
8 cooked whole crayfish, or shrimp

Ask your fishmonger to scale and gut the salmon, leaving the head, tail, and fins attached. Sprinkle the inside of the body cavity with salt and pepper and fill it with the next 5 ingredients. Close cavity with skewers or toothpicks. Rub salt and pepper over the outside of the fish, wrap it in a large piece of cheesecloth, tie at each end, and place it on a rack in a 17¼-by-11½-by-2¼-inch roasting pan. Pour in boiling water until it just reaches the top of the rack. Cover and steam on the stovetop over surface heat or in a preheated moderate oven (375°F) 30 to 50 minutes (the time depends upon the size of the fish), or only until the fish flakes when tested with a fork. Remove from heat and cool. Discard the stuffing. Strip off and discard the skin from the middle portion of the salmon's body and coat the whole fish with aspic. Chill until the aspic is set. Pour a thin layer of aspic in the bottom of a long fish platter and chill until aspic is set. Transfer fish to the platter and decorate the head and the lines on the body where the unskinned portion meets the skinned portion with thick mayonnaise put through a pastry tube fitted with a thin nozzle. Meanwhile, marinate the artichoke bottoms and asparagus tips in Vinaigrette. Arrange 2 asparagus tips on each artichoke bottom, garnish with bits of truffle and coat with aspic. Chill until aspic is set, then arrange on the platter around the fish. Decorate Deviled Hard-Cooked Egg halves with bits of truffle, coat with aspic, and chill until aspic is set. Place eggs on the platter around the artichoke bottoms and asparagus. If crayfish are used as a garnish, leave heads attached, dip crayfish in aspic, and place them along the lengthwise center of the back. Serve for a cold buffet. Makes 12 to 15 servings.

Cold Whole Salmon d'Orsay

4 cups aspic
1 (3½- to 4-pound) poached salmon
    or salmon trout
18 peeled cooked shrimp, heads on

3 hard-cooked eggs
Caviar
3 medium-sized tomatoes, halved
Green Mayonnaise

Coat the bottom of a tray with a layer of aspic ½ inch thick. Chill. Remove the skin from the back of the fish and place fish on the bed of jellied aspic. Garnish the top center line of the salmon with a row of shrimp with their heads stuck into the salmon Coat shrimp and fish with aspic. Cut eggs in half, remove yolks and save for another use, fill whites with caviar, and place around the fish on the tray, alternating with tomato halves. Coat with aspic. Chill. Serve Green Mayonnaise separately. Makes 6 servings.

Cold Salmon with Shrimp

2 (3½- to 4-pound) dressed salmon
    or salmon trout
Fish stock
Aspic
About 18 peeled cooked shrimp
18 slices truffle, or black olive slices
1 envelope unflavored gelatin
¼ cup water
Mayonnaise

6 medium-small tomatoes
1 cup mixed cooked vegetable salad
4 hard-cooked eggs, sliced
2 gherkin pickles, sliced
6 baked 1½-inch pastry shells
24 cooked asparagus tips, 1 inch long
⅓ cup thick Velouté Sauce
6 thin slices cucumber

Poach the fish (with head attached) in stock. Remove from heat and allow fish to cool in the stock. Coat a long platter with aspic and chill until aspic is set. Remove fish from the stock, drain well, and remove the skin. Place fish on the aspic-coated platter. Arrange a row of shrimp down the center of the back. Garnish each shrimp with a slice of truffle or black olive. Soften gelatin in the ¼ cup water and set in a pan of hot water to melt. Add to 1 cup Mayonnaise, mix well, and push the mixture through a pastry bag, using a small nozzle, to decorate the fish around the head and around the shrimp. Cut tomatoes in half and scoop out the centers. Drain well and fill with vegetable salad. Top each with a slice of egg and garnish with a little tomato and a slice of gherkin pickle. Coat with aspic. Fill pastry shells with asparagus tips. Cover with Velouté Sauce. Top each with a thin slice of cucumber and a slice of hard-cooked egg. Garnish with bits of tomato. Coat with aspic. Arrange the tomatoes and pastry shells around the fish. Serve additional Mayonnaise separately in a sauceboat. Makes 6 to 8 servings.

Salmon Cutlets Pojarsky

1¼ pounds boned, skinned salmon
2 cups soft white breadcrumbs
½ cup milk
4 eggs
6 tablespoons softened butter

1 teaspoon lemon juice
Salt and freshly ground black pepper
Fine dry breadcrumbs
6 servings cooked vegetables (peas, carrots,
    green beans, and so on)

Very finely chop salmon or put it through a food chopper, using the finest blade. Soak soft breadcrumbs in milk, squeeze dry, and add crumbs to the salmon. Beat in 2 of the eggs. Add 3 tablespoons of the butter and the lemon juice. Mix well. Season with salt and pepper. Shape the mixture into 6 large or 12 small cutlets on a floured board. Beat the 2 remaining eggs together with 2 tablespoons water and dip cutlets into the egg mixture, then roll in fine dry breadcrumbs. Cook over lower heat in the remaining butter, adding more butter as needed. Arrange cutlets in a ring on a warmed dish. Toss cooked vegetables in butter and spoon into the center of the dish. Makes 6 servings.

Salmon Mousse

1 quart aspic
Sliced hard-cooked egg, tomato,
    and truffles
1 cup finely flaked cooked salmon
½ cup (1 stick) softened butter

⅓ cup heavy cream
¼ cup thick Béchamel Sauce
Freshly squeezed lemon juice
Salt and ground black pepper

Pour a ¼-inch layer of aspic in an 8-inch square pan. Chill until firm and set aside for later use. Coat the bottom and sides of a 1-quart charlotte mold or ring mold with aspic. Chill until almost firm. Decorate as desired with eggs, bits of tomato, and truffles. Cover with a thin layer of aspic and chill until firm and ready to use. Let remaining aspic stand at room temperature until ready to use later. Blend salmon with butter until smooth. Gradually beat in cream and Béchamel Sauce. Season to taste with lemon juice, salt, and pepper. Turn into the prepared mold. Finish filling the mold with the liquid aspic. Chill until the mousse is set. Unmold on a round serving plate. Cut triangles from the firm aspic and arrange on the plate around the mold. Makes 6 servings.

Salmon Mousseline Chantilly

1¼ pounds boned raw salmon
2 large egg whites
1¾ cups heavy cream
1 teaspoon salt
¼ teaspoon freshly ground black pepper
Dash cayenne

Hollandaise Sauce
Whipped cream
6 whole cooked shrimp or crayfish tails
2 cups cooked buttered mushroom caps
Chopped chervil or parsley

Put salmon through a food chopper, using the finest blade. Pound and beat the salmon with a spoon. Set the bowl in a pan of cracked ice. Gradually beat in egg whites, using a wooden spoon. Gradually beat in cream. Add salt, pepper, and cayenne. Spoon into well-buttered custard cups, place cups in a pan of hot water, and bake in a preheated oven (350°F) 20-30 minutes, or until a knife inserted in the center comes out clean. Unmold the timbales onto a serving dish. Combine equal parts Hollandaise Sauce and whipped cream. Serve over the timbales. Garnish each with a shrimp or a crayfish tail. Fill center of the dish with mushrooms. Sprinkle with chopped chervil or parsley. Makes 6 servings.

Salmon Loaf Valois

1¼ pounds boned raw salmon
1 egg
3 egg yolks
¾ cup Béchamel Sauce
½ cup heavy cream

1 teaspoon salt
¼ teaspoon freshly ground black pepper
1½ teaspoons chopped fresh thyme
Parsley
Béarnaise Sauce

Put salmon through a food chopper, using the finest blade. Pound and beat the salmon with a wooden spoon. Beat in whole egg and egg yolks. Stir in Béchamel Sauce, cream, salt, pepper, and thyme. Push through a sieve. Spoon into buttered custard cups. Place cups in a pan of hot water and bake in a preheated oven (350°F) 20-30 minutes, or until a knife inserted in the center comes out clean. Turn the loaf out onto a platter and garnish with parsley. Serve Béarnaise Sauce in a sauceboat. Makes 6 servings.

SHAD (ALOSE)

SHAD RESEMBLES HERRING but is larger. As with herring, the roe of the shad is highly prized.

English Grilled Whole Shad

3½ to 4 pounds dressed shad
Pure vegetable oil
½ teaspoon salt
¼ teaspoon freshly ground black pepper
Flour

2 slices bacon
2 tablespoons butter, melted
6 servings buttered boiled potatoes
Lemon wedges
Parsley

Score the fish, oil lightly, rub with salt and pepper, and roll in flour. Place the bacon on the shad and put the fish in a baking dish and bake in a preheated oven (325°F) 40 to 50 minutes, or until fish is flaky when tested with a fork. Baste with melted butter and place under the broiler 4 inches from the heat source to brown. Transfer shad to a serving platter and pour the pan juices over it. Serve, with buttered boiled potatoes, garnish with lemon wedges and parsley. Makes 6 servings.

Whole Shad with Sorrel

¼ cup olive oil
2 tablespoons lemon juice
1 small bay leaf
1 teaspoon chopped fresh thyme
1 tablespoon chopped parsley
½ teaspoon salt

⅛ teaspoon freshly ground black pepper
3½ to 4 pounds dressed shad
3 pounds sorrel, stemmed
2 tablespoons butter
Salt and freshly ground black pepper

Combine oil, lemon juice, and seasonings. Pour over shad and marinate for 2 hours. Broil 4 inches from the heat source for 12 to 15 minutes, turning carefully to brown both sides. Fish is done when it is flaky when tested with a fork. Wash sorrel and cook it in butter with the water that clings to the leaves, until it is very soft. Drain, press out all the water possible, and push through a sieve. Add salt and pepper. Serve over shad. Makes 6 servings.

SOLE

THE TRUE EUROPEAN OR "DOVER" SOLE is considered the finest of the flat fish. It is found in most European waters but not in American waters, though it is sometimes imported. In the United States, "sole" is usually flounder or other flat fish. Other fish that can be filleted and poached in the same way as sole include whiting, pollack, dab, and freshwater trout.

Sole Meunière

Allow 1 (½-pound) sole per person. Fry as directed for Fried Fish. Place on a warm platter. Serve very hot, with wedges of lemon.

Sole à l'Anglaise

This name is applied to three methods of cooking sole:
- Broil sole as directed in the recipe for Broiled Fish. Serve with melted butter or Maître d'Hôtel Butter and boiled potatoes.
- Simmer sole in equal parts milk and lightly salted water 8 minutes, or until the fish flakes when tested with a fork. Serve with melted butter and boiled potatoes.
- Dip serving-size pieces of sole in egg beaten together with water (1 tablespoon water to each egg), roll in fine dry breadcrumbs, and brown in butter. Serve with soft Maître d'Hôtel Butter.

Allow 2 pounds fillets for 6 servings.

Deep-Fried Sole with Lemon

Allow 1 (½-pound) sole per person. Dip fish in lightly salted milk, roll in flour, and shake off surplus. Fry until golden brown in deep fat preheated to 375°F. Drain on paper towels. Sprinkle salt and pepper lightly on both sides of fish. Put a handful of thoroughly dried washed parsley in the hot fat and remove it immediately with a perforated spoon or skimmer. Arrange this around the fish as a garnish, along with lemon slices.

Deep-Fried Sole

Allow 1 (½-pound) sole per person. Fry in deep fat as directed for Deep-Fried Fish. Serve very hot on a warm platter, garnished with fried parsley and lemon slices.

Whole Sole Saint-Germain

6 (½-pound) dressed sole
Salt
Freshly ground black pepper
Flour
½ cup (1 stick) butter, melted

Fine white breadcrumbs
12 small (1½ inches in diameter)
    parboiled potatoes
Béarnaise Sauce

Pat sole dry. Sprinkle lightly with salt and pepper, dredge in flour, dip in ¼ cup of the melted butter, and then roll in breadcrumbs. Press the fish down well with a spatula. Place on a buttered broiler rack and sprinkle with 3 tablespoons melted butter. Cook in a broiler 4 to 5 inches from heat source until browned, turning to brown both sides. (Or, if desired, bake in a well-buttered baking dish in a preheated oven [350°F] 25 minutes, or until fish has browned.) Roll potatoes in remaining butter. Arrange in a baking pan and bake in a preheated oven (350°F) 25 minutes, or until browned. (If fish is baked, the potatoes may be baked at the same time.) Transfer fish to a warmed platter, and place potatoes around fish. Serve Béarnaise Sauce separately. Makes 6 servings.

Fillets of Sole Bercy

2 shallots, chopped
¼ cup chopped parsley
¼ cup dry white wine
¼ cup fish stock
2 pounds fillet of sole

Salt and ground white pepper
1 tablespoon freshly squeezed lemon juice
3 tablespoons butter
Parsley sprigs
Lemon wedges

Sprinkle chopped shallots and parsley in the bottom of a well-buttered baking dish. Add wine and stock. Rub both sides of sole fillets lightly with salt and white pepper, and arrange over shallots. Sprinkle with lemon juice and dot with butter. Cook, uncovered, in a preheated oven (350°F) 20 minutes, basting twice with the pan liquid. Place under broiler heat to brown. Arrange on a warm platter and garnish with parsley and lemon wedges. Makes 6 servings.

Whole Sole Mornay

6 (½-pound) sole
Salt and freshly ground black
    pepper

1½ cups dry white wine
1 cup Mornay Sauce
¼ cup grated Gruyère cheese

Sprinkle sole lightly with salt and pepper. Heat wine in a skillet, add fish, and simmer 8 to 10 minutes, or until fish flakes when tested with a fork. Transfer sole to a buttered heatproof platter. Cook the wine until reduced by half, add to Mornay Sauce, and spread over fish. Sprinkle with cheese. Brown under broiler. Makes 6 servings.

Whole Sole Colbert

6 (½-pound) sole
1 cup milk
½ teaspoon salt
Flour
2 eggs, beaten with 2 tablespoons water
Fine white breadcrumbs

Oil for frying
½ cup softened butter
½ teaspoon chopped parsley
½ teaspoon chopped fresh tarragon
½ teaspoon melted beef extract
Salt and freshly ground black pepper

Split the sole along the side from which the dark skin has been removed. Raise the fillets so that the backbone can be loosened. Cut or break the backbone in two or three places so that it can be removed easily after cooking. (If your fishmonger knows how to do this, ask him to do it for you.) Soak the sole 10 minutes in milk to which salt has been added, drain, roll in flour, dip in beaten egg, and then roll in fine dry breadcrumbs. Fry in deep fat preheated to 375°F until fish has browned. Drain on paper towels. Remove the backbone. Combine remaining ingredients and place in the backbone cavity. Serve on a platter. Makes 6 servings.

Fillets of Sole Bonne Femme

6 (½-pound) fillets of sole
Salt and freshly ground black
    pepper
1 shallot, minced
¼ cup finely chopped mushrooms
½ cup hot fish stock
½ cup hot dry white wine

1 small bay leaf
2 tablespoons chopped parsley
½ teaspoon chopped thyme
18 small mushroom caps
3 tablespoons butter
1 tablespoon flour
1 tablespoon butter

Sprinkle fillets lightly with salt and pepper. Arrange in the bottom of a well-buttered baking dish and sprinkle with shallots and chopped mushrooms. Add stock, wine, bay leaf, parsley, and thyme. Cover and bake in a preheated oven (350°F) 15 to 20 minutes, or until the fish flakes when tested with a fork. Drain the liquid into a small saucepan. Cook until the liquid has been reduced to 1 cup. Transfer fish to a heatproof platter. Cook mushroom caps in 2 tablespoons of the butter about 5 minutes and place 3 on each serving of fish. Blend the flour with the remaining 1 tablespoon butter and add to the reduced liquid. Bring to the boiling point and cook 2 minutes, stirring constantly. Pour the sauce over the fillets, covering them completely. Place the dish under the broiler just until the top is glazed. Serve hot. Makes 6 servings.

Fillets of Sole in Red Wine Sauce

3 (1-pound) fillets of sole
Salt and freshly ground black
  pepper
2 shallots, finely chopped
1 cup dry red Burgundy

½ cup Demi-Glace Sauce
1 tablespoon flour
3 tablespoons butter
24 glazed pearl onions
24 small mushroom caps sautéed in butter

Sprinkle fillets lightly with salt and pepper and place in a well-buttered flameproof baking dish. Add shallots and wine. Cover and simmer 8 to 10 minutes, or until the fish flakes when tested with a fork. Drain off the cooking liquid, strain into a saucepan, and cook until reduced by half. Add Demi-Glace Sauce and cook 30 seconds. Blend flour with 2 tablespoons of the butter. Mix with the sauce and stir and cook 1 minute. Add the rest of the butter. Transfer fillets to a platter and cover with the sauce. Garnish with onions and mushroom caps. Makes 6 servings.

Fillets of Sole with Almonds

6 fillets of sole
Salt and freshly ground black
  pepper
6 tablespoons butter

¼ cup slivered blanched almonds
Lemon wedges
Parsley

Sprinkle fillets lightly with salt and pepper. Sauté in butter over medium heat until lightly browned. Transfer fish to a warm platter and set aside in a warm place. In the butter that is left in the skillet, cook almonds until golden. Pour almonds and butter over the fillets of sole. Garnish with lemon wedges and parsley. Makes 6 servings.

Fillets of Sole with Quenelles, Artichokes, Truffles, and Lobster Sauce Herriot

3 (1-pound) fillets of sole
Salt and freshly ground black
  pepper
1 shallot, chopped
2 tablespoons freshly squeezed
  lemon juice
¾ cup fish stock
¾ cup dry white wine

18 Fish Quenelles
12 small artichoke hearts, quartered
1 truffle
1 cup Lobster Sauce

Sprinkle fillets lightly with salt and pepper. Fold fillets in half and place in a buttered flameproof baking dish. Sprinkle with shallot and lemon juice. Add stock. Cover and simmer 5-8 minutes, or until the fish flakes when tested with a fork. Drain cooking liquid into a small saucepan, add wine, and cook until it has reduced to ⅓ cup. Add quenelles to the sauce and keep warm. Sauté artichoke hearts until tender but not mushy. Season with salt and pepper. Arrange fish fillets down the center of a platter, having them overlap. Top each with a slice of truffle. Cover with Lobster Sauce. Garnish with quenelles at one end of the platter and artichokes at the other. Makes 6 servings.

Fillets of Sole with Shrimp and Hollandaise Montcalm

2 pounds fillets of sole
Salt and ground white pepper
½ cup dry white wine
¾ cup Hollandaise Sauce

6 medium-sized boiled potatoes
⅓ cup diced cooked shrimp
⅔ cup fish Velouté Sauce

Sprinkle fillets lightly with salt and white pepper. Simmer in wine in a covered saucepan 8 to 10 minutes, or until the fish flakes when tested with a fork. Transfer fish to a warmed platter and set aside in a warm place. Cook the liquid until reduced by half, then blend with the Hollandaise Sauce. Arrange potatoes on a platter around the fish and coat them with the sauce. Mix shrimp with Velouté Sauce and spread over fish. Makes 6 servings.

Fillets of Sole with Crayfish and Truffles Paillard

1 pound boned whiting
½ cup heavy cream
2 egg whites
Salt and freshly ground black
    pepper
12 whole crayfish
Dry white wine

6 fillets of sole
1½ cups fish Velouté Sauce
2 tablespoons butter
1 cup sliced mushrooms,
    sautéed in butter
Chopped truffle
6 thin slices truffle

Puree the whiting with 2 tablespoons of the cream through a food chopper, using the finest blade. Stir and beat fish with a wooden spoon, beating in the egg whites. Set the bowl in a pan of ice water. Gradually beat the remaining cream into the fish. Beat well. Season with salt and pepper. Cook the crayfish in a little wine until they turn red, about 5 minutes. Peel crayfish and remove the meat from the shells. Empty the heads, reserving 6 heads for decoration. Set the crayfish aside. Pat the sole fillets dry, spread with a layer of the whiting mixture and fold them over in half. Arrange fillets down the center of a heatproof platter and place a crayfish head at the pointed end of each. Fill the space between them with remaining forcemeat to hold the heads in place. Pour in ½ cup of the wine in which the crayfish was cooked. Cover and bake 15 to 20 minutes in a preheated oven (350°F). Drain the wine from the platter into a small saucepan, and cook until it has reduced to ⅓ cup. Mix with ½ cup of the Velouté Sauce. Heat, adjust seasonings, stir in butter and truffles, and spoon over the cooked rolled fillets. Combine the remaining Velouté Sauce, the crayfish meat, and mushrooms. Add salt and pepper to taste and pour the mixture around the fillets. Garnish each serving with a slice of truffle, if desired. Makes 6 servings.

Fillets of Sole with Anchovies Monte Carlo

2 pounds fillets of sole	¼ cup olive oil
Salt and freshly ground black pepper	2 tablespoons mashed anchovies
Flour	½ cup (1 stick) butter, melted
	6 anchovies

Cut fillets into 6 equal portions. Sprinkle lightly with salt and pepper. Roll in flour. Fry in hot oil over medium heat until fillets have browned on both sides. Transfer to a warmed platter. Combine mashed anchovies and butter and pour over fish. Garnish as desired with whole anchovy fillets. Makes 6 servings.

Fillets of Sole with Artichokes and Potatoes Murat

2 pounds fillets of sole	5 medium-sized potatoes, peeled and diced
1 teaspoon salt	6 tablespoons butter
¼ teaspoon freshly ground black pepper	6 raw artichoke bottoms
½ cup milk	3 firm, ripe tomatoes, thickly sliced
Flour	Chopped parsley
¼ cup oil or shortening	

Cut fillets in half lengthwise. Add ½ teaspoon of the salt and ⅛ teaspoon of the pepper to the milk, dip fish in seasoned milk, and roll it in flour. Fry in oil until crisp and brown. Set aside in a warm place. Parboil potatoes 2 to 3 minutes, drain off water, toss in 2 tablespoons of the butter, and cool. Fry potatoes until brown in butter, using as little as possible. Set aside in a warm place. Dice artichoke bottoms, and cook in butter. Mix lightly with potatoes and fish, and put all into a serving dish. Fry tomatoes in butter and arrange on top of the dish. Sprinkle lightly with salt, pepper, and parsley. Makes 6 servings.

Fillets of Sole with Shrimp Venini

10½ pounds sole
1 quart cold water
⅓ cup chopped onion
⅔ cup dry white wine
Salt
9 tablespoons butter

¼ cup Béchamel Sauce
½ cup heavy cream
30 peeled and deveined shrimp
2 tablespoons brandy
¾ cup Tomato Sauce

Fillet the sole. Put the bones, skins, and heads in a saucepan with water, onion, ⅓ cup of the wine, and 1 teaspoon salt. Cover, bring to the boiling point, reduce heat, and simmer 30 minutes. Strain the stock and cool until reduced to 3 cups. Poach the sole fillets in the stock and the remaining wine until the fish flakes when tested with a fork. Arrange the fillets, overlapping, around the bottom of a serving dish and keep them warm. Strain the cooking liquor into a saucepan and cook until reduced by half. Add 4 tablespoons of the butter and bring to the boiling point. Beat in Béchamel Sauce and simmer until of sauce consistency. Stir in cream and 3 tablespoons of the butter and beat with a whisk. Keep warm. Cook shrimp in remaining 2 tablespoons butter in a skillet until shrimp turns red. Flame with the brandy. Remove shrimp and keep them warm. Add Tomato Sauce to the skillet and cook 5 minutes. Adjust seasonings. Cover the sole with the Béchamel Sauce mixture. Arrange the shrimp in a circle inside the circle of sole fillets in the dish and pour the Tomato Sauce in the center. Makes 10 servings.

Paupiettes of Sole with Shrimp and Mussels Daumont

3 pounds boned whiting
1 cup heavy cream
4 egg whites
Salt and freshly ground black pepper
2 pounds fillets of sole
18 crayfish tails or shrimp
½ cup dry white wine

¼ cup finely chopped mushrooms
2 cups Béchamel Sauce
¼ cup (½ stick) butter
1 tablespoon flour
2 quarts Herbed Steamed Mussels

Puree whiting through a food chopper with 4 tablespoons of the cream, using the finest blade. Stir and beat in the egg whites, using a wooden spoon or an electric mixer. Set the bowl in a pan of ice water. Gradually beat in the remaining cream. Beat well. Season with salt and pepper. Cut sole fillets into 12 pieces of uniform size and shape, pat them dry, spread each with a layer of whiting mixture, and fold each over in half. Arrange the fillets in a ring in a buttered baking dish. Put crayfish in a saucepan, cover with water, and add ½ teaspoon salt. Bring to the boiling point, reduce heat, and simmer 5 minutes, or until the crayfish turn red. Drain off water, reserving 1 cup for later use. Peel the crayfish and set aside. Add wine to crayfish cooking water, heat, and pour over the fillets. Add mushrooms. Cover and bake in a preheated oven (350°F) 15 to 20 minutes, or until the fish flakes when tested with a fork. Drain off the stock, strain it through a fine sieve, cook until reduced to ½ cup, and add Béchamel Sauce. Very finely mash 6 of the crayfish and blend with the butter and flour. Add to the sauce and cook until of desired thickness. Pour over fillets of sole. Place a crayfish or shrimp between each pair of fillets. Remove the steamed mussels from their shells and put them in the center of the dish. Makes 6 servings.

Paupiettes of Sole in Cream

1½ cups mushrooms, finely chopped	½ cup milk
3 tablespoons butter	Fritter Batter
½ cup each chopped onion, chives, and parsley	Fine white breadcrumbs
	4 to 6 tablespoons butter
Salt and freshly ground black pepper	3 tablespoons flour
	1 cup dry white wine
6 fillets of sole	1 cup heavy cream
2 eggs, beaten	⅓ cup grated Parmesan cheese

Cook mushrooms in butter 5 minutes. Add onion, chives, and parsley and cook 2 to 3 minutes, or until vegetables are soft enough to spread. Add salt and pepper. Sprinkle fish lightly with salt and pepper and spread uniformly with the cooked mushroom mixture. Roll up, jelly-roll fashion, and fasten the seams with toothpicks. Beat eggs together with milk and dip the fish rolls into the mixture. Then dip them in Fritter Batter, roll in breadcrumbs, and set aside for 10 minutes for coating to dry. Brown on all sides in butter. Transfer to a warm heatproof platter and set aside in a warm place. Blend flour with the butter left in the skillet. Stir and cook 1 minute. Add wine. Stir and cook until sauce is smooth and thickened. Add cream, mix well, and heat. Pour the sauce into the platter around the fish. Sprinkle with cheese and brown under the broiler. Makes 6 servings.

Vol-au-Vent of Sole Fillets with Shrimp and Crayfish la Vallière

8 (3-ounce) fillets of sole	1 cup cooked mussels
1 cup whiting forcemeat	3½ cups Nantua Sauce
½ cup fish stock	Salt and freshly ground black pepper
½ cup dry white wine	
1 cup sautéed sliced mushrooms	1 large (8-inch) hot puff pastry case (vol-au-vent)
1 cup peeled, deveined cooked shrimp	
8 crayfish tails	8 slices truffle

Pound the fillets lightly with a spatula. Spread each with a layer of whiting force-meat, fold in half, and poach in stock and wine until the fish flakes when tested with a fork, 8 to 10 minutes. Combine mushrooms, shrimp, crayfish, mussels, and Nantua Sauce. Season with salt and pepper. Place the hot vol-au-vent on a serving plate. Fill with the shellfish and mushroom mixture, arrange the fillets over the top, slightly overlapping, and garnish each with a truffle slice. Serve very hot. Makes 8 servings.

Chaud-Froid of Sole Fillets with Vegetable Salad

4 (4-pound) fillets of sole
Salt and freshly ground black
    pepper
Freshly squeezed lemon juice
⅓ cup dry white wine
¼ cup chopped onion
1 cup each cooked peas, diced cooked
    carrots, diced cooked potatoes,
    and diced raw celery

2 teaspoons unflavored gelatin
3 tablespoons cold water
¾ cup Mayonnaise
Chaud-Froid Sauce
Chervil leaves
Aspic

Fold fillets in half. Trim them uniformly and place them in a buttered baking dish. Sprinkle with salt, pepper, 3 tablespoons lemon juice, and the wine. Cover and bake in a preheated oven (350°F) 15-20 minutes, or until the fish flakes when tested with a fork. Transfer fish to a flat surface and cool under slight pressure. Combine vegetables with salt, pepper, and lemon juice to taste. Soften gelatin in water, set in a pan of hot water to melt, mix with the Mayonnaise, and add to the vegetable salad. Mix lightly and turn the salad into a flat round dish. Chill. Arrange sole fillets on a wire rack and coat with Chaud-Froid Sauce. Before the sauce sets, decorate each fillet with a chervil leaf dipped in liquid aspic. Chill until the coating is set. Coat with semi-liquid aspic and chill until set. Turn out the vegetable salad into the center of a large round serving plate and arrange the fillets over it with the tips pointing toward the center. Fill between the fillets with chopped aspic. Surround the salad with diced aspic. Makes 8 servings.

Fillets of Sole in Aspic

2 pounds fillets of sole
Salt and freshly ground black
    pepper
Freshly squeezed lemon juice
1 cup dry white wine

1 truffle, sliced
Aspic
Mayonnaise or Ravigote or
    Green Mayonnaise

Cut sole fillets into 6 equal portions. Sprinkle with salt, pepper, and lemon juice. Place in a skillet, add wine, bring to the boiling point, reduce heat, and simmer 8 to 10 minutes, or until the fish flakes when tested with a fork. Cool the fillets in the stock under slight pressure. Trim edges uniformly and place fish on a platter. Garnish with truffle, coat with almost-set aspic, and chill. Surround with chopped aspic. Serve with a cold sauce—plain Mayonnaise, or Ravigote, or Green Mayonnaise. Makes 6 servings.

Chaud-Froid of Sole Fillets Floralies

12 fillets of sole (4 pounds total)	3 cups aspic
Fish stock	4 cups macédoine of cooked vegetables
Chaud-Froid Sauce	4 firm ripe tomatoes
Pimiento	Thick Mayonnaise
Cucumber pickle	13 black olives

Fold fillets in half, trim them uniformly, and poach in stock according to directions for Poached Fish. Transfer fish to a flat surface, cover with aluminum foil, and place a large plate on the foil in order to give a little pressure to the fish as it cools. Place a wire cooling rack on a baking sheet and arrange the cold sole fillets on the rack. Coat with Chaud-Froid Sauce. Before the sauce sets, simulate flowers on each fillet with small pieces of pimiento. Make stems and leaves with thin slices of cucumber pickle. Chill. Glaze with aspic. Chill again until aspic is set. Pour a thin layer of aspic on a large serving plate and chill until aspic is firm. Turn the cooked vegetables into the center of the tray and spread them to form a circle. Place the fillets of sole on the vegetables, forming a ring with the small ends pointed inward. Encircle with sliced tomatoes. Using a pastry bag and a leaf nozzle, pipe enough Mayonnaise around the vegetables to cover the edges and a portion of the tomato slices. Place olives between the large ends of the fillets. Serve cold. Makes 12 servings.

STURGEON (ESTURGEON)

STURGEON IS OFTEN CUT INTO THICK STEAKS, larded and braised, and served with vegetables. Sturgeon is also served with sauces, such as Curry, Hongroise, Velouté, or Mushroom Sauce.

Sturgeon Braised in White Wine

2½ pounds sturgeon	Butter
Thin narrow strips fatty salt pork (lardoons)	1 large carrot
	1 medium-sized onion
Salt and freshly ground black pepper	1 cup dry white wine

Remove skin and bones from sturgeon and lard one side with lardoons. Sprinkle lightly with salt and pepper. Brown on both sides in butter. Peel and slice carrot and onion and add. Pour in wine. Cover and braise in a preheated oven (325°F) 25 to 30 minutes, or until the fish flakes when tested with a fork. Transfer sturgeon and vegetables to a warmed platter. Cook the braising stock until reduced by three-fourths. Pour over fish. Makes 6 servings.

Sturgeon Fillets with Lemon

2½ pounds sturgeon
Salt and freshly ground black
  pepper
Flour

6 tablespoons butter
Freshly squeezed lemon juice
Chopped parsley

Remove skin and bones from the sturgeon and cut fish into slices weighing about 4 ounces each. Sprinkle lightly with salt and pepper. Roll the pieces in flour and brown on both sides in 3 tablespoons of the butter. Remove fish to a warm platter. Sprinkle with lemon juice. Melt remaining butter and pour over the fish. Garnish with parsley. Makes 6 servings.

TROUT (TRAIL DE RIVIERE)

THERE ARE MANY VARIETIES OF FRESHWATER TROUT, all delicious, though trout caught in mountain streams is particularly prized. Char is a related species, found in deep lakes. Recipes calling for salmon or salmon trout can usually be used for freshwater trout.

Whole Trout with Almonds

1 teaspoon salt
1 cup milk
6 (½-pound) dressed trout

Flour
Butter
⅓ cup sliced blanched almonds

Add salt to milk and dip trout into it. Roll in flour. Brown on both sides in butter over medium heat. Transfer trout to a warm platter. Put 2 more tablespoons butter in a skillet. Add almonds and stir and cook until almonds are brown. Pour over the trout. Makes 6 servings.

Fried Whole Trout

In the recipe for Trout with Almonds, omit the almonds and serve the browned trout with sizzling browned butter. Sprinkle with lemon juice. Garnish with parsley and lemon wedges. Allow 1 (½-pound) trout per person.

Fried Trout with Mushrooms Mantua

Fry 6 (½-pound) trout, as directed in Whole Trout with Almonds, omitting the almonds. Meanwhile, cook 1 teaspoon chopped shallot and 2 peeled, seeded, chopped tomatoes in ¾ cup Marsala until tomatoes are soft and the sauce is reduced by half. Cook 3 tablespoons finely chopped mushrooms in 1 tablespoon butter and add. Stir in 2 tablespoons finely chopped cooked lean ham, and salt, pepper, and lemon juice to taste. Serve over fish. Sprinkle with chopped parsley. Makes 6 servings.

Whole Trout Glazed in Red Wine

1 medium-sized onion, sliced
Salt and freshly ground black
    pepper
6 (½-pound) dressed trout
1¾ cups dry red wine

Heart-shaped fried white-bread
    Croutons

Scatter onion slices in the bottom of a large flameproof baking dish. Sprinkle salt and pepper lightly over trout and arrange them over the onion. Pour wine over the fish. Bring to the boiling point, reduce heat, and cook until the fish flakes when tested with a fork. Drain the wine into a small saucepan and reduce by half. Pour over trout. Quickly glaze under the broiler. Serve on a platter garnished with croutons. Makes 6 servings.

Glazed Whole Trout Hussarde

3 tablespoons chopped onion
4 tablespoons butter
1 cup sliced onion
3 cups soft breadcrumbs
½ cup milk
¼ teaspoon chopped thyme

1 tablespoon chopped parsley
Freshly ground black pepper
Salt
1 egg, beaten
6 (½-pound) dressed trout
¾ cup dry white wine

Cook chopped onion in 2 tablespoons of the butter until onion is transparent. Transfer the onion to a mixing bowl. In the same skillet, add 2 more tablespoons of the butter and the sliced onion. Cook until onion is transparent, then place in the bottom of a baking pan. Soak breadcrumbs in milk, squeeze them dry, fluff them with a fork, and add to the chopped onion. Stir in fresh herbs, ⅛ teaspoon pepper, salt, and egg. Spoon into the body cavities of trout. Close cavities with toothpicks. Place fish on the cooked onion slices in the baking pan. Sprinkle with salt and pepper.

Pour in wine. Place in a preheated oven (350°F) and bake 25 to 30 minutes, or until the fish flakes when tested with a fork. Pour off stock into a saucepan and boil until reduced by half. Season with salt and pepper to taste. Pour over trout. Glaze quickly under the broiler. Makes 6 servings.

Baked Whole Trout Mâcon

6 (½-pound) dressed trout	Bouillon
1¾ cups red wine	Salt
2 cups sliced onions	2 cups small mushroom caps
6 tablespoons butter	1 rounded teaspoon meat glaze

Place trout in a baking pan. Pour in wine. Bake in a preheated oven (350°F) 30 minutes, or until the fish flakes when tested with a fork. Set aside and keep warm. Brown the onions in 3 tablespoons of the butter. Add enough bouillon to cover the onions by more than half. Add ½ teaspoon salt. Simmer until the liquid has evaporated and onions are glazed. Set aside and keep warm. Sauté mushrooms in 3 tablespoons of the butter until tender. Drain the wine from the trout into a saucepan and boil it down a little more than half. Add meat glaze. Adjust seasonings. Transfer trout to a platter and pour the sauce over it. Pile mushrooms at one end of the platter and onions at the other end.

Boned Whole Trout Renato

6 (½-pound) dressed boned trout	1 cup dry white wine
Salt and freshly ground black pepper	6 servings steamed potatoes
6 teaspoons capers	1 whole large tomato, peeled
6 anchovies, diced	Chopped parsley
¼ cup olive oil	Lemon slices, cut in half
	Black olives

Open trout flat like a book and sprinkle lightly with salt and pepper. Scatter 1 teaspoon capers and 2 diced anchovy on each. Fold the tail toward the head. Pour oil and wine in a skillet and add trout. Cover, bring to the boiling point, reduce heat, and simmer 10 minutes, or until the fish flakes when tested with a fork. Transfer trout to a round serving dish and keep hot. Cook and reduce the liquid. Season to taste with salt and pepper and pour over fish. Arrange the potatoes around the fish. Cut the tomato into 6 wedges and place it in the center of the dish in its original shape. Sprinkle with parsley. Place lemon slices around the edge of the dish. Garnish with olives. Makes 6 servings.

Trout in Aspic

Red wine may be substituted for white wine in this recipe, and the fish decorated with truffles and small balls of turnip and carrot instead of the shrimp and herbs.

8 (½-pound) trout
Salt and freshly ground black
    pepper
2 teaspoons chopped fresh thyme
1 small bay leaf
1 small onion, sliced

1 cup dry white wine
2 cups fish aspic
¼ pound peeled cooked shrimp
Blanched tarragon leaves or parsley
    or watercress

Cook the trout in seasonings and wine as in the recipe for Glazed Trout Andréa. Cool in the stock. Arrange trout on a large platter that has been coated thinly with aspic, then coat the trout with aspic. Decorate as desired with shrimp and tarragon leaves. Makes 6 servings.

Glazed Whole Trout in Aspic Andréa

6 (½-pound) trout
1 cup dry white wine
1 cup fish stock
2 teaspoons chopped fresh tarragon
Radishes, sliced

Whole tarragon leaves and stems
6 baked 2-inch pastry shells, cooled
1½ cups Shrimp Mousse
6 peeled cooked shrimp
Parsley

Ask the fishmonger to clean the trout through the gills without cutting open the stomach. Cut off fins, remove scales, and wash. Place the fish in a large buttered baking pan. Add wine, stock, and chopped fresh tarragon. Bake in a preheated oven (325°F) 10-15 minutes, or until the fish flakes when tested with a fork. Remove from the oven and cool in the stock. Transfer fish to a large platter. Set aside. Make aspic from the stock, using the recipe in this book. Garnish the fish with radishes, and tarragon leaves and stems. Coat lightly with semiliquid aspic. Chill until aspic is set. Fill the pastry shells with Shrimp Mousse; garnish each with a whole shrimp. Coat with aspic. Chill until set. Just before serving arrange the tarts on the tray with the fish. Garnish with parsley. Makes 6 servings.

Salmon Trout in Aspic Vladimir

1 (4- to 5-pound) dressed salmon trout
Fish stock
Fish aspic
8 large hard-cooked eggs
½ cup (1 stick) softened butter
¼ cup Mayonnaise

Salt and freshly ground black pepper
Spinach puree
Tomato puree
1 lemon
Green Mayonnaise

Poach trout in fish stock. Remove from heat and cool in the stock. Remove skin, and chill the fish. Cut out the fillets, slice them, and place them, with the rest of the fish, in the original shape on a large tray. Coat with aspic. Cut eggs in half and remove yolks. Push the yolks through a sieve, blend with butter, add Mayonnaise, and season to taste with salt and pepper. Divide the mixture into two equal parts. Add spinach puree to one half and tomato puree to the remaining half, until the mixtures are the desired colors. With pastry bags, pipe the Mayonnaise mixtures into the cavities of the egg whites, filling half with green and half with red. Brush with aspic. Place the stuffed egg halves on the tray around the fish. Decorate the top of the fish with green and red rosettes, using the rest of the Mayonnaise mixtures. Garnish the tray at each end with a notched lemon half. Chill. Serve with Green Mayonnaise in a separate bowl. Makes 6 servings.

Trout in Aspic Palace Hotel

8 (½-pound) trout	3 tomatoes, peeled, seeded, and diced
16 medium-small potatoes	Salt and freshly ground black pepper
Court bouillon	¼ cup olive oil
30 cooked crayfish tails, or	1½ tablespoons vinegar
30 cooked shrimp (leave tails	2 cups fish aspic
attached to 16 shrimp)	Dill or parsley
1 cup diced cooked asparagus tips	Vinaigrette Sauce
1 cup cooked green beans	

Remove the 2 fillets from each trout, leaving them attached to the head. Roll each fillet around a potato on either side of the head. Poach in court bouillon to cover, then cool and remove the potatoes (save potatoes for potato salad). Reserve 16 crayfish tails or shrimp with tails attached. Dice the remainder and mix with the asparagus, beans, tomatoes, salt, pepper, oil, and vinegar. Marinate 1 hour. Drain the marinade from the vegetables and add aspic to the vegetables. Chill until the mixture begins to set. Drain the trout well and arrange them on a large tray. Fill the openings in the poached trout with the vegetable mixture and brush the trout with semiliquid aspic. Chill until set. Fill the center of the tray with crayfish tails or shrimp with tails attached. Garnish with dill or parsley. Serve with Vinaigrette Sauce in a separate dish. Makes 8 servings.

TUNA (THON)

Grilled Tuna Maître d'Hôtel

Sprinkle thick slices of tuna lightly with salt and ground black pepper. Dredge in flour, shake off surplus, and cook until browned in oil or shortening over medium heat, turning to brown both sides. Blend 2 tablespoons lemon juice and 1 teaspoon chopped parsley with ½ cup (1 stick) softened butter. Season with a little salt and freshly ground black pepper. Serve over fish. Allow ⅓ pound fish per person.

Tuna with Tomatoes and Mushrooms Bordelaise

1½ pounds tuna	5 medium-sized tomatoes, peeled,
Salt and freshly ground black	seeded, and quartered
pepper	⅓ cup Demi-Glace Sauce
2 tablespoons oil	⅓ cup dry white wine
4 tablespoons butter	2 cups quartered mushrooms
½ cup thinly sliced onion	Chopped parsley
2 shallots, chopped	

Rub fish lightly with salt and pepper. Brown on both sides in oil and 2 tablespoons of the butter. Add onion, shallots, tomatoes, Demi-Glace Sauce, wine, and salt and pepper. Cover and cook over medium heat until the fish flakes when tested with a fork. Transfer fish to a platter. Set aside in a warm place. Return the skillet to the heat and cook the sauce until reduced by one-fourth. Meanwhile, sauté mushrooms in remaining 2 tablespoons butter and add to the sauce. Heat 30 seconds. Pour over fish. Sprinkle with chopped parsley. Makes 6 servings.

Housewife's Tuna Steaks

2 pounds tuna, cut ¼ inch thick	3 tablespoons tomato puree
Salt and freshly ground black	2 tablespoons freshly squeezed
pepper	lemon juice
4 tablespoons (¼ stick) butter	1½ cups sliced mushrooms cooked
⅓ cup chopped onion	in butter, or
1 tablespoon flour	1 cup diced, peeled, and seeded tomatoes
⅓ cup each wine and water	cooked in butter

Place fish in a saucepan, cover with cold water, bring to the boiling point, reduce heat, and simmer 4 to 5 minutes. Remove fish from the water, drain, season lightly with salt and pepper, and brown on both sides in 2 tablespoons of the butter. Melt remaining butter in a casserole. Add onion, mix well, sprinkle with flour, and stir and cook 1 minute. Add wine and water. Cook until the sauce has reduced by one-fourth. Stir in tomato puree and lemon juice. Add the tuna, cover, and cook in a preheated moderate oven (350°F) 15 minutes, or until the fish flakes when tested with a fork. Transfer fish to a platter. Set aside in a warm place. Add mushrooms or tomatoes to the sauce and bring to the boiling point. Adjust seasonings and pour around fish. Makes 6 servings.

TURBOT

THE TURBOT IS A LARGE EUROPEAN FLAT FISH with very delicate flesh and considered by many to be the finest fish.

Broiled Turbot Steaks Maître d'Hôtel

Cut 2 pounds turbot into serving-size pieces. Sprinkle lightly with salt and ground black pepper. Roll in flour and brush with salad oil. Place on a preheated oiled broiler pan and broil 4 inches from the heat source 5 to 8 minutes. Turn fish carefully and brush again with oil. Cook 5 to 8 minutes, or until the fish flakes when tested with a fork. Blend 2 tablespoons lemon juice and 1 tablespoon chopped parsley with ½ cup (1 stick) butter. Serve on the fish. Makes 6 servings.

Deep-Fried Turbot with Tartar Sauce

2 pounds boned turbot	¼ teaspoon freshly ground black pepper
½ cup milk	Flour
½ teaspoon salt	Tartar Sauce

Cut fish into serving-size pieces. Dip in milk seasoned with salt and pepper, and then in flour. Fry until browned in deep fat preheated to 375°F. Drain on paper towels. Serve with Tartar Sauce. Makes 6 servings.

Poached Turbot with Hollandaise Sauce

4 slices turbot (1 pound, 5 ounces each)	Parsley
Fish stock or boiling salted water	Lemon wedges
1 whole onion	Tomatoes
1 whole clove	Hollandaise Sauce
1 bay leaf	

Poach fish in fish stock or boiling salted water as directed in recipe for Poached Fish, adding onion, clove, and bay leaf. Garnish with parsley and lemon wedges and serve with tomatoes and Hollandaise Sauce in separate dishes. Makes 4 servings.

Boned Turbot Aida

2-pound turbot	Grated nutmeg to taste
Salt and freshly ground black pepper	1 cup Mornay Sauce
1½ cooked fresh spinach	1 teaspoon paprika
¼ cup (½ stick) butter	¾ cup grated Parmesan cheese

Fillet the turbot. Make stock from the bones and strain the stock. Cut each fillet in half, sprinkle lightly with salt and pepper, and cook 8 to 10 minutes in the strained stock. Remove fish and set aside. Drain out all the liquid from the spinach. Season spinach with salt, pepper, and nutmeg to taste. Cook the fish stock almost to a glaze, add Mornay Sauce and paprika, and adjust seasonings. Spread spinach in the bottom of a well-buttered baking dish. Top with the fish and cover with the sauce. Sprinkle with cheese and dot with butter. Cook in a preheated oven (450°F) 10 minutes, or until browned. Makes 6 servings.

Cooked Turbot au Gratin

Duchess Potatoes	1½ cups flaked cooked turbot
1 cup sliced mushrooms	Salt and freshly ground black pepper
3 tablespoons butter	⅓ cup grated Gruyère cheese
2 cups Mornay Sauce	½ cup fresh breadcrumbs

Using a pastry bag and a star-shaped nozzle, pipe a high border of Duchess Potatoes around the top of a casserole. Brown lightly in the oven. Sauté mushrooms in 1 tablespoon of the butter and add to Mornay Sauce, along with the fish. Add salt and pepper. Turn into the baking dish inside the potato ring. Sprinkle with cheese and breadcrumbs. Dot with the remaining 2 tablespoons butter. Bake in a preheated oven (350°F) 10 minutes, or until browned. Makes 6 servings.

WHITEFISH (LAVARET)

WHITEFISH IS THE NAME GIVEN TO a dozen or more species of freshwater fish. The largest American species, common in the Great Lakes, attains a length of about 2 feet. Lavaret is a European species; it resembles féra, which is a lake fish belonging to the salmon family, in the delicacy and flavor of its flesh. Féra is cooked in the same ways as whitefish or salmon. North American landlocked salmon can be prepared by the same methods.

Broiled Whole Whitefish

Sprinkle dressed whitefish lightly with salt and ground black pepper. Dip in flour, brush with olive oil or pure vegetable oil, and place on an oiled preheated broiler rack. Cook under broiler until the fish flakes when tested with a fork, turning to brown both sides. Transfer fish to a platter. Sprinkle with browned butter, capers, and chopped parsley. Or, if desired, omit browned butter and capers, and serve with Béarnaise Sauce. Allow 1 (½-pound) dressed fish per person.

Fried Fillets of Whitefish

6 (½-pound) whole whitefish
Salt and freshly ground black
   pepper
Flour
Butter and pure vegetable oil

Freshly squeezed lemon juice
Browned butter
Chopped parsley
Lemon slices

Cut the fish with a sharp knife down the back. Cut off heads and remove bones. Wash and pat dry. Sprinkle lightly with salt and pepper. Dip in flour and cook in shortening or oil until golden brown on both sides. Arrange fish on a warmed platter. Sprinkle with lemon juice. Pour sizzling hot browned butter over the fish. Sprinkle with parsley. Garnish with lemon slices. Makes 6 servings.

Whitefish Colbert

6 (½-pound) whole whitefish
Flour
1 egg, beaten
¾ teaspoon salt
½ teaspoon freshly ground black pepper

Fine white breadcrumbs
Butter and oil
6 tablespoons butter, melted
1 tablespoon chopped parsley
1 teaspoon chopped thyme

Remove heads from fish. Split the fish down the back (do not open along the belly) and remove the bones in such a way that the fillets remain attached. Keep the fish opened flat. Wash and pat dry. Dredge in flour, dip in beaten egg seasoned with salt and pepper, and roll in breadcrumbs. Let fish stand 10 minutes for crumbs to dry. Fry in equal parts butter and oil until browned on both sides. Combine the melted butter and the herbs and serve over fish. Makes 6 servings.

Whitefish Fillets with Mushrooms and Tomatoes

12 (3-ounce) fillets of whitefish
   or landlocked salmon
2 cups sliced mushrooms
1½ cups peeled, seeded, diced tomatoes
1 teaspoon salt
¼ teaspoon freshly ground black pepper
⅛ teaspoon grated nutmeg

¼ teaspoon each chopped thyme,
   marjoram, and sage
½ cup dry white wine
1 cup Velouté Sauce
1 egg yolk
¼ cup heavy cream
Medallions of baked pastry dough (optional)

Place the fillets, overlapping, in a well-buttered baking dish. Cover with mushrooms and tomatoes. Sprinkle with salt, pepper, nutmeg, and herbs. Add wine. Cover and cook in a preheated oven (325°F) 30 to 40 minutes, or until the fish flakes when tested with a fork. Transfer fillets to a serving dish. Strain the liquid into a saucepan, mix with Velouté Sauce, and simmer 1 to 2 minutes. Blend egg yolk with cream and add. Cook 30 seconds. Spoon over the fillets. If desired, garnish with medallions of baked pastry. Makes 6 servings.

Whole Whitefish in White Wine

1 (4-pound) whitefish
Salt and freshly ground black
  pepper
1 shallot, chopped

½ cup dry white wine
1 cup Velouté Sauce
Freshly squeezed lemon juice to taste
1 tablespoon butter

Ask your fishmonger to scale and gut fish, leaving head, tail, and fins attached if desired. Sprinkle with salt and pepper. Scatter shallot in a baking dish and put fish on top. Heat wine and pour over fish. Cover the dish with aluminum foil and cook in a preheated oven (350°F) until the fish flakes when tested with a fork. Transfer fish to a warmed platter. Cook the liquid around the fish until reduced to ¼ cup and then blend it with the Velouté Sauce. Heat, add lemon juice, salt, and pepper, and stir in the butter. Pour the sauce over the fish. Makes 6 servings.

WHITING (MERLAN)

THE EUROPEAN WHITING IS CAUGHT mainly in the Atlantic. Various American fish, including the silver hake, are also called whiting.

Whiting Colbert

6 (½-pound) whiting
½ teaspoon salt
¼ teaspoon freshly ground black pepper
1 cup cold boiled milk
Flour
2 eggs, beaten with 2 tablespoons water

Fine white breadcrumbs
Oil for frying
½ cup (1 stick) softened butter
½ cup chopped parsley
½ teaspoon chopped fresh tarragon
½ teaspoon melted beef glaze

Split whiting along the backbone and lift out the bones. Add salt and pepper to the milk and pour over fish. Soak 10 minutes. Remove fish from milk and drain well. Roll in flour, dip in egg mixture and roll in breadcrumbs. Fry in deep fat preheated to 375°F until fish has browned. Drain on paper towels. Blend together the remaining ingredients. Serve on fish. Makes 6 servings.

Coiled Deep-Fried Whiting

Dress the whiting and with scissors cut off all the fins except the tail fin. With a smooth, firm motion, remove the skin on both sides of the fish by pulling it toward the tail. Sprinkle fish lightly with salt and ground black pepper. Stick the tail in the fish's mouth and secure with toothpicks. This forms a circle. Dip fish in egg beaten together with water (1 tablespoon water for each egg), then roll in fine dry breadcrumbs. Fry until browned in deep fat preheated to 375°F. Drain on paper towels. Remove toothpicks. Serve on a platter and garnish with fried parsley and lemon slices. Pass Tomato Sauce in a separate bowl. Allow 1 (½-pound) fish per person.

English Whiting

Prepare and cook whiting as directed for Whiting Colbert. Transfer to a platter and serve with melted butter and boiled potatoes. Allow 1 (½-pound) fish per person.

Poached Whole Whiting Dieppoise

4 (½-pound) dressed whiting
Salt and freshly ground black
    pepper
¾ cup dry white wine
¾ cup fish stock
2 shallots, chopped

½ pound cooked shrimp
½ pound steamed mussels (without shells)
1 tablespoon flour
1 tablespoon butter
Chopped parsley

Sprinkle fish lightly with salt and pepper. Simmer in a covered skillet in wine and stock, along with the shallots, 8 to 10 minutes, or until the fish flakes when tested with a fork. Transfer fish to a platter and garnish with shrimp and mussels. Blend flour with butter, add to the liquid in which the fish was cooked, and mix well. Stir and cook 1 to 2 minutes. Adjust seasonings and spread over fish, shrimp, and mussels. Sprinkle with parsley. Makes 4 servings.

Baked Whole Whiting

1½ cups chopped mushrooms
3 shallots, chopped
2 tablespoons oil
⅓ cup dry white wine
1 cup Demi-Glace Sauce
Chopped parsley

2 tablespoons tomato puree
6 (½-pound) dressed whiting
Salt and freshly ground black pepper
¼ cup fine white breadcrumbs
¼ cup (½ stick) butter
Lemon wedges

Cook mushrooms and shallots in oil 5 minutes. Add wine and simmer until most of the liquid has evaporated. Stir in Demi-Glace Sauce, 2 tablespoons parsley, and tomato puree and bring to the boiling point. Cover the bottom of a baking dish with a little of the sauce. Sprinkle whiting lightly with salt and pepper, and place over the sauce. Spread the fish with the remaining sauce. Sprinkle with breadcrumbs and dot with butter. Bake in a preheated oven (350°F) 30 minutes, or until crumbs have browned. Garnish with chopped parsley and lemon wedges. Makes 6 servings.

Deep-Fried Whiting Fillets Orly

Carefully fillet 6 (½-pound) whitings. Add 1 teaspoon salt, ¼ teaspoon ground black pepper, 2 tablespoons each chopped parsley and lemon juice, and marinate 1 hour. Dip fish in Fritter Batter and fry until browned in deep fat preheated to 375° F. Drain on paper towels. Serve with Tomato Sauce. Makes 6 servings.

FISH STEWS

BOUILLABAISSE AND OTHER REGIONAL FISH STEWS are among the greatest examples of fish cookery. Since they all contain a variety of fish and sometimes shellfish, they are grouped together here.

Marseilles Bouillabaisse

2 cups chopped onions	1 pound each red snapper, perch, cod,
2 leeks (white parts only), sliced	bass, and eel, and 2 pounds
1 clove garlic, crushed	Spanish mackerel, all sliced
½ cup olive oil	1 inch thick
2 sprigs parsley	2½ pounds whole lobsters or
1 bay leaf	lobster tails, shells included
4 or 5 medium-sized tomatoes,	2 quarts Rich Fish Stock
peeled, seeded, and diced	¼ teaspoon crumbled saffron threads
Dried zest of ½ orange	1 tablespoon chopped fresh thyme
½ cup sliced fresh fennel	½ teaspoon freshly ground black pepper
1 tablespoon salt	2 cups dry white wine
	12 (¼-inch-thick) slices French bread

In a large kettle, cook onions, leeks, and garlic in hot oil until onions are transparent. Add parsley, bay leaf, tomatoes, orange zest, fennel, salt, fish, lobster, and stock. Cover and bring to the boiling point. Add saffron, thyme, pepper, and wine. Boil 8 to 10 minutes. Adjust seasonings. To serve, remove fish and lobster to a serving dish. Pour the broth into soup plates over French bread. Serve fish in a separate dish. Makes about 12 servings.

Bouillabaisse Provençale

This regional dish is made with eel and a variety of fish, such as bass, cod, flounder, haddock, perch, and red snapper, and always includes dried orange zest.

1 cup sliced onion
1 leek (white part only), sliced
1 clove garlic, crushed
½ cup olive oil
2 ribs celery, sliced
1 rib fennel, sliced, or
⠀⠀¼ teaspoon fennel seeds
2 sprigs parsley
Dried zest of ¼ orange

1 pound each eel, cod, haddock, bass,
⠀⠀red snapper, and perch or
⠀⠀flounder, all cut into 2-inch pieces
1½ quarts cold water
2 teaspoons salt
1 bay leaf
3 egg yolks
6 to 8 (¼-inch-thick) slices
⠀⠀French bread, toasted

Cook onion, leek, and garlic in hot oil until onion is transparent. Add celery, fennel, parsley, orange zest, fish, water, salt, and bay leaf. Boil 10-15 minutes. Remove fish with a perforated spoon or skimmer. Beat egg yolks together with a little of the liquid and add them to the rest of the liquid. Heat 1 minute. Adjust seasonings. Put some of the fish and a slice of toast in each soup plate and fill with hot fish stock. Makes 6 to 8 servings.

Freshwater Fish Stew or Pauchouse

4 pounds freshwater fish (eel, carp,
⠀⠀perch, pike) dressed, heads reserved
2 small onions, sliced
Bouquet garni
4 whole peppercorns
Salt
¼ pound salt pork, diced

1 clove garlic, finely chopped
⅓ cup brandy
2 cups dry white wine
2 cups sliced mushrooms
2 tablespoons butter
3 egg yolks
¾ cup heavy cream

Cook fish heads, along with 1 of the onions, the bouquet garni, peppercorns, 1 teaspoon salt, and enough cold water to barely cover them, 30 minutes. Cool. Strain and set aside. Cut fish into 6 portions, rub lightly with salt, and set aside. Brown diced salt pork with garlic in a large skillet. Add fish and brandy. Ignite. Add the wine and enough stock to barely cover the fish and cook slowly until the fish flakes when tested with a fork. Meanwhile sauté mushrooms and the remaining onion in the butter. Arrange the cooked fish over the mushrooms. Cook the stock until reduced by half. Beat egg yolks together with cream, add to the stock, and cook slowly 1 minute. Pour sauce over the fish and heat (do not boil). Serve in timbales or patty shells, accompanied with slices of French bread, rubbed with garlic and dried in the oven. Makes 6 servings.

Flemish Freshwater Fish Stew or Waterzoi

4½ pounds dressed fish
  (eel, pike, trout)
Salt and freshly ground black pepper
2 cups sliced celery

¼ cup chopped parsley
½ cup (1 stick) butter
2 or 3 grated rusks
Brown bread, thinly sliced and buttered

Cut fish into serving-size pieces. Sprinkle lightly with salt and pepper. Set aside. Scatter celery and parsley in the bottom of a well-buttered skillet and arrange the fish on top. Pour in hot water to cover. Dot with butter. Bring to the boiling point, reduce heat, and simmer 10 minutes. Transfer fish to a warm serving dish and keep hot. Cook the stock until reduced by half. Thicken only to sauce consistency with grated rusks. Pour over fish. Serve very hot with thinly sliced brown bread and butter. Makes 6 servings.

SHELLFISH, FROGS' LEGS, AND SNAILS

THE TERM *SHELLFISH (FRUITS DE MER)* in this chapter covers the various saltwater and freshwater crustaceans (lobster, shrimp, prawns, crayfish, and crabs), mollusks (oysters, scallops, mussels, clams, and snails), and one amphibian—the frog.

Other recipes for shellfish are covered in the hot and the cold hors d'oeuvre and pasta and rice chapters.

When buying shellfish, make sure that they are unmistakably alive, from clean waters and a reputable source.

CRABS (CRABES)

CRABS ARE DESIGNATED AS HARD-SHELL OR SOFT-SHELL. Soft-shell crabs are crabs that are molting—that is, they are throwing off the hard shells, leaving soft ones underneath.

Fresh crabmeat can be purchased by the pound or half-pound. Before it is used, the bits of shell and cartilage should be removed from the meat by flaking through it with one's fingers.

One pound of fresh crabmeat is about 3 cups.

Boiled Hard-Shell Crabs

Wash crabs in plenty of cold water and scrub with a brush. Plunge the crabs head first into enough rapidly boiling water to completely cover them. Add 1 tablespoon of salt to 1 quart water. Boil 15 minutes, or until the shells turn red. Drain and hold under cold running water. Drain again and let them cool, resting on the claws. Break off the claws and legs close to the body. Crack claws with a nutcracker and remove the meat. Break off the tail or pointed apron. With both hands, pull the upper and lower shells apart, beginning at the tail. Remove membranous covering along the edges. Using a pointed knife, remove the meat between the sections and the cartilage. Keep the pieces whole if possible. Save roe and liver to garnish crabmeat salad. Six crabs yield about 1 cup meat.

Dressing Soft-Shell Crabs

Wash crabs in cold water. Place the live crabs on a board, face down. With scissors, make an incision straight across the crabs just behind the eyes and cut out the face. Lift the pointed ends of the shells and scrape out the spongy portion. Turn crabs on their backs and cut off their tails. Allow 2 crabs per person.

Deep-Fried Soft-Shell Crabs

12 dressed soft-shell crabs
Salt and freshly ground black pepper

Flour
2 large eggs, beaten with 2 tablespoons water

Sprinkle crabs with salt and pepper and roll in flour. Dip floured crabs into eggs, and then roll in flour again. Fry in deep fat preheated to 370°F until golden brown. Drain on paper towels. Serve hot. Makes 6 servings.

Crab Mornay

1⅓ cups cooked crabmeat
2 cups Mornay Sauce
Salt and freshly ground black
    pepper

1 teaspoon freshly squeezed lemon juice
½ cup grated Parmesan cheese
4 tablespoons butter
1 cup soft white breadcrumbs

Add crabmeat to Mornay Sauce. Stir in salt, pepper, and lemon juice. Spoon into 6 well-buttered cleaned crab shells, scallop shells, or gratin dishes. Sprinkle with cheese. Melt butter, add breadcrumbs, mix well, and sprinkle over the cheese. Bake in a preheated oven (350°F) 30 minutes, or until crumbs are browned. Makes 6 servings.

Crab with Rice Pilaf

4 cups Rice Pilaf
1⅓ cups cooked crabmeat
2 cups Shrimp Sauce
Salt and freshly ground black
    pepper

1 teaspoon freshly squeezed lemon juice
Parsley

Pack Rice Pilaf into an oiled 1-quart ring mold, place mold in a pan of hot water, and bake in a preheated oven (375°F) 30 to 40 minutes, or until hot. Combine crabmeat, Shrimp Sauce, salt, pepper, and lemon juice and heat only until hot. Unmold Rice Pilaf onto a round serving dish and pile the crabmeat mixture in the center of the ring. Garnish with parsley. Makes 6 servings.

English Cold Crabmeat with Mayonnaise

1 teaspoon English-style dry mustard
1 tablespoon water
1 cup Mayonnaise

6 medium-sized crabs, cooked
2 large hard-cooked eggs, chopped
Chopped parsley

Soak mustard in water 5 minutes and blend with Mayonnaise. Remove meat from crabs, dice, and add to Mayonnaise mixture. Spoon the mixture into the crab shells, or into coquilles. Sprinkle with the eggs. Garnish with parsley. Chill and serve. Makes 6 servings.

LOBSTER (HOMARD)

ALTHOUGH AMERICAN AND EUROPEAN LOBSTERS belong to different, but very similar, species, the same methods of preparation can be used for both. Lobsters should be bought alive. They may be killed by severing the spinal cord with a sharp pointed knife at the point where the tail joins the body. Lobster cooked 10-15 minutes (according to size) in simmering water or court bouillon may be served with hot melted butter or with Mayonnaise, or used in the preparation of more elaborate lobster dishes. If the lobster meat is to be reheated, cook the lobster 5-8 minutes or just until the meat can be removed from the shell.

Lobster à l'Américaine

Since this is strictly a French dish, with its tomatoes seemingly characteristic of Provence in its preparation, the origin of its name is a mystery. According to some authorities, it was probably once "à l'Amoricaine," from the old name for Brittany, Amorica, and was miscopied.

2 (2-pound) live lobsters	New Igredient
	¼ cup chopped parsley
¼ cup olive oil	1 teaspoon chopped fresh tarragon
Salt to taste	1 small bay leaf
¼ cup warmed brandy	¾ cup dry white wine
¼ cup finely chopped onion or shallots	Fish stock
1 small clove garlic, finely chopped	Cayenne
2 tablespoons butter	Ground white pepper
2 pounds (6 medium-sized) tomatoes	

Sever the spinal cord at the base of each lobster's neck. Remove the tail section from the body and cut it into 3 or 4 crosswise slices. Cut the body section in half lengthwise, clean it, and reserve the coral and liver to use in the sauce. Heat the oil. Season the lobster meat with salt and cook it in the hot oil until the shells turn red. Flame with the brandy. Remove the meat from the shells and set aside. Save shells to use in sauce to give it more flavor. Cook onion and garlic in butter until onion is limp. Peel, seed, and dice tomatoes and add to onion. Stir in herbs, and the shells, the wine, and stock. Cover and simmer 30 minutes. Add cayenne, salt, and white pepper. Transfer lobster meat to the sauce, cover, and simmer 5 minutes. Just before serving, remove shells and mix in liver and coral. Makes 6 servings.

Lobster Bordelaise

2 (2-pound) live lobsters
6 tablespoons butter
¼ cup warmed brandy
¼ cup chopped shallots
1 clove garlic, crushed
1 cup dry white wine
1½ cups fish stock

1½ cups Sauce Espagnole
1½ cups Tomato Sauce
1 tablespoon chopped fresh tarragon
1 tablespoon chopped fresh chervil
    and parsley
Salt and freshly ground black pepper
Parsley

Cut up the lobsters as directed for Lobster à l'Américaine. Cook them in a skillet in 4 tablespoons of the butter until shells begin to turn red. Pour in the brandy and ignite. Add shallots and garlic. Stir and cook until shallots are transparent. Add wine, stock, Sauce Espagnole, and Tomato Sauce. Mix well. Cook, uncovered, 10 minutes. Transfer the lobster to a serving dish and keep hot. Cook the liquid until reduced by half. Stir in the remaining 2 tablespoons butter, the herbs, and salt and pepper. Simmer 1 minute. Pour the sauce over the lobster. Garnish with parsley. Makes 6 to 8 servings.

Lobster à l'Indienne

2 (1½-pound) cooked lobsters
¼ cup (½ stick) butter
1¾ cups Curry Sauce

Salt and freshly ground black
    pepper
4 cups hot cooked rice

Remove meat from lobsters, cut into nice slices, and heat 2 to 3 minutes in a bit of the butter. Add the Curry Sauce and heat. Season with salt and pepper. Meanwhile, toss rice lightly with remaining butter. Place in a preheated oven (350°F) to dry, about 10 minutes. Spoon rice into an oiled 1-quart ring mold. Turn out onto a serving dish. Fill center with lobster and a little of the sauce. Serve remaining sauce in a separate dish. Makes 6 servings.

Lobster Newburg

2½ cups cooked lobster meat
3 tablespoons butter, melted
¼ cup fine sherry
4 large egg yolks
1 cup light cream

Dash each cayenne and grated nutmeg
½ teaspoon paprika
Salt to taste
Toasts
Lobster coral

Put lobster and butter in the top of a double boiler with the sherry and warm. Blend egg yolks with ¼ cup of the cream and add to the lobster. Stir in remaining cream and cook over hot water (not boiling) until the sauce is of medium thickness. Remove from heat and add seasonings. Serve on toast, topped with a little lobster coral. Makes about 6 servings.

Lobster Thermidor

3 (1¼-pound) live lobsters	1 teaspoon mustard
Fish stock	2 cups Mornay Sauce
2 shallots, chopped	Salt and freshly ground black pepper
3 tablespoons butter	1 tablespoon whipped cream
½ cup dry white wine	½ cup grated Parmesan cheese

Boil lobsters in fish stock 5 minutes, reduce heat and simmer 8-10 minutes When lobsters are cool enough to handle, remove meat from the claws and bodies, keeping the bodies intact. Coarsely chop the meat and set aside. Cook shallots in butter until transparent, add wine and cook until reduced by three-fourths. Add the mustard to the shallot mixture, along with Mornay Sauce. Stir and cook only to heat the ingredients. Add salt and pepper. Mix the lobster meat with two-thirds of the sauce. Put a little of the remaining sauce in each of the shells and fill them with the lobster mixture. Blend whipped cream with the remaining sauce and spread over the tops. Sprinkle with cheese. Brown under the broiler.

Instead of using lobster shells, this may be served in a casserole or in coquilles (deep-sea scallop shells). Makes 6 servings.

Lobster Medallions in Aspic Niçoise

2 (1-pound) cooked lobsters	4 anchovies, diced
12 tomato slices	2 teaspoons unflavored gelatin
1 quart aspic	3 tablespoons cold water
6 pitted green or black olives	⅓ cup Mayonnaise
1½ cup cold cooked diced potatoes	Freshly ground black pepper
1 cup cold cooked green beans	12 baked 3-inch pastry shells, cooled
cut into 1-inch pieces	Parsley
1 small tomato, diced	

Cut 12 (1½-inch thick) medallions from lobster tails. Reserve the remaining lobster meat for another use. Dip tomato slices in aspic and place one on each lobster medallion. Decorate each with half of a pitted olive, round side up, and glaze with aspic. Chill until aspic is set. Combine potatoes, beans, diced tomato, and anchovies. Soften gelatin in cold water. Set in a pan of hot water to melt. Blend with Mayonnaise and add to the vegetables. Season to taste with pepper. Spoon into the tart shells, smooth the tops, and coat with aspic. Chill until set. Chill remaining aspic until set. To serve, put a lobster medallion on top of each filled tart shell, arrange the tart on a serving plate, and surround them with chopped aspic. Garnish the center of the plate with parsley. Makes 6 servings.

Lobster in Aspic with Truffles

3½ pints fish aspic
2 truffles
6 hard-cooked eggs, sliced

Meat of 2 (1½ pound) cooked lobsters
Watercress

Coat the inside of a 1½-quart mold with aspic. Chill until set. Decorate the bottom with alternating slices of truffle and slices of hard-cooked eggs. Arrange thin slices of lobster tails, each decorated with a slice of truffle, vertically against the side of the mold. Coat with cold liquid aspic. Chill until set. Repeat with a second row of sliced lobster tails and coat with aspic. Chill until aspic is set. Continue until the mold is full. Chill until ready to serve. To unmold, briefly dip the mold in very hot water and turn out on a round serving plate. Shake the mold to release the aspic. Garnish with watercress. Makes 6 to 8 servings.

Lobster Medallions in Aspic Duke of Windsor

1 (2-pound) cooked lobster
8 slices large black olives
3 cups aspic
2 cups diced celery root or celery
Whites of 2 hard-cooked eggs, diced
1 tablespoon wine vinegar

3 tablespoons olive oil
½ teaspoon salt
⅛ teaspoon freshly ground black pepper
1 teaspoon curry powder
½ cup Mayonnaise
8 baked 2-inch pastry shells, cooled

Cut lobster tail into 8 good slices and top each with an olive slice. Glaze with aspic, chill, and set aside. Cook celery root 1 minute in boiling water, drain, and rinse in cold water. Dice the meat from the lobster claws and the tail trimmings. Add to the celery root, along with egg whites. Combine vinegar, oil, and seasonings. Mix lightly with the salad. Marinate 1 hour in the refrigerator. Reserve ⅓ cup aspic. Chill the remaining aspic until set. Drain salad, adjust seasonings, mix with Mayonnaise, and fill tart shells to the top edge. Glaze with aspic. Chill. Just before serving, top each with a lobster medallion and place on a large serving plate. Surround with chopped jellied aspic. Makes 8 scrvings.

Cold Lobster Soufflé

2 (1¼-pound) lobsters, cooked and
  cooled in court bouillon
1 cup fish Velouté Sauce
1 teaspoon freshly squeezed lemon juice
Dash cayenne

¼ cup fino sherry
3 cups liquid aspic
Salt and ground white pepper
1 cup heavy cream, whipped
1 truffle, sliced

Extend the height of a 1½-quart soufflé dish 1 to 2 inches with a band of aluminum foil or parchment paper, folded to a width of 3 or 4 inches and long enough to reach around the dish. Tie the band in place with a string, and pin or staple the seam together. Set dish aside. Remove meat from lobster shells, keeping the flesh intact so that 6 nice slices can be cut from it. Finely chop the meat, mix with a little Velouté Sauce, and push the mixture through a sieve Add lemon juice, cayenne, sherry and remaining sauce. Add 2½ cups of the aspic. Season with salt and white pepper. Chill until the mixture begins to set. Fold in whipped cream. Turn into the prepared soufflé dish. Smooth and flatten the top. Chill until firm and ready to use. Remove the paper band from the dish. Arrange lobster and truffle slices alternately over the top of the soufflé. Coat with aspic. Chill. Coat again with aspic. Chill. Serve cold. Makes 8 servings.

ROCK LOBSTER (LANGOUSTE)

ROCK LOBSTERS RESEMBLE THE LARGER LOBSTERS but lack the large claws of the latter and have less flavor. They can be prepared in the same way as cold lobster dishes.

Rock Lobster Bouquetière

1 (2½-pound) lobster, cooked and
  cooled in court bouillon
Truffles
Pimiento
4 cups aspic
2 teaspoons unflavored gelatin
3 tablespoons cold water

½ cup Mayonnaise
4 cups mixed cooked vegetables
Salt and freshly ground black
  pepper
Hard-cooked eggs

Remove the tail from the lobster and take out the meat without damaging the shell. Reserve the shell, claws, and feelers. Cut the lobster meat into medallions and decorate them with truffle and pimiento. Glaze with aspic. Chill. Soften gelatin in cold water, set in a pan of hot water to melt, then blend with the Mayonnaise and add to cooked vegetables. Season with salt and pepper. Turn onto a serving plate and shape into a dome. Chill. Reserve ½ cup aspic; pour remaining aspic into small molds and chill until set. Slice eggs, garnish with truffles and pimiento, glaze with aspic, and chill. To serve, arrange lobster medallions over the dome of salad. Unmold aspics and place them around half of the salad. Place egg slices around the aspic molds. Decorate the dish with the lobster tail, claws, and feelers. Glaze the shells with aspic and chill a few minutes to set the glaze. Makes 6 servings.

SHRIMP (CREVETTES)

THERE ARE MANY VARIETIES OF EDIBLE SHRIMP, ranging in size from the very tiny ones to those that average only a dozen or less to the pound. Large shrimp are sometimes called prawns, but the name *prawn* in Europe properly applies to a different crustacean (French *langoustine;* Italian *scampi)*. Prawns are prepared in the same ways as shrimp, and either can be used in many of the same ways as crayfish.

Shrimp à l'Indienne

⅓ cup chopped onion
3 tablespoons butter
About 2 teaspoons curry paste

2 cups Fish Velouté Sauce
1½ pounds shrimp, peeled and deveined
Rice à l'Indienne

Cook onion in butter over low heat until transparent. Stir in curry powder. Stir and cook 1 minute. Add Velouté Sauce and bring to the boiling point and simmer 20 minutes, skimming. Add shrimp, stir, and cook until shrimp turns red (do not boil). Serve over Rice à l'Indienne. Makes 6 servings.

Fried Shrimp

1½ pounds shrimp, peeled
    and deveined
½ cup olive oil
Salt

Dash cayenne
Parsley

Fry shrimp quickly in hot oil. Drain on paper towels. Season with salt and a little cayenne. Garnish with parsley. Makes 6 servings.

(See other Fried Shrimp recipes in chapter 10.)

Scampi Thermidor

1 cup Béchamel Sauce
¾ cup milk
1 cup heavy cream
⅓ cup plus ½ cup grated
    Parmesan cheese
1 teaspoon mustard
1 tablespoon water

6 tablespoons butter
¼ cup olive oil
2½ pounds cooked scampi or
    large prawns, peeled and deveined
¼ cup warmed brandy
12 thin slices truffle, or
    ½ cup sautéed mushrooms

Combine Béchamel Sauce, milk, cream, and ⅓ cup cheese in a 1-quart saucepan. Stir and cook 3 to 4 minutes over medium-low heat, or until sauce has thickened. Add the mustard to the sauce. Stir in 3 tablespoons of the butter. Strain. Put the remaining 3 tablespoons butter and the oil in a skillet. Heat and add scampi. Stir and cook 4 minutes. Add brandy and ignite. Heat 30 seconds. Add sauce, and truffle slices, if using. Turn into a heatproof serving dish. Sprinkle with remaining ½ cup cheese. Brown under broiler. Makes 6 servings.

Brochettes of Prawns or Shrimp

24 medium-large prawns or
    very large shrimp
Salt and freshly ground black
    pepper
Flour

Oil for frying
Butter or Herb Butter
Lemon wedges
Parsley

Peel and devein the prawns; remove tails. Rinse in cold water and pat dry. Sprinkle lightly with salt and pepper. Roll in flour and thread 4 on each of 6 short skewers. Fry until browned in deep fat preheated to 375°F. Drain on paper towels. Serve hot with butter or Herb Butter and a lemon wedge for each serving. Garnish with parsley. Makes 6 servings.

Italian Brochettes of Scampi or Prawns

24 peeled scampi or large prawns
Salt and freshly ground black
    pepper
24 small mushroom caps
24 slices raw lean ham
24 squares mozzarella cheese,
    1 by 1 by ½ inch

½ teaspoon chopped thyme
½ cup (1 stick) butter, melted
3 cups Rice Pilaf
1 tablespoon freshly squeezed lemon juice

Pat scampi dry and sprinkle with salt and pepper. Thread on each of 12 skewers 2 each of the following: shrimp, mushroom, ham slice folded in four, and cheese. Add thyme to butter and brush over the skewered food. Place skewers in a shallow pan. Cook in a preheated oven (350°F) 10 to 15 minutes, basting 2 times with butter. Carefully remove the skewers and arrange the shrimp and other foods in a ring in a round dish. Fill the center with a mound of cooked rice or Rice Pilaf. Sprinkle scampi with lemon juice. Makes 6 servings.

Prawn Cocktail Belleville

3 pounds prawns
Court bouillon
Cooked-vegetable salad

Chopped parsley
Mayonnaise

Cook prawns in court bouillon 5 minutes, or until they turn pink. Remove from the stock, and when cool enough to handle, peel and devein them, leaving the tails attached. Fill a large goblet or round bowl with vegetable salad and hang the shrimp by the tails around the edges. Sprinkle the salad with parsley. Serve Mayonnaise separately. Makes 6 servings.

CRAYFISH (ECREVISSES)

CRAYFISH (ALSO CALLED *CRAWFISH*) are small freshwater crustaceans that look like miniature lobsters. They are interchangeable with shrimp in many recipes. Other recipes for crayfish appear throughout this book.

Crayfish in Court Bouillon or à la Nage

1 cup each sliced celery and carrots
1 onion, sliced
1 shallot, sliced
2 sprigs parsley
½ bay leaf
¼ teaspoon whole peppercorns

½ teaspoon thyme
2 quarts cold water
1 teaspoon salt
1 cup dry white wine
6 to 8 crayfish per person

Place all ingredients except crayfish in a 6-quart stockpot. Bring slowly to the boiling point, reduce heat, and simmer, uncovered, 25 minutes. Strain stock through cheesecloth into a saucepan. Bring to the boiling point. Wash crayfish thoroughly. Remove the intestinal tract by inserting a knife tip under the intestine in the middle of the tail and pulling the intestine out gently, holding it between the knife and one finger. Immediately throw the crayfish into the boiling court bouillon. Simmer 5 to 10 minutes, or until the crayfish turn red. Serve in a tureen as one would serve soup. Makes 6 to 8 servings.

OYSTERS (HUITRES)

Oysters on the Half Shell

Allow 6 raw oysters per person. Open the shells at the last minute, leaving each oyster on the deep half of the shell but cut away from the muscle attaching it to the shell. Arrange on a bed of cracked ice. Serve as an hors d'oeuvre with a dish of freshly squeezed lemon juice and freshly ground black pepper.

Baked Oysters Florentine

20 oysters with their liquor
1 cup drained cooked spinach
5 tablespoons butter
½ cup Béchamel Sauce

¹⁄₁₆ teaspoon grated nutmeg
Salt and freshly ground black pepper
¼ cup grated Parmesan cheese

Cook oysters in their liquor over very low heat or over hot water only until the edges curl. Cook spinach until dry in 2 tablespoons of the butter. Add Béchamel Sauce, nutmeg, and salt and pepper. Put an oyster in each shell and top with 1 teaspoon spinach sauce. Sprinkle with cheese. Melt remaining 3 tablespoons butter and drizzle over the tops. Bake in a hot (400°F) oven for 5-8 minutes or until heated through. Serve hot. Makes 4 servings.

Baked Oysters Mornay

20 to 24 oysters in their liquor
¾ cup Béchamel Sauce
1 large egg yolk

½ cup grated Gruyère cheese
Salt and freshly ground black pepper
Freshly squeezed lemon juice

Cook oysters in their liquor over very low heat or over hot water only until edges curl. Drain off the liquor and add ¼ cup to the Béchamel Sauce. Beat in egg yolk and ¼ cup of the cheese. Season to taste with salt, pepper, and lemon juice. Place 1 teaspoon sauce in each of 4 heatproof dishes and add 5 to 6 oysters. Cover with sauce. Sprinkle with remaining cheese. Brown quickly under the broiler. Serve at once. Makes 4 servings.

Oysters Villeroi

24 oysters with their liquor
1 cup Béchamel Sauce
2 large egg yolks

1 cup fine white breadcrumbs
Butter

Cook oysters in their liquor over very low heat only until edges curl. Drain off liquor and add ¼ cup to Béchamel Sauce. Beat in egg yolks. Pat the oysters dry between paper towels. Dip them into the sauce and roll them in breadcrumbs. Let stand a few minutes to dry the crumbs. Fry in butter until golden brown on both sides. Serve at once. Makes 4 to 6 servings.

CLAMS (PALOURDES)

MANY VARIETIES OF CLAMS are known and eaten; the two most common on the Atlantic coast of North America are round or hard clams and long or soft clams or "steamers." The small hard clams are eaten raw in the same way as oysters, and they can also be cooked in some of the same ways as oysters or mussels. Large hard clams are used in chowders and stews. Soft clams are usually steamed or shelled and fried in deep fat.

MUSSELS (MOULES)

IT IS ESSENTIAL THAT MUSSELS BE ABSOLUTELY FRESH; to ensure freshness the shells must be tightly closed. As a safety measure, test the mussels by attempting to slide the two halves of the shells across each other. Discard any that are open or slide, even slightly.

How to Wash Mussels

Put the mussels in a colander and hold them under cold running water to rinse off all the loose dirt and mud. Scrub the shells with a stiff brush and scrape them with a knife to remove all the seaweed, slime, and dirt that has adhered to the shells. Soak mussels 2 hours in cold water to rid the interior of possible sand and to get rid of some of the salty flavor. Put mussels in a colander and rinse again under cold running water. Pull off the beard that protrudes from the closed shell.

Steamed Mussels

Put mussels in a large kettle with only enough water or white wine to create steam. Add a little parsley, chopped shallots, and fresh thyme. Cover the kettle tightly and cook over high heat 3-5 minutes, or only until shells open, shaking the kettle occasionally up and down and sideways to cook all the mussels uniformly. Transfer mussels to another pan and cover tightly to keep hot. Strain the broth through a very fine sieve or through 2 layers of cheesecloth.

To serve, put mussels in a soup plate, heat the broth with butter or olive oil, and pour it over them. With your fingers or an oyster fork, pick the mussels out of the shells and discard shells in a dish provided for that purpose. Provide each guest with a soup spoon for the broth, a large napkin, and a finger bowl or a finger towel wrung out in hot water for cleaning the fingers. Allow 1 quart mussels per person when served steamed.

Herbed Steamed Mussels

⅓ cup olive oil or butter
1 clove garlic
½ cup chopped parsley
1 tablespoon chopped fresh thyme

Dash cayenne
3 quarts scrubbed and cleaned mussels
Salt and freshly ground black pepper

Heat together in a large kettle the first 5 ingredients. Add mussels and mix until the shells are well coated with oil. Cover the kettle and steam until all the shells open, 8 to 10 minutes. Season the sauce with salt and pepper to taste. Serve the mussels in their shells and the sauce together in soup plates. Makes 3 servings.

Mussel Salad with Mayonnaise Francillon

3 quarts scrubbed and cleaned mussels
1 cup dry white wine
¾ cup Mayonnaise

1 teaspoon mustard
3 medium-large cooked potatoes dressed in Vinaigrette

Cook the mussels in the wine 3-5 minutes, or until all the shells open. Remove the mussels, and allow mussels to cool. Cook the liquid until it has reduced to almost the thickness of syrup. Cool and blend with Mayonnaise. Mix the mustard with the Mayonnaise. Remove mussels from shells, combine with the Mayonnaise mixture, and place in the center of an hors d'oeuvre dish. Slice the potatoes and arrange them around the mussels. Makes 4 servings.

Steamed Mussels Marinière

4 to 5 quarts scrubbed and cleaned mussels
1 cup dry white wine
3 shallots, sliced

1 sprig parsley
½ teaspoon chopped thyme
3 whole peppercorns
Chopped parsley

Put mussels in a large kettle with wine, shallots, parsley, thyme, and peppercorns. Cover and steam over low heat 3-5 minutes, or until all the shells open. Transfer mussels to soup plates. Strain liquid, heat 30 seconds, and pour over the mussels. Sprinkle with parsley. Makes 4 to 5 servings.

Mussels in Poulette Sauce

3 quarts mussels, scrubbed and cleaned
1 shallot, chopped
1 sprig parsley
1 cup dry white wine
1 cup fish Velouté Sauce

2 egg yolks
¼ cup heavy cream
Salt and freshly ground black
   pepper

Cook mussels, shallot, and parsley in the wine 3-5 minutes, or until all the shells open. Drain off the liquor and save the liquid. Let it stand a few minutes, then strain through 2 layers of cheesecloth. Blend with Velouté Sauce and egg yolks. Remove mussels from the shells, debeard them if necessary, and add to the sauce, along with the cream. Stir and cook 1 minute, or only until hot. Add salt and pepper. Serve in baked pastry shells or bread cases, or over toast points or cooked rice. Makes 6 servings.

Mussels Villeroi

3 to 4 quarts cooked mussels in
   their shells
2 egg yolks, lightly beaten
2 cups thick Velouté Sauce
2 whole eggs

⅛ teaspoon freshly ground black pepper
2 tablespoons water
Fine white breadcrumbs
Oil for frying

Remove mussels from their shells, remove beards, and pat the mussels dry. Blend egg yolks with Velouté Sauce. Stir and cook over very low heat (do not boil) until sauce has thickened and reduced to 1½ cups. Beat whole eggs together with pepper and water. Dip mussels in the sauce and let stand 1 to 2 minutes. Dip them in the egg mixture, then roll them in breadcrumbs. Dip in egg and crumbs again and fry until brown in deep fat preheated to 375°F. Drain on paper towels. Serve as a main dish, or use to garnish other seafood dishes. Makes 6 servings.

SCALLOPS

IN FRANCE SCALLOPS ARE CALLED *COQUILLES SAINT-JACQUES* and are sold in their shells. The shells (*coquilles*) are often saved and used to cook and serve various seafoods and other foods (see recipes in chapter 5). In the United States scallops are usually sold without the shells.

FROGS' LEGS

ONLY THE LEGS OF FROGS ARE EATEN IN FRANCE. The meat resembles chicken in texture and is regarded as a delicacy. About 6 frogs' legs should be allowed per serving.

Frogs' legs may be obtained ready to cook. If you prepare them yourself, cut off the hind legs close to the frog's body. Wash the legs in cold water and strip off the skin as you would pull off a glove. Cut off the feet and soak the legs 2 hours in very cold water, changing the water often, then drain and dry thoroughly.

Fried Frogs' Legs

Dip cleaned frogs' legs in milk and dredge in flour seasoned with salt and freshly ground black pepper. Pan-fry in hot butter or olive oil 8 to 10 minutes, until browned on all sides.

Frogs' Legs Fritters

36 cleaned frogs' legs	¼ teaspoon freshly ground black pepper
2 tablespoons lemon juice	1 recipe Fritter Batter
¼ cup olive oil	Oil for frying
1 tablespoon chopped parsley	Fried parsley
1 teaspoon salt	Lemon slices

Marinate frogs' legs 1 hour in lemon juice, oil, and seasonings. Pat the legs dry, dip in Fritter Batter, and fry until brown in deep fat preheated to 375°F. Drain on paper towels. Serve as an entrée or as a hot hors d'oeuvre. Garnish with fried parsley and lemon slices.

Frogs' Legs in Poulette Sauce

36 cleaned frogs' legs	¼ cup light cream
5 tablespoons butter	2 egg yolks
⅓ cup finely chopped mushrooms	Salt to taste
2 shallots, finely chopped	1 teaspoon freshly squeezed lemon juice
1 cup chicken stock	4 tablespoons chopped parsley

Cook frogs' legs slowly in half the butter, without letting them brown, until they are tender. Remove from the skillet and keep hot. Add the remaining butter to the skillet. Stir in mushrooms and shallots. Cook, stirring frequently, over low heat 5 minutes, or until shallots are transparent. Beat stock and cream with the egg yolks and add to the sauce. Stir and cook gently until sauce has thickened. Blend in salt and lemon juice. Add frogs' legs and bring to the boiling point. Serve immediately, sprinkled with chopped parsley.

Frogs' Legs with Fine Herbs

Fry frogs' legs in very hot butter until browned on all sides. Toss with chopped parsley and a little lemon juice.

SNAILS (ESCARGOTS)

Although fresh snails are rarely available in the United States, canned snails imported from Europe may be purchased. Allow 12 snails per serving.

Snails in Chablis

2 cups Chablis
1½ teaspoons finely chopped shallot
⅓ cup meat glaze
2 tablespoons chopped ham

1 teaspoon chopped thyme
Snail Butter (see recipe for Baked Snails)
6 dozen canned snails, rinsed

Boil wine with shallot until the wine is reduced to ⅔ cup. Add meat glaze, ham, and thyme, and whisk in the butter. Put the snails in little ramekins and pour the sauce over the snails. Bake in a preheated oven (450°F) 10 minutes. Makes 6 servings.

Spanish Sautéed Snails

½ cup chopped onion
½ cup short julienne strips green
   bell pepper
1 cup chopped raw ham
1 clove garlic, crushed
¼ cup olive oil

6 dozen canned snails,
   drained and rinsed
Salt and freshly ground black
   pepper
2 tablespoons chopped parsley

Cook onion, green pepper, ham, and garlic in oil 2 to 3 minutes. Add snails. Season to taste with salt and pepper. Sauté until snails start to brown. Add parsley and toss gently. Serve very hot in a deep dish. The snails must be highly seasoned.

Baked Snails in Garlic-Parsley Butter Bouguignonne

3 cups dry white wine
1 teaspoon finely chopped shallot
   or onion
½ cup softened butter

¼ cup finely chopped parsley
½ teaspoon minced garlic
Salt and freshly ground black pepper
6 dozen canned snails, rinsed, and shells

Boil the wine with shallot until the wine is reduced by half. Strain. Blend butter with parsley, garlic, salt, and pepper. Pour about ½ to 1 teaspoon wine into each snail shell, insert a snail, and top with a little of the herbed butter (Snail Butter). Bake in a preheated oven (450°F) 10 minutes. Serve hot. Makes 6 servings.

MEATS

IN THIS CHAPTER, THE RECIPES AND DISCUSSION ARE of the meat of beef, veal, lamb and mutton, and pork, as well as the variety meats of those animals. And whereas the methods of butchering and the names of the various cuts of meat may vary around the country, the general principles are the same: the tender cuts are separated from the less tender so that each cut is appropriate for a certain method of cooking.

Beef (BOEUF)

As with all the meats covered in this chapter, beef has the whole range of cuts of meat and their appropriate cooking processes, from a few minutes of grilling or broiling for tournedos and filet mignon steaks (like Grilled Châteaubriand and Fillet of Beef Richelieu), to five or six hours for stews and braises of the rump, chuck and shin (like Spoon Beef and Braised Rump of Beef).

Lamb and Mutton (AGNEAU AND MOUTON)

The youngest lamb (at 2 to 3 months old) is called "milk-fed" and appears only in early spring. It has its own rules of cooking, since it must be cooked to medium without any pink showing or it will be tough. As soon as lamb ages to the next stage (5 to 9 months), the same rules as for all meat apply: the tender cuts from the loin and ribs are grilled, broiled, sautéed, or roasted quickly and served medium-rare, and the other cuts are stewed or braised and served with their cooking juices. When the animal approaches 2 years old it becomes mutton, a meat very scarce now. If one can find it, a grilled thick mutton chop or a roasted saddle of mutton is one of the glories of cooked meats.

Pork (PORC)

Pork is probably the most versatile of all the meats, cooked either from the fresh, raw state, or salted and smoked and made into all kinds of hams, sausages, and charcuterie. But whatever the preparation, fresh pork benefits enormously, and will be more tender and more flavorful, if it is marinated either in a dry rub (a simple mixture of coarse salt, herbs, and spices) or in a wet brine (the same but dissolved in water), before cooking.

When cooking pork, always leave on a ⅛-inch layer of fat to improve the flavor and help keep the meat moist and tender. The best flavor and texture of roast pork is achieved when the meat is cooked to an internal temperature of 180°F and then allowed to rest for 20 minutes. The juices should have the slightest tinge of pink. When the meat reaches 137°F, though still rare, it is safe to eat because any trichinae will have been killed, but the best flavors are reached at 150°F.

BEEF

Roast Fillet of Beef

Trim the fat and connective tissue from a beef fillet roast and lard it with larding pork, or tie thin strips of fatty salt pork or beef suet around it. If a meat thermometer is used, insert it in the thickest part of the roast. Place the roast in a preheated oven (450°F). Cook as directed in the introduction or until 120–125 degrees for rare and 140 degrees for medium rare. Allow the roast to stand 15 minutes in a warm place before carving it. Serve with the pan juices or spread with meat glaze or beef extract. Allow about ½ pound per serving.

Fillet of Beef Bouquetière

2 to 3 pounds fillet of beef	½ cup (1 stick) butter
About 2 tablespoons oil	1 cup Demi-Glace Sauce
1 cup sliced carrots	Sherry or cognac (optional)
½ cup sliced onion	12 cooked potato "olives"
½ cup sliced celery	1 small head cooked cauliflower
Salt and freshly ground black	2 cups each cooked green beans and
pepper	cooked cubed turnips

Ask your butcher to lard the roast for you. Brown it on all sides in hot fat in a Dutch oven. Remove the meat and set aside. Add carrots, onion, and celery. Cover and cook 5 minutes over low heat without browning the vegetables. Return the roast to the pot. Sprinkle with salt and pepper. Melt half the butter and pour it over the meat. Cover and cook in a preheated oven (450°F) about 30 minutes. Shortly before the meat is done, remove the cover to finish browning. Transfer meat to a platter and let it stand in a warm place 15 to 20 minutes. Skim and discard the fat from the pan juices. Add the Demi-Glace Sauce, strain, bring to the boiling point, and simmer until reduced by one-fourth. Bring to the boiling point. Stir in sherry or cognac to taste, if desired. Serve with the meat. Toss the hot cooked vegetables in the remaining butter and arrange them on the platter around the meat. Serve hot. Makes 4 to 6 servings.

Roast Fillet of Beef Girondine

2 to 3 pounds fillet of beef	1 pound mushrooms
1 cup Demi-Glace Sauce	2 tablespoons cooking oil
6 artichoke bottoms	Salt and freshly ground black
4 tablespoons (½ stick) butter	pepper

Cook the beef fillet as directed for Fillet of Beef Bouquetière. Transfer the meat to a platter. Keep warm. Degrease the pan, add Demi-Glace Sauce and bring to the boiling point. Strain and keep warm. Cut artichoke bottoms into quarters and cook in half the butter. Cut mushrooms into thick slices and cook in the remaining butter and the oil 5 minutes, or until tender. Season artichokes and mushrooms with salt and pepper, and arrange around the platter. Coat with the sauce, and serve remaining sauce separately. Makes 4 to 6 servings.

Roast Fillet of Beef with Madeira Sauce

2 to 3 pounds fillet of beef
1 cup Madeira Sauce
1 pound mushrooms

3 tablespoons butter
Salt and freshly ground black
  pepper

Roast the beef fillet according to the directions for Roast Fillet of Beef. Transfer meat to a platter and keep warm. Degrease the pan and add the Madeira Sauce (or deglaze with Madeira and add 1 cup of Brown Sauce). Bring to the boiling point. Meanwhile, remove mushroom caps from the stems (save stems for another use) and sauté caps in butter until all the moisture has evaporated and the caps are tender. Add salt and pepper. Place around the meat and coat with the sauce. Serve remaining sauce separately. Makes 4 to 6 servings.

Roast Fillet of Beef Richelieu

3½ pounds fillet of beef
¼ cup chopped onion
3 tablespoons butter
2 cups chopped mushroom stems
⅔ cup Demi-Glace Sauce
About ¾ cup white breadcrumbs

Salt and freshly ground black pepper
8 medium-sized firm, ripe tomatoes
24 sautéed mushroom caps
8 servings braised lettuce
Parsley

Roast the beef according to directions for Roast Fillet of Beef, and let it stand 15 minutes in a warm place before carving. Sauté the onion in 1 tablespoon of the butter until limp. Add the mushroom stems and stir and cook 5 minutes. Add the Demi-Glace Sauce and enough of the breadcrumbs to make a smooth mixture. Season with salt and pepper. Cut a slice from the top of each tomato and scoop out the insides, leaving the shells intact. Sprinkle the cavities with salt and pepper and fill them with the mushroom mixture. Melt the remaining butter, mix with the rest of the breadcrumbs, and sprinkle them over the tomatoes. Bake the tomatoes in an 8-by-8-by-2-inch baking pan in a preheated oven (325°F) 25 minutes, or until crumbs are brown. To serve, slice the roast and arrange the slices, overlapping, down the center of a warmed platter. Garnish the dish with the stuffed tomatoes, sautéed mushroom caps, braised lettuce, and parsley. Makes 8 servings.

Baked Fillet of Beef in Puff Pastry Wellington

1 (4-pound) fillet of beef
1 cup (1 stick) butter
Salt and freshly ground black
    pepper
½ cup each sliced celery and onion
1 cup sliced carrots
⅓ cup chopped parsley
1 bay leaf

2 teaspoons chopped fresh rosemary
¼ cup Cognac
Puree or mousse of foie gras
1 cup mushroom Duxelles
Puff Pastry
Milk
1 cup Madeira Sauce
1 truffle, or ¼ cup mushrooms, chopped

It is unnecessary to lard the roast for this dish. Spread the meat generously with butter. Sprinkle with salt and pepper. Spread all the vegetables, bay leaf, and rosemary in a shallow baking pan, and place the roast on top. Cook in a preheated oven (450°F) 15 to 20 minutes, or 120 degrees on a meat thermometer, until rare. Remove roast from the oven, flame with the Cognac, and let cool completely. When roast is cold, spread with foie gras over the entire surface and then pat the Duxelles on top. Roll puff pastry ⅛ inch thick and wrap it around the roast. Trim the edges of the pastry, moisten with water, and seal by pressing the edges together. If desired, decorate with strips of pastry cut ½ inch wide and laid in lattice fashion over the crust. Place in a baking pan, seam side down. Brush the crust with milk (or with an egg yolk beaten with 1 teaspoon milk). Prick the crust in a few places to allow the steam to escape. Bake in a preheated oven (425°F) 20-30 minutes, or until browned and the meat is a little more cooked. Transfer to a platter and keep warm. Add Madeira Sauce, ¼ cup foie gras, and chopped truffle or mushrooms to the roasting pan. Simmer 3 minutes. Slice the beef and serve with the sauce in a separate bowl. Makes 6 servings.

Fillet of Beef in Aspic with Foie Gras and Truffles Rothschild

3 pounds cold roast fillet of beef
½ pound foie gras puree

1 fresh black truffle, sliced
1 cup port-flavored aspic

Cut beef into slices ¼ inch thick. Spread one side of each slice with foie gras puree. Arrange the slices on a long dish, overlapping. Place a slice of truffle on each. Cover with half-set aspic. Chill. Serve cold. Makes 6 servings.

Russian Fillet of Beef in Aspic

3 pounds cold roast fillet of beef
3½ cups port-flavored aspic
Truffles

6 cooked artichoke bottoms
1 cup Russian or Mixed Vegetable Salad
1 cup Tartar Sauce

Cut beef into slices ¼ inch thick. Place slices in an upright position, in a 9-by-5-by-3-inch loaf pan. Fill with half-set aspic, tilting the pan so the aspic runs between the slices, coating them well. Decorate with truffle slices. Chill until aspic is firm and ready to serve. Turn out onto a platter. Garnish with the artichoke bottoms filled with the salad. Serve with Tartar Sauce. Makes 6 servings.

Fillet of Beef in Aspic with Tongue and Foie Gras

1 quart aspic, port-flavored
20 slices truffle
¾ pound pickled or smoked beef tongue
¾ pound cooked foie gras

¼ pound (1 stick) softened butter
1 (3-pound) roast fillet of beef,
    slightly underdone

Coat bottom and sides of a 9-by-5-by-3-inch loaf pan with aspic. Chill until almost set. Decorate the bottom with truffle slices and beef tongue cut into juliennes. Cover with half-set aspic. Chill until aspic is firm. Combine foie gras with butter, mixing well. Slice cold fillet of beef about ¼ inch thick. Spread both sides of each slice with the pâté-and-butter mixture, and place the slices in an upright position in the mold. Fill with half-set aspic. Refrigerate until firm and ready to serve. Turn out onto a platter and, if desired, garnish with additional aspic cut into cubes. Makes 8 servings.

Fillet of Beef with Tomatoes, Mushrooms, and Sauce Béarnaise Charlemagne

¼ cup (½ stick) butter
2 shallots, finely chopped, or
    2 tablespoons chopped onion
½ pound mushrooms finely chopped
1 tablespoon finely chopped parsley
½ teaspoon salt

Freshly ground black pepper
1 cup Tomato Sauce
2 pounds roasted fillet of beef
    (rare or medium rare)
Béarnaise Sauce

Melt butter in a 1½-quart saucepan. Add shallots and mushrooms. Stir and cook until the moisture has evaporated. Season with parsley, salt, and pepper, and add to Tomato

Sauce. Slice the hot beef and arrange the slices in a baking dish with mushroom-tomato sauce between the slices. Cover with Béarnaise Sauce. Cook under broiler until glazed. Makes 5 to 6 servings.

Grilled Châteaubriand

Châteaubriand is cut from the middle of the fillet, and the cooking is tricky because of its thickness. If it is sealed at high temperature too quickly, a hard crust forms which will impede further cooking, leaving the beef raw on the inside. Therefore the Châteaubriand should be cooked a bit more slowly than the other cuts of the beef filet.

1 Châteaubriand steak, 3 inches thick
Salt
Butter

Sprinkle both sides of meat lightly with salt. Spread generously with butter and cook about 6 minutes under the broiler. Transfer steak to a pan; reduce oven temperature to 350°F, and cook about 15 minutes for rare, 20 minutes for medium-rare. Serve with Béarnaise Sauce and Pommes Soufflés or French Fried Potatoes. Makes 2 servings.

Broiled Filet Mignon

Filets mignon are cut from the very tip of the whole filet of beef at the small (or rib) end.

4 filet mignon steaks, 1½ to
**   2 inches thick**
Salt

Melted butter
Ground black pepper
Béarnaise Sauce

Sprinkle meat lightly on both sides with salt and brush both sides with butter. Broil 3 inches from the heat source in a preheated broiler 6 minutes on each side, or until cooked as desired, brushing with butter. Sprinkle with pepper and serve with Béarnaise Sauce or Beef Marrow Sauce. Makes 4 servings.

TOURNEDOS

TOURNEDOS ARE CUT FROM THE SECTION next to the filet mignon, or the small, thinner (rib) end of the whole filet of beef. They are cut usually in 3½- to 4-ounce portions or 1 per person. They are usually broiled, grilled, or sautéed and then sauced and garnished in many ways.

Broiled Tournedos with Béarnaise Sauce

Tie string around each to hold it in shape. Sprinkle both sides of tournedos with salt and spread with butter. Broil on each side 3 minutes for rare, 4 to 5 minutes for medium-rare, in a preheated broiler. Remove the strings before serving. Cut pieces of white bread slightly larger than the tournedos and fry them in butter. Put each steak on a slice of fried bread and spoon on a border around the steak of very thick Béarnaise Sauce. Garnish with boiled potatoes and watercress. Allow 1 tournedos per serving.

Broiled Tournedos with Beef Marrow

6 tournedos	1 cup Brown Sauce
2 shallots, finely chopped	6 slices poached beef marrow
½ cup dry red wine	Chopped parsley

Broil tournedos as directed in the recipe for Broiled Tournedos. Cook the shallots in the wine until liquid is reduced by three-fourths. Stir in Brown Sauce and simmer 4 to 5 minutes, or until sauce is of desired thickness. Transfer steaks to a platter and cover with the sauce. Top each with a slice of poached marrow. Sprinkle with parsley. Makes 6 servings.

Broiled Tournedos Choron

6 tournedos	1 cup Choron Sauce
Butter	6 cooked artichoke bottoms
6 fried rounds white bread cut to fit meat and fried in butter	Boiled or French fried potato balls

Broil tournedos as directed in recipe for Broiled Tournedos. Place each on a round of fried bread and arrange on a hot platter. Keep hot. Put a tablespoon of Choron Sauce on each artichoke bottom, and place them on the platter around the steaks. Pass the rest of the sauce. Garnish with boiled or French fried potato balls. Makes 6 servings.

Broiled Tournedos Henri IV

18 tiny new potatoes	6 rounds bread cut to fit meat and fried in butter
6 tablespoons butter	
1 teaspoon salt	6 large cooked artichoke hearts
Ground white pepper	¾ cup Béarnaise Sauce
6 tournedos	

Scrape potatoes, wash, and pat dry. Cook, covered, very slowly in butter with salt and white pepper about 30 minutes, or until potatoes are tender. Meanwhile, broil tournedos as directed in the recipe for Broiled Tournedos. Place each tournedos on a slice of fried bread and place them on a platter. Pile 3 potatoes on each artichoke heart and arrange on the platter around the steaks. Pass Béarnaise Sauce in a sauce-boat. Makes 6 servings

Sautéed Tournedos Clamart

6 tournedos
Butter
6 rounds white bread cut to fit the
    meat and fried in butter

6 baked 2-inch tart shells
1½ cups buttered cooked Peas French Style
Château Potatoes
½ cup Veal Stock

Season and sauté the tournedos in butter 3 minutes on each side. Place each on a round of fried bread and place them on a hot platter. Keep hot. Fill tart shells with peas and serve with the steaks, along with the potatoes. Pour all the fat out of the pan, and deglaze with the stock. Reduce 3 minutes and pour over the steaks. Makes 6 servings.

Sautéed Tournedos Colbert

6 tournedos
6 round flattened chicken croquettes
6 small French Fried Eggs

6 slices truffle, or 6 mushroom caps
    sautéed in butter

Sauté tournedos (or broil as directed in recipe for Broiled Tournedos). Place each on a chicken croquette. Top with a French Fried Egg and garnish with a truffle slice or sautéed mushroom cap. Makes 6 servings.

Tournedos Masséna

2 shallots, finely chopped
2 tablespoons finely chopped onion
1 tablespoon butter
1 teaspoon flour
¼ cup Bouillon
¾ cup dry white wine
1 tablespoon brandy

1 truffle, finely chopped
6 tournedos
6 rounds white bread cut to fit
    meat and fried in butter
12 slices poached beef marrow
6 large cooked artichoke bottoms
½ cup Béarnaise Sauce

Cook shallots and onion in butter until transparent. Blend in flour. Stir and cook until browned. Add Bouillon. Mix well and set aside. In another saucepan, heat wine. Warm brandy, ignite, and add to wine; then add wine and brandy to the first mixture. Cover and simmer over very low heat 30 minutes, stirring frequently. Strain. Add truffle and cook 1 minute. Broil tournedos as directed in the recipe for Broiled Tournedos. Place each on a round of fried bread and arrange them on a hot platter. Top each with 2 slices marrow and coat with the sauce. Fill artichoke bottoms with Béarnaise Sauce and arrange on the platter around the meat. Serve at once. Makes 6 servings.

Sautéed Tournedos Rossini

½ pound goose foie gras	6 rounds white bread cut to fit
1 truffle	meat and fried in butter
¼ cup Madeira	¾ cup Demi-Glace Sauce
6 tournedos	1 tablespoon butter

Cut goose liver into 6 thick slices. Cut truffle into 6 thin slices. Marinate liver and truffle in Madeira in a covered dish 1 to 2 hours. Sauté tournedos. Place each on a round of fried bread. Keep hot. Degrease the pan and deglaze with the marinade, add Demi-Glace Sauce, and simmer 4 minutes. Add truffle slices and heat 30 seconds. Fry liver in butter, place a slice on each tournedos, top each with a truffle slice, and pour sauce over them. Serve at once. Makes 6 servings.

Filet of Beef Stroganoff

2 pounds thin end (filet mignon) fillet of beef	1 teaspoon prepared Dijon mustard
Salt and freshly ground black pepper	½ cup sour cream
4 tablespoons (½ stick) butter	1 teaspoon each chopped chervil,
1 cup hot Brown Stock	parsley, chives

Trim meat of all fat, skin, and nerves. Cut meat across the grain into strips 2-by-½-by-½ inches. Sprinkle lightly with salt and pepper and refrigerate 2 hours. Heat the butter in a large skillet. Add the meat. Brown quickly on all sides. Pour off the butter, add the Brown Stock, mustard, cream, chervil, parsley, and chives. Heat just to a boil, season, toss together, and serve at once.

Sautéed Sirloin Pepper Steaks or Steak au Poivre

4 eight-ounce sirloin steaks	4 tablespoons melted butter
Salt	½ cup brandy
1 tablespoon whole white peppercorns, coarsely crushed	2 tablespoons Demi-Glace Sauce

Rub salt into both sides of the meat. Dip meat into the crushed peppercorns, pressing the pepper into both sides with your hand. Fry the steaks in a heavy skillet in 2 tablespoons of the butter to desired doneness, turning to brown both sides. Transfer steaks to a hot platter and keep hot. Tip out all the fat from the pan. Add brandy to the skillet, boil, and flame. Add Demi-Glace Sauce, mix with a wooden spoon, and bring to the boiling point. Stir in the remaining butter and pour over the steaks. Serve at once. Makes 4 servings.

Fondue Bourguignonne

2 pounds sirloin steak
1½ cups pure vegetable oil
Salt and freshly ground black pepper

Assorted cold sauces (Mayonnaise,
    Aurora, Rémoulade, Vinaigrette)

Cut the meat into 1½-inch cubes. Skewer the cubes, using wooden skewers. (Do not use forks or metal skewers.) Heat oil in a heatproof dish and place in the center of the table on a hotplate, or over an alcohol lamp. Have your guests dip their own pieces of skewered meat into the hot oil and cook them as desired (rare, medium, or well-done). Provide salt, pepper in pepper mills, and a selection of sauces, each in a separate bowl. The pieces of meat are removed from the skewers and speared with forks for dipping into the desired sauce. Makes 6 servings.

Entrecôte Steak with Mushrooms

2 (1-pound) entrecôte steaks (or center
    cut rib steaks) 1 inch thick
5 tablespoons butter
2 tablespoons olive oil
½ pound blanched mushrooms
    (cooking liquid reserved)

½ cup Demi-Glace Sauce
Salt and freshly ground black pepper
Parsley

Trim any excess fat from steaks and make a small incision around them, in the layer of gristle between the fat and the meat. This prevents the steak from curling. Pat dry thoroughly. Heat 3 tablespoons of the butter and the oil in a skillet. When the butter foam begins to subside, add steaks and sauté on each side 3 to 4 minutes, regulating the heat so the fat does not burn. The steak is medium rare when bubbles of red juice begin to appear on the surface. Transfer steaks to a hot platter and keep hot. Skim off and discard fat from the pan juices, and add a little of the liquid used for blanching mushrooms to the pan. Mix well. Cook 30 seconds. Stir in Demi-Glace Sauce and mushrooms, mix well, then add remaining 2 tablespoons butter. Bring to the boiling point. Season with salt and pepper. Sprinkle steaks with salt and pepper and cover them with mushroom sauce. Garnish with parsley. Makes 6 servings.

Broiled Entrecôte Mirabeau

2 (1-pound) entrecôte steaks (center
    cut rib steaks), 1 inch thick
Melted butter
Salt and freshly ground black
    pepper
Anchovies
Pitted green and black olives
Watercress

Trim the steaks. Brush with butter and sprinkle lightly with salt. Place in a preheated broiler 3 inches from the heat source. Broil 5 minutes on each side for rare, 7 to 8 minutes for medium-rare. Sprinkle with pepper. Transfer to a hot platter. Dip anchovies in oil and place in lattice fashion over the top of the steaks. Garnish platter with pitted green olives and watercress. Serve with Soufflé Potatoes or French Fried Potatoes. Makes 4 servings.

Broiled Entrecôte Lyonnaise

3 cups sliced onions
3 tablespoons butter
Salt and freshly ground black pepper
1 teaspoon wine vinegar
1 tablespoon meat glaze
¼ cup dry white wine
4 (⅓-pound) entrecôte steaks (or sirloin
    or rib steaks), 1 inch thick
Chopped parsley

Fry onions in butter until golden brown. Season with salt and pepper to taste. Add vinegar, meat glaze, and wine. Simmer 2 to 3 minutes. Broil steaks as directed in the recipe for Entrecôte Mirabeau. Transfer steaks to a hot platter; pour onions over them. Sprinkle with chopped parsley. Serve at once. Makes 4 servings.

One-Minute Entrecôte

Cut entrecôte steaks ½-inch thick. Season both sides lightly with salt and ground black pepper. Fry very quickly, about 2 minutes on each side, in a little butter and oil (in equal amounts). Serve at once with Herb Butter. Allow 1 steak per serving.

Beef à la Mode

12 lardoons (long strips fatty salt pork)
Salt and freshly ground black pepper
1 tablespoon chopped parsley
1 clove garlic, minced
(4-pound) beef round roast
⅛ teaspoon grated nutmeg
3 tablespoons olive oil
¼ cup warmed brandy
1 cup dry red wine
1 cup beef stock
1 calf's or pig's foot (if available)
12 small carrots, pared
18 pearl white onions
3 tablespoons butter
1 tablespoons potato flour
3 tablespoons water
Parsley

Roll lardoons in salt, pepper, parsley, and garlic, and with a larding needle lard the meat. Rub the outside of the meat with salt, pepper, and nutmeg. Brown it on all sides in hot shortening or oil in a Dutch oven. Pour warmed brandy over the meat and ignite. Add wine, stock, and calf's foot (if using). Cover and cook in a preheated oven (325°F) 1½ hours. Brown carrots and onions in butter over low heat and add to the meat. Cover and cook 1 hour longer, or until meat and vegetables are tender. Skim off and discard all fat from the gravy. Transfer meat to a warmed platter. Surround with vegetables. Blend starch with water and add to the gravy. Bring to the boiling point, strain, and spoon some over the meat. Serve the remainder in a sauceboat. Garnish meat with parsley. Makes 6 to 8 servings.

Beef à la Mode in Aspic

4 to 5 pounds eye round of beef	1 large onion
6 lardoons (strips fatty salt pork)	5 carrots
Salt and freshly ground black pepper	2 shallots, chopped
½ cup brandy	2 ribs celery, sliced
2 to 3 tablespoons rendered beef suet	Parsley
or bacon fat	1 bay leaf
2 calf's feet	1 whole clove
3 cups dry white wine	12 small onions

Lard the beef with the lardoons, or ask your butcher to do it for you. Season with salt and pepper. Place meat in a bowl, pour brandy over it, and marinate 3 to 4 hours, turning meat occasionally. Remove beef (reserve marinade), pat dry, and brown on all sides in hot fat in a heavy saucepan. Transfer meat to another pan and keep warm. Split the calf's feet and parboil 10 minutes in hot water. Remove from water, dry, chop into coarse pieces, and brown in the same saucepan in which the beef was browned. Pour in the reserved marinade. Cook 3 to 4 minutes, scraping up all the browned bits from the bottom of the saucepan. Add wine. Peel the large onion, cut in half, and add. Peel 2 of the carrots, quarter, and add, along with the celery, 2 sprigs parsley, bay leaf, and clove. Return meat to the saucepan, cover, and simmer 4 hours, or until meat is tender, turning occasionally. Transfer meat and calf's feet to a bowl and cool. Slice meat and set aside. Cut meat from the calf's feet and slice it into juliennes. Set aside. Skim off and discard fat from the stock and strain the stock through a fine sieve. Pour enough of the stock into a mold or large pan, about 2 inches deep, to coat the bottom and sides. (Reserve remaining stock.) Chill until coating is almost set.

Meanwhile, peel the small onions, cut in half, and cook in water until tender. Peel remaining carrots, leave whole, and cook separately until tender. Cool. Cut 2 inches from the small ends of carrots. Split and arrange them in the center bottom of the mold to simulate a daisy. Finish covering the bottom with the rest of the carrots, sliced, and the onions. Cover with semiliquid aspic from stock. Chill until firm. Finish filling mold with sliced beef and meat cut from the calf's feet. Pour in enough of reserved stock to cover the meat and fill the mold. Chill until firm and ready to serve. Unmold on a platter. Garnish with parsley. Makes 8 to 10 servings.

Sauerbraten Berlin Style

1 clove garlic	1½ cups wine vinegar
½ cup sliced onion	2 cups beer
2 carrots, sliced	1 teaspoon salt
1 rib celery, diced, or ¼ cup diced celery root	3 to 4 pounds round of beef
	⅓ cup olive oil
¼ cup chopped parsley	2 tablespoons shortening or oil
1 bay leaf	1 cup beef stock
8 whole peppercorns	¾ cup sour cream

Combine the first 10 ingredients and bring to the boiling point. Place beef in a bowl and pour the mixture and then the oil over it. Cover and marinate in the refrigerator 3 days, turning meat occasionally.

Remove meat and vegetables from marinade. Reserve marinade. Dry meat with paper towels and brown on all sides in oil in a Dutch oven or a heavy 4-quart saucepan, along with the vegetables. Add marinade and stock. Cover and cook in a preheated oven (325°F) 2½ to 3 hours, or until meat is tender. Transfer meat to a serving dish and keep warm. Strain stock and cook until reduced by half. Stir in sour cream and heat. Adjust seasonings. Cut meat into slices and serve with the gravy, Red Cabbage with Apples, and mashed potatoes. Makes 6 to 8 servings.

Spoon Tender Braised Beef

5 pound eye round of beef	2 cups Brown Stock
Salt and freshly ground black pepper	1 cup diced carrots
Flour	½ cup chopped onion
1 to 2 tablespoons oil	¹⁄₁₆ teaspoon minced garlic
1 cup dry white wine	1 tablespoon tomato puree

Rub the beef with salt and pepper. Dredge meat lightly in flour and brown slowly on both sides in oil in a heavy skillet. Add wine, stock, carrots, onion, and garlic. Cover. Cook over low heat or in a preheated oven (300°F) for 2-3 hours or until meat is so well done that it will fall apart when you attempt to slice it. Transfer meat to a platter. Remove all the fat from the braising liquid, add tomato puree and reduce by half. Adjust seasonings, strain, and pour over meat. Makes 6 servings.

Braised Beef Bourguignonne

3 pounds boneless beef (rump or chuck)	1½ teaspoons salt
Flour	3 sprigs parsley
3 tablespoons olive oil or bacon fat	2 slices bacon
1 clove garlic, finely chopped	1 cup pearl onions
2 cups red Burgundy	18 medium-sized mushroom caps
Brown Stock	¼ teaspoon freshly ground black pepper
1 small bay leaf	2 tablespoons butter

Cut beef into large cubes and roll them in flour. Brown on all sides in hot oil or bacon fat. Add garlic and fry with the meat 15 seconds. Turn into a 2-quart casserole. Add wine and enough stock to barely cover the meat, along with bay leaf, salt, and parsley. Cover and cook in a preheated oven (300°F) 2 hours. Dice bacon and fry briefly, then add onions and cook until onions are lightly browned and bacon is crisp. Add mushrooms and fry 2 minutes. Add onions and the bacon to the meat and cook 20 minutes, or until meat and vegetables are tender. Drain off the sauce from the meat and vegetables, degrease, simmer 5 minutes, add meat and vegetables and reheat. Serve hot with bread triangles fried in butter. Makes 6 servings.

Italian Braised Beef

3 pounds boneless rump or other lean roast, larded with fatty salt pork	½ cup chopped onion
2 whole carrots	½ cup chopped carrots
2 ribs celery	½ cup chopped celery
1 cup red wine	¼ cup tomato puree
½ cup olive oil	1 cup water
½ teaspoon sage	8 braised onions
½ teaspoon dried rosemary	8 braised potatoes

Roll the meat up the long way, rolling it around the whole carrots and the ribs of celery. Make a marinade with the red wine, ⅓ cup of the oil, and the sage and rosemary, and marinate the meat in this for 48 hours. Remove the meat, reserving the marinade. Brown the meat on all sides in the remaining oil, adding the chopped vegetables to the pan a few minutes before the meat is all browned. Pour the marinade over the meat and cook, uncovered, until the liquid is reduced by half. Add the tomato puree and water. Cover and cook slowly 2½ to 3 hours, turning the meat 2 or 3 times. Remove the meat to a warm serving platter and keep warm. Skim off the excess fat from the cooking liquid, strain the liquid, and reduce if necessary. Arrange the braised onions and potatoes on the platter around the meat. Serve the gravy separately. Makes 6 to 8 servings.

Braised Rump of Beef

3 pounds boneless rump or other lean
    roast, larded with fatty salt pork
Salt and freshly ground black pepper
2 tablespoons lard or olive oil
½ cup sliced onion
½ cup sliced carrots
2 cups dry white wine, stock, or water

1 cup Demi-Glace Sauce
2 sprigs parsley
1 rib celery, quartered
6 braised potatoes
12 braised carrots
½ pound braised white onions
Watercress (optional)

Rub the outside of the meat with salt and pepper and brown it on all sides in lard or oil along with the sliced onion and carrots. Pour off the excess fat, add wine, stock, or water, and cook the meat, uncovered, until the liquid has reduced by half. Pour the Demi-Glace Sauce over the meat. Add parsley and celery. Cover and cook slowly 2½ to 3 hours, turning the meat 3 or 4 times. Transfer meat to a warmed platter and keep it warm until ready to serve. Skim off excess fat from the cooking liquid and discard. Strain the liquid; if it is not thick enough, boil it a few minutes to reduce it to desired consistency. Slice the meat, and arrange the slices, overlapping, on a platter. Garnish with the braised vegetables. Decorate the platter, if desired, with watercress. Makes 6 to 8 servings.

Marseilles Daube or Braised Beef with Tomatoes and Olives

3 pounds shoulder or rump of beef,
    cut into large cubes
Lardoons (strips fatty salt pork)
2½ cups dry red wine
1 cup brandy
1 cup sliced carrots
1½ cups sliced onions
1 clove garlic

6 whole peppercorns
½ teaspoon salt
2 sprigs parsley
3 tablespoons olive oil
¼ pound fresh pork rind
1 cup diced, peeled, seeded tomatoes
12 pitted black olives

Lard each cube of meat with a lardoon. Add wine, brandy, carrots, onions, garlic, peppercorns, salt, and parsley. Pour oil over the top. Cover and marinate in the refrigerator overnight. Rinse pork rind in water, and put in the bottom of a Dutch oven. Place the meat on the pork rind and pour in the marinade. Add tomatoes. Cover tightly and cook in a preheated oven (325°F) 2 to 3 hours. Remove the meat, degrease the juices and reduce for a few minutes. Pour back over the beef, add the olives, and simmer for 10 minutes. If desired, use a whole piece of meat without cubing it. The method of cooking is the same but the cooking time may need to be increased by 30 minutes. Makes 6 servings.

Braised Beef Birds or Paupiettes

6 thin large slices rump or round of beef	2 tablespoons olive oil
	1 cup sliced carrots
Salt and freshly ground black pepper	½ cup sliced onion
6 slices bacon	½ cup dry white wine
6 thin slices raw ham	2 cups diced fresh tomatoes

Sprinkle both sides of meat slices lightly with salt and pepper. Place a slice of bacon and a slice of ham on each. Roll up and tie with strings. Brown on all sides in oil, along with carrots and onions. Pour off fat. Add wine and cook 1 to 2 minutes. Add tomatoes, cover, and cook over low heat 1 hour, or until meat is tender. Transfer meat to a serving dish and remove strings. Strain the braising liquid and skim off fat, adjust seasonings, and serve over meat. Garnish with any desired vegetables. Makes 6 servings.

Beef Birds or Paupiettes Provençale

In the recipe for Beef Birds, replace the bacon and ham with ¾ pound sausage meat mixed with 2 tablespoons chopped parsley and 1⁄16 teaspoon finely chopped garlic. Add 12 pitted green olives to the final cooking process of the sauce.

Beef Birds or Paupiettes Milanese

In the recipe for Beef Birds Provençale, omit the garlic and the olives. Serve with boiled macaroni or Risotto Milanese.

English Beefsteak Pie

2 pounds round steak	4 hard-cooked eggs
Salt and freshly ground black pepper	4 slices bacon
6 tablespoons flour	Water or stock
½ cup chopped parsley	1 tablespoon Worcestershire sauce
¼ pound sliced mushrooms	Puff Pastry or Plain Pastry Dough
2 cups sliced onions	Milk

Cut steak into thin 2-inch pieces. Sprinkle lightly with salt and pepper, roll in flour, and put half the meat into a buttered casserole with half the parsley, mushrooms, and onions. Cut eggs in half and place over meat. Repeat layering, using remaining meat, parsley, bacon, and onion. Pour in enough water or stock and Worcestershire sauce to cover the meat. Top with Puff Pastry Dough rolled ¼ inch thick, or Plain Pastry Dough rolled ⅛ inch thick. Trim, turn under, and flute the edge. Cut 2 or 3 vents in the pastry to allow steam to escape. Brush crust with milk. Bake in a preheated oven (450°F) 10 minutes. Reduce heat to 350° and continue cooking 30 to 40 minutes, or until meat is tender. Makes 6 servings.

Polish Meat Balls with Herbs or Bitokes

1 pound lean beef, ground	2 tablespoons each finely chopped
¾ pound lean pork, ground	chervil, dill, parsley, tarragon, mixed
½ cup finely chopped onion	¼ pound (1 stick) butter
1½ teaspoons salt	¾ cup Demi-Glace Sauce
⅛ teaspoon freshly ground black pepper	½ cup sour cream

Combine the first 5 ingredients. Shape into 1½-inch balls and roll in the mixture of herbs. Cook in butter over low heat until done; do not allow meat balls to brown. Add Demi-Glace Sauce and cook 3 to 4 minutes. Serve with sizzling Brown Butter poured over and with sour cream in a separate bowl. Makes 6 servings.

Hamburger Steak

FOR EACH SERVING:

⅓ pound ground beef sirloin	Salt and freshly ground black pepper
1 teaspoon finely chopped lightly cooked onion	Brown Butter
1 egg yolk	Chopped parsley

Mix meat with onion, egg yolk, salt, and pepper. Shape into a steak ½ inch thick. Brown on both sides in butter, keeping the inside slightly underdone, if desired. Serve with Brown Butter poured over and garnish with the parsley.

Salt Brisket of Beef Belle Flamande

3 to 4 pounds salted or corned beef	6 servings green beans, cooked
Cold water	Chopped parsley
6 each medium-sized carrots, potatoes, and turnips, quartered	½ pound sausage, cooked
Heart of 1 head cabbage	Vincent Sauce

Place beef, with cold water to cover, in a Dutch oven. Bring to the boiling point and skim. Cover and simmer (do not boil) 4 hours, or until meat is tender. Add carrots, potatoes, and turnips 20 minutes before cooking time is up, and cabbage 10 minutes before meat is done. To serve, slice enough meat for one meal and put it on a hot platter, arranging vegetables and sausage around the meat. Sprinkle vegetables with parsley. Serve Vincent Sauce separately. Makes 6 servings sliced corned beef with vegetables, and enough beef for hash for another meal.

Vincent Sauce

Blanch equal amounts parsley, watercress, and chives in hot water. Drain well and puree. Add 2 tablespoons puree to each ½ cup Mayonnaise. Mix well. Stir in the chopped white of 1 hard-cooked egg. Serve with salt beef.

VEAL

VEAL HAS A DELICATE FLAVOR AND TEXTURE and therefore has a wonderful capacity to absorb the flavors of herbs and sauces.

Roast Loin of Veal

1 (5-pound) boned veal loin roast
Salt and freshly ground black pepper

Thin strips salt port
Mushrooms (optional)

Sprinkle veal with salt and pepper. Cover with salt pork. Put roast on a rack, fat side up. Cook, uncovered, in a preheated oven (375°F) 15 minutes per pound, or until meat registers 165°F on a meat thermometer. Add a little water to the pan if the fat tends to scorch. Transfer meat to a hot platter and keep warm for 20 minutes while making the sauce. Make gravy from pan drippings, adding sautéed mushrooms if desired. Makes 10 to 12 servings.

Roast Boned Loin of Veal with Kidneys or Rognonade

Have the butcher cut a 5-pound boned loin of veal with the kidneys attached and roast it as directed for Roast Loin of Veal. Serve with sautéed fluted mushrooms. Makes 10 to 12 servings.

Veal Rib Roast with Vegetables

1 veal rib roast, allowing 2 ribs
    per serving, chinebone removed
Salt and freshly ground black pepper

Buttered cooked vegetables: carrots,
    cauliflower, potatoes, and tomatoes
Chopped chives

Sprinkle meat lightly with salt and pepper and wrap it in buttered paper or aluminum foil. Roast on a spit or in a preheated oven (350°F) 1 hour. Remove the paper or foil and continue cooking until the meat is golden brown. (Allow total cooking time of 20 minutes per pound.) Transfer roast to a warm platter. Serve with cooked vegetables. Sprinkle potatoes with chopped chives. Allow 2 ribs per serving.

Roast Veal Nivernaise

3 pounds rolled rump veal roast,
   larded with fatty salt pork
Salt and freshly ground black pepper
2 cups brown stock
2 cups turnips cut in the shape
   of large olives

30 pearl white onions
½ pound fresh peas
1 pound potato olives
3 tablespoons butter

Rub salt and pepper over the surface of the meat, and place it on a rack in a heavy saucepan or Dutch oven. Cook meat, uncovered, in a preheated oven (500°F) 10 to 15 minutes, or until browned. Reduce heat to 350°F. Add 1 cup stock, cover, and cook 20 minutes per pound, or until meat is tender. Transfer meat to a warm platter and keep warm. Strain the juices, skim off fat, and reduce by half. Cook turnips, onions, peas and potatoes separately, drain, and toss with the butter. Slice the meat and arrange the vegetables on the platter around the roast. Serve sauce separately. Makes 6 servings.

Jellied Veal Pot Roast

4 pounds rolled rump veal roast,
   larded with fatty salt pork
Salt and freshly ground black pepper
Butter
2 cups Plain White Stock

12 medium-small carrots
2 small white turnips
12 pearl onions
½ pound string beans

Sprinkle surface of roast with salt and pepper. Put it in a Dutch oven over medium heat and brown on all sides in butter, adding butter as needed. Drain the butter from the pan. Slip a rack under the meat. Add stock, not more than 1 cup at a time. Cover and cook slowly until meat is tender, adding remaining stock as needed. Peel carrots and turnips and cut into large juliennes. Brown in butter, along with onions. After meat has cooked 1 hour, add these vegetables to the meat. Cover and cook until meat and vegetables are tender. Cook string beans in a separate saucepan and add to the veal at the last moment. If liquid tends to evaporate too fast, add more stock. Place veal and vegetables in a deep bowl. Skim fat from the braising liquid and pour into the bowl over meat and vegetables. Chill. Serve in the jellied aspic. Makes 6 to 8 servings.

Roast Saddle of Veal

Ask your butcher to trim and lard a saddle of veal. Fold the long ends under and tie in place with strings. Sprinkle with salt and freshly ground black pepper. Place on a rack in a large baking pan. Cook in a preheated oven (350°F) 20 minutes per pound. Make sauce from pan defatted juices and veal stock.

Cold Saddle of Veal

Cold Roast Saddle of Veal
6 hard-cooked eggs
20 thin slices truffle
Small baked pastry tart shells

Marinated cold cooked asparagus tips
Parsley

Slice as much of the roast as needed and place it in its original shape on a large tray. Slice 5 of the eggs, cover the yolks with truffle slices, and arrange the egg slices in a row in the center of the roast for two-thirds of its length. Finish the row with baked tart shells filled with asparagus tips. Fill additional baked pastry tart shells with asparagus tips and arrange them on the tray. Garnish tray with parsley.

Veal Medallions with Mushrooms

6 medallions of veal tenderloin,
    ¾ inch thick
Salt and freshly ground black pepper
6 tablespoons butter

1 cup Brown Veal Stock
6 large fluted mushroom caps,
    sautéed in butter
Chopped parsley

Sprinkle veal with salt and pepper. Sauté in butter over medium-low heat until browned and thoroughly done. Place chops in a serving dish and cover with hot sauce made from deglazing the defatted pan juices with the Brown Stock. Top each with a sautéed mushroom cap. Garnish with chopped parsley. Serve with boiled potatoes. Makes 6 servings.

Sautéed Veal Grenadins in White Wine

A grenadin is a piece of veal cut from the rump, like escalopes or cutlets, but smaller and thicker.

6 veal loin or kidney chops, boned
¾ teaspoon salt
⅛ teaspoon freshly ground black pepper
Flour

About ½ cup (1 stick) butter
½ cup dry white wine
6 slices bread

Rub chops with salt and pepper. Dredge in flour. Brown on both sides, over medium heat, in butter, adding butter as needed. Add wine, cover, and simmer 15 minute. Cut slices of bread to fit the chops and fry in butter. Serve the chops on the bread on a hot platter. Garnish with cooked vegetables such as cauliflower, green beans, peas, and carrots. Makes 6 servings.

⌀ Sautéed Veal Medallions or Noisettes

Noisettes are small nuggets of veal cut from the shoulder, but since there are so few, the word has come to mean small rounds (2 inches thick) cut from the filet, and are also called "medallions" when larger, rounder, and thicker pieces cut from the loin. Loin or kidney chops can be substituted for noisettes.

6 loin medallions	About ½ cup (1 stick) butter
¾ teaspoon salt	12 fresh sage leaves
⅛ teaspoon freshly ground black pepper	½ cup dry white wine
Flour	

Rub veal with salt and pepper. Dredge in flour. Brown on both sides, over medium heat, in butter, adding butter as needed. Place 2 leaves of sage on each chop. Add wine, cover, and simmer 15 minutes. Transfer chops to a hot platter. Add butter to the cooking liquid. Heat and strain over chops. Serve with French fried or boiled potatoes. Makes 6 servings.

⌀ Sautéed Veal Loin Chops in Aspic Molière

6 veal loin chops	Mayonnaise
Salt and freshly ground black pepper	1 slice cooked tongue or ham
Butter	1 hard-cooked egg white
6 cauliflower florets	Aspic
Boiling water	Truffles
3 medium-sized tomatoes	Parsley

Sprinkle chops with salt and pepper and fry them in butter until brown on both sides. Add butter as needed. Cool chops under a weight to flatten them. Cook cauliflower in 1 inch boiling water with ½ teaspoon salt until barely tender, about 5 minutes. Cool and chill. Peel and cut tomatoes in half and scoop out centers. Sprinkle with salt and pepper and place a piece of cauliflower in each. Cover carefully with Mayonnaise. Chill until ready to serve. Cut tongue or ham and egg white into small daisy-petal shapes and arrange them in daisy fashion on each chop. Glaze with aspic and chill. Cut tongue or ham into ½-to ¾-inch disks and place one on each cauliflower. Cut truffle slices into four-leaf-clover shapes and place one on each disk of ham or tongue. Coat a round tray with aspic and chill until aspic is set. Place chops on the tray, with the bone ends toward the center. Place a piece of parsley in the center, partially covering the ends of the bones. Arrange tomatoes and cauliflower between the chops near the rim of the tray. Makes 6 servings.

Sautéed Veal Cutlets Chenonceaux

A veal cutlet is cut from the leg ½-inch thick, preferably with the round bone included, or from the loin with the rib bone attached.

6 (6-ounce) veal cutlets
Salt and freshly ground black pepper
¼ pound (1 stick) butter
12 slices pickled or boiled beef tongue
½ cup sherry

½ cup Brown Stock
6 teaspoons slivered, toasted
    blanched almonds
Macaire Potatoes

Sprinkle cutlets lightly with salt and pepper. Brown on both sides in butter, adding butter as needed. Transfer cutlets to a platter and keep hot. In the same skillet, heat the tongue in the butter that is left, adding more if necessary. Place 2 slices on each cutlet. Remove fat from the skillet and pour sherry into the skillet. Simmer 1 minute, add stock and bring to the boiling point, and boil 1 to 2 minutes. Pour over meat. Sprinkle with almonds. Serve with Macaire Potatoes. Makes 6 servings.

Sautéed Veal Cutlets with Onions and Cheese Foyot

2 cups sliced onions
2 tablespoons butter
6 (6-ounce) veal cutlets
Salt and freshly ground black pepper
1 cup grated Gruyère cheese

½ cup white breadcrumbs
4 tablespoons (½ stick) butter
½ cup dry white wine
¾ cup veal stock

Cook onions in butter until transparent. Place half in the bottom of a baking pan. Sprinkle cutlets with salt and pepper, put on top of onions and cover with remaining onions. Mix cheese with breadcrumbs and sprinkle over onions. Dot with butter. Combine wine and stock and pour over the top. Bake in a preheated oven (325°F) 1 hour. Makes 6 servings.

Sautéed Viennese Veal Cutlets or Wiener Schnitzel

2 pounds veal loin boneless cutlets
1 teaspoon salt
¼ freshly ground black pepper
1 egg, beaten

2 tablespoons flour
6 tablespoons white breadcrumbs
4 tablespoons (½ stick) butter
6 thin slices lemon

Cut veal into 6 equal portions. Season the cutlets, dip in beaten egg, then in flour mixed with breadcrumbs. Brown on both sides in butter, adding butter as needed. Transfer veal to a hot platter and top each cutlet with a lemon slice. Makes 6 servings.

Sautéed Veal Cutlets with Watercress

4 (6-ounce) veal loin cutlets
Salt and freshly ground black pepper
2 tablespoons butter, melted
3 tablespoons softened butter

1 tablespoon chopped parsley
1 tablespoon chopped watercress
Watercress
Matchstick Potatoes

Rub both sides of cutlets with salt and pepper. Brush with melted butter. Brown on both sides over medium-low heat . Meanwhile, blend softened butter with parsley and chopped watercress. Chill and shape into a cylinder. Cut 4 slices and place one on each cutlet. Transfer cutlets to a platter. Garnish with watercress. Serve with Matchstick Potatoes. Makes 4 servings.

Sautéed Veal Scaloppine Valdostana

A scallop (*escalope* or *scaloppine*), is cut from the sirloin and pounded very thinly. They can be cut from the loin, but have less flavor even if they are more tender and cook instantly.

2 pounds veal sirloin cut into
    6 thin uniform scallops
Salt and freshly ground black pepper
Flour
1 egg, beaten
3 tablespoons olive oil

3 tablespoons butter
½ pound mushrooms, sliced
6 thin slices Val d'Aosta Fontina cheese
Stuffed Eggplant
Stuffed Tomatoes
Browned Sliced Potatoes

Flatten steaks to ¼ inch thick with a mallet. Season with salt and pepper, dredge in flour, dip in egg, and brown on both sides in the oil and 2 tablespoons of the butter. Transfer veal to an 11-by-7-by-1½-inch baking dish. Add remaining butter and the mushrooms. Stir and cook 3 to 4 minutes and spoon over veal. Top each steak with a slice of cheese. Cook in a preheated oven (400°F) 10 minutes, or until cheese has melted. Serve with Stuffed Eggplant, Stuffed Tomatoes, and Browned Sliced Potatoes. Makes 6 servings.

Jellied Veal Cutlets

4 (6-ounce) veal cutlets
Salt and freshly ground black pepper
Butter
4 cups liquid aspic

8 small carrots
12 pearl onions
2 medium-sized tomatoes, halved
Chervil or parsley

Trim cutlets to make them of uniform size. Sprinkle with salt and pepper. Brown on both sides in butter over medium heat. Place cutlets in an 8-by-8-by-2-inch oven-proof dish. Pour ⅓ cup of the aspic over them. Brown carrots and onions in butter, and place them over the cutlets. Top each cutlet with half a tomato, and chervil or parsley leaves. Pour remaining aspic over the cutlets and vegetables. Chill until aspic is set and the dish is ready to be served. Serve in the baking dish. Garnish with chervil or parsley. Makes 4 servings.

Veal Scaloppine with Marsala

2 pounds veal sirloin cut into
    6 thin uniform scallops
Salt and freshly ground black pepper
Flour

3 tablespoons olive oil or salad oil
3 tablespoons butter
¼ cup veal or chicken stock
¼ cup Marsala

Pound steaks to ¼ inch thick with a mallet. Sprinkle with salt and pepper, dredge in flour, and fry quickly in oil and butter. Add stock and half the wine. Cover and simmer 10 minutes. Transfer meat to a hot platter. Pour remaining wine into the skillet and cook to reduce the liquid by half. Adjust seasonings and pour over the meat. Makes 6 servings.

Saltimbocca alla Romana

2½ pounds veal sirloin steaks,
    ¾ inch thick
Salt freshly ground black pepper
6 slices raw ham
6 fresh sage leaves
Flour

2 tablespoons olive oil
3 tablespoons butter
⅓ cup dry white wine
Buttered diced potatoes
Chopped parsley

Cut steaks into 12 pieces of equal size. Flatten with a mallet until ⅛ inch thick, and season lightly with salt and pepper. Place on each of 6 steaks 1 ham slice, 1 sage leaf, and another veal steak (sandwich fashion). Hold in place with half-toothpicks. Dredge in flour. Brown in a heavy skillet in oil and 2 tablespoons of the butter. Transfer to a hot platter and keep warm. Put remaining 1 tablespoon butter and the wine in the skillet. Bring to the boiling point and boil 30 seconds. Strain sauce over the meat. Serve with buttered diced potatoes sprinkled with parsley. Makes 6 servings.

Sautéed Scallops of Veal with Ham, Tongue, Mushrooms, and Madeira Zingara

6 veal scallops	¼ cup Madeira
Salt and freshly ground black pepper	½ cup shredded cooked or pickled beef tongue
Flour	½ cup shredded cooked ham
Butter	½ cup shredded poached mushrooms
½ cup Demi-Glace Sauce	Veal stock

Season veal with salt and pepper. Dredge in flour. Brown on both sides over medium heat in butter, adding butter as needed. Transfer meat to a hot platter and keep warm. Combine next 2 ingredients in a separate saucepan, mix well, and heat. Stir in all remaining ingredients except stock and heat. Use as a garnish for the top of the scallops. Make sauce from the defatted veal pan juices and veal stock. Makes 6 servings.

Stuffed Breast of Veal

3 to 4 pounds boned breast of veal	2 tablespoons minced parsley
Salt and freshly ground black pepper	1½ teaspoons chopped fresh marjoram
½ cup finely chopped onion	Flour
½ clove garlic, crushed	2 tablespoons butter
½ pound sausage meat	¾ cup Bouillon
2 cups soft white breadcrumbs	

Cut a pocket in the veal. Sprinkle inside and out lightly with salt and pepper. Cook onion and garlic with sausage until sausage begins to brown. Add breadcrumbs, herbs, and salt and pepper to taste. Mix well and stuff lightly into the pocket of the veal. Close opening with skewers and lace tightly with string. Dredge meat in flour and brown on all sides in butter in a Dutch oven. Add ¾ cup water or bouillon, cover, and simmer 2 hours, or until meat is tender. Transfer meat to a platter and keep hot. Defat the cooking juices and reduce by half. Serve over the sliced veal. Makes 6 to 8 servings.

Garnished Riblets, Tenders, or Tendrons of Veal

Tendron of veal is sliced breast of veal at the small end of the ribs. They are cut with the full width of the breast across the bone. They are usually braised, like short ribs, in very little liquid.

3 pounds veal riblets	Veal stock
Salt and freshly ground black pepper	20 boiled pearl onions
Flour	6 small cooked new carrots
Pure vegetable oil	1½ cups each cooked green peas and
½ cup sliced onion	green beans cut into 1-inch pieces
1 cup sliced carrots	4 tablespoons (¼ stick) butter

Season riblets with salt and pepper and dredge in flour. Brown on both sides in 2 tablespoons oil over medium heat. Transfer to another pan and keep hot. In the first skillet, cook sliced onion and carrots, adding more oil as needed. Sprinkle with salt and pepper and place in the bottom of an 11-by-7-by-1½-inch baking dish. Top with browned riblets. Add enough stock to half-cover the meat. Cook in a preheated oven (300°F) 1 hour, or until meat is tender, basting frequently. Remove meat to a platter and keep hot. Skim off and discard fat from the juices. If necessary add a little more stock. Simmer 5 minutes. Pour over the meat. Toss hot cooked onions with 1 tablespoon of the butter and scatter over the veal. Mix carrots, peas, and green beans lightly with remaining butter. Serve with the veal in a separate dish. Makes 6 servings.

Blanquette of Veal

2¼ pounds shoulder or breast of veal	12 pearl onions, peeled
Water	4 carrots, peeled and quartered
1 large onion	2 large egg yolks
2 sprigs parsley	½ cup heavy cream
6 whole peppercorns	½ pound small mushroom caps,
2 teaspoons salt	sautéed in butter
1 clove garlic	

Cut meat into 2-inch pieces and parboil 5 minutes in a saucepan in water to cover. Drain. Add the large onion, parsley, peppercorns, salt, and garlic, with water to cover (about 4 cups). Bring to the boiling point, reduce heat, and simmer 1½ hours, or until veal is tender. Add pearl onions and carrots 30 minutes before cooking time is up. Using a perforated spoon, transfer meat, carrots, and pearl onions to a serving dish and keep hot. Strain stock and cook until reduced by about one-third. Lightly beat egg yolks together with cream and stir into the stock. Stir and heat until sauce thickens. (Do not boil.) Adjust seasonings. Pour over the meat, carrots, and onions. Garnish with mushroom caps. Serve with rice or boiled potatoes. Makes 6 servings.

Veal Marengo

2½ pounds shoulder of veal
Salt and freshly ground black pepper
Butter
Olive oil or salad oil
1½ tablespoons flour
1 small clove garlic, crushed
⅓ cup dry white wine

Bouillon or water
2 sprigs parsley
1 tomato
24 pearl onions
½ pound mushrooms
12 to 16 toast points
Chopped parsley

Cut meat into 2-inch pieces. Sprinkle with salt and pepper and brown in a Dutch oven in 2 tablespoons each butter and oil, adding butter and oil as needed. Sprinkle with flour; stir and cook until flour has browned. Add garlic and wine and cook until most of the wine has evaporated. Pour in enough bouillon or water to barely cover the meat. Add parsley sprigs, cover, and cook in a preheated oven (325°F) 1 hour, or until meat is tender. Meanwhile, peel and seed tomato and mix with a little oil, pick out seeds, and mix tomatoes with oil. Peel onions and cook in a little bouillon. When meat is tender, transfer it to a casserole, strain gravy over meat, and add tomatoes, onions, and mushrooms. Put casserole back into 325° oven, cover, and cook 30 minutes. Fry toast points in hot oil. Transfer contents of casserole to a serving dish and garnish with toast points and chopped parsley. Makes 6 to 8 servings.

Veal Shanks Milanese or Osso Buco alla Milanese

6 shank cross cuts on the bone,
    2 inches thick
Salt and freshly ground black pepper
Flour
2 tablespoons olive oil or salad oil
3 tablespoons butter
1 carrot, sliced
1 rib celery, sliced
¾ cup diced onion

1 small clove garlic, crushed
½ cup tomato puree
½ cup dry white wine
1 cup veal stock
2 tablespoons chopped parsley
1 tablespoon grated lemon zest
2 teaspoons cornstarch
2 tablespoons water

Sprinkle veal with salt and pepper, then dredge in flour. Brown meat on both sides in a heavy skillet in equal parts oil and butter, adding more oil and butter as needed. Add vegetables, garlic, and remaining 1 tablespoon butter. Stir and cook until vegetables have lightly browned. Add tomato puree and wine. Cover and simmer until the liquid has reduced by half. Pour in stock, cover, and simmer 2 hours until veal is tender. Add parsley and lemon zest. Adjust seasonings. Turn into a serving dish. Serve with cooked rice or Risotto. Makes 6 servings.

Paupiettes of Veal à la Grecque

Paupiettes are thin slices of meat spread with a stuffing, rolled, and tied.

6 thin veal scallops	½ teaspoon chopped thyme
Salt and freshly ground black pepper	6 thin slices raw ham
1 cup chopped onion	1 small onion, sliced
5 tablespoons butter	1 small carrot, sliced
2¼ cups soft breadcrumbs	1 cup veal stock
2 tablespoons chopped parsley	Rice à la Grecque

Sprinkle veal with salt and pepper. Set aside. Cook chopped onion in 3 tablespoons of the butter until limp. Add breadcrumbs, herbs, and salt and pepper to taste. Spread over the meat. Cover each scallop with a thin slice of ham. Roll up and tie with strings at both ends. Cook, along with sliced onion and carrot, in remaining 2 tablespoons butter. Add stock. Cook in a preheated oven (325°F) 1 hour, basting occasionally with the stock. Arrange paupiettes on a mound of Rice à la Grecque. Skim fat from gravy. Bring to the boiling point, and pour over the paupiettes. Makes 6 servings.

LAMB AND MUTTON

Lamb is the flesh of young sheep and mutton that of older sheep, the dividing line being set at an age of about one year. Most of the sheep sold in the United States is lamb. Mutton is delicious, but scarce in the United States. The color of the meat is a good indication of the age of the animal. Young lamb has bright pinkish flesh and reddish bones. As the age of the animal increases its flesh becomes darker in color and its bones and fat become lighter.

Roast Leg of Lamb Boulangère

1 (6- to 7-pound) leg of lamb	4 medium-sized onions, sliced
Salt and freshly ground black pepper	2 cups lamb stock or water
8 medium-sized potatoes, quartered	

Trim off all but a thin layer of fat from the roast. Rub it with salt and pepper and place on a rack, fat side up, in a baking pan. Roast, uncovered, using one of the following methods:

FRENCH TWO-TEMPERATURE METHOD. Cook meat in a preheated oven (450°F) 20 minutes, then reduce heat to 325°F. For medium-rare, cook 10 to 12 minutes per pound; for well-done, cook 13 to 15 minutes per pound. It should reach an internal temperature of 140°F for medium rare and then let sit to rest.

AMERICAN LOW-TEMPERATURE OR ONE-TEMPERATURE METHOD. Cook meat in a preheated oven (325°F). For medium-rare cook 30 minutes per pound, or to 140°F on a meat thermometer.

Parboil potatoes 5 to 7 minutes in boiling water to cover. Drain and add to the roasting pan, along with onions, about 45 minutes before cooking time is up. Transfer meat and vegetables to a hot platter and keep warm. Skim off and discard fat from pan drippings. Add stock or water to the pan and simmer, scraping all the browned bits from the bottom of the pan. Serve with the roast. Makes 8 to 10 servings.

Roast Rack of Lamb with Parsley

1 loin lamb roast (rack), allowing 2 to 3 ribs per serving, chine bone removed	¼ cup finely chopped parsley
	½ cup white breadcrumbs
	Watercress
Salt and freshly ground black pepper	Broiled Whole Tomatoes
1 tablespoon Dijon mustard	Asparagus tips, steamed

Season roast with salt and pepper, and stand it on the ribs in a large shallow pan. Cook in a preheated oven (375°F) 20 minutes per pound, or until a meat thermometer registers 140°F. After the meat has been in the oven for three-fourths of the cooking time, spread with the mustard, mix the parsley with the breadcrumbs and spread over the roast. Continue cooking until meat is done. Transfer roast to a hot platter. Garnish with watercress, Broiled Whole Tomatoes, and asparagus tips. Allow 2 to 3 ribs per serving.

Sautéed Lamb Rib Chops or Cotelettes Cyrano

In France, rib lamb chops are called *côtelettes*, and the loin chops *côtes*.

12 rib lamb chops	12 small slices fried goose foie gras
Salt and freshly ground black pepper	Chateaubriand Sauce
2 tablespoons butter	12 truffle slices
12 cooked artichoke bottoms	

Sprinkle chops with salt and pepper and brown on both sides in butter. Heat artichoke bottoms in butter and place a chop on each. Top each with a slice of fried goose liver, coat lightly with Chateaubriand Sauce, and decorate with a truffle slice or a sautéed mushroom. Makes 6 servings.

Châteaubriand Sauce

Simmer ¾ cup dry white wine with 1 finely chopped shallot, ¼ bay leaf, and ⅛ teaspoon ground thyme until wine is slightly reduced. Add 2 tablespoons meat glaze or meat extract, and reduce by one-fourth. Add 2 tablespoons butter, 1 teaspoon fresh tarragon, 2 teaspoons chopped parsley, and a dash cayenne. Season with salt and pepper to taste.

Saddle of Lamb French Style

Saddle of lamb is not generally available in the United States but can usually be obtained by placing a special order with the butcher. Ask the butcher to saw across the ribs close to the backbone so the roast can be carved easily.

1 saddle of lamb roast
Salt and freshly ground black pepper
3 cups Duchess Potatoes
2 eggs, beaten with 2 tablespoons water

White breadcrumbs
Oil for frying
Parsley

Season the meat with salt and pepper and stand it on the ribs in a large shallow pan. Cook in a preheated oven (375°F) 20 minutes per pound, or until a meat thermometer registers 140°F. Transfer the roast to a warm platter. Meanwhile, shape Duchess Potatoes into cylindrical croquettes 2½ inches long and 1½ inches in diameter. Dip in the egg mixture, then roll in breadcrumbs. Fry until brown in deep fat preheated to 375°F. Drain on paper towels. Place on the platter on either side of the roast. Garnish the platter with parsley. Allow 2 to 3 ribs per serving.

Italian-Style Lamb Rib Chops

12 rib lamb chops
Salt and freshly ground black pepper
2 large eggs, beaten with
      2 tablespoons water
1 cup white breadcrumbs

1 cup grated Parmesan cheese
6 tablespoons butter
¾ pound tiny zucchini
1½ pounds cooked asparagus tips
2 tablespoons browned butter

Trim excess fat from lamb chops and rub them with salt and pepper. Dip in egg mixture, then in breadcrumbs mixed with some of the cheese. Pan-fry in butter, adding butter as needed. Peel zucchini and cut into slices ¼ inch thick. Sprinkle with salt and pepper. Dip in egg mixture, then in breadcrumb-cheese mixture. Pan-fry in butter, adding butter as needed. Place lamb chops and fried zucchini on a hot platter, with the chops and zucchini slices overlapping in a circle. Place asparagus tips in the center and pour browned butter over them. Sprinkle with cheese. Serve hot. Makes 6 servings.

Baked Lamb Rib Chops Madelon

12 rib lamb chops
Salt and freshly ground black pepper
2 tablespoons butter
1 cup finely chopped cooked
      chicken or veal

1 cup sautéed chopped mushrooms
1 cup Béchamel Sauce
1 cup soft white breadcrumbs
¼ cup (½ stick) butter, melted
Madeira Sauce

Sprinkle lamb chops with salt and pepper and brown in butter only on one side. Place chops in a 13-by-9-by-2-inch baking dish. Combine chicken, mushrooms, and Béchamel Sauce. Adjust seasonings and put a heaping tablespoonful of the mixture on each chop. Mix the breadcrumbs with the butter and sprinkle over the tops. Bake in a preheated oven (350°F) 15 minutes, or until crumbs are brown. Serve with Madeira Sauce. Makes 6 servings.

Sautéed Lamb Chops Saint-Michel

12 rib or loin lamb chops	Boiling water
Salt and freshly ground black pepper	6 parboiled artichoke bottoms, quartered
Flour	1 cup Béchamel Sauce
4 tablespoons butter	6 baked 2-½-inch pastry shells
½ cup finely chopped onion	

Sprinkle chops with salt and pepper, dredge in flour, and cook on both sides in 3 tablespoons of the butter. Arrange on a hot platter and keep warm. Meanwhile, parboil onion 2 to 3 minutes in boiling water to cover, then drain well. Cook in butter, along with artichoke bottoms, 2 to 3 minutes (do not brown). Add to Béchamel Sauce. Spoon the mixture into pastry shells. Arrange these on the platter around the chops. Makes 6 servings.

Pan-Fried Noisettes of Lamb or Mutton

For an explanation of "noisettes," see Sautéed Veal Medallions.

Rub a heated heavy skillet with a little butter, or with some of the fat trimmed from the steaks. Lay noisettes in the skillet and cook over medium heat until well browned on one side. Pour off any fat that accumulates in the pan. Turn steaks to brown the other side. Sprinkle with salt and ground black pepper. Cut slices of bread to fit the noisettes, fry in butter, and place one under each chop. Transfer to a hot platter. Serve with potatoes, creamed asparagus tips in artichoke bottoms, or in baked pastry shells, with buttered peas or other vegetables. Garnish with parsley. Allow 1 to 2 steaks per serving.

Mutton Boned Loin Chops or Noisettes Niçoise

4 medium-sized potatoes	1 clove garlic, crushed
2 tablespoons olive oil	2 medium-sized tomatoes
4 tablespoons (½ stick) butter	½ cup pitted black olives
6 loin mutton or lamb boned loin chops	Diced anchovies
Salt and freshly ground black pepper	2 tablespoons chopped parsley
2 shallots, chopped	

Peel and cube potatoes and fry in the oil and half of the butter. Drain potatoes on paper towels and keep warm. Sprinkle mutton or lamb chops with salt and pepper and fry in the same skillet and fat in which potatoes were fried. Transfer chops to another dish and keep warm. In the same skillet and the same fat, cook shallots and garlic about 1 minute. Drain off and discard fat. Coarsely chop tomatoes and add to the shallots and garlic. Bring to the boiling point, reduce heat, and simmer 5 minutes, or until tomatoes are cooked. Add olives and anchovies, adjust seasonings, add potatoes, and toss together. Turn out onto a platter and arrange the chops over the mixture. Sprinkle with chopped parsley. Serve with buttered green beans. Makes 6 servings.

Epigrammes of Lamb or Mutton Saint-Germain

Epigrammes are slices of breast of lamb or mutton, or chops or cutlets, dipped in beaten egg and breadcrumbs and broiled or fried.

3½ pounds breast of lamb or mutton	3 whole cloves
Water	1 teaspoon salt
Bouquet garni	1 egg
1 carrot, sliced	White breadcrumbs
1 rib celery, sliced	Oil for frying
1 medium-sized onion, sliced	Bearnaise Sauce
6 whole peppercorns	

Place meat in a Dutch oven or heavy saucepan. Pour in enough water to barely cover the meat. Add the next 7 ingredients. Cover, bring to the boiling point, and simmer 1½ hours, or until meat is tender. Transfer meat to a board, pull out bones, cover with foil, top with a heavy weight, and cool. Cut into heart-shaped cutlets, dip in egg beaten with 1 tablespoon water, and then in breadcrumbs. Broil, pan-fry, or fry in deep fat preheated to 375° F. Serve with Bearnaise Sauce. Makes 6 to 8 servings.

Stuffed Breast of Lamb

2 slices bread	Salt and freshly ground black pepper
Water	1 tablespoon pure vegetable oil
½ pound pork sausage meat	½ cup sliced onion
2 tablespoons chopped onion	½ cup sliced celery
1 tablespoon chopped parsley	½ cup sliced carrots
1 egg, beaten	1 cup Brown Stock
1 (3-pound) boned breast of lamb	

Soak bread in water, squeeze dry, and fluff with a fork. Mix with sausage, onion, parsley, and egg. Spread over lamb. Roll up jelly-roll fashion and tie with a string at each end.

Sprinkle with salt and pepper. Brown the roll in oil in a heavy skillet or Dutch oven. Put the vegetables in the pan around the meat. Pour in ½ cup water, cover, and cook in a preheated oven (325°F) 2 hours, or until meat is fork tender. Transfer meat to a warm platter and keep hot. Remove all fat from the pan. Add stock and cook until reduced by half. Strain, boil 1 minute, and serve in a sauceboat alongside the lamb. Makes 6 servings.

Stuffed Breast of Lamb Florentine

1 (3-pound) boned breast of lamb	2 fresh tomatoes, diced
Salt and freshly ground black pepper	½ cup lamb stock
2 pounds fresh spinach	6 cups Dauphine Potatoes
5 tablespoons butter	1 cup Demi-Glace Sauce

Flatten breast of lamb with a mallet or with the side of a heavy knife. Season with salt and pepper. Set aside. Cook spinach, drain, chop, toss with 2 tablespoons of the butter, and season to taste with salt and pepper. Spread one-third of it over breast of lamb. Heat tomatoes with 1 tablespoon of the butter until hot. Season to taste with salt and pepper, and spread over spinach. Roll up the breast jelly-roll fashion. Hold in place with strings tied near each end. Brown the lamb roll in the remaining 2 tablespoons butter in a Dutch oven. Add stock. Cover and cook in a preheated oven (325°F) 1½ hours, or until meat is tender, adding more stock if needed. Transfer lamb to a hot platter, and cut into as many slices as needed. Spoon remaining spinach onto the platter around lamb and surround with Dauphine Potatoes. Keep hot. Add Demi-Glace Sauce to the defatted pan juices and bring to the boiling point. Adjust seasonings and strain. Serve separately. Makes 6 servings.

Indian Lamb Korma

Korma is a dry curry, made with meat marinated in yogurt.

2 pounds boneless leg of lamb	1 teaspoon ground ginger
¾ cup yogurt	½ teaspoon ground cinnamon
2½ teaspoons salt	½ teaspoon freshly ground black pepper
1 teaspoon ground cumin	¼ to ½ teaspoon cayenne
1½ teaspoons ground turmeric	⅛ teaspoon ground cloves
½ teaspoon ground cardamom	1 cup water
¼ cup peanut oil or ghee	1 teaspoon freshly squeezed lemon juice
1½ cups chopped onions	2 tablespoons grated fresh or packaged
1 clove garlic, crushed	flaked coconut
1 teaspoon dry mustard	3 cups cooked rice

Trim off and discard excess fat from lamb. Cut meat into 1-inch pieces. Mix with the next 5 ingredients and marinate for 2 or more hours. Brown in 1 tablespoon of the oil or ghee. Pour off excessive fat. In another skillet, cook onions and garlic until golden in remaining oil or ghee. Add next 6 ingredients, stir and cook 2 minutes. Add lamb, cover tightly, and simmer 20 minutes. Pour in water and mix well. Cover and simmer 30 minutes, or until lamb is tender, adding water if needed. Stir in lemon juice and coconut just before serving. Serve over rice. Makes 6 servings.

Creole Lamb Stew

2½ pounds boned shoulder of lamb,
    cut into 1½-inch cubes
3 tablespoons butter
1½ cups chopped onions
2 to 3 teaspoons curry powder
3 tablespoons flour

3 cups Bouillon
1 teaspoon salt
1 Bouquet Garni
½ cup grated fresh coconut
½ teaspoon freshly ground black pepper
3 cups Creole Rice

Trim off and discard excess fat from lamb. Brown meat on all sides in butter in a Dutch oven. Add onions and curry powder. Stir and cook until onions are limp. Sprinkle with flour; stir and cook until flour has browned. Add bouillon, salt, and Bouquet Garni. Cover and cook slowly in a preheated oven (325°F) 1¼ hours. Remove and discard parsley, add coconut, and cook 30 minutes or until meat is tender. Skim off fat, add pepper, and adjust seasonings. Serve with rice. Makes 6 servings.

Hungarian Paprika Lamb

2½ pounds boned shoulder of lamb
⅓ cup diced fat salt pork
1 cup sliced onion
1 small clove garlic, crushed
2 teaspoons paprika
¾ cup tomato puree

1 cup water
2 teaspoons salt
Dash cayenne
1½ cups sour cream
3 cups Rice Pilaf

Trim off fat and cut lamb into 1½-inch cubes. Set aside. Fry salt pork with onion until lightly browned. Add lamb and garlic and brown lightly. Stir in paprika. Add tomato puree, water, and salt. Cover and cook slowly 1¾ hours or until meat is very tender and the water has evaporated. Stir in cayenne and sour cream, and heat only until hot. Serve with Rice Pilaf. Makes 6 servings.

Stewed Lamb with Peas

2½ pounds boneless shoulder of lamb,
    cut into 1½-inch cubes
3 tablespoons flour
6 tablespoons butter
Bouillon
1 teaspoon salt

2 sprigs parsley
2 tablespoons tomato puree
12 pearl onions
2 cups cooked green peas
½ teaspoon freshly ground black pepper

Trim off and discard excess fat from lamb. Dredge the meat in flour and brown on all sides in 3 tablespoons of the butter in a Dutch oven. Add enough bouillon to come halfway to the top of the meat. Add the next 3 ingredients. Cover and cook in a preheated oven (325°F) 1 hour. Brown onions in remaining 3 tablespoons butter and add to the meat. Cover and cook 30 minutes, or until meat and onions are tender. Remove and discard parsley. Add peas and pepper. Adjust seasonings. Serve hot. Makes 6 servings.

 Turkish Lamb Sausage or Kefta

5 slices white bread
Water
1½ pounds ground lamb or mutton
2 eggs
1½ teaspoons salt

¼ teaspoon freshly ground black pepper
¹⁄₁₆ teaspoon ground cinnamon
¹⁄₁₆ teaspoon finely chopped garlic
2 tablespoons olive oil or salad oil

Trim crusts from bread. Break bread into pieces and soak in enough water to cover until bread is wet. Squeeze bread dry and fluff with a fork. Add to meat, along with all the remaining ingredients except the oil. Mix well. Divide the mixture into 18 pieces of equal size. Form, on waxed paper, into little sausage-shaped rolls 1 inch in diameter. Fry in oil until browned on all sides. Serve very hot. Makes 6 servings.

PORK

Fresh pork should be just beyond medium rare at 150°F so that its rich flavor may be fully developed. Roasted pork should reach 160°F internal temperature and let sit 20 minutes in a warm place. Also the flavor and texture are even better when the meat is wet or dry brined.

Pork is the most versatile of all meats and may be made into salt pork or cured or smoked ham and bacon and sausage.

FRESH PORK

Roast Loin of Pork

1 (5-pound) center-cut loin pork roast
   on the bone
1½ teaspoons salt
¼ teaspoon freshly ground black pepper
¼ teaspoon ground ginger

Stock
Parsleyed potatoes
Buttered green peas

Ask the butcher to remove the chine bone of the loin to make carving easier. Combine salt, pepper, and ginger and sprinkle over the meat. Place meat on a rack in a roasting pan, fat side up. Cook in a preheated oven (350°F) 30 minutes per pound, or until a meat thermometer registers 160°F. Transfer roast to a warm platter and let it rest 20 minutes in a warm place. Pour off and discard the fat from the pan drippings. Deglaze the pan with the stock. Bring to a boil, stirring and scraping the browned bits from the bottom of the pan. Adjust seasonings. Garnish the roast with parsleyed potatoes and buttered green peas. Makes about 10 servings.

Roast Stuffed Suckling Pig

1 (12- to 15-pound) suckling pig
2 tablespoons salt
¾ teaspoon freshly ground black pepper
¾ teaspoon ground ginger

Liver and Pork Stuffing
3 tablespoons butter, melted
2 cups boiling water
Stock

Wash pig under running water, drain, and wipe dry with paper towels. Mix salt, pepper, and ginger and rub the inside of the pig with this mixture. Fill the cavity loosely with Liver and Pork Stuffing. Close opening with skewers and lace tightly with string. Wipe the skin and rub with the butter. Place a small block of wood in the pig's mouth to brace it for the apple, which will be inserted when the pig is cooked. Place pig, in kneeling position, on a rack in a large shallow pan. Pour boiling water in the pan and cover pig with foil. Roast in a preheated oven (325°F) 5 to 6 hours, basting every 45 minutes with the hot water and fat that is in the pan. Add more water if needed. Remove pig to a large warm platter. Replace wooden block with apple. Place parsley in or around the pig's ears. Serve with a sauce made from deglazing the pan with the stock after all the fat has been removed from the juices. Makes 12 to 15 servings.

Liver and Pork Stuffing for Suckling Pig

The pig may be stuffed with whole sausages and black (blood) puddings.

½ pound suckling pig's liver
Butter
½ pound ground lean pork
8 tablespoons (1 stick) butter
1 cup chopped onion
1 cup diced celery
1 cup diced mushrooms

2½ tablespoons chopped fresh thyme
3 tablespoons minced parsley
½ teaspoon freshly ground black pepper
1 tablespoon salt
2 quarts (8 cups) toasted bread cubes
    (croutons)

Season and slice liver and cook in butter until it is tender. Put through a food chopper, using the finest blade. Set aside. (Reserve the cooking water.) Cook pork in 1 tablespoon of the butter until pork loses its pink color, in a kettle large enough for mixing the stuffing. Add onion and remaining butter. Stir and cook until onion is limp. Add celery and mushrooms, stir, and cook 5 minutes. Add liver, the pan juices, and remaining ingredients. Mix well. Spoon loosely into the body cavity of the pig. Makes sufficient stuffing for a 12- to 15-pound pig.

Loin of Pork in Pastry Belle Fermière

3½ to 4 pounds cured boneless
    loin of pork, ¾ cooked
Plain Pastry Dough Triple batch
Butter
6 medium-sized carrots, cooked

4 medium-sized turnips, cooked
2 pounds red cabbage, cut into wedges, cooked
1 cup cooked spinach
6 slices bacon, cooked
Parsley

Cool cooked roast and trim off fat if the layer is thick. Roll three-quarters of the pastry ⅛ inch thick in an oblong large enough to cover the meat and allow 3 inches in length and 2 inches in width to overlap. Place the cold loin in the center of the dough. Bring the dough from the two sides to the top, overlapping about ¾ inch, then bring the two ends to the top of the loin, pressing the edges together. Place the roll on an ungreased baking sheet, seam side down. Roll the remaining dough ⅛ inch thick. Cut strips ¼ inch wide and place them in lattice fashion over the roll. Bake in a preheated oven (425°F) 10 to 15 minutes. Reduce oven temperature to 350°F and continue baking until pastry is brown. Cut off a few slices and place on a tray. Garnish with buttered carrots and turnips cut into short strips, buttered cabbage, and rolls of buttered spinach wrapped in strips of cooked bacon. Makes 8 to 10 servings.

Pork Tenderloin with Apple Brandy

2 pork tenderloins
1 teaspoon salt
¼ teaspoon freshly ground black pepper
½ teaspoon ground cumin
Butter

2 tablespoons apple brandy
¾ cup light cream
1 tablespoon meat glaze
½ pound cooked noodles

Cut the pork tenderloins into slices about ½ inch thick, weighing about 2 ounces each. Mix salt, pepper, and cumin and rub over meat. Cook slowly in butter 1 minute each side. Transfer meat to a warm platter. Pour off the fat from the pan, add brandy to the skillet, swirl it around the bottom, heat, and ignite. Add cream and meat glaze and simmer to reduce the liquid by one-quarter. Pour over tenderloins. Serve with buttered noodles. Makes 6 servings.

Pork Chops with Apples

6 rib pork chops, cut 2 inches thick	Large tart baking apples
Salt and freshly ground black pepper	1 cup Demi-Glace (optional)
3 tablespoons butter	

Trim off and discard excess fat and sprinkle pork with salt and pepper. Brown in a heavy skillet over medium-low heat in 1 tablespoon of the butter. Transfer chops to a 12-by-7½-by-2-inch baking dish. Pour off all the fat in the pan. (Set unwashed skillet aside for later use.) Wash and core apples, and cut into crosswise slices ½ inch thick. Place one slice on each chop. Melt remaining 2 tablespoons butter and brush over apples. Bake in a preheated oven (350°F) 30 minutes or until chops and apples are tender, basting apples with butter twice. Transfer the chops to a warm platter. If desired, add 1 cup Demi-Glace to the skillet, bring to the boiling point, strain, and serve separately in a sauceboat. Makes 6 servings.

Pork Chops Bonne Femme

6 pork chops, 2 inches thick	12 small parboiled new potatoes
Salt and freshly ground black pepper	2 slices bacon, diced
Flour	30 glazed pearl onions
Butter, lard, or shortening	Parsley

Trim off and discard excess fat from pork chops. Sprinkle with salt and pepper and dredge in flour. Brown on both sides in lard or shortening over medium-low heat. Reduce heat and cook slowly until tender. Transfer chops to a warm platter and keep warm. Finish cooking potatoes in 1 tablespoon butter with the bacon. Place on platter with the chops, along with glazed onions. Sprinkle chops with chopped parsley and garnish the platter with sprigs of parsley. Makes 6 servings.

Italian Pork Chops

6 pork chops, 2 inches thick	½ pound medium-wide noodles
Salt and freshly ground black pepper	⅛ teaspoon grated nutmeg
Butter	Sauce Italienne

Trim off and discard all but ⅛ inch fat from chops. Rub salt and pepper into the meat on both sides. Brown chops over low heat in butter, adding butter as needed. Cook slowly until pork is tender. Cook noodles as directed on the package. Drain. Add 2 tablespoons butter and the nutmeg to the noodles and toss lightly. Transfer the chops to the center of a warm platter and arrange the noodles around them. Spoon Sauce Italienne over the chops. Makes 6 servings.

Pork Chops with Sauce Robert

6 loin pork chops, 2 inches thick
Salt and freshly ground black pepper
Butter

Sauce Robert
Noisette Potatoes

Trim off all but ⅛ inch of fat from chops. Rub with salt and pepper. Brown chops over low heat in butter, adding butter as needed. Cook slowly until chops are tender. Transfer meat to a warm platter and cover with Sauce Robert. Serve with Noisette Potatoes. Makes 6 servings.

Noisette Potatoes

Peel potatoes and with a French melon-baller scoop out balls about the size of hazelnuts. Fry in a heavy skillet in butter. Season with salt and freshly ground black pepper to taste. Allow 6 balls per serving.

Ragoût of Pork

2 pounds boneless shoulder of pork
2 tablespoons butter
2 tablespoons flour
2 sprigs parsley
5 whole peppercorns
1 small clove garlic, crushed
2 teaspoons salt

3 cups water
18 pearl onions
4 carrots
3 turnips
3 potatoes
¾ teaspoon freshly ground black pepper

Cut the meat into 1½-inch cubes and brown in butter in a Dutch oven. Sprinkle with flour and stir and cook until flour has browned. Add parsley, peppercorns, garlic, salt, and water. Cover, bring to the boiling point, and simmer 1½ hours. Peel all the vegetables. Leave onions whole, slice carrots thickly, quarter turnips and potatoes, and add vegetables to the stew. Cover and cook 30 minutes, or until vegetables are tender. Add pepper and adjust salt. Makes 6 to 8 servings.

Indonesian Pork Satés

2 pounds lean pork
¼ cup soy sauce
1 tablespoon brown sugar
2 tablespoons minced onion
3 tablespoons freshly squeezed
    lemon juice
1 small clove garlic, crushed

2 tablespoons ground coriander seeds
½ teaspoon freshly ground black pepper
⅛ teaspoon cayenne
1 teaspoon salt
¼ cup ground Brazil nuts or
    unblanched almonds
Pure vegetable oil

Cut away and discard excess fat from pork. Cut into 1½-inch cubes. Combine all remaining ingredients except oil. Pour over meat, mix well, and marinate about 4 hours or overnight. String meat on skewers and cook over slow-burning charcoal 25 to 30 minutes, or until meat is browned on all sides and is well-done, basting with oil and turning frequently. Serve hot. Makes 6 servings.

Choucroute Garnie

Bacon rinds
2½ pounds sauerkraut
6 slices bacon
6 Bratwurst
Boiling water
1½ pounds pickled spareribs,
  cooked ham, or goose
1 sprig parsley

2 medium-sized carrots, sliced
2 whole medium-sized onions
2 whole cloves
1 cup dry white wine
Boiled potatoes

Line a 2-quart casserole with bacon rinds. Wash sauerkraut and squeeze it well by hand. Place half of it in the casserole. Blanch bacon and Bratwurst in boiling water, drain, and place over the sauerkraut. Put the remaining sauerkraut on top. Cut spareribs, ham, or goose into serving-size pieces, and place over the sauerkraut, along with parsley and carrots. Stud each onion with a clove and add. Pour in wine. (Do not add salt.) Cover and cook in a preheated oven (325°F) 2 hours. To serve, place sauerkraut and meat in the center of the dish and arrange bacon, Bratwurst, and carrots around it. Serve boiled potatoes in a separate dish. Makes 6 servings.

SAUSAGE

Fried Pork Sausages with Cabbage

12 links pork sausage
Boiling water
1 head cabbage (2 pounds)

½ teaspoon sugar
½ teaspoon salt
Freshly ground black pepper

Prick sausage with a fork and arrange in a 10-by-6-by-2-inch baking pan. Pour in 2 tablespoons boiling water. Cook in a preheated oven (400°F) 15 minutes, or until sausages are brown. (Reserve fat.) Meanwhile, coarsely chop cabbage and cook with the sugar and salt in ½ inch boiling water in a covered saucepan 8 to 10 minutes, or only until cabbage is crisp-tender. Toss lightly with pepper to taste and 2 tablespoons of the sausage fat. Serve cabbage in a shallow dish with sausage around it. Makes 6 servings.

Pork Sausages in White Wine with Mashed Potatoes

12 links pork sausage
⅓ cup dry white wine
¾ cup Demi-Glace Sauce

6 portions mashed potatoes
Cooked peas, string beans, or spinach

Prick sausage with a fork, place in a baking pan, and pour in wine. Bake in a preheated oven (400°F) 15 minutes, or until sausages are thoroughly cooked. Drain the wine into a saucepan, add Demi-Glace Sauce, and bring to the boiling point. Skim off fat. Transfer sausage to a platter and pour the sauce over it. Serve with mashed potatoes and one or more green vegetables. Makes 6 servings.

Spanish Sausage or Chorizo

3 pounds lean pork
¼ cup vinegar
3 teaspoons salt
1 teaspoon sweet paprika
¾ teaspoon crushed hot red pepper

1½ teaspoons freshly ground black pepper
1½ teaspoons dried oregano
¼ teaspoon ground allspice
1½ yards sausage casing or cloth bags

Put meat through a meat grinder, using the coarse blade. Add all remaining ingredients except casing and mix well. Fill the sausage casing, using the attachment to the meat grinder known as a sausage stuffer. When ready to use, turn back the casing and cut into slices ¼ to ½ inch thick. Store sausage in refrigerator or other cold place. It will keep for several weeks. This sausage may be fried or used in any recipe specifying chorizos sausage. Makes 3 pounds.

Rillettes

Rillettes are made of lean and fat pork cut into fine dice, cooked slowly in lard, and seasoned with salt, black pepper, and herbs. The mixture is then cooled and ground very fine or pounded in a mortar.

3 pounds boneless shoulder butt of pork
About 1 cup boiling water
1 bay leaf
1 whole clove

½ teaspoon chopped marjoram
½ teaspoon chopped sage
½ teaspoons salt
1 teaspoon coarsely ground black pepper

Cut pork, both lean and fat, into ½-inch dice. Place in a saucepan with the next 3 ingredients. Cook slowly, stirring occasionally, until water has evaporated. Continue cooking until the fat begins to brown, but not until the meat is dry. Remove from heat and transfer meat to a strainer. Set the strainer over the saucepan in which the meat was cooked until most of the fat has drained out of the meat. Reserve fat. Remove and discard bay leaf and cloves. Put meat through a food chopper, using the finest blade, or very finely chop and pound in a mortar or wooden bowl. Gradually blend in all the fat except 1 cup, add the herbs, salt, and pepper, and mix well. Pack the meat mixture into small jars or crocks, and pour a layer of the remaining fat, ½ inch thick, over the top. Cover jars with lids. Store in the refrigerator until ready to use. To serve, remove fat layer from the top and spread the mixture on toast, crusty rolls, or crackers. Makes about 2 pounds.

Braised Ham

1 (8- to 10-pound) boiled ham	Demi-Glace Sauce
1½ cups Madeira, Marsala, port, or sherry	Salt and freshly ground black pepper

Place ham in a roasting pan just big enough to fit it. Remove skin and trim the fat layer if it is thick. Score the fat. Pour wine over the ham. Cover and cook in a preheated oven (350°F) 1 hour. Remove cover, baste with cooking liquid, and transfer ham to a platter and keep hot. Let the ham rest 20 to 30 minutes before carving. Skim off and discard fat from the cooking liquid. Add Demi-Glace Sauce to the pan and cook until the sauce has reduced to the desired consistency, stirring occasionally. Season with salt and pepper to taste. Serve with the ham. Makes 16 to 20 servings.

Medallions of Ham with Sauce Bordelaise Cézanne

6 thin slices ham	6 baked 4-inch buttered white crustless bread
¼ cup chopped onion	½ cup well-drained, chopped, cooked spinach
4 tablespoons butter	Melted butter
1 cup diced mushrooms	Grated Gruyére or Parmesan cheese
2 tablespoons chopped parsley	6 wide pieces celery 2 inches long, braised
1 cup Mornay Sauce	6 slices beef marrow
Salt and freshly ground black pepper	Sauce Bordelaise

Cut medallions from the ham slices with a 4-inch cookie cutter. Save trimmings. Cook onion in 2 tablespoons of the butter until limp; add mushrooms and parsley and cook until mushrooms are tender. Add ½ cup ham trimmings and combine blend with all but 2 tablespoons of the Mornay Sauce. Season to taste with salt and pepper. Spread over baked bread rounds. Top each with a ham medallion. Mix spinach with reserved 2 tablespoons Mornay Sauce, using only enough to bind the spinach, and spoon about ½ teaspoon onto the center of each medallion. Brush with melted butter, sprinkle with grated cheese, and put under broiler until cheese is melted. Transfer medallions to a warm platter and keep them warm. Top each piece of celery with a piece of beef marrow, cover with Sauce Bordelaise, and arrange around the medallions. Makes 6 servings.

Medallions of Ham Polignac

12 slices baked ham	2 truffles
½ pound foie gras puree	3 pints Madeira-flavored aspic
¼ cup (½ stick) softened butter	1 quart Mimosa or Russian Salad

Cut medallions from the ham slices with a 3-inch cookie cutter. Save trimmings. Blend foie gras puree with the butter, spread on 6 of the ham rounds, and cover each with another ham round. Garnish the center of each "sandwich" with a slice of truffle and glaze with half-set aspic. Coat a large round tray with melted aspic and chill until firm. Put the salad in a mound in the center of the tray. Garnish with slices of truffle and small rounds of ham cut from the trimmings from the large medallions. Coat with liquid aspic and chill until set; there will be some aspic left. Chill remaining aspic until firm. Just before serving, dice the firm aspic, spoon it onto the tray around the salad, and arrange the ham sandwiches in a circle on top of the aspic around the edge of the tray. Serve at once. Makes 6 servings.

Ham Glazed with Aspic

1 (10- to 12-pound) cold cooked ham	2 tomatoes, finely chopped and drained
1 quart Madeira-flavored aspic	2 truffles, finely chopped
3 hard-cooked egg whites	Watercress

Peel the rind from the cold cooked ham, and trim the fat if the layer is very thick. Saw the end of the shank bone smooth. Place the ham on a tray, rounded side up. Slice the top thinly, cutting down to the bone. Slip the long, thin blade of a sharp knife between the bone and the slices to loosen them so they may be served easily. Glaze the remaining ham with half-set aspic. Put the egg whites, tomatoes, and truffles in separate bowls and mix each with a little half-set aspic. Use to decorate the ham in any desired pattern. Chill until aspic is set. Serve on a large tray and garnish with watercress. Makes about 20 servings.

Ham in Aspic with Riesling and Foie Gras

3 pints Alsatian Riesling-flavored aspic	12 slices cooked ham
1 truffle	6 slices cooked goose foie gras

Pour about ½ cup liquid aspic into a chilled, lightly oiled 1½-quart mold. Swirl the mold around to coat the bottom and sides completely. Chill until aspic is almost set. Decorate the bottom and sides with thin slices of truffle, gently pushing the slices into the aspic to hold them in place. Pour in another cup of aspic, swirling the mold to cover the truffles completely. Chill until aspic is set. Fill the mold with alternate layers of sliced ham and sliced goose foie gras and chill. Chill remaining aspic until it begins to set, then pour enough into the mold to cover the ham and liver completely. Chill until firm and ready to serve. Chill remaining aspic. Unmold ham and liver mold onto a tray. Cut jellied aspic into cubes and spoon it onto the tray around the mold. Serve at once. Makes 6 to 8 servings.

Ham à la Rothschild

½ pound foie gras puree
¼ cup (½ stick) softened butter
12 slices ¼-inch thick baked ham

1 truffle
2 cups port-flavored aspic

Mix foie gras puree with butter. Spread over one side of each ham slice. Arrange the slices, overlapping, on a platter. Decorate with slices of truffle. Glaze with half-set aspic. Chill until aspic is set. Makes 6 servings.

Ham Mousse

3 envelopes unflavored gelatin
¾ cup cold water
1 cup cold Velouté Sauce
1 cup Mayonnaise

¾ cup heavy cream
¾ teaspoon salt
⅛ teaspoon ground white pepper
4½ cups or more finely diced ham

Soften gelatin in water. Add softened gelatin to the Veloluté. Combine Mayonnaise, ¼ cup of the cream, the salt, and white pepper and add to the sauce. Chill until mixture begins to set. Fold in ham. Whip remaining cream and gently fold into the mousse. Turn mousse into a lightly oiled 10-by-10-by-2-inch pan. Chill until firm. Makes 12 servings.

Ham Mousse for a Cold Buffet

12 slices baked lean ham,
    cut ¼ inch thick
½ pound foie gras puree
1 cup Chaud-Froid Sauce
½ cup julienned celery root

Vinaigrette Dressing
1 recipe Ham Mousse
1 quart sherry-flavored aspic
6 tomatoes, peeled

Trim ham slices into pear-shaped pieces 3½ inches long and 2½ inches wide at the widest part. Cut 3 triangles from the trimmings and reserve; reserve remaining trimmings to add to the mousse. Top each pear-shaped slice with a dome-shaped mound of foie gras puree. Chill. Cover with some of the Chaud-Froid Sauce and chill again. Marinate celery root in Vinaigrette Dressing.

When Ham Mousse is firm, unmold and carve it into the shape of a small ham. Cover with Chaud-Froid Sauce and brush the shank end with a little aspic. Chill. Coat the triangles of ham with Chaud-Froid Sauce and chill, glaze with aspic, then chill again, then arrange in a collar below the simulated shank bone. Chill. Glaze with semiliquid aspic and chill until firm. Cut tomatoes in half, remove seeds, drain, and top with the marinated celery root. Glaze a large platter with aspic and chill until firm. Place the "ham" in the center, with 3 pear-shaped slices at each end and 2 tomato halves at each side. Use the remaining pear-shaped ham slices and tomato halves to replenish the platter as required. Makes 12 servings.

Chessboard Ham Mousse

2 cups sherry aspic	1 recipe Ham Mousse, not yet set
Truffles	Russian or Mimosa Salad I
Hard-cooked egg whites	

Coat a lightly oiled 10-by-10-by-2-inch pan with aspic, swirling the pan to coat the bottom and sides completely. Chill until aspic is almost set. Cover the bottom in a chessboard pattern with squares of truffle and egg whites. Decorate the sides of the pan with egg-white crescents. Cover with another thin layer of aspic. Chill until firm. Fill the pan with Ham Mousse. Chill until the mousse is firm.

To serve, unmold the mousse onto a tray and surround it with piles of the Russian or Mimosa Salad. Garnish with fancy shapes cut from firm aspic. Makes 12 servings.

VARIETY MEATS

BRAINS

Brains are obtained from veal, beef, lamb, and pork, veal brains being the most desirable. Brains should be used as soon as purchased—precooked in simmering water as described below, refrigerated in a covered container, and used within 24 hours.

Veal brains weigh about ½ pound each; beef brains about ¾ pound each; lamb and pork brains about ¼ pound each. Allow 1 pound for each 4 servings.

How to Prepare Brains for Cooking

Soak brains 15 to 20 minutes in cold salted water (1 teaspoon salt to 1 quart water). Rinse under running water and drain. Drop brains in boiling salted acidulated water (1 teaspoon salt and 1 tablespoon lemon juice or vinegar to 1 quart water). Cover, reduce heat, and simmer 8 minutes (do not boil). If brains are not to be served immediately, refrigerate in a covered jar with the membrane on and use within 24 hours. When ready to use, remove membrane with a pointed knife. Precooked brains may be prepared according to the following recipes.

Sautéed Brains

Cut brains in thick slices, season, dip in flour, and fry in browned butter. Garnish with capers and chopped parsley.

Sautéed Brain Fritters

Season thick slices of brains, dip in beaten egg, then in fine dry breadcrumbs. Sauté in hot oil or butter until browned on both sides. Serve with parsley and lemon wedges.

Deep-Fried Brain Fritters

Season slices of brains, dip in Fritter Batter, and fry in deep fat preheated to 375°F. Drain on paper towels. Serve with Tomato Sauce.

Coquille of Brains

Put seasoned sliced or diced brain in coquilles, or in individual casseroles. Cover with Mornay Sauce or Sauce Italienne, sprinkle with buttered soft white breadcrumbs, and brown in a hot oven.

Broiled Brains

Season and brush brains generously with melted butter. Broil 10 to 15 minutes, or until browned, under the broiler, turning to brown both sides. Serve with Black Butter, or with crisp bacon and grilled tomatoes.

Calf's Brains in Black Butter

4 calves' brains	Ice-cold water
Cold water	Flour
Simmering water	1 cup (2 sticks) butter
2 tablespoons freshly squeezed	4 teaspoons capers
lemon juice	2 tablespoons vinegar
1 teaspoon salt	Chopped parsley

Soak the brains in cold water to cover 1 hour. Drain and put them in boiling water to cover. Add lemon juice and salt. Bring to the boiling point, reduce heat, and simmer 8 minutes. Drain, cover the brains with ice water, and let stand until brains are cold, then remove brains from the water and pat them dry with a clean towel. Season and roll brains in flour and sauté them in 4 tablespoons of the butter, adding butter as needed. When brains have nicely browned, transfer them to a warmed platter, sprinkle with capers, and keep warm. Add remaining butter to the skillet. As the butter begins to brown, remove the skillet from the heat, add the vinegar, and give the skillet a few good shakes to mix the vinegar with the butter. Heat the butter and vinegar to the foaming point and pour over the brains. Sprinkle with parsley. Serve at once. Makes 4 servings.

Brains with Scrambled Eggs

Finely chop 1 veal brain (precooked or raw). Season and cook in a little melted butter. Add beaten eggs and 2 tablespoons milk. Stir and cook over medium-low heat until eggs are set. Season to taste with salt and freshly ground black pepper. Serve on toast garnished with chopped parsley. Makes 4 servings.

HEAD

Calf's Head Vinaigrette

Meat from 1 calf's head, including tongue and brains	1 large leek
	A few green celery leaves
Water	4 sprigs parsley
2 whole onions	2 carrots, sliced
4 whole cloves	Vinaigrette Sauce
½ teaspoon whole peppercorns	2 hard-boiled eggs, coarsely chopped
2 lemons, flesh removed and chopped	1 tablespoon each chopped tarragon,
2 teaspoons salt	parsley, chervil
1 bay leaf	2 tablespoons capers, rinsed

Place the calf's head, tongue, and brains in a large saucepan, cover with cold water, and let stand 2 hours. Place the next 10 ingredients in a large saucepan with 2 quarts water and bring to the boiling point. Add the meat from the calf's head and simmer 35 minutes. Skim. Add the tongue and simmer 1 hour, or until tongue is tender. Then add the brains and simmer 10 minutes. Transfer the brains to a bowl to cool. Cool the tongue and meat in the broth. Remove the skin and membrane from the brains. Dice the brains and set aside. Take the tongue and meat out of the broth. Remove the gristle and skin from the tongue. Slice both tongue and meat and arrange the slices on a platter. Add the diced brains to the Vinaigrette Sauce with the eggs, herbs, and capers, and serve over the slices. Allow ½ pound calf's head per serving.

Head Cheese

1 calf's head or pig's head	1 clove garlic
Water	1 large onion, quartered
Dry white wine	5 whole cloves
2 teaspoons salt	5 whole allspice
1 carrot, sliced	¼ teaspoon whole peppercorns
3 ribs celery, sliced	1 bay leaf
3 sprigs parsley	Dash cayenne
4 shallots, quartered	¾ teaspoon dried sage

Ask the butcher to clean the head, removing snout and reserving the brains and tongue. Place the well-washed head and the tongue in a large kettle. Cover with equal parts water and wine. Add salt. Tie the next 10 ingredients in a cheesecloth bag and add. Bring to the boiling point and skim the surface. Reduce heat, cover, and simmer 4 hours, or until meat falls off the bones. Remove the tongue from the water after it has cooked 1½ hours or is tender. Remove the root portion and skin and cut the tongue into 1-inch pieces. Pour a little stock over the tongue and set it aside. Remove the head from the stock and trim off the rind. Cut the meat into 1-inch pieces and add to the pieces of tongue. Set aside. Simmer the brains in a little of the cooking water, covered, 8 minutes, or until they are done. Lift from the cooking water, cut into pieces, and add to tongue and meat. Add cayenne and sage to meat. Mix well. Pack the meat into a 9½-by-5-by-3-inch loaf pan. Pour in ¾ cup of the cooking liquid. Cover with foil and place a weight on top to keep the meat submerged in the stock. Cool and refrigerate at least 2 days before using. Serve sliced and well chilled. Makes 1 loaf 9½ by 5 by 3 inches.

HEART

Veal heart, due to its delicate flavor and tenderness, is preferred to heart of lamb, pork, or beef, and is tender enough to slice thinly and sauté. Beef heart is the least desirable and the largest, usually weighing 3½ to 4 pounds.

When buying heart, allow 2 pounds beef heart and 1½ pounds veal, lamb, or pork heart for 6 servings.

To prepare heart for cooking, wash it and cut out the arteries and veins at the top of and inside the heart. Soak in sour milk or in water to which a little vinegar has been added. This helps to tenderize the tissues. To cook heart, use one of the following methods:

Sautéed Veal Hearts

2 (1-pound) veal hearts	About 3 tablespoons butter
Salt and freshly ground black pepper	Assorted cooked vegetables
Flour	

Cut hearts into thin slices, sprinkle with salt and pepper, and dredge in flour. Fry over medium heat in butter, adding butter as needed. Serve with buttered boiled onions, string beans, and sautéed potatoes, or with other vegetables if desired. Makes 6 servings.

Braised Stuffed Veal Hearts

2 veal hearts
2 slices salt pork
2 cups soft white breadcrumbs
½ cup diced onion
1½ teaspoons salt

¼ teaspoon freshly ground black pepper
½ teaspoon ground thyme
1 tablespoon chopped parsley
3 tablespoons flour
2-3 cups Chicken Stock

Dice the salt pork and fry until crisp in a Dutch oven. Set aside. Combine breadcrumbs, onion, ¼ teaspoon of the salt, ⅛ teaspoon of the pepper, the thyme, and parsley. Stuff into the cavity of the heart. Close opening with skewers and lace with twine. Sprinkle heart with remaining salt and pepper, dredge in flour, and brown in the rendered salt pork. Add stock, cover, and simmer over medium-low heat or cook in a preheated oven (350°F) 2 hours, adding more stock if needed. Makes 6 servings.

Lamb Heart Casserole

3 lamb hearts
Flour
2 tablespoons butter or bacon drippings
½ cup sliced onion
1 small clove garlic, crushed
½ cup chopped celery

2 cups skinned, seeded, chopped tomatoes
1 small bay leaf
½ teaspoon sugar
1 teaspoon salt
¼ teaspoon freshly ground black pepper
Chopped parsley

Prepare hearts for cooking as directed above. Cut them in half, dredge in flour, and brown on all sides in butter or bacon drippings. Add onion and garlic and cook until onion is limp. Turn the mixture into a casserole and add all remaining ingredients except the parsley. Cover and cook in a preheated oven (350°F) for 2 to 2½ hours, or until hearts are tender, adding a little water if needed. Sprinkle with parsley. Makes 6 servings.

Braised Pork Hearts

3 pork hearts
1 teaspoon salt
⅛ teaspoon freshly ground black pepper
Flour

3 tablespoons olive oil
¾ cup sliced onion
½ cup boiling water
½ teaspoon dried thyme

Prepare pork hearts for cooking as directed above. Cut hearts into quarters, rub with salt and pepper, and dredge in flour. Brown all sides in oil. Add onion and cook until onion is limp. Pour in boiling water. Cover and simmer 2 to 2½ hours, or until hearts are tender, adding thyme 30 minutes before cooking time is up. Makes 6 servings.

KIDNEYS

The size, flavor, and tenderness of a kidney are largely determined by the type and the age of the animal from which it comes and its freshness (must be very fresh). In general, the kidneys from small young animals are more delicate in flavor than those from larger, older animals. For example, veal kidney, which makes 1 serving, is more tender and has a more delicate flavor than a kidney from a steer, which is large enough to make 4 servings.

Veal, lamb, or pork kidney should be cooked for only a short time over medium heat. Beef kidney needs to be cooked slowly in moist heat until tender.

Sautéed Kidneys

Allow 1 veal kidney or 2 lamb kidneys per serving. Remove the membrane from kidneys and split them in half lengthwise, or slice ¼ inch thick. Cut out the fat and the white veins. Season and sauté in hot bacon fat or melted butter 10 to 15 minutes, turning frequently. Add a little sherry, Madeira, or port to deglaze the pan. Serve on toast for lunch or supper with scrambled eggs.

Broiled Kidneys

4 lamb kidneys, or 2 veal kidneys
French dressing or ¼ cup melted butter
Salt and freshly ground black pepper
8 broiled buttered mushroom caps

4 grilled tomatoes
8 slices bacon, cooked until crisp
Parsley

Remove the membrane from kidneys and cut each kidney in half. Pour a little French dressing in a bowl and dip kidneys into it, or if preferred, dip them into melted butter. If butter is used, sprinkle kidneys with salt and pepper. Place kidneys on a baking sheet and broil 7 or 8 minutes 3 inches from the heat source. Turn and broil 5 minutes or until kidneys are browned. Serve hot with mushroom caps, tomatoes, and bacon. Garnish kidneys with parsley. Makes 4 servings.

Sautéed Kidneys and Mushrooms

3 veal kidneys
Salt and ground black pepper
4 tablespoons butter
¾ cup finely chopped shallots

2 tablespoons sherry
½ cup Demi-Glace
½ pound sliced mushrooms
Chopped parsley

Skin the kidneys, slice thinly, season, and cook in hot butter (2 tablespoons) for a few seconds on each side. Put aside on a platter and keep warm. Sauté shallots in the same butter until transparent and add the sherry. Reduce by half. Add the Demi-Glace and mushrooms. Cook 5 minutes or until the mushrooms are tender. Pour any kidney juices into the sauce, and cook over high heat for 2 minutes. Add the remaining butter, cook 30 seconds, and add the kidneys. Warm through. Sprinkle with parsley and serve on toast or rice. Makes 6 servings.

Steak and Kidney Pie

1 pound round steak	2 tablespoons pure vegetable oil
3 veal kidneys, or 6 lamb kidneys	1 teaspoon prepared mustard
5 tablespoons flour	2 cups sliced onions
1½ teaspoons salt	1¼ cups beef stock
⅛ teaspoon freshly ground black pepper	2 cups water
¼ teaspoon ground ginger	1 recipe Plain Pastry Dough or Puff Pastry
2 tablespoons butter	

Cut steak into 1-inch cubes. Wash kidneys and remove the membranes, fat, and tubes. Cut kidneys into quarters. Combine flour and seasonings and dredge kidneys in mixture, reserving leftover flour mixture. Brown kidneys briefly in butter and oil. Remove from heat and add the reserved flour, the mustard, onions, stock, and water. Add the beef, bring to the boiling point, reduce heat, and simmer 1 hour. Turn the beef and kidney mixture into a 10-by-6-by-2-inch baking dish. Cover with pastry dough or puff pastry. Trim, turn under, and flute edges. Cut 2 or 3 gashes in top of crust to allow steam to escape. Bake in a preheated oven (425°F) 30 minutes, or until browned. Makes 6 servings.

Sautéed Veal Kidneys Bordelaise

6 veal kidneys	2 shallots, finely chopped
2 tablespoons butter	1 cup Brown Sauce
2 tablespoons olive oil	12 slices blanched marrow
3 cups sliced mushrooms	Chopped parsley
1 cup dry red wine	

Remove the outer membrane from kidneys and split them in half, lengthwise, or slice them ¼- to ½-inch thick crosswise. Remove fat and veins. Wash and pat dry. Fry in a heavy skillet in half of the butter and half of the oil 2 minutes on each side. Sauté mushrooms separately in remaining butter and oil and mix with the kidneys. Transfer to a serving dish and keep hot. Add wine and shallots to the skillet juices and cook until the liquid has almost evaporated. Add Brown Sauce, bring to the boiling point, and pour over kidneys and mushrooms. Garnish with slices of marrow and the parsley. Makes 6 servings.

LIVER

All kinds of liver are highly nutritious. Calf's liver is the most popular, since it is the tenderest and has the mildest flavor.

Calf's Liver en Brochette

24 pieces calf's liver cut into 1½-inch squares, ¼ inch thick
Butter
24 pieces lean bacon, cut into 1½-inch squares

Fine dry breadcrumbs
2 eggs, beaten with 2 tablespoons water
Salt and freshly ground black pepper
Herb Butter

Fry liver lightly in butter. Dip bacon in hot water and drain well. Thread liver and bacon alternately on short skewers. Roll in breadcrumbs, dip in egg mixture, and roll in crumbs again. Fry in deep fat preheated to 375°F. Drain on paper towels and sprinkle lightly with salt and pepper. Serve with Herb Butter or Bearnaise Sauce. Makes 6 servings.

Sautéed Calf's Liver English Style with Bacon and Watercress

6 slices calf's liver ¾ inch thick
Flour
4 tablespoons butter
Salt and freshly ground black pepper
2 tablespoons bacon fat

Chopped parsley
6 slices crisp bacon, cooked until crisp
Watercress
6 boiled potatoes

Remove arteries and ligaments from liver, dredge in flour, and cook 2 minutes on both sides in butter in a heavy skillet. Sprinkle with salt and pepper. Transfer liver to a platter. Add bacon drippings to the skillet, blend with the butter already in the skillet, heat, and pour over liver. Sprinkle with parsley. Garnish with bacon, watercress, and boiled potatoes. Makes 6 servings.

Sautéed Calf's Liver with White Wine and Parsley Bercy

6 slices calf's liver, ¾ inch thick
Salt and freshly ground black pepper
Flour
7 tablespoons butter

2 shallots, chopped
⅓ cup dry white wine
1 teaspoon chopped parsley

Season liver with salt and pepper and dredge in flour. Cook 2 minutes on both sides in 3 tablespoons of the butter. Let the remaining butter soften. Cook shallots in wine until most of the liquid has evaporated. Cool. Blend the parsley with the softened butter and add to the cooled shallots. Season to taste with a little salt and pepper. Pour the sauce over the browned liver, heat, and serve. Makes 6 servings.

OXTAIL

Braised Oxtail Bourgeoise

3 oxtails	12 small carrots, quartered
Salt	1 clove garlic
Flour	¼ cup chopped parsley, plus additional
¼ cup pure vegetable oil or lard	1 leek chopped
Beef broth	1 teaspoon chopped sage leaves
Red Burgundy	Chopped parsley
12 small mushrooms	
18 pearl onions	
18 small new potatoes	

Wash oxtails and cut each into 6 pieces, or ask the butcher to cut them for you. Sprinkle with salt and dredge in flour. Brown on all sides in shortening or lard in a Dutch oven. Drain off fat. Pour in equal amounts of broth and wine, enough to barely cover the oxtails. Cover and cook in a preheated oven (325°F) 3 to 4 hours, or until tender. Remove the oxtail, strain the juices, defat and reduce by ¼. Pour back over oxtails in the Dutch oven. Add mushrooms, small onions, potatoes, carrots, garlic, parsley, leek, and sage, and simmer 30 minutes. Adjust seasonings. Serve hot, sprinkled with more parsley. Makes 6 to 8 servings.

Braised Oxtail

4 pounds oxtail, disjointed	1¼ cups dry white wine
Salt	1 small bay leaf
Flour	2 sprigs parsley
¾ cup pure vegetable oil	1 cup sliced mushrooms
2 cups chopped onions	1 tablespoon butter
1¾ cups sliced carrots	¾ teaspoon freshly ground black pepper
1 clove garlic	Chopped parsley
1¼ cups beef stock	

Sprinkle oxtail with salt and dredge in flour. Brown in shortening or lard in a Dutch oven. Add onions, carrots, and garlic to the pan and cook until browned. Add stock, wine, bay leaf, and parsley sprigs. Season with ½ teaspoon salt. Cover and cook in a preheated oven (325°F) 3 to 4 hours, or until meat is done. Sauté mushrooms in butter and add to the oxtails 30 minutes before cooking time is up.

Stir in pepper. Degrease the braising liquid and serve hot, sprinkled with chopped parsley. Makes 6 servings.

Pigs' Feet or Trotters

Preparation for Cooking

Place cleaned pigs' feet in a saucepan with water to cover, 1 teaspoon salt, 1 each sliced carrot and onion, 2 sprigs parsley, and 2 whole cloves. Cover, bring to the boiling point, reduce heat, and simmer 2½ hours. Serve plain, with a sauce, or dip pigs' feet in melted butter, roll in fine dry breadcrumbs, and fry in oil preheated to 375°F. Allow 1 pig's foot per serving.

Pigs' Feet Sainte-Menehould

6 pigs' feet	Coarsely ground black pepper
Water	¼ cup (1 stick) butter, melted
1 cup dry white wine	Fine white breadcrumbs
1 carrot, sliced	6 servings mashed potatoes
1 medium-sized onion, sliced	6 servings cooked green peas
2 sprigs parsley	

Cook pigs' feet as above. Remove from the stock and pull out the bones. Arrange the feet between two boards and place a weight on top. Let stand in a cool place overnight. Sprinkle with pepper, dip in butter, and roll in breadcrumbs, pressing them down. Fry in a heavy skillet in butter until browned on both sides. Serve with mashed potatoes and green peas. Makes 6 servings.

Baked Pigs' Feet with Truffle Sauce

Prepare pigs' feet as for Pigs' Feet Sainte-Menehould except for the cooking and let stand overnight. Place in a buttered 13-by-9-by-2-inch baking dish. Cook in a preheated oven (325°F) 1 hour, or until the feet have browned. Transfer the feet to a platter and pour Madeira Sauce with chopped fresh truffles around them. Serve with any vegetables desired. Allow 1 pig's foot per serving.

Sweetbreads

Sweetbreads are either the thymus or pancreas glands of young beef, calves, and lambs. The pancreas gland (located by the stomach) is rounder than the elongated thymus (located in the throat) and is considered the finer tasting of the two.

All sweetbreads are prepared for cooking in the same way as brains (see How to Prepare Brains for Cooking, page 410).

Sautéed Sweetbreads in Cream Sauce

3 pairs calves' or lambs' sweetbreads
Court Bouillon
Salt and freshly ground black pepper
Flour
4 tablespoons (½ stick) butter

½ cup heavy cream
Brandy
Freshly squeezed lemon juice
1 cup poached sliced mushrooms

Soak sweetbreads according to the directions in How to Prepare Brains for Cooking. Poach in simmering Court Bouillon 15 minutes. Cool, trim, and slice ½ inch thick. Season the slices lightly with salt and pepper and roll in flour. Cook in a skillet in butter 2 minutes on each side. Transfer sweetbreads to a hot platter and keep hot. Tip out the butter and add the cream to the skillet and mix well with the pan residue. Simmer until the sauce is slightly thick. Season to taste with salt, pepper, brandy, and lemon juice. Add mushrooms, heat, and pour sauce over sweetbreads. Makes 6 servings.

Baked Sweetbreads Florentine

3 pairs calves' or lambs' sweetbreads
Salt and freshly ground black pepper
Flour
6 tablespoons (¾ stick) butter

2 pounds fresh spinach, cooked and drained
Dash grated nutmeg
1 cup Mornay Sauce
⅓ cup grated Parmesan cheese

Soak sweetbreads according to the directions in How to Prepare Brains for Cooking. Poach in simmering water or stock 15 minutes. Cool, trim, and slice ½ inch thick. Sprinkle slices lightly with salt and pepper and roll in flour. Cook in 2 tablespoons of the butter for 2 minutes on each side. Sauté spinach in 1 tablespoon of the butter. Season to taste with salt and pepper, and add nutmeg. Spread in a buttered 8-by-8-by-2-inch baking dish. Arrange sweetbreads over the spinach. Cover with Mornay Sauce. Sprinkle with cheese. Dot with the remaining 3 tablespoons butter. Brown under the broiler 4 inches from the heat source. Makes 6 servings.

Broiled Sweetbreads with Ham and Béarnaise Sauce

3 pairs calves' sweetbreads
Salt and freshly ground black pepper
½ cup (1 stick) butter, melted
1 cup fine white breadcrumbs

6 slices broiled ham
6 slices buttered toast
6 mushroom caps, sautéed in butter
Béarnaise Sauce

Soak and precook sweetbreads in water or stock according to the directions in How to Prepare Brains for Cooking. Drain, cool in ice water, and remove connective tissue and outer covering. Split sweetbreads and season with salt and pepper. Dip in butter and roll in breadcrumbs. Sprinkle with more melted butter. Broil 4 inches from heat source until well browned, about 5 minutes on each side. Place a slice of ham on each slice of toast. Top each with a sweetbread and a mushroom cap. Serve with Béarnaise Sauce. Makes 6 servings.

Sweetbreads in Pastry Cases

3 pairs veal sweetbreads
2 cups sweetbread braising liquid
Velouté Sauce
1 cup diced cooked ham

Salt and ground white pepper
6 small baked puff-pastry cases of
　　plain pastry tart shells
Parsley

Soak sweetbreads and cook in water or stock according to the directions in How to Prepare Brains for Cooking, saving 2 cups of the cooking broth. Cool the cooked sweetbreads in ice water. Remove connective and covering tissue and cut sweetbreads into cubes. Set aside. Add sweetbreads and ham to the hot Velouté. Season to taste with salt and white pepper. Serve in pastry shells. Garnish with parsley. Makes 6 servings.

Sliced Sweetbreads Graziella

3 pairs calves' or lambs' sweetbreads
Salt and freshly ground black pepper
Flour
5 tablespoons butter
6 rounds fried bread

3 firm, ripe tomatoes
1 cup Soubise Sauce
6 mushroom caps, sautéed
6 tablespoons Madeira Sauce

Soak sweetbreads according to the directions in How to Prepare Brains for Cooking. Cool, trim, and slice ½ inch thick. Season with salt and pepper to taste, and roll in flour. Cook in 4 tablespoons of the butter 2 minutes on each side. Place each slice on a round of fried bread and place on a warm platter. Keep hot. Cut tomatoes in half. Season and fill with the Soubise. Dot with remaining 1 tablespoon butter and broil until tomatoes are brown. Remove from oven. Top each with a mushroom cap. Cover with Madeira Sauce and place on the platter around the sweetbreads. Serve with potatoes. Makes 6 servings.

Braised Sweetbreads Comtesse

3 pairs calves' or lambs' sweetbreads
¼ cup sliced onion
½ cup sliced carrots
3 tablespoons butter
1 tablespoon flour
½ cup dry white wine
1 cup veal or chicken stock

Salt and freshly ground black pepper
2 tablespoons sherry
1 teaspoon cornstarch
Braised lettuce
Quenelles, made with veal
　　Mousseline Forcemeat
Truffle slices

Soak and precook sweetbreads according to the directions in How to Prepare Brains for Cooking. Remove all connective and covering tissue. Cook onion and carrots in butter until onion is golden. Sprinkle with flour. Add sweetbreads, wine, stock, salt, and pepper, and heat to simmering. Cover and bake in a preheated oven (350°F) 20 minutes. Remove cover and bake 10 minutes more. Place sweetbreads in the center of a warm platter. Mix sherry with cornstarch and add to the pan liquids. Mix well and heat until the sauce has thickened slightly and is transparent. Pour over sweetbreads. Serve with braised lettuce and veal quenelles garnished with truffle slices. Makes 6 servings.

TONGUE

Beef tongue (called ox tongue in England) is the most commonly used. If calves' and lambs' tongues are available, they are also delicious and may be braised or served in ragoûts. Cooked ready-to-serve tongue and pickled tongue can be obtained. If using pickled or salted tongue, soak it for 5 hours in two changes of cold water—and then do not salt the finished dish, or salt lightly.

Broiled Tongue with Madeira Sauce

1 (3- to 4-pound) beef tongue	1 clove garlic
Cold water	½ cup sliced carrots
Bouquet garni	5 whole peppercorns
3 whole cloves	1 small bay leaf
1 medium-sized onion	Madeira Sauce

Put tongue in a 6-quart kettle and cover with cold water. Add all remaining ingredients except Madeira Sauce. Bring to the boiling point and simmer 3 hours, or until tongue is tender. Cool in the broth for 30 minutes. Cut off the tongue root or muscle and peel off the skin. Slice diagonally and serve with Madeira Sauce. Makes 6 to 8 servings.

Tongue in Aspic with Asparagus and Truffles Princesse

2½ cups aspic	1 pickled ox tongue
36 asparagus tips, cooked	6 hard-cooked egg whites
¼ cup Vinaigrette	1 truffle, sliced
Cucumber pickle	

Coat a large platter with aspic and chill until aspic is set. Marinate the cooked asparagus tips 1 hour in Vinaigrette. Remove asparagus from the marinade, drain well, and arrange in bundles of 3 tips in the center of the aspic-coated platter. Cut pickle into narrow strips and drape one of each across each asparagus bundle. Coat with aspic. Chill until aspic is set. Cut the tongue into thin slices. Fold each slice in half and decorate as desired with the egg whites and truffle slices Arrange tongue slices on the aspic-coated tray around the asparagus, coat them with aspic, and chill until aspic is set. Makes 12 servings

Beef Tongue Saint-Germain

1 (3- to 4-pound) hot cooked smoked
    beef tongue
1¾ cups Madeira Sauce
3 cups cooked green peas, pureed

⅛ teaspoon sugar
Salt and freshly ground black
    pepper
2 tablespoons butter

Slice tongue and arrange slices overlapping, down the center of a platter. Coat with some of the Madeira Sauce. Heat pea puree. Add seasonings and butter. Serve separately. Serve remaining sauce in a separate dish. Makes 6 to 8 servings.

TRIPE

Tripe is the walls of the stomachs of cud-chewing animals. There are three kinds: plain or blanket or double (*gras double)* tripe—because the interior and the exterior surfaces are quite distinct—from the smooth first stomach; honeycomb tripe, which is the most tender and desirable for most tripe dishes; and the third type from the fourth stomach (sometimes called the rennet stomach) which is called "leaf"*(feuille)*, book, or Bible tripe, and is the least useful for cooking.

Beef tripe is the most popular, but pork and sheep tripe are also used in some places. Sheep tripe is used in Scotland, and pork tripe is used in the southern part of the United States. Both France and Italy are famous for their tripe dishes.

To make tripe from the raw state is a long and laborious task, so it is best to use the precooked fresh tripe that is available in the markets today, although it needs further cooking. Pickled tripe is also available but must be soaked for several hours before using.

Tripe Braised with Apple Brandy and Cider *or* Tripe à la Mode de Caen

This is the most famous tripe dish in France.

3 pounds precooked fresh tripe
2 calves' feet
2 medium-sized onions, sliced
2 large carrots, sliced
2 ribs celery, sliced
2 leeks, sliced
2 sprigs parsley
¼ pound chopped beef-kidney suet
1 tablespoon chopped fresh thyme

1 bay leaf
2 cloves garlic
6 whole peppercorns
1 whole clove
1 teaspoon salt
¼ cup brandy
2 cups hard cider
Beef or veal stock
2 cups flour

Wash tripe and cut into 2-inch squares. Set aside. Wash and split calves' feet. Set aside. In a 3-quart earthenware casserole, put all the ingredients, in this order: vegetables, tripe, calf's feet, suet, seasonings. Pour in brandy, cider, and enough stock or water to barely cover the ingredients. Cover the casserole and seal it with a roll of dough made by mixing flour with enough cold water to make a very stiff paste. Bring the liquid to the boiling point. Put the casserole in a preheated oven (300°F) and cook 10 to 12 hours, or overnight. (Never open the casserole or disturb the tripe while it cooks.) Transfer the tripe to another casserole. Remove calves' feet, pick off meat, discard bones, and return meat to the casserole. Skim fat from the liquid and discard. Strain the stock over the tripe. Heat. Serve very hot from the casserole, accompanied by boiled or baked potatoes. Makes 8 servings.

Braised Tripe in Poulette Sauce

3 pounds precooked fresh tripe	2 cups Supreme Sauce
2 large onions, sliced	2 egg yolks
2 large carrots, sliced	½ cup heavy cream
2 sprigs parsley	1 tablespoon fresh lemon juice
1 bay leaf	1 tablespoon chopped parsley
6 whole peppercorns	5 mushroom caps, cooked in butter
½ teaspoon salt	
Water	
1 cup sliced mushrooms	
¼ cup fino sherry	

Wash tripe and cut into 1-inch pieces. Place in a saucepan with onions, carrots, parsley, bay leaf, peppercorns, salt, and water to barely cover. Cover and simmer 3 hours. Remove tripe and strain the stock. Sauté tripe and mushrooms until mushrooms are tender, being careful not to brown the tripe. Add the sherry and cook another 3 minutes. Mix egg yolks with cream and add to the Supreme Sauce. Cook for 2 minutes, stirring, or until it reaches desired consistency. (Do not boil.) Mix in lemon juice and parsley. Serve over tripe and mushrooms. Adjust seasonings. Garnish with mushroom caps. Makes 8 servings.

POULTRY

Chicken

The French word for poultry is *volaille*, but it is used in a general way also for chicken *(poulet, poularde)*. Some of the most glorious dishes in the repertoire of French cuisine have been created for it. Because the success of any dish depends on the quality of the ingredients, with chicken it is essential that one knows which kind of chicken to choose so that it is the right kind for the dish. From the smallest (and youngest) to the largest (and oldest), the types of chicken and their most appropriate cooking methods are:

Poussin or squab chicken	1 pound	Grill, broil, or roast
Broiler	1½ to 2½ pounds	Grill, broil, or roast
Fryer	2 to 3 pounds	Fry, fricassee, or bake in a casserole
Roaster	3 to 5 pounds	Roast, poach, or bake in a casserole
Capon	4 to 6 pounds	Roast or poach
Fowl or stewing chicken	3 to 5 pounds	Stew or fricassee
Old Hen/Rooster	3 to 6 pounds	Fricassee, use for stock or use as forcemeat

The old hen *(vieille poule)* makes the best broth, and the rooster, if not too old and tough, is what the great dish *coq au vin* is all about—very flavorful and otherwise tough meat that benefits from a long braise and does not dry out as a younger bird would. The capon (castrated male) or *chapon* makes the best poached or spit-roasted chicken one could ever have.

It is important to use the best chicken available, and now that there are organic, free-range, and "natural" chickens on the market, one should buy those. Wash the chicken, pat it dry, and store it for a day, *uncovered*, in the refrigerator before using it.

Trussing a chicken is more for its appearance at the table than for anything else; use whatever method, with or without trussing needles, that you can remember and with which you feel comfortable.

To test chicken for doneness, pierce deep into the thick part of the thigh with a skewer and see what color the juices run. Since a whole chicken should rest in a warm place for 15 minutes before it is carved and therefore will continue cooking, the juices should be very slightly pink when the cooking is terminated. A meat thermometer should read 175° to 180°F.

Duck (CANARD and the younger CANETON)

In America only the young birds—up to 6 months old, weighing 4 to 5 pounds—are readily available. These are most likely to be the White Pekin ducks. In France, that duck is available, as are the small and ubiquitous *nantais*, which are roasted whole, the *rouennais*, which is cooked whole without having been bled and so gives the famous pressed duck of Tour d'Argent fame, and the large *barbarie* duck, which is used for braising and in casserole dishes.

Goose (OIE)

Only the young birds, about 6 months old, are used for roasting, but if the goose is older or larger they are very good for braised dishes and for making *confit d'oie* or goose cooked in its own rendered fat.

Guinea Fowl (PINTADE and the younger PINTADEAU)

Guinea fowl tastes like a cross between chicken and pheasant, and the meat looks the same way. Any cooking technique for chicken is suitable for guinea fowl, but the most successful way to treat the larger birds is to serve the legs braised and the breast meat roasted.

Pigeon & Squab (PIGEON and PIGEONNEAU)

Again the younger birds or squabs are suitable for grilling, broiling, and roasting, either whole or flattened out, and the older pigeons for braising and in casseroles. The flesh of both is all dark meat, and becomes more strongly flavored as the bird ages.

CHICKEN

Roast Chicken with Oyster Dressing

1 (4- to 5-pound) roasting chicken	Softened butter
Salt and freshly ground black pepper	Parsley
Oyster Dressing	Radishes

Wash chicken, and pat dry. Sprinkle inside of neck and body cavities with salt and pepper. Fill with Oyster Dressing. Close cavities with skewers and lace tightly with twine. Sprinkle skin with salt and pepper and rub with butter. Place chicken on a rack in a shallow baking pan. Bake in a preheated oven (375°F) 1½ hours or until the juices, when tested with a fork or skewer at the thickest part of the thigh, still run slightly pink, basting with butter and pan drippings occasionally. If breast, wings, and legs are browning too quickly, cover them with foil. Remove from oven, put on a warm platter, and let stand in a warm place 20 minutes before carving. Garnish with parsley and trimmed radishes. Serve with sauce made from the degreased pan juices. Makes 6 to 8 servings.

Oyster Dressing

2 cups diced bread, toasted	¼ cup chicken broth
¼ cup (½ stick) butter, melted	2 tablespoons minced onion
1 teaspoon salt	¼ cup finely diced celery
¼ teaspoon freshly ground black pepper	1 cup well-drained oysters
½ teaspoon chopped thyme	

Combine all ingredients except oysters and mix lightly. Pick over oysters and remove all bits of shell. Chop coarsely and add. Mix well, using a fork. This amount will stuff one 4- to 5-pound chicken.

Chaud-Froid Chicken Lambertye

Truss a fat hen or capon and place it in a large saucepan with enough well-seasoned, rich chicken stock to cover it, aromatic vegetables, and fresh herbs. Cover the saucepan, bring the stock to the boiling point, reduce heat, and cook slowly about 1½ hours, or until chicken is tender. (The cooking time depends upon the size and the age of the chicken.) Uncover the saucepan and cool the chicken in the stock. Transfer chicken to a pastry board or other flat surface and pat it dry with paper towels. Bone the chicken by slicing off the breast meat. Cut (with scissors) away the entire breast bone down to the level of the tops of the legs and thighs by making a circular incision around the breast and removing it. Discard the bones. Remove the skin from the two pieces of breast meat. Fill the chicken's cavity with Foie Gras Mousse, rounding the top nicely to re-form the shape of the chicken. Cut the chicken breast into slices and place them over the mousse. Coat the whole chicken with white Chaud-Froid Sauce and chill until sauce has set. Coat with aspic and chill again until aspic is firm. Decorate as desired with shapes cut from truffles or cold cooked tongue. Glaze with aspic again and chill. If desired, cut cooked ham slices into oval-shaped pieces the size of a goose egg. Cover each with a dome of Foie Gras Mousse. Coat with white Chaud-Froid Sauce and chill until sauce has set. Decorate as desired with shapes cut from truffles or cold cooked tongue, and coat them with aspic. Chill until aspic is set. Cover the bottom of a large serving tray with chopped jellied aspic and arrange the chicken and the simulated eggs on the aspic. Makes about 6 servings.

Andalusian Whole Poached Chicken

1 (4-pound) chicken	2 teaspoons freshly squeezed lemon juice
Water to cover	¹⁄₁₆ teaspoon ground white pepper
1¼ teaspoons salt	12 small slices Fried Eggplant
2 egg yolks	¾ cup Tomato Fondue
3 tablespoons dry sherry	3 cooked, peeled red bell
⅓ cup heavy cream	peppers, halved
1 cup Velouté Sauce	Rice à la Grecque

Wash chicken and leave whole. Cook in water to cover with 1 teaspoon of the salt until it is tender but still holds its shape—40 to 50 minutes. Combine egg yolk, sherry, cream, Velouté Sauce, lemon juice, the remaining ¼ teaspoon salt, and the white pepper. Bring almost to the boiling point, but do not boil. Transfer chicken to a warm platter and cover with the sauce. Top Fried Eggplant with Tomato Fondue and arrange on the platter. Stuff bell peppers with Rice à la Grecque and place on the platter. Makes 6 servings.

Harlequin Chaud-Froid Chicken

1 5-pound capon or roasting chicken
2 ribs celery, sliced
⅓ cup sliced onion
1 teaspoon salt
¼ teaspoon freshly ground black pepper
2 envelopes unflavored gelatin
½ cup cold water

1 cup foie gras puree or mousse
⅔ cup heavy cream, whipped
1 cup finely ground cooked or pickled tongue
2 cups Chaud-Froid Sauce
1 tablespoon thick tomato puree
1 truffle
2 slices cooked tongue
12 baked 2-inch tart shells (optional)

Cook chicken or capon as for Chaud-Froid Chicken Lambertye, cool in the stock, and when cool, bone in the same manner.

Soften 1 envelope of the gelatin in ¼ cup cold water and melt over hot water (not boiling). Mix the melted gelatin into the foie gras. Fold in half of the cream. Stuff into the body cavity of the cold cooked chicken, filling one side only. Make tongue mousse with the ground tongue, remaining gelatin, water, and cream. Stuff into the other side of the chicken's body cavity. Chill.

Divide Chaud-Froid Sauce into two parts. Coat the side of the chicken filled with foie gras mousse with plain white Chaud-Froid Sauce. Stir tomato puree into the remaining sauce and use it to coat the side of the chicken filled with tongue mousse. Slice truffle and cut into ¾-inch circles. Cut in half and place a row lengthwise down the center of the pink side of the chicken. Repeat on the white side of the chicken with tongue circles of the same size and shape. Chill.

If desired, fill 6 of the tart shells with any remaining foie gras mousse and 6 with any remaining tongue mousse. Coat half with white Chaud-Froid Sauce and the remainder with pink Chaud-Froid Sauce. Chill. Place on the platter around the chicken. Makes 6 servings.

Glazed Chicken Muguette

Prepare exactly as for the Harlequin Chaud-Froid Chicken but instead of tongue use ham.

Chicken Sauté with Chambertin

1 (3- to 4-pound) whole chicken,
   or 3 to 4 pounds chicken legs,
   thighs, and breasts
2 teaspoons salt
½ teaspoon freshly ground black pepper
2 tablespoons olive oil
3 tablespoons butter

½ pound small mushroom caps
12 pearl onions, peeled
2 shallots, chopped
1 cup Chambertin
½ cup heavy cream
Chopped parsley

Wash chicken and cut into 12 serving-size pieces. Rub pieces with salt and pepper and brown on all sides in oil and butter. Add mushroom caps and onions. Cover and cook in a preheated oven (325°F) 30 to 40 minutes, or until chicken is tender. Transfer chicken and vegetables to a warm serving dish and keep warm. Put shallots in the chicken pan and cook 1 to 2 minutes; do not brown. Add wine and simmer until reduced by half. Stir in cream and cook until sauce is thick. Pour over chicken. Sprinkle with parsley. Makes 6 servings.

Baked Deviled Spring Chicken or Poussin

1 (1¼- to 2-pound) young chicken
½ teaspoon salt
⅛ teaspoon freshly ground black pepper
Dash cayenne
¼ teaspoon dry mustard

3 tablespoons fine white breadcrumbs
3 tablespoons butter
4 slices bacon, cooked until crisp
Parsley
Sauce Diable

Cut chicken in half lengthwise, trim off the vertebrae, and spread chicken out flat. Pull out any bones that can be easily removed. Beat chicken with a mallet or the flat side of a cleaver. Sprinkle with salt and pepper. Place in a buttered baking pan skin side up in a preheated oven (450°F) and cook 10 minutes, or until about half done. Remove from oven. Mix cayenne and mustard with breadcrumbs, spread over chicken, and dot with butter. Place under broiler heat for about 10 minutes to finish cooking. Transfer to a warm platter and top with bacon. Garnish platter with parsley. Serve Sauce Diable in a sauceboat. Makes 2 servings.

Sautéed Chicken Portuguese Style

1 (3- to 3½-pound) young chicken
Salt and freshly ground black pepper
6 tablespoons butter
½ cup dry white wine
1½ cups small mushrooms

1 tablespoon chopped onion
1 cup chopped tomatoes
3 Mushroom-Duxelles Stuffed Tomatoes
Chopped parsley

Cut chicken into serving-size pieces and rub with salt and pepper. Place in a baking dish and brush with 4 tablespoons of the butter. Pour the wine around. Cook in a preheated oven (350°F) 1 hour, or until tender, basting frequently. Remove from oven and cool in the cooking liquid. Sauté mushrooms and onion in the remaining 2 tablespoons butter. Add tomatoes and season with salt and pepper to taste. Cook 5 minutes. Reheat the chicken in the cooking liquid and remove to a warm platter. Cover with the mushroom and tomato mixture. Arrange Mushroom-Duxelles Stuffed Tomatoes on the platter and garnish the platter with parsley. Makes 6 servings.

Mushroom-Duxelles Stuffed Tomatoes

2 tablespoons chopped onion
1 tablespoon butter
¼ pound finely chopped mushrooms
2 shallots, finely chopped

Salt and freshly ground black pepper
3 medium-sized tomatoes
½ cup buttered soft breadcrumbs

Lightly brown onion in butter. Add mushrooms and shallots. Stir and cook over a medium-high heat to evaporate all moisture left in the mushrooms. Season with salt and pepper. Cut tomatoes in half. Scoop out centers, sprinkle cavities with salt and pepper, and invert on a plate to drain. Fill with the mushroom mixture. Sprinkle with breadcrumbs. Brown in a preheated oven (400°F) 10 to 12 minutes. Makes 6 servings.

Sautéed Chicken with Wild Mushrooms or Forestière

1 (3- to 4-pound) young chicken,
    cut into serving pieces
1½ teaspoons salt
½ teaspoon freshly ground black pepper
1 tablespoon flour
6 tablespoons butter

1 tablespoon chopped garlic
½ pound morels or other wild
    mushrooms, sliced
½ cup dry white wine
¾ cup Demi-Glace Sauce
Chopped parsley

Rub chicken with salt and pepper, dust with flour. Add 2 tablespoons butter to a pan. Brown the chicken pieces on both sides. Cover and cook 15 minutes, turning the pieces once. Remove the chicken pieces and keep warm. Add the remaining butter, garlic, and the mushrooms. Cook 5 minutes and add the chicken. Cover and cook another 15 minutes or until the chicken is tender.

Pour wine and Demi-Glace Sauce into the pan. Stir and cook until the liquid has thickened to sauce consistency. Adjust seasonings. Sprinkle with parsley. Makes 6 servings.

Sautéed Chicken with Curry and Mushrooms Stanley

2 cups sliced onions
¼ cup (½ stick) butter
1 (3-pound) chicken, cut into
    serving pieces
2 cups heavy cream
¼ cup tomato puree
1 teaspoon curry powder

1 teaspoon hot paprika
1½ cups sliced mushrooms
1 tablespoon freshly squeezed lemon juice
1 truffle, sliced
Puff pastry small crescents (optional)

Season and cook onions in butter about 5 minutes. Add chicken and cream, cover, and cook slowly for 15 minutes. Add the tomato puree, curry powder, paprika, mushrooms, and lemon juice. Cook another 10 minutes or until the mushrooms and chicken are tender. Turn into a warm platter. If desired, serve with the little crescents and garnish with black truffle slices. Makes 6 servings.

Viennese Fried Chicken

1 (2½-pound) chicken
4 chicken livers
2 teaspoons salt
¼ teaspoon freshly ground black pepper

2 eggs, beaten
½ cup fine white breadcrumbs
6 tablespoons butter
Tomato Sauce
Fresh peaa

Cut chicken into quarters, wash, and pat dry. Flatten the pieces and remove the thigh bones. Season chicken and chicken livers with salt and pepper and dip in egg and then in breadcrumbs. Fry chicken pieces in 4 tablespoons of the butter until browned, then fry chicken livers. Drain on paper towels. Put on a warm platter covered with Tomato Sauce finished with the remaining 2 tablespoons of butter. Serve a quarter of chicken and a chicken liver to each person and cooked fresh peas tossed in butter and seasoned. Makes 4 servings.

Chicken Pilaf Asian Style

1 (3-pound) chicken, with neck
Salt and freshly ground black pepper
6 tablespoons butter
¼ cup chopped onion
1 cup long-grain converted rice

2½ cups hot chicken stock or water
¼ teaspoon crumbled saffron threads
1 large green bell pepper, cut into strips
2 tomatoes, quartered, peeled, and seeded

Cut chicken into 10 pieces and rub all pieces, including neck, with salt and pepper. Brown on both sides over medium heat in 4 tablespoons of the butter, along with the onion. Meanwhile, soak rice 30 minutes in cold water to cover. Drain and cook in remaining 2 tablespoons butter until it begins to stick to the bottom of the pan. Add to the chicken, along with 1 teaspoon salt and the remaining ingredients. Turn into a 2-quart casserole. Cover and bake in a preheated oven (350°F) 20 to 25 minutes, or until chicken and rice are tender and the rice has absorbed most of the liquid. Serve with the chicken arranged over the rice. Makes 6 servings.

Chicken Fricassée

1 (4-pound) chicken, with neck and gizzard	1 small bay leaf
1 teaspoon salt	12 peeled pearl onions
Flour	¼ pound mushrooms
3 to 4 tablespoons butter	½ teaspoon chopped marjoram
2 cups chicken broth	¼ teaspoon chopped rosemary
1 carrot, pared and sliced	2 egg yolks
1 rib celery, sliced	⅓ cup heavy cream
1 sprig parsley	1 teaspoon freshly squeezed lemon juice
5 whole peppercorns	Heart-shaped croutons fried in butter

Wash chicken and cut into 10 pieces. Rub pieces, including neck and gizzard, with salt and dredge in flour. Brown lightly over medium heat in butter in a large casserole. Heat broth and pour over chicken. Add the next 5 ingredients. Cover and simmer 45 minutes, or until chicken is tender. Transfer chicken to a warm platter and keep hot. Strain stock and return it to the saucepan. Degrease. Add onions, cover, and cook 15 minutes. Meanwhile wash mushrooms, chop stems, and leave caps whole. Add to the broth and cook another 10 minutes. Return chicken to saucepan, add marjoram and rosemary, and cook 5 minutes. Blend egg yolks with cream, add to the broth, and heat 1 minute. Add lemon juice. Adjust salt. Put chicken in a serving dish, pour sauce over it, and garnish with croutons. Makes 6 servings.

Browned Boned Breasts of Chicken

3 chicken breasts, with wings attached	⅓ cup butter
Salt and freshly ground black pepper	
Flour	

Skin, bone, and halve chicken breasts and remove wing tips but not the main wing bones. Sprinkle with salt and pepper and dredge lightly in flour. Cook in butter in a heavy skillet until chicken is browned, 20 to 25 minutes, adding butter as needed. Makes 6 servings.

Chicken Breasts with Curry Sauce

1 recipe Browned Boned Breasts of Chicken
3 cups fluffy cooked rice
1½ cups Curry Sauce

Arrange the cooked chicken breasts in a crown on a heated platter. Fill center with rice. Heat Curry Sauce and spoon over the breasts. Makes 6 servings.

Butter-Steamed Boned Breasts of Chicken

3 chicken breasts, with wings attached
Salt and freshly ground black pepper
½ butter, melted
Juice of ½ lemon
Chopped parsley

Skin, bone, and halve the chicken breasts and remove wing tips but not the main wing bones. Season with salt and pepper. Arrange breasts in a sauté pan just large enough to hold them. Pour over the melted butter. Sprinkle with freshly squeezed lemon juice. Cover and cook 10 to 12 minutes, or until breasts are tender. Sprinkle with parsley. Makes 6 servings.

Breasts of Chicken with Mushrooms

12 mushroom caps
1 recipe Butter-Steamed Boned
Breasts of Chicken
2 tablespoons butter
1½ cups Allemande Sauce
Salt and freshly ground black pepper

Wash mushroom caps. Sauté the caps in butter and arrange 2 on each chicken breast. Place the breasts on a warm platter. Set aside and keep warm. Drain the butter that was left in the pan in which chicken was cooked into the liquid left from sautéeing mushrooms. Add the Allemande Sauce and season with salt and pepper to taste. Heat and spoon over chicken. Makes 6 servings.

Creamed and Truffled Breasts of Chicken with Asparagus

3 chicken breasts, with wings attached
Salt and freshly ground black pepper
1½ teaspoon chopped fresh thyme
Flour
¼ cup (½ stick) butter
¼ cup brandy
1 cup heavy cream
1¼ teaspoons paprika
Toast points
Cooked asparagus tips
1 truffle, chopped (optional)

Skin, bone, and halve chicken breasts and remove wing tips but not the main wing bones. Season with salt, pepper, and thyme and dredge in flour. Cook breasts in a heavy skillet in butter, only until lightly browned (not cooked through the center). Heat brandy, pour over chicken, and ignite. Add cream, cover, and simmer 15 minutes, turning the breasts once. Add paprika and adjust seasonings. Arrange the breasts on a warm platter and surround with toast points. Garnish with hot asparagus tips. Strain sauce over chicken and asparagus. Sprinkle with truffle, if desired. Makes 6 servings.

Chicken Breasts Florentine

1½ pounds spinach, cooked
4 tablespoons (½ stick) butter
¹⁄₁₆ teaspoon grated nutmeg
⅛ teaspoon freshly ground black pepper
Salt

1 recipe Butter-Steamed Boned
  Breasts of Chicken
Mornay Sauce
½ cup grated Parmesan cheese

Toss the spinach with 2 tablespoons of the butter and the seasonings and spread it in the bottom of an 11-by-7-by-1½-inch baking dish. Put the cooked chicken breasts on top. Spread with Mornay Sauce, sprinkle with the cheese, and dot with bits of butter, using the remaining 2 tablespoons. Place under broiler heat to warm and melt cheese. Makes 6 servings.

Chicken Kiev

3 boned chicken breasts, with or
  without wings attached
Salt and freshly ground black pepper
½ cup (1 stick) butter
6 teaspoons chopped chives

Flour
2 eggs, lightly beaten
About 1 cup soft white breadcrumbs
Oil for frying

Cut chicken breasts in half lengthwise and place each between pieces of waxed paper. Pound with a mallet or the flat side of a cleaver until they are thin, being careful not to break through the meat. Remove and discard waxed paper. Season with salt and pepper. Cut butter into 6 pieces of equal length and width. Freeze or chill until very firm. Place one piece in the middle of each chicken breast half. Sprinkle each with 1 teaspoon chopped chives. Roll up envelope style, sides and ends overlapping. Dredge rolls in flour, dip in egg, and roll in breadcrumbs. Refrigerate at least 1 hour so crumbs will adhere. Fry 2 rolls at a time in deep fat preheated to 370°F until browned. Drain on paper towels. Serve at once. Makes 6 servings.

Breasts of Chicken Sandeman

3 boned breasts of chicken, with
 wings attached
Salt and freshly ground black pepper
6 tablespoons butter
¼ cup Cognac

2 tablespoons sherry
1 cup heavy cream
1 tablespoon meat glaze
1 canned pimiento
Cooked rice

Skin, bone, and halve chicken breasts and remove wing tips but not the main wing bones. Season with salt and pepper. Cook breasts in a heavy skillet in 2 tablespoons of the butter until browned. Transfer chicken to a warm platter. Add Cognac to the skillet, heat, and ignite. Pour in sherry and cook 1 minute. Add cream and meat glaze and simmer about 5 minutes. Pour over chicken. Garnish the center with pimiento cut into juliennes. Serve with rice in a separate bowl. Makes 6 servings.

Breasts of Chicken Spanish Style

2 chicken breasts
Salt and freshly ground black pepper
8 tablespoons (1 stick) butter
1 cup long-grain rice
Water
½ cup chopped onion

¼ teaspoon crumbled saffron threads
¼ cup each sliced red and green bell peppers
1 cup green peas
2½ cups chicken stock
2 cups chicken Velouté
1½ cups Tomato Fondue

Rub chicken breasts with salt and pepper. Melt 3 tablespoons of the butter and brush some of it over the chicken. Place chicken in a buttered baking pan and bake in a preheated oven (350°F) 50 minutes, or until breasts are tender, basting frequently with melted butter. Meanwhile, soak rice 30 minutes in water to cover. Drain off water and cook rice in 2 tablespoons of the butter until it is dry and sticks to the bottom of the pan. Add 2 more tablespoons butter and the onion. Stir and cook until onion is limp. Add saffron, ½ teaspoon salt, green and red peppers, peas, and 2½ cups stock. Cover and cook 12 to 15 minutes. Slice chicken breasts into 6 servings and place on a warm platter. Heat Velouté and spoon over chicken. Serve remaining sauce in a separate dish. Garnish the dish with the rice mixture and Tomato Fondue. Serve hot. Makes 6 servings.

Stuffed Chicken Breasts

3 chicken breasts, boned and halved
Salt and freshly ground black pepper

1½ cups chicken or veal forcemeat with panada
Butter

Place chicken breasts between waxed paper and pound with a mallet or the flat side of a cleaver until thin, being careful not to break through the meat. Remove waxed paper.

Sprinkle breasts with salt and pepper and place ¼ cup forcemeat in the middle of each breast. Roll up envelope style. Place rolls in a generously buttered baking dish and top each with a pat of butter. Cover and cook in a preheated oven (350°F) 35 minutes, basting with pan juices, and with additional butter if chicken starts to become dry. Remove cover and cook 15 minutes, or until breasts are golden brown. Makes 6 servings.

Stuffed Chicken Breasts with Wine

In recipe for Stuffed Chicken Breasts, baste chicken with ½ cup dry white wine during the first 35 minutes of cooking.

Chicken Breasts with Savory Stuffing

3 chicken breasts, boned and halved	3 tablespoons butter
Salt and freshly ground black pepper	1 cup chicken stock
1 recipe Savory Stuffing	¼ cup heavy cream
Flour	

Place chicken breasts between waxed paper and pound with a mallet or the flat side of a cleaver until thin, being careful not to break through the meat. Remove waxed paper. Sprinkle breasts with salt and pepper and place ¼ cup Savory Stuffing in the middle of each breast half. Roll up envelope style, overlapping the sides and ends of meat. Sprinkle both sides with salt and pepper and dredge in flour. Brown on all sides in butter over medium heat. Arrange chicken breasts in a buttered 11-by-7-by-1½-inch baking dish and pour stock over them. Cover and bake in a preheated oven (350°F) 10 minutes, basting with stock that is in the baking dish. Remove cover and bake 15 minutes. Add cream and heat. Adjust seasonings. Serve over chicken. Makes 6 servings.

Savory Stuffing

Combine 2 cups soft white breadcrumbs with ¼ teaspoon each chopped savory, thyme, and marjoram, ⅛ teaspoon freshly ground black pepper, ¼ teaspoon salt, 1 tablespoon each finely chopped onion and parsley, ¼ cup butter, melted, and 3 tablespoons water or chicken stock. Makes enough for 6 servings.

Chicken and Ham Aspic Mercédès

1½ quarts chicken aspic	1 cup heavy cream, whipped
1 (3-pound) chicken, poached and boned	2 truffles
Baked ham slices	2 hard-cooked egg whites
Salt	Aspic triangles
⅛ teaspoon ground white pepper	

Coat the inside of a 1½-quart mold with liquid aspic and chill until set. Cut chicken into crosswise slices about ¼ inch thick. Trim an equal number of ham slices to the same size. Set aside. Reserve trimmings. Cut enough of the remaining chicken into small pieces to make 2 cups when added to ham trimmings. Put through a food chopper, using the finest blade, and add to 2 cups of the liquid aspic. Add salt and white pepper. Chill until mixture just begins to set. (If mousse does not set, add 1 envelope unflavored gelatin, softened in ¼ cup cold water and melted over hot water.) Fold in whipped cream. Decorate the center of the bottom of the mold with truffles and hard-cooked egg whites cut into petal shapes. Using a pastry bag, pipe the mousse on enough ham and chicken slices to surround the egg and truffle decoration, and place them mousse side up, alternating ham and chicken slices. Chill until set. Pour in a layer of aspic and chill. Arrange alternating chicken and ham slices topped with aspic around the sides of the mold. Finish filling mold with half-set aspic. Chill until firm and ready to use. Unmold on a large tray. Garnish with aspic triangles. Makes 8 servings

Truffled Chaud-Froid of Chicken Breasts with Ham Salad

3 chicken breasts, boned	1 truffle
Water	1 quart aspic
½ teaspoon salt	6 cucumber cups filled with ham salad
1 quart white Chaud-Froid Sauce	1 tomato cup filled with ham salad

Poach chicken breasts in salted simmering water until they are tender, 7-10 minutes. Cool. Remove skins from the breasts, cut in half, and trim the meat into uniform ovals. Coat breasts with half-set Chaud-Froid Sauce and chill until the sauce is set. Decorate each oval as desired with truffle cutouts. Glaze with half-set aspic. Chill until set. To serve, arrange the ovals of chicken breasts on a serving dish and surround with diced aspic, and fill cucumber cups with ham salad and place on the tray. Garnish center of tray with tomato filled with salad. Makes 6 servings.

Russian Chicken Cutlets Pojarski

1 cup soft white breadcrumbs	1½ teaspoons chopped fresh thyme
½ cup milk	½ cup (1 stick) plus about
3 cups ground raw chicken breasts	4 tablespoons butter
1 teaspoon salt	¼ cup heavy cream
¼ teaspoon ground white pepper	Flour

Soak bread in milk 15 minutes. Drain and squeeze out the excess milk. Fluff the crumbs with a fork and mix well with the chicken, salt, white pepper, thyme, ½ cup butter, and the cream. Divide the mixture into 6 equal portions and mold into shapes resembling chicken breasts. (Chill mixture before shaping.) Dredge in flour and brown over medium heat, in butter, adding butter as needed. Makes 6 servings. Serve with lemon wedges.

Curried Chicken

1⅓ cups chopped onions
1 clove garlic, crushed
¼ cup peanut oil or ghee
1 teaspoon ground turmeric
1 teaspoon ground cumin
½ teaspoon ground ginger
½ teaspoon freshly ground black pepper
½ teaspoon ground mustard seeds, toasted

3 teaspoons ground coriander seeds, toasted
⅛ to ¼ teaspoon ground hot red pepper
1 (2-inch) stick cinnamon
3 pounds chicken legs and thighs
3 teaspoons salt
1 cup hot water
1 teaspoon freshly squeezed lemon juice
3 to 4 cups fluffy hot cooked rice

Stir and cook onions and garlic in hot oil 2 to 3 minutes. Add turmeric and cook over medium-low heat about 10 minutes, or until onions are very soft, stirring constantly to prevent the turmeric from scorching. Add remaining spices and stir and cook 2 to 3 minutes. Rub chicken with 2 teaspoons of the salt, add to onion mixture, cover, and cook over medium heat 20-25 minutes, or until chicken is barely tender. Add remaining salt and 1 cup hot water, cook 10 minutes, or until the sauce thickens. Remove and discard the cinnamon stick. Stir in lemon juice just before serving. Serve with rice. Makes 6 servings.

Anglo-Indian Chicken Curry

1 cup chopped onion
1 small clove garlic, crushed
¼ cup butter or peanut oil
1 teaspoon ground turmeric
1 teaspoon ground ginger
1½ teaspoons ground cumin
½ teaspoon freshly ground black pepper
½ teaspoon ground cardamom
¼ teaspoon ground hot red pepper

3 pounds chicken legs and thighs
2 cups water
1½ teaspoons salt
2 tablespoons ground coriander seeds
¼ cup Coconut Milk
1 teaspoon freshly squeezed lemon juice
Rice à l'Indienne
¼ cup toasted sliced blanched almonds

Stir and cook onion and garlic in butter or peanut oil until onion is soft. Add the next 6 ingredients. Stir and cook 10 minutes over medium heat. Add chicken, a few pieces at a time, and brown lightly on all sides, adding more butter or oil if needed. Add water, salt, and coriander. Cover and cook 30 minutes, or until chicken is tender. The sauce should be well reduced; if it is not, remove cover and cook over low heat until the sauce has thickened. Add Coconut Milk and lemon juice just before serving. Heat but do not boil. Serve on Rice à l'Indienne. Garnish with toasted almonds. Makes 6 servings.

Coconut Milk

Heat a whole coconut in a a preheated oven (275°F) 30 minutes. Punch holes in the eyes, drain out coconut water, crack the shell, and remove the coconut meat with a pointed paring knife. Trim off the brown coat. Grate coconut meat or put it through a food chopper and soak 1 cup in 1 cup boiling water 30 minutes. Strain through cheesecloth, squeezing out all the liquid. Makes 1 cup coconut milk.

Rice à l'Indienne

1 cup long-grain converted rice	1 (1-inch) stick cinnamon
Water	5 whole peppercorns
2 tablespoons butter	3 little black seeds from a cardamom seed pod
¼ cup chopped onion	2¼ cups chicken stock
½ small bay leaf	

Soak rice 30 minutes in water to cover. Drain and cook in butter, without browning, until the rice is dry and sticks to the bottom of the pan. Add onion and cook until limp. Add remaining ingredients. Cover and cook over low heat about 12 minutes, or in a preheated oven (350°F) 15 to 17 minutes. The rice is done when it has absorbed all the stock and every grain separates. Remove spices before serving. Serve with curry. Makes 6 servings.

Tuscan Fried Chicken

3 pounds chicken legs and breasts	¾ cup grated Parmesan cheese
2 teaspoons salt	⅓ cup olive oil
½ teaspoon freshly ground black pepper	6 slices lemon
2 large eggs, beaten	Parsley
¾ cup fine white breadcrumbs	

Wash chicken parts and pat dry. Rub with salt and pepper. Dip in eggs and then in mixture of breadcrumbs and cheese. Fry in hot oil until chicken is browned on all sides and is tender. Serve garnished with lemon slices and parsley. Makes 6 servings.

Spanish Chicken and Rice Valenciana with Lobster and Frogs' Legs

2½ pounds chicken thighs, drumsticks, and breasts	½ teaspoon crumbled saffron threads
	4 cups chicken stock
½ pound lean pork, cut into cubes	½ pound raw lobster meat
4 tablespoons olive oil	12 sautéed frogs' legs (optional)

¾ cup chopped onion
1 small clove garlic, crushed
1½ cups long-grain rice
3 tablespoons salt
½ teaspoon freshly ground black pepper

½ cup fresh peas
8 artichoke bottoms, quartered
Parsley
1 tomato

Brown chicken and pork in 1 tablespoon of the oil in a heavy skillet over medium heat. Transfer to a 9-by-13-by-2-inch baking dish. Add onion and garlic. Meanwhile, wash rice in water, drain, and cook in remaining 3 tablespoons oil until rice is dry and sticks to the bottom of the pan. Add to the baking dish. Add seasonings to stock and pour over chicken, pork, and rice. Cover and cook in a preheated oven (325°F) 1 hour. Add lobster, frogs' legs (if using), peas, and artichoke bottoms. Mix very gently with the rice, tossing with a fork. Cover and bake 10 minutes. Garnish with parsley and tomato strips. If the dish begins to get too dry, add a little stock. Makes 8 servings.

Chicken Marengo

About 3½ pounds chicken legs
    and thighs
Salt and freshly ground black pepper
Flour
¼ cup olive oil
3 tablespoons butter
1 cup chicken stock
12 pearl onions, peeled

4 fresh tomatoes, peeled, seeded,
    and quartered
½ cup pitted black olives
⅛ teaspoon ground allspice
¼ pound sliced mushrooms
½ cup dry white wine
Cooked rice

Rub chicken with 1 teaspoon salt and ½ teaspoon black pepper. Dredge in flour. Brown in oil and 2 tablespoons of the butter. Add the next 6 ingredients. Cover and simmer 45 minutes, or until chicken is tender. Sauté mushrooms in remaining 1 tablespoon butter and add to chicken, along with wine, 5 minutes before cooking time is up. Adjust seasonings. Serve with rice. Makes 6 servings.

Baked Chicken Legs with Cream, Truffles, and Asparagus Archduke

6 chicken legs with thighs
    (about 3 pounds total)
2 teaspoons salt
½ teaspoon freshly ground black pepper
¼ cup (½ stick) butter
⅓ cup white port
½ cup brandy

½ cup Béchamel Sauce
½ cup heavy cream
6 slices truffle
6 servings cooked asparagus tips
1 tablespoon butter, melted
6 strips pimiento

Rub chicken legs with salt and half of the pepper. Cover and cook in the butter in a heavy skillet, without browning, 45 minutes over low heat until chicken is tender. Transfer chicken to a warm platter and keep hot. Pour off the butter and add the port and brandy, and cook 2 to 3 minutes. Add Béchamel Sauce and cream. Stir and cook until the sauce has thickened slightly. Add remaining pepper and adjust salt. Spoon over chicken. Garnish with truffle slices. Pour melted butter over asparagus and heat. Arrange it in serving-size portions on the platter around the chicken. Garnish asparagus with pimiento. Makes 6 servings.

Stuffed Boned Chicken Legs with Truffled Madeira Sauce Régence

6 large chicken legs	¾ cup heavy cream
2 cups Quenelle Forcemeat with Panada	Salt and freshly ground black pepper
½ cup julienned boiled tongue or pickled tongue	6 artichoke bottoms, sautéed
	½ cup sautéed mushrooms
Rich Veal Stock	6 pitted green olives, rinsed
2 tablespoons butter	Madeira Sauce
2 tablespoons flour	6 slices truffle

Bone the chicken legs or have the butcher do it for you. Stuff them with Quenelle Forcemeat and tongue strips. Wrap each leg separately in cheesecloth. Simmer the stuffed chicken legs in the stock very gently, allowing 10 minutes per pound of chicken. Set aside and keep warm. Melt the butter in a saucepan, remove from heat, and blend in flour. Stir and cook 1 minute, remove from heat, and add ¾ cup of the stock in which the chicken legs were cooked. Cook sauce for 30 minutes, skimming. Strain and add the cream, and salt and pepper to taste. Unwrap the chicken legs and put in the stock sauce. Fill the artichoke bottoms with the mushrooms. Top each with a pitted olive, heat, and cover with some of the Madeira Sauce. Arrange artichoke bottoms in the center of a serving platter. Place the chicken around the artichokes, spoon some of their sauce over them, and put a truffle slice on each. Makes 6 servings.

Vol-au-Vent of Truffled Chicken Ragoût

Double recipe Puff Pastry
2 eggs, beaten
Chicken Ragoût

Roll one-fourth of the Puff Pastry dough into a 10-inch circle ⅛ inch thick. Cut out a 9-inch circle, using a round 9-inch cake pan as a guide. (Save all the trimmings of the dough to use later.) Place the dough on a baking sheet and prick it all over with a fork so it will rise uniformly. Make a ball of paper 6 inches in diameter, wrap it in tissue paper or foil, and tie it with string. Place the ball in the center of the circle of dough. Brush the edges of the dough with water. Roll half of the remaining dough into a 13-inch circle ⅛ inch thick and cut it into a 12-inch circle, using a 12-inch plate as a guide. Fit the dough over the paper ball and press the edges down well all around the circle. Brush the entire surface with beaten egg. Roll half of the remaining dough ⅛ inch thick. Cut out strips ½ inch wide and long enough to reach across the top of the dome and to the edges on both sides. Roll the rest of the dough into a 10-inch circle. Cut out a 9-inch circle, from which cut a ring 1 inch wide. Place this ring around the dome. Roll all the reserved trimmings of the dough ⅛ inch thick and cut into circles, crescents, and rings, using scalloped cookie cutters and a pastry cutter. Place these cutouts as desired on the Puff-Pastry dome and around the edge. Prick with a fine needle in several places. Brush the entire surface with beaten egg.

Bake the vol-au-vent in a preheated oven (400°F) 20 to 25 minutes. If the pastry begins to brown too quickly, cover it with foil or brown paper. Remove the vol-au-vent from the oven and cool. Using a sharp pointed knife, cut around the edge of the dome, being careful not to cut the base crust. Carefully lift up the dome and set it aside. Remove and discard the paper ball. Fill the center of the vol-au-vent with Chicken Ragoût. Cover with the pastry dome. Makes 8 servings.

Chicken Ragoût

2 cups sliced mushrooms
1 tablespoon finely chopped onion
2 tablespoons butter
3 cups cubed cooked chicken

2 tablespoons chopped parsley
2 cups Mornay Sauce
½ truffle, diced
Salt and freshly ground black pepper

Sauté mushrooms and onion in butter 5 minutes. Add remaining ingredients. Stir and cook the mixture until it is hot. Serve on rice or in patty shells or use to fill a large vol-au-vent. Makes 8 servings.

Chicken Sukiyaki

2 cups scallions, cut into 1-inch pieces
1 cup white meat from broiler-size
    chicken, cut into thin julienne
1 tablespoon chicken fat or butter
1 tablespoon soy sauce
2 cups sliced celery

1 cup thinly sliced water chestnuts
1 cup thinly sliced bamboo shoots
1 cup sliced mushrooms
¼ pound young whole spinach leaves
Rice wine, sherry, or chicken broth
Fluffy cooked rice

Cook scallions and chicken in chicken fat or butter about 5 minutes over high heat. Sprinkle with soy sauce. Toss. Add all remaining ingredients except wine or broth.

Toss. Cook 4 to 5 minutes, adding wine or broth as needed to prevent the ingredients from becoming too dry. There should be very little liquid in the pan. Serve hot with rice. Makes 4 servings.

Chicken Quenelles with Truffle and Tongue Isabella

2½ cups Chicken Forcemeat
with Panada
Chicken or veal stock, or
lightly salted water
Croutons
2 cups Sauce Supreme

¼ cup heavy cream
½ teaspoon salt
Dash ground white pepper
½ teaspoon meat glaze
2 tablespoons chopped cooked tongue
1 small truffle, finely chopped

Pass forcemeat through a fine sieve and shape into quenelles, either with tablespoons, by rolling on a floured board, or by filling buttered small barquette molds (oval-shaped tart pans) with the forcemeat. Poach 15 to 20 minutes in a deep skillet containing barely simmering stock or lightly salted water, never allowing the liquid to boil. Remove quenelles from the liquid and drain well. Arrange on croutons the same size and shape as the quenelles. Heat the Sauce Supreme and mix in cream, salt, white pepper, and meat glaze. Heat and spoon over quenelles. Sprinkle with tongue and truffle. Makes 6 servings.

Chicken Quenelles in Tarragon Sauce

1 recipe Chicken Quenelles Isabella,
omitting tongue and truffles
1¼ teaspoons chopped fresh tarragon

12 slices sautéed mushrooms
Tarragon or parsley leaves

Make the recipe for Chicken Quenelles Isabella, and place the quenelles on croutons as directed. Arrange on a warm platter. Mix the chopped tarragon into the Sauce Supreme, and spoon over quenelles. Decorate each with a mushroom slice and a cross of tarragon or parsley leaves. Makes 6 servings.

Livers, Giblets, and Hearts with Mushrooms

½ cup sliced onion
3 cups sliced mushrooms
¼ cup (½ stick) butter
½ pound chicken livers or turkey livers
½ pound cooked chicken or
turkey gizzards and hearts

Salt and freshly ground black
pepper
½ cup dry white wine
5 slices toasted white bread
Parsley

Sauté onion and mushrooms in butter until vegetables are tender, stirring frequently. Cut chicken livers in half, or cut turkey livers into quarters, and add. Slice gizzards and hearts very thinly, and add. Stir and cook 2 minutes. Season to taste with salt and pepper. Add wine and cook 3 minutes. Spoon onto toast. Garnish with parsley and serve at once. Makes 6 servings.

Giblets with Rice

½ pound chicken or turkey gizzards and hearts	2¾ cups chicken stock
1 cup chopped onion	1 cup long-grain rice
4 tablespoons (½ stick) butter	¼ teaspoons salt
1 sprig parsley	Chopped parsley

Cut gizzards and hearts into small dice and cook with onion in 2 tablespoons of the butter until browned. Add parsley and stock and cook over low heat 30 minutes, or until giblets are tender. Meanwhile, soak rice 30 minutes in water to cover. Drain and cook in remaining 2 tablespoons butter until rice is dry and sticks to the bottom of the pan. Add to giblets, along with salt. Cover and cook 12 to 15 minutes. Turn off heat and let stand 5 to 10 minutes, or until rice has absorbed all liquid. Sprinkle with parsley. Makes 6 servings.

TURKEY

TURKEY IS TRUSSED, STUFFED, AND ROASTED in the same way as chicken, and young turkeys may also be broiled. When buying turkey, if the ready- to-cook weight is less than 12 pounds, allow ¾ pound to 1 pound per serving; if it is over 12 pounds, allow ½ to ¾ pound. In France, turkeys are known as *dindon* (turkey cock), *dinde* (hen turkey), and *dindonneau* (young turkey); recipes usually call for *dindonneau*, and if *dinde* is specified, a young, small bird is usually meant. The most perfect size and type to cook is a "natural," or organic, 10-12 pound turkey. Allow turkey to stand 20 to 30 minutes after it comes out of the oven to make sure the meat is juicy and tender.

Roast Turkey

Lay the bird on its side on a rack in a roasting pan. Spread generously with melted butter and lay thin slices of salt pork over the breast. Roast, uncovered, in a preheated oven (425°F) 15 minutes; turn on the other side and roast 15 minutes longer. Reduce oven temperature to 350°F and cook until turkey is done, turning from side to side and basting with pan drippings every 20 minutes, and allowing 20 minutes per pound total cooking time. Place the bird on its back for the last 15 minutes of cooking. If the pan drippings begin to burn, add a little water to the pan but be careful not to add enough to create steam. To test for doneness, pierce the thigh with a fork: If the juice runs out clear without a trace of pink, the bird is done.

6 to 8 pounds	1½ to 2 hours
8 to 12 pounds	3 hours
12 to 16 pounds	3-4 hours
16 to 20 pounds	4 hours
20 to 25 pounds	4-5 hours

If a meat thermometer is used stuck into the thickest part of the thigh, when it registers 175°F, the turkey should be done. If the breast and legs brown too quickly, cover with aluminum foil. To test for doneness pierce the thigh and if the juices run very slightly pink, the turkey is ready to sit in a warm place for 20-30 minutes, depending on its size.

Sausage and Chestnut Stuffing

1 cup chopped onion
1 cup (2 sticks) butter
2 pounds sausage meat
2 pounds cooked, shelled, peeled,
 very coarsely chopped chestnuts
½ cup Cognac
10 cups partially dried bread cubes

3 teaspoons each chopped sage and thyme
¼ cup chopped parsley
¾ teaspoon freshly ground black pepper
¾ cup turkey or chicken stock

Cook onion in butter until limp. Add all the remaining ingredients and mix gently but thoroughly. Stuff, truss, and roast turkey. Makes enough stuffing for one 12- to 15-pound bird.

Mushroom Stuffing

To the preceding recipe, add ½ pound chopped mushroom caps. Cook mushrooms with the onions.

Oyster Stuffing

Mix 1 cup finely chopped oysters, well drained, with other ingredients for Sausage and Chestnut Stuffing, omitting the chestnuts.

Broiled Young Turkey

1 (5- to 6-pound) young turkey
3 tablespoons butter, melted
1 teaspoon salt

¼ teaspoon freshly ground black pepper
Chopped parsley

Ask the butcher to split the turkey into 2 lengthwise halves and remove the backbone. Fold the wings under the back. Place the turkey, skin side down, in a buttered or oiled broiler pan. Brush well with melted butter or oil. Mix salt and pepper and season the turkey. Place the broiler pan 9 inches from the heat source. (If the oven is a gas oven, set thermostat at 350°F). Broil 40 minutes, brushing with melted butter, oil, or pan drippings. Turn and cook 40 to 50 minutes, or until turkey is done, basting 2 to 3 times with pan drippings. To serve, cut each half into 4 pieces. Makes 8 servings.

DUCK

DOMESTICATED DUCK IS ALL DARK MEAT (unlike chicken or turkey) and a smaller proportion of meat in relation to bone. The average ready-to-cook weight of duck on the American market is 4 to 5 pounds; in Europe the weight ranges from 3½ to 6 pounds, depending on the breed. Duck may be roasted (stuffed or unstuffed), braised, grilled, or fricasseed.

Only young ducks should be cooked; French recipes usually specify *caneton* (duckling) rather than *canard* (duck).

For wild duck, see chapter 13.

Roast Duck

1 (4-pound) duck
Salt and freshly ground black pepper
2 sprigs fresh thyme

1 lemon, chopped
1 onion, chopped
1¼ cups chicken or veal stock

Wash duck, pat dry, season the cavity and stuff it with thyme, lemon, and onion. Place on a rack in a baking pan. Truss and roast in a preheated oven (375°F) 1 hour, or until duck is tender. Transfer duck to a warm platter and keep hot. Pour off fat from the pan drippings. Mix stock with the juices in the pan. Stir and cook 2 minutes. Adjust seasonings. Serve in a separate sauceboat. Makes 4 servings.

Roast Duck with Orange Bigarade

This dish can be presented chilled in aspic as well as hot.

1 (4-pound) duck
2 tablespoons sugar
¼ cup vinegar
½ cup veal stock
½ cup Demi-Glace Sauce

1 tablespoon freshly squeezed lemon juice
½ cup freshly squeezed orange juice
2 tablespoons julienned orange zest, blanched
8 peeled, seeded orange slices

Wash duck and pat dry. Place on a rack in a baking pan. Cook in a preheated oven (375°F) 1 hour . Transfer duck to another pan to keep warm. Skim off and discard fat from pan drippings. Stir and cook sugar in a very small saucepan until it is brown or caramelized, being careful not to burn it. Add vinegar, mix well, and add to pan juices along with next 4 ingredients. Simmer 2 minutes. Add orange zest. Cut duck into serving pieces and arrange on a warm platter. Garnish with orange slices. Serve sauce in a sauceboat. Makes 4 servings.

Duck with Chipolata Sausages and Chestnuts

Chipolatas are little sausages similar to American breakfast sausages. If these are not available, use other small sausages.

1 (4-pound) duck
24 pearl onions, peeled
1½ cups Demi-Glace Sauce
½ pound mushrooms

12 chipolata sausages
Salt and freshly ground black pepper
½ pound Braised Chestnuts

Wash duck and pat dry. Place in a rack in a shallow casserole in a preheated oven (475°F) 15 minutes. Remove duck from the pan and let it cool. Cut into serving pieces. Sauté onions in the pan drippings. Drain off fat and add Demi-Glace Sauce to pan. Return duck to the casserole. Cover and cook in a preheated oven (350°F) 40 minutes. Add mushrooms and sausages and cook 10 minutes. Remove from oven and transfer duck, sausages, onions, and mushrooms to a warm platter. Skim off fat from pan drippings, and season the drippings to taste with salt and pepper. Spoon over duck. Garnish with Braised Chestnuts. Serve any remaining sauce in a separate dish. Makes 4 servings.

Duck with Figs

24 fresh almost ripe figs
Sauternes
1 (4-pound) duck

Salt and freshly ground black pepper
2 tablespoons brandy

Wash figs and soak in wine to cover in a covered jar for 24 hours. Wash duck and pat dry. Season with salt and pepper. Place duck in a casserole. Bake, uncovered, in a preheated oven (375°F) 30 minutes. Drain off fat from pan. To pan drippings, add fig marinating wine, reserving the figs. Return duck to oven and continue cooking 30 minutes, or until duck is tender, basting with wine occasionally. Skim off fat and discard. Add figs and cook 10 minutes. Transfer duck to a warm platter, and place figs around it. Add brandy to pan drippings, heat, and spoon over duck. Serve remaining sauce in a sauceboat. Makes 4 servings.

Duck Niçoise

1 (4-pound) duck
Salt and freshly ground black pepper
1 small clove garlic, crushed
6 medium-sized tomatoes, peeled,
    seeded, and quartered
½ cup pitted green olives

½ cup pitted black olives
2 tablespoons chopped parsley
½ cup dry white wine
¼ cup brandy
¼ cup Bouillon

Wash duck, pat dry, and rub with salt and pepper. Truss and place on a rack in a roasting pan. Cook in a preheated oven (375°F) 1 hour. Put duck on a warm platter and keep warm. Drain fat from the pan. Add all remaining ingredients to the pan drippings. Stir and cook 10 minutes, or until most of the liquid has evaporated. Adjust seasonings. Spoon sauce onto platter around the duck. Makes 4 servings.

Duck with Mushrooms, Truffles, and Madeira Mistral

1 (4-pound) duck
½ pound chicken livers
1 duck liver
4 tablespoons butter
2 shallots, chopped
1 pound mushrooms
Salt and freshly ground black pepper
¼ cup Madeira

3 tablespoons bacon drippings
1 carrot, pared and sliced
1 onion, sliced
1 rib celery, sliced
½ cup chicken or veal stock
1½ cups Demi-Glace Sauce
1 truffle, sliced

Wash duck, pat dry, and set aside. Coarsely dice chicken livers and duck liver and brown them in 2 tablespoons of the butter. Add shallots. Chop half the mushrooms and add, along with 1 teaspoon salt, ½ teaspoon pepper, and the wine. Simmer 5 minutes. Drain and push the mixture through a sieve or put it through a food mill. Season to taste with salt and pepper. Rub inside of duck's body cavity with salt and pepper and stuff with liver puree mixture. Close openings with skewer and lace tightly with twine. Brown the duck on all sides in a casserole in 2 tablespoons of the bacon drippings. Remove duck and add vegetables. Cover and cook 5 minutes without browning. Return duck to casserole. Sprinkle with salt and pepper. Cover and cook in a preheated oven (375°F) 1 hour, or until duck is tender. Transfer duck to a warm platter and keep warm. Pour off fat from the casserole, keeping all the juices. Add stock and Demi-Glace Sauce to the casserole. Bring to the boiling point and boil 5 minutes. Mix in the truffles. Spoon a little of the sauce over the duck. Serve remaining sauce separately in a sauceboat. Poach 4 mushroom caps in boiling water. Decorate breast of duck with poached mushroom caps. Slice remaining mushrooms, sauté in remaining butter, and spoon onto the platter around duck. Makes 4 servings.

Braised Duck with Peas

1 (4-pound) duck
2 tablespoons butter
4 slices salt pork
24 pearl onions
½ cup chicken or veal broth

1 cups Demi-Glace Sauce
Bouquet garni
1 teaspoon salt
½ teaspoon freshly ground black pepper
2 cups shelled fresh green peas

Wash duck and pat dry. Brown on all sides in butter in a Dutch oven. Transfer duck to another pan. Fry salt pork in the Dutch oven. Add onions and cook until they begin to color. Drain off fat. Add broth, Demi-Glace Sauce, bouquet garni, salt, and pepper. Return duck to the Dutch oven, cover, and cook over low heat (350°F) 1 hour, or until duck is tender. Add peas, and cook 10 minutes. Transfer duck and vegetables to a serving dish. Serve the sauce separately in a sauceboat. Makes 4 servings.

Casserole of Duck in Chambertin or Pinot Noir Wine

1 (4-pound) duck
1 teaspoon salt
½ teaspoon freshly ground black pepper
2 tablespoons olive oil
2 tablespoons butter
½ pound pearl onions

½ pound mushrooms
2 cups Chambertin wine
1 shallot, chopped
½ cup heavy cream
Chopped parsley

Wash duck, pat dry, and cut into quarters. Sprinkle with salt and pepper and brown on all sides in oil and butter in a casserole. Add onions. Cover and cook in a preheated oven (350°F) 40 minutes. Wash mushrooms, remove stems, and add caps to the duck. Cover and cook 10 minutes, or until duck is tender. Transfer duck, onions, and mushrooms to a platter. Skim off excess fat and discard. Add wine and shallot to the pan juices. Simmer until the liquid has reduced by half. Stir in cream. Heat sauce and spoon over the duck. Sprinkle with parsley. Serve remaining sauce in a sauceboat. Makes 4 servings.

Romanian Duck with Pickled Cucumbers

1 (4-pound) duck
Salt
¼ cup butter or lard
1 cup chopped onion
1½ cups thin Demi-Glace Sauce

1 tablespoon tomato puree
¼ teaspoon freshly ground black pepper
4 (3-inch) pickled cucumbers
½ cup sour cream

Cut duck into quarters and rub with 1 teaspoon salt. Brown in butter or lard in a heavy skillet over medium heat. Add onion after one side of the duck has browned and cook as the other side browns. Drain off excess fat. Add 1 teaspoon salt and next 3 ingredients. Cover and cook over low heat until duck is tender, about 60 minutes. Peel pickled cucumbers, cut into quarters, remove seeds, slice, and add to duck. Cook 10 to 15 minutes. If sauce is too thick, add a little bouillon. Adjust seasonings. Arrange in a serving dish. Serve sour cream separately. Makes 4 servings.

Boned and Chilled Stuffed Duck or Ballotine Charles Vaucher

2 (4-pound) ducks
3 pounds boneless lean shoulder of pork
1 cup dry white wine
¼ cup cognac
1 teaspoon chopped thyme
½ teaspoon chopped rosemary

1 teaspoon salt
½ teaspoon freshly ground black pepper
2 truffles
Hard-cooked egg whites
Aspic
½ pound foie gras puree

Split the ducks lengthwise along the back without breaking the skin and remove all bones except those in the drumsticks (or have the butcher do this for you). Remove the meat, being careful to keep the skin in one piece. Cut the meat into cubes and discard excess fat. Make brown stock with the bones. Cut the pork into cubes, trimming off and discarding excess fat. Mix the next 6 ingredients, pour over the duck meat and pork, and marinate 24 hours. Remove meat from marinade, drain, and put it through a food chopper twice, using the finest blade. Dice 1 of the truffles and add, mixing well. Stuff the duck skins with the mixture, forming them into their original shape. Sew up the openings. Braise in 2 cups of the brown stock for 2 hours, keeping the heat very low to prevent steam from bursting the skins. Cool and then chill. Thinly slice the front half of each duck. Decorate the rear halves and the slices of duck with thin strips of egg white. Coat with aspic and chill. Very finely chop remaining truffle. Shape the foie gras puree into 1-inch balls and roll them in chopped truffle. Place the duck halves on one side of a chilled tray. Arrange the slices of duck in front and garnish the tray with foie gras balls. Serve cold. Makes 15 or more servings.

Glazed Duckling Marivaux

1 (4-pound) duck
2 cups aspic
1 cup cooked green peas
½ cup cooked diced carrots
½ cup cooked diced potatoes
¼ cup diced celery

3 tablespoons Mayonnaise
Salt and freshly ground black pepper
½ pound foie gras puree
6 tablespoons softened butter
1 truffle, sliced
Lettuce

Roast the duck, keeping it slightly underdone. Cool. Remove the breast meat, cut it into long, thin slices, and coat with aspic. Chill. Remove breastbone. Combine vegetables, Mayonnaise, and salt and pepper to taste and spoon into the breast cavity in a dome. Place strips of the breast meat vertically around the vegetable dome. Cover with semiliquid aspic. Mix foie gras with butter and use to fill small molds (duck-shaped molds, if available). Chill until firm. Unmold and decorate with truffle. Coat with aspic. Cover the bottom of a tray with aspic and chill until set. Place the duck in center of the tray and arrange duck slices and molded foie gras mixture around it. Garnish with lettuce. Makes 6 servings.

GOOSE

GOOSE (FRENCH *OIE*) MAY BE ROASTED, BRAISED, and otherwise cooked in the same manner as duck.

Since goose older than 10 months is apt to be tough, select a younger bird, weighing 6 to 10 pounds, for roasting. It may be roasted stuffed or unstuffed. If a stuffing is used, allow ½ cup per pound of goose. Braising is the recommended method of cooking a goose weighing over 10 pounds.

Allow 1 to 1½ pounds ready-to-cook goose per serving.

Roast Goose with Chestnut Stuffing

2 pounds chestnuts
Water
Chicken stock
1 pound sausage meat
½ teaspoon dried thyme leaves
½ teaspoon dried marjoram leaves
¼ cup cognac

1 (8- to 10-pound) goose
Goose fat or chicken fat
1 cup hot water
¼ cup Madeira
Salt and freshly ground black pepper
Watercress or parsley

Using a sharp pointed knife, slit the shells of chestnuts on the convex side. Place in a saucepan, cover with water, and bring to the boiling point. Remove pan from heat (do not drain off water), remove chestnuts one at a time from the water, and peel off shells and inner skins while nuts are hot. Cook in stock to cover 30 minutes, or until they are barely tender. Drain chestnuts and mix gently with sausage meat, thyme, marjoram, and cognac. Stuff chestnut mixture into the neck and body cavities of the goose. Close openings with skewers and lace tightly with twine. Truss. Rub body of goose with goose fat or chicken fat. Place goose on a rack in a large baking pan. Pour hot water into pan. Roast in a preheated oven (375°F) 2 hours, or until goose is tender and browned, adding more water to the pan as it evaporates. Siphon off the fat that accumulates in the pan and baste the goose with it. Transfer goose to a warm platter and keep warm. Discard the fat in the pan, leaving the juices. Add the Madeira and simmer 5 minutes, stirring in all the brown bits from the bottom of the pan. Season sauce with salt and pepper. Garnish goose with watercress. Serve sauce in a sauceboat. Makes 8 to 10 servings.

Roast Goose English Style

1 (8- to 10-pound) goose	2 teaspoons dried ground sage
Salt	Freshly ground black pepper
3 cups chopped onions	½ teaspoon ground mace
3 tablespoons butter	3 tablespoons flour
1½ one-pound loaves white bread	2 cups stock
Milk	Watercress
2 eggs, beaten	Applesauce

Wash goose and pat dry. Rub inside of body cavity with salt. Set aside. Sauté onions in butter. Cut bread into cubes, add milk to cover, and soak until bread has absorbed most of the milk. Squeeze dry and fluff bread with a fork. Add sautéed onions, 1 teaspoon salt, the eggs, sage, pepper to taste, and mace. Mix well and stuff into the neck and body cavities of the goose. Close openings with skewers and lace with twine. Truss. Place goose on a rack in a baking pan. Bake in a preheated oven (375°F) 2 hours. Transfer goose to a warm platter and keep warm. Skim off and discard fat from pan drippings. Blend flour with stock and add to pan juices. Stir and cook until thickened. Add salt and pepper to taste. Serve in a sauceboat. Garnish goose with watercress. Serve with applesauce in a separate sauceboat. Makes 8 to 10 servings.

German Roast Goose with Apple Stuffing

1 cup chopped onion	1½ teaspoons salt, or to taste
½ cup (1 stick) butter	½ teaspoon freshly ground black pepper
1 quart peeled diced apples	1 teaspoon dried ground sage
1 quart cooked chestnuts, chopped	1 teaspoon grated nutmeg
1½ cups diced cooked potatoes	Dash ground cloves
1 goose liver, chopped	1 (8- to 10-pound) goose
Boiling water	1 cup Riesling
1 cup dark raisins	2 cups stock made from giblets
½ cup chopped parsley	

Cook onion in 2 tablespoons of the butter until limp. Add remaining butter and next 4 ingredients; pour boiling water over raisins, drain, and add, along with next 6 ingredients. Mix well. Wash goose and pat dry. Sprinkle inside neck and body cavities with salt. Stuff, close openings with skewers, and lace tightly with twine. Truss goose and place on a rack in a large baking pan. Pour 1 cup hot water into the roasting pan. Cook in a preheated oven (375°F) 2 hours, or until goose is tender and brown, basting frequently with the liquid in the pan. Add more water to the pan as it evaporates. Siphon off the fat as it accumulates in the pan and baste the goose while it is cooking. Transfer goose to a warm platter. Discard all the fat in the pan, reserving the juices. Add the Riesling and stock. Stir and cook until slightly thickened, scraping all the brown bits from the bottom of the pan. Season with salt and pepper to taste. Makes 8 to 10 servings.

Braised Goose Lyonnaise

1 (6- to 7-pound) goose	3 tablespoons butter
Salt and freshly ground black pepper	20 peeled chestnuts
½ cup dry white wine	½ pound mushrooms
1¾ cups Demi-Glace Sauce	½ pound chipolatas or other small sausages
20 pearl onions, peeled	

Wash goose and pat dry. Rub inside of neck and body cavities with salt and pepper. Truss. Place in a casserole. Cook in a preheated oven (450°F) 20 minutes to brown. Pour off fat. Add wine and Demi-Glace Sauce. Cook onions in butter until they begin to brown. Place in the roasting pan around the goose, cover, reduce oven temperature to 375°F and cook 1 hour. Add chestnuts and continue cooking 30 minutes. Wash mushrooms and add, along with sausages. Continue to cook until goose is tender. Transfer goose and vegetables to a warm platter. Skim off fat from the pan sauce and discard. Adjust seasonings and serve sauce in a sauceboat. Makes 6 to 7 servings.

Fricasseed Goose Giblets

Neck, wing tips, gizzard, and heart of 1 goose	½ cup sliced celery
	½ cup sliced carrots
2 cups water or chicken bouillon	¼ teaspoon freshly ground black pepper
Salt	2 tablespoons chopped parsley
2 medium-sized potatoes	2 egg yolks
8 small white onions	¼ cup heavy cream

Cut neck into 3 parts and wing tips into 2 parts each; cut gizzard and heart into slices ¼ inch thick. Put in a saucepan with water or bouillon and 1 teaspoon salt, cover, bring to the boiling point, reduce heat, and simmer 1 hour, or until meat is tender. Remove from stock and cut the meat from the neck and wing bones. Strain the stock. Peel and dice potatoes; peel onions, leaving them whole. Add potatoes, onions, celery, and carrot to the stock, cover, and cook 20 minutes, or until vegetables are tender. Return the goose meat and giblets to the stock. Add pepper, parsley, and salt to taste. Blend the egg yolks with the cream, add, and cook 1 minute to thicken. Makes 4 servings.

Cassoulet of Goose Toulousaine

2⅓ cups (1 pound) dried white beans (Great Northern)
5 cups boiling water
2 medium-sized onions
2 whole cloves
1 carrot, cut in half
1 small clove garlic, crushed
1 sprig parsley
1 rib celery
¼ cup finely diced salt pork
¼ pound garlic pork sausage
2 teaspoons salt

2 tablespoons goose or duck drippings, or cooking oil
¾ pound boneless lean pork, cut into cubes
¾ pound boneless lean lamb, cut into cubes
4 shallots, chopped
2 cups diced, peeled, seeded tomatoes
1 tablespoon chopped parsley
½ cup dry white wine
½ teaspoon freshly ground black pepper
2 pounds goose or duck confit
1 cup soft breadcrumbs
2 tablespoons butter, melted

Wash the beans, add the boiling water, cover, and boil 2 minutes. Remove from heat and soak in the cooking water 1 hour. Stud 1 of the onions with the cloves and add to the beans. Add the next 7 ingredients. Bring to the boiling point, uncovered. Skim off the foam from the surface, cover, and simmer 30 minutes. Remove the sausage and set aside. Cover the pan and continue to simmer the beans 30 minutes longer. Heat the goose or duck drippings or cooking oil in a skillet, add the pork and lamb, and sauté over heat 10 to 15 minutes, or until meat has browned. Transfer the meat to the bean mixture, leaving the fat in the skillet. Chop the remaining onion and add to the fat, along with the shallots. Cook over medium heat 5 minutes, or until onion is lightly browned, stirring constantly. Add the tomatoes, chopped parsley, and wine (if using). Stir and cook 5 minutes, then add to the bean mixture. Cover and simmer 1 hour, or until beans are tender, adding more boiling water if the beans become too dry. Remove and discard the whole onion, carrot, parsley sprig, and celery. Add the pepper, and additional salt to taste. (If you have any leftover goose or duck juices, add it to the beans.) Fill a 2-quart earthenware casserole with alternating layers of beans, goose or duck, and the sausage, with beans as the bottom and top layers. Combine the breadcrumbs with the butter and sprinkle over the beans. Bake in a preheated oven (350°F) 40 minutes, or until the crumbs are brown. Makes 6 to 8 servings.

GUINEA FOWL

ALL FOUR OR FIVE SPECIES OF GUINEA FOWL (French *pintade* or *pintadeau*) are native to Africa. It is now farm-raised in many parts of the world. The flesh is delicate, resembling that of pheasant. Young Guinea fowl can be prepared in any way suitable for chicken.

Roast Guinea Hen

2 (2-pound) guinea hens
2 teaspoons salt
1 teaspoon freshly ground black pepper
2 medium-sized onions
2 ribs celery, sliced

2 carrots, pared and quartered
2 sprigs parsley
Softened butter
8 thin strips salt pork

Wash guinea hens and pat dry. Rub the body cavities with some of the salt and pepper. Put 1 each of the vegetables and parsley sprigs into the body cavity of each guinea hen. Close openings with skewers and lace tightly with twine. Truss. Rub the skin of the hens with remaining salt and pepper and with softened butter. Place birds, breast side down, on a rack in a shallow baking pan. Place 2 salt pork strips across the back of each bird. Bake, uncovered, in a preheated oven (375°F) 20 minutes. Turn the birds over and place 2 salt pork strips across the breast of each. Bake 20 minutes, or until the birds are tender. Serve with gravy made from defatted pan juices. Makes 4 to 6 servings.

Sautéed Guinea Fowl à l'Africaine

2 young guinea fowl
Salt and freshly ground black pepper
Flour
6 tablespoons butter
2 tablespoons olive oil
2 chopped shallots
1 clove garlic, chopped

⅓ cup dry white wine
½ cup chopped tomato
¾ cup hot water
8 slices sweet potatoes
4 bananas, peeled
Freshly squeezed lemon juice

Cut guinea fowl into serving-size pieces as for fried chicken, season with 2 teaspoons salt and ½ teaspoon pepper, and dredge in flour. Brown lightly in 2 tablespoons each butter and oil in a heavy skillet over medium heat. Add shallots, garlic, wine, tomato, and water. Cover and cook 20 minutes. Place sweet potato slices in a buttered baking pan, sprinkle with salt, and dot with 2 tablespoons of the butter. Cover and cook in a preheated oven (350°F) until tender. Cut bananas into thick diagonal slices, sprinkle with lemon juice, and sauté in remaining 2 tablespoons butter. Arrange pieces of guinea fowl on a platter, with sweet potatoes and bananas around them. Skim off and discard fat from pan in which guinea fowl was cooked, cook to reduce pan liquid to sauce consistency, and pour over guinea fowl. Makes 8 servings.

Guinea Fowl with Lychee Nuts

3 small young guinea fowl
½ cup sherry
¾ cup chicken stock
¾ cup Demi-Glace Sauce
¼ cup freshly squeezed orange juice
½ teaspoon ground ginger

½ teaspoon ground coriander seeds
Dash ground cloves
Salt
1 cup peeled, pitted lychee nuts
Rice a l'Indienne

Roast guinea fowl as directed in recipe for Roast Guinea Hen. Remove breasts and legs. Bone the legs. Add a little sherry to the breasts and legs and keep warm. (Save the rest of the fowl for another meal.) Discard all the fat from the pan, leaving the juices, and pour the remaining sherry and the stock into the roasting pan and scrape the pan thoroughly with a wooden spoon. Cook until reduced by half over medium-high heat. Stir in Demi-Glace Sauce, orange juice, and spices. Bring to the boiling point. Remove from heat, strain, and add salt if needed. Add the lychee nuts. Arrange guinea legs and breasts on a platter and pour sauce and lychee nuts over. Serve with Rice a l'Indienne. Makes 6 servings.

Fried Breasts of Guinea Hen

Breasts of young guinea hens
Salt and freshly ground black pepper
Butter or salt pork drippings

Buttered cooked mushroom caps
Chicken stock
Cream

Allow 1 breast per serving. Rub breasts with salt and pepper. Fry in butter or salt pork drippings in a heavy skillet over medium heat until browned and tender. Transfer to a warm platter and garnish with mushroom caps. Pour off the fat and deglaze with the white wine. Add stock. Stir and cook 5 minutes. Add cream, and salt and pepper to taste. Heat 30 seconds. Serve sauce in a sauceboat.

PIGEON AND SQUAB

VERY YOUNG PIGEONS ARE CALLED SQUABS or *pigeonneau*. The average weight is about 1 pound and they are tender and delicious. Allow 1 squab or pigeon per serving.

Broiled Pigeon or Squab

6 young pigeons (or squabs)
Salt and freshly ground black pepper
¼ cup (½ stick) butter, melted

Buttered toast
Watercress

Split pigeons down each side of the backbone without separating the halves and flatten them with the broad side of a cleaver. Sprinkle with salt and pepper. Brush with butter. Arrange pigeons skin side down on a broiler rack. Broil 8 minutes on one side, brush both sides of pigeons again with melted butter, turn and cook 8 minutes, or until skin is brown and crisp and pigeons are still slightly pink. Serve on buttered toast. Garnish with watercress. Makes 6 servings.

Sautéed Pigeon

Split pigeons or squabs in half lengthwise. Sprinkle with salt and freshly ground black pepper. Brown on both sides in butter in a heavy skillet over medium heat. If squabs brown before they are well-done, lower heat and cook until done. Allow 1 bird per person.

Roast Pigeon Stuffed with Mushrooms, Almonds, and Chestnuts

4 young pigeons
2 tablespoons freshly squeezed
    lemon juice
Salt and freshly ground black pepper
12 chicken livers, cut in half
4 tablespoons butter
⅔ cup finely chopped mushrooms

½ cup ground lean cooked ham
½ cup chopped blanched almonds
    and chopped chestnuts
½ teaspoon chopped thyme
8 thin slices fatty salt pork
Watercress

Rub the inside of the body cavities of pigeons with some of the lemon juice, salt, and pepper. Set aside. Cook chicken livers in 2 tablespoons of the butter until just barely done. Transfer to a wooden bowl and finely chop. In the same skillet, sauté mushrooms in remaining butter. Add to livers, along with ham, almonds and chestnuts, and thyme. Season to taste with salt and pepper. Stuff loosely into the body cavities of pigeons. Close openings with skewers and lace tightly with twine. Tie legs of each pigeon together. Rub skin with lemon juice, salt, and pepper. Place pigeons on a rack, breast side up, in a shallow baking pan. Cover breasts with salt pork. Roast in a preheated oven (375°F) 25 minutes, or until pigeons are done, basting occasionally with pan drippings. Serve hot or cold, garnished with watercress. Makes 4 servings.

Pigeons with Little Peas

4 pigeons (or squabs)
Salt and freshly ground black pepper
4 tablespoons (½ stick) butter
6 thin slices salt pork
Chopped parsley
⅓ cup dry white wine

1 cup Demi-Glace Sauce
20 pearl onions
¼ cup chicken stock or water
3 cups buttered cooked little peas

Rub the skin and inside of the body cavities of pigeons with salt and pepper. Brown them lightly in butter in a heavy skillet over medium heat. Remove the birds, reserving the butter, and place them breast side up in a large casserole. Place a slice of salt pork over the breast of each and sprinkle with parsley. Dice remaining salt pork and add it to the casserole. Pour the butter that was left in the skillet over the pigeons. Add wine, Demi-Glace Sauce, and onions. Cover and cook in a preheated oven (375°F) 20 minutes, or until pigeons and onions are tender. Transfer pigeons to a serving platter and arrange the onions around them. Skim off and discard excess fat from the pan liquid. Add stock or water and cook 5 minutes. Serve the sauce in a sauceboat. Serve pigeons with peas in a separate dish. Makes to 8 servings.

Braised Pigeons with Turnips and Onions

6 young pigeons
Salt and freshly ground black pepper
2 tablespoons butter
1 tablespoon olive oil
1 cup Demi-Glace Sauce

2 tablespoons tomato puree
12 pearl onions, peeled
3 medium-sized white turnips
Chopped parsley

Sprinkle pigeons with salt and pepper. Brown on all sides in 1 tablespoon each butter and oil in a heavy deep skillet. Add next 3 ingredients. Peel turnips, cut them to resemble large olives, brown in remaining 1 tablespoon butter, and add to pigeons. Cover, bring to the boiling point, reduce heat, and simmer 20-30 minutes, or until pigeons and vegetables are done. Skim excess fat off the cooking juices, and adjust seasonings. Serve in a large deep dish. Sprinkle with parsley. Makes 6 servings.

Squabs on Fried Croutons

6 squabs
Salt and freshly ground black pepper
2 tablespoons butter, melted
6 thin strips salt pork
6 pigeon livers

¼ pound foie gras puree
6 slices bread, fried in butter
2 tablespoons brandy
½ cup chicken stock
½ cup dry white wine

Rub the skin and the inside of body cavities of squabs with salt and pepper. Brush the skin with melted butter. Place squabs on a rack in a shallow baking pan. Place a strip of salt pork over the breast of each squab. Cook in a preheated oven (375°F) 20 minutes, or until squabs are done. Cook pigeon livers in melted butter until they are barely done. Finely chop, mix with foie gras puree, and adjust seasonings. Spread the mixture over one side of each slice of fried bread, and top each with a roasted squab. Skim off fat from the roasting pan drippings. Add brandy, ignite, and deglaze. Add stock and wine. Stir and cook until sauce is slightly thickened. Serve in a sauceboat to spoon over squab. Makes 6 servings.

FEATHERED
AND
FURRED
GAME

THE TERM *GAME (GIBIER)* COVERS ALL wild birds and furred animals that are eaten. In this chapter there is a selection of recipes for both.

The best results and easiest cooking comes from using fresh game that has been "hung" or kept in a cool and well-ventilated space for one to several days to tenderize it and to develop the flavors. The only exception to the hanging rule is quail, which are generally best when eaten soon after they are killed.

GAME BIRDS

All young birds are best cooked at high temperatures and served while the meat is still pink (and after the bird has rested in a warm place for 10 minutes)—again the only exception being quail, which are cooked *just* to the point where the pink has turned white. Older birds are braised in fricassees or casseroles.

All the game birds, but especially partridge and woodcock, are best simply roasted and served with their juices soaked into a piece of country-style bread as the only sauce.

Wild Duck (CANARD SAUVAGE)

Wild ducks can be either freshwater or brackish water ducks, or surface-feeding ones, and saltwater or diving ducks, although with the latter one has to choose wisely so they don't taste of fish. Mallards are the most common, but there are many other suitable ducks—like canvasback, pintail, pochard, wigeon, and gadwall—that are worth seeking out. Teal duck, for example, may be the finest.

Grouse (GELINOTTE)

Grouse, another large family of birds, includes red grouse in England and the willow grouse or ptarmigan in America. There is also the black grouse, ruffed grouse, and capercaillie. Most recipes for pheasant will suit grouse as well.

Partridge (PERDREAUX when young, and PERDRIX when older*)*

Partridge is also a very large family of different birds living in North America, Europe, and Asia, such as gray and red-legged partridges.

Pheasant (FAISAN)

Probably the most commercially important game bird, the pheasant is like other feathered game as far as cooking techniques go: young and female birds are best roasted and served plain, older birds braised, served with cabbage or in soups.

Quail (CAILLE)

Quail belongs to the same family as the partridge, but has a milder flavor. In America, the varieties eaten include mountain quails, the bobwhite, and the California quail. Unlike other game birds, their eggs are highly prized.

Woodcock (BECASSE)

This bird, that ranges from Britain and northern Spain all the way to Japan and Siberia, is bigger than the American woodcock, but both are held by most to be the finest eating game bird in the world. It is the only bird that is cooked with its entrails still intact, since they give the fullest flavor to the roasted or grilled meat.

GAME ANIMALS

With furred game, the same rules apply as to domesticated animals, so that meats high on the hog, as it were, like the loin meats, are grilled, broiled, baked, or roasted at high heat and for a short time, while low on the hog (the tougher meats) are poached or braised at low temperatures for a long time.

Hare and Rabbit (LIEVRE and LAPEREAU for young rabbit and LAPIN for older)

The best way to describe the difference in America between the two animals, other than size, is that the cottontail is the rabbit and jackrabbit is the hare. The difference in cooking them is that rabbit is a white and mild-tasting meat, suitable for grilling, broiling, and roasting, or for use in galantines and terrines, while the hare is dark, can be quite strongly flavored, and is usually marinated in wine and then braised or "jugged," or made into a forcemeat with other meats for a game pie.

Venison (CHEVREUIL)

Venison is the general term for the meat of any animal in the deer family. In addition to deer, antelope and elk are very good eating. Venison is always cleaned and bled immediately after killing and then hung for up to three weeks. The meat has very little fat and needs larding or a covering of bacon or pork fat.

Wild Boar (MARCASSIN when young, and SANGLIER when older)

Most of the recipes for venison can be used for wild boar, and the older animals, as with the tougher cuts of deer, are marinated for a day or so before being cooked. Superb sausages and hams are made from wild boar.

GAME BIRDS

The kinds of game birds available vary in different parts of the world and in different sections of the United States. However, all can be roasted in the same way, and other methods of preparation can also used for different birds.

WILD DUCK (CANARD SAUVAGE)

Wild duck (mallard, teal, canvasback) is one of the most popular of game birds. There are many other species of wild duck and related waterfowl, and all can be cooked in the same ways. Most ducks improve in flavor and tenderness if hung in a cool place for two days.

Roast Wild Duck

1 (1½-pound) wild duck
½ teaspoon salt
1⁄16 teaspoon freshly ground
    black pepper
1 medium-sized carrot, sliced

1 rib celery, sliced
1 small white onion, sliced
3 juniper berries (optional)
2 slices fatty salt pork
½ cup dry white wine

Sprinkle surface of duck and body cavity with salt and pepper. Stuff the cavity with the next 4 ingredients. Close opening with skewers and lace tightly with twine. Truss. Place duck on a rack in a shallow roasting pan. Cover breast with salt pork slices. Roast 20 minutes in a preheated oven (450°F), basting frequently with wine. Let duck sit 10 minutes. Remove skewers and twine. Cut duck into serving-size pieces and place on a warm platter. Makes 2 servings.

Roast Marinated Wild Duck

3 (1½-pound) wild ducks
Salt and freshly ground black pepper
Lemon juice
Port
1 bay leaf
1 whole clove

1 small onion, sliced
1 carrot, sliced
1 rib celery, sliced
Sliced fatty salt pork
Marinade Sauce

Rub the ducks inside and out with salt, pepper, and lemon juice. Truss. Put the ducks in a deep dish and pour in port to cover. Add the next 5 ingredients. Marinate 24 hours. Remove ducks from marinade, reserving it. Place ducks on a rack in a shallow roasting pan. Cover breasts with slices of salt pork. Roast in a preheated oven (450°F) 20 minutes, basting with the marinade 3 times. If well-done duck is desired, roast 10 to 20 minutes longer. Cut duck into serving-size pieces and serve with Marinade Sauce. Makes 6 servings.

Broiled Wild Duck

1 (1½-pound) wild duck, halved
¼ cup (½ stick) butter, melted
½ teaspoon salt

Freshly ground black pepper
2 tablespoons currant jelly, melted

Combine butter, salt, and pepper and brush over the entire surface of the duck. Place duck on a broiler rack, skin side down. Broil 6 inches from heat source; or, if a gas broiler, set thermostat to 400°F and broil 5 to 8 minutes, depending on desired doneness, brushing occasionally with the melted butter mixture. Turn duck and broil 5 to 8 minutes longer, brushing with butter mixture. In the last 3 minutes of cooking brush the skin side with melted currant jelly. Makes 2 servings.

Marinade Sauce

1½ cups strained marinade from
    Roast Marinated Wild Duck
1 teaspoon minced shallot
1 rib celery
⅔ cup freshly squeezed orange juice

½ teaspoon lemon juice
1 cup veal or chicken stock
Dash cayenne
½ teaspoon grated orange zest
Salt

Combine the first 6 ingredients and cook until the liquid has reduced by half. Strain. Add the remaining ingredients. Simmer 5 minutes. Serve over duck. Makes about 1½ cups.

GROUSE

Grouse, of which there are various species, is highly prized in England and the United States. In France, where it is known as *gelinotte*, it is much less common, and the meat is inferior to that of the English and American species. Grouse, partridge, and pheasant can all be prepared in many of the same ways; see the following recipes for partridge and pheasant.

Roast Grouse

Grouse
Salt and freshly ground black pepper
Melted butter
Slices salt pork

½ cup hot water
1 tablespoon butter
2 or 3 juniper berries

Allow 1 bird per serving. Rub the skin with salt, pepper, and melted butter. Place slices of salt pork across the breast. Roast, uncovered, in a preheated oven (450°F) 15 minutes, or until juices run pale pink when the thigh is pierced with a skewer. Remove from oven, place on a warm platter, and keep warm. Add ½ cup hot water to the roasting pan, bring to the boiling point, and simmer until liquid is reduced by half. Add 1 tablespoon butter and juniper berries. Serve sauce over grouse. Grouse may also be served with Bread Sauce.

Bread Sauce

2 cups milk
2 shallots, left whole
2 whole cloves
¼ teaspoon salt

$\frac{1}{16}$ teaspoon freshly ground black pepper
1 cup fresh white breadcrumbs
1½ tablespoons butter

Combine the first 5 ingredients in a saucepan. Bring to the boiling point, reduce heat, and simmer 5 to 6 minutes. Strain. Add breadcrumbs and butter. Serve over grouse or other birds. Makes 2 cups.

PARTRIDGE

In French, young partridges are *perdreaux* (usually roasted), older ones *perdrix* (usually braised).

Partridges with Oranges and Grapes Titania

2 partridges
Salt and freshly ground black pepper
4 slices bacon
¼ cup sliced carrot
¼ cup sliced celery
1 small onion, sliced

½ cup (1 stick) butter, melted
Segments from 2 oranges
1 cup green seedless grapes
¼ cup freshly squeezed orange juice
¼ cup chicken stock

Truss partridges, rub skin with salt and pepper, and lay bacon slices over the breasts. Place vegetables in the bottom of a Dutch oven and lay partridges on the vegetables. Spoon 2 tablespoons of the butter over each partridge. Cover and cook in a preheated oven (400°F) 20 to 30 minutes, or until partridges are tender, removing the vegetables and adding orange segments and grapes for the last 5 minutes of cooking. Remove the birds and fruit to an ovenproof platter. Add orange juice and stock. Boil 1 minute. Pour over the partridges Serve at once. Makes 4 servings.

Roast Partridges on Foie Gras Toasts

4 partridges
Salt and freshly ground black pepper
½ cup (1 stick) softened butter
4 slices bread
4 partridge livers
1 truffle (optional)

¼ pound foie gras
1 tablespoon chopped parsley
2 tablespoons brandy
4 Baked Whole Tomatoes
Parsley

Truss partridges. Rub the skin with salt, pepper, and some of the butter. Place on a rack in a large roasting pan and cook in a preheated oven (400°F) 8 minutes on each side, then breast side up for another 8 minutes, or until partridges are tender. Drain the butter from the roasting pan into a skillet, and fry the bread in it, adding remaining butter as needed. Remove bread, and in the same skillet and butter sauté the partridge livers. Chop livers and the truffle, if using, and mix with foie gras and chopped parsley. Spread the mixture on the fried bread. Arrange on a round tray. Place a partridge on each slice of bread, with the feet pointing toward the center of the tray. Rinse the roasting pan with brandy and pour over partridges. Garnish tray with Baked Whole Tomatoes and parsley. Makes 8 servings.

Baked Whole Tomatoes

Place medium-sized whole tomatoes in a baking pan and bake in a preheated oven (350°F) 20 minutes, or until tomatoes are soft. Allow 1 tomato per serving.

PHEASANT (FAISAN)

Braised Pheasant with Wild Rice

1 (2- to 3-pound) pheasant
Salt and freshly ground black pepper
⅓ cup sliced celery
½ small white onion
2 tablespoons butter

¼ cup Madeira
1 cup chicken stock
1 cup cooked Wild Rice

Rub pheasant inside and out with salt and pepper. Stuff celery and onion into the body cavity. Brown the bird in butter in a casserole. Pour over Madeira and heat 2 minutes. Add stock. Cover, bring to the boiling point, and simmer 45 minutes, or until bird is tender. Serve the bird with Wild Rice and any other vegetable of choice. Makes 2 servings.

Roast Pheasant

1 (2- to 3-pound) pheasant
Salt and freshly ground black pepper
1 slice lemon

4 slices fatty salt pork
Melted butter
Madeira Sauce (optional)

Sprinkle pheasant inside and out with salt and pepper. Place the lemon slice in the body cavity. Truss. Cover the breast with the slices of salt pork. Cut cheesecloth large enough to cover the bird completely, soak it in melted butter, and spread over the pheasant. Place covered bird on a rack in a shallow baking pan. Roast in a preheated oven (350°F) 30 minutes per pound, or until bird is done, basting occasionally with melted butter. Transfer pheasant to a warm platter. In the roasting pan, make Madeira Sauce or pan gravy (see following recipe) and serve with the bird. Makes 2 servings.

Madeira Sauce for Roast Pheasant

Remove the pheasant, discard the fat but not the juices, and add to the roasting pan 1 cup chicken stock. Cook over medium heat, scraping all the browned bits from the bottom of the pan. Add ½ cup Madeira and simmer 10 minutes. Chop the pheasant liver and add, along with salt and pepper to taste.

Casserole of Pheasant

1 (2- to 3-pound) pheasant
Salt and freshly ground black pepper
1 tablespoon butter
2 tablespoons olive oil
4 slices fatty salt pork

1½ cups sliced mushrooms
¼ pound pearl onions, peeled
¼ cup Madeira
Chopped parsley

Season the pheasant inside and out with salt and pepper. Brown on all sides in butter and oil. Cover the breast of the pheasant with salt pork. Place bird in a casserole, cover, and cook in a preheated oven (400°F) 30 minutes, or until pheasant is tender. The meat should be a little on the pink side; otherwise it will be dry. Add mushrooms and onions when pheasant is half done. Sprinkle them with salt and pepper. When pheasant and vegetables are done, add Madeira and cook 3 to 4 minutes over medium heat, stirring. Serve in the casserole, sprinkled with parsley. Or transfer pheasant to an oval platter, arrange mushrooms on one side and onions on the other, and garnish with fried bread. Makes 2 servings.

Salmis of Pheasant

1 pheasant
2 tablespoons olive oil
¼ cup chopped onion
1 shallot, chopped
¼ small clove garlic, crushed
1½ tablespoons flour
1 cup dry white or red wine
1 sprig parsley

4 whole peppercorns
½ bay leaf
½ teaspoon salt
1 cup chopped tomatoes
8 mushroom caps
2 tablespoons butter
2 slices toast
Puree of foie gras

Braise pheasant (preferably an older bird) the day before serving, leaving it slightly underdone. Cool in the pan. The day the dish is to be served, remove the bird from the pan, put the oil in the pan, and add onion. Stir and cook until onion is golden. Add the next 3 ingredients; stir and cook 1 minute. Add wine, parsley, peppercorns, bay leaf, and salt. Stir and cook until thickened. Add tomatoes. Meanwhile, cut breasts and legs from the pheasant, remove and discard skin, and slice meat. Then cut up the carcass and add to the sauce, along with the leg bones. Cover and simmer 1 hour. Place the slices of meat in a skillet and strain sauce over them. Heat through. Sauté mushroom caps in butter and arrange over the meat. Serve on toast spread with puree of foie gras. Makes 2 servings.

Pheasant Auge Valley Style

Cook pheasant as in the recipe for Casserole of Pheasant but omit mushrooms and onions, and substitute apple brandy or hard cider for the Madeira. When pheasant is half done, add 2 peeled, cored, and quartered tart apples. Add ¾ cup cream 5 minutes before the pheasant is cooked and simmer over medium-low heat. Makes 2 servings.

Chaud-Froid of Pheasant with Foie Gras and Walnuts Marie-Jeanne

1 (3-pound) pheasant	Salt and freshly ground black pepper
2 tablespoons butter	½ pound chestnuts, cooked
2 tablespoons olive oil	1 pound cooked foie gras
1 cup game or brown stock	10 walnut halves, peeled, toasted
1 cup Demi-Glace Sauce	Truffle slices
3 pints aspic	Cashew nuts, toasted
	Green seedless grapes

The day before serving, brown pheasant in butter and oil in a heavy saucepan. Add stock, cover, and cook 1 hour or until pheasant is tender. Cool. Make a Chaud-Froid Sauce from the sieved and degreased pan juices, the Demi-Glace Sauce, and 1 cup of the aspic. Adjust seasonings. Remove the breast and bones from the pheasant and discard bones; set breast aside. Put chestnuts through a food chopper twice, using the finest blade. Put foie gras through the food mill, and mix with chestnuts. Push mixture through a sieve. Fill the cavity left by the removal of the breast with some of the foie gras mixture. Cut breast into strips and lay them over the top of the foie gras mixture. Cover lightly with Chaud-Froid Sauce and decorate with a row of walnut halves in the center and a row of truffle slices on each side. Glaze with aspic. Line small molds with aspic and chill until set. On the bottom of each of 8 molds put 3 bits of truffle and cashew nut halves in a design, fill some of the molds with remaining foie gras mixture, cover with aspic, and chill. Put green seedless grapes and several small slices of pheasant breast in the bottom of each remaining mold, fill with the rest of the sauce, cover with aspic, and chill until set. Arrange pheasant on a large oval tray. Turn out the molds and arrange them around the pheasant. Makes 6 to 8 servings.

Broiled Quail with Foie Gras Toasts

Quail	Toast
Salt and freshly ground black pepper	Cooked foie gras (optional)
Softened butter	Parsley

Allow 1 quail per serving. Split dressed quail and sprinkle with salt and pepper. Spread with butter. Place the bird, skin side down, on a preheated broiler pan. Broil 5 to 6 minutes. Turn and broil 5 to 6 minutes longer, or until quail is tender and browned. Serve on toast spread with butter or foie gras. Garnish with parsley.

Quails Bonne-Maman

3 carrots, pared	Salt and freshly ground black pepper
3 ribs celery	6 quails
3 small white onions	¾ cup rich veal stock
5 tablespoons butter	Chopped parsley

Cut carrots and celery into short juliennes. Thinly slice onions. Cook vegetables in 1 tablespoon of the butter until almost done. Season with salt and pepper to taste. Sprinkle quails, inside and out, with salt and pepper. Brown in remaining 4 table-spoons butter. Add to vegetables, along with stock. Cover and simmer 10 minutes. Sprinkle with parsley. Makes 6 servings.

If this dish is to be served cold, the stock should be rich enough to jelly; if not add 1½ teaspoons unflavored gelatin softened in 2 tablespoons cold water to the strained and degreased cooking juices.

Roast Quail

Quail	Slices fatty salt pork
Salt and freshly ground black pepper	½ cup water or stock
Softened butter	¼ cup dry sherry

Allow 1 quail per serving. Rub quail, inside and out, with salt and pepper, then rub with butter. Cover each breast with 2 slices salt pork and place bird in a buttered shallow roasting pan. Roast, uncovered, 20 minutes, or until done, in a preheated oven (400°F). If the bird has not browned sufficiently, place under the broiler for a few minutes to brown. Transfer bird to a serving dish. Degrease the pan, leaving the juices, and add the sherry. Cook over high heat 1 minute, and then add water or stock to the pan. Stir and cook 1 to 2 minutes, scraping the browned bits from the bottom of the pan. Season to taste with salt and pepper.

Quail in Pilaf Turque

1 cup raw long-grain rice	Freshly ground black pepper
2 tablespoons olive oil	¼ cup (½ stick) butter
2 cups boiling chicken stock	¾ cup Tomato Sauce
6 quails	1 tablespoon chopped onion
Salt	

Wash rice in water. Drain and cook in oil until rice is dry and begins to stick to the pan. Add stock and ½ teaspoon salt. Season quails inside and out with salt and pepper. Brown quickly in butter and press into the rice. Cover and cook 15-20 minutes, or until rice is tender and the quails are cooked. Combine Tomato Sauce and onion in a small saucepan. Rinse the degreased skillet in which the quails were browned with ¼ cup of the stock and add to Tomato Sauce. Stir and cook 2 to 3 minutes. Spoon over quails. Makes 6 servings.

Quails in Wine

6 quails	½ cup diced mushrooms
Salt and freshly ground black pepper	2 medium-sized pieces orange zest
3 tablespoons butter	1 tablespoon flour
½ cup diced carrots	1 cup chicken stock
2 tablespoons diced onion	½ cup dry white wine

Sprinkle quails with salt and pepper, and brown them lightly in butter. Transfer to a buttered casserole. To the skillet in which the quails were browned, add the next 3 ingredients. Blanch orange zest in hot water, drain, and add to the vegetables. Cook over low heat 5 to 6 minutes. Add flour and mix well. Gradually stir in stock. Stir and cook until sauce has thickened. Season with salt and pepper to taste. Simmer 10 minutes. Pour wine over the quails and cook in a preheated oven (350°F) 10 to 15 minutes. Add the vegetable sauce. Cover and cook 25 minutes, or until birds are tender. Makes 6 servings.

WILD TURKEY

The largest of American upland game birds, wild turkey is found only in North America. The average weight of a young hen turkey is about 8 pounds; a young tom is about 12 pounds.

Roast Wild Turkey

Dress, stuff, and truss as for domestic turkey. Cover breast with fatty salt pork slices, or spread the body generously with butter and cover with a clean cloth or 3 layers of cheesecloth (large enough to drape over the bird) that has been lightly wrung out in hot water. Roast in a preheated oven (350°F) 15 minutes per pound. Allow 1 pound turkey per person. Serve with Wild Rice and any of the garnishes for goose.

WOODCOCK (BECASSE)

Woodcock is regarded as the choicest of game birds. One or two birds serves one person.

Roast Woodcock

Woodcock	½ cup hot water or stock
Salt and freshly ground black pepper	1 tablespoon butter
Melted butter	3 juniper berries, crushed
Slices salt pork	Toast

Allow 1 bird per serving. Rub woodcock with salt and pepper. Rub the skin with melted butter. Place slices of salt pork across the breast. Roast, uncovered, in a preheated oven (450°F) 10 minutes. Remove from oven, place on a warm platter, and keep warm. Add hot water or stock to the roasting pan. Bring to the boiling point and simmer until the liquid has reduced by half. Add 1 tablespoon butter and juniper berries. Serve on toast with the sauce.

Chaud-Froid of Woodcock with Foie Gras Strasbourg

2 cold roasted woodcocks	1 truffle
¼ pound poached goose liver	2½ cups game aspic
Brown Chaud-Froid Sauce flavored with game stock	

Remove breasts from the woodcocks. With scissors, cut out the breastbone. Fill the cavity with goose liver. Cut the breasts diagonally into 3 slices and place them in their original position over the cavities of the birds. Coat the birds completely with Brown Chaud-Froid Sauce. Chill. Garnish with slices of truffle or olive. Coat with aspic. Chill the woodcocks and some of the the remaining aspic until set. Coat a platter with aspic, chill until set, and place the birds on it. Break up the jellied aspic with a fork and spoon it onto the platter around the birds. Makes 2 servings.

Mousse of Woodcock and Foie Gras in Aspic Diplomat

3 roasted woodcocks
¾ pound poached goose liver
Salt and freshly ground black pepper

2 truffles, sliced
2½ cups game aspic

When woodcocks are cold, remove skin and cut out the breasts and slice them. Remove the meat from the legs and put it through a food chopper twice, using the finest blade. Blend with the goose liver and season to taste with salt and pepper. Spread a layer of the liver mixture in the bottom of a 10-by-6-by-2-inch dish. Cover with sliced woodcock breasts and spread with remaining liver mixture. Garnish the top with slices of truffle or olive. Cover completely with cold but still liquid game aspic. Chill until set. Serve, sliced, on a chilled tray. Makes 6 servings.

FURRED GAME

HARE AND RABBIT

German Creamed Hare Braised in Red Wine or Hasenpfeffer

1 large (4-pound) hare
1½ cups wine vinegar
1 cup water
1 cup dry red wine
2 cups sliced onions
2 teaspoons salt
1 tablespoon mustard
1 teaspoon freshly ground black pepper

1 teaspoon ground allspice
1 whole clove
Flour
¼ cup (½ stick) butter
1 cup sour cream

Cut rabbit into serving-size pieces. Let it marinate 48 hours in the next 9 ingredients in the refrigerator. Remove rabbit from marinade, pat dry, dredge in flour, and brown in butter in a heavy saucepan. Pour marinade over rabbit. Cover, bring to the boiling point, reduce heat, and simmer 45 minutes, or until rabbit is tender. Transfer rabbit to a warm platter. Strain the broth. Blend ⅓ cup flour with a little water, add to the broth, and stir and cook 30 minutes. Add rabbit and sour cream, and heat but do not boil. Adjust seasoning. Serve with Potato Dumplings or buttered noodles. Makes 6 servings.

Braised Rabbit

2 (1-pound) rabbits
1½ teaspoons salt
½ teaspoon freshly ground black pepper
3 slices fatty salt pork
1 small onion, sliced
1 clove garlic, crushed

1 cup chopped tomatoes
½ teaspoon chopped basil
½ teaspoon chopped oregano
½ cup port
Chopped parsley

Cut rabbit into serving-size pieces. Season with salt and pepper. Fry salt pork until barely crisp, remove slices, and drain on paper towels. In the salt pork fat, brown the rabbit on all sides. Add crumbled salt pork, along with next 3 ingredients. Cover and bring to the boiling point, reduce heat, and simmer 45 minutes, or until rabbit is tender. Add herbs and wine 10 minutes before cooking time is up. Serve in a warm platter. Garnish with parsley. Makes 6 servings.

Jugged or Civet of Hare

1 (4½-pound) hare
2½ cups dry red wine
⅓ cup fat rendered from salt pork
2 tablespoons flour
¾ cup brandy
Water
1 tablespoon tomato puree

1 sprig parsley
1 clove garlic, crushed
1 teaspoon salt
¼ teaspoon freshly ground black pepper
20 pearl onions, peeled
½ pound mushrooms
½ cup heavy cream

Clean the hare, reserving the liver and blood. Cut hare into pieces and marinate 48 hours in wine. Reserve the marinade. Pat the pieces dry and brown over high heat in 3 tablespoons of the salt pork fat. Sprinkle with flour and let it brown. Add brandy, heat, and ignite. Add red wine marinade and an equal amount of water and the next 5 ingredients. Cover, bring to the boiling point, reduce heat, and simmer 20 minutes. Brown onions in remaining salt pork fat and add to the hare. Simmer 20 minutes. Wash mushrooms and add. Cover and cook 10 minutes, or until hare is tender, adding the diced liver 5 minutes before cooking time is up. Mix the hare's blood with a few spoonfuls of the sauce and stir into the mixture. Remove parsley. Add cream and heat (do not boil). Adjust salt and turn into a deep dish, heaping the mushrooms in the center. Makes 6 to 8 servings.

Jugged Hare with Chestnuts

Make the recipe for Jugged Hare, replacing the mushrooms with 1 pound chestnuts, scored, peeled, and cooked in the oven until done.

Jugged Hare German Style

2½ pounds hare forelegs
1½ teaspoons salt
¼ teaspoon freshly ground black pepper
3 tablespoons bacon drippings
1 cup claret or port
2½ cups Demi-Glace Sauce

¾ cup hare's blood
½ pound small white onions
¼ cup (½ stick) butter
½ pound mushrooms
Stewed apples

Toss hare forelegs with salt and pepper. Brown on all sides in bacon drippings. Add wine and cook until reduced by half. Add Demi-Glace Sauce, cover, and simmer until hare is tender. Transfer meat to a warm serving dish. Thicken the sauce with the hare's blood. Heat but do not boil. Adjust salt and pepper. Meanwhile, parboil onions, sauté in half of the butter, and arrange in the dish with hare. Quarter the mushrooms, cook in remaining butter until tender, and arrange in the serving dish. Strain the sauce over the rabbit. Serve with stewed apples. Makes 6 servings.

Marinated and Roasted Whole Hare or Rabbit with Grapes

2 young hares or rabbits
½ cup water
½ cup brandy
2 tablespoons olive oil
2 small onions, sliced
½ cup sliced carrots
1 clove garlic, crushed
2 sprigs parsley

1 bay leaf
1 teaspoon salt
½ teaspoon poultry seasoning
¼ teaspoon freshly ground black pepper
⅔ cup peeled green grapes
2 hare livers
Butter

Place hares or rabbits in a deep dish. Add the next 11 ingredients and marinate in the refrigerator 2 days, turning rabbits in the marinade occasionally. Place the rabbits, along with marinade, in a casserole or Dutch oven. Cover and cook in a preheated oven (350°F) 1½ hours, or until rabbits are tender, basting frequently with marinade. Transfer rabbits to a warm serving dish. Add grapes to the cooking liquid. Sauté livers in butter, mash, and add. Bring sauce only to the boiling point. Pour around the hare. Makes 6 servings.

Roasted Saddle of Hare

The saddle is the back of the hare from the first ribs to the legs. It should be roasted medium-rare.

| 2 (1½-pound) saddles of hare | Slices fatty salt pork, or lardoons |
| Salt and freshly ground black pepper | Olive oil |

Rub the saddles of hare with salt and pepper. Cover with slices of salt pork Pour enough oil into a roasting pan to cover the bottom generously. Heat in a preheated oven (450°F) until the oil is almost smoking, then put in the saddles, turning them to brown on all sides, for 5 minutes. Roast 10 minutes. Transfer meat to a board and carve. Makes 6 servings.

Roast Saddle of Hare with Chestnuts and Sauce Diane

2 (1½-pound) saddles of hare	Watercress
Salt and freshly ground black pepper	Chestnut Puree
Slices salt pork, or lardoons	Sauce Diane
Olive oil	

Rub saddles of hare with salt and pepper. Cover with slices of salt pork. Pour enough oil into a roasting pan to cover the bottom generously. Heat in a preheated oven (450°F) until oil is almost smoking, then put in the saddles and brown, on all sides, for 5 minutes. Roast 10 minutes. Transfer meat to a warm platter. Garnish with watercress. Serve with Chestnut Puree and Sauce Diane. Makes 6 servings.

Chestnut Puree

| 1 pound shelled and cooked chestnuts | Salt and freshly ground black pepper |
| 2 tablespoons butter | Heavy cream |

Put chestnuts through a food chopper, using the finest blade, then force through a sieve. Add butter, salt, and pepper. Thin with heavy cream to consistency desired. Makes about 1½ cups.

VENISON

Venison is the meat of any kind of deer. Like beef, it should be aged for a period of 2 to 4 weeks before cooking. Since the meat lacks fat, venison roasts should be larded with strips of fatty salt pork or covered with slices of salt pork, and venison steaks should be cooked in a generous amount of butter or oil. The less tender cuts of venison should always be marinated. The tender saddle of young venison, however, should not. Saddle should be cooked only to the rare stage. A saddle weighing to 6 pounds will cook in 45 minutes to 1 hour in a very hot oven (450°F).

Roast Leg of Venison with Black Pepper Madeira Sauce

1 (6- to 7-pound) leg of venison	3 juniper berries
4 cups red wine	1 teaspoon salt
1 cup beef bouillon	6 slices fatty salt pork
1 medium-size onion, sliced	Madeira Sauce
1 clove garlic, crushed	2 teaspoons cracked black peppercorns
1 bay leaf	

If the lower part of the leg is used, remove the shank bone. Place meat in a large bowl and refrigerate for 24 hours in the next 7 ingredients. Remove meat from marinade and tie it into a compact shape. Strain marinade and set aside. Place the meat on a rack in a shallow roasting pan. Arrange salt pork slices over the top. Roast, uncovered, in a preheated oven (450°F) 20 minutes. Reduce oven temperature to 325°F and cook 15 to 18 minutes per pound, or to an internal temperature of 130°F. Baste meat occasionally with marinade while it is cooking. Transfer meat to a warm platter. Remove and discard fat from pan cooking juices. Strain. Add to Madeira Sauce, reduce, add 2 teaspoons freshly cracked black peppercorns, and serve hot with the roast. Makes 10 to 12 servings.

Roast Saddle of Venison

1 (5- to 6-pound) saddle of venison	½ pound mushrooms, fluted
Salt and freshly ground black pepper	Cream Pan Sauce for Venison
Slices of fatty salt pork	

Wipe meat with a damp cloth. Rub with salt and pepper. Place meat on a rack in a shallow roasting pan. Cover top with slices of salt pork. Place in a preheated oven (450°F) and cook, uncovered, 45 minutes to 1 hour, or until the internal temperature is 140°F. About 15 minutes before meat is done, add mushrooms that have been simmered 5 minutes in a little stock. Remove meat to a warm platter. Garnish with the mushrooms, new potatoes parboiled and sautéed in butter, and chestnuts cooked until tender and sautéed lightly in butter. Serve with Cream Pan Sauce. Makes 6 to 8 servings.

Cream Pan Sauce for Venison

1 shallot, finely chopped	1½ cups heavy cream
2 tablespoons butter	Salt and freshly ground black pepper

Remove and discard fat from the venison roasting pan. Add shallot and butter. Stir and cook about 2 minutes. Add cream. Mix well. Stir and cook until sauce thickens. Add salt and pepper. Serve over roast venison. Makes enough for 6 to 8 servings.

Sautéed Venison Steaks with Cherries

12 small (2-ounce) round venison
    steaks or medallions
Butter

¾ cup pitted ripe Bing cherries
½ cup dry sherry

Pan-fry meat in butter in a skillet over medium-high heat to desired doneness. Keep warm. Place cherries and sherry in a saucepan, bring to the boiling point, reduce heat, and simmer 2 to 3 minutes. Strain, reserving cherries. Transfer meat to a heated round platter and arrange in a circle. Put cherries in the center. Pour sauce over steaks and cherries. Serve at once. Makes 6 servings.

Saddle of Venison with Mushrooms

1 saddle of venison
Salt and freshly ground black pepper
Slices fatty salt pork
Butter
½ cup brown stock
½ cup Demi-Glace Sauce

½ cup heavy cream
½ cup chopped onion
3 cups sliced white mushrooms
3 cups sliced fresh porcini (optional)
6 to 8 servings boiled potatoes
Chopped parsley

Wipe meat with a damp cloth and rub with salt and pepper. Place meat on a rack in a shallow roasting pan. Cover top with slices of salt pork. Cook in a preheated oven (450°F) 30 to 45 minutes, or until the internal temperature is 130°F. Baste several times with melted butter while cooking. Let rest 20 minutes. Transfer meat to a warm platter and keep warm. Remove and discard fat from pan drippings. Add stock and boil 3 minutes. Add Demi-Glace Sauce and cream. Cook until the sauce has reached the desired consistency. Adjust salt and pepper. Brown onion in 1 tablespoon butter, then add white mushrooms and 2 tablespoons butter. Stir and cook until mushrooms are done. Sauté porcini if using, in 2 tablespoons butter. Arrange onion and mushrooms on the platter around the roast. Spoon sauce over the meat. Cut salt pork into julienne and sprinkle along the top as a garnish. Serve remaining sauce in a sauceboat. Serve potatoes in a separate dish. Sprinkle with parsley. Makes 6 to 8 servings.

Mushroom Stuffed Venison Medallions or Noisettes

These steaks are cut either from the loin fillet or from the topside of the leg. They are cut fairly thick, averaging 2½ to 3 inches.

6 large venison steaks	Flour
Salt and freshly ground black pepper	Eggs, beaten
5 tablespoons butter	1 cup fine white breadcrumbs
Rich mushroom Duxelles	2 tablespoons olive oil

Rub steaks with salt and pepper and fry in 3 tablespoons of the butter over high heat, keeping them very underdone. Cool slightly. Cut the steaks open but not through. Fill with Rich Duxelles. Press the top slightly, dredge in flour, dip in eggs, and roll in breadcrumbs. Fry until golden brown on both sides in remaining 2 tablespoons butter and 2 tablespoons oil. Makes 6 servings.

Medallions of Venison with Ginger Pilaf and Madeira Sauce Madame Lacroix

1 cup long-grain rice	Freshly ground black pepper
6 tablespoons butter	6 large mushroom caps, sautéed
2 tablespoons chopped onion	in butter
Salt	¼ cup heavy cream
2 tablespoons chopped candied ginger	1 cup Madeira Sauce
2 cups hot bouillon	1 teaspoon cracked black pepper
6 steaks cut from the fillet saddle	1 tablespoon currant jelly
of venison	

Cook rice 10 minutes in water to cover. Drain and cook rice in 2 tablespoons of the butter until it is dry and begins to stick to the bottom of the pan. Cook onion in 1 tablespoon of the butter until limp; add onion and ½ teaspoon salt to rice. Add ginger and bouillon. Cover, bring to the boiling point, reduce heat, and simmer 12 to 15 minutes. Remove from heat and let stand about 5 minutes. Fry steaks in remaining 3 tablespoons butter, browning both sides. Sprinkle with salt and pepper. To serve, place rice in a mound in the center of a warm round serving platter, and arrange steaks around it. Top each steak with a mushroom cap. Rinse skillet with cream, add Madeira Sauce, pepper, and jelly, and cook 1 to 2 minutes. Pour a little sauce over the steaks. Serve remaining sauce in a sauceboat. Makes 6 servings.

Venison Stew Hungarian Style

2 pounds boneless venison	1 clove garlic, crushed
3 tablespoons flour	3 cups beef or veal stock
2 teaspoons salt	½ cup tomato puree
3 tablespoons fat rendered	½ teaspoon freshly ground black pepper
from salt pork	3 teaspoons paprika
¾ cup sliced onion separated into rings	1 cup sour cream

Cut venison into 1½-inch cubes. Dredge in flour mixed with salt, pressing it in well. Brown meat in salt pork fat. Add onion and garlic. Stir and cook until onion is limp. Add stock. Cover, bring to the boiling point, reduce heat, and simmer 2 hours, or until meat is tender. Add tomato puree and cook 10 minutes. Add remaining ingredients. Heat but do not boil. Serve with buttered noodles, boiled new potatoes, and red cabbage cooked with apples. Makes 6 servings.

WILD BOAR

Young Wild Boar Cutlets

12 cutlets of young wild boar	6 whole peppercorns
¾ cup dry white wine	½ teaspoon dried thyme
½ cup wine vinegar	½ teaspoon salt
1 small onion, sliced	12 narrow strips fatty salt pork (lardoons)
1 carrot, sliced	3 tablespoons olive oil
1 sprig parsley	3 tablespoons butter
1 small bay leaf	

Trim cutlets neatly and marinate 2 hours in the next 9 ingredients. Drain cutlets and pat dry. Lard each cutlet with a lardoon. Brown on both sides in hot oil and butter. Cook in a preheated oven (350°F) 10 minutes, or until meat is cooked. Serve with wild rice and currant jelly. Makes 6 servings.

PATES, TERRINES, GALANTINES, AND FOIE GRAS

THIS CHAPTER SHOULD REALLY BE CALLED "pastry, terrine, and galantine forcemeats and foie gras," because that is what the word *pâté* originally meant: some kind of pork, veal, beef, fowl, game (furred or feathered), fish, shellfish or vegetables, ground up with herbs, spices, and pork fat (although pork fat was not used with vegetables) or eggs, shaped, wrapped in some kind of pastry (puff, brioche, suet, or short), and baked. Now it is called a *pâté en croûte,* like a game pie or pâté enclosed in pastry or with just a cover or top.

That ground-up mixture is called a forcemeat and when baked in an earthenware dish it is called a terrine. When it's stuffed back into the boned meat of a whole fowl or game bird, or even a whole suckling pig, the dish is called a galantine. Any of the mixtures can be coarse and simple like a "country pâté," or quite elaborate, with various fillings in layers, or interlaced with strips of meat and livers, or studded with nuts and whole truffles.

However the forcemeat is cooked and whatever form it takes, it will always benefit in flavor if left to cure for a few days, and if it is eaten neither too hot nor too cold. A terrine is always weighted while it cools to make sure the end result holds together and will slice easily. Very often, if a forcemeat has been baked in a pastry crust (enclosed or covered in a dish), aspic is poured into a hole in the top of the pastry as it cools, so that when it is served at room temperature a delicious jelly (preferably made from the bones of the meats used) will accompany it.

For forcemeats you should use only the finest, freshest (never frozen) meats. Mixing should be done by hand when the meats are cold and as minimally as possible; a combination of ground and hand-chopped meats gives the best results.

Use foie gras, or "fattened liver," from ducks and geese obtained from whole, fresh livers. The canned varieties are rarely, if ever, good substitutes, though the livers cooked and preserved in jars in the rendered fat of ducks and geese are the real thing.

PATES IN PASTRY OR *EN CROUTE*

❧ *Pastry for Pâté en Croûte*

4 cups sifted all-purpose flour
1 teaspoon salt
1 cup (2 sticks) butter
½ cup lard

About ½ cup cold water
1 egg, beaten
2 tablespoons milk

Sift flour and salt together into a mixing bowl. Add butter and lard and cut in until the dough has a coarse crumb consistency. Sprinkle in just enough water to make a dough that can be gathered together into a smooth ball. Chill at least 2 hours.

How to Line a Pâté Mold

Use a loaf pan or a 9½-by-5-by-3-inch mold. Roll out pastry dough ¼ inch thick, flour lightly, and mark out the shape of the bottom of the loaf pan or terrine on the pastry 4 times. Cut off one of the imprints to make the top, set aside, and cover with a cloth. Butter the pan and lightly dust it with flour. Fit the pastry dough into the bottom and sides of the pan, pressing it firmly into the corners with a piece of pastry dough or with your fingers. Trim the edges evenly, leaving a ½-inch border. Fill with forcemeat as specified in the recipe you are making, packing it in well. Press the edges of the pastry inward upon the filling. Roll the reserved piece of pastry ⅛ inch thick, cut it to fit the top of the pan, moisten under the edges, and lay it over the filling. Crimp the edges with a pastry crimper or with a fork. Decorate the top as desired with pastry leaves or flowers made from leftover dough. With a fork, prick the crust in several places. Make a small hole in the center, into which insert a funnel of waxed paper or foil to allow steam to escape. Beat the egg together with the milk and brush the top crust with the mixture.

How to Bake and Cool Pâté en Croûte

Bake pâté in a preheated oven (350°F) 30 to 35 minutes per pound or until the center of the forcemeat reads 180°F on a meat thermometer. The pâté is done when the fat that rises is perfectly clear. If crust begins to brown too quickly, cover with aluminum foil or buttered brown paper. Remove pâté from the oven and pour aspic through the funnel to fill air spaces and the space between the filling and crust formed during baking. Cool slowly to room temperature, then refrigerate at least 24 hours. To serve, turn out onto a tray and cut into slices.

Cold Veal and Ham Loaf in Pastry

¾ pound lean veal, in one piece
¾ pound lean ham
¾ cup port or claret
½ cup sliced carrots
¼ cup sliced onion
5 whole peppercorns
¼ teaspoon chopped thyme
1 bay leaf
½ pound fatty salt pork, diced
2 pounds finely ground lean veal

1 tablespoon chopped parsley
2 shallots, finely chopped
1½ teaspoons salt
⅓ cup heavy cream
2 large eggs, beaten
Pastry for Pâté en Croûte
2 chopped truffles (optional)
Pistachio nuts
1 egg, beaten with 1 tablespoon milk
Sherry-flavored aspic

Slice veal and ham 1 inch thick and cut into strips 4 inches long. Add the next 6 ingredients and marinate in the refrigerator overnight. Put the next 7 ingredients in a bowl and mix well. Set this forcemeat aside. Line the pan or mold with Pastry for Pâté en

Croûte as directed in How to Line a Pâté Mold. Spread a layer of the forcemeat 1 inch thick over the bottom of the pastry-lined pan. Press strips of marinated ham and veal onto the forcemeat, laying them lengthwise, 3 abreast. Strew truffles between the strips, if desired, and sprinkle with pistachio nuts. Repeat with another layer of forcemeat and another of veal and ham strips, truffles, and pistachio nuts. Cover with remaining forcemeat. Top with pastry and brush with egg mixture, bake, add aspic, and cool according to directions in How to Bake and Cool Pâté. To serve, turn out onto a tray and slice. Garnish the tray with jellied aspic broken up with a fork, and with grilled or raw stuffed tomatoes. Makes about 15 servings.

Chicken Pâté

In the recipe for Cold Veal and Ham Loaf, replace the ham with chicken. Following previous directions, make Pastry Pâté en Croûte, line the pâté pan or mold, fill with layers of forcemeat and of sliced chicken and veal, bake, and cool. Serve sliced, on a tray garnished with aspic broken up with a fork, and with cheese and black olive canapés and chicken and grape canapés. If desired, cook without the pastry and when cool turn out and coat with Chaud-Froid Sauce. Chill and coat with clear aspic. Chill again. Place a row of halved pitted black olives and pistachio nuts down the center. Makes about 15 servings. Duck may be used instead of chicken.

Salmon Mousse in Pastry or en Croûte

2 pounds salmon, boned and skinned	2 large egg whites
1 teaspoon salt	2 cups heavy cream
¼ teaspoon freshly ground black pepper	Pastry for Pâté en Croûte
¼ teaspoon grated nutmeg	1 egg, beaten with 1 tablespoon milk
	Aspic

Put 1 pound of the salmon through a food chopper twice, using the finest blade. Add half of the salt, half of the pepper, and the nutmeg. Gradually beat in the egg whites, beating vigorously with a wooden spoon, or mix in an electric mixer. Place the mixing bowl in a pan of cracked ice and gradually beat in the cream. Set this forcemeat aside.

Line a pâté mold or loaf pan with Pastry for Pâté en Croûte, following instructions in How to Line a Pâté Mold. Spread the pastry-lined bottom with a layer of salmon forcemeat 1 inch thick. Sprinkle remaining salt and pepper over the rest of the salmon and place half of it in the mold over the forcemeat layer. Cover with a layer of forcemeat. Repeat, using remaining salmon and forcemeat, having forcemeat as the top layer. Top with pastry, brush top with egg mixture, and bake one hour. Add aspic after removing the pâté from the oven. Cool slowly to room temperature, then refrigerate at least 24 hours. To serve, unmold onto a tray and slice. Makes about 15 servings. Sole or trout may be used instead of salmon.

Truffled Venison Pâté in Pastry

1¾ pounds boneless venison	1 pound boneless lean fresh pork
¼ pound fatback	½ pound fatty salt pork
¼ pound goose liver	2 shallots, finely chopped
1 large truffle	⅓ cup heavy cream
3 tablespoons cognac	2 large eggs, beaten
¹⁄₁₆ teaspoon freshly ground black pepper	Pastry for Pâté en Croûte
¼ teaspoon chopped thyme	Pistachio nuts
1 small bay leaf	1 egg, beaten with 1 tablespoon milk
2 teaspoons salt	Port-flavored game aspic

Slice ¾ pound of the venison, the fatback, and the goose liver 1 inch thick and cut into strips 4 inches long (cut the liver strips the length of the liver). Dice truffle, if using. Marinate sliced venison, fatback, liver, and truffle in the cognac, pepper, thyme, bay leaf, and ½ teaspoon salt 4 hours.

Put the remaining 1 pound venison, the fresh pork, and the salt pork through a food chopper twice, using the finest blade. Add remaining 1½ teaspoons salt, the shallots, cream, and the 2 beaten eggs and mix well. Set this forcemeat aside.

Line a loaf pan or mold with Pastry for Pâté en Croûte and line a loaf pan or mold, following previous directions. Spread a layer of forcemeat 1 inch thick on the bottom. Spread half the marinated strips of venison, fatback, and liver over it and sprinkle with half the truffle (if using) and with pistachio nuts. Repeat with another layer of forcemeat and then the remaining venison, fatback, liver, truffle, and pistachio nuts. Cover with the remaining forcemeat. Following previous directions, top with pastry, brush with egg mixture, bake, add aspic, and cool.

To serve, turn out onto a tray, slice, and garnish tray with jellied aspic, broken up with a fork. Makes about 15 servings.

Pâté of Wild Rabbit or Hare in Pastry

1 (3- to 4-pound) rabbit or hare, dressed	1 pound fatty pork
Boneless lean pork	1 teaspoon salt
Boneless lean veal	½ teaspoon each chopped thyme and sage
2 tablespoons olive oil	1 onion, sliced
¼ cup chopped parsley	4 sprigs parsley
¼ cup sliced onion	Pastry for Pâté en Croûte
½ cup sliced carrots	2 truffles, chopped (optional)
1 clove garlic, quartered	1 egg, beaten with 1 tablespoon milk
¾ cup dry white wine	Port-flavored game aspic
2 tablespoons cognac	

Remove the sinews from the rabbit or hare, if this has not been done. Cut the meat from the loin and the tender part of the legs into narrow slices. Weigh this meat and add equal amounts of lean pork and veal, also cut into narrow strips. Add the next 5 ingredients, ¼ cup of the wine, and 1 tablespoon of the cognac to the rabbit, pork, and veal strips, and marinate in the refrigerator overnight.

Cut the rest of the rabbit meat from the bones and put it, along with the liver and heart, ¾ pound lean pork, and the fatty pork, through a food chopper twice, using the finest blade. Add the remaining ½ cup wine and 1 tablespoon cognac, the salt, and herbs and mix well. Cover with slices of onion and the parsley sprigs. Cover bowl tightly and refrigerate this forcemeat overnight. When ready to bake the pâté, remove and discard the onion and parsley, drain the marinade from the sliced meat into the forcemeat, and mix well.

Line a loaf pan or mold with Pastry for Pâté en Croûte following previous directions. Spread a layer of forcemeat 1 inch thick over the bottom. Lay half the strips of rabbit, pork, and veal on the forcemeat. Sprinkle with truffle, if using. Repeat with another layer of forcemeat and then the remaining strips of meat and the truffle. Cover with the remaining forcemeat. Following previous directions, top with pastry, brush with egg mixture, bake, add aspic, and cool. To serve, turn pâté out onto a tray, slice, and garnish tray with jellied aspic, broken up with a fork. Or, if desired, remove crust and coat pâté with half-set aspic, smoothing the aspic with a spatula dipped in hot water. Chill until set. Garnish the top with a row of orange segments, each topped with a pistachio nut; glaze with aspic and chill. Decorate the tray with tomato halves topped with Mayonnaise. Makes about 15 servings.

TERRINES

How to Bake and Cool a Terrine

Use a terrine mold or other earthenware casserole that has a tight-fitting cover. Line the bottom and sides with thin slices of pork fatback or bacon slices. After filling with the desired mixture, cover completely with thin slices of fatback or bacon and lay a bay leaf on top. Cover with the lid and tie 2 layers of aluminum foil over it. Place mold in a pan of hot water, with the water about halfway up the sides of the mold, and place in a preheated low-temperature (325°F) oven to bake. Add more hot water to the pan as it evaporates. For temperatures and baking times, see individual recipes.

The terrine is done when, after 40-50 minutes, the juices just run clear and the mixture begins to shrink from the sides of the mold. Take it out of the oven, remove the mold from the pan of water, and take off the lid. Weight the top of the terrine with a heavy plate or a wooden block cut to fit the mold. Cool slowly to room temperature, several hours or overnight, then chill in the refrigerator 12 to 24 hours, keeping the weight on top.

How to Unmold and Serve a Terrine

While the terrine can be served directly from its dish without unmolding, it may also be unmolded by dipping the dish quickly into very hot water, loosening the edges with a spatula, and inverting the dish onto a platter. Remove the slices of salt pork and wipe off the excess fat. The terrine may then be sliced for serving. Or, return it to the mold and pour aspic flavored with sherry, Madeira, or port over it. Chill again until aspic is firm, then turn out onto a platter and slice.

Chicken Liver Terrine Chagny

1 pound chicken livers
¾ pound pork sausage
3 tablespoons sherry, plus additional
    if desired
1½ tablespoons cognac
½ teaspoon chopped thyme
¾ teaspoon salt
2 large eggs, well beaten
Thin slices fatty salt pork
1 bay leaf

Very finely chop livers and mix with the sausage, 3 tablespoons sherry, the cognac, thyme, and salt. Beat in the eggs and continue beating the mixture with a wooden spoon until well blended. Line the bottom and sides of a 1½-quart terrine mold or casserole with salt pork and fill with the mixture. Following directions in How to Bake and Cool a Terrine, cover, seal, bake in a preheated oven (325°F) 1 hour, cool, and refrigerate. If desired, pour a little sherry over the pâté before refrigerating. Serve from the mold, or unmold and slice. Makes 10 to 12 servings.

Pork Liver Terrine

1½ pounds pork liver
½ pound boneless lean veal
½ pound fatback, cut into cubes
½ cup flour
2 eggs
1 teaspoon chopped parsley
½ teaspoon salt
½ teaspoon chopped thyme
¼ teaspoon chopped marjoram
    2 tablespoons finely chopped onion
1 shallot, finely chopped
Thin slices fatback or bacon
1 bay leaf
Port-flavored aspic
Parsley
Black olives

Put liver, veal, and fatback through a food chopper, using the finest blade. Add flour and mix about 5 minutes with a wooden spoon, or blend in an electric mixer. Beat in eggs, one at a time. Add the next 6 ingredients. Mix well.

    Line the bottom and sides of a heavy 1½-quart terrine or casserole mold with fatback or bacon and pack in the pâté mixture. Following previous directions, cover, seal, and bake in a preheated oven (325°F) 1½ hours; open, cool, refrigerate, and unmold. Return the pâté to the casserole. Either serve it from the casserole, or turn out onto a tray, pour aspic over the pâté, chill again, and slice. Garnish with parsley and black olives. Makes 12 to 15 servings.

Pork Forcemeat and Liver Pâté

2 pounds pork, lamb, or beef liver
¾ pound lean pork
¾ pound fatty pork
2 teaspoons chopped parsley
¼ teaspoon chopped thyme
¼ teaspoon chopped marjoram

½ teaspoon salt
2 shallots, finely chopped, or
   2 tablespoons chopped onion
1½ tablespoons flour
2 large eggs
Thin slices fatback or bacon

Put liver and both lean and fatty pork through a food chopper twice, using the finest blade. Add the next 6 ingredients, stir, and beat 5 to 6 minutes. Beat in eggs, one at a time, mixing well. Line a 9½-by-5-by-3-inch loaf pan with fatback or bacon. Put in the pâté mixture and pack it in well. Cover top with fatback or bacon and cover pan with 2 layers of aluminum foil, tying it down. Following previous directions, bake in a preheated oven (325°F) 1 ½ hours; open, cool, and refrigerate. Unmold according to previous directions, slice, and serve. Makes a 9½-by-5-by-2-inch loaf.

Pork and Veal Terrine with Truffles

1¼ pounds boneless lean veal
¼ pound boneless lean ham
¼ cup cognac
¼ teaspoon salt
⅛ teaspoon freshly ground black pepper
¼ teaspoon chopped thyme
¼ teaspoon grated nutmeg
1 tablespoon finely chopped shallot
   or onion
2 truffles, finely chopped

¾ pound lean fresh pork
½ pound fatback or bacon
2 large eggs, beaten
¼ teaspoon ground ginger
¼ teaspoon each chopped thyme and sage
1 clove garlic, crushed
Thin slices fatback or bacon
1 bay leaf
Sherry- or Madeira-flavored aspic (optional)

Slice ½ pound of the veal and the ham ¼ inch thick and cut into strips 4 inches long. Marinate 2 to 3 hours in the cognac, along with the salt, pepper, thyme, nutmeg, shallot, and 1 of the truffles. Put fresh pork, ½ pound fatback or bacon, and remaining ¾ pound veal through a food chopper twice, using the finest blade. Add the next 4 ingredients. Drain the marinade from the veal and ham strips and add the marinade to the ground meat mixture. Mix well.

Line the bottom and sides of a 2-quart terrine mold or casserole with slices of fatback or bacon. Put one-third of the meat mixture on the bottom. Cover with half of the veal and ham strips. Sprinkle with truffle (if using). Repeat with the second third of the meat mixture and the remaining veal and ham strips and truffle. Cover with the rest of the meat mixture. Following previous directions, cover, seal, and bake in a preheated oven (325°F) 1½ hours, or until the pâté shrinks from the sides of the mold and the juices are clear yellow with no trace of pink; open, cool, refrigerate. Return the pâté to the terrine. Serve it from the mold, or pour aspic over it and chill again, then turn it out on a tray and slice. Garnish the tray, if desired, with parsley and diced jellied aspic. Makes about 20 servings.

GALANTINES

MANY BELIEVE THAT THE WORD *GALANTINE* originates with the old French word for chicken ("géline" or "galine"). Certainly they are cooked in a rich stock and then jellied (the other possible origin of the word as in "galandine") in their own juices. Galantines were originally made only of chicken, but now other fowl and gamebirds are also used, as well as breast of veal and other meats.

How to Roll and Cook a Galantine

Generously butter a large clean cloth or several layers of cheesecloth and spread on a flat surface. Lay the skin of the fowl on the cloth with the outside down and spread with other ingredients as directed in the individual recipe. By lifting the edge of the cloth and pulling gently, carefully shape the arrangement into a firm roll, drawing the edges of the skin together to form a sausage-shaped roll. Sew the skin together along the length of the roll and at the ends. Wrap the roll tightly in the cloth, making sure it is smooth and even, and tie it in the middle and at the ends with string.

Place the roll and other ingredients as specified in a large kettle and pour in rich stock to cover. Cover the kettle, bring to the boiling point, reduce heat, and simmer according to individual recipes. Let the galantine cool in the stock, then remove it, unroll, and roll again in a clean cloth. Weight it with a heavy plate and let stand for 2 hours or longer.

Make a clear aspic from the stock in which the galantine was cooked. Remove the cloth and the threads with which the skin was sewn. Glaze the roll with Chaud-Froid Sauce and the aspic, or with the aspic alone. Chill until firm and cut into thin slices for serving.

Galantines may be served at a cold buffet or as a first course accompanied by buttered toast.

Galantine of Chicken

1 (6-pound) roasting chicken
2 pounds veal shank
1 calf's foot (optional)
½ pound boneless lean fresh pork
½ pound boneless lean veal
½ pound pork fatback, cut into cubes
3 tablespoons cognac, sherry, or Madeira
1½ teaspoons salt
¼ teaspoon ground mace
1 teaspoon ground thyme
¼ cup heavy cream

¼ pound fatback
¼ pound cooked tongue or ham
1 truffle, chopped (optional)
½ cup pistachio nuts
1 sprig parsley
1 carrot
½ cup sliced onion
½ cup sliced celery
Chicken stock
Chaud-Froid Sauce (optional)

Have the butcher bone the chicken (or bone it yourself). Make a rich stock from the chicken bones, veal shank, and the calf's foot, if using. Set aside.

Split the boned chicken down the length of the back and open it out flat, skin side up. Starting at the back, with a sharp knife carefully cut the skin away from the meat, removing the skin in one piece. Be careful not to pierce the skin. Trim skin at the legs and wings, leaving enough to cover the openings. Cut the meat of the breast and the tenderloin under the breast and that of the drumsticks into thin slices and set aside. Put the remaining chicken meat and the fresh pork and the veal through a food chopper twice, using the finest blade. Add the next 6 ingredients and mix well.

Place the chicken skin, outside down, on a buttered cloth (see preceding directions) and spread it with the meat mixture. Cut fatback and tongue into strips and arrange them in alternate layers over the meat. Sprinkle truffle (if using) between the slices. Sprinkle with pistachio nuts. Cover with the slices of chicken.

Following the preceding directions, shape the arrangement into a roll and place it, with the parsley, carrot, onion, and celery, in a large kettle. Pour in stock to cover. Cover the kettle, bring to the boiling point, reduce heat, and simmer 1¼ hours. Cool, glaze, or cover with Chaud-Froid Sauce, chill, and slice according to preceding directions. Makes about 8 servings.

Galantine of Duck

1 (4- to 5-pound) duck
2 pounds veal shank
1 calf's foot (optional)
¾ pound veal cutlets
¼ cup cognac or sherry
¾ pound boneless lean veal
½ pound boneless lean pork
¼ pound fatback
1½ teaspoons salt
¼ teaspoon freshly ground black pepper
¾ teaspoon each chopped thyme and sage

⅓ cup heavy cream
1 truffle, finely chopped (optional)
¼ cup pistachio nuts
½ cup sliced carrots
½ cup sliced onions
2 sprigs parsley
2 whole cloves
8 whole peppercorns
Stock
Chaud-Froid Sauce (optional)

Have the butcher bone the duck and reserve the carcass and the liver. Make a rich stock from the duck carcass, veal shank, and the calf's foot, if available. Set the stock aside.

Detach the duck meat from the skin as in Galantine of Chicken. Cut the breast and leg meat into thin strips, removing and discarding sinews. Cut the veal cutlets into strips 4 inches long and 1 inch wide. Marinate the strips of veal and the strips of duck meat in cognac 2 hours. Put the remaining duck meat, the duck liver, the boneless veal and pork, and fatback through a food chopper twice, using the finest blade. Drain the cognac or sherry from the veal strips into the ground meat, add seasonings and cream, and mix well.

Lay the duck skin, outside down, on a buttered cloth (see How to Roll and Cook a Galantine) and spread with the meat mixture. Over this lay the marinated strips of veal and duck. Sprinkle with truffle (if using) and pistachio nuts.

Following the previous directions, shape the arrangement into a roll and place it in a kettle, along with the carrots, onion, parsley, cloves, and peppercorns. Pour in stock to cover. Cover the kettle, bring to the boiling point, reduce heat, and simmer 1½ hours. Cool, glaze, or cover with Chaud-Froid Sauce, chill, and slice according to the previous directions. Makes 6 to 8 servings.

Galantine of Turkey

Use the recipe for Galantine of Chicken, but replace the chicken with one 12- to 15-pound turkey and double all the other ingredients. Increase the simmering time to 1¾ hours. Makes 12 to 15 servings.

Galantine of Veal

3½ pounds breast of veal	1 carrot, sliced
Salt and freshly ground black pepper	⅓ cup sliced onion
1 teaspoon poultry seasoning	1 rib celery, sliced
¼ teaspoon chopped rosemary	2 pounds veal shank
1¾ pounds sausage meat	Hot stock
¾ pound lean ham, sliced	Chaud-Froid Sauce (optional)
3 tablespoons pistachio nuts	

Ask the butcher to bone the veal and reserve the bones. Make a rich stock from the bones and set it aside.

Spread the meat out flat on a buttered cloth (see How to Roll and Cook a Galantine) and sprinkle it with salt, pepper, poultry seasoning, and rosemary. Spread the sausage over the veal, leaving a 1-inch border all around. Cut the ham into strips 4 inches long and 1 inch wide and arrange these in rows down the length of the veal. Sprinkle with pistachio nuts.

Following the previous directions, shape the arrangement into a roll and place it, with the vegetables and veal shank, in a large kettle. Pour in hot stock to cover. Cover the kettle, bring to the boiling point, reduce heat, and simmer 2 hours. Cool, glaze, chill, and slice according to previous directions. Makes 12 to 15 servings.

FOIE GRAS

LITERALLY TRANSLATED, *FOIE GRAS* MEANS "FAT LIVER," since the term is used for the livers of geese and ducks that have been fattened by special feeding. Traditionally the finest French foie gras comes from geese raised in Alsace and southwestern France, but excellent livers are now produced in other countries like Hungary and the United States.

Scallops of Foie Gras Lucullus

1 pound raw foie gras	12 slices truffle
¼ teaspoon salt	Flour
¹⁄₁₆ teaspoon freshly ground	8 tablespoons (1 stick) butter
black pepper	¾ cup Demi-Glace Sauce
¼ cup sherry	12 (2-inch) rounds bread

Cut foie gras diagonally into 12 fairly thick slices. Season with salt and pepper and marinate 2 hours in the sherry and the truffle slices. Remove foie gras slices from the marinade, pat dry, dredge in flour, and sauté over medium heat in 3 tablespoons of the butter, for 1 minute on each side. Remove and keep warm. Tip out the butter, and add the Demi-Glace Sauce with sherry and truffles and cook over low heat about one minute. Fry the rounds of bread in the remaining butter. Put a slice of foie gras on each round and cover with the sauce, being careful to get a truffle slice on top of each. Makes 6 servings.

Small Eclairs or Carolines with Goose Liver Puree

Make small éclairs with Choux Paste. Cool. Make an opening, and with a pastry bag and round ¼-inch tube fill them with foie gras puree. If desired, coat the éclairs with white or light brown Chaud-Froid Sauce; or serve plain. Serve as an hors d'oeuvre. Allow 3 or 4 per person.

Friandises of Foie Gras

Double recipe Plain Pastry Dough (Pâté Brisée) (using 2 cups flour), or Puff Pastry
1½ cups (10 ounces) foie gras puree
1 egg yolk, beaten with 1 teaspoon milk

Roll pastry ⅛ inch thick on a lightly floured board. Cut into rounds with a 2-inch cookie cutter. Top the center of each with a heaping ½ teaspoon foie gras puree.

Moisten the edges slightly and fold the dough over. Crimp edges with a fork and brush with egg yolk mixture. Bake in a preheated oven (400°F) 5 to 8 minutes, or until browned. Serve as a hot hors d'oeuvre. Makes about 4 dozen.

Truffled Whole Foie Gras in Aspic

1 whole foie gras or goose liver denerved
White semi-dry wine
Rich Veal Stock
Semiliquid chicken aspic

6 slices truffle
Melba toast
Watercress or parsley

Poach the liver in wine and Rich Veal Stock. When cool place whole liver on a chilled tray. Cover the liver with several layers of aspic, chilling after each layer is applied. On each side of the liver place 3 truffle slices. Coat again with several layers of aspic, chilling after each layer. Chill until serving time. Slice and serve on Melba toast. Garnish with watercress or parsley. Makes 6 servings.

Jellied Truffled Surprises

1 pound foie gras or goose liver,
    poached in sherry
½ cup (1 stick) softened butter

Truffles, or truffle peel, finely chopped
1 cup sherry-flavored aspic

Puree the liver and blend in the butter. Cool and chill. Shape into walnut-sized balls and roll them in truffles or truffle peel until well coated. Dip in aspic and chill until set. Arrange in a pyramid on a tray or use to garnish cold meat, poultry, or game dishes. Makes 6 servings.

Jellied Foie Gras Loaf

1 large foie gras or goose liver
1 cup Madeira
3 truffles
1 tablespoon meat glaze
2 large egg yolks

¼ cup (½ stick) softened butter
¼ cup hazelnuts, chopped
Salt and freshly ground black pepper
4 cups aspic

Poach liver in Madeira with truffles the day before you plan to serve loaf, and let it cool in the wine. Pour off the liquid, skim off fat, and boil, with the meat glaze, until only 2 tablespoons remain. Place in a small bowl and beat together with egg yolks, and cook in a bain-marie, stirring constantly until a thick cream. Let cool slightly and blend in butter. Pound hazelnuts, or chop them through an electric blender, and add. Push liver through a sieve and mix thoroughly with the egg and nut mixture. Slice 2 of the truffles and add. Season to taste with salt and pepper. Line a 1-quart mold with aspic. Chill until set. Slice remaining truffle and arrange in the bottom and around the sides of the mold. Coat again with aspic. Chill until set. Pack in the liver mixture. Chill until set. Finish filling the mold with aspic. Chill until set. Chill remaining aspic until set. Unmold the loaf onto a chilled tray. Break up additional aspic with a fork and spoon it around the loaf. Makes one 1-quart mold.

Small Molds of Foie Gras in Wine Aspic

1 quart Madeira- or port-flavored aspic
2 truffles, sliced

8 (2-inch) cubes foie gras or goose liver
Parsley

Coat eight 4-ounce molds with aspic and chill. Place a truffle slice in the bottom of each and put a cube of foie gras on top. Fill the molds with aspic. Chill until set. Chill remaining aspic. Just before serving, unmold in a circle on a chilled tray. Break up chilled aspic with a fork and spoon it around the molds. Garnish with parsley and slices of remaining truffle. Makes 8 servings.

Molded Foie Gras Mousse

3½ pints chicken aspic
2 truffles
2 envelopes unflavored gelatin

¾ cup water
3 cups foie gras puree
½ cup heavy cream, whipped

Place a pâté mold or a 9½-by-5-by-3-inch loaf pan in a pan of cracked ice. Pour in aspic and roll the pan from side to side to coat evenly with aspic. Cut ½-inch circles from truffles and arrange them in a row ½ inch apart down the lengthwise center of the mold. Affix each circle with a few drops of aspic and let it stand a few minutes to set.

Soften the gelatin in water in a small bowl. Place over hot water (not boiling) to melt. Push foie gras puree through a fine sieve. Stir in melted gelatin. Fold in whipped cream. Pack the foie gras mixture into the mold or pan, filling it half full. Cut truffles into small pieces and place a row lengthwise down the center of the pâté. Pack in remaining foie gras mixture, filling the mold or pan to within ½ inch of the top. Chill until the mousse is set. Finish filling the mold with cool but still liquid aspic. Chill until aspic is firm.

To serve, unmold the mousse on a large tray. Cut into slices ¼ inch thick. Decorate the tray with jellied aspic broken up with a fork. Makes about 15 servings.

VEGETABLES

THE INVIOLABLE RULE OF THUMB WITH VEGETABLES is to buy them as fresh as possible and in perfect condition. Seasonality still makes a huge difference, even though most vegetables and fruits are now available from somewhere all year long. Local asparagus are still the best, tomatoes need the summer to be their best, apples need the fall in order to retain their wonderful snap of freshness, blueberries are at their peak only briefly once a year—all of this will be obvious in your local farmers' market.

There are two main ways to cook vegetables: either they take a long time to cook and are intended to be eaten cooked through and probably at room temperature, or they should be cooked quickly at the last minute and served up immediately. Either way, if different vegetables are cooked together, cut each of them into the size that will ensure that they all cook at the same rate, or add them to the cooking medium at different times. Boiled vegetables should be cooked in a very large pot of boiling salted water so that the water does not go off the boil (or does so only for a minute) when the vegetables are added. Only then will they cook in the shortest amount of time and retain their color, flavor, and nutrients.

ARTICHOKES (ARTICHAUTS)

Whole Artichokes

Allow 1 large artichoke or 2 small ones per serving. Wash artichokes, cut off stems even with the base, and remove and discard tough outer leaves. Cut off and discard the top third of each artichoke; if any prickly ends of leaves are left, trim them off. Stand artichokes upright in a saucepan just large enough for them to fit snugly, or tie a string around each one to hold it in shape. To prevent discoloration, rub lemon juice over the cut surfaces. Pour in boiling water to cover and add 1 teaspoon salt. Cover and cook 20 minutes, or until artichokes are tender. They are done when a leaf will pull out easily. Remove strings and place artichokes upside down to drain. Using a sharp knife, remove the prickly choke in the center that covers the heart; discard. Serve hot artichokes with melted butter, Hollandaise or Mousseline Sauce, or one of the following:

- *Lemon Butter*. Melt ½ cup (1 stick) butter and add 1½ tablespoons lemon juice and a dash of freshly ground black pepper.
- *Parsley Butter*. Melt ½ cup (1 stick) butter and add 2 tablespoons chopped parsley, 1 teaspoon lemon juice, and a dash of freshly ground black pepper.

Whole Artichokes with Vinaigrette Sauce

Cook artichokes as in preceding recipe. Open the leaves at the top, reach down and remove the choke, and arrange them on a serving platter and put a large sautéed mushroom cap in the opening of each. Garnish platter with parsley and wedges of peeled tomato. Serve Vinaigrette Sauce in a sauceboat. Either hot or cold artichokes may be served with Vinaigrette Sauce.

Braised Whole Artichokes with Tomatoes Mireille

12 small artichokes	½ teaspoon salt
½ cup olive oil	⅛ teaspoon freshly ground black pepper
1 cup hot chicken bouillon	¼ teaspoon sugar
12 pearl onions	Chopped parsley
4 medium-sized tomatoes	

Cut off the stems and tops of artichokes and trim off the tips of the leaves. Wash well. Put in a casserole with oil, bouillon, and onions, and cook 10 minutes. Peel tomatoes, cut into quarters, and add. Sprinkle with salt, pepper, and sugar. Cover casserole and bake in a preheated oven (425°F) 20 minutes, or until vegetables are tender. Sprinkle with parsley and serve from the casserole. Makes 6 servings.

Roman Braised Whole Artichokes with Garlic and Mint

12 small or 6 large artichokes	1 teaspoon salt
1 clove garlic	6 whole peppercorns
½ cup chopped parsley	⅓ cup olive oil
½ cup chopped mint leaves	2 cups dry white wine
	⅔ cup chicken or veal stock

Prepare artichokes for cooking as instructed for Whole Artichokes. Scoop out the choke with a pointed teaspoon. Finely chop garlic, mix with parsley and mint, and stuff into the centers of the artichokes. Stand artichokes in an upright position in a saucepan or flameproof casserole just big enough for them to fit snugly. Add salt, peppercorns, and oil. Cover and cook over medium heat 10 minutes. Add wine and stock. Cover and cook in a preheated oven (375°F) 30 minutes, or until the leaves pull out easily and the sauce is well reduced. Makes 6 servings.

Artichoke Bottoms in Brown Butter

6 large artichokes	1 quart water
Lemon juice	1 teaspoon salt
1 tablespoon flour	2 tablespoons butter

Wash artichokes and cut off stems even with the base. Trim the bottoms and rub them with lemon juice to prevent discoloration. Using a sharp knife, cut off leaves about ½ inch from the base. Cut each artichoke into 6 pieces. Mix flour with a little of the water in a 1½-quart saucepan. Add remaining water, salt, and 1 teaspoon lemon juice. Bring to the boiling point and add artichoke pieces. Cover and cook over medium heat 20 minutes, or until artichokes are tender. Drain well. Remove and discard the prickly chokes. Brown the butter lightly in a skillet. Add artichoke bottoms and heat a few minutes on each side. Serve hot. Makes 6 servings.

Artichoke Bottoms with Creamed Asparagus Argenteuil

6 cooked large artichoke bottoms
4 to 5 tablespoons butter
Salt and freshly ground black pepper
1½ pounds asparagus tips, cooked

1 cup Béchamel Sauce

Prepare and boil artichoke bottoms as for Artichoke Bottoms in Brown Butter. Cook in 2 to 3 tablespoons butter a few minutes, but do not brown. Meanwhile add asparagus to the Béchamel Sauce and season. Fill the artichoke bottoms with the creamed asparagus. Place under the broiler to brown. Makes 6 servings.

Sautéed Artichoke Bottoms Colbert

6 cooked large artichoke bottoms
Flour
⅛ teaspoon freshly ground black pepper
2 eggs, beaten
White breadcrumbs

10 tablespoons butter (1¼ sticks) or more
½ teaspoon lemon juice
1 teaspoon chopped parsley
½ teaspoon chopped fresh tarragon
½ teaspoon meat glaze

Prepare and boil artichoke bottoms as for Artichoke Bottoms in Brown Butter, drain well, and remove chokes. Mix flour and pepper and dredge artichoke bottoms in the mixture. Dip in eggs and then roll in breadcrumbs. Fry in 2 to 3 tablespoons butter, browning all sides. Drain on paper towels and transfer to a serving dish. Melt remaining butter, add all other ingredients, mix, and pour over artichoke bottoms. Serve hot. Makes 6 servings.

Artichoke Bottoms Stuffed with Mushrooms

1 cup Mushroom Puree
¼ cup Béchamel Sauce
1 large egg, separated
Salt and freshly ground black pepper

¼ cup grated Parmesan cheese
6 cooked large artichoke bottoms
3 tablespoons butter, melted

Combine Mushroom Puree, Béchamel Sauce, egg yolk, and salt and pepper to taste. Mix well and bring to the boiling point. Remove from heat and let cool while beating egg white. Beat egg white until it stands in soft stiff peaks, then fold it into the mushroom mixture, along with 2 tablespoons of the cheese. Stuff into the bottoms of cooked artichokes. Arrange in a buttered baking dish. Sprinkle tops with remaining cheese and the butter. Bake in a preheated oven (350°F) 15 minutes, or until the mushroom stuffing has puffed and browned. Serve hot. Makes 6 servings.

Artichoke Bottoms Stuffed with Foie Gras and Mushrooms

6 large artichokes
Lemon juice
Boiling water
Salt
6 teaspoons chopped cooked foie gras

6 tablespoons sautéed chopped mushrooms
6 teaspoons butter
Freshly ground black pepper
¼ cup Madeira

Wash artichokes and cut off stems even with the base. Cut off leaves ½ inch above the bottom; if there are any prickly tips left on, trim them off. Rub lemon juice over cut surfaces to prevent discoloration. Place in a saucepan, pour in boiling water to cover, and add 1 teaspoon salt and 1 teaspoon lemon juice. Cover and cook 20 minutes, or until the bottoms are tender. Drain well. Remove the chokes from the centers. In the center of each artichoke bottom put 1 teaspoon foie gras and 1 tablespoon mushrooms. Dot each with 1 teaspoon butter. Sprinkle with salt and pepper. Pour the Madeira over the tops of all. Bake in a preheated oven (400°F) 15 to 20 minutes. Makes 6 servings.

Artichoke Bottoms Stuffed with Spinach Florentine

6 large artichokes
½ cup well-drained cooked spinach
3 tablespoons butter
Salt and freshly ground black pepper

1 cup Béchamel Sauce
2 egg yolks
¼ cup heavy cream
2 tablespoons grated Parmesan cheese

Prepare and cook artichoke bottoms as for Artichoke Bottoms Stuffed with Foie Gras. Drain well and remove chokes. Combine spinach, 1 tablespoon of the butter, and salt and pepper to taste. Spoon into the cooked artichoke bottoms. Beat egg yolks lightly, mix with cream, and add to the Béchamel. Stir and cook over low heat 1 to 2 minutes. Add ½ teaspoon salt and a dash of freshly ground black pepper. Spoon over stuffed artichokes. Sprinkle with cheese. Brown under broiler heat.

Other cooked vegetables such as peas, carrots, mushrooms, asparagus tips, or green beans, or a mixture of vegetables, tossed in a little butter, may be used in place of spinach. Makes 6 servings.

ASPARAGUS (ASPERGES)

How to Cook Asparagus

The French method of cooking asparagus is to peel the spears, tie them in serving-size bundles, and cook them 10 to 18 minutes, or only until barely tender, in a large amount of boiling salted water, using 1½ teaspoons salt to 1 quart water. Then the asparagus is drained immediately and placed on a dish covered with a clean towel or put in a special asparagus dish equipped with a rack to permit thorough draining. Asparagus may be served hot or cold with various sauces. Peeled asparagus cooks more quickly than unpeeled. The spears can be eaten down to the stem end, and they retain their natural green color and texture.

To cook asparagus, lay cleaned asparagus in a skillet, add ½ teaspoon salt, and pour in boiling water to a depth of at least 1 inch. Bring to the boiling point, uncovered, and cook 5-8 minutes; the time depends upon the size and natural tenderness of the asparagus. Remove from the water.

Asparagus cooked by any of these methods may be served with melted butter, Brown Butter, Egg Butter, Almond Butter, Maître d'Hôtel Butter, Mustard Butter, or with Antiboise, Béarnaise, Caper, or Mousseline Sauce. (See chapter 3.)

Asparagus in Brown Butter Milanese

2½ pounds asparagus, cooked
½ cup grated Parmesan cheese

Brown Butter
Chopped parsley

Arrange asparagus in overlapping rows in a shallow baking dish, having the tips visible. Sprinkle with cheese and spoon the Brown Butter over. Cook in a preheated oven (400°F) 5 to 10 minutes to melt cheese. Sprinkle with parsley. Makes 6 servings.

Asparagus Polish Style

2½ pounds asparagus, cooked
2 hard-cooked eggs, chopped
Chopped parsley

6 tablespoons butter
¼ cup white breadcrumbs

Arrange asparagus in overlapping rows in a shallow serving dish, having the tips visible. Sprinkle with eggs and parsley. Melt butter in a small skillet or saucepan, add breadcrumbs, and stir and fry until crumbs are brown. Sprinkle over asparagus and serve immediately. Makes 6 servings.

Asparagus with White Wine

2½ pounds asparagus, cooked
½ cup butter, melted
½ cup dry white wine

Salt and freshly ground black pepper
½ cup grated Parmesan cheese

Arrange asparagus in a shallow baking dish and pour butter and wine over it. Sprinkle lightly with salt, pepper, and cheese. Place in a preheated oven (425°F) 5 to 10 minutes, or until cheese browns lightly. Makes 6 servings.

BEANS

Green Beans or Haricots Verts in Cream Sauce

In classic French cooking, "green beans" are always *haricots verts,* or the very thin young beans about 4 inches long and ⅛ inch wide.

1 pound young green beans
1 teaspoon salt
Boiling water
2 tablespoons butter

½ cup heavy cream
Dash freshly ground black pepper

Wash beans, cut off tips. Cook in ample salted, boiling water, uncovered, 5 to 8 minutes or only until beans are crisp-tender. Drain off water. Shake the pan over low heat 1 to 2 minutes to dry the beans. Add butter and mix well. Add cream and pepper. Cook until the cream has thickened slightly. Makes 6 servings.

Green Beans in Béchamel Sauce

1 pound green beans
1 teaspoon salt
 Boiling water

Béchamel Sauce
Chopped parsley

Cook beans in salted boiling water as instructed in the recipe for Green Beans in Cream Sauce. Drain and shake the pan over low heat 1 to 2 minutes. Add Béchamel Sauce and heat. Turn into a serving dish. Sprinkle with parsley. Makes 6 servings.

Green Beans à la Paysanne

1 pound green beans
10 small new potatoes
1 teaspoon salt

Boiling water
3 tablespoons butter
¹⁄₁₆ teaspoon freshly ground black pepper

Wash beans and remove tips. Wash and scrape new potatoes and cut into quarters. Put the beans and potatoes in salted, boiling water and cook 10 minutes, or until beans are crisp-tender and potatoes are done. Drain off water and shake the pan over low heat 1 to 2 minutes. Melt butter in a small saucepan and cook until it is golden brown. Pour over beans, add pepper, toss lightly, and serve immediately. Makes 6 servings.

Portuguese-Style Green Beans

¼ pound fat bacon
1 pound green beans
2 medium-sized tomatoes
¾ cup Bouillon

½ teaspoon salt
½ teaspoon freshly ground black pepper
Chopped parsley

Finely dice fat bacon and put it in a flameproof 1½-quart casserole. Wash green beans, cut off tips, and place in the casserole over the fat bacon. Peel, seed, and dice tomatoes. Scatter over beans. Add Bouillon, salt, and pepper. Bring to the boiling point over high heat. Cover and cook in a preheated oven (350°F) 8 minutes, or until beans are tender. Sprinkle with parsley. Serve hot. Makes 6 servings.

Broad or Fava Beans

2 cups shelled young broad beans,
    or lima beans, peeled
Boiling water
1 teaspoon salt

1 tablespoons butter
¼ cup heavy cream
⅛ teaspoon freshly ground black pepper

Wash beans and place them in a saucepan. Cover with boiling water and salt. Bring to the boiling point, and cook 5 minutes, or until beans are tender. Drain and toss with butter and cream. Boil 30 seconds. Add pepper. Adjust salt. Makes 4 servings.

Red Beans in Wine

2 cups dried red kidney beans
4 cups cold water
1 teaspoon salt
½ cup chopped onion
1 tablespoon butter

¼ pound lean salt pork
¼ teaspoon freshly ground black pepper
2 tablespoons flour
1 cup dry red wine

Wash beans and soak 2 hours in enough cold water to cover. Drain and add the 4 cups cold water. Cover, bring to the boiling point, and cook 2 hours, or until beans are tender, adding more water if necessary Drain. Add salt. Cook onion in butter until limp. Dice salt pork, add to onion, and cook until onion and pork are lightly browned. Add pepper, sprinkle with flour, and add wine. Add beans and simmer 10 minutes. Adjust salt. Makes 6 servings.

Dried Beans Breton Style

2 cups dried beans
4 cups cold water
1 teaspoon salt
½ cup chopped onion

3 tablespoons butter
1 cup thick Tomato Sauce
⅛ teaspoon freshly ground black pepper
Chopped parsley

Wash beans and soak 2 hours in enough cold water to cover. Drain and add the 4 cups cold water. Cover and cook 2 hours, or until beans are tender. Drain. Add salt. Cook the onion in the butter until limp. Add to the beans, along with Tomato Sauce and pepper. Mix lightly and cook 5 to 10 minutes over medium low heat. Adjust salt. Sprinkle with parsley. Serve hot. Makes 6 servings.

Dried Beans in Cream Sauce

2 cups dried beans
4 cups cold water
1 teaspoon salt
½ cup chopped onion
1 cup diced carrots

3 tablespoons butter
3 tablespoons chopped parsley
¾ cup heavy cream
¾ cup thin Béchamel Sauce

Wash beans and soak 2 hours in enough cold water to cover. Drain, add the 4 cups cold water, cover, bring to the boiling point, and cook 2 hours, or until beans are tender. Drain. Add salt. Cook onion and carrots in the butter until carrots are soft. Add to the beans, along with the parsley, cream, and Béchamel Sauce. Mix lightly and cook 10 minutes. Adjust salt. Makes 6 servings.

Flageolet Beans

Flageolet beans, fresh or dried, may be prepared in the same ways as other fresh and dried beans.

BROCCOLI (CHOUX BROCOLIS)

How to Cook Broccoli

Allow 2 pounds broccoli for 6 servings. Wash broccoli and peel the tough portion of the stems. Place broccoli in a saucepan of ample salted boiling water and cook 8 minutes or only until broccoli is tender. Drain. Serve with melted butter or Brown Butter, or Anchovy, Almond, Maître d'Hôtel, Mustard, or Tomato Butter, or Anchovy Sauce, Béarnaise, Caper, Mornay, or Vinaigrette Sauce.

BRUSSELS SPROUTS (CHOUX DE BRUXELLES)

English Brussels Sprouts

1½ pounds Brussels sprouts	⅛ teaspoon freshly ground black pepper
Boiling water	2 tablespoons butter
2 teaspoons salt	

Wash and trim Brussels sprouts. Rinse in cold water. Boil in ample salted, boiling water for 10 minutes, or until Brussels sprouts are barely tender. Drain. Toss lightly with the pepper and butter. Makes 6 servings. If desired, serve with grated Parmesan cheese, or with Anchovy, Béarnaise, Caper, Egg, Hollandaise, or Mornay Sauce.

Fried Brussels Sprouts

1½ pounds Brussels sprouts, cooked	6 tablespoons butter
Freshly ground black pepper	Chopped parsley

Sprinkle Brussels sprouts with pepper. Fry in butter, turning to brown all sides. Sprinkle with parsley. Serve immediately. Makes 6 servings.

Brussels Sprouts au Gratin

1½ pounds Brussels sprouts, cooked	1 tablespoon butter, melted
2 cups Béchamel Sauce	½ cup grated Parmesan cheese

Mix Brussels sprouts with 1⅓ cups of the Béchamel Sauce. Turn into a 1-quart casserole. Cover with remaining sauce. Sprinkle with butter and cheese. Brown in a preheated oven (450°F). Serve hot. Makes 6 servings.

CABBAGE (CHOUX)

Braised Red or Green Cabbage

1 head (1½ pounds) cabbage	1 teaspoon salt
1 cup sliced carrots	⅛ teaspoon freshly ground black pepper
1 cup sliced onion	1 cup stock or Bouillon
4 slices lean salt pork	

Remove and discard damaged leaves from cabbage. Cut cabbage into 6 wedges and remove core. Place carrots and onion in a buttered 2-quart casserole. Cover with salt pork and then with cabbage wedges. Combine seasonings with Bouillon and pour over cabbage. Cover and cook in a preheated oven (350°F) 60 minutes, or until cabbage is tender. Makes 6 servings.

Green Cabbage au Gratin

1 head (1½ pounds) cabbage	1½ cups Béchamel Sauce
½ teaspoon salt	⅛ teaspoon freshly ground black pepper
Boiling water	½ cup grated Parmesan cheese

Remove and discard damaged leaves from cabbage. Cut cabbage into quarters. Cut out the core and shred cabbage coarsely. Put the cabbage in ample boiling salted water and cook 5 to 8 minutes, or only until cabbage is barely tender. Drain. Add 1 cup of the Béchamel Sauce and the black pepper. Adjust salt. Turn into a shallow baking dish. Spoon the remaining Béchamel Sauce over the top. Sprinkle with cheese. Place in a preheated oven (400°F) to melt and brown the cheese. Makes 6 servings.

Whole Stuffed Savoy Cabbage

1 large (2-pound) head Savoy cabbage	2 tablespoons chopped parsley
Salt	½ clove garlic, crushed
Boiling water	⅛ teaspoon freshly ground black pepper
3 slices bread	1 large egg, beaten
Milk	6 slices bacon
½ pound pork sausage	Beef stock or consommé
¼ cup chopped onion	¼ cup buttered white breadcrumbs
2 tablespoons butter	

Remove and discard damaged leaves from cabbage. Scoop out the center and reserve it for slaw or salad. Place the head and 1 teaspoon salt in a deep saucepan and add boiling water to cover completely. Bring to the boiling point, uncovered, and boil 10 minutes. Remove cabbage, shock in cold water, and invert in a bowl to drain thoroughly.

Crumble bread and soak it in enough milk to cover until bread is thoroughly wet. Squeeze dry and fluff with a fork. Crumble sausage and brown it over medium heat. Drain off fat and add the sausage to the bread. Cook onion in butter until limp and add to the bread, along with salt to taste. Add the next 4 ingredients. Mix well. Stuff mixture into the cavity of the cabbage. Place bacon over the cabbage and place cabbage in a saucepan. Pour in stock to a depth of 1 inch. Cover and cook over medium-low heat 30 minutes. Transfer cabbage to a baking pan, sprinkle with buttered breadcrumbs, and brown in a preheated oven (400°F). Remove and discard string and transfer the cabbage to a serving dish. Makes 6 servings.

Red Cabbage Limousin Style

6 cups coarsely shredded red cabbage
2 cups peeled, chopped chestnuts
½ teaspoon salt
⅛ teaspoon freshly ground black pepper

1 cup beef stock or consommé

Fill a buttered 2-quart casserole with alternating layers of cabbage and chestnuts, beginning and ending with cabbage. Combine remaining ingredients and pour over cabbage. Cover and cook in a preheated oven (350°F) 1½ hours, or until cabbage and chestnuts are very tender. Serve hot. Makes 6 servings.

Turkish Stuffed Cabbage Leaves or Dolmas

Boiling water
12 large outside cabbage leaves
1 teaspoon salt
1 teaspoon paprika
½ cup chopped onion
Olive oil
2 cups minced cooked lamb
1 cup cooked rice
¼ cup (½ stick) softened butter
½ teaspoon chopped oregano

¼ teaspoon ground cumin
¼ teaspoon freshly ground black pepper
½ small clove garlic, crushed
½ cup sliced carrots
½ cup sliced onion
1 cup beef, veal, or mutton stock
¼ cup tomato puree
12 thin slices lemon
Lemon juice

Pour boiling water over cabbage leaves and let them stand 10 minutes, or until leaves are pliable. Remove leaves from water, spread out on a clean towel, and with scissors cut out the thick ribs. Season with salt and paprika. Cook onion until limp in 2 tablespoons oil, and combine with the next 8 ingredients. Put a rounded tablespoonful of the stuffing on each cabbage leaf. Fold the edges of the leaf over the filling, roll securely, and fasten with toothpicks. Place 2 tablespoons oil, the carrots, and sliced onion in a baking dish and arrange the cabbage rolls, seam side down, on top. Bake in a preheated oven (350°F) 15 to 20 minutes, or until cabbage begins to brown. Blend stock with tomato puree and pour over the dolmas. Cover and return to the oven to cook 25 to 30 minutes. Transfer dolmas to a serving dish and garnish each with a lemon slice. Cook the stock until reduced by half, then season to taste with lemon juice. Serve over dolmas. Makes 6 servings.

Braised Red Cabbage with Apples

1 head (1½ pounds) red cabbage
2 to 3 tablespoons wine vinegar
½ teaspoon salt
2 medium-sized onions
3 medium-sized apples, sliced
1 cup water or Bouillon

⅛ teaspoon freshly ground black pepper
Dash ground cloves

Remove and discard damaged leaves from cabbage. Finely shred cabbage, mix with vinegar and salt, and let stand 30 minutes. Thickly slice onions, place them in a 1½-quart casserole, and cover with half of the cabbage. Add the apples. Top with remaining cabbage. Pour in water or Bouillon. Place a heatproof plate upside down on the cabbage to weight it down. Cover and cook in a preheated oven (350°F) 2 hours, or until done. Blend the remaining ingredients and add to cabbage 10 minutes before cooking time is up. Serve hot. Makes 6 servings.

Red Cabbage in Red Wine

1 cup thinly sliced onion
4 slices lean salt pork, diced

4 cups coarsely shredded red cabbage
½ teaspoon salt
1/16 teaspoon freshly ground black pepper
½ cup dry red wine

Cook onion with salt pork until the onion begins to soften. Add cabbage, salt, and pepper and mix well. Cover and cook in a preheated oven (350°F) 20 minutes. Bring wine to the boiling point, pour over cabbage, and cook 60 minutes. Makes 6 servings.

CARDOONS (CARDONS)

THE CARDOON IS A THISTLELIKE PLANT related to the artichoke that grows in the Mediterranean area. Only the peeled stems are eaten.

Baked Cardoons with Beef Marrow and Madeira

2 cardoons
Lemon juice
2 quarts boiling water
1 tablespoon flour
1 whole clove
1 carrot, pared

1 medium-sized onion
1 small bay leaf
2 teaspoons salt
Madeira Sauce
Sliced beef marrow, poached 5 minutes
    in simmering water

Remove and discard tough outside stalks of the cardoons. Separate the other stalks from the hearts (as in preparing celery). Wash the stalks, peel off the strings, and cut stalks into 3- to 3½-inch lengths, leaving the hearts whole. Rub cardoons with lemon juice and place in a 3-quart saucepan. Add boiling water. Blend flour with 1½ table-spoons lemon juice and add to the water. Stir in the next 5 ingredients. Cover and cook 1 hour. Drain and rinse cardoons in hot running water. Transfer cardoons to a serving dish. Cover with Madeira Sauce. Garnish with slices of hot beef marrow. Makes 6 servings.

CARROTS (CAROTTES)

Carrots Chantilly

1 pound young tender carrots
Salt
Boiling water
¼ cup heavy cream

Freshly ground black pepper
2 cups hot cooked peas
2 tablespoons butter

Wash and pare carrots. Put the carrots in salted, boiling water and cook 7 to 10 min-utes, or only until carrots are crisp-tender. Drain and add cream and cook until the sauce thickens. Add pepper and adjust salt. Turn carrots into the center of a serving dish. Toss peas with butter, season to taste with salt and pepper, and turn them into the dish around the carrots. Makes 6 servings.

Carrots in Cream Sauce

1 pound young tender carrots
3 tablespoons butter, melted

Salt and freshly ground black pepper
½ cup heavy cream

Wash carrots, trim both ends, and leave whole. Blanch in boiling water 5 minutes. Rinse under cold running water and slip off the skins. Place in a skillet with butter.

Sprinkle with salt, pepper. Simmer 5 minutes. Add cream, cover, and cook until carrots are tender. Makes 6 servings.

 Glazed Carrots

3 dozen young tender carrots
2 tablespoons sugar
½ teaspoon salt

¼ cup (½ stick) butter
Boiling water
Chopped parsley

Wash and pare carrots. Leave whole if small, or cut in half lengthwise if medium-sized or large. Place them in a saucepan with the next 3 ingredients and enough boiling water to barely cover them. Cook, uncovered, until carrots are crisp-tender and the liquid is reduced to a syrupy consistency, giving the carrots an attractive glaze. Turn into a serving dish and sprinkle with parsley. Makes 6 servings.

Carrots Vichy

2 dozen young tender carrots
½ teaspoon salt
2 tablespoons butter

Boiling water
Ground white pepper
Chopped parsley

Pare carrots, thinly slice, and place in a saucepan with salt and butter. Add boiling water to a depth of ½ inch. Cover, bring to the boiling point, and cook 5 to 6 minutes, or only until carrots are barely tender and the water has evaporated. Add white pepper and parsley. Makes 6 servings.

CAULIFLOWER (CHOU-FLEUR)

Boiled Cauliflower

1 large head cauliflower
Salt
Boiling water

Cut off and discard the coarse leaves surrounding the cauliflower head, leaving only the young tender leaves that adhere to the head. Wash the cauliflower well and soak it 20 minutes in cold water with 1 teaspoon salt per quart of water. Drain and rinse under cold running water. Cook in ample boiling, salted water for 10 minutes, or until cauliflower is barely tender. Drain. Serve with melted butter and freshly ground black pepper to taste, or serve with Anchovy, Béarnaise, Caper, Cream, Egg, Hollandaise, Mornay, or Mousseline Sauce (see chapter 3). Makes 6 servings.

Cauliflower au Gratin

1 large head cauliflower
2 tablespoons butter
2 cup heavy cream
4 tablespoons grated Parmesan cheese

4 tablespoons grated Gruyère cheese
1 cup chicken Velouté Sauce
Salt
Freshly ground black pepper

Cook cauliflower as instructed in the recipe for Boiled Cauliflower. Meanwhile, melt butter in a 1-quart saucepan. Add cream and 2 tablespoons of each kind of cheese to the hot Velouté, and the salt and pepper. Pour ¼ cup sauce in the bottom of a casserole and put in the cooked cauliflower, rounded side up. Cover with remaining sauce. Sprinkle with the rest of the cheese. Brown in a preheated oven (400°F). Makes 6 servings.

Cauliflower Milanese

1 large head cauliflower
Freshly ground black pepper

½ cup grated Parmesan cheese
6 tablespoons butter

Break cauliflower into flowerets and cook as for Boiled Cauliflower. Drain. Transfer the florets to a buttered shallow baking dish. Sprinkle with pepper and cheese. Melt half of the butter and sprinkle over the cheese. Brown in a preheated oven (450°F). Dot with the remaining butter. Makes 6 servings.

Cauliflower Polish Style

1 large head cauliflower
2 hard-cooked eggs, chopped
2 tablespoons chopped parsley

½ cup soft white breadcrumbs
6 tablespoons butter

Cook cauliflower as instructed in the recipe for Boiled Cauliflower. Remove from water and drain well. Place in a serving dish, rounded side up. Sprinkle with eggs and parsley. Brown breadcrumbs in a skillet in half of the butter; sprinkle on cauliflower. Melt remaining butter and pour over cauliflower. Serve at once. Makes 6 servings.

CELERY AND CELERY ROOT (CELERIS AND CELERI-RAVE)

Braised Celery Hearts

3 stalks celery
½ cup sliced carrots
¼ cup sliced onion
Boiling stock or water

½ teaspoon salt
1 tablespoon butter
½ cup Demi-Glace Sauce

Remove outside ribs from the stalks of celery and cut off tops. Save these for soup, stock, and stew. Do not separate the celery ribs forming the heart. Split hearts lengthwise, parboil them 5 minutes, then put them in cold water. Spread the ribs apart and hold them under cold running water to rinse out any dirt that might be lodged between the ribs. Spread carrots and onion in a flameproof baking dish and place the celery hearts on top, all lying in the same direction. Pour in boiling stock or water to a depth of ½ inch. Sprinkle celery with salt and dot with butter. Cut a piece of waxed paper the size of the baking dish, making a small hole in the center, and place it over the top. Bring liquid to the boiling point, cover, and bake in a preheated oven (400°F) 30 minutes, or until celery is tender. Remove celery to a serving dish. Bring cooking liquid to the boiling point and cook until stock has reduced to ½ cup. Add Demi-Glace Sauce and cook 3 to 4 minutes. Pour over celery. Makes 6 servings.

Celery à la Menagère

2 stalks celery	½ teaspoon salt
2 medium-sized onions	⅛ teaspoon freshly ground black pepper
2 tablespoons butter	¼ teaspoon sugar
1 cup sliced carrots	½ cup bouillon
2 medium-sized tomatoes	

Remove and discard the big outer ribs of celery stalks. Cut the remaining ribs into 2-inch pieces. Set aside. Peel onions, cut into slices ¼ inch thick, and brown lightly in butter, along with carrots, in a flameproof baking dish. Place celery over the top. Peel, seed, and quarter tomatoes and arrange over celery. Sprinkle with salt, pepper, and sugar. Add bouillon. Cover and cook in a preheated oven (350°F) 40 minutes, or until celery is tender. Serve with veal. Makes 6 servings.

Celery with Parmesan Cheese

4 cups celery cut into 1-inch pieces	2 tablespoons butter
Boiling chicken or veal stock,	½ cup grated Parmesan cheese
or boiling water and	Dash ground white pepper
½ teaspoon salt	

Place celery in a saucepan and pour in stock or water to a depth of ¼ inch. Add salt if water is used. Cover, bring to the boiling point, and cook 10 minutes, or only until celery is crisp-tender. Drain, add butter, half of the cheese, and the white pepper. Toss. Serve with remaining cheese sprinkled over the top. Makes 6 servings.

Boiled Celery Root

Celery root or celeriac (*céleri-rave*) is a variety of celery with a large edible root. It is sliced and either served raw with salt, pepper, and vinegar or cooked in various ways.

To boil celery root, trim off leaves and root fibers, pare root, and slice ½ inch thick, or cut into dice. Pour in boiling water to a depth of ½ inch and add ½ teaspoon salt. Cover and cook 15 minutes, or until tender. Drain and serve with melted butter, Hollandaise Sauce, or Béchamel Sauce. Allow 3 roots for 6 servings.

Celeriac Fritters

Celery root	1 egg beaten with 1 tablespoon milk
Boiling water	Fine dry breadcrumbs
Salt	Oil for frying, or butter
Flour	Tomato Sauce

Pare celery root and cut into slices ½ inch thick. Place in a saucepan with boiling water and salt, adding ½ teaspoon salt for each 2 cups water. Cover and boil until celery root is soft, being careful not to overcook. Drain well. If slices are very large, cut them into halves or quarters. Dredge in flour, dip in egg mixture, and roll in breadcrumbs. Deep fry until brown in fat preheated to 375°F, or shallow-fry in butter. Serve with Tomato Sauce. Allow 3 roots for 6 servings.

CHESTNUTS (MARRONS)

How to Peel Chestnuts

Four methods of peeling chestnuts follow.

- *Skillet.* Slit each chestnut with a sharp knife and put them in a skillet with enough oil to coat them. Stir and cook over medium heat about 10 minutes. When cool enough to handle, remove shells and skins with a sharp knife.
- *Oven.* Slit chestnuts and coat them with oil as in the skillet method. Bake in a preheated oven (450°F) 20 minutes. Cool. Remove shells and skins with a sharp knife.
- *Deep fry.* Cut all around the chestnuts with a sharp knife. Place a few of them at a time in a wire basket or sieve and immerse them in fat preheated to 375°F until the peel opens of its own accord. Drain chestnuts well on paper towels. When cool enough to handle, remove shells and skins.
- *Boiling.* Slit each shell and place in boiling water to cover. Boil 20 minutes. Drain and cool. Peel off shells and skins.

Braised Chestnuts

2 pounds chestnuts, peeled
Boiling beef, chicken, or veal stock

Freshly ground black pepper
2 tablespoons butter

Place chestnuts in a saucepan. Add boiling stock to a depth of 1 inch. Cover, bring to the boiling point, reduce heat, and simmer 10 to 15 minutes, or until just tender. Add pepper and butter. Toss and serve. Makes 6 servings.

Creamed Chestnuts

Braise chestnuts as in the recipe for Braised Chestnuts. Drain. Omit butter. Heat with ½ cup Bechamel Sauce and 1 cup heavy cream.

Chestnut and Celery Root Puree

2 pounds chestnuts, shelled
   and skinned
1 slice celery root, or ¼ cup
   sliced celery

Boiling bouillon, or boiling water
   and ½ teaspoon salt
2 tablespoons butter
Stock, milk, or heavy cream

Place chestnuts and celery root and 1 inch boiling bouillon or water in a saucepan. Add salt if water is used. Cover. Bring to the boiling point and cook 15 to 20 minutes, or until chestnuts are very soft. Push through a sieve or food mill. Add butter. Thin with stock, milk, or cream to consistency desired. Serve hot. Makes 6 servings.

CUCUMBERS (CONCOMBRES)

Cucumbers in Butter

3 cucumbers
Salt
Boiling water
¼ cup (½ stick) butter, melted

⅛ teaspoon freshly ground black pepper
1 tablespoon lemon juice
Chopped parsley

Peel cucumbers, cut them lengthwise into quarters, then cut each quarter into 1-inch pieces. Place in a saucepan with ½ teaspoon salt and boiling water to cover. Cover and simmer 3 minutes. Drain. Pour butter into a 1-quart flameproof casserole and add cucumbers. Sprinkle with ¼ teaspoon salt and ⅛ teaspoon pepper. Cover and cook over very low heat 15 to 20 minutes. Sprinkle with lemon juice and parsley. Serve in the casserole. Makes 6 servings.

Creamed Cucumbers

Prepare cucumbers as in the recipe for Cucumbers in Butter. When they are about three-fourths done, add 1 cup hot cream. Finish cooking them in the cream. Omit the lemon juice. Sprinkle with chopped parsley.

EGGPLANT (AUBERGINES)

Stuffed Eggplant

3 medium-small eggplants
½ cup olive oil
⅓ cup Béchamel Sauce
1 egg, lightly beaten

Salt and freshly ground black pepper
1 cup grated Gruyère cheese
⅓ cup heavy cream

Wash eggplants and cut them lengthwise into halves. Cut the meat crosswise several times with a knife without piercing the skin. Pour the oil into a baking pan large enough to accommodate the eggplants and heat. Place the eggplant halves, cut side down, in the hot oil and bake until the meat can be easily scooped out, leaving the shell intact. Chop the eggplant meat and mix well with Béchamel Sauce, egg, salt and pepper to taste, and half of the cheese. Stuff the shells with this mixture, sprinkle with remaining grated cheese, and place in a baking pan. Brown in a preheated oven (400°F). Salt the cream lightly, and just before serving pour a little over the top of each eggplant half. Makes 6 servings.

Eggplant Provençale

2 pounds eggplant
Salt
Flour
½ cup olive oil

6 medium-sized tomatoes
Freshly ground black pepper
1 small clove garlic, crushed
Chopped parsley

Wash eggplant, peel, cut into large dice, and sprinkle with ½ teaspoon salt. Let stand 20 minutes. Wipe the salt off the eggplant, dredge in flour, and sauté in ¼ cup of the hot oil. Meanwhile, peel, seed, and quarter tomatoes. Sauté them quickly in remaining hot oil in another saucepan. When both vegetables are done, toss them together and season with salt and pepper to taste and garlic. Cook the vegetables together 5 minutes. Sprinkle with parsley, if desired. Makes 6 servings.

Or, instead of dicing the eggplants, cut them in half lengthwise, remove the meat, and reserve the shells. When the eggplant and tomatoes have been tossed together, divide the mixture and put into the shells, then bake in a preheated oven (350°F) 5 minutes.

Eggplant Carlton Hotel

3 medium-sized eggplants
2 medium-sized tomatoes
¼ pound Gruyère cheese, diced
2 tablespoons minced onion

Salt and freshly ground black pepper
Olive oil
¾ cup hot water

Wash eggplants and tomatoes. Cut eggplants in half lengthwise, scoop out the meat, and cut it into small dice. Peel, seed, and dice tomatoes, and mix with eggplant, cheese, and onion. Add salt and pepper to taste. Stuff the eggplant shells with the mixture and sprinkle with oil. Pour ¼ cup each oil and hot water into a baking pan large enough to accommodate the eggplant. Put in eggplant and bake in a preheated oven (350°F) 40 minutes, or until eggplant is done. Transfer eggplant to a platter. Serve hot. Makes 6 servings.

Stuffed Eggplant with Saffron

3 medium-small eggplants
½ cup olive oil
½ cup chopped onion
¼ cup (½ stick) butter
3 medium-sized tomatoes

1 cup cooked rice
¼ teaspoon crumbled saffron threads
¼ cup hot beef or veal stock
Salt and freshly ground black pepper
½ cup grated Parmesan cheese

Wash eggplants, peel, and cut in half lengthwise. Scoop out and reserve the meat, being careful to leave shell ¼ inch thick. Cook eggplant shells in oil in preheated (350°F) oven without allowing them to become too soft. Cook the onion until limp in half of the butter. Add the reserved eggplant meat. Peel, seed, and dice tomatoes and add to eggplant and onion, along with rice. Dissolve saffron in hot stock and add. Season to taste with salt and pepper. Cook 2 to 3 minutes. Stuff the mixture into the eggplant shells. Sprinkle with cheese and dot with remaining butter. Bake in a preheated oven (450°F) until tops have browned. Makes 6 servings.

Tuscan Stuffed Eggplant

6 small eggplants
2 tomatoes, coarsely chopped,
    and 6 slices of tomato
¼ cup soft white breadcrumbs
1 teaspoon salt

¼ teaspoon freshly ground black pepper
½ pound mozzarella
¼ cup chopped onion
2 tablespoons olive oil

Wash eggplants, cut them in half lengthwise, and scoop out the meat, leaving the shells intact. Divide meat into two equal portions. Chop one portion and mix with the chopped tomatoes, the breadcrumbs, ¼ teaspoon salt, and ⅛ teaspoon pepper. Stuff into the shells, filling them about half full. Place a slice of cheese on each. Cook onion in the oil until limp. Chop remaining eggplant and add, along with remaining salt and pepper. Stir and cook about 5 minutes. Finish filling eggplant shells with this mixture. Cut tomato slices in half and put a half slice on each stuffed eggplant half. Cover with cheese. Arrange on a large baking sheet and bake in a preheated oven (350°F) 30 minutes. When the stuffed eggplants are cooked, arrange them around the edge of a large round serving tray. Makes 6 to 12 servings.

ENDIVE

THE WHITE BLEACHED HEADS of Belgian endive are used for salads, or as a cooked vegetable. Endive may be braised, gratinéed with cheese, or served with a sauce.

Braised Belgian Endive

12 medium-sized heads Belgian endive	1 teaspoon sugar
5 tablespoons butter	1 tablespoon lemon juice
½ teaspoon salt	½ cup boiling water
⅛ teaspoon freshly ground black pepper	Chopped parsley

Trim off and discard the base and any wilted leaves of endive. Wash heads one at a time under cold running water. Arrange the heads in the same direction in 2 layers in a generously buttered flameproof casserole, dotting each layer with 2 tablespoons butter and sprinkling with salt, pepper, sugar, and lemon juice. Pour in boiling water. Cut a piece of waxed paper the size of the casserole, cut a small hole in the center, and lay over the endive. Bring the water to the boiling point, reduce heat, and simmer 45 minutes. Remove endive to a serving dish. Cook until the liquid has been reduced to about ½ cup, add remaining 1 tablespoon butter, and pour the sauce over endive. Sprinkle with parsley. Serve hot. If desired, this dish may be cooked in a preheated oven (350°F) 45 minutes. Makes 6 servings.

Belgian Endive with Brown Butter

Cook Braised Belgian Endive as in preceding recipe, but instead of thickening the cooking liquid to make a sauce, brown 2 tablespoons butter and pour over the endive. This recipe uses 6 tablespoons butter in all, instead of 5 as in preceding recipe.

Belgian Endive Flemish Style

Cover Braised Endive with 1 cup hot Demi-Glace Sauce.

Belgian Endive au Gratin with Ham

Spread ⅔ cup Béchamel or Mornay Sauce in a casserole. Wrap each head of Braised Endive in a thin slice of boiled ham and arrange over the sauce in two layers. Cover with 1⅓ cups Béchamel or Mornay Sauce. Sprinkle with grated Gruyère, Swiss, or Cheddar cheese. Put casserole in a preheated oven (425°F) or under the broiler, until cheese is lightly browned. Makes 6 servings.

JERUSALEM ARTICHOKES OR SUNCHOKES (TOPINAMBOURS)

JERUSALEM ARTICHOKES ARE TUBERS of firm consistency that resemble globe artichokes in flavor, although they are an entirely different vegetable.

To prepare them, peel the tubers carefully and drop them in cold water immediately to prevent discoloration. Blanch briefly in boiling water, drain, and simmer in butter until tender. Season to taste with salt and freshly ground black pepper. Or, if desired, serve with Béchamel Sauce.

Large Jerusalem artichokes may be sliced, blanched, dipped in Fritter Batter, and fried in hot deep fat. They may also be cooked in boiling water until tender, drained, and pureed. Sliced cooked Jerusalem artichokes may be chilled and put into vegetable salads.

Jerusalem Artichokes Baked with Cream

18 Jerusalem artichokes
1 teaspoon salt
Boiling water

2 tablespoons butter
Freshly ground black pepper
Heavy cream

Wash and peel Jerusalem artichokes and cut them into olive shapes, dropping them in cold water as they are peeled to prevent discoloration. Place them in a saucepan with salt and enough boiling water to cover. Cover, bring to the boiling point, and cook 15 minutes. Drain. Turn tubers into a buttered baking dish. Dot with butter. Sprinkle with pepper. Pour in enough heavy cream to barely cover and bake in a preheated oven (425°F) 15 minutes. Makes 6 servings.

KOHLRABI (CHOUX-RAVES)

KOHLRABI IS A MEMBER OF THE CABBAGE FAMILY with an edible turnip-shaped stem and a cabbagelike leaf. When the leaves are young and tender they may be used in salads. The tuberous stems may be stuffed; boiled and served with butter, cream sauce, or Hollandaise Sauce; made into an au gratin dish; or served cold with Vinaigrette Sauce. They may also be cooked in the same ways as turnips or celery root.

Boiled Kohlrabi

Cut the leaves off the kohlrabi. (If the leaves are young and tender, reserve them for use in salads.) Wash and pare the kohlrabi and cut into ½-inch cubes, or slice ¼ inch thick. Place in a saucepan with salt and 1 inch boiling water, using ½ teaspoon salt to 2 cups water. Cover, bring to the boiling point, and cook 25 minutes, or until barely tender. Drain. Season to taste with salt and freshly ground black pepper and toss with butter. Allow 1 medium-sized kohlrabi per serving; use 2 tablespoons butter for 6 servings.

LEEKS (POIREAUX)

Boiled Leeks

4 bunches leeks	3 tablespoons butter
½ teaspoon salt	Freshly ground black pepper
Boiling water	Chopped parsley

Cut off and discard the green tops and whiskers from the root ends of leeks. Remove one or two layers of their white skin. Wash and rinse under cold running water to make sure all sand is removed. Drain. Place leeks in a saucepan with salt. Pour in boiling water to a depth of 1 inch. Cover and cook 10 minutes, or until tender. Drain well. Add butter, and pepper to taste. Cover and let stand 2 to 3 minutes, or until butter melts. Transfer to a serving dish and sprinkle with parsley. Makes 6 servings.

Braised Leeks

4 bunches leeks	¼ teaspoon grated nutmeg
½ cup sliced carrots	½ teaspoon ground dried thyme
⅓ cup sliced onion	2 to 3 cups rich beef stock or bouillon
½ cup coarsely chopped celery tops	2 tablespoons flour
¼ cup diced salt pork	3 tablespoons butter
¼ teaspoon salt	⅔ cup buttered soft breadcrumbs
⅟₁₆ teaspoon freshly ground black pepper	

Prepare leeks for cooking as in recipe for Boiled Leeks. Cover the bottom of a well-buttered baking dish with carrots, onion, celery tops, and salt pork, and arrange leeks on top. Sprinkle with the seasonings and pour in enough stock to barely cover the leeks. Cut a piece of waxed paper the size of the baking dish, make a tiny hole in the center, and place over the leeks. Cover and cook in a preheated oven (350°F) 35 to 40 minutes, or until leeks are tender and have absorbed most of the stock. Remove and discard the waxed paper. Blend flour with butter and add to 1¼ cups of the stock. Stir and cook until sauce has thickened. Pour over leeks. Sprinkle with buttered bread-crumbs. Brown under the broiler. Makes 6 servings.

Creamed Leeks on Toast or Fried Bread

Arrange 5 Boiled Leeks on each piece of toast or fried bread, and spoon Velouté Sauce or Béchamel Sauce over them. Garnish each serving with chopped parsley.

LENTILS (LENTILLES)

Lentils

2 cups dried lentils	2 tablespoons butter
4 cups cold water	3 slices lean salt pork, diced
2 medium-sized onions	1 small clove garlic, crushed
1 medium-sized carrot	2 teaspoons salt
1 sprig parsley	⅛ teaspoon freshly ground black pepper

Wash lentils and soak 1 hour in 4 cups cold water. Peel and dice onions and carrot. Add half of the onions, the carrot, and the parsley to the lentils and the water in which they have soaked. Cover, bring to the boiling point, reduce heat, and simmer 45 minutes, or until lentils are almost tender, adding more water if needed. Remove and discard parsley. Sauté remaining onion in 2 tablespoons of butter, along with the salt pork. Add to the lentils. Stir in garlic, salt, and pepper. Serve hot. Makes 6 servings.

LETTUCE (LAITUE)

Braised Lettuce with Ham

2 medium-small heads lettuce	Boiling water or stock
½ teaspoon salt	6 very thin slices fried, boiled, or baked ham
2 tablespoons bacon or ham fat	2 tablespoons Madeira wine
1 small onion, sliced	2 tablespoons Demi-Glace
¼ cup sliced carrot	

Remove and discard wilted outside leaves from the lettuce. Wash the lettuce well under cold running water. Cut each head into 3 wedges and place them in a deep 10-inch skillet with the next 4 ingredients. Pour in boiling water or stock to a depth of 1 inch. Cover with buttered parchment paper and simmer 20 minutes. Transfer lettuce wedges to a round serving dish, arranging them in a ring, alternating with slices of ham the same size. Keep warm. Cook the cooking liquid until reduced to 1¼ cups. Pour in Madeira and Demi-Glace. Stir and cook 1 to 2 minutes, or until sauce has thickened. Adjust the salt. Pour over lettuce. Makes 6 servings.

MUSHROOMS (CHAMPIGNONS)

Mushrooms in Cream Sauce

1½ pounds small mushrooms
2 tablespoons butter, melted
1 tablespoon lemon juice

1 cup Béchamel Sauce
¾ cup heavy cream
Salt and freshly ground black pepper

Remove stems from mushrooms and save for sauces and soups. Wash mushroom caps and simmer 5 minutes in butter and lemon juice. Add Béchamel Sauce, cream, salt, and pepper. Simmer until mushrooms are tender and sauce has thickened. Makes 6 servings.

Baked Mushrooms

12 large mushroom caps
½ cup olive oil
½ teaspoon salt

Room temperature Maître d'Hôtel
or Snail Butter

Wash mushroom caps and drain well. Pour oil into a baking pan and heat it in a preheated oven (450°F). Add mushrooms and stir to coat them thoroughly with oil. Sprinkle with salt. Return the pan to the oven and cook 10 minutes, or until the mushrooms are done. Remove mushrooms from the oven and fill the cavities with the butter. Serve at once. Makes 6 servings.

Mushrooms in Chervil Cream Sauce

1½ pounds mushrooms
2 tablespoons chopped onion
4 tablespoons (½ stick) butter
¼ cup heavy cream

1½ teaspoons chopped fresh chervil
1 teaspoon salt
⅛ teaspoon freshly ground black pepper
Chopped parsley

Remove stems from mushrooms and reserve for another use. Wash the caps and set aside. Cook onion until limp in half of the butter. Add mushroom caps and cook over medium-low heat 10 minutes. Add cream and chervil and cook another 5 minutes. Add salt and pepper. Turn into a serving dish. Sprinkle with parsley. Makes 6 servings.

Mushroom Puree

1½ pounds mushrooms
3 tablespoons butter
1 tablespoon lemon juice

Salt and freshly ground black pepper
½ to ¾ cup very thick hot Béchamel Sauce

Wash mushrooms thoroughly, leaving stems attached, and put them through a food mill. Melt butter in a saucepan. Add mushrooms and lemon juice. Stir and cook until all the moisture has evaporated. Season with salt and pepper to taste, and add hot Béchamel Sauce. Heat, but do not boil. Serve as an accompaniment to meat dishes, or to fill tartlets, barquettes, or artichoke bottoms. Makes 6 servings.

Russian Stewed Wild Mushrooms

1½ pounds wild mushrooms
    like fresh cèpes
3 tablespoons butter
¾ teaspoon salt (or to taste)
¼ teaspoon fennel seeds, or
    1 teaspoon chopped fresh fennel

¼ teaspoon dill seeds or 1 teaspoon
    chopped fresh dill
2 tablespoons chopped chives
⅛ teaspoon freshly ground black pepper
4 tablespoons sour cream

Wash mushrooms. Slice and place in a 10-inch skillet with butter and next 4 ingredients. Stir and cook until mushrooms are tender. Transfer mushrooms to a serving dish. Cook the liquid until it has reduced by one-fourth. Add pepper and sour cream. Heat about 1 minute. Pour over mushrooms. Serve immediately. Makes 6 servings.

Sautéed Wild Mushrooms or Cèpes

1½ pounds wild mushrooms or cepes
2 small cloves garlic

½ cup olive oil
½ cup chopped parsley

Wash the mushrooms and cut them into thin slices. Cook the garlic very lightly in the oil and remove and discard garlic. Put mushrooms into the oil and sauté 3 minutes, or until limp. Add half the parsley and sauté 1 minute longer. Remove to a serving dish and sprinkle with remaining parsley. Makes 6 servings.

OKRA

How to Cook Okra

Wash okra and cut off the stems. Leave the pods whole. Place in a saucepan with ½ teaspoon salt. Pour in boiling water to a depth of ½ inch. Bring to the boiling point, uncovered, and cook 5 minutes. Cover and cook 5 minutes, or only until okra is tender. Drain. Add 2 tablespoons butter to the saucepan. Simmer 2 to 3 minutes. Sprinkle with ground black pepper. Serve hot. Allow 5 medium-sized pods per serving.

ONIONS (OIGNONS)

Glazed Pearl Onions

1½ pounds pearl onions	2 tablespoons butter
½ cup boiling water	1 tablespoon sugar
½ cup chicken or veal stock	

Drop unpeeled onions into rapidly boiling water and let them stand about 10 seconds, or just long enough to loosen the skins from the onions. Drain and hold a few seconds under cold running water. Cut off a thin slice from the bottom and the top, then slip off the outside skin and the first layer of onion with your fingers. Cut a cross in the root end of each onion to prevent the onion from bursting. Place onions in a saucepan with ½ cup boiling water, the stock, 1 tablespoon of the butter, and the sugar. Bring to the boiling point, reduce heat, and simmer, uncovered, 15 minutes, or until the onions are tender and all the liquid has evaporated. Add the remaining 1 tablespoon butter. Shake and cook over low heat until onions take on a glaze. Makes 6 servings.

Deep-Fried Onions

4 large mild very fresh onions	½ teaspoon salt
Coarse sea salt	½ teaspoon freshly ground black pepper
½ cup milk	Oil for frying
½ cup flour	

Peel onions, wash, and cut into slices ¼ inch thick. Separate the rings, and cover with sea salt. Let stand 20 minutes and wipe off salt. Dip them in milk and then in flour seasoned with salt and pepper. Place a few rings at a time in a wire basket or large sieve and immerse in deep fat preheated to 375°F. Fry until onions are golden brown. Remove from fat and turn out onto paper towels to drain. Serve hot. Makes 6 servings.

Stuffed Onions

6 large sweet Spanish onions	1 cup chopped cooked meat
Boiling water	½ cup cooked rice
Salt	Freshly ground black pepper
2 tablespoons butter or olive oil	6 tablespoons buttered soft breadcrumbs
1 small clove garlic, crushed	6 teaspoons grated Parmesan cheese
½ teaspoon dried marjoram	Stock or Boullion

Peel onions and parboil 10 minutes in boiling water to cover, with ½ teaspoon salt. Remove the centers and set the onion shells aside. Chop centers and cook in butter or oil, along with the garlic, until onions begin to turn golden. Add marjoram, meat, and rice. Stir and cook 2 minutes. Season to taste with salt and pepper. Stuff mixture into the onion shells. Top each with 1 tablespoon buttered breadcrumbs and 1 teaspoon grated Parmesan cheese. Place in a 9-by-9-by-2-inch baking pan. Pour in stóck or Bouillon to a depth of 1 inch. Cook in a preheated oven (400°F) 30 to 40 minutes, or until tops are brown. Serve each onion in an individual serving dish and pour a little of the stock around it. Makes 6 servings.

PEAS (POIS)

GREEN PEAS IN FRANCE ARE EATEN when they are still small and tender, and are known as *petits pois*.

Peas Bonne Femme

3 pounds green peas, shelled	¼ cup chopped onion
¼ pound lean salt pork	Stock or water
2 tablespoons butter	12 pearl onions

Wash peas and set them aside to drain. Rinse salt pork in hot water and dice. Place in a 1½-quart saucepan with butter and chopped onions. Stir and cook until onions and pork are soft. Add stock or water and salt. Mix well, bring to the boiling point, and add pearl onions. Cover and cook 5 minutes. Add peas and continue cooking until onions and peas are tender, about 10 minutes. Makes 6 servings.

Peas Steamed in Lettuce

3 pounds green peas, shelled	¼ teaspoon chopped chervil
3 tablespoons butter	1 teaspoon sugar
6 pearl onions	½ teaspoon salt
6 lettuce leaves, shredded	¼ cup water
1 sprig parsley	¹⁄₁₆ teaspoon freshly ground black pepper

Place peas in a sieve, wash under cold running water, and set aside to drain. Melt 2 tablespoons of the butter in a saucepan. Add peas and the next 7 ingredients. Cover, bring to the boiling point, reduce heat, and simmer only until peas are barely tender and only 2 to 3 tablespoons of water remain in the pan, 5-10 minutes. Remove and discard parsley. Remove the cover, turn up the heat for 1 minute and shake the pan and cook until the liquid has thickened slightly. Season. Makes 6 servings.

Peas with Mint

3 pounds green peas, shelled
2 tablespoons minced fresh mint leaves
1 tablespoon salt
Boiling water

2 tablespoons butter
Dash freshly ground black pepper
6 whole fresh mint leaves

Wash peas and place them in a 1½-quart saucepan with minced mint and salt. Pour in boiling water to a depth of ½ inch. Bring to the boiling point, cover, and boil briskly 5 minutes, or until almost done. Drain off water, add butter, cover, and simmer 3 to 4 minutes, or until peas are tender. Add pepper and toss lightly. Turn into a serving dish and garnish with whole mint leaves. Makes 6 servings.

Peas à la Paysanne

3 pounds green peas, shelled
4 tablespoons (½ stick) butter
12 pearl onions, peeled
12 small young carrots, pared
12 very small new potatoes, peeled
2 sprigs parsley

2 teaspoons sugar
1 teaspoon salt
½ cup boiling water
2 medium-small heads lettuce
1 teaspoon freshly ground black pepper

Wash peas and set them aside to drain. Melt 3 tablespoons of the butter in a saucepan. Add peas and the next 7 ingredients. Remove and discard wilted outside leaves from the lettuce. Cut each head into 3 wedges and tie them at each end and in the center with twine to hold them in shape. Place over the vegetables. Cover, bring the water to the boiling point, reduce heat, and simmer only until vegetables are done, 8 to 10 minutes. Remove and discard parsley. Transfer vegetables to a serving dish. Remove twine from lettuce. Season the juices and pour over the vegetables. Makes 6 servings.

Split-Pea Puree

2 cups dried split peas
4 cups cold water
¾ pound lean salt pork
¾ cup diced onion

½ cup diced carrots
½ teaspoon salt (or to taste)
¾ teaspoon freshly ground black pepper
2 tablespoons butter

Wash peas and place them in a saucepan with 4 cups cold water. Dice salt pork, brown, and add to the peas, along with onion and carrots. Cover, bring to the boiling point, reduce heat, and simmer 1½ hours. Put the peas through a sieve or food mill, and stir in salt, pepper, and butter. This puree should be very thick. Makes 6 servings.

PEPPERS (POIVRONS)

Spanish Stuffed Peppers with Ham and Rice

6 large green or red bell peppers	1 teaspoon capers
Salt	½ small clove garlic, crushed
Boiling water	⅛ teaspoon freshly ground black pepper
½ cup chopped onion	2 tablespoons chopped parsley
About 5 tablespoons olive oil	1 cup tomato sauce
2 cups finely diced ham	½ cup water or Bouillon
1 cup cooked rice	

Wash peppers and cut a slice from the stem ends, saving the slices. Remove seeds and pith. Place peppers and the slices cut from the stem ends in a saucepan with ½ teaspoon salt and enough boiling water to cover. Cover and parboil 5 minutes. Remove peppers from water and drain well. Sauté onions in 2 tablespoons of the oil. Add ham, rice, capers, garlic, black pepper, parsley, and salt to taste. Stuff the mixture into the peppers. Replace top slices and brush peppers with oil. Arrange peppers in a baking pan. Combine 2 tablespoons oil, the tomato sauce, and water or Bouillon, and pour into the pan around the peppers. Bake in a preheated oven (350°F) 35 minutes, or until peppers are done. Transfer peppers to a serving dish. Season pan sauce to taste with salt and pepper and serve in a sauceboat. Makes 6 servings.

POTATOES (POMMES DE TERRE)

Potatoes Anna

This dish can be cooked also with rendered duck or goose fat.

6 cups thinly sliced potatoes	1 teaspoon salt
1 cup butter	⅛ teaspoon freshly ground black pepper

Peel potatoes, then wash them, pat dry, and thinly slice. Pat slices dry between clean towels. Generously butter the bottom and sides of a 12-inch round heavy skillet. Season potatoes with salt and pepper and arrange them over the bottom and around the sides of the pan, having the slices slightly overlapping. Finish filling pan with layers of potatoes. Melt remaining butter and heat until it has browned very lightly. Pour over potatoes. Bake in a preheated oven (425°F) 40 to 50 minutes, or until potatoes are tender when tested with a pointed knife. Turn potatoes out onto a large heatproof serving plate. Place under broiler to brown. Serve hot. Makes 6 to 8 servings.

Potatoes Voisin

In the recipe for Potatoes Anna, sprinkle grated Gruyère cheese between the layers of potatoes.

Potatoes Baden Style

2 pounds hot boiled potatoes	Salt
2 tablespoons butter	⅛ teaspoon freshly ground black pepper
2 eggs, separated	½ cup grated Gruyère cheese
¼ cup milk	

Push potatoes through a sieve and mix with the butter. Beat egg yolks, blend with milk, and add to potatoes, along with the next 3 ingredients. Mix well. Beat egg whites until they stand in soft peaks, and gently fold them into the potato mixture. Turn into a buttered 1-quart casserole, reserving 1 cupful. Put the reserved potatoes into a pastry bag fitted with a fluted nozzle and pipe a border of potatoes around the edge of the casserole. Bake in a preheated oven (350°F) until potatoes have puffed like a soufflé and browned over the top. Makes 6 servings.

Potatoes Boulangère

6 medium-large potatoes	¼ teaspoon freshly ground black pepper
6 medium-sized onions	1 cup boiling Bouillon, or beef or
1 teaspoon salt	veal stock

Peel potatoes and onions. Slice potatoes ½ inch thick and onions ¼ inch thick. Mix together, along with salt and pepper, and put into a well-buttered 2-quart baking dish. Pour in Bouillon or stock. Cover and cook 15 minutes in a preheated oven (400°F). Remove cover and continue cooking until the liquid has evaporated and the vegetables begin to brown. Serve hot with beef, veal, or pork roasts. Makes 6 servings.

Château Potatoes

2 pounds potatoes	3 tablespoons butter
1 teaspoon salt	⅛ teaspoon freshly ground black pepper
Cold water	Chopped parsley

Peel potatoes and cut them in the size and shape of large olives. Place them in a saucepan with salt and enough cold water to cover. Bring the water to the boiling point and cook 1 to 2 minutes. Drain and pat dry thoroughly. Heat butter in a skillet. Add potatoes, and cook in a very hot oven or sauté until golden. Sprinkle with pepper and parsley. Makes 6 servings.

Potato Chips

Peel potatoes, cut them into cylinders about 1 inch in diameter, and thinly slice. Place a few slices at a time in a wire basket or medium-large sieve and deep fry in fat preheated to 375°F about 1 minute, or until golden. Drain on paper towels. Allow 1 medium-sized potato per serving.

Dauphine Potatoes

½ cup butter
1 cup water
2 teaspoons salt
1 cup sifted all-purpose flour
4 large eggs

2½ pounds (7 to 8 medium-sized) potatoes
1 teaspoon grated nutmeg
⅛ teaspoon freshly ground black pepper
Oil for frying

Place first 3 ingredients in a 1-quart saucepan, bring to the boiling point, and add all the flour at one time. Stir and cook over low heat 1 to 2 minutes, or until the mixture leaves the sides of the pan and forms a ball. Cool slightly. Beat in one egg at a time. (This is choux paste.) Peel potatoes, boil, and mash until fluffy (do not add milk or butter). Add to choux paste and mix well. Stir in nutmeg and pepper. Shape mixture into 1-inch balls, or drop it from a tablespoon, or put it into a pastry bag and pipe 2-inch lengths. Fry in deep fat preheated to 375°F 2 to 3 minutes, or until browned. Drain on paper towels. Makes 6 to 8 servings.

Lorette Potatoes

Make the recipe for Dauphine Potatoes, adding ½ cup grated Gruyère cheese to the mashed potatoes.

Stuffed Baked Potatoes

6 medium-sized baking potatoes
Salt and freshly ground black
    pepper
About ¾ cup milk

About ¼ cup heavy cream
2 tablespoons butter, melted
Grated Parmesan cheese

Wash and dry potatoes. Bake in a preheated oven (400°F) until potatoes are soft. Cut off a thick lengthwise slice from each potato. Scoop out potatoes, leaving shell, about ¼ inch thick, intact. Place potato shells in the oven to dry and crisp. Mash the scooped-out portion of the potatoes, add salt, pepper, and enough milk and cream to give a fluffy consistency. Spoon into the shells, rounding over the tops. Brush with butter and sprinkle with cheese. Brown in a preheated oven (400°F), or place under the broiler to brown. Makes 6 servings.

Lyonnaise Sautéed Potatoes

2 pounds (6 medium) potatoes
¼ cup (½ stick) butter
½ pound onions

Salt and freshly ground black pepper
Chopped parsley

Cook unpeeled potatoes in salted, boiling water until they are done. Peel, slice, and fry slices in hot butter until golden brown. Peel onions, thinly slice, and sauté in a separate skillet. Add to the potatoes and cook another 8 minutes. Sprinkle with salt and pepper and mix lightly. Turn into a serving dish. Sprinkle with parsley. Makes 6 servings.

Macaire Potatoes

6 large baking potatoes
½ teaspoon salt

⅛ teaspoon freshly ground black pepper
6 tablespoons butter

Wash potatoes and bake in a preheated oven (400°F) until done. Remove from oven, cut in half, and scoop out the flesh. Add salt, pepper, and half of the butter and mash coarsely with a fork. Heat 2 tablespoons of the remaining butter in a skillet, add potatoes and press them down to ½-inch thickness. Brown on both sides, adding remaining butter as needed. Serve hot. Makes 6 servings

Maître d'Hôtel Potatoes

6 medium-large potatoes
¾ cup bouillon
Salt and freshly ground black pepper
½ teaspoon grated nutmeg

2 tablespoons butter
⅓ cup milk
Chopped parsley

Cook potatoes in their jackets until they are done. Peel, thinly slice, and place in a 10-inch skillet. Add bouillon, salt and pepper to taste, nutmeg, and butter. Bring to the boiling point and cook, uncovered, 5 minutes. Add milk and simmer (do not boil) until the sauce is creamy and has slightly thickened. Turn into a serving dish. Sprinkle with parsley. Makes 6 servings.

Matchstick Potatoes

Peel potatoes and cut them into strips the size of matchsticks. Wash in cold water, drain, and pat dry thoroughly between clean towels. Put a few potatoes at a time in a wire basket or medium-large sieve and immerse in deep fat preheated to 370°F. Fry 2 to 3 minutes, or until browned. Drain on paper towels. Sprinkle with salt and serve hot. Allow 1 medium-large potato per serving. These are also called shoestring potatoes or straw potatoes.

Gratin of Potato Puree Mont d'Or

6 medium-sized potatoes
1 teaspoon salt
Boiling water
2 tablespoons butter
¼ teaspoon grated nutmeg

⅛ teaspoon freshly ground black pepper
3 eggs, beaten
¼ cup grated Gruyère cheese
½ cup thin slices Gruyère

Wash, peel, and quarter potatoes. Put them in a saucepan with salt. Pour in boiling water to a depth of 1 inch. Cover, bring to the boiling point, and cook until potatoes are soft. Drain well and put through a potato ricer or push through a coarse sieve. Add butter, nutmeg, pepper, and eggs and mix well. Stir in grated cheese. Turn the mixture into a heatproof serving dish and make irregular rows mounded to the center, like a little mountain. Place the slices of cheese on top. Brown in a preheated oven (400°F). Makes 6 servings.

Noisette Potatoes

With a French melon-baller, cut peeled potatoes into balls the size of hazelnuts. Fry in butter until golden. Cover and keep in a warm place until ready to serve.

Potato Olives

Cut peeled potatoes into oval shapes the size of olives, using a French oval-shaped scoop. Fry in butter until golden. Cover and keep in a warm place until ready to serve. Allow 4 medium-sized potatoes for 6 servings.

Potatoes Paysanne

12 pearl onions
¼ pound lean salt pork
2 tablespoons butter
1 tablespoon flour
1½ cups bouillon or beef stock

2 pounds (6 medium-sized) potatoes
Freshly ground black pepper
Salt
Chopped parsley

Peel onions and put into a 10-inch skillet. Cut salt pork into strips ½ inch wide and add to onions, along with butter. Cook over medium heat until onions are golden, stirring occasionally. Sprinkle flour over onions; stir and cook until flour has browned lightly. Add bouillon and mix well. Peel potatoes and add. Cover and cook 25 minutes, or until potatoes are tender. Season to taste with pepper and salt. Turn into a serving dish and sprinkle with parsley. Makes 6 servings.

Snow Potatoes

6 medium-large potatoes	1 teaspoon salt
¼ cup (½ stick) butter	Boiling water

Peel potatoes, cut them into large pieces, and put them in a saucepan. Add butter and salt. Pour in boiling water to a depth of ¼ inch. Cover and bring to the boiling point. Remove cover and cook until potatoes are soft and all the water has evaporated. Put potatoes through a potato ricer or push through a coarse sieve. Serve hot. Makes 6 servings.

Soufflé Potatoes

Peel baking potatoes of uniform size and trim the surface so that they will be smooth and regular. Cut potatoes into long narrow slices a scant ⅛ inch thick. Or, if desired, cut them into long pointed ovals a scant ⅛ inch thick. For best results use a potato slicer. Wash the potatoes in cold water and pat them dry thoroughly. Fill a deep-fat frying kettle half full of cooking oil or salad oil, or rendered beef suet. Preheat to 275°F. Drop a few slices of potatoes at a time into the hot fat. With a large perforated spoon, raise the slices, one at a time, from the hot fat for a few seconds and return them to the kettle until they begin to puff, about 7 to 8 minutes. Using a sieve, remove the potatoes from the hot fat, drain them on paper towels, and cool them at least 5 minutes. The second frying may follow immediately, or, if desired, the potatoes may be finished later in the day or even chilled and finished the next day. The potatoes will deflate but will puff again in the second frying.

For final frying, preheat fat to 400°F. Put a few slices at a time into a wire basket or medium-large sieve and lower it into the hot fat. Potatoes will puff into small oval-shaped balloons. Turn the puffs to brown them on all sides. Remove from the fat and drain them on paper towels. Sprinkle with salt and serve immediately. Allow 2 pounds large potatoes for 6 servings.

Swiss Potato Pancake, Roesti, or Potatoes Yvette

1 pound (3 medium-sized) potatoes	½ teaspoon salt
½ cup (1 stick) butter	⅟₁₆ teaspoon freshly ground black pepper

Wash potatoes, peel, cut into juliennes, and rinse under cold running water. Drain well and dry thoroughly between clean towels. Melt butter in a shallow 9-inch skillet. Add potatoes, sprinkle with salt and pepper, mix with the butter, and spread over the bottom of the skillet. Cook until potatoes are brown on the underside. Press potatoes down slightly with a spatula. Slip the spatula under the potatoes and slide them onto a large plate or thin flat lid with the unbrowned side up. Invert the skillet over the unbrowned side, and turn plate and skillet over, letting the potatoes drop into the skillet, with the browned side up. Continue cooking until potatoes are brown. Serve at once. Makes 3 servings.

New Potatoes with Bacon

18 pearl onions, peeled
2 tablespoons butter, melted
2 slices lean bacon
1 cup bouillon
2 tablespoons tomato puree

18 small new potatoes
½ teaspoon salt
½ teaspoon freshly ground black pepper
Chopped parsley

Cook onions in butter until they are lightly browned. Dice bacon, add to onions, and cook until browned. Add bouillon and tomato puree and cook 3 to 4 minutes. Peel potatoes and add to onions, along with salt. Cover and cook 20 minutes, or until potatoes and onions are tender. Add pepper. Serve hot, sprinkled with parsley. Makes 6 servings.

New Potatoes with Hollandaise Sauce

2 pounds small new potatoes
Boiling water
1 teaspoon salt

Ground white pepper
¾ cup Hollandaise Sauce

Pare potatoes and rinse under cold running water. Cook in a saucepan with boiling water and the salt. Cover, bring to the boiling point, and boil 10 to 15 minutes, or until potatoes are tender. Drain and season with pepper to taste. Serve with Hollandaise Sauce. Makes 6 servings.

Potato Croquettes

2 pounds (6 medium-sized) potatoes
Boiling water
1 teaspoon salt
¼ teaspoon freshly ground
    black pepper

3 whole eggs
2 egg yolks
Flour
Fine white breadcrumbs
Oil for frying

Pare and quarter potatoes. Cook until soft in a covered saucepan with boiling water and the salt. Drain potatoes well and put them through a ricer or food mill. Add pepper. Beat

2 of the whole eggs and the egg yolks together until light and foamy, and add to potatoes. Whip the mixture until fluffy. Sprinkle a pastry board lightly with flour and shape the potatoes into pear-shaped croquettes or into balls, using 2 rounded tablespoons of the mixture for each croquette. Beat the remaining egg lightly. Dip croquettes in egg and then roll them in breadcrumbs. Let them stand about 20 minutes and then fry in deep fat preheated to 375°F. Drain on paper towels. Serve hot. Makes 6 servings.

Potato Croquettes with Almonds

Make the recipe for Potato Croquettes. Form the mixture into pear-shaped croquettes or balls, dip them in beaten egg, then roll them in thin blanched almond shavings. Fry in deep fat preheated to 375°F until browned. Drain on paper towels.

Potato Croquettes with Currants and Almonds

Place ½ cup dried currants in a sieve and steam them over boiling water until they are plump. Cool and pat dry thoroughly between towels. Make the recipe for Potato Croquettes and stir in currants. Shape mixture into cakes 2½ inches in diameter and ½ inch thick. Dip cakes in 1 beaten egg, then roll them in ½ cup finely chopped blanched almonds. Let stand 20 minutes. Fry in deep fat preheated to 375°F until browned. Drain on paper towels. Serve with game. Makes 6 servings.

Potato Fritters

3 cups Duchess Potatoes
1 cup Choux Paste
Salt and freshly ground black pepper

Combine the Duchess Potatoes and the Choux Paste, mix well, and add salt and pepper if needed. Put the mixture in a pastry bag with a plain tube and pipe it in rings on buttered paper or buttered aluminum foil. Holding the paper or foil by a corner, slide it into deep fat preheated to 375°F. The rings will slip off; take the paper or foil out. Fry the rings 2 to 3 minutes, or until puffed and brown. Makes about 24 rings.

Potato Gnocchi

The potatoes should be dry and mealy.

1 pound (3 medium-sized) potatoes
3 large egg yolks
½ teaspoon salt
½ cup sifted all-purpose flour

¼ cup (½ stick) butter, melted
1½ cups grated Parmesan cheese
2 quarts boiling water
¼ cup melted butter

Boil potatoes in their jackets, then peel and mash until smooth. Beat in egg yolks and salt. Continue beating until potatoes are fluffy. Stir in flour, butter, and ½ cup of the cheese. Shape into 1½-inch balls on a lightly floured board. Flatten them slightly. Poach about one-fourth of the balls at a time in 2 quarts boiling water 5 minutes. As they are cooked, arrange them in layers in a buttered 1½-quart casserole, sprinkling grated cheese between the layers and over the top. Drizzle with melted butter. Bake in a preheated oven (400°F) 10 to 15 minutes, or until top is browned. Makes 6 servings.

Potato Dumplings with Cheese or Knepfes

Make the recipe for Potato Gnocchi. Shape the mixture into balls and fry in butter until golden brown. Serve sprinkled with grated Gruyère or Parmesan cheese. Makes 6 servings.

Potato Pancakes or Galettes

Potato pancakes should be cooked as soon as they are mixed to prevent the batter from turning dark.

¼ cup all-purpose flour	⅛ teaspoon freshly ground black pepper
1½ pounds potatoes	1 large egg
1 tablespoon grated onion	1 tablespoon chopped parsley (optional)
1 teaspoon salt	Olive oil, salad oil, or butter

Put flour into a mixing bowl. Peel the potatoes and grate over the flour, using a fine grater. Add onion, salt, pepper, egg, and parsley, if desired. Mix quickly and well. Grease a heavy-bottomed 9- or 10-inch skillet with oil or butter and heat until hot. Drop 2 heaping tablespoons of the mixture at a time on the hot skillet. Fry until pancakes are brown on the underside. Turn and brown the other side, adding more oil or butter as needed. Drain on paper towels. Serve hot as a vegetable with roasts. Makes about 15 pancakes.

Potato Soufflé

2 cups smooth mashed potatoes	2 teaspoons water
½ cup hot milk	¾ cup grated Gruyère
¾ teaspoon salt	1 large whole egg
¼ teaspoon freshly ground black pepper	2 large eggs, separated
1 tablespoon minced onion	

Combine mashed potatoes with the next 5 ingredients. Beat until fluffy. Add the cheese. Beat whole egg and egg yolks together and add to potato mixture. Mix well. Beat the 2 egg whites until they stand in soft peaks, and carefully fold into the potatoes. Butter only the bottom of a 1-quart casserole and put in the mixture. Bake in a preheated oven (350°F) 45 minutes, or until the soufflé is well puffed and the top is flecked with brown. Serve at once. Makes 6 servings.

SALSIFY (SALSIFIS)

Salsify, of which the root is the edible portion, is also called oyster plant.

Deep-Fried Salsify

2 pounds salsify
White Court Bouillon for Vegetables
2 tablespoons chopped parsley
2 tablespoons lemon juice
1 tablespoon olive oil

½ teaspoon salt
⅛ teaspoon freshly ground black pepper
Fritter Batter
Fried parsley

Wash and pare salsify, dropping them into the court bouillon as they are scraped to prevent discoloration. Remove and cut into 3-inch pieces. Bring court bouillon to the boiling point, return the salsify to the court bouillon, and cook about 5 minutes. Transfer salsify to a bowl, add the next 5 ingredients, mix well, and marinate 30 minutes. Drain. Dip pieces of salsify in Fritter Batter, and deep fry until brown in fat preheated to 375°F. Drain on paper towels. Garnish with dried parsley. Makes 6 servings.

White Court Bouillon for Vegetables

Mix 2 tablespoons flour with ½ cup water to a smooth paste. Add 4 cups vegetable stock, mix, and strain through a fine sieve. Add 1 teaspoon salt, and 1½ tablespoons lemon juice. Boil 3 to 4 minutes.

Salsify with Herbs

2 pounds salsify
White Court Bouillon for Vegetables
¼ cup (½ stick) butter

2 teaspoons chopped fresh thyme
Salt and freshly ground black pepper
2 tablespoons chopped parsley

Wash, pare, and cut salsify and cook in White Court Bouillon for Vegetables, as instructed in the recipe for Deep-Fried Salsify. Rinse well in water. Sauté in hot butter. Toss with thyme, salt, and pepper. Turn into a serving dish and sprinkle with parsley. Makes 6 servings.

SORREL (OSEILLE)

SORREL CAN BE COOKED or the young leaves used in salads.

Buttered Sorrel

Wash 2 pounds sorrel, changing the water several times. Finely shred. Melt 3 tablespoons butter in a 2-quart saucepan, add sorrel, cover, and cook until wilted, using only the water that clings to the leaves. Remove cover, and shake the pan over medium-low heat until all liquid has evaporated. Season to taste with salt and freshly ground black pepper and ½ teaspoon sugar. Add a little heavy cream if sorrel is too acid. Makes 6 servings.

SPINACH (EPINARDS)

Creamed Spinach with Hard-Cooked Eggs

2 pounds fresh spinach	¼ teaspoon grated nutmeg
4 tablespoons (½ stick) butter	1 teaspoon lemon juice
¼ teaspoon salt	1 cup Soubise Sauce
½ teaspoon sugar	½ cup milk or light cream
¼ teaspoon freshly ground black pepper	2 hard-cooked eggs

Wash and cook the spinach in salted, boiling water only until spinach is wilted. Remove cover, press out water from spinach, and shake the pan over medium-low heat to evaporate liquid. Finely chop spinach and heat with 2 tablespoons of the butter 2 to 3 minutes. Stir. Season with the next 5 ingredients. Add the spinach to the Soubise and cream and heat. Transfer spinach to a serving dish. Cut eggs into quarters or eighths and arrange over the top. Makes 6 servings.

Spinach Loaf with Velouté Sauce

2 pounds cooked fresh spinach	1½ teaspoons chopped fresh thyme
1 cup soft white breadcrumbs	½ teaspoon freshly ground black pepper
2 cups Soubise Sauce	2 hard-cooked eggs, sliced
2 eggs, separated	Velouté Sauce
1 teaspoon salt	

Press the water out of the spinach, draining it into a cup, and reserve. Finely chop spinach, add breadcrumbs, and set aside. Add spinach and crumbs to the Soubise. Beat egg yolks lightly and add, along with the salt, thyme, and pepper. Mix well. Beat egg whites until they stand in soft peaks, and fold them into the mixture. Turn into a buttered 9-by-5-by-3-inch loaf pan. Bake in a preheated oven (375°F) 40 minutes, or until a knife inserted in the center comes out clean. Let stand in the pan 10 minutes. Unmold onto a serving platter and garnish with hard-cooked eggs. To serve, cut into ½-inch slices. Serve with Velouté Sauce in a separate bowl. Spinach Loaf may also be served with Cheese Sauce. Makes about 8 servings.

TOMATOES (TOMATES)

Tomatoes Algerian Style

8 medium-large tomatoes	1 medium-sized eggplant
Olive or salad oil	¼ to ⅓ cup olive oil
Salt and freshly ground black pepper	1 small clove garlic, crushed

Wash tomatoes, cut them in half, and scoop out the centers, leaving the shells intact. (Save centers for salad.) Sprinkle the cavities with oil, salt, and pepper. Place shells in a baking pan and cook in a preheated oven (350°F) 12 to 15 minutes, being sure that they do not lose their shape. Wash eggplant, peel, and cut into slices ½ inch thick. Sprinkle with salt and set aside for 30 minutes. Wipe salt and moisture from eggplant and fry in hot oil, browning both sides. Finely chop the cooked eggplant. Cook garlic in a little oil about 2 minutes and add to eggplant. Season to taste with salt and pepper. Stuff into the tomato shells. Arrange in a baking pan and heat 5 to 10 minutes in a preheated moderate oven (350°F). Makes 8 servings.

Tomato and Eggplant Casserole

2 medium-sized eggplants	1 small clove garlic, crushed
Salt	⅛ teaspoon freshly ground black pepper
Flour	1 cup soft white breadcrumbs
⅓ cup olive oil	3 tablespoons butter, melted
6 medium-sized tomatoes	½ cup grated Parmesan cheese

Wash and peel eggplant and cut into crosswise slices ½ inch thick. Sprinkle with salt and set aside for 30 minutes. Wipe salt off the slices, dredge them in flour, and fry in oil, browning both sides. Wash, peel, seed, and dice the tomatoes, and cook in 1 tablespoon oil, along with the garlic, pepper, and salt to taste. Arrange alternating layers of eggplant slices and tomato mixture in a 10-by-6-by-2-inch baking dish, having eggplant on the bottom and tomatoes on the top. Blend soft breadcrumbs with butter and sprinkle over the top. Sprinkle with cheese. Bake in a preheated oven (375°F) 25 minutes, or until crumbs are brown. Makes 6 servings.

Tomatoes Mireille

1 medium-sized eggplant	1 small clove garlic, crushed
Salt	2 tablespoons chopped parsley
Flour	2 fresh basil leaves
About ½ cup olive oil	¹⁄₁₆ teaspoon freshly ground black pepper
6 medium-sized tomatoes	

Wash eggplant, peel, and slice ¼ inch thick. Sprinkle the slices with salt and set aside for 30 minutes. Wipe salt off the slices and dredge them in flour. Sauté in oil, browning both sides. Keep warm. Wash, peel, quarter, and seed tomatoes and cook them 5 to 8 minutes in a separate saucepan in 1 tablespoon of the oil, along with the garlic, parsley, and basil. Add pepper and salt to taste. Arrange eggplant slices in a circle in a round serving plate. Pour the tomato mixture into the center. Sprinkle with additional chopped parsley, if desired. Makes 6 servings.

Duchess Tomatoes

6 medium-sized tomatoes
Salt and freshly ground black pepper
Duchess Potatoes made from
    1 pound (4 medium) potatoes

¼ cup grated Parmesan cheese
1 tablespoon melted butter

Wash and dry tomatoes and cut in half. Scoop out the centers and sprinkle the cavities lightly with salt and pepper. Invert on a tray to drain well. Fill a pastry bag with Duchess Potatoes and pipe into the tomatoes, heaping them over the top. Sprinkle with cheese. Brush with melted butter. Brown in a preheated oven (450°F). Makes 6 servings.

Tomatoes Stuffed with Meat

6 medium-large tomatoes
Salt and freshly ground black pepper
2 slices crustless bread, crumbled
Water
½ cup chopped onion
2 tablespoons butter
1½ cups finely chopped cooked beef,
    veal, or mutton

2 tablespoons chopped parsley
1 small clove garlic, crushed
1 cup soft breadcrumbs
½ cup grated Parmesan cheese
Olive oil

Wash tomatoes, cut in half, and scoop out centers. Reserve ½ cup of the centers for use in the stuffing and save the rest for another use. Sprinkle inside of the tomato shells with salt and pepper and invert them to drain well. Soak bread in water about 5 minutes, squeeze it dry, and fluff it with a fork. Cook onion in butter until limp. Add bread, ½ cup tomato centers, the meat, parsley, garlic, and salt and pepper to taste. Stuff into the tomato shells. Sprinkle tops with breadcrumbs, cheese, and a few drops of oil. Arrange in a baking pan and bake in a preheated oven (350°F) 30 to 40 minutes, or until done. Makes 6 servings.

Mushroom-Stuffed Tomatoes Hussarde

6 medium-large tomatoes
Salt and freshly ground black pepper
½ cup chopped onion
Olive oil, pure vegetable oil, or butter
½ cup soft breadcrumbs

1 cup chopped cooked ham
1½ cups finely chopped mushrooms
2 tablespoons chopped parsley
Parsley leaves

Wash tomatoes, cut in half, and scoop out centers. (Save centers for another use.) Sprinkle inside of tomato shells with salt and pepper and invert them to drain well. Cook onion in 2 tablespoons oil or butter, add breadcrumbs, stir, and cook 1 minute. Add next 3 ingredients and salt and pepper to taste. Mix well and cook 2 to 3 minutes. Stuff into tomato shells. Sprinkle the top of each with a little oil. Arrange tomatoes in a large baking dish. Bake in a preheated oven (350°F) 15 minutes, or only until tomatoes are heated through. Garnish each with a parsley leaf. Makes 6 servings.

Tomatoes Portuguese Style

3 pounds (8 medium-large) tomatoes
2 tablespoons olive oil or salad oil
2 shallots, chopped
1 small clove garlic, crushed
1 tablespoon meat glaze

Salt
Freshly ground black pepper
½ cup soft white breadcrumbs
Chopped parsley

Wash tomatoes. Peel or not, as desired. Remove seeds and sauté tomatoes in hot oil 5 to 8 minutes. Add the next 6 ingredients and cook 1 minute. Turn into a serving dish and sprinkle with parsley. Makes 6 servings.

Tomatoes Stuffed with Spinach

6 medium-sized firm tomatoes
½ teaspoon salt
1 pound spinach
2 tablespoons butter
¾ teaspoon salt

⅛ teaspoon freshly ground black pepper
1 tablespoon minced onion
¼ cup soft white breadcrumbs
Hollandaise Sauce

Wash tomatoes, cut in half crosswise, and scoop out centers. (Save centers for another use.) Sprinkle tomato cavities with salt. Invert tomatoes on a tray to drain well. Wash spinach and cook with butter in a covered saucepan until spinach wilts. Remove spinach from heat and chop medium-fine. Add the next 4 ingredients, mix well, and stuff into the tomato cavities. Place tomatoes in an 11-by-7-by-1½-inch baking pan. Bake in a preheated oven (350°F) 15-20 minutes. Serve with Hollandaise Sauce. Makes 6 servings.

TURNIPS (NAVETS)

Turnips in Cream Sauce

2¼ pounds turnips
Salt
Boiling water
2 tablespoons butter

¼ cup light cream
⅛ teaspoon freshly ground black pepper

Wash, peel, and slice turnips. Cook in boiling, salted water for 10 minutes or until tender. Drain off water. Toss turnips gently in the butter. Add cream and boil gently for 2 minutes or until the sauce thickens. Add salt to taste and the pepper. Makes 6 servings.

Glazed Turnips

2½ pounds turnips
½ teaspoon salt
Boiling water
1 cup boiling beef bouillon or stock

3 tablespoons butter
⅛ teaspoon ground white pepper
Chopped parsley

Wash, peel, and slice turnips. Place in a saucepan with the salt and enough boiling water to cover. Bring to the boiling point and boil, uncovered, 5 minutes. Drain off water. Add boiling bouillon or stock. Cover and cook 10 minutes. Remove cover and cook until all but 2 to 3 tablespoons of the liquid has evaporated. Add 2 tablespoons of the butter. Shake the pan over medium-low heat until turnips are glazed. Add remaining 1 tablespoon butter and the white pepper. Toss lightly. Sprinkle with parsley. Serve around a roast. Makes 6 servings.

Stewed Turnips

2½ pounds turnips
2 to 3 tablespoons butter
1 tablespoon flour
½ cup chopped onion

1 cup bouillon or beef stock
¼ teaspoon freshly ground black pepper
Salt
1 tablespoon butter

Wash and peel turnips and cut into crosswise slices ¼ inch thick. Brown slices on both sides in hot butter. Sprinkle with flour and onion. Cook over medium-low heat until onion is limp, stirring frequently. Add bouillon or stock. Cook, uncovered, 5 minutes. Add pepper, salt to taste, and butter. Makes 16 servings.

Yellow Turnip Balls with Salt Pork

4 thin slices salt pork
1½ cups water
1 pound yellow turnips

½ teaspoon salt
2 tablespoons butter
Dash freshly ground black pepper

Cook salt pork in water in a covered saucepan 15 minutes. Peel turnips, cut into balls with a French melon-baller and add to the salt pork. Add salt. Cook, uncovered, 15 to 20 minutes, or until turnips are tender. Drain off water and toss the turnip balls lightly with butter and pepper. Serve with the salt pork. Makes 4 servings.

ZUCCHINI (COURGETTES)

Fried Zucchini

Select small zucchini, wash, and cut into lengthwise slices ½ inch thick. Sprinkle with salt and let stand 15 minutes. Dry the slices with a towel, dredge them in flour, and fry until brown in deep fat preheated to 375°F. Drain on paper towels and serve immediately. Allow 3 or 4 slices per person.

Zucchini Fritters

3 small zucchini
Salt
1 cup sifted all-purpose flour
1 egg, lightly beaten

¾ cup milk
1 tablespoon butter, melted
Oil for frying

Wash zucchini and cut into crosswise slices ½ inch thick. Sprinkle with salt and let stand 15 minutes. Drain and pat dry with a clean towel. Meanwhile, sift flour with ½ teaspoon salt into a mixing bowl. Add egg, milk, and butter and mix well. Dip zucchini slices in the batter, one by one, and fry until browned in deep fat preheated to 375°F. Drain on paper towels. Serve hot. These fritters may be fried ahead of time and reheated in the oven just before serving. Makes 6 servings.

Milanese Stuffed Zucchini

5 small zucchini
½ cup chopped onion
2 tablespoons butter
1 cup Béchamel Sauce

¼ pound bitter-almond macaroons
Salt and freshly ground black pepper
Grated Parmesan cheese

Wash zucchini, cut in half lengthwise, and cook 6 minutes in 1 inch boiling water and ½ teaspoon salt. Drain off water and rinse with cold water. Invert zucchini on a tray to drain well. Scoop out centers, being careful not to damage the skins. Chop centers. Cook onion in the butter until limp. Mix with zucchini centers. Stir and cook the mixture 3 minutes. Add Béchamel Sauce and simmer 1 to 2 minutes. Heat macaroons in a preheated oven (300°F) 10 minutes. Cool. Roll a few at a time in a paper or plastic bag with a rolling pin to form fine crumbs. Mix the crumbs with the zucchini mixture. Season to taste with salt and pepper. Put mixture in a pastry bag fitted with a star tube and pipe into the zucchini shells. Sprinkle with cheese. Brown in a preheated oven (450°F). Makes 10 servings.

Zucchini Stuffed with Mushrooms

6 small zucchini	2 tablespoons chopped parsley
Salt	Freshly ground black pepper
Oil for frying	1 cup soft white breadcrumbs
Chopped mushrooms	Grated Parmesan cheese
½ small clove garlic, crushed	Tomato Sauce
3 tablespoons olive oil	

Cut zucchini in half lengthwise. Make small cuts about ¼ inch deep and ½ inch wide all around the edge and a few in the cut surface. Sprinkle with salt and allow to stand 15 minutes. Drain, wipe off the salt, and fry in deep fat preheated to 350°F. Drain on paper towels. Scoop out centers, being careful not to break the skins. Measure the scooped-out centers and then measure an equal amount of mushrooms. Cook mushrooms and garlic in 1 tablespoon oil until mushrooms are tender. Add to the scooped-out zucchini, along with parsley. Season to taste with salt and pepper. Stuff the mixture into the zucchini shells. Mix breadcrumbs with 2 tablespoons oil and sprinkle over the tops. Sprinkle with cheese. Brown in a preheated oven (375°F). Serve Tomato Sauce in a sauceboat. Makes 6 servings.

Stuffed Zucchini Orientale

⅓ cup finely chopped onion	1 clove garlic, crushed
4 to 5 tablespoons olive oil	4 medium-sized tomatoes
½ cup long-grained rice	1 cup diced cooked lamb
1 cup chicken or veal stock	6 small zucchini
½ teaspoon salt	Grated Parmesan cheese
¼ teaspoon freshly ground	1 cup soft white breadcrumbs
black pepper	2 tablespoons butter, melted

Cook onion until limp in 2 tablespoons of the oil. Add rice and stir and cook 3 to 4 minutes. Add the next 4 ingredients. Peel, seed, and dice tomatoes and add. Cover, bring to the boiling point, reduce heat, and simmer 12 to 15 minutes. Add lamb and set aside. Wash zucchini, cut in half lengthwise, and remove and discard seeds. Place zucchini, cut side down, in a baking pan. Pour 2 to 3 tablespoons oil in the pan. Bake in a preheated oven (400°F) 10 minutes, or until about halfway done. Remove from the oven. Carefully scoop out the centers and add them to the rice and lamb. Spoon the mixture into the zucchini shells, mounding it over the top. Sprinkle with grated cheese. Blend breadcrumbs and butter and sprinkle over squash. Arrange in baking pan and bake in a preheated oven (350°F) 20 minutes, or until crumbs are brown. Makes 6 servings.

Zucchini Vaucluse Style

3 small zucchini	1 small clove garlic, crushed
Salt	2 tablespoons chopped parsley
Flour	⅛ teaspoon freshly ground black pepper
Olive oil	½ teaspoon chopped oregano
4 medium-sized tomatoes	1 cup soft breadcrumbs

Wash, peel, and cut zucchini lengthwise into quarters. Sprinkle with salt and let stand 15 minutes. Wipe off salt, dredge in flour, and fry in shallow hot oil, turning to brown all sides. Place zucchini side by side in rows in a 10-by-6-by-2-inch baking dish. Peel, seed, and dice tomatoes, and cook 5 minutes in 2 tablespoons hot oil, adding salt to taste, garlic, parsley, pepper, and oregano. Spread over zucchini. Mix breadcrumbs with 2 tablespoons oil and sprinkle over the tomatoes. Cook in a preheated oven (350°F) 30 minutes, or until crumbs are brown. Makes 6 servings.

Ratatouille Niçoise

2 small zucchini	¼ cup olive oil
1 small eggplant	1 clove garlic, crushed
4 medium-sized tomatoes	¼ teaspoon freshly ground black pepper
2 red or green bell peppers	Salt
½ cup sliced onions	Chopped parsley

Cut zucchini and eggplant into slices ⅛ inch thick. Peel and dice tomatoes. Remove seeds and pith from peppers and cut them into strips. Sauté onion in oil until onion begins to turn golden. Add tomatoes and cook 1 minute, then add zucchini, eggplant, peppers, garlic, and seasonings. Cover, bring to the boiling point, and cook 1 to 2 minutes. Remove cover and cook until all the liquid has evaporated, stirring occasionally. Turn into a serving dish and sprinkle with parsley. Makes 6 servings.

SALADS

THERE ARE TWO GENERAL CLASSES OF FRENCH SALADS: those made with predominantly leafy greens, and those made up of a combination of several raw or cooked ingredients, which is called a "composed" salad.

Whatever the leaves being used—Boston or romaine, endives or chicory (green chicory, curly endive, Belgian endive, radicchio and Treviso, escarole, and so on), the leaves should be washed in cold water (iced water for greens from the summer garden), spun dry, and stored first in towels and then in a plastic bag in the refrigerator to become crisp. One should avoid any leaves of the cabbage or kale family or arugula rocket in fresh salads unless that is the dominant taste one wants to achieve. And one does not need, however occasionally fashionable, a chilled bowl or, even less necessary, chilled salad-tossing implements. A wooden bowl, though tactile and visually pleasing, is not good for salads in the long run, since they will sooner or later turn rancid. Use glass, which has the added advantage of more visual appeal.

All the leaf salad needs is the addition of fresh herb leaves, a simple sauce, and perhaps some hard-cooked eggs or little garlic toasts. The guidelines for saucing are quite simple: the power of the sauce must match the strength of the flavor of the greens. For example, hazelnut, walnut, and almond oils and any of the family of chicory or endive, and arugula is a marriage made in heaven. For the dressing, the general rule of three parts oil to one part acid is not fixed; rather it is a formula that ranges from three to five parts oil to one part acid. A salad of delicate Boston lettuce needs little acid in relation to the oil used (five parts oil to one part acid) and it should be a mild oil at that—not one of the green, peppery oils that are more suited to bitter greens, tomatoes, bread, and grilled or roasted vegetables. The leaves should always be tossed with the sauce or dressing at the last moment. The tastes achieved by pouring the sauce over the greens set on individual plates can never reach the satisfaction level of greens tossed with a dressing in a large bowl and then served out onto individual plates.

The rules for saucing compound salads are to let the power of the oils and acids used match the strength of the flavor of the foods in the salad and, most important, to dress and marinate all the ingredients. The preparation of a Salade Niçoise is a perfect example. Assembling the potatoes, eggs, green beans, lettuce leaves, olives, anchovies, and tuna and then pouring some vinaigrette over them can never achieve the potential of this glorious salad. But if you use the juices from the best-quality tuna (cooked at home or from the jar or can) to make a dressing, then pour it over the hot potatoes just after they are drained from boiling, and let the potatoes marinate in some of that sauce for a few hours as they cool, and then use that same dressing to toss with all the other ingredients separately before assembling the salad, you will have a truly sublime and wonderful Niçoise.

If the salad comes at the beginning of a menu, and is to be followed by other dishes, it should be milder in flavor than what follows it. If, on the other hand, the salad follows a rich roast or braised meat, the dressing and salad ingredients can be more strongly flavored.

Andalusian Rice Salad

2 cups cold cooked rice
4 tablespoons Vinaigrette Sauce
1 teaspoon paprika
1 tablespoon finely chopped onion
2 tablespoons chopped parsley

A very small bit of crushed garlic
2 medium-sized roasted red bell pepper,
   seeded, skinned, and julienned
3 medium-sized tomatoes, quartered
Chopped chervil

Toss rice lightly in 3 tablespoons of the Vinaigrette and the next 5 ingredients. Arrange in a mound in the center of a serving dish. Toss in the remaining Vinaigrette with the tomatoes, and arrange in clusters around the rice, alternating with tomato wedges. Sprinkle rice with chervil. Makes 6 servings.

Potato and White Asparagus Salad Argenteuil

2 cups finely diced cooked potatoes
½ cup cooked peas
½ cup Mayonnaise
2 tablespoons chopped chervil
Salt and freshly ground black pepper

12 cooked white asparagus tips, 2 inches long
2 tablespoons Vinaigrette Sauce
Shredded lettuce
3 hard-cooked eggs, quartered

Mix potatoes and peas lightly with Mayonnaise and chervil. Season to taste with salt and pepper. Arrange in a mound in the center of a serving dish. Marinate asparagus tips in Vinaigrette and arrange them over the top of the mound. Surround with shredded lettuce and the eggs. Makes 6 servings.

Artichoke Salad à la Grecque

12 small tender artichokes
Freshly squeezed lemon juice or
   lemon slices
Boiling water
12 small tender carrots
12 pearl onions, peeled
2 cups water
¾ cup wine vinegar
¼ cup freshly squeezed lemon juice
½ cup olive oil

1 teaspoon salt
1 small bay leaf
6 whole peppercorns
6 coriander seeds
1 tablespoon chopped fresh thyme
18 small mushroom caps
Black olives
Pimento-stuffed green olives

Cut off and discard the top third of each artichoke. Pull off and discard all tough outer leaves. Trim off prickly ends of the leaves. Cut stems even with the base and rub lemon juice over the cut surfaces to prevent discoloration. Place artichokes in a saucepan with enough boiling water to cover them generously. Add carrots and onions. Bring to the boiling point and cook 5 minutes. Drain vegetables and set them aside. Place 2 cups water and next 5 ingredients in a 1½-quart saucepan. Tie spices in a cheesecloth bag and add to the vinegar mixture. Bring mixture to the boiling point and pour over blanched vegetables. Cover and cook over low heat 25 minutes. Wash mushroom caps and add to hot mixture. Continue cooking 10 minutes, or until all the vegetables are done. Cool vegetables in marinade. Remove and discard the spice bag. Cut artichokes into quarters and remove and discard the chokes. Slice carrots thickly. Transfer vegetables to a salad bowl. Arrange onions and black and green olives around the edge and on top. Chill and serve as an hors d'oeuvre. Makes 6 servings.

Green Bean Salad Beatrice

1½ pounds green beans, cooked	Watercress
¼ cup Vinaigrette Sauce	2 hard-cooked egg yolks, chopped
3 medium-large tomatoes	

Mix green beans with ¾ of the Vinaigrette. Turn into a serving dish. Slice tomatoes, toss with the remaining sauce, and place the slices on small bunches of watercress, and arrange them around the beans. Sprinkle with egg yolk. Makes 6 servings.

Chicory and Dandelion Warm Salad with Bacon

Chicory and Belgian endive are related though very different-looking plants, of which the nomeclature is badly confused. The salad plant with crisp curly green and white leaves is called endive in England and *chicorée* in France and is usually known as chicory in the United States, while the plant known as endive in the latter two countries is called chicory in England; and in Belgium, where it is widely grown (hence Belgian endive), it is called *chicorée de Bruxelles*. To confuse the situation further, the two names are sometimes reversed, both in the United States and in England.

6 slices bacon or salt pork, diced	1 quart washed and dried chicory
2 tablespoons wine vinegar	1 quart washed and dried dandelion greens
Freshly ground black pepper	

Cook bacon or salt pork until lightly browned. Drain off and discard half of the drippings. Add vinegar and pepper to bacon and remaining drippings. Heat 30 seconds. Mix the greens in a salad bowl and toss lightly but thoroughly with the bacon mixture. Serve immediately. Makes 6 servings.

Truffled Celery Root Salad Beaucaire

Boiling water
2 cups coarsely julienned celery root
½ teaspoon salt, plus additional
2 cups thinly sliced celery
2 medium-sized potatoes, cooked
⅓ cup Mayonnaise
1 truffle, chopped

Ground white pepper
1 medium-sized beet, cooked
4 tablespoons Vinaigrette Sauce
2 medium-sized tomatoes, sliced
Lettuce hearts
Walnut halves

Blanch the celery root in enough boiling water to cover, with ½ teaspoon salt. Drain and rinse under cold running water and drain again. Pat dry and add to celery. Finely dice potatoes and add to celery, along with Mayonnaise, truffle, and salt and white pepper to taste. Mix gently but thoroughly. Turn into a salad bowl and shape into a mound. Cut beet into long, narrow strips, toss in 2 tablespoons of the Vinaigrette, and arrange them in pairs around the mound. Dress the tomatoes in the remaining sauce and arrange them overlapping, in a circle in the top center of the salad. Top tomatoes with a heart of lettuce. Garnish the top of the salad with walnut halves. Makes 6 servings.

Potato and Cauliflower Salad Marguerite

2 cups diced cooked potatoes
1 cup cooked cauliflower, small pieces
1 cup cooked green beans cut
    into 1-inch pieces
1 cup cooked asparagus tips

9 tablespoons Vinaigrette Sauce
Salt and freshly ground black pepper
Mayonnaise
3 hard-cooked eggs

Put each vegetable in a separate bowl and mix with Vinaigrette, using 3 tablespoons for the potatoes and 2 tablespoons each for the other vegetables. Marinate 1 hour. Season vegetables with salt and pepper to taste. Put the potatoes in a salad bowl and arrange the other vegetables in separate layers on top of the potatoes. Cover the top layer completely with Mayonnaise. Make a large daisy for the center of the top and smaller daisies in a circle around the mound of salad by cutting strips of egg whites to simulate the petals and mixing the mashed egg yolks with a little Mayonnaise to make the centers. Makes 8 servings.

Curly Endive Salad Mercédès

4 cups creamy-white centers of
    curly endive or chicory
2 hard-cooked eggs
⅓ cup olive oil
2 tablespoons freshly squeezed
    lemon juice

½ teaspoon salt
⅛ teaspoon freshly ground black pepper
2 tablespoons chopped parsley
1 tablespoon chopped fresh chervil
1½ cups julienned celery
1½ cups julienned cooked beets

Tear chicory into small pieces and place in a salad bowl. Finely chop eggs and mix with the next 6 ingredients. Pour over chicory and toss lightly. Wipe the sides of the salad bowl. Arrange celery and beets in alternating nests in a circle over the top of the chicory. Makes 6 servings.

Russian Salad Mimosa

1 cup cooked green beans cut into 1-inch pieces	10 tablespoons Mayonnaise
1 cup diced cooked potatoes	Salt and freshly ground black pepper
1 cup diced cooked carrots	1 hard-cooked egg, chopped
1 cup diced cooked turnips	Chopped parsley
1 cup cooked green peas	Truffles or black olives, chopped
	Shredded raw beet

Mix each vegetable separately with 2 tablespoons Mayonnaise, and salt and pepper to taste. Mound each vegetable separately in one salad bowl. Sprinkle the beans with chopped egg white; the potatoes with chopped egg yolk; the carrots with parsley; the turnips with truffles or black olives; the peas with beets. Makes 8 to 10 servings.

Lettuce Salad Mimosa

In France, a small crust of bread rubbed with garlic is sometimes mixed with salad greens to impart a delicate flavor of garlic to the salad. This is called a *chapon*.

½ head romaine lettuce	Salt and freshly ground black pepper
½ head iceberg lettuce	⅓ cup Vinaigrette Sauce
1 head Boston lettuce	3 hard-cooked egg yolks
Chapon	

Wash, drain, and dry all the lettuce thoroughly. Tear into bite-size pieces, place in a salad bowl with the chapon, and sprinkle with salt and pepper to taste. Add Vinaigrette and toss. Sprinkle with hard-cooked egg yolk rubbed through a coarse sieve. Makes 6 to 8 servings.

Mixed Vegetable Salad Macedoine

1 cup cooked green beans cut into 1-inch pieces	2 cooked artichoke bottoms, diced
1 cup diced cooked carrots	½ cup Mayonnaise
½ cup diced cooked turnip	Salt and freshly ground black pepper
½ cup cooked green peas	2 medium-sized beets, cooked
1½ cups diced cooked potatoes	2 hard-cooked eggs, sliced

Combine the first 7 ingredients. Season to taste with salt and pepper. Turn mixture into a salad bowl and round it over the top. Peel and slice beets. Arrange beet slices and egg slices over the top as desired. Makes 8 to 10 servings.

Waldorf Salad

2 cups diced celery
Boiling and cold water
2½ cups diced apples
1 teaspoon freshly squeezed
    lemon juice

Dash salt
½ cup Mayonnaise
½ cup hazelnuts or English walnuts, toasted

Blanch celery in boiling water 1 minute. Shock in cold water. Drain thoroughly. Add to apples, along with lemon juice and salt and let the mixture stand 1 hour. Add Mayonnaise and mix well. Turn into a salad bowl. Slice nuts and sprinkle them over the top. Makes 6 servings.

Salad Niçoise

2 cups diced cold cooked potatoes
2 cups cold cooked green beans cut
    into 1-inch pieces
Vinaigrette Sauce
Salt and freshly ground black pepper
1 clove garlic

3 tomatoes, quartered
3 hard-cooked egg, quartered
1 (6-ounce) can tuna chunks
Pitted ripe olives
6 to 12 anchovies

Toss the potatoes and green beans with the Vinaigrette and season to taste with salt and pepper. Rub the inside of a salad bowl with a cut clove of garlic. Turn potatoes and beans into the bowl. Decorate the salad with tomato quarters interspersed with egg, chunks of tuna, olives, and anchovies, all tossed individually in a little Vinaigrette and juices of the tuna. Makes 6 servings.

Parisian Lobster and Green Bean Salad

1 cup diced cooked carrots
1 cup cooked green beans cut into
    1-inch pieces
½ cup cooked green peas
1 cup diced cooked lobster meat
½ cup Mayonnaise

1 teaspoon freshly squeezed lemon juice
Salt and freshly ground black pepper
1 cup chopped tomato
4 tablespoons Vinaigrette Sauce
2 hard-cooked eggs, sliced
4 lettuce hearts, washed, thoroughly dried

Combine the first 6 ingredients. Add salt and pepper to taste. Turn the mixture into a salad bowl and round it over the top. Toss the tomato in some Vinaigrette and place in the center of the mound. Arrange the slices of egg around the edge. Dress the lettuce hearts in Vinaigrette and arrange them in a circle over the top of the salad, alternating with slices of egg. Makes 8 servings.

Asparagus, Artichoke and Mushroom Salad Rachel

½ pound mushrooms, poached
6 artichoke bottoms, cooked
½ pound asparagus
6 tablespoons olive oil

6 teaspoons white wine vinegar
Salt
Freshly ground black pepper
3 tablespoons port

Thinly slice mushrooms and artichoke bottoms and set them aside in separate bowls. Cut asparagus, except the tips, into small pieces and cook in boiling, salted water, with the tips, until crisp-tender. Drain and turn into a small bowl. Marinate each vegetable separately in 2 tablespoons oil, 2 teaspoons vinegar, salt, dash pepper, and 1 tablespoon port. Arrange all the vegetables in separate mounds in a salad bowl. Garnish the top of each mound with an asparagus tip. Makes 6 servings.

SALAD DRESSINGS

THE TRUE BASIC SALAD DRESSING *assaisonnement* of France is Vinaigrette Sauce, which consists of a mixture of three parts olive oil and one part good wine vinegar seasoned with salt and pepper and, sometimes, with mustard and herbs. To this base other ingredients, such as capers, anchovies, olives, and so on, may be added to create a wide variety of interesting dressings. The use of garlic in French salad dressings is usually confined to southern France.

The recipes for Mayonnaise and related dressings used in combination salads appear in chapter 3.

Vinaigrette Sauce

The wine vinegar here may be replaced with freshly squeezed lemon juice.
2 tablespoons wine vinegar
¼ teaspoon salt
⅛ teaspoon freshly ground black pepper
1 teaspoon Dijon mustard (optional)

6 tablespoons light olive oil, or pure vegetable oil
1 tablespoon chopped parsley and/or other fresh herbs, such as chervil, hives, basil, tarragon, thyme, marjoram

Place vinegar, or lemon juice, salt, pepper, and, if desired, mustard mixture in a small mixing bowl. Beat vigorously with a fork or wire whip. Gradually whisk in the oil. If using fresh herbs, add them just before tossing the dressing with the salad. Makes about ½ cup.

Anchovy Vinaigrette

To ½ cup Vinaigrette made without salt, add 1 anchovy, finely chopped, 1 teaspoon minced shallot, and 1 tablespoon minced chives. Mix well. Use with salad greens, endive, celery, or cold cooked vegetables. Makes about ⅔ cup.

Lorenzo Vinaigrette

To 1½ cups Vinaigrette add ¼ cup chile sauce, ⅓ cup finely chopped watercress leaves, and 2 teaspoons finely chopped onion. Mix well and let stand 30 minutes before using. Makes a generous 2 cups.

New Orleans Vinaigrette

To ½ cup Vinaigrette, add 1 teaspoon hot Creole mustard and ½ teaspoon Worcestershire sauce. Mix well and let stand at least 30 minutes before using. Makes a generous ½ cup.

Vinaigrette Niçoise

To ½ cup Vinaigrette, made without salt, add 1 teaspoon each capers, chopped anchovies, and chopped green olives, and 1 small clove garlic, quartered. Mix well and let stand at least 30 minutes. Remove garlic before using. Makes a generous ½ cup.

Roquefort Vinaigrette

Beat 1 tablespoon finely crumbled Roquefort cheese together with 2 tablespoons heavy cream. Mix thoroughly with ½ cup Vinaigrette made without salt. Makes a generous ⅔ cup.

Ravigote Vinaigrette

1 teaspoon chopped capers
1 teaspoon minced shallot or scallion
1 hard-cooked egg, finely chopped
1 tablespoon minced parsley or other
    finely chopped fresh herb, such as
    chervil, tarragon, or chives

1 cup Vinaigrette Sauce
Salt and freshly ground black pepper

Stir the first 4 ingredients into the Vinaigrette. Add salt and pepper to taste. Serve over vegetables, poached fish, poached calves' brains, hot or cold boiled beef or chicken, or pigs' feet. Makes about 1¼ cups.

Russian Vinaigrette with Mayonnaise

To ¼ cup Vinaigrette, add 1 tablespoon Mayonnaise, 1 teaspoon chile sauce, and 1 teaspoon ground ginger. Beat vigorously with a rotary beater. Serve on head lettuce or with cooked vegetable salads. Makes a scant ⅓ cup.

Vinaigrette Rémoulade

1 cup light olive oil
⅓ cup wine vinegar
½ teaspoon salt
⅛ teaspoon freshly ground black pepper

2 anchovies, finely chopped
2 teaspoons capers, chopped
1 small clove garlic, crushed

Combine all ingredients in a mixing bowl and beat vigorously with a fork or wire whip. Toss with salad greens, mix with cold cooked vegetables for salads, or serve over tomatoes and seafood salads. Makes about 1⅓ cups.

Sour Cream Sauce

1 egg yolk
¼ cup sour cream
½ cup Vinaigrette Sauce
1 teaspoon freshly squeezed
    lemon juice

1 tablespoon chopped fresh dill,
    or 1 teaspoon dried dill weed
1 tablespoon chopped parsley

Beat egg yolk and cream together in a bowl. Gradually beat in Vinaigrette, as in making Mayonnaise. Add lemon juice, dill, and parsley. Serve over cold or hot fish, or cold egg or vegetable dishes. Makes about ¾ cup.

Mustard Cream Sauce

2 teaspoons sugar
2 teaspoons Dijon prepared mustard
2 tablespoons freshly squeezed
    lemon juice

Salt
1 cup heavy cream, whipped

Combine the first 4 ingredients and fold into cream. Makes about 1¾ cups.

Tarragon Mustard Sauce Thermidor

2 teaspoons chopped fresh tarragon
2 teaspoons Dijon prepared mustard

2 tablespoons freshly squeezed lemon juice
1 cup heavy cream, whipped

Combine the first 3 ingredients and gradually fold into cream. Makes about 1¾ cups.

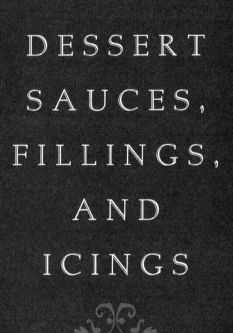

DESSERT
SAUCES,
FILLINGS,
AND
ICINGS

IT MIGHT SEEM ODD THAT PAIRING a relatively rich sauce with a rich dessert makes it seem lighter and far less rich, and the explanation to this conundrum lies in the kind of sauce you use. If, for example, you serve a steamed and aged, very rich Christmas pudding by itself, you would have mainly the sensation of its density and weight. But put a rich cooked custard sauce with it, and suddenly the starchy heaviness is smoothed and glossed over by the sauce, as they both lose their richness and textures in each other, creating a lighter overall sensation. Add whipped cream to the sauce to make it lighter and mousselike, and the effect is even more dramatic. Whipped or Chantilly Cream on a pie, or ice cream with Apple Charlotte, creates the same results.

The most important thing to remember when making fresh fruit purees (only blueberries and their kin have to be cooked) to be mixed with alcohols or sugar syrups to make a sauce, is that you should puree the fruit by hand, by pushing it through a sieve. Machine-made purees diminish the brilliant flavors, aromas, and appearance of fresh fruit, and result in a watery texture.

For convenience, a number of sauces, pastry creams, frostings, and other basic preparations for building desserts are grouped in this chapter; others are given in connection with the dessert recipes in chapters 18 to 21.

SAUCES

Cooked Fruit Sauce

1½ cups unsweetened fruit juice
(cherry, orange, plum, raspberry,
or strawberry)
⅓ cup sugar

2 teaspoons cornstarch
¹⁄₁₆ teaspoon salt
2 tablespoons freshly squeezed
lemon juice

Pour fruit juice into a 1-quart saucepan. Combine the next 3 ingredients and add to the juice. Stir and cook until the juice has thickened slightly and is transparent. Add lemon juice and cook about 30 seconds. Serve over puddings or plain cake. Makes about 1 ⅔ cups.

Apricot Sauce

½ pound dried apricots
2 cups water
½ cup sugar

¹⁄₁₆ teaspoon salt
Kirsch, cognac, or apricot brandy

Simmer apricots in 2 cups water for 10 minutes or until just soft. Drain. Put the cooked apricots through a food mill. Add sugar and salt. Stir and cook 4 to 5 minutes over medium heat. Add kirsch, cognac, or apricot brandy. Serve over puddings or plain cake.

To store: Turn the sauce into a jar and add 1 to 2 tablespoons kirsch, cognac, or apricot brandy. Cover tightly and place in the refrigerator. Makes about 1½ cups.

Quick Apricot Sauce

1½ cups apricot jam
½ cup water
2 tablespoons sugar

6 teaspoon salt
1 tablespoon kirsch, cognac,
   or apricot brandy

Combine the first 4 ingredients in a 1-quart saucepan. Mix well. Heat to the boiling point, stirring constantly. Stir and cook over low heat 5 to 8 minutes. Strain. Stir in kirsch, cognac, or apricot brandy . Serve hot or cold over puddings, vanilla ice cream, or plain cake.

To store: Turn the sauce into a jar and add 1 to 2 tablespoons apricot brandy, kirsch, or cognac. Cover the jar tightly and place in the refrigerator. Makes about 1¾ cups.

Bing Cherry Sauce

2 cups Bing cherries, pitted
Pinch salt
1 cup water

½ teaspoon vanilla extract
1 teaspoon freshly squeezed lemon juice

Combine the first 3 ingredients in a 1-quart saucepan. Simmer 15 minutes. Remove from heat. Add remaining ingredients and puree through a food mill. Cool and serve over plain cake, puddings, or ice cream. Makes about 2½ cups.

American Sherry Cranberry Sauce

1 pound (4 cups) fresh cranberries
1 cup dry sherry

1¾ cups sugar
Dash salt

Wash cranberries and place in a saucepan with the sherry. Cover and cook 8 to 10 minutes, or only until the skins pop. Add the sugar and salt, mix well, and cook 1 minute. Serve as a dessert sauce, or with meat or poultry. Makes about 3½ cups.

Cooked Lemon Sauce

½ cup sugar
1 tablespoon cornstarch
1/16 teaspoon salt
1 cup water

2 tablespoons freshly squeezed lemon juice
1 teaspoon grated lemon zest
2 tablespoons (¼ stick) butter
¼ teaspoon vanilla extract

Combine the first 3 ingredients in a 1-quart saucepan. Add the water. Stir and cook until the mixture has thickened and is clear. Remove from heat and stir in the remaining ingredients. Serve over plain cake, puddings, and so on. Makes about 1¼ cups.

Lemon Mousseline Sauce

Make Cooked Lemon Sauce and cool it. Fold in 1 cup whipped heavy cream. Serve on cake or cold puddings.

Lingonberry or Blueberry Sauce

Lingonberries are grown in the arctic regions, and in Minnesota and New England.

2 cups lingonberries or blueberries	¼ cup water
¾ cup sugar	Dash salt

Wash lingonberries and place them in a 1-quart saucepan with remaining ingredients. Bring to the boiling point and cook 10 minutes. Serve as a sauce for Dessert Crêpes or over puddings. Makes about 2 cups.

Apple-Lingonberry Sauce

Make Lingonberry Sauce, increasing the sugar to 1 cup. While sauce is hot, add 1 cup grated raw apples. Serve as a dessert sauce, or with meat or poultry. Makes about 2¾ cups.

Fresh Raspberry Sauce

2 cups raspberries	1 teaspoon freshly squeezed lemon juice
¼ cup medium sugar syrup	

Crush the raspberries and push them through a sieve, discarding the seeds. Add syrup and lemon juice. Mix well. Serve over ice cream, plain cake, or puddings. Makes about 1½ cups.

Fresh Strawberry Sauce

1 cup strawberries, crushed	Kirsch to taste (optional)
2 tablespoons sugar	
1 cup strawberries, sliced	

Combine crushed strawberries and sugar. Fold in sliced strawberries and kirsch, if using. Serve over ice cream, cake, puddings, Bavarian Creams, or other cream desserts. Makes 2 cups.

Cooked Orange Sauce

½ cup sugar
1 tablespoon cornstarch
¹⁄₁₆ teaspoon salt
1 cup freshly squeezed orange juice

1 tablespoon grated orange zest
1 teaspoon grated lemon zest
2 tablespoons (¼ stick) butter
¼ teaspoon vanilla extract

Combine the first 3 ingredients in a 1-quart saucepan. Add the orange juice. Stir and cook until the mixture has thickened and is clear. Remove from heat and stir in the remaining ingredients. Serve over plain cake, puddings, sweet waffles, and so on. Makes about 1¼ cups.

Cooked Pineapple Sauce

2 tablespoons sugar
2 tablespoons cornstarch
⅛ teaspoon salt
2 cups crushed fresh pineapple

1 tablespoon butter
½ teaspoon grated lemon zest
1½ teaspoons vanilla extract

Combine the first 4 ingredients in a 1-quart saucepan. Stir and cook over medium heat until the sauce has thickened. Remove from heat and add remaining ingredients. Puree through a food mill or sieve. Serve over plain cake. Makes about 2 cups.

Cooked Pineapple-Rum Sauce

⅓ cup sugar
1 tablespoon cornstarch
⅛ teaspoon salt
1 cup fresh pineapple juice

¼ teaspoon grated lemon zest
2 tablespoons light or dark rum, or to taste
2 tablespoons butter

Combine the first 3 ingredients in a 1-quart saucepan. Gradually stir in pineapple juice. Stir and cook until the sauce is of medium thickness. Remove from heat and add remaining ingredients. Makes 1 generous cup.

Apricot Brandy Cream Sauce

1 large egg, separated
About ¾ cup sifted confectioners' sugar
Dash salt

½ cup heavy cream, whipped
3 tablespoons apricot brandy or
peach brandy

Beat the egg white until it stands in soft peaks. Gradually beat in confectioners' sugar. Add salt and egg yolk and beat well. Fold in whipped cream and brandy. Chill until the sauce is cold. Serve over hot or cold puddings or plain cake. Makes about 1½ cups.

Apricot Brandy Whipped Cream or Chantilly

1 cup heavy cream
½ cup apricot brandy or peach brandy

Whip the cream until it stands in soft peaks. Fold in the brandy. Makes about 3 cups.

Custard Sauce or Crème Anglaise

2 cups milk   ⅓ cup sugar
2 large eggs   ¼ teaspoon salt

Heat 1¾ cups of the milk until tiny bubbles appear around the edges (do not boil). With a fork, lightly beat the eggs, then add to them the remaining ¼ cup cold milk, the sugar, and the salt. Mix well. Stir in hot milk. Stir and cook over low heat or hot water only until the custard coats a metal spoon. Strain through a sieve. Serve over plain cake, puddings, or cooked fruits. Makes about 2 cups.

Vanilla or Almond Custard Sauce

Add 1 teaspoon pure vanilla or almond extract to Custard Sauce after it is cooked.

Coconut Custard Sauce

Add ¼ cup flaked coconut to Custard Sauce.

Brandy Custard Sauce

Add apricot or peach brandy, sherry, kirsch, or other liqueur to taste to Custard Sauce.

Rich Custard Sauce

In Custard Sauce recipe, replace 1 cup of the milk with 1 cup heavy cream and replace the 2 whole eggs with 2 large egg yolks.

Chocolate Custard Sauce

Add 1 square (1 ounce) unsweetened chocolate to the hot Custard Sauce. Stir until chocolate is melted.

Butterscotch Sauce

1¼ cups light brown sugar
⅔ cup light corn syrup
¼ cup (½ stick) butter

⅓ cup heavy cream
⅓ cup milk
1 teaspoon vanilla extract

Combine the first 3 ingredients in a 1-quart saucepan. Mix well. Stir and cook over medium heat until the boiling point has been reached. Continue cooking until a candy thermometer shows 230°F, or until ½ teaspoon of the mixture dropped into cold water forms a very soft ball. Remove from heat and add remaining ingredients. Mix well. Serve over ice cream or plain cake.

To store: Turn the sauce into a jar. Cover tightly and refrigerate. If the sauce stiffens on standing, add 1 to 2 tablespoons hot water to it and mix well.

Makes about 2 cups.

Coffee Sauce

1½ cups sugar
2 tablespoons espresso coffee
⅛ teaspoon salt

¾ cup boiling water
1 tablespoon butter
1 teaspoon vanilla extract

Combine the first 4 ingredients in a saucepan. Stir and cook 10 minutes. Add butter. Cool. Add vanilla extract. Makes 1⅔ cups.

Chocolate Sauce

2 ounces unsweetened chocolate
1 cup sugar syrup
¹⁄₁₆ teaspoon salt

2 tablespoons butter
1 teaspoon vanilla extract

Melt chocolate in a double boiler over hot water. Remove from heat, add the next 2 ingredients, and mix well. Stir and cook over low heat 4 to 5 minutes, or until the sauce has thickened. Remove from heat and add butter and vanilla extract. Serve over ice cream, puddings, or plain cake.

To store: Turn the sauce into a jar. Cover tightly and refrigerate. If the sauce stiffens on standing, stir in 1 to 2 tablespoons hot water.

Makes about 1¼ cups.

Foamy Egg Sauce

¼ cup (½ stick) softened butter
1 cup sifted confectioners' sugar
1 large egg, well beaten

1 tablespoon hot water
Dash salt
1¼ teaspoons vanilla extract

Stir butter until fluffy in the top of a 1-quart double boiler. Gradually blend in confectioners' sugar. Beat in egg, hot water, and salt. Stir and cook over hot water (not boiling) until mixture is glossy and smooth. Remove from heat and add vanilla extract. Serve over plain cake or puddings. Makes about 1 cup.

Chocolate Foamy Sauce

Melt 1 square (1 ounce) unsweetened chocolate and blend with the butter, sugar, and egg in Foamy Egg Sauce. Omit the 1 tablespoon hot water.

Lemon Foamy Sauce

Add 1 teaspoon grated lemon zest and 2 teaspoons freshly squeezed lemon juice to Foamy Egg Sauce.

Orange Foamy Sauce

Replace the 1 tablespoon hot water in Foamy Egg Sauce recipe with 1 tablespoon freshly squeezed orange juice. Add 1 tablespoon grated orange zest.

Rum Foamy Sauce

Replace the 1 tablespoon hot water in Foamy Egg Sauce with 1 tablespoon rum, or other alcohols, sherry, or liqueur.

Grand Marnier Custard Sauce

4 large egg yolks	¼ teaspoon salt
½ cup sugar	½ teaspoon vanilla extract
¾ cup heavy cream	3 tablespoons Grand Marnier
1 cup scalded milk	

Place the egg yolks in the top of a 1-quart double boiler and beat them until they are light. Gradually beat in the sugar. Stir in the cream, milk, and salt. Stir and cook over hot (not boiling) water until the mixture coats a metal spoon. Remove the sauce from the heat and beat in vanilla extract and Grand Marnier. Makes about 2 cups.

Hard Sauce

½ cup softened sweet butter	1 tablespoon brandy, rum, or liqueur
1 to 1¼ cups sifted confectioners' sugar	

Stir butter until it is fluffy. Gradually beat in confectioners' sugar and brandy, rum, or liqueur. Serve over warm puddings. Makes about 1 cup.

Coffee Hard Sauce

Make Hard Sauce, replacing brandy, rum, or liqueur with 1 tablespoon strong brewed coffee. Add ½ teaspoon vanilla extract.

Orange Hard Sauce

Make Hard Sauce, replacing brandy, rum, or liqueur with 1 tablespoon freshly squeezed orange juice. Add 2 teaspoons grated orange zest and ¼ teaspoon grated lemon zest.

Jelly Glaze

Put an 8-ounces of red currant, apricot, peach, or other jelly into a small saucepan. With a fork, break up the jelly and mix with 3 tablespoons hot water. Stir the mixture over low heat until the jelly has melted and blended with the water. Strain. Makes 1 generous cup.

Sabayon Sauce

Sabayon Sauce may be served hot over hot puddings and soufflés or served chilled as a dessert. For chilled sabayon, whisk it when hot in its cooking pan immersed in water with ice. Continue whisking until thoroughly cold. Store, covered, for up to 3 days.

4 large egg yolks
⅔ cup sugar
1 cup white wine or Marsala

Place egg yolks and sugar in top of a 1½-quart double boiler and beat with a wire whip until the mixture is light and fluffy. Gradually stir in wine. Cook over hot (not boiling) water, stirring constantly, until the mixture is thick and creamy. (Cooking too long or at too high a temperature causes the mixture to curdle.) Makes about 1⅔ cups.

Vanilla Sauce

½ cup sugar
4 teaspoons cornstarch
¼ teaspoon salt
1 cup water

2 tablespoons butter
2 tablespoons heavy cream
1 teaspoon pure vanilla extract

Combine the first 3 ingredients in a 1-quart saucepan. Mix well. Add water. Stir and cook 5 minutes, or until the sauce is clear and has thickened. Remove from heat and stir in butter. Add the cream and vanilla extract. Serve over plain cake or puddings. Makes about 2 cups.

Vanilla-Bourbon Sauce

Add 2 tablespoons bourbon to Vanilla Sauce.

Lemon-Vanilla Sauce

Omit the cream in the Vanilla Sauce recipe and add 1½ tablespoons freshly squeezed lemon juice and 1 teaspoon grated lemon zest.

Vanilla-Rum Sauce

Add 2 tablespoons rum to Vanilla Sauce.

Vanilla Cream Sauce

¼ cup sugar
2 teaspoons cornstarch
⅛ teaspoon salt
2 large egg yolks

1½ cups milk
1½ teaspoons vanilla extract
½ cup heavy cream, whipped

Combine the first 3 ingredients in a 1-quart saucepan, or in the top of a double boiler. Add egg yolks and mix well. Stir in the milk. Cook, stirring constantly, over low heat or over hot water until the custard coats a metal spoon. Remove from heat and cool completely. Fold in vanilla extract and whipped cream. Makes about 2½ cups.

Whipped or Chantilly Cream

This cream may be flavored to taste with rum, brandy, kirsch, Cointreau, or other liqueur, if desired.

1 cup heavy cream
¼ cup confectioners' sugar, or
   2 tablespoons granulated sugar

1 teaspoon vanilla extract (optional)

Place all ingredients in a mixing bowl and beat mixture until it stands in soft peaks. Makes about 2 cups.

Coffee Whipped Cream

Mix 1 teaspoon strong coffee infusion with the sugar in Whipped Cream.

Mocha Whipped Cream

Mix 1 teaspoon strong coffee infusion and 1 tablespoon cocoa with the sugar in Whipped Cream.

Coconut Whipped Cream

Fold ¼ cup flaked coconut into Whipped Cream Topping.

Orange Whipped Cream

Fold 2 tablespoons grated orange zest and ¼ teaspoon grated lemon zest into Whipped Cream.

Whipped Cream with Almonds and Kirsch

3 tablespoons sifted confectioners' sugar
Dash salt
½ cup heavy cream

1 tablespoon sliced, blanched almonds
2 tablespoons kirsch, or to taste

Put the first 3 ingredients in a bowl and beat the mixture until it stands in soft peaks. Fold in almonds and kirsch. Serve on fruit or plain cake. Makes about 1 cup.

OTHER CREAMS

French Pastry Cream or Crème Patissière

½ cup sugar
4 tablespoons cornstarch
¹⁄₁₆ teaspoon salt
2 cups milk

4 large egg yolks
1½ teaspoons vanilla extract
1 tablespoon butter

Combine first 3 ingredients in the top of a double boiler, or in a 1-quart saucepan. Add ¼ cup of the milk and mix well. Heat 1½ cups milk and gradually add to the mixture, stirring constantly. Stir and cook over medium direct heat until the mixture is very thick. Beat egg yolks, blend with remaining ¼ cup milk, and add to the cooked mixture. Cook over hot water or very low heat, stirring constantly, until the cream is about as thick as mayonnaise. Remove from heat and mix in vanilla extract and butter. Cool completely before using, stirring occasionally to prevent a crust from forming. Makes 2 cups, or filling for 8 tarts.

Chocolate Pastry Cream

Make French Pastry Cream, adding 2 squares (2 ounces) melted unsweetened chocolate to the cooked sugar, cornstarch, salt, and milk mixture. Continue as directed in the recipe.

Coffee Pastry Cream

In the recipe for French Pastry Cream, blend 2 teaspoons instant coffee with the sugar, cornstarch, and salt. Continue as directed in the recipe.

Mocha Pastry Cream

Follow the recipe for Chocolate Pastry Cream, adding 2 teaspoons strong coffee infusion along with the chocolate.

Cream Saint-Honoré

Soften 2 teaspoons unflavored gelatin in 2 tablespoons cold water, and stir into 2 cups hot French Pastry Cream (or Chocolate or Coffee Pastry Cream). Beat 4 egg whites until they stand in soft peaks but are not dry, then beat in ¼ cup sugar, 1 tablespoon at a time, and fold the mixture into the hot cream.

Frangipane Cream

2 cups milk	2 large whole eggs
1 (3-inch) piece vanilla bean, or	2 large egg yolks
1 teaspoon pure vanilla extract	2 tablespoons butter
5 tablespoons flour	4 macaroons, crumbled
¾ cup sugar	(see Macaroon Crumbs, page 573)
Dash salt	

Heat milk, with vanilla bean (if using), only until milk is hot. Combine the next 3 ingredients in a 1½-quart saucepan. Add whole eggs and egg yolks. Mix well.

Gradually stir in hot milk. Cook over medium low heat until the boiling point is reached, stirring vigorously. Cook 2 more minutes, without boiling, stirring constantly. Remove saucepan from heat and discard the vanilla bean. (If using vanilla extract, add it now.) Add butter and Macaroon Crumbs. Mix well. Cool, stirring occasionally to prevent a skin from forming over the top of the cream. Makes 2 cups.

Almond Pastry Cream

1 cup blanched almonds
½ cup sifted confectioners' sugar
3 tablespoons softened butter

2 large egg yolks
1 tablespoon kirsch or rum

Put almonds through a food chopper twice, using the finest blade. Add confectioners' sugar and mix well. Set aside. Mix butter until creamy, then beat in one egg yolk at a time and the kirsch or rum. Blend into the almond mixture. Makes about 1¼ cups.

Thick Custard Filling

½ cup sugar
2 tablespoons cornstarch
1 tablespoon flour
Dash salt

3 large egg yolks
1 cup light cream
1 cup milk
1 teaspoon pure vanilla extract

Combine the first 4 ingredients in either a saucepan or a double boiler. Beat in egg yolks and ¼ cup of the cream. Heat the remaining cream with the milk only until hot. (Do not boil.) Add to the sugar and egg mixture. Stir and cook over low heat or hot water (not boiling) until the custard is very thick. Cool before using, stirring frequently to prevent a skin from forming over the top. Use as a filling for cakes, pastries, and so on. Makes 2 cups.

Sweet Chestnut Puree

1 pound chestnuts
1 (2-inch) piece vanilla bean
1 cup hot milk
½ cup sugar

¼ cup water
Dash salt
1 tablespoon softened butter

Shell and peel chestnuts. Coarsely chop and cook them, along with the vanilla bean, in hot milk 20 to 30 minutes, or until chestnuts are very soft. Remove vanilla bean. Force chestnuts through a ricer, or puree them in an electric blender. Put sugar, water, and salt in a small heavy saucepan. Stir and cook slowly until the mixture begins to boil. Cover and cook 3 minutes, or until the steam has washed off any sugar crystals that may have formed around the sides of the pan. Cook, without stirring, until a soft ball forms when a little of the syrup is dropped into cold water (or to 234°F on a candy thermometer). Blend the syrup with the chestnut puree, beating vigorously until a thick paste is formed. Cool to lukewarm and stir in the butter. Store in a tightly covered jar in the refrigerator and use as needed. Makes ¾ to 1 cup.

ICINGS AND FILLINGS

Cooked Butter-Cream

This butter-cream method makes a firm mixture that is not as delicate as the custard version (see page 568) but is better in hot weather. It is used to fill pastries, tart shells, to fill layers between cakes, and to ice them. It is easier to make with an electric mixer, since a lot of beating is required. If all of it is not used at one time, store remainder in a covered jar in the refrigerator for use on another cake.

½ cup sugar	8 tablespoons (1 stick) butter
2 tablespoons water	1½ teaspoons vanilla extract
2 tablespoons water	

Combine the first 2 ingredients in a 3-cup saucepan. Bring to the boiling point over medium-low heat, stirring constantly to dissolve the sugar. Cook rapidly, without stirring, until a candy thermometer shows 244°F, or until the syrup spins a long thread. Cool syrup about 1 minute. Beat egg yolks in a bowl with a small bottom until they are very thick and lemon-colored. Gradually beat in the syrup, beating well after each addition. Beat in 1 tablespoon of the butter at a time. Add vanilla extract and beat well until the frosting is cool. Chill until medium-stiff, then beat again with a spoon. Chill until of spreading consistency. Use as frosting and filling for cakes, or as filling for pastries. Cakes or pastries frosted or filled with this frosting must be stored in a cool place. Makes 2 cups.

Chocolate Butter-Cream

Put 2 squares (2 ounces) unsweetened chocolate in a cup and set in a pan of hot water over low heat. When it is melted, stir it into Butter-Cream along with the vanilla extract.

Coffee Butter-Cream

Replace the water in the recipe for Butter-Cream with 3 tablespoons strong brewed coffee. Or beat in 1 teaspoon strong coffee infusion along with the vanilla extract.

Kirsch Butter-Cream

Add 1 tablespoon kirsch, or to taste, to Butter-Cream along with the vanilla extract.

Mint Butter-Cream

Add 2 tablespoons crème de menthe, or to taste, to Butter-Cream along with the vanilla extract.

Mocha Butter-Cream

To Coffee Butter-Cream, add 1 square (1 ounce) melted unsweetened chocolate.

Praline Butter-Cream

Add ¼ cup Praline Powder and kirsch to taste to Butter-Cream along with the vanilla extract.

Rum Butter-Cream

Add 2 tablespoons dark rum, or to taste, to Butter-Cream along with the vanilla extract.

Rum-Chocolate Butter-Cream

Add 1 square (1 ounce) melted unsweetened chocolate to Rum Butter-Cream.

Uncooked Butter-Cream

This recipe and its variations may be used if desired in any recipe calling for Butter-Cream Filling and Frosting.

3 egg yolks	½ cup (1 stick) softened butter
¼ cup sugar	½ cup (1 stick) firm butter (not hard)
1 teaspoon vanilla extract	

Place the first 3 ingredients in a bowl and beat by hand (or in an electric mixer) until well mixed. Add the softened butter a little at a time and blend until well mixed. Blend in the firm butter, a small piece at a time, until the mixture is creamy and thick. Makes about 1¼ cups.

Any of the following additions may be made if desired, before adding the butter. Chill if the mixture becomes soft.

- Chocolate: Add 1 square (1 ounce) melted and cooled unsweetened chocolate.
- Coffee: Add 1 teaspoon strong coffee infusion, or to taste.
- Lemon: Add 1 teaspoon each freshly squeezed lemon juice and grated lemon zest.
- Liqueur or brandy: Add 2 tablespoons Cointreau, Grand Marnier, kirsch, or cognac.
- Nuts: Add ¼ cup finely ground toasted almonds, hazelnuts, pecans, or walnuts.
- Orange: Add 1 tablespoon each grated orange zest and frozen concentrated orange juice.

Walnut-Rum Butter-Cream

2 tablespoons rum
1¼ cups finely ground walnuts
1 large egg white

¼ cup sugar
¾ cup (1½ sticks) softened sweet butter

Mix rum with walnuts and set aside. Break egg white into the top of a double boiler, place over boiling water, and gradually beat in sugar. Continue beating until the meringue is the consistency of heavy cream. Beat in butter, 1 tablespoon at a time. Stir in walnut mixture. Use as filling for cakes. Makes about 1½ cups.

Custard Butter-Cream

This version of butter-cream has the finest and lightest texture and is best in cold weather.

1 recipe Vanilla Custard
1 cup butter

Remove the cooked and strained custard from heat and, when tepid, beat in the butter, 1 tablespoon at a time. Continue beating until butter is thoroughly blended. Chill the butter-cream. This filling will keep several days if stored in a tightly covered jar in the refrigerator. Makes 2 cups.

Chocolate Butter-Cream

Add 2 squares (2 ounces) unsweetened chocolate to the hot Butter-Cream along with the vanilla extract. Stir and beat until chocolate is melted. Continue as directed in the recipe.

Chocolate-Rum Butter-Cream

Beat 2 tablespoons dark rum (or other rum), or to taste, into Chocolate Butter-Cream. Continue as directed in the recipe for Butter Filling and Frosting.

Coffee Butter-Cream

In the recipe for Butter-Cream, replace the water with ¾ cup brewed strong coffee. Continue as directed in the recipe.

Mint Butter-Cream

Beat 2 tablespoons crème de menthe into hot Butter-Cream. Continue as directed in the recipe.

Mocha Butter-Cream

Add 1 square (1 ounce) unsweetened chocolate and 1 teaspoon instant coffee to the hot Butter-Cream. Stir and beat until chocolate is melted. Continue as directed in the recipe.

Rum Butter-Cream

Beat 2 tablespoons dark rum, or to taste, into hot Butter-Cream. Continue as directed in the recipe.

Uncooked Butter-Cream

This method is the fastest and easiest, but the texture is not as smooth as the other two kinds of cooked butter-creams.

1½ cups softened butter
2 cups sifted confectioners' sugar

1 teaspoon vanilla extract
2 large egg yolks

Stir butter until it is creamy. Blend in 1 cup of the confectioners' sugar and the vanilla extract. Beat well. Beat in egg yolks for a couple of minutes. Chill. Makes enough butter-cream for top and sides of two 8-inch cake layers.

Fondant Cake Icing

1 cup cooked Fondant
1 to 2 tablespoons liquid (water,
    simple syrup, maple syrup, strong
    coffee, freshly squeezed orange juice,
    or freshly squeezed lemon juice)

Flavoring to taste (almond extract,
    vanilla extract, any liqueur, or
    grated orange or lemon zest)
1 teaspoon egg white (optional)

Warm the Fondant in a heavy-bottomed saucepan over very low heat, or in the top of a double boiler over hot (not boiling) water, stirring constantly. (Be very careful not to overheat.) Add the liquid gradually, using only enough to thin the Fondant to pouring consistency while keeping it thick enough to mask the cake. Add desired flavoring. To give more sheen to the icing, if desired, add the unbeaten egg white just before using the icing. Brown-Sugar Fondant may be treated in the same way. Makes enough icing for the top and sides of an 8- or 9-inch cake.

Easy Caramel Filling

1 cup white granulated sugar
1 cup brown sugar
½ cup milk

½ cup (1 stick) butter
1½ teaspoons vanilla extract
½ cup chopped toasted nuts (optional)

Combine the first 4 ingredients in a 1½-quart saucepan. Mix well. Stir and cook until mixture begins to boil. Cook, without stirring, exactly 2 minutes over medium heat. Remove from heat, add vanilla extract, and beat until filling is of spreading consistency. Add nuts, if desired, just before the filling is stiff enough to spread. Makes filling for two 8-inch cake layers.

Chocolate Cream Icing

¼ cup (½ stick) butter
1 square (1 ounce) unsweetened
    chocolate

2 to 2½ cups sifted confectioners' sugar
2 to 3 tablespoons heavy cream
1 teaspoon vanilla extract

Brown butter lightly in a saucepan large enough for mixing the frosting. Add chocolate and stir until it has melted. Add confectioners' sugar and cream alternately, stirring until frosting is smooth and stiff enough to hold its shape when the spoon is raised. Stir in vanilla extract. Spread frosting over the top of an 8-inch square cake, or put it through a cake-decorating tube to decorate Petits Fours and other cakes. Makes enough frosting for the top of an 8-inch-square cake.

 Coffee Cream Icing

2 teaspoons strong coffee infusion
3 tablespoons softened butter
1 pound sifted confectioners' sugar

5 to 6 tablespoons sour cream
1 teaspoon vanilla extract

Blend instant coffee with the butter. Add confectioners' sugar alternately with sour cream, using only enough cream to make a frosting that is of smooth spreading consistency. Stir in vanilla extract. Makes about 2 cups.

Royal Icing or Glace Royale

3 large egg whites
About 2 cups sifted confectioners' sugar
Pinch salt

Beat the egg whites together with ⅔ cup of the confectioners' sugar until the mixture is creamy. Gradually beat in the remaining sugar. If the icing is to be used for spreading, it should have the consistency of heavy cream. If it is to be used for decorating purposes (put through a cake-decorating tube), it should stand in stiff peaks. Since this icing thickens as it is beaten, beating it with an electric beater saves time and energy. Add additional sugar if necessary to make the icing the consistency desired. Use immediately. Makes about 2 cups.

GLAZES AND OTHER DESSERT PREPARATIONS

Caramel

Heat 1 cup sugar in a small, heavy saucepan over low heat, stirring constantly with a wooden spoon for 8 to 10 minutes until the sugar is melted and straw colored. Remove from heat and add 1 cup water. Return to heat and simmer until the syrup is thick and smooth and the desired color. This syrup may be stored in a covered jar and kept to use as needed. Makes about ¾ cup.

Caramel Glaze

Melt 1 cup sugar in a small saucepan over low heat. Add 1½ tablespoons butter and stir until the mixture is golden brown. Makes enough glaze for the top of a 9- or 10-inch cake.

Chocolate Glaze

6 squares (6 ounces) semisweet chocolate
¼ cup light corn syrup

3 tablespoons water
2½ tablespoons sweet butter

Chop the chocolate into small pieces and set it aside. Place the remaining ingredients in a small saucepan. Stir and cook the mixture over medium heat until the boiling point has been reached. Remove from heat and stir in chocolate. Continue stirring the mixture until the chocolate has completely melted. Use this glaze to frost-glaze cakes, cookies, or Petits Fours. Makes about ¾ cup.

Glazing Syrup

2 cups sugar
⅔ cup water

⅛ teaspoon cream of tartar
Dash salt

Combine all the ingredients in the top of a double boiler. Stir and cook until the boiling point has been reached. Cook, without stirring, until a candy thermometer shows 300°F, or until a little of the mixture dropped into cold water separates into threads. Remove pan from the heat and quickly set it in a pan of cold water to prevent further cooking; then set pan containing mixture over hot water to prevent syrup from hardening. Use for glazing nuts and for glazing other confections. Makes about 1¼ cups.

Sugar Syrup

One-quarter cup of alcohols like rum, Cognac, kirsch, Cointreau and Grand Marnier may be added to the syrups after they are cooked and let cool.

HEAVY (MAKES ABOUT 3 CUPS):
1½ cups sugar
2 cups water

LIGHT (MAKES ABOUT 3 1/4 CUPS):
1 cup sugar
2 cups water

Combine sugar and water in a 1½-quart saucepan. Mix well and bring to the boiling point. Simmer 5 minutes. Cool to lukewarm and add rum, kirsch, or other liqueur, if desired. Use as directed in specific recipes in this book. This syrup may be stored in a covered jar in the refrigerator to use as needed.

Vanilla Sugar

Bury a vanilla bean in 5 pounds granulated sugar in a canister equipped with a tight-fitting lid. Store at least 1 week before using. Replenish the sugar as it is used. Vanilla sugar may be used in any recipe specifying sugar and vanilla extract or vanilla bean. Makes 5 pounds vanilla sugar.

If vanilla beans are unavailable, any recipe that specifies them can be made with pure vanilla extract, using ½ teaspoon for each 1 inch of vanilla bean.

Vanilla Syrup

¾ cup sugar
2 cups water
Dash salt

1 (2-inch) piece vanilla bean,
or 1 teaspoon vanilla extract

Combine the sugar, water, salt, and vanilla bean (if using) in a 1-quart saucepan and mix well. Bring to the boiling point and boil 2 minutes. Remove the vanilla bean, if used, or add the vanilla extract now. Makes 2¼ cups.

Chocolate Curls

Let a large and thick piece of chocolate stand at room temperature until warmed. Using a vegetable parer or a sharp paring knife, shave thin curls from the top of the square.

How to Melt Chocolate for Decorating Purposes

Melt semisweet chocolate over warm water (not hot). Cool it until chocolate is stiff enough to be piped through a decorating tube. A little sifted confectioners' sugar may be added if the chocolate is too thin.

Macaroon Crumbs

Heat macaroons in a preheated oven (350°F) 10 minutes. Remove from oven and cool. Place the macaroons in a plastic bag or paper bag and roll into crumbs with a rolling pin.

Praline Powder

1 cup sugar
1 cup blanched almonds
½ teaspoon vanilla extract

Put the sugar and almonds in a heavy skillet. Stir and cook over medium heat until the sugar is well caramelized. Add the vanilla extract. Turn out onto a buttered platter and cool until the mixture hardens, then break it into pieces and put them in a plastic bag or paper bag. With a heavy rolling pin, roll and pound the pieces to a powder. Store in a tightly closed container. Use as needed. Makes about 1 cup.

DESSERTS

IT IS HARD TO THINK OF A DESSERT THAT, if well made and with perfect ingredients, will not be well liked by your guests. The difficulty is knowing which dessert to serve within a certain menu or for a specific occasion. Now that the dessert course is the last in a meal (it used to come after the cheese and, in England, before the savory), it has to be in balance with what has been served before it. There is no point, no matter how wonderful the dessert is, in weighing down your guests so they can barely move after the meal. Blockbuster desserts should be saved for when they can be the main element of a meal, like a weekend lunch when the only course before the dessert is a big salad; then the dessert can take center stage.

It is important to consider what kind of wine to drink with desserts. The rule to follow is that the wine must always be sweeter than the dessert, or the wine will taste sour and flat. One should stay away from chocolate desserts with wine, and instead choose fruit desserts, like Peach Charlotte, or mild cream ones, like Blancmanger.

CREAMS AND CUSTARDS

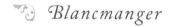 ## Blancmanger

1 cup blanched almonds	½ envelope unflavored gelatin
2 bitter almonds or pure extract, if available	½ cup milk
	½ cup heavy cream
Water	⅔ cup sugar

Pound almonds and extract in a mortar until they are thoroughly crushed, or put a few at a time in an electric blender and blend until very fine. Gradually work a little water at a time into the almonds until 2 cups water has been added and the liquid is milky. Strain through a sieve lined with cheesecloth, extracting as much of the almond milk as possible. Combine the gelatin, ¼ cup cold water, milk, and the cream in a 1½-quart saucepan and let them stand 5 minutes for gelatin to soften. Add sugar and the almond milk. Stir and cook over low heat 4 to 5 minutes, or until liquid is hot. Never allow mixture to boil. Pour into an oiled 3-cup ring mold. Chill until firm.

Blancmanger with Strawberries

Wash the strawberries and reserve a few whole unhulled ones to use as decoration. Slice remaining berries, sprinkle with remaining sugar and 2 tablespoons kirsch, and marinate at least 30 minutes. Just before serving, unmold the Blancmanger on a serving plate. Fill center with sliced strawberries. Decorate dish with whole unhulled berries. Makes 6 servings.

Chocolate Blancmanger

Prepare Blancmanger, adding to the hot liquid 1½ squares (1½ ounces) unsweetened chocolate melted in a custard cup in a pan of hot water. Replace kirsch with 2 teaspoons vanilla extract, or heat 1 (3-inch) piece vanilla bean with the liquid mixture. Continue as instructed in the recipe. Serve with Chantilly Cream.

Hazelnut Blancmanger

In the Blancmanger recipe, replace the almonds with toasted fresh hazelnuts. Continue as directed in the recipe.

Liqueur Blancmanger

Prepare Blancmanger with either almonds or hazelnuts, and add 2 tablespoons Cointreau, curaçao, kirsch, maraschino, or any other liqueur desired.

Caramel Baked Crème Brûlée

1 cup granulated white sugar
1 tablespoon water
2 cups light cream
1 (2-inch) piece vanilla bean, or
    1 teaspoon vanilla extract

4 large eggs, lightly beaten
½ teaspoon salt
¼ cup light brown sugar

In a small saucepan over low heat, melt ½ cup of the white sugar, stirring constantly to prevent burning. Add the water and stir and cook until all the lumps disappear. Pour the syrup into a 10-by-6-by-1½-inch baking dish decorative enough to bring to the table, coating the bottom of the dish completely. Set the dish aside to cool. Heat the cream, with vanilla bean (if using), in the top of a double boiler over hot water until bubbles form around the edge. Combine the remaining ½ cup white sugar, the eggs, salt, and vanilla extract (if vanilla bean was not used) in a mixing bowl. Gradually beat in the hot cream. Beat vigorously. Strain the mixture into the prepared baking dish and place the dish in a pan of hot water. Bake in a preheated oven (325°F) 40 minutes, or until a knife inserted in the center comes out clean. Remove the dish from the water and cool. Refrigerate 4 to 5 hours or overnight. Before serving, sift the brown sugar uniformly over the top of the crème. Place the dish under the broiler 4 inches from the heat source. Broil 3 to 4 minutes, or until the brown sugar melts and forms a glaze. Watch carefully to prevent burning. Cool. Refrigerate 3 to 4 hours, or until well chilled. Serve from the dish. Makes 6 servings.

Orange Harlequin Cream

1 envelope unflavored gelatin
¼ cup cold water
½ cup sugar
⅛ teaspoon salt
¾ cup hot water
¾ cup dry white wine
¾ cup strained freshly squeezed
    orange juice

1 (2-inch) piece vanilla bean, or
    1 teaspoon vanilla extract
6 large egg yolks
1 cup heavy cream, whipped
Royal Icing
Shaved semisweet chocolate
Pistachio nuts
¾ cup white wine jelly

Soften gelatin in cold water and set aside. Combine sugar and salt in a 1½-quart saucepan or in the top of a double boiler. Add the next 3 ingredients and the vanilla bean (if using). Mix well. Cook over medium heat until liquid has thickened. Beat egg yolks, stir a little of the hot mixture into them, and then add them to the remaining hot mixture. Cook over hot water (not boiling) or very low heat about 4 minutes, stirring constantly. Remove custard from heat and strain it into a bowl. Add softened gelatin and the vanilla extract (if vanilla bean was not used). Mix well. Chill in a pan of ice water until mixture begins to set. Fold in whipped cream. Pour into a glass bowl and chill until the cream is set. Decorate with Royal Icing, shaved chocolate, and pistachio nuts. Heat wine jelly until about halfway melted and spread it over the frosting and nuts. Makes 6 to 8 servings.

Sherry Custard

1 envelope unflavored gelatin
¼ cup cold water
½ cup sugar
1 cup milk
1 (2-inch) piece vanilla bean, or
    1 teaspoon vanilla extract

3 large egg yolks
⅓ cup sweet sherry
¾ cup heavy cream, whipped
1⅛ teaspoon salt
2 large egg whites
Chantilly Cream

Soften gelatin in cold water and set aside. Combine ⅓ cup of the sugar, milk, and vanilla bean (if using) in the top of a double boiler. Stir and cook over medium heat until thickened. Beat egg yolks, stir a little of the hot mixture into them, and then add them to the remaining hot mixture. Cook over hot water (not boiling) or very low heat, about 4 minutes, stirring constantly. Remove from heat and strain into a bowl. Add softened gelatin, vanilla extract (if vanilla bean was not used), and sherry. Chill in a pan of ice water until the custard begins to set. Fold in whipped cream. Meanwhile, add salt to egg whites and beat until they stand in soft stiff peaks. Beat the remaining sugar into the egg whites and fold them into cream mixture. Pour into champagne glasses and decorate each with Chantilly Cream. Makes 6 servings.

Praline Floating Island

1/16 teaspoon salt	6 tablespoons Praline Powder
4 large egg whites	Custard Sauce
½ cup sugar	Whole toasted blanched almonds
¾ teaspoon vanilla extract	

Add salt to egg whites and beat them until stiff. Beat in sugar, 1 tablespoon at a time. Beat in vanilla extract and Praline Powder. Butter a 1-quart round mold and sprinkle lightly with granulated sugar, or coat it with caramel. Fill with the egg white mixture. Place the mold in a pan of hot water and bake in a preheated oven (275°F) 25 to 35 minutes, or until the meringue is firm. Cool. Unmold it in a glass bowl and pour Custard Sauce around it. Decorate with almonds. Makes 6 servings.

Molded Chestnut Puree

1 pound chestnuts	2 cups milk
Boiling water	4 tablespoons cognac
2 large eggs	1½ teaspoons pure vanilla extract
½ cup granulated sugar	2 tablespoons confectioners' sugar
¼ teaspoon salt	1 cup heavy cream, whipped
1 square (1 ounce) unsweetened chocolate	

Cut a slit in the pointed end of each chestnut. Cover chestnuts with boiling water and boil 35 to 40 minutes. Drain off water and cool the chestnuts until they can be handled. Remove the brown inner skin. Puree chestnuts, a few at a time, through a food mill. Break the eggs into the top of a double boiler and gradually beat in the granulated sugar. Add salt, chocolate, and milk. Mix well. Stir and cook over hot water (not boiling) until the chocolate is melted and the mixture coats a metal spoon. Add 2 tablespoons of the cognac and the vanilla extract to the chestnut puree. Add the puree to the cooked mixture. Cool. Pour the mixture into a well-buttered 8-inch tube cake pan. Chill overnight or until cake is firm. Unmold onto a serving plate. Fold the remaining cognac and the confectioners' sugar into the whipped cream. Spread over the cake as a frosting. Makes 8 to 10 servings.

Chilled Sabayon with Strawberries

6 large eggs, separated	2 cups sliced strawberries
⅔ cup sugar	8 whole unhulled strawberries
¾ cup sweet sherry	
¼ teaspoon salt	

Combine egg yolks and sugar in the top of a 1½-quart double boiler. Beat with a rotary beater until sugar and egg yolks are well blended. Beat and cook over hot water (not boiling) until the mixture is fluffy and has thickened. (The water in the bottom of the double boiler should never boil.) Gradually beat in sherry and continue beating until mixture is the consistency of thick cream. Cool quickly by beating the sabayon in the top of the double boiler that has been immersed in water with ice. Beat until quite cold. Just before serving, add salt to egg whites and beat them until stiff but not dry. Fold into the custard and turn it into a crystal bowl. Arrange the sliced strawberries over the top and garnish with whole unhulled strawberries. Makes 8 servings.

Chilled Zabaglione Gritti Hotel

2 teaspoons unflavored gelatin	1 cup Marsala
3 tablespoons cold water	Chantilly Cream
9 large egg yolks	6 glacé cherries
9 tablespoons sugar	Unsweetened chocolate

Soften the gelatin in the cold water and melt over hot water. Beat egg yolks in the top of a double boiler and gradually beat in sugar and Marsala. Place the mixture over hot water and beat vigorously with a wire whisk until the custard is quite foamy and begins to thicken. Add the softened gelatin and continue beating as the mixture cools in an ice bath (see Chilled Sabayon with Strawberries). Pour into serving dishes and chill. Just before serving, garnish each serving with a dollop of Chantilly Cream, a cherry, and a few shavings of chocolate. Makes 6 servings.

BAVARIAN CREAMS

A Bavarian Cream is made with soft custard, gelatin, whipped cream, and any desired flavoring, such as vanilla, coffee, or chocolate. It is usually molded, sometimes with Macaroon Crumbs, Ladyfingers, or chunks of sponge cake soaked in a liqueur, sherry, or rum. Nuts and fruit may also be added. These ingredients must be folded in after the mixture is thick enough to hold them in suspension so that the added ingredients will be evenly distributed throughout the custard to give the finished dessert a smooth, uniform texture. If the cream has become too firm before these ingredients are added, place the bowl in a pan of warm water and stir until cream is soft.

Rub the dry mold lightly with almond or pure vegetable oil, or rinse it in cold water, before pouring in the gelatin mixture. Chill for several hours or overnight, until the dessert is firm. Just before serving, loosen edges with a small spatula and turn the dessert out onto a serving plate. If the dessert does not slip out of the mold readily, briefly dip it in very hot water, or wrap the mold in a cloth wrung out in water as hot as your hands can stand.

Jellied Custard

This is the basis of all Bavarian Creams.

1 envelope unflavored gelatin	3 large egg yolks
¼ cup cold water	½ cup sugar
1 (2-inch) piece vanilla bean	Dash salt
1 cup milk	

Soften gelatin in cold water and set aside. Add vanilla bean to milk and heat only until hot, stirring to prevent a skin from forming over the surface. Lightly beat eggs in the top part of a double boiler, or in a 1-quart saucepan. Gradually beat in sugar. Add salt. Gradually add hot milk, including the vanilla bean. Stir and cook the custard over hot water (not boiling) or over very low heat until custard coats a metal spoon. Remove from heat. Remove vanilla bean, rinse it, and save it for use in another dessert. Strain custard into a bowl and stir in softened gelatin. Cool the custard, stirring occasionally to prevent a skin from forming over the surface. Makes 4 servings.

Vanilla Bavarian Cream

1 recipe Jellied Custard
1 cup heavy cream, whipped
Fresh Strawberry Sauce

Chill Jellied Custard in a bowl of ice water or in the refrigerator until the mixture begins to thicken and hold its shape. Fold in whipped cream. Turn into an oiled 1-quart mold. Chill until firm and ready to serve. Unmold onto a serving plate and serve with Strawberry Sauce. Makes 6 to 8 servings.

Cherry Bavarian Cream

Prepare Vanilla Bavarian Cream and fold in ½ cup pitted brandied cherries and 2 tablespoons kirsch along with the whipped cream. Continue as instructed in the recipe. Unmold onto a serving plate and decorate with glacéed cherries and angelica.

Chocolate Bavarian Cream

Prepare Vanilla Bavarian Cream, adding 2 squares (2 ounces) unsweetened chocolate to the hot custard, and stirring until chocolate is melted and well mixed. Continue as directed in the recipe. Serve with rum-flavored whipped cream.

Coffee Bavarian Cream

Prepare Jellied Custard, heating 1 tablespoon strong coffee infusion with the milk. Continue as directed in the recipe for Vanilla Bavarian Cream. Unmold the dessert on a serving plate and serve with Chantilly Cream.

Bavarian Cream Diplomat

Fill an oiled 6-cup mold with alternate layers of Vanilla Bavarian Cream and finely chopped mixed candied fruit, using ½ cup fruit total, and 12 Ladyfingers broken into pieces and sprinkled with 3 tablespoons kirsch. Chill until set. Just before serving, unmold onto a serving plate. Garnish with glacéed cherries, angelica, and whipped cream.

Bavarian Cream with Liqueurs

Prepare Vanilla Bavarian Cream. Before folding in the whipped cream, add 3 tablespoons of one of the following: Benedictine, Chartreuse, Cointreau, crème de menthe, curaçao, kirsch, rum, sherry, or other liqueur. Continue as instructed in the recipe. Just before serving, unmold onto a serving plate and decorate with candied or glacéed fruit and/or whipped cream.

Pistachio Bavarian Cream

Prepare Vanilla Bavarian Cream, adding ¼ cup finely ground or chopped pistachio nuts and 2 tablespoons kirsch along with the gelatin. Continue as instructed in the recipe. Unmold onto a serving plate, serve with Chantilly Cream, and sprinkle with pistachio nuts.

Ginger Bavarian Cream

1 envelope unflavored gelatin
¼ cup cold water
¼ cup sugar
⅛ teaspoon salt
2 large egg yolks
1 cup milk
1 (2-inch) piece vanilla bean, or
   1 teaspoon vanilla extract

2 tablespoons syrup drained from
   preserved ginger
¼ cup finely diced preserved ginger
1 cup heavy cream, whipped
Strips of preserved ginger
Angelica

Soften the gelatin in the cold water and set aside. Combine the next 3 ingredients in the top of a double boiler, or in a 1-quart saucepan. Mix well. Heat milk with vanilla bean (if using) and gradually stir into the sugar and egg mixture. Stir and cook over hot water (not boiling) or over very low heat 12 to 15 minutes, or until custard coats a metal spoon. Remove from heat. Strain and stir in softened gelatin and the ginger syrup. Chill until the custard begins to thicken, stirring occasionally. Fold in diced preserved ginger, vanilla extract (if vanilla bean was not used), and whipped cream; turn into an oiled 1-quart mold. Chill until set and ready to serve. Unmold onto a serving plate. Decorate with strips of preserved ginger and angelica. Makes 6 servings.

Nesselrode Bavarian Cream

In Ginger Bavarian Cream, replace ginger syrup and chopped preserved ginger with ¼ cup syrup drained from glacéed chestnuts and ¼ cup finely chopped glacéed chestnuts. Flavor with 1 to 2 tablespoons rum, if desired. Decorate with whipped cream, glacéed chestnuts, and glacéed cherries.

Orange Bavarian Cream

1 envelope unflavored gelatin
½ cup freshly squeezed orange juice
½ cup sugar
4 large egg yolks
⅛ teaspoon salt
1½ cups milk
1 (2-inch) piece vanilla bean, or
    1½ teaspoons vanilla extract

1 tablespoon grated orange zest
1 teaspoon grated lemon zest
1½ cups heavy cream, whipped
Orange sections
Glacéed cherries

Soften the gelatin in the orange juice and set aside. Combine the next 3 ingredients in the top of a double boiler or in a 1-quart saucepan and mix well. Heat milk with the vanilla bean (if using) and gradually stir it into egg and sugar mixture. Stir and cook over hot water (not boiling) or over very low heat 12 to 15 minutes, or until custard coats a metal spoon. Remove from heat and strain into a bowl. Add softened gelatin and mix well. Add orange and lemon zests. Mix well. Chill until mixture begins to thicken. Fold in 1 cup of the whipped cream, adding vanilla extract if vanilla bean was not used. Turn into an oiled 6-cup mold. Chill until the cream is set and ready to serve. Turn out onto a large plate. Decorate with remaining whipped cream, the orange sections, and glacéed cherries. Makes 8 servings.

Cold Souffles and Dessert Mousses

These so-called soufflés are not actually soufflés but light molded gelatin desserts, often containing fruit.

Cold Mocha Soufflé

2 envelopes unflavored gelatin
½ cup cold water
½ square (½ ounce) unsweetened
    chocolate
3 squares (3 ounces) semisweet
    chocolate
2 tablespoons strong coffee infusion
4 large whole eggs

3 large egg yolks
½ cup sugar
1½ teaspoons vanilla extract
2 tablespoons rum or brandy
1¼ cups heavy cream
Shaved semisweet chocolate,
    or chocolate decorettes

First prepare the soufflé dish: Fold a 26-inch piece of aluminum foil in half lengthwise and tie it around the outside of a 1-quart soufflé dish as a collar. This extends the capacity of the dish. Set aside.

    Soften the gelatin in the cold water and place it in a pan of hot water (not boiling) to melt. Set aside to cool slightly. Melt the chocolate with the coffee over hot water (not boiling). Beat whole eggs and egg yolks together with sugar with an electric beater about 15 minutes, or beat vigorously by hand over hot water. Add the melted gelatin, the chocolate, vanilla extract, and rum or brandy and mix well. Let cool slightly. Whip ¾ cup of the cream and fold it into mixture. Pour the mixture into the prepared soufflé dish. Chill until soufflé is firm. Remove foil collar and carefully press shaved chocolate or chocolate decorettes around the exposed sides of the soufflé. Whip remaining ½ cup cream, put it into a pastry bag with a fluted nozzle, and make rosettes over the top of the soufflé. Makes 6 to 8 servings.

Cold Apricot Soufflé

2 envelopes unflavored gelatin
¼ cup cold water
2 tablespoons freshly squeezed
    lemon juice
4 large whole eggs
3 large egg yolks
½ cup granulated sugar

1 cup apricot puree (made from
    dried apricots)
1 tablespoon cognac
½ teaspoon vanilla extract
1 cup heavy cream
2 teaspoons confectioners' sugar

Prepare a 1-quart soufflé dish as directed in the recipe for Cold Mocha Soufflé. Set aside. Soften the gelatin in the cold water and lemon juice and place it in a pan of hot water (not boiling) to melt. In a mixing bowl, combine whole eggs, egg yolks, and sugar and beat with an electric beater, or beat by hand over hot water, until eggs are thick and lemon-colored. Drain the apricot puree well and add it to the egg mixture, along with the cognac, vanilla extract, and melted gelatin. Mix well. Whip ⅔ cup of the cream and fold it into the egg mixture. Pour the mixture into the prepared soufflé dish. Chill until the soufflé is firm and spongy. Remove the foil band. Add the confectioners' sugar to the remaining cream and beat until soft peaks form. Press the cream through a pastry bag fitted with a fluted nozzle to decorate the top of the soufflé. Makes 6 to 8 servings.

Cold Lemon Soufflé

1½ envelopes unflavored gelatin	1 teaspoon grated lemon zest
⅓ cup cold water	1 teaspoon vanilla extract
4 large eggs, separated	1⅓ cups heavy cream
½ cup freshly squeezed lemon juice	2 teaspoons confectioners' sugar
¼ teaspoon salt	Toasted blanched almonds, slivered
1 cup granulated sugar	6 to 8 fresh whole strawberries

Prepare a 1-quart soufflé dish as directed in the recipe for Cold Mocha Soufflé. Set aside.

Soften the gelatin in the cold water. Set aside. In the top of a double boiler, combine egg yolks, lemon juice, salt, and ½ cup of the granulated sugar. Stir and cook over hot water (not boiling) until mixture is of custard consistency. Stir in gelatin mixture, lemon zest, and vanilla extract and turn into a 2-quart mixing bowl. Cool. Beat egg whites until they stand in soft stiff peaks, then gradually beat in the remaining ½ cup sugar. Continue beating until mixture stands in stiff peaks. Whip 1 cup of the cream until it stands in soft peaks. Pile both the egg whites and the cream over the lemon custard and gently fold them into the mixture. Pour into the prepared soufflé dish. Chill until firm and spongy. Remove the foil band. Combine the remaining ⅓ cup cream and the confectioners' sugar and whip until the cream stands in soft peaks. Spread it over the top of the soufflé. Sprinkle with almonds. Arrange strawberries around the edges. Makes 6 to 8 servings.

Cold Orange Soufflé

1½ envelopes unflavored gelatin	¾ cup granulated sugar
¼ cup cold water	1½ teaspoon grated lemon zest
1 tablespoon freshly squeezed lemon juice	1 tablespoon grated orange zest
	1 tablespoon Triple Sec
4 large eggs, separated	1⅓ cups heavy cream
½ cup freshly squeezed orange juice	2 teaspoons confectioners' sugar
¼ teaspoon salt	Mandarin orange sections

Prepare a 1-quart soufflé dish as directed in the recipe for Cold Mocha Soufflé. Set aside.

Soften gelatin in cold water and lemon juice. Set aside. In the top of a double boiler, combine egg yolks, orange juice, salt, and ½ cup of the granulated sugar. Stir and cook mixture over hot water (not boiling) until it is of custard consistency. Stir in gelatin mixture, lemon and orange zests, and Triple Sec. Turn the mixture into a mixing bowl. Cool. Beat egg whites until they stand in soft peaks, then gradually beat in remaining ¼ cup sugar. Continue beating until the mixture stands in stiff peaks. Whip 1 cup of the cream until it forms soft peaks. Pile both the egg whites and the cream over the orange custard and gently fold them into the mixture. Pour into the prepared soufflé dish. Chill until soufflé is firm and spongy. Remove the foil band. Combine the remaining ⅓ cup cream and the confectioners' sugar and beat until cream stands in soft peaks. Press the whipped cream through a cake-decorator's tube fitted with a fluted nozzle to decorate the top of the soufflé. Garnish with Mandarin orange sections. Makes 6 to 8 servings.

Chocolate Mousse

6 squares (6 ounces) semisweet chocolate, or 1 (6-ounce) package semi-sweet chocolate pieces
¼ teaspoon salt
2 tablespoons water

4 large eggs, separated
2 teaspoons vanilla extract
¾ cup heavy cream
1½ teaspoons sugar, or to taste

Combine the first 3 ingredients in the top part of a double boiler. Place over hot water and stir until chocolate is melted. Beat egg yolks until light and lemon-colored, then gradually beat in melted chocolate. Stir in vanilla extract. Beat egg whites until they stand in soft stiff peaks, then fold them into the chocolate mixture. Whip ½ cup of the cream and fold it in. Spoon the mousse into a decorative serving dish or into sherbet glasses and chill until ready to serve. Garnish with the remaining ¼ cup cream, whipped and sweetened with sugar to taste. Makes 6 to 8 servings.

Strawberry Mousse

1 quart strawberries
12 tablespoons sugar
1⁄16 teaspoon salt

3 large egg whites
½ cup heavy cream

Wash and hull strawberries. Reserve 6 for use as a garnish. Crush the remaining strawberries and mix with 5 tablespoons of the sugar. Set aside. Add salt to egg whites and beat until they stand in soft peaks. Gradually beat in 6 tablespoons of the sugar. Fold in the strawberry puree . Turn into a glass bowl and chill. Just before serving, add the remaining 1 tablespoon sugar to the cream and beat it until it stands in soft peaks. Pipe the cream through a pastry bag, or spoon it, as desired, over the top of the Strawberry Mousse. Decorate with the reserved whole strawberries. Makes 6 servings.

Raspberry Mousseline

1 quart fresh raspberries	2 envelopes unflavored gelatin
1 tablespoon freshly squeezed	½ cup cold water
lemon juice	1½ cups heavy cream, whipped
¾ cup sugar	Whole raspberries
Pinch salt	Ladyfingers (optional)

Crush raspberries and push them through a sieve, discarding the seeds. Add lemon juice, sugar, and salt. Stir until sugar has completely dissolved. Soften the gelatin in the cold water in a custard cup. Set in a pan of hot water (not boiling) to melt. Add to the raspberry puree. Place the bowl in a pan of cracked ice and stir until raspberries begin to thicken. Fold in the whipped cream. Rinse a 1½-quart mold in cold water and pour in the raspberry cream. Chill several hours or overnight, or until the cream is firm. To serve, unmold onto a large chilled serving plate and garnish the top with whole raspberries or strawberries. If desired, split Ladyfingers and arrange them around the sides of the mold. Makes 8 servings.

Strawberry Mousseline

In the recipe for Raspberry Mousseline, replace the raspberries with strawberries. Continue as directed in the recipe. Makes 8 servings.

BAKED CUSTARDS

Baked Vanilla Custard

3 cups milk	4 egg yolks
1 (3-inch) piece vanilla bean, or	½ cup sugar
2 teaspoons vanilla extract	⅛ teaspoon salt
4 whole eggs	⅓ cup heavy cream, whipped (optional)

Scald milk, with vanilla bean (if using), and let cool slightly. Beat whole eggs and egg yolks together, and beat in sugar and salt. Add a little of the hot milk to the eggs and then add them to the remaining milk. Mix well, adding vanilla extract if vanilla bean was not used. Strain into a lightly buttered 1½-quart casserole, or into 8 lightly buttered custard cups. Place casserole or cups in a pan of hot water. Bake in a preheated oven (325°F) 50 to 60 minutes, or until a knife inserted in the center comes out clean. Cool. Serve topped with whipped cream, if desired. Makes 8 servings.

ᐦ Baked Coffee Custard

Make the recipe for Baked Vanilla Custard, replacing ¾ cup of the milk with ¾ cup strong coffee infusion. Continue as directed in the recipe. Makes 8 servings.

ᐦ Baked Praline Custard

Make the recipe for Baked Vanilla Custard, adding 3 tablespoons Praline Powder to the hot mixture. Mix well. Continue as directed in the recipe. Makes 8 servings.

ᐦ Baked Caramel Custard

1 cup sugar	Baked Vanilla Custard
½ cup water	Chantilly Cream

Heat sugar in a heavy skillet until it melts. Gradually stir in water. Cook until the sugar is a deep chestnut brown or caramel. Pour the caramel syrup into a 6-cup ring mold and tilt the mold until the inside is coated. (Or coat the inside of 8 custard cups.) Chill a few minutes for caramel to set. Make the recipe for Baked Vanilla Custard and pour it into the 6-cup mold or the custard cups. Place mold or cups in a pan of hot water and bake in a preheated oven (325°F) 50 to 60 minutes, or until a knife inserted in the center of the custard comes out clean. Cool. If the ring mold is used, turn the custard out onto a serving plate and set a bowl of Chantilly Cream in the center. If custard cups are used, unmold onto individual serving dishes. Top with Chantilly Cream. Makes 8 servings.

ᐦ Baked Chocolate Custard

3 cups milk	4 large whole eggs
1 (3-inch) piece vanilla bean, or	4 large egg yolks
2 teaspoons vanilla extract	½ cup sugar
3 squares (3 ounces) unsweetened	⅛ teaspoon salt
chocolate	½ cup Chantilly Cream

Heat milk, with vanilla bean (if using). Melt chocolate over hot water and gradually stir in ½ cup of the hot milk. Beat whole eggs and egg yolks together and beat in sugar and salt. Add a little of the hot milk to the eggs and then add them to the remaining hot milk. Stir in the chocolate and milk mixture and add vanilla extract if vanilla bean was not used. Strain into a lightly buttered 6-cup casserole, or into 8 lightly buttered custard cups. Place casserole or cups in a pan of hot water. Bake in a preheated oven (325°F) 50 to 60 minutes, or until a knife inserted in the center of the custard comes out clean. Cool. Serve with Chantilly Cream. Makes 8 servings.

Baked Coconut Custard

2 cups milk
1 (2-inch) piece vanilla bean
3 large eggs, beaten

¼ cup sugar
¾ cup flaked coconut or grated fresh coconut
Grated nutmeg

Heat 1¾ cups of the milk with the vanilla bean. Combine eggs, sugar, and the remaining ¼ cup milk. Add to the hot milk. Stir in coconut. Turn into a buttered 1-quart casserole. Sprinkle the top with nutmeg. Place the casserole in a pan of hot water. Bake in a preheated oven (300°F) 1 hour, or until a knife inserted in the center of the pudding comes out clean. If vanilla bean is not available, add 1½ teaspoons vanilla extract along with the eggs and sugar. Makes 6 servings.

Baked Lemon Custard

2 teaspoons grated lemon zest
1 (3-inch) piece vanilla bean, or
    2 teaspoons vanilla extract

3 cups milk
6 large eggs
½ cup sugar

Heat lemon zest and vanilla bean (if using) with 2⅔ cups of the milk. Beat eggs until foamy, then gradually beat in the sugar and the remaining ⅓ cup milk. Add to the hot mixture. Add vanilla extract (if vanilla bean was not used). Strain into a buttered 1-quart mold. Place mold in a pan of hot water. Bake in a preheated oven (325°F) 1 hour, or until a knife inserted in the center comes out clean. Serve warm or cold. Makes 6 servings.

PETITS POTS DE CREME

Petits Pots de Crème are rich custards baked and served in small individual ceramic pots designed especially for this purpose.

Vanilla Pots de Crème

2 cups light cream
1 (3-inch) piece vanilla bean, or
    1½ teaspoons vanilla extract
6 egg yolks

½ cup sugar
⅛ teaspoon salt
Chantilly Cream (optional)

Heat 1¾ cups of the cream with the vanilla bean (if using). Beat egg yolks until light and lemon-colored. Gradually beat in sugar and salt, the remaining ¼ cup cream, and the vanilla extract (if vanilla bean was not used). Gradually beat in the hot cream. Strain mixture into crème pots or custard cups. Place pots in a baking pan. Pour in hot water to depth of 1 inch. Cover the pots with crème pot covers or aluminum foil. Bake in a preheated oven (325°F) 20 to 25 minutes, or until a knife inserted in the center comes out clean. Cool and chill before serving. Garnish with Chantilly Cream, if desired. Makes 6 servings.

Almond Pots de Crème

Make the recipe for Vanilla Pots de Crème. Put ⅓ cup blanched almonds through a food chopper, using the finest blade. Mix well with 2 tablespoons kirsch and add to the uncooked custard mixture just before pouring it into the crème pots or cups. Bake as directed in the recipe. Makes 6 servings.

Coffee Pots de Crème

Make the recipe for Vanilla Pots de Crème, but heat 1½ teaspoons strong coffee infusion with the cream and vanilla bean. Continue as directed in the recipe. Makes 6 servings.

Crème de Cacao Pots de Crème

Make the recipe for Vanilla Pots de Crème, and add 2 tablespoons crème de cacao to the sugar and eggs along with the ¼ cup cold cream. Continue as directed in the recipe. Makes 6 servings.

Praline Pots de Crème

Make the recipe for Vanilla Pots de Crème. Add 3 tablespoons sifted Praline Powder to the hot cream and mix well. Continue as directed in the recipe. Chill. Garnish with Chantilly Cream sprinkled with Praline Powder. Makes 6 servings.

Rum and Chocolate Pots de Crème

2 cups light cream
1 (4-inch) piece vanilla bean, or
   3 teaspoons vanilla extract
4 squares (4 ounces) semisweet
   chocolate

6 egg yolks
¼ cup sugar
⅛ teaspoon salt
2 tablespoons rum
Chantilly Cream

Combine 1¾ cups of the cream and the vanilla bean (if using) in a saucepan. Heat, add chocolate, and stir until chocolate is melted and thoroughly blended with the cream. Beat egg yolks until light and lemon-colored. Gradually beat in sugar and salt. Add the remaining ¼ cup cold cream and the rum. Mix well. Stir in the hot cream and the vanilla extract (if vanilla bean was not used). Strain into crème pots or custard cups. Arrange the pots in a baking pan. Pour hot water into the pan to a depth of 1 inch. Cover pots with crème pot covers or with aluminum foil. Bake in a preheated oven (325°F) 20 to 25 minutes, or until a knife inserted in the center comes out clean. Cool and chill. If desired, serve with Chantilly Cream that has been flavored to taste with a little rum. Makes 6 servings.

Chocolate Pots de Crème

Make the recipe for Rum and Chocolate Pots de Crème, omitting the rum. Continue as directed in the recipe. Makes 6 servings.

CHARLOTTES

CHARLOTTES ARE CYLINDER-SHAPED DESSERTS consisting of an outer shell of bread, ladyfingers, or cake and a cold or hot filling.

To make a cold charlotte, line a charlotte mold or a springform pan with Ladyfingers or strips of sponge cake or Génoise. Pour into it a filling consisting of Jellied Soft Custard, Bavarian Cream, French Pastry Cream, or ice cream, with or without fruits or nuts. Chill until firm, then unmold onto a serving plate and garnish with whipped cream and glacéed or candied fruit, or small fresh fruit, such as strawberries. Serve cold.

For hot charlottes, the mold is lined with butter-soaked bread strips and filled with sweetened very thick stewed fruit. The fruit may or may not be flavored with liqueur or rum. The charlotte is baked and then turned out onto a serving plate. Unless the stewed fruit is very thick, the charlotte is apt to collapse at this point.

Apple Charlotte

Firm-textured bread, sliced
  ¼ inch thick
1 cup (2 sticks) butter, melted
6 to 8 large cooking apples
¼ cup water
¼ cup (½ stick) butter
About ½ cup plus 2 tablespoons sugar

¼ teaspoon salt
1 tablespoon freshly squeezed
  lemon juice
½ teaspoon vanilla extract
½ cup apricot marmalade or jam
¼ cup dark rum

For best results, use bread 2 to 3 days old. Remove crusts. Cut 1 slice of bread into 4 semicircles and dip them in the butter. Sauté until golden brown on each side, adding a little more butter if needed. Fit them into the bottom of a 6-cup charlotte mold or deep casserole. Cut bread slices in strips 1¼ inches wide, enough to line the inside of the mold. Dip them in melted butter and fit them, overlapping, around the inside sides of the mold. Trim off all protruding ends. Peel, quarter, and core apples and cut into thin slices. Place them in a pan with the water and ½ stick butter. Cover and cook over very low heat until apples are soft and all the water has evaporated. Add ½ cup sugar (or to taste) and the next 3 ingredients. Mix well. Heat again if apples seem watery; they should be thick enough to remain in a solid mass in a spoon. Turn the mixture into the prepared mold. Dip in melted butter enough bread strips to cover the top and arrange them over the mold. Pour all remaining butter over the top of the mold. Place the mold on a baking sheet in order to catch any butter that drips over the sides and to prevent the bottom from browning too much. Bake in a preheated oven (400°F) 40 minutes, or until top is browned. Remove from the oven and let stand 20 minutes, then remove from the mold. Place marmalade, rum, and 2 tablespoons sugar in a saucepan, bring to the boiling point, and cook 1 minute. Serve spooned over the warm Apple Charlotte. Makes 6 to 8 servings.

Chocolate Charlotte

12 Ladyfingers, or
    12 strips sponge cake
½ cup milk
4 squares (4 ounces) semisweet
    chocolate
7 tablespoons sugar
2 envelopes unflavored gelatin

½ cup water
4 large eggs, separated
2 tablespoons Praline Powder, or
    1 tablespoon rum
⅛ teaspoon salt
1 cup heavy cream, whipped

Line a 7-inch springform pan, or 1-quart bowl, with waxed paper and then with split Ladyfingers or sponge cake strips. Set aside. Heat the milk in the top of a double boiler. Add chocolate, stir, and heat until chocolate is melted and smooth. Add 4 tablespoons of the sugar. Soften the gelatin in the water and add to the hot milk mixture. Lightly beat egg yolks. Stir in a little of the hot milk and gradually add to the remaining hot mixture. Stir and cook over hot water (not boiling) until custard coats a metal spoon, 10 to 12 minutes. Remove from heat and blend in the Praline Powder or rum. Cool, stirring occasionally, until custard begins to thicken. Add salt to the egg whites and beat them until they stand in soft peaks, then beat in 2 tablespoons of the sugar. Carefully fold into the custard. Whip ½ cup of the cream and fold into mixture. Turn into the prepared pan or bowl. Chill until firm. Just before serving, unmold and decorate with the rest of the cream beaten with remaining 1 tablespoon sugar and put through a pastry tube fitted with a rosette nozzle. Makes 6 servings.

Charlotte Malakoff

12 Ladyfingers
⅓ cup orange liqueur
⅔ cup water
½ cup fine granulated sugar
½ cup (1 stick) softened butter

½ cup finely ground blanched almonds
4 tablespoons kirsch
1½ teaspoons vanilla extract
2½ cups heavy cream
1 tablespoon confectioners' sugar

Oil a 1-quart charlotte mold and cover the bottom with a piece of waxed paper cut to fit it. Split the Ladyfingers and dip them in a mixture of the orange liqueur and water. Arrange them vertically around the sides of the mold. Gradually blend granulated sugar into butter and beat the mixture until it is fluffy. Add almonds, kirsch, and vanilla extract. Whip 2 cups of the cream until stiff, fold into the mixture, and turn it into the prepared mold. Chill several hours or overnight. If the Ladyfingers extend beyond the top of the charlotte, trim them even with it. Unmold onto a serving plate. Remove waxed paper. Whip the remaining ½ cup cream together with confectioners' sugar and put through a pastry bag fitted with a rosette tube to decorate the top. Makes 6 to 8 servings.

Peach Charlotte

12 Ladyfingers
Kirsch or framboise
1 envelope unflavored gelatin
¼ cup cold water
1 cup crushed fresh peaches
2 teaspoons freshly squeezed
    lemon juice
¾ cup granulated sugar
2 large egg yolks

1 large whole egg
⅛ teaspoon salt
¾ cup milk
1 (2-inch) piece vanilla bean, or
    1 teaspoon vanilla extract
1½ cups heavy cream
1 tablespoon confectioners' sugar
Raspberry Puree

Line bottom and sides of a lightly oiled charlotte mold with split Ladyfingers dipped in kirsch or framboise, and set aside. Soften gelatin in water and set aside. Combine peaches with lemon juice and ¼ cup of the granulated sugar and set aside. Beat egg yolks and whole egg in the top of a double boiler or in a 1-quart saucepan. Beat in remaining ½ cup granulated sugar, the salt, milk, and vanilla bean (if using). Cook over hot water (not boiling) or very low heat until the custard coats a metal spoon. Strain through a fine sieve into a bowl. Stir in softened gelatin. Chill in a pan of ice water until the custard begins to thicken and set. Whip 1 cup of the cream and fold it into the custard, along with the peach mixture. If vanilla extract is used instead of vanilla bean, add it with the peaches and cream. Turn into the prepared mold and refrigerate until charlotte is firm and ready to serve. Unmold onto a serving dish. Decorate with remaining ½ cup cream, whipped together with confectioners' sugar and put through a pastry bag fitted with a star tube. Serve with Raspberry Puree. Makes 6 servings.

Raspberry Puree

Crush 2 cups fresh raspberries and push them through a sieve, discarding the seeds. Add a dash of salt, 1 teaspoon freshly squeezed lemon juice, and ⅓ cup medium sugar syrup. Makes about 1 cup.

Charlotte Royale

1 (15½-by-10½-by-1-inch)   Charlotte Cream
  Jelly-Roll Sponge Cake Layer   Petits Fours

Make the sponge cake layer and line a charlotte mold as directed in the following recipe. Fill the mold with Charlotte Cream and chill as directed in the Charlotte Cream recipe. Unmold onto a cake plate, surround with Petits Fours, and serve. Makes 8 to 10 servings.

Jelly-Roll Sponge Cake Layer

4 large eggs   1 teaspoon vanilla extract
¾ teaspoon double-acting   ¾ cup sifted cake flour
  baking powder   Confectioners' sugar
¼ teaspoon salt   Currant jelly
¾ cup granulated sugar   Apricot jam

Place the first 3 ingredients in a mixing bowl and set the bowl over a pan of hot water (not in it). Beat with a wire whip or rotary beater until the eggs are foamy. Gradually beat in the granulated sugar and continue beating until the mixture is very thick. Beat in vanilla extract. Remove bowl from over the hot water. Add flour all at once and carefully fold it into the mixture. Line a lightly greased 15½-by-10½-by-1-inch jelly-roll pan with waxed paper (or brown paper) cut to fit. Grease the paper. Pour the batter into the pan and spread it uniformly over the bottom. Bake in a preheated oven (400°F) 12 to 13 minutes, or until cake springs back when touched in the middle with your index finger. Turn cake upside down on a clean dish towel that has been dusted with confectioners' sugar. Quickly remove paper, trim off browned edges, and set cake aside to cool. Split cake in half horizontally and put the 2 layers together with currant jelly. Spread apricot jam over the top layer. Let layers stand 1 hour or more so that they will hold together.

Line a charlotte mold with the cake as follows: cut the cake into 1-by-10-inch strips as needed—the number used depends on the diameter of the mold. (Save leftover cake for making Petits Fours.) Place the first strip, cut side against the mold, across the center bottom, having the strip extend up both sides, dividing the mold in half. Cut the second strip in half and butt one end of each against the first strip in the center bottom of the mold to make a cross, dividing the mold into quarters. Cut 2 more strips of cake in half, pointing one end of each, and place this end in the center of each of the four sections. This divides the mold into eighths. Fill in remaining space with as many half strips of cake as needed to cover the bottom and sides completely, shaping the ends that are placed in the center so that they will fit snugly.

Charlotte Cream

¾ cup mixed glacéed fruit
½ cup maraschino liqueur
2 envelopes unflavored gelatin
½ cup water
4 eggs, separated
⅓ cup sugar

¹⁄₁₆ teaspoon salt
1 (3-inch) piece vanilla bean, or
    2 teaspoons vanilla extract
1½ cups milk
1½ cups heavy cream, whipped

Soak the glacéed fruit in liqueur until ready to use. Soften the gelatin in the water and set aside. Beat egg yolks in the top of a double boiler or in a 1-quart saucepan. Gradually beat in sugar. Add salt, vanilla bean (if using), and milk. Stir and cook over hot water or very low heat until mixture coats a metal spoon. Remove from heat and strain the custard into a mixing bowl. Add the glacéed fruit and the vanilla extract (if vanilla bean is not used). Chill in a pan of ice water until the custard begins to set. Fold in whipped cream. Pour into a sponge-cake-lined mold (see preceding recipe). Chill until the Charlotte Cream is firm and ready to serve.

Petits Fours for Charlotte Royale

Cut the sponge cake that was left from lining the mold into small cakes of any desired shape. Cover tops and sides with a thin layer of Apricot Glaze, let stand 30 minutes or more for the glaze to set, then frost with Coffee Fondant Frosting for Petits Fours (see page 680). Decorate as desired with Chocolate Cream Frosting put through a cake-decorator's tube.

Charlotte Russe

1 small round sugar cookie
18 Ladyfingers
1 envelope unflavored gelatin
¼ cup cold water
4 large egg yolks

½ cup sugar
1 (2-inch) piece vanilla bean
1 cup milk
1 cup heavy cream, whipped
Chantilly Cream

In a 1-quart charlotte mold or a 1-quart bowl, place the cookie in the center bottom. Finish covering bottom of mold with ends of Ladyfingers cut into triangles, placing them close together and radiating them from the round cookie in the center to simulate the petals of a daisy. Place remaining Ladyfingers (full size) upright and close together around the sides of the mold. Set aside.

Soften gelatin in water and set aside. Beat egg yolks in the top of a double boiler or in a 1-quart saucepan and gradually add the sugar. Mix well. Heat vanilla bean with milk and gradually beat the milk into the eggs and sugar, stirring rapidly. Stir and cook over hot water (not boiling) or very low heat until the custard coats a metal spoon. Remove from heat and strain into a bowl. Chill in a pan of ice water until mixture begins to thicken and set. Fold in whipped cream and pour into the prepared mold. Chill until firm and ready to serve. Unmold onto a serving dish and decorate with Chantilly Cream that has been put through a pastry bag fitted with a star tube. Makes 6 servings.

Marquise Alice

1 envelope unflavored gelatin	3 tablespoons Praline Powder
¼ cup cold water	¾ cup heavy cream, whipped
1 cup milk	12 Ladyfingers
½ cup sugar	Kirsch
¼ teaspoon salt	Chantilly Cream
2 eggs, separated	6 ounces warm red currant jelly
1½ teaspoons vanilla extract	

Soften the gelatin in the water and set aside. Beat the milk, ¼ cup of the sugar, the salt, and the egg yolks together in a saucepan or in the top of a double boiler. Stir and cook over very low heat, or over hot water (not boiling), until the custard coats a metal spoon. Stir in softened gelatin. Strain the custard into a mixing bowl. Add vanilla extract. Chill until custard begins to set. Beat egg whites until they stand in soft peaks, then gradually beat in the remaining ¼ cup sugar and Praline Powder. Fold into the gelatin mixture. Fold in whipped cream.

Meanwhile, split the Ladyfingers, sprinkle them with kirsch, and arrange a layer over the bottom and around the sides of a 7-inch springform pan. Add half of the gelatin mixture and put a layer of kirsch-sprinkled Ladyfingers over it. Pour in the remaining gelatin mixture. Chill until firm and ready to serve. Remove the sides from the springform pan and place the dessert on a serving plate. Spread Chantilly Cream evenly and smoothly over the top. Put the currant jelly in a plastic bag, cut a small hole in one corner, and pipe parallel lines of jelly over the cream. A very pretty decoration can be made by lightly drawing the point of a knife across the lines at intervals. Makes 8 servings.

MERINGUES

A MERINGUE IS A FOAM MADE FROM EGG WHITE, sugar, and air, plus salt and flavoring. To the American cook, the word *meringue* generally means the topping for a pie, which is a soft meringue. However, to the French cook, it more often means a hard meringue used as the base or container for a dessert. Hard meringues require more sugar and more beating than do soft meringues and are baked at a lower temperature for a longer time. Hard meringue is usually piped through a pastry bag or shaped with the bowl of a large spoon to form shells for tarts and pies or layers for meringue cakes. After hard meringues have been baked and cooled, they are filled with fruit, ice cream, pastry cream, whipped cream, or a combination of whipped cream and fruit. Hard meringue shells may be made several days before using and stored in a tightly closed container in a dry place.

Italian meringue is still another type, which is made by beating hot sugar syrup into stiffly beaten egg whites. It is not as stiff as hard meringue and does not require baking, since the egg whites are cooked by the hot sugar syrup. However, if desired, it may be browned lightly in a slow to moderate oven. Italian meringue is used to frost cakes, is spread over pastry fillings, and is added to certain types of sherbets to give them a fluffier, lighter texture.

Soft Meringue

¼ teaspoon salt	6 tablespoons sugar
3 large egg whites	½ teaspoon vanilla extract

Add salt to egg whites and beat them until the egg whites stand in soft peaks. Gradually beat in sugar and vanilla extract. Continue beating until the egg whites stand in stiff peaks. Spread the meringue over the top of any pie specifying meringue topping, and seal it to the inside edges of the crust. Bake in a preheated oven (325°F) 15 minutes. Cool on a cooling rack away from drafts. Makes enough meringue for one 9-inch pie.

Italian Meringue

1 cup sugar	¹⁄₁₆ teaspoon salt
¼ teaspoon cream of tartar	3 large egg whites
½ cup water	1½ teaspoons vanilla extract

Combine the sugar and cream of tartar in a 1-quart saucepan. Add the water. Stir and cook slowly until sugar has dissolved and water begins to boil. Cover and boil 3 minutes, or until the steam has washed down any crystals that may have formed on the sides of the pan. Remove cover and boil rapidly, without stirring, to 242°F on a candy thermometer, or until syrup spins a thread 6 to 8 inches long. Add the salt to the egg whites and beat them until they stand in stiff peaks. Using an electric or rotary beater, gradually beat in the hot syrup. Add the vanilla extract and continue beating until the meringue stands in very stiff peaks. Use as a pie or pudding topping, to frost cakes, and to make sherbets and frozen parfaits. Makes about 2½ cups.

Caramel Italian Meringue

In Italian Meringue recipe, replace white sugar with caramel.

Chocolate Italian Meringue

Add 2 squares (2 ounces) melted and cooled unsweetened chocolate to Italian Meringue just before serving.

Coffee Italian Meringue

In Italian Meringue recipe, replace water with strong coffee infusion.

Fruit Italian Meringue

Fold ¾ cup pureed fruit (peaches, raspberries, strawberries, cooked apples) into Italian Meringue just before using.

Nut Italian Meringue

Fold ½ cup finely chopped toasted almonds, pecans, pistachios, or walnuts into Italian Meringue just before using.

Peppermint Italian Meringue

Fold ½ cup crushed peppermint candy into Italian Meringue just before using.

Hard Meringue

¼ teaspoon salt
¼ teaspoon cream of tartar
4 large egg whites

1 cup fine granulated sugar
½ teaspoon vanilla extract

Add salt and cream of tartar to egg whites. Beat with an electric beater at high speed until the whites are stiff enough to hold their shape. Beat in the sugar, 2 tablespoons at a time, at low speed. Beat the whites until they stand in very stiff peaks and are shiny and moist.

Individual Meringue Shells

Make the recipe for Hard Meringue. Mark twelve 3-inch circles on a piece of brown paper. Butter the paper lightly and dust it with cornstarch. Using a pastry bag, spread each circle with a layer of the meringue mixture ¼ inch thick. Build a border with more meringue to a height of 1½ inches, leaving the center unfilled. Place paper on a cookie sheet. Bake in a preheated oven (200°F) 1¼ hours. Turn off heat and cool in the oven 30 minutes. Remove from the oven. When cold, remove to a tin box and cover tightly. Use as needed for cream fillings, fruits, and ice cream. Makes twelve 3-inch shells.

Meringue Pie Shell

Make the Hard Meringue recipe, using only 2 egg whites and half the quantities of the other ingredients. Using a round 9-inch layer cake pan as a guide, mark a 9-inch circle on brown paper. Butter it lightly and dust with a little cornstarch. Spread the circle with a layer of meringue ¼ inch thick. Build a border with remaining meringue to a height of 1½ inches. Place paper on a cookie sheet. Bake in a preheated oven (200°F) 2 hours. Cool in the oven 30 minutes. Remove from oven and cool. Remove the shell from the paper. Fill with a cream filling, fruit, or ice cream. Makes one 9-inch meringue shell.

Meringue Cake Layers

Make the Hard Meringue recipe. Using an 8-inch layer cake pan as a guide, trace two 8-inch circles on each of 2 large pieces of baking parchment paper. Butter lightly and dust with a little cornstarch. Spread each circle with a layer of meringue about ⅓ inch thick. Bake as directed for the Meringue Pie Shell. Spread cream fillings and fruit or ice cream mixtures between the layers. Makes four 8-inch layers.

FILLINGS FOR HARD MERINGUES

Lime Cream

4 large egg yolks
½ cup sugar
1⁄16 teaspoon salt
¼ cup fresh lime juice

¼ teaspoon grated lemon zest
½ cup heavy cream, whipped
½ teaspoon vanilla extract

Beat the egg yolks in the top of a double boiler. Gradually beat in sugar and salt. Add lime juice and mix well. Stir and cook over hot water (not boiling) until mixture is thick and smooth. Remove from heat and cool. Fold in remaining ingredients. Pile the mixture in 6 Individual Meringue Shells or in a 9-inch Meringue Pie Shell. Makes 6 servings.

Lemon Cream

Make the recipe for Lime Cream, replacing the lime juice with freshly squeezed lemon juice, and the ¼ teaspoon grated lime zest with ½ teaspoon grated lemon zest. Continue as directed in the recipe. Makes 6 servings.

Peach Chantilly Cream

2 cups diced peaches	⅛ teaspoon salt
½ cup sifted confectioners' sugar	2 cups heavy cream

Combine peaches, ¼ cup of the confectioners' sugar, and the salt. Whip cream until almost stiff, then gradually beat in the remaining ¼ cup sugar . Fold in the peaches. Use as a filling for Meringue Shells. Makes 8 servings.

Raspberry Chantilly Cream

In the recipe for Peach Chantilly Cream, replace diced peaches with the same amount of whole fresh raspberries. If desired, flavor to taste with kirsch or framboise. Makes 8 servings.

Strawberry Chantilly Cream

In the recipe for Peach Chantilly Cream, replace diced peaches with the same amount of sliced strawberries. If desired, flavor to taste with kirsch or framboise. Makes 8 servings.

Vanilla Whipped-Cream Filling

1½ teaspoons unflavored gelatin	2 tablespoons sugar
1½ tablespoons cold water	1 teaspoon vanilla extract
1 cup heavy cream	Chocolate Curls (optional)

Soften the gelatin in the water in a custard cup and place the cup in a pan of hot water to melt the gelatin, stirring frequently. Combine the cream and sugar and beat until the cream stands in soft peaks. Fold in the melted gelatin and the vanilla extract. Makes enough filling for 8 Individual Meringue Shells or 4 Meringue Cake Layers. After filling the meringues, garnish the tops, if desired, with Chocolate Curls.

Coffee Whipped-Cream Filling

In the recipe for Vanilla Whipped-Cream Filling, mix 2 tablespoons strong coffee infusion with the melted gelatin, replacing the vanilla extract, and fold into the whipped cream.

Fruit in Meringue Cases

1 recipe Hard Meringue
2 cups diced peaches, sliced strawberries, or whole raspberries
⅓ cup confectioners' sugar

1 teaspoon vanilla extract
2 tablespoons kirsch (optional)
⅔ cup Chantilly Cream

Butter the bottoms of six 2½-inch muffin pans and line them with unglazed brown or white paper cut to fit. Make the recipe for Hard Meringue and pipe or spoon the mixture into the muffin pans, filling them. Bake in a preheated oven (200°F) 1 to 1¼ hours. Remove the meringues from the pans while warm and scoop out and discard the soft centers from the underside. Cool. Combine fruit, confectioners' sugar, vanilla extract, and kirsch, if using. Macerate 30 minutes. Just before serving, fill the meringue nests with the fruit. Place on a serving plate with tops of meringues up. Top with Chantilly Cream. Makes 6 servings.

Meringues Glacées

12 (3-inch) Individual Meringue Shells
6 scoops ice cream (any desired flavor)
1 tablespoon confectioners' sugar

Kirsch or Cointreau to taste
½ cup heavy cream

Press a meringue shell on each side of a scoop of ice cream, using 2 shells per serving. Combine the last 3 ingredients and beat until the cream stands in peaks. Put the cream in a pastry bag fitted with a fluted nozzle and decorate edges of shells with a fluted design of whipped cream. Makes 6 servings.

Meringue Cake

⅓ cup sugar
2 cups raspberries, sliced strawberries, or sliced peaches
1½ teaspoons vanilla extract
2 tablespoons kirsch (optional)

1 cup heavy cream
4 Meringue Cake Layers
Raspberries, whole strawberries, or diced peaches

Combine the sugar, 2 cups fruit, the vanilla extract, and kirsch (if using). Set aside to macerate 30 minutes. Whip the cream until it stands in stiff peaks, being careful not to overbeat it. Save 1 cup of it for decorating the cake. Fold the fruit mixture into the remaining cream and spread it between the Meringue Cake Layers in layer-cake fashion. Spread it over the top and sides of the cake. There should be some left. Put remaining cream in a pastry bag fitted with a rosette nozzle and pipe rosettes over the top and sides of the cake as desired. Garnish the plate with raspberries, whole strawberries, or diced peaches. Makes 8 servings.

Meringue Vacherin

¹⁄₁₆ teaspoon salt	1½ teaspoons vanilla extract
6 large egg whites	Strawberry Chantilly Cream
1½ cups sifted confectioners' sugar	8 whole unhulled fresh strawberries

On each of 2 pieces of baking parchment paper, cut to fit a cookie sheet, mark two 8-inch circles, using an 8-inch cake pan as a guide. Lay the sheets of paper on 2 well-buttered cookie sheets and press down well so that the butter will seep through the papers and grease the cookie sheets. Sprinkle the papers lightly with cornstarch. Set aside.

Add the salt to the egg whites and beat them until stiff but not dry. Sift 1¼ cups of the confectioners' sugar over them all at one time, add the vanilla extract, and with a rubber spatula gently fold in sugar and vanilla extract. Fill a pastry bag fitted with the largest nozzle (¾ to 1 inch in diameter) with egg white mixture and pipe it into 4 rings or wreaths, using the marked circles as a guide. Sift remaining ¼ cup confectioners' sugar lightly over the wreaths. Set leftover meringue mixture aside. Bake in a preheated oven (200°F) about 1 hour, or until meringues are dry. Turn off heat and let meringues remain in the oven 30 minutes. Strip off the paper, and invert the meringues to allow them to dry. Using reserved meringue mixture, put the meringue wreaths together in layer-cake fashion, on a heatproof plate. Trim the edges smooth with a sharp knife, and cover the top and sides with the meringue mixture. Put the rest of the meringue mixture in a pastry bag fitted with a rosette nozzle and pipe rosettes as desired around the top and sides, reserving any leftover meringue. Return meringue wreath to a preheated oven (275°F) and bake 40 to 45 minutes, or until dry. Cool. Fill center with Strawberry Chantilly Cream. Garnish with strawberries. Makes 8 servings.

Snow Eggs or Oeufs à la Neige

¹⁄₁₆ teaspoon salt	1 (2-inch) piece vanilla bean, or
4 large egg whites	1½ teaspoons vanilla extract
¾ cup plus 2 tablespoons sugar	4 egg yolks
2 cups milk	

Add the salt to the egg whites and beat them until they are stiff. Gradually beat in ¾ cup sugar, beating well after each addition. Heat the milk, 2 tablespoons sugar, and the vanilla bean (if using) in a shallow saucepan. Bring to the boiling point and reduce heat to simmering. (If vanilla bean was not used, add vanilla extract now.) Using a soup spoon, shape the meringue into ovals the size and shape of an egg and drop them into the simmering milk. After poaching 2 minutes, turn them carefully with a fork and poach 2 more minutes. (If the meringue eggs are cooked longer they will collapse.) Remove the meringue eggs from the milk with a perforated spoon and drain them on a dry cloth or paper towels. Set aside. Reserve the milk. Beat the egg yolks well. Strain the hot milk and gradually beat it into the egg yolks. Stir and cook over hot water or very low heat until the custard begins to thicken. Remove from heat and chill.

To serve, strain the custard into a glass bowl, and float the meringue eggs on it. Makes 6 servings.

 Snow Eggs with Berries

Garnish with whole strawberries or raspberries. Combine crushed strawberries or raspberries with sugar to taste and serve in a separate bowl

Snow Eggs with Chocolate Custard

2 cups milk	4 large egg yolks
1 (3-inch) piece vanilla bean	2 squares (2 ounces) unsweetened chocolate
½ cup sugar	6 Snow Eggs
⅛ teaspoon salt	Praline Powder

Heat 1¾ cups of the milk with the vanilla bean until hot. Combine sugar and salt in the top of a double boiler or in a saucepan. Add egg yolks and mix well. Stir in the remaining ¼ cup cold milk, then add the hot milk and stir and cook over hot water or low heat until custard coats a metal spoon. Add the chocolate and stir until it is melted. Cool. Place the Snow Eggs in a glass bowl. Strain the chocolate custard around them and sprinkle with Praline Powder. Makes 6 servings.

Mon Rêve

6 Snow Eggs	½ cup cold Chocolate Sauce
Custard for Snow Eggs	2 tablespoons Praline Powder
1½ cups heavy cream	Kirsch to taste

Make the Snow Eggs and custard according to the recipe for Snow Eggs. Cool the custard. Whip the cream and fold the Chocolate Sauce and the Praline Powder into it. Turn it into a serving bowl and shape it into a smooth dome. Arrange the Snow Eggs on top. Add kirsch to the cooled custard and pour it around. Makes 6 servings.

PUDDINGS

Apple Pudding

¾ cup (1½ sticks) softened butter
2 large egg yolks
2 large whole eggs
2 tablespoons flour
17 almond macaroons
(6 ounces total)

2 cups sweetened applesauce
¹⁄₁₆ teaspoon salt
1 teaspoon vanilla extract
Whipped cream
Confectioners' sugar

Beat the butter until fluffy. Beat in the egg yolks and whole eggs, one at a time. Stir in the flour. Break the macaroons into fine pieces, mix with the applesauce, salt, and vanilla extract, and blend with the butter and egg mixture. Turn into 7 buttered 6-ounce custard cups. Place them in a pan of hot water. Bake in a preheated oven (350°F) 40 minutes, or until puddings are firm. Cool 10 minutes. Turn out into dessert dishes. Sweeten whipped cream with confectioners' sugar to taste and serve it as desired over the puddings. Makes 7 servings.

Bread and Butter Pudding

2 cups finely diced bread
3 to 4 tablespoons butter
1¾ cups hot milk
¼ cup finely chopped glacéed
orange peel
¼ cup currants or raisins

1 teaspoon grated lemon zest
1 teaspoon vanilla extract
3 large eggs, separated
½ cup plus 1 tablespoon sugar
1 cup sweet sherry
3 tablespoons apricot jam

Sauté the bread in butter, adding more butter as needed. Add the sautéed bread to the hot milk. Stir in the next 4 ingredients. Beat the egg yolks, gradually beat in ¼ cup of the sugar, and gently blend with the milk and bread mixture. Beat the egg whites until they stand in soft stiff peaks, and beat into them ¼ cup sugar. Fold into the egg yolk mixture. Turn into a buttered 1-quart mold. Place the mold in a pan of hot water. Bake in a preheated oven (325°F) 1 hour, or until a knife inserted in the center of the pudding comes out clean. Let the pudding stand 20 to 30 minutes before unmolding it onto a serving dish. Combine the sherry, 1 tablespoon sugar, and the jam in a small saucepan. Bring to the boiling point and cook 2 minutes. Serve over the pudding. Makes 6 servings.

Breadcrumb Pudding

2 cups milk	½ cup sugar
1 (2-inch) piece vanilla bean, or	2 whole eggs
1 teaspoon vanilla extract	3 large eggs, separated
2½ cups soft white breadcrumbs	Sabayon Sauce or Vanilla Sauce

Scald the milk, with the vanilla bean (if using). Add breadcrumbs. Beat ¼ cup of the sugar with the whole eggs and the egg yolks and gently blend with the milk and breadcrumbs. Rub the mixture through a sieve. Add vanilla extract (if vanilla bean was not used). Beat the egg whites until they stand in soft peaks; gradually beat in the remaining ¼ cup sugar. Fold into the custard mixture and turn it into a buttered 1-quart mold. Place the mold in a pan of hot water. Bake in a preheated oven (325°F) 50 to 60 minutes, or until a knife inserted in the center comes out clean. Let the pudding stand 20 to 30 minutes before unmolding it. Serve warm with Sabayon Sauce or Vanilla Sauce. Makes 6 servings.

English Rolypoly Jam Pudding

¼ pound beef suet	Marmalade or apricot, strawberry,
2 cups sifted all-purpose flour	gooseberry, raspberry, or plum jam
2 teaspoons double-acting	Boiling water
baking powder	Jam sauce
½ teaspoon salt	
About ½ cup water	

Put suet through a food chopper, using the finest blade, or finely chop it with a knife. Sift the next 3 ingredients together. Add the suet and mix well. Gradually add enough water to the mixture to make a soft, stiff dough that can be rolled. Knead about 20 seconds. Roll dough ¼ inch thick on a lightly floured board. Spread the dough with marmalade or jam. Roll up jelly-roll fashion. Moisten the edge and press down to seal thoroughly. Rinse a clean towel in cold water and wrap it around the roll. Tie the roll tightly at both ends and tie again in the middle. Place it in a large saucepan containing enough boiling water to cover it generously. Cover and boil 2½ hours, adding more water as needed. Cut into slices ½ inch thick and serve with jam sauce. Makes 6 servings.

English Plum Pudding

½ pound (1¼ cups) chopped
  pitted dates
½ pound (1¼ cups) glacéed
  lemon peel
½ pound (1¼ cups) chopped
  glacéed orange peel
1 pound (2½ cups) chopped
  glacéed citron
1 (15-ounce) package dried currants
1 (15-ounce) package seedless raisins
1 (15-ounce) package seeded raisins
1 cup slivered blanched almonds
2 cups apricot or peach brandy
2 cups sifted all-purpose flour
½ cup light brown sugar

1 teaspoon ground cinnamon
1 teaspoon ground ginger
1 teaspoon grated nutmeg
¼ teaspoon ground cloves
1 teaspoon salt
1 cup fine dry white breadcrumbs
1 pound beef suet
4 large eggs, well beaten
1 (6-ounce) glass red currant jelly
Boiling water
2 or 3 lumps sugar
Brandy or rum
Hard Sauce, Chantilly Cream,
  or Sabayon Sauce

Soak fruit and almonds in brandy for 4 days. Sift flour, sugar, spices, and salt together into a large mixing bowl. Add breadcrumbs and mix well. Put beef suet through a food chopper, using the finest blade, and mix well with the flour mixture. Add the brandied fruit and almonds, the eggs, and the jelly. Mix well. Turn the dough into 2 greased and floured 2-quart molds. Cover with the lids, or with 2 layers of heavy-duty aluminum foil tied tightly to hold it in place. Place the molds in large kettles and pour in enough boiling water to come halfway up the sides of the molds. Cover the kettles and boil 4 hours from the time the water starts to boil. Remove from water and cool. Store the puddings in a cool place for at least a month before serving. If desired, unmold the puddings and wrap in cloth wrung out in sherry, rum, or brandy. Before serving, steam the pudding for 1½ to 2 hours in the mold in which it was cooked. Unmold onto a serving plate. Soak sugar lumps in brandy or rum and heat ¼ cup brandy or rum. Pour heated liquor into sweetened liquor, ignite and quickly pour over the pudding. Bring the pudding to the table flaming. Serve with Hard Sauce, Chantilly Cream, or Sabayon Sauce. Makes two 2-quart puddings (10 servings each).

Tapioca Pudding

3 cups milk
1 (2-inch) piece vanilla bean, or
  1½ teaspoons vanilla extract
2 large eggs, separated
½ cup plus 2 teaspoons sugar

¼ teaspoon salt
¼ cup tapioca
½ teaspoon grated lemon zest
⅓ cup heavy cream

Heat 2¾ cups of the milk, with the vanilla bean (if using). Beat the egg yolks and add the remaining ¼ cup milk, ¼ cup of the sugar, and the salt. Mix well. Add to the hot milk, along with the tapioca. Stir and cook over very low heat until the mixture has thickened and the tapioca is transparent, 20 to 30 minutes. Remove from heat and remove vanilla bean if used. Beat egg whites until they stand in soft peaks, then beat in ¼ cup sugar. Fold into the hot mixture, along with the lemon zest and the vanilla extract (if the vanilla bean was not used). Combine the cream and the 2 teaspoons sugar and beat until cream stands in soft stiff peaks. Serve over pudding. Makes 6 servings.

 Rhubarb Tapioca Pudding

6 cups diced rhubarb
2 tablespoons tapioca
1 teaspoon grated lemon zest
¼ teaspoon salt
1½ teaspoons vanilla extract

6 tablespoons butter
2½ cups soft white breadcrumbs
2 teaspoons sugar
⅓ cup heavy cream

Combine the first 5 ingredients and set aside. Melt the butter in a saucepan. Add breadcrumbs and mix well. Fill a buttered 1½-quart casserole with alternating layers of breadcrumbs and the rhubarb mixture, having breadcrumbs as the bottom and top layers. Cover and bake in a preheated oven (400°F) 25 minutes. Remove cover and bake the pudding 10 minutes, or until crumbs are brown. Combine sugar and cream and beat until the cream stands in soft peaks. Serve over warm pudding. Makes 6 servings.

RICE DESSERTS

Rice Condé

¾ cup long-grain converted rice
Hot water
½ teaspoon salt
3 cups milk
¾ cup sugar
1 (2-inch) piece vanilla bean, or
    1 teaspoon vanilla extract

4 large egg yolks
2 tablespoons butter
2 tablespoons heavy cream
Glacéed cherries
Angelica
Apricot Sauce

Place rice in a 1½-quart saucepan and add enough hot water to cover. Soak 30 minutes. Drain off all the water from the rice. Add the next 3 ingredients and the vanilla bean (if using), cover, and cook 20 to 25 minutes, or until rice is tender but not mushy. Remove and discard vanilla bean, or if using vanilla extract add it now. Beat the egg yolks until they are light and foamy, then add them to the rice. Add the butter and cream. Mix well, being careful not to crush the rice. Heat 1 to 2 minutes, or only enough to cook the egg yolks. Turn the mixture into a 5-cup mold. Let stand until the mixture takes the shape of the mold. Unmold onto a serving platter. Garnish as desired with glacéed cherries and angelica. Serve with Apricot Sauce. Makes 6 to 8 servings.

Apples Condé

1 cup sugar	1 (1-inch) piece vanilla bean
2 cups water	¼ teaspoon salt
1 (2-inch) piece vanilla bean	3 large egg yolks
3 medium-sized tart apples	1 tablespoon butter
2 tablespoons rum	Glacéed cherries
½ cup long-grain rice	Angelica
2 cups milk	Apricot Sauce

Combine ¾ cup of the sugar, the water, and 2-inch piece vanilla bean in a saucepan large enough for poaching apples. Bring to the boiling point and simmer 5 minutes. Peel, halve, and core apples. Add them to the syrup and cook, uncovered, until apples are tender when pierced with a toothpick but still hold their shape. Add rum and let apples stand in the syrup until ready to use. Soak the rice 30 minutes in enough hot water to cover. Drain well. Add the milk, with 1-inch vanilla bean, salt, and remaining ¼ cup sugar. Cover and cook over very low heat 20 to 25 minutes, or until rice is tender but not mushy. Beat the egg yolks until light and foamy, then gradually stir them into the rice, along with the butter. Press the rice into a round mold or pan 8 inches in diameter and 2 inches deep, and let stand until the rice takes the shape of the mold. Unmold onto a warm platter. Remove the apples from the syrup, drain them well, and arrange them over the top of the rice. Garnish with glacéed cherries and angelica. Serve warm with Apricot Sauce. Makes 6 servings.

Apricots Condé

Use the recipe for Apples Condé, replacing the apples with 9 poached apricots, or with 18 canned apricot halves. Garnish with glacéed cherries and citron. Makes 6 servings.

Peaches Condé

Use the recipe for Apples Condé, replacing the apples with peaches. Makes 6 servings.

Pineapple Condé

Use the recipe for Apples Condé, replacing the apples with thin slices fresh pineapple. Serve with Apricot Sauce flavored with rum to taste. Makes 6 servings.

Praline Condé

Use the recipe for Rice Condé, but reduce the amount of sugar to ⅓ cup and add ¼ cup Praline Powder. Continue as directed in the recipe. When ready to serve the condé, unmold it onto a serving plate and sprinkle it with toasted slivered blanched almonds. Serve with Chantilly Cream. Makes 6 to 8 servings.

Stuffed Apricots Colbert

24 poached apricot halves	2 tablespoons water
Vanilla Syrup	Fine white breadcrumbs
3 cups hot Rice Condé	Oil for frying
Flour	Confectioners' sugar
2 eggs, beaten	Apricot Sauce

Poach the apricot halves in Vanilla Syrup only until they are firm-tender. Remove from syrup, drain well, and pat dry with paper towels. Prepare the rice as instructed in the recipe for Rice Condé and spoon it into the centers of 12 of the apricot halves. Cover each with one of the remaining apricot halves. Roll them in flour. Beat the eggs together with the water. Dip the floured apricots into beaten eggs, roll in breadcrumbs, and fry 2 to 3 minutes (or until browned) in deep fat preheated to 375°F. Drain on paper towels. Sprinkle with confectioners' sugar. To serve, place apricots in individual dessert dishes and spoon Apricot Sauce over them. Serve warm. Makes 8 servings.

Orange Rice Mold Maltaise

1 cups long-grain rice	2 teaspoons grated orange zest
3½ cups hot milk	½ teaspoon grated lemon zest
½ teaspoon salt	½ cup freshly squeezed orange juice
1 (2-inch) piece vanilla bean, or	1 cup heavy cream, whipped
1½ teaspoons vanilla extract	2 cups fresh orange sections
⅔ cup sugar	¼ cup Grand Marnier

Soak rice 30 minutes in water to cover. Drain well. Add the rice to the hot milk, along with salt and vanilla bean (if using). Cover and simmer (do not boil) 30 minutes. Remove from heat and let the rice stand 10 minutes with cover on. Remove vanilla bean, if used, or add vanilla extract if vanilla bean was not used. Stir in sugar, orange and lemon zest, and orange juice. Fold in whipped cream. Pour into a lightly oiled 9-inch ring mold. Chill several hours or overnight. To serve, unmold onto a chilled serving plate and fill center with orange sections marinated in Grand Marnier. Makes 8 servings.

Pears with Rice à l'Imperiale

½ cup mixed glacéed fruit
3 tablespoons kirsch
½ cup long-grain rice
2 cups milk
¼ teaspoon salt
3 tablespoons sugar

1 (2-inch) piece vanilla bean, or
   1½ teaspoons vanilla extract
6 large halves of pears, poached
   in Vanilla Syrup
½ cup red currant jelly

Macerate the glacéed fruit in 2 tablespoons of the kirsch while preparing the other ingredients. Soak the rice 30 minutes in hot water to cover. Drain well and add the milk, salt, sugar, and vanilla bean (if using). Cover and cook over low heat 20 to 25 minutes, or until rice is tender but not mushy. Remove vanilla bean, or, if vanilla bean was not used, fold in vanilla extract, along with the glacéed fruit. Turn this mixture into a shallow serving bowl. Arrange the poached pear halves over the top. Melt the jelly in a small saucepan Add the remaining kirsch. Spoon the sauce over the pears, covering them completely. Serve warm. Makes 6 servings.

Pears with Rice Marie-Anne

6 medium-small pears
½ cup sugar
2 cups water
1 teaspoon freshly squeezed lemon juice
¹⁄₁₆ teaspoon salt
1 (2-inch) piece vanilla bean, or
   1½ teaspoon vanilla extract

2 tablespoons kirsch
½ cup long-grain rice
1 (8-inch) round Génoise layer
Soft Meringue, using 2 egg whites
Glacéed cherries
Angelica

Wash and peel the pears, leaving them whole with stems attached. Combine the sugar, water, lemon juice, salt, and vanilla bean (if using) in a saucepan. Bring to the boiling point and simmer 5 minutes. Add the pears and cook 10 minutes, or until pears are tender when pierced with a toothpick. Add kirsch and set aside. Cook the rice as directed in the recipe for Apples Condé. Place the Génoise in the bottom of an oven-proof bowl and spoon the cooked rice over it, shaping it in the form of a pyramid, leaving space around the edge of the cake to place the pears in upright position later. Cover the rice with Soft Meringue forced through a pastry bag fitted with a star noz-zle. Place the bowl in a preheated oven (275°F) 25 to 30 minutes, or until meringue is dry. Drain the pears well and pat dry with paper towels. Arrange them on the cake around the pyramid of rice in the space left for them. Decorate as desired with glacéed cherries and angelica. Makes 6 servings.

Singapore Pineapple with Rice

¾ cup long-grain rice
4 cups milk
1 cup sugar
½ teaspoon salt
1 (2-inch) piece vanilla bean, or
    1½ teaspoons vanilla extract
2 envelopes unflavored gelatin

½ cup cold water
1 cup heavy cream, whipped
1 cup water
3 cups fresh pineapple wedges
¼ cup maraschino liqueur
Apricot Sauce

Wash the rice, drain well, and add it to the milk. Stir in ½ cup of the sugar and the salt, and add the vanilla bean (if using). Cover and cook over low heat 20 to 25 minutes, or until rice is very soft and creamy. Push the rice through a sieve. Soften the gelatin in ½ cup cold water and add to the hot rice. Add vanilla extract (if vanilla bean was not used), and stir until gelatin has melted. Chill until the rice begins to set. Fold in the whipped cream and turn into a lightly oiled 6-cup ring mold. Chill until cream is firm, 5 to 6 hours or overnight. Meanwhile, combine remaining ½ cup sugar and 1 cup water in a saucepan, bring to the boiling point, reduce heat, and simmer 3 to 4 minutes. Add the pineapple, cover, and cook over low heat 10 minutes. Remove from heat and cool in the syrup. Drain off syrup and add liqueur. Macerate at least 1 hour. To serve, unmold the rice cream onto a large chilled serving plate or tray. Fill the center with the pineapple wedges. Serve with Apricot Sauce flavored to taste with some of the liqueur in which the pineapple was macerated. Makes 8 servings.

Rice à l'Imperatrice

½ cup finely chopped glacéed fruit
3 tablespoons kirsch
½ cup long-grain rice
3 cups milk
¼ teaspoon salt
1 (3-inch) piece vanilla bean, or
    1½ teaspoons vanilla extract
1½ teaspoons unflavored gelatin

2 tablespoons water
¼ cup sugar
2 large egg yolks
½ cup heavy cream, whipped
Glacéed cherries
Angelica
½ cup red currant jelly

Combine the glacéed fruit and 2 tablespoons of the kirsch and macerate while preparing the rest of the ingredients. Soak the rice in hot water 30 minutes. Drain well. Add 2 cups of the milk, the salt, and the vanilla bean (if using). Cover and cook 20 to 25 minutes, or until rice is tender but not mushy. If rice becomes too dry before it has finished cooking, add a little more milk. Soften the gelatin in 2 tablespoons water. Combine the sugar and egg yolks and mix well. Stir in the remaining 1 cup milk. Stir and cook over low heat or hot water (not boiling) until custard coats a metal spoon. Add the gelatin and stir until it is dissolved. Strain the custard into the rice. Mix well and chill until the mixture begins to set. Fold in the macerated fruit, the vanilla extract (if vanilla bean was not used), and the whipped cream. Turn the mixture into a lightly oiled 1-quart mold. Chill until the rice mixture is set. Unmold onto a serving plate. Decorate as desired with glacéed cherries and angelica. Warm the jelly together with the remaining 1 tablespoon kirsch and serve over the dessert. Makes 6 servings.

Strawberry Rice à l'Imperatrice

Replace the glacéed fruit in the recipe for Rice à l'Impératrice with 1½ cups sliced strawberries. Macerate them in 3 tablespoons kirsch. Continue as directed in the recipe. When the cream is unmolded on a serving plate, decorate it with whole unhulled strawberries. Omit the currant jelly and serve with whipped cream flavored to taste with sugar and kirsch. Makes 8 servings.

Chestnut Frou-Frou

Rice à l'Impératrice	½ cup heavy cream, whipped
2 tablespoons thick Sweet Chestnut Puree	Almond Wafer Cornets
½ teaspoon vanilla extract	Chantilly Cream

Prepare and mold Rice à l'Impératrice as directed in the preceding recipe. Fold Sweet Chestnut Puree and vanilla extract into the whipped cream and pipe it into the cornets, using a pastry bag with a star nozzle. Unmold the Rice à l'Impératrice onto a large serving plate. Fill the center with Chantilly Cream and surround the mold with the filled Almond Wafer Cornets. Makes 8 servings.

HOT DESSERT SOUFFLES

A HOT DESSERT SOUFFLE IS PREPARED WITH A BASE OF BUTTER, milk, flour, egg yolks, sugar, and flavoring, other than the type of egg-white-only soufflés used with fresh fruit purees. The three standard methods of preparation are:

- *Béchamel Sauce or Cream Sauce method.* Make a Béchamel Sauce or Cream Sauce, starting with a cooked roux. Cool slightly and beat in egg yolks. Carefully incorporate stiffly beaten egg whites.
- *Bouilli method.* Mix flour, milk, and sugar together and cook until the mixture has thickened. Cool slightly and beat in butter and egg yolks. Then gently

fold in the stiffly beaten egg whites. This method is preferred by some because it requires less butter and makes a lighter soufflé.

- *French Pastry Cream method* with its cooked eggs. The egg yolks are beaten into the pastry cream and the stiffly beaten egg whites are then folded into the mixture.

No matter which method of preparation is used, the size of a soufflé depends upon the amount of air beaten into the egg whites and upon maintaining this air during the baking period. Therefore, it is essential that the egg whites be beaten correctly and that they be folded into the cooked mixture carefully. If the egg whites are beaten insufficiently, too little air is enclosed in the egg white foam and the air cells do not expand sufficiently during baking, with the result that the soufflé will be smaller and less stable than it should be. If the egg whites are overbeaten, the cell walls will lose their elasticity and break; the egg whites will have a dry, lumpy appearance; and the soufflé will collapse.

How to Beat Egg Whites for a Soufflé

To beat egg whites to the greatest volume and stability, have them at room temperature, make sure that they and all the utensils are free of fat in any form (for example, particles of egg yolk or grease on the beater or bowl), and beat them with a fine wire whip.

Two ingredients that may be added to egg whites to increase their stability are cream of tartar (for its acidity) and sugar. Add ¼ teaspoon cream of tartar to 4 to 6 egg whites after they have been beaten until foamy. Continue beating until they glisten and stand in soft peaks when the beater is raised. Then beat in 1 tablespoon sugar (reserved from the total amount specified in the recipe) and continue beating until the egg whites stand in sharp, stiff, moist-looking peaks when the beater is withdrawn. The addition of these ingredients permits the air bubbles to swell along with the expansion of the air they contain.

Fold the egg whites into the soufflé mixture as soon as they have been beaten sufficiently. First mix 2 tablespoons of the beaten whites into the soufflé preparation to thin it so that the remaining whites can be folded in more easily. Then, using a rubber spatula and a light folding motion, never stirring, fold in the remaining egg whites. This operation should be done quickly and with a light hand. If a few particles of foam are not fully incorporated this will not interfere with the success of the soufflé.

How to Prepare a Soufflé Dish

Soufflés may be baked in a charlotte mold (a cylindrical metal mold commonly used in France), or in a straight-sided ovenproof casserole. The charlotte mold is usually tall enough to accommodate the soufflé after it has baked, but the average casserole will need to have its sides extended with a collar made of 2 layers of aluminum foil or brown paper folded to a width of 6 inches and tied around the dish so it will extend

4 inches above the top of the dish. (As the soufflé bakes it will puff and rise up the sides of the collar. Remove the collar after the soufflé has baked.) Butter the bottom and sides of the dish and the inside of the collar generously and sprinkle with granulated sugar. Spoon the soufflé mixture into the dish, filling it three-fourths full.

How to Give a Soufflé a "Top Hat"

Smooth the top of the soufflé mixture. Using a knife with a rounded tip, the tip of a teaspoon, or your index finger, trace a circle ½ inch deep around the top of the soufflé 1 inch from the edge. The crust will break at this point and form a taller center. This permits the soufflé to rise evenly.

How to Bake a Soufflé

Place the soufflé in a preheated oven (400°F) and immediately set the oven control to 375°F. Bake a 1½-pint mold 20 minutes; a 1½-quart mold 30 to 35 minutes; a 2-quart mold 45 minutes. The center of a soufflé baked at this temperature is rather soft and creamy. The soufflé will start to fall in a few minutes; therefore serve it *immediately*.

How to Serve a Soufflé

Serve the soufflé in the dish in which it was baked. Break the top with a fork and with a fork and spoon (holding them vertically) spread it apart, using the same technique as for tearing an angel food cake into slices with two forks. Each serving should include some of the center and some of the bottom, top, and side crusts.

Hot Vanilla Soufflé, Bouilli Method

3 tablespoons flour
¾ cup milk
7 tablespoons sugar
4 large egg yolks
2 tablespoons butter
2½ tablespoons vanilla extract

¼ teaspoon salt
5 large egg whites
¼ teaspoon cream of tartar
Cream and Brandy Sauce, Lemon Sauce,
  or Chocolate Sauce

Prepare a 1½-quart soufflé dish or casserole according to previous directions and set aside. In a saucepan, combine the flour and ¼ cup of the milk and mix until the mixture is smooth. Beat in remaining milk and 6 tablespoons of the sugar. Stir and cook until the mixture is very thick. Remove the saucepan from the heat and beat mixture vigorously for 2 minutes. Beat in egg yolks one at a time. Beat in butter and vanilla extract. Transfer the mixture to a large mixing bowl. Set aside. Add salt to egg whites and beat them until they are foamy. Add cream of tartar and continue beating until the egg whites glisten and stand in soft peaks when the beater is raised. Add the remaining 1 tablespoon sugar and beat until the egg whites stand in sharp stiff peaks. Stir 2 tablespoons of the beaten whites into the soufflé mixture. Carefully fold in remaining egg whites. Spoon the mixture into the prepared casserole or soufflé dish. Trace a circle around the top of the soufflé (see How to Give a Soufflé a "Top Hat"). Bake (see previous directions). Serve immediately with Cream and Brandy Sauce, Lemon Sauce, or Chocolate Sauce. Makes 6 servings.

Hot Almond Soufflé

Make Hot Vanilla Soufflé, adding ½ cup finely ground toasted blanched almonds and ¼ teaspoon almond extract to the cooked mixture just before folding in the beaten egg whites.

Hot Coffee Soufflé

Make Hot Vanilla Soufflé, blending 1 tablespoon strong coffee infusion with the flour.

Hot Macaroon Soufflé

Make Hot Vanilla Soufflé, adding ½ cup Macaroon Crumbs to the cooked mixture just before folding in the beaten egg whites.

Hot Vanilla Soufflé, Pastry Cream Method

5 large eggs, separated
2 tablespoons sugar
½ cup French Pastry Cream
¼ teaspoon vanilla extract

¼ teaspoon salt
¼ teaspoon cream of tartar
Sabayon Sauce or Cream and
　　Brandy Sauce

Prepare a 1½-quart soufflé dish or casserole according to previous directions and set it aside. Beat egg yolks well, then beat in 1 tablespoon of the sugar. Add French Pastry Cream and vanilla extract. Mix well. Add salt to the egg whites and beat them until they are foamy. Add cream of tartar and continue beating until the egg whites glisten and stand in soft peaks. Add the remaining 1 tablespoon sugar and continue beating until the egg whites stand in sharp stiff peaks. Stir 2 tablespoons of the egg whites into the soufflé mixture. Carefully fold in the remaining egg whites. Spoon the mixture into the prepared soufflé dish or casserole. Trace a circle around the top (see previous directions). Bake (see previous directions). Serve immediately with Sabayon Sauce or Cream and Brandy Sauce. Makes 6 servings.

Hot Chocolate Soufflé

2 squares (2 ounces) unsweetened chocolate	3 large eggs, separated
3 tablespoons butter	2 teaspoons vanilla extract
¼ cup flour	¼ teaspoon salt
1 cup milk, scalded	¼ teaspoon cream of tartar
6 tablespoons sugar	Vanilla Sauce, Rum Sauce, Chantilly Cream, or whipped cream

Prepare a 1-quart soufflé dish or casserole according to previous directions and set it aside. Melt the chocolate in a 1-quart saucepan over hot water (not boiling). Add the butter and stir over hot water until it has melted. Blend in the flour. Stir and cook over low heat 1 minute to form a roux. Remove from heat and stir in the hot milk and 5 table-spoons of the sugar. Stir and cook mixture until it is very thick. Remove the saucepan from heat and beat the mixture 1 minute. Beat in egg yolks, one at a time, and vanilla extract. Stir and cook about 30 seconds. Transfer the mixture to a large mixing bowl and set aside. Add the salt to egg whites and beat them until they are foamy. Add the cream of tartar and beat them until they glisten and stand in soft peaks. Add the remaining 1 tablespoon sugar and continue beating until the egg whites stand in sharp stiff peaks. Stir 2 tablespoons of the beaten egg whites into the cooked mixture. Carefully fold in the remaining egg whites. Spoon the mixture into the prepared soufflé dish or casserole. Trace a circle around the top (see previous directions). Bake (see previous directions). Serve immediately with Vanilla Sauce, Rum Sauce, Chantilly Cream, or whipped cream. Makes 5 servings.

Hot Chocolate-Rum Soufflé

Add 1 to 2 tablespoons rum to the Hot Chocolate Soufflé mixture along with the vanilla extract.

Hot Lemon Soufflé

2 tablespoons butter	4 large eggs, separated
2 tablespoons flour	1 tablespoon grated lemon zest
½ cup water	½ teaspoon vanilla extract
¾ cup sugar	¼ teaspoon salt
¼ cup freshly squeezed lemon juice	Whipped cream

Prepare a 1½-quart soufflé dish or casserole according to previous directions and set aside. Melt the butter in a 1-quart saucepan. Remove from heat and blend in the flour. Stir and cook 1 minute to form a roux. Add the water. Reserve 1 tablespoon sugar and add the rest to the mixture. Mix well. Stir and cook until the mixture is very thick. Add lemon juice, mix well, and cook 1 to 2 minutes, stirring constantly. Remove from heat.

Beat the egg yolks, beat in a little of the hot mixture, and then stir into the remaining hot mixture. Add lemon zest and vanilla extract. Transfer the mixture to a large mixing bowl. Set aside. Add salt to egg whites and beat them until they glisten and stand in soft peaks, then beat in the reserved 1 tablespoon sugar. Continue beating until the egg whites stand in sharp stiff peaks. Stir 2 tablespoons of the egg whites into the cooked mixture. Carefully fold in the remaining egg whites. Spoon the mixture into the prepared soufflé dish or casserole. Trace a circle around the top of the soufflé (see previous directions). Bake (see previous directions). Serve immediately, with whipped cream. Makes 6 servings.

Hot Orange Soufflé

¼ cup (½ stick) butter	4 large eggs, separated
⅓ cup flour	1 tablespoon grated orange zest
1 cup freshly squeezed orange juice	1 teaspoon grated lemon zest
2 tablespoons freshly squeezed	½ teaspoon vanilla extract
lemon juice	¼ teaspoon salt
6 tablespoons sugar	Foamy Egg Sauce or whipped cream

Prepare a 1½-quart soufflé dish or casserole according to previous directions and set it aside. Melt the butter in a 1-quart saucepan. Remove from heat and blend in the flour. Stir and cook 1 minute to form a roux. Add orange juice, lemon juice, and 5 tablespoons of the sugar. Mix well. Stir and cook until the mixture is very thick. Remove from heat. Beat the egg yolks, beat in a little of the hot mixture, and then stir into the remaining hot mixture. Add orange and lemon zests, and vanilla extract. Transfer the mixture to a large mixing bowl. Set aside. Add salt to the egg whites and beat them until they glisten and stand in soft peaks. Beat in the remaining 1 tablespoon sugar and continue beating until egg whites stand in sharp stiff peaks. Stir 2 tablespoons of the beaten egg whites into the cooked mixture. Carefully fold in the remaining egg whites. Spoon mixture into the prepared soufflé dish or casserole. Trace a circle around the top of the soufflé (see previous directions). Bake (see previous directions). Serve immediately with Foamy Egg Sauce or whipped cream. Makes 6 servings.

Hot Grand Marnier Soufflé

2 tablespoons butter	¼ teaspoon salt
2 tablespoons flour	5 large egg whites
½ cup light cream	¼ teaspoon cream of tartar
½ cup sugar	6 Ladyfingers or 6 macaroons
4 large egg yolks	¼ cup Grand Marnier
1 tablespoon grated orange zest	Whipped cream

Prepare a 1½-quart soufflé dish or casserole according to previous directions and set it aside. Melt the butter in a 1-quart saucepan. Remove from heat and blend in the flour. Stir and cook 1 minute to form a roux. Add the cream. Reserve 1 tablespoon of the sugar and add the remaining sugar. Mix well. Stir and cook until the mixture is very thick. Remove from heat. Beat the egg yolks, beat in a little of the hot mixture, and then stir into the remaining hot mixture. Stir and cook 1 minute over low heat. Add orange zest. Transfer the mixture to a large mixing bowl and set it aside. Add the salt to the egg whites and beat them until they are foamy. Add cream of tartar and continue beating until the egg whites stand in soft peaks. Beat in the reserved 1 tablespoon sugar. Continue beating until the egg whites stand in sharp stiff peaks. Stir 2 tablespoons beaten egg whites into the cooked mixture. Carefully fold in the remaining egg whites. Spoon half of the mixture into the prepared soufflé dish or casserole. Dip the Ladyfingers or macaroons in Grand Marnier and place them over the top, then spoon the remaining soufflé mixture over them. Trace a circle around the top of the soufflé and bake (see previous directions). Serve immediately with whipped cream flavored to taste with Grand Marnier. Makes 6 servings.

If desired, replace the Grand Marnier in this recipe with Cointreau or Triple Sec. Or omit the orange zest and dip the Ladyfingers in crème de cacao or other liqueur.

Hot Banana Soufflé

3 large firm, ripe bananas
Freshly squeezed lemon juice
⅓ cup sugar
1 tablespoon cornstarch
¼ teaspoon salt
½ teaspoon grated lemon zest
¾ cup milk

3 large eggs, separated
3 tablespoons butter
1 teaspoon vanilla extract
Heavy cream, whipped
Sugar
Grated nutmeg

Peel the bananas, slice them, and dip them in lemon juice to prevent discoloration. Combine the next 4 ingredients. Add the milk and mix well. Stir and cook over medium heat until mixture has thickened. Beat the egg yolks, beat in a little of the hot mixture, then mix with the remaining hot mixture. Stir in the butter and vanilla extract. Fold in the bananas. Beat the egg whites until they stand in soft stiff peaks, then fold them into the mixture. Butter only the bottom of a 1½-quart soufflé dish and turn the mixture into it. Place the dish in a pan of hot water. Bake in a preheated oven (375°F) 45 minutes, or until the soufflé is soft-firm in the center when pressed with your index finger. Serve with whipped cream sweetened to taste with sugar. Garnish the cream with a dash of grated nutmeg. Makes 6 servings.

Fruit Sauce

Combine 1 cup coarsely crushed strawberries, peaches, or apricots with 1 tablespoon kirsch. Mix. Makes a scant 1¼ cups.

Hot Fruit Soufflé

Mix 1 cup crushed strawberries, peaches, or apricots with 1 tablespoon kirsch or to taste, and 2 tablespoons sugar. Add to the beaten egg whites whipped as meringue. Bake in buttered and sugared metal soufflé dishes at 375°F for 20 minutes and serve immediately with fresh fruit sauces made with the same or a different fruit.

PUDDING SOUFFLES

Soufflé puddings are denser and richer than other soufflés, and are made with a Choux Paste base and will puff again if reheated after they become cold. The baked, unmolded, cold pudding should be placed in a pan of hot water and baked in a pre-heated oven (350°F) 30 to 40 minutes, or until it has puffed.

Chocolate Pudding Soufflé

2 squares (2 ounces) unsweetened
    chocolate
6 tablespoons butter
⅔ cup sifted all-purpose flour
⅔ cup milk, heated
6 tablespoons sugar

2 teaspoons vanilla extract
4 large eggs, separated
¼ teaspoon salt
¼ teaspoon cream of tartar
Vanilla-Rum Sauce

Melt the chocolate in a 1-quart saucepan over hot water (not boiling). Add the butter and stir until butter is melted. Gradually blend in the flour. Stir in the hot milk, a little at a time, mixing well after each addition. Stir and cook over low heat until the mixture leaves the sides of the pan clean and forms a ball. Remove from the heat. Beat in 5 tablespoons of the sugar and the vanilla extract. Continue beating until the mixture is creamy. Stir and cook about 1 minute. Transfer the mixture to a large mixing bowl and set aside. Add the salt to the egg whites and beat them until they are foamy. Add the cream of tartar and continue beating until the egg whites glisten and stand in soft peaks. Add the remaining 1 tablespoon sugar. Continue beating until the egg whites stand in sharp stiff peaks. Stir 2 tablespoons of the beaten whites into the cooked mixture. Carefully fold in the remaining egg whites. Generously butter a 5-cup ring mold, sprinkle it with sugar, and spoon the soufflé mixture into it. Place the mold in a pan of hot water. Bake in a preheated oven (350°F) 45 to 50 minutes, or until the pudding has puffed and a toothpick inserted in the center comes out clean. Unmold onto a serving plate and serve immediately with Vanilla-Rum Sauce. Makes 6 servings.

Saxon Pudding Soufflé

¾ cup milk
1 (2-inch) piece vanilla bean, or
   1½ teaspoons vanilla extract
3 tablespoons butter, melted
6 tablespoons flour
4 large eggs, separated

6 tablespoons sugar
1⁄16 teaspoon salt
Custard Sauce, kirsch-flavored
   Apricot Sauce, or white wine
   Sabayon Sauce

Heat milk, adding vanilla bean (if using). Combine butter and flour and mix and cook until flour is well blended, forming a thick roux. Remove vanilla bean from milk and pour in all the milk at one time. Stir, beat, and cook mixture over low heat until it pulls away from the sides of the pan. Use a wire whisk during the first part of the cooking period, then use a wooden spoon, beating vigorously. (This mixture is similar to Choux Paste.) Transfer the dough to a 2-quart mixing bowl, and while it is still hot beat in the egg yolks, one at a time, being sure that each yolk is thoroughly incorporated before adding another. Beat in vanilla extract (if vanilla bean was not used) and 5 tablespoons of the sugar, one at a time. Add salt to egg whites and beat them until they stand in soft peaks, then beat in remaining 1 tablespoon sugar and continue beating until egg whites stand in sharp stiff peaks. Stir 2 tablespoons of the beaten egg whites into the dough mixture to thin it a little so that the egg whites can be folded in more easily, then gently fold in remaining egg whites, avoiding a beating or stirring motion. Butter a 1½-quart soufflé dish or a mold with a tube in the center, and sprinkle the bottom and sides lightly with sugar. Pour in the soufflé mixture. Place mold in a pan of hot water. Bake the soufflé in a preheated oven (350°F) 40 to 50 minutes, or until a cake tester or toothpick inserted in the center comes out clean. Let stand a few minutes before unmolding, then unmold onto a round serving plate. Serve with Custard Sauce, kirsch-flavored Apricot Sauce, or white wine Sabayon Sauce. Makes 6 servings

Royal Pudding Soufflé

1 (15½-by-10½-by-1-inch)
   Jelly-Roll Sponge Cake
1½ cups apricot jam or
   red currant jelly

1 recipe Saxon Soufflé Pudding
Glacéed cherries
Apricot Sauce flavored with
   Madeira or Muscatel

While Jelly-Roll Sponge Cake is still warm, spread it with a thin layer of apricot jam or red currant jelly. Roll it up quickly and let it stand wrapped in a clean towel for at least 1 hour. Cut the roll into slices ½ inch thick and arrange them on the bottom and around the sides of a buttered 1½-quart mold. Make the recipe for Saxon Soufflé Pudding and pour the mixture over the jelly-roll slices. Place mold in a pan of hot water and bake in a preheated oven (350°F) 40 to 50 minutes, or until a cake tester or toothpick inserted in the center comes out clean. Cover the soufflé with brown paper or foil if it begins to brown too quickly. Take the soufflé out of the oven, run a small spatula around the inside rim of the mold, and place a round platter upside down over the soufflé. Holding the mold and platter together firmly, invert them. Tap the platter lightly on the table and remove the mold. Decorate the top of the pudding with glacéed cherries. Serve with Apricot Sauce. Makes 8 servings.

FROZEN DESSERTS

FROZEN DESSERTS RANGE FROM SIMPLE FRUIT ICES made with a sugar syrup to such elaborate preparations as Baked Alaska.

ICES

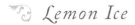 *Lemon Ice*

4 cups cold water	1 cup freshly squeezed lemon juice
2 cups sugar	1 tablespoon grated lemon zest
⅛ teaspoon salt	1 teaspoon vanilla extract

Combine the water, sugar, and salt in a saucepan. Bring to the boiling point and boil, uncovered, for 5 minutes. Remove from heat and cool 2 to 3 minutes. Stir in the remaining ingredients. Pour the mixture into 2 freezer trays or into an 8-by-2-inch square baking pan and freeze until it is a firm mush. Turn the mixture into a large mixing bowl and beat with an electric beater until it is fluffy, starting with the beater at low speed and increasing the speed to the highest as the mixture softens. (Do not beat long enough to melt the mixture.) Return the mixture to the trays or pan and freeze until firm, stirring it twice while it is freezing. If the ice is frozen too hard to serve, let it stand 10 to 15 minutes at room temperature to soften. Makes 1½ quarts.

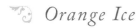 *Orange Ice*

4 cups cold water	¼ cup Cointreau or Triple Sec
2 cups sugar	1 teaspoon grated lemon zest
2 cups freshly squeezed orange juice	Dash salt
¼ cup freshly squeezed lemon juice	

Combine the water and sugar in a saucepan, bring to the boiling point, and boil 5 minutes. Cool 10 minutes. Stir in the remaining ingredients. Strain and pour the mixture into 2 freezer trays. Freeze until the mixture is mushy, then turn it into a bowl and beat it with an electric beater until smooth and fluffy. Return the ice to the freezer trays and freeze until firm, stirring twice without removing it from the trays. Before serving, let the ice stand at room temperature 10 to 15 minutes to soften. Makes 1¾ quarts.

🍃 Raspberry Ice

4 cups cold water
⅛ teaspoon salt
2 cups raspberry puree

2 tablespoons freshly squeezed lemon juice
½ teaspoon grated orange zest

Put the water in a 2-quart saucepan, bring to the boiling point, and boil gently 5 minutes. Add the remaining ingredients and strain. Pour the mixture into 2 freezer trays and freeze until it is a firm mush. Turn it into a large mixing bowl and beat with an electric beater until it is fluffy. Return the mixture to the freezer trays and freeze until it is firm, stirring it twice in the trays. If the ice is frozen so hard that it is difficult to serve, let it stand 10 to15 minutes at room temperature to soften. Makes 2 quarts.

🍃 Strawberry Ice

Use the recipe for Raspberry Ice, but replace the raspberry puree with 2 cups strawberry puree. Makes 2 quarts.

SHERBETS

🍃 Melon Sherbet

1⅔ cups sugar
2 cups water
3 tablespoons kirsch
2 cups mashed very ripe melon

¼ teaspoon grated lemon zest
Dash salt
2 large egg whites
½ teaspoon vanilla extract

Combine the sugar and water in a 1½-quart saucepan, mix well, bring to the boiling point, and cook without stirring 5 minutes. Remove from heat and cool slightly. Stir in kirsch. Pour the mixture into 2 freezer trays, place them in the freezer, and freeze to a firm mush. Turn the mixture into a large bowl. Add remaining ingredients and beat the mixture with an electric beater until it is fluffy. Return it to the freezer trays, freeze it to a firm mush, stir without removing from the trays, and then freeze until firm. Remove the sherbet from the freezer and let it stand 10 minutes at room temperature before serving. Makes 2 quarts.

🍃 Lemon Milk Sherbet

1 envelope unflavored gelatin
2 cups cold milk
1 cup sugar
⅓ cup freshly squeezed lemon juice

1½ cups milk
Dash salt
2 large egg whites

Soften the gelatin in ½ cup of the milk and place it over hot water (not boiling) to melt. Combine the sugar, lemon juice, and remaining 1½ cups milk and stir until the sugar is dissolved. Add the melted gelatin and pour the mixture into a freezer tray. Freeze until the mixture is almost firm. Turn it into a mixing bowl, add the salt and egg whites, and beat with an electric beater until the mixture is fluffy. Return the mixture to the freezer tray and freeze until firm. Remove the sherbet from the freezer and let it stand at room temperature about 20 minutes to soften before it is served. Makes 1 quart.

ICE CREAMS

The old-fashioned crank freezer made a smoother ice cream than can usually be achieved by other ice-cream makers, but with the availability of commercial ice creams that method of making ice cream is practically extinct. The following recipes result in excellent, smooth ice creams.

Vanilla Ice Cream

1¼ cups sugar
¼ teaspoon salt
3 teaspoons vanilla extract

2 cups milk
2 cups heavy cream

Combine the first 4 ingredients in order and stir until the sugar is dissolved. Add the cream and mix well. Pour the mixture into 2 freezer trays or into an 8-by-8-by-2-inch baking pan. Freeze until the mixture is a firm mush. Turn it into a large mixing bowl and beat with an electric beater until the mixture is fluffy, starting with the beater at low speed and increasing the speed to the highest as the mixture softens. (Do not beat so long that the mixture melts.) Return the mixture to the trays or pan and freeze until the ice cream is firm, stirring once before it is completely frozen. Makes 1½ quarts.

Ginger Ice Cream

Add 2¼ teaspoons ground ginger and mix it with the sugar before adding the milk. Or, if desired, use ¼ cup chopped candied ginger and 2 tablespoons syrup drained from the ginger and fold into the beaten mixture just before returning it to the trays for freezing.

Fruit Ice Cream

Mix 1 cup coarsely crushed strawberries, peaches, or apricots with 2 tablespoons sugar and 1 tablespoon kirsch. Fold into the beaten mixture just before returning it to the trays for freezing.

 Pistachio Ice Cream

Fold ¼ to ⅓ cup finely ground pistachio nuts into the beaten mixture just before returning it to the trays for freezing.

FROZEN MOUSSES

Frozen Melon Mousse

1 envelope unflavored gelatin	½ cup sugar
¼ cup cold water	1 tablespoon freshly squeezed lemon juice
2 cups mashed ripe melon,	½ teaspoon vanilla extract
like honeydew or cantaloupe	1 cup heavy cream, whipped

Soften the gelatin in the cold water and set it aside. Combine the next 3 ingredients and cook only until the mixture is hot and the sugar has dissolved. Stir in the softened gelatin. Chill until the mixture begins to thicken. Fold in the vanilla extract and whipped cream. Turn the mixture into a freezer tray and freeze until it is firm. Remove the mousse from the refrigerator and let it stand 10 minutes at room temperature before serving. Makes 1 quart.

Frozen Peach Mousse

Use the recipe for Frozen Melon Mousse, replacing the melon with 2 cups mashed ripe peaches. Makes 1 quart.

Frozen Strawberry Mousse

2 cups (1 pint) fresh strawberries	1 tablespoon kirsch, or to taste
¾ cup sugar	1 cup heavy cream, whipped
⅛ teaspoon salt	

Wash and hull the strawberries, crush them, and mix with the next 3 ingredients. Fold in whipped cream. Turn the mixture into a freezer tray and freeze until firm. Remove mousse from the freezer 20 minutes before serving to soften slightly. Makes 6 servings.

PARFAITS

 Angel Parfait

⅔ cup sugar	2 cups heavy cream, whipped
¾ cup water	1½ teaspoons vanilla extract
3 large egg whites	

Combine the sugar and water in a 1-quart saucepan. Stir and cook until the boiling point is reached. Cover and cook 3 minutes. Remove cover and continue to cook, without stirring, to 234°F on a candy thermometer, or until ½ teaspoon syrup forms a soft ball when dropped into cold water. Beat the egg whites until they stand in soft peaks, then gradually beat in the hot syrup. Continue beating until mixture is cool. Fold in the cream and vanilla extract. Pour into a 9-by-9-by-2-inch pan or into 2 freezer trays. Freeze without stirring until firm. This may be frozen in a crank-type freezer if desired. Makes 1½ quarts.

Anisette Parfait

1¼ cups sugar	2 tablespoons anisette
1 cup water	2½ cups heavy cream
Dash salt	2 tablespoons confectioners' sugar
8 large egg yolks, beaten	Glacéed cherries

Combine the first 3 ingredients in a 1½-quart saucepan. Stir and cook the mixture until the boiling point is reached. Cook, without stirring, to 234°F on a candy thermometer, or until ½ teaspoon of the syrup forms a soft ball when dropped into cold water. Remove the saucepan from the heat and cool until the syrup stops bubbling. Pour the syrup in a fine stream into the beaten egg yolks, beating all the while. Place the bowl in cracked ice and beat the mixture until it is quite cold. Beat in the anisette. Whip 2 cups of the cream until stiff and fold into the beaten egg mixture. Rinse a 5-cup mold with cold water and fill it with the parfait. Freeze until firm, 4 to 5 hours. To serve: Turn the mold out onto a serving plate. Add confectioners' sugar to the remaining ½ cup cream and beat until stiff, then put it in a pastry bag and pipe a design over the top and sides. Decorate with glacéed cherries. Makes 1¼ quarts.

Coffee Parfait

1 cup sugar	3 large egg whites
¾ cup strong coffee infusion	1½ teaspoons vanilla extract
¼ teaspoon salt	2 cups heavy cream, whipped

Combine the sugar and coffee in a 1-quart saucepan. Bring to the boiling point, stirring all the time. Continue boiling rapidly, without stirring, about 5 minutes, or until mixture reaches the soft-ball stage (234°F on a candy thermometer). Remove syrup from the heat and cool about 1 minute. Meanwhile, add the salt to the egg whites and beat until they stand in soft peaks. Pour the hot syrup in a fine stream over the beaten egg whites, beating the mixture all the while. Add the vanilla extract and continue beating until mixture is thick and cool. Fold in the whipped cream. Turn the mixture into 2 freezer trays, or into a 9-by-9-by-2-inch baking pan. Freeze without stirring until mixture is firm. Makes 1½ quarts.

Coffee-Rum Parfait

Make Coffee Parfait and fold 2 to 3 tablespoons dark or light rum into the mixture along with the whipped cream.

Crème de Menthe Parfait

1 cup sugar
¾ cup water
¼ teaspoon salt
3 large egg whites

2 tablespoons crème de menthe, or to taste
2 cups heavy cream, whipped
A few drops green food coloring

Combine the sugar and water in a 1-quart saucepan. Bring to the boiling point, stirring all the while, and boil rapidly, without stirring, about 5 minutes, or until mixture reaches the soft-ball stage (234°F on a candy thermometer). Remove from heat and cool about 1 minute. Meanwhile, add the salt to the egg whites and beat until they stand in soft peaks. Pour the hot syrup in a fine stream over the beaten egg whites, beating the mixture all the while. Continue beating until mixture is thick and cool. Beat in the crème de menthe. Fold in the whipped cream and food coloring. Turn the mixture into 2 freezer trays, or into a 9-by-9-by-2-inch baking pan. Freeze until firm, without stirring. This mixture may also be flavored with vanilla, cognac, kirsch, rum, or other flavoring. Makes 1½ quarts.

Mocha Parfait

1 (9-by-5-by-1-inch) layer Génoise
  or Jelly-Roll Sponge Cake
Heavy Sugar Syrup flavored with rum
1 pint chocolate ice cream, softened
3 tablespoons rum
1 pint Coffee Parfait, softened

2 tablespoons sugar
1½ teaspoons strong coffee infusion
1 teaspoon vanilla extract
1 cup heavy cream
Shaved sweetened or unsweetened
  chocolate, or chocolate cigarettes

Line the bottom and sides of a 9-by-5-by-3-inch loaf pan with heavy waxed paper, having the paper extend 2 to 3 inches above the top of the pan. Place the cake in the bottom of the pan and sprinkle it with the rum-flavored Sugar Syrup. Freeze 1 hour. Combine the chocolate ice cream with the rum, spread over the cake, and freeze until firm. Spread Coffee Parfait over the chocolate layer and freeze until it is firm. The day before or several hours before serving, remove the mold from the pan by running a metal spatula around the sides between the paper and the pan. Lift the mold up by the waxed paper, place it on a serving tray, and remove paper. Add the sugar, coffee, and vanilla extract to the cream and whip until the cream stands in soft peaks. Spread some cream over top and sides of the mold. Put the remaining whipped cream into a pastry bag fitted with a plain or rosette nozzle, and pipe crosswise rows of rosettes over the top of the mold. Garnish with shaved chocolate or with chocolate cigarettes. Cut into 1-inch slices. Makes 9 servings, or one 9-by-3-inch mold.

Peach Parfait Chantilly

1 pint Vanilla Ice Cream	4 to 5 medium-sized ripe peaches, sliced
1⅓ cups heavy cream	2 teaspoons confectioners' sugar
⅔ cup toasted slivered almonds	3 drops vanilla extract

Remove the ice cream from the freezer and let it stand at room temperature until it begins to soften. Whip 1 cup of the cream and fold it into the ice cream, along with ½ cup of the almonds. Turn the mixture into freezer trays and freeze until the ice cream is soft-firm. Spoon into parfait glasses, alternating with peaches. Combine the remaining cream, the confectioners' sugar, and the vanilla extract. Beat the mixture until it stands in soft peaks. Serve as a topping over the parfait. Sprinkle with the remaining almonds. Makes 8 servings.

ICE CREAM WITH FRUIT OR COUPES GLACEES

These combinations of ices or ice creams with fruit (usually marinated in a liqueur and sometimes with Chantilly Cream) are traditionally served in silver or crystal coupes or in short-stemmed saucer-shaped champagne glasses. The following recipes represent only a few of the many possible variations.

Coupe Frou-Frou

Fill each coupe or glass half-full with Vanilla Ice Cream. Cover the ice cream with chopped fresh peaches which have been marinated in curaçao. Garnish with Chantilly Cream and top each serving with a glacéed cherry.

Coupe Jacques

Put a large spoonful of Lemon Ice in the bottom of each coupe or glass. Add a spoonful of any desired fresh fruit or combination of fruits marinated in kirsch. Fill with Strawberry Ice Cream.

Pineapple Coupe

Put chopped pineapple marinated in kirsch in the bottom of the coupe or glass. Add a scoop of pineapple ice or ice cream. Garnish with Chantilly Cream and top with a piece of glacéed pineapple.

Coupe Vanderbilt

Fill the coupe or glass half-full with Orange Ice. Cover with chopped fresh wild strawberries marinated in Grand Marnier. Just before serving, pour in champagne.

BOMBES

How to Make a Bombe

Use a round decorated mold or charlotte mold, preferably with a tight cover. Place the mold in a bowl of ice. Line the mold with any desired ice cream, coating the bottom thickly and spreading the ice cream evenly around the sides up to the edge, leaving a hollow space in the center for the filling. Fill with any desired parfait, frozen mousse, or other filling and smooth off the top. Cover with waxed paper and then with the cover of the mold (or cover tightly with aluminum foil tied around the top) and put the bombe in the freezer. These operations must be performed as rapidly as possible to avoid melting. Freeze until firm. At least 1 hour before serving, take the mold out of the refrigerator, dip it quickly into hot water, dry, and unmold onto a round serving dish. Decorate as desired and return the bombe to the freezer until ready to serve. Cut into slices for serving. A 1½-quart mold makes 10 servings.

Bombes can be made with a wide variety of ice creams, fillings, and decorations, according to the taste and ingenuity of the maker.

Bombe Diane

1 quart Vanilla Ice Cream	Glacéed cherries
Crème de Menthe Parfait	Shaved unsweetened chocolate
Whipped cream	Thin deer-shaped cookies
Sugar	

Line a chilled 1½-quart dome-shaped mold with vanilla ice cream. Fill the center with Mint Parfait. Spread vanilla ice cream over the top. Cover with the lid that fits the mold, or with aluminum foil tied around the top of the mold. Freeze until firm. At least 1 hour before serving, unmold the bombe onto a serving tray. Sweeten whipped cream to taste with sugar, put it in a decorator's tube fitted with a rosette nozzle, and decorate the bombe with rosettes as desired. Return to the refrigerator until ready to serve. Garnish with glacéed cherries, shaved chocolate, and cookies. Makes 10 servings.

Bombe Marinette

Line a mold with Vanilla Ice Cream and fill the center with Strawberry Mousse, following the previous directions.

Bombe Esperanza

Marinate chopped glacéed fruit with curaçao and mix with 1 pint Orange Ice. Line a mold as previously directed, using Pistachio Ice Cream. Fill the center with the fruit and ice mixture. Cover and refrigerate as previously directed.

SPECIAL ICE-CREAM DESSERTS

Baked Alaska

1 (9-inch) square Génoise layer, ¾ inch thick	¼ teaspoon cream of tartar
1 teaspoon salt	10 tablespoons sugar
5 large egg whites	½ teaspoon vanilla extract
	1 (1-quart) brick ice cream

Place cake on a cutting board. Make it into an oval or oblong shape by cutting a strip 2 inches wide from each side and trimming the ends if desired. Set cake aside. Add the salt to the egg whites and beat them until they are foamy. Add the cream of tartar and beat until soft peaks form. Beat in the sugar, 1 tablespoon at a time. Continue beating until the egg whites stand in stiff peaks. Beat in the vanilla extract. Set the meringue aside. Cut the brick of ice cream into slices 1 inch thick and arrange them over the cake. Trim the ice cream at the edges to conform to the shape of the cake. Cover completely with a thick layer of meringue. Put the leftover meringue in a pastry bag fitted with a star nozzle and pipe it over the top and sides in any pattern desired. Store the meringue-covered cake in the freezer until ready to serve. Just before serving, place it in a preheated oven (450°F) 4 to 5 minutes, or until delicately browned. Serve at once. Makes 8 servings

Neapolitan Cassata

½ cup glacéed fruit	1 pint coffee ice cream
2 tablespoons rum	1 cup heavy cream, whipped
1 quart Vanilla Ice Cream	Citron
1½ pints Raspberry Ice	1 glacéed cherry

Soak glacéed fruit in rum while preparing the other ingredients. Line a 6-cup dome-shaped mold with a 1-inch layer of Vanilla Ice Cream. (Return leftover ice cream to the freezer for use later.) Cover this with a 1-inch layer of Raspberry Ice. Cover the Raspberry Ice with a 1-inch layer of coffee ice cream, leaving a space in the center. Soften the reserved Vanilla Ice Cream and fold it into the rum-soaked fruit and half of the whipped cream. Spoon this mixture into the mold to finish filling it. Cover the mold with a lid or with aluminum foil and freeze until the ice cream is very firm.

About 1 hour before serving, unmold onto a serving plate and frost with the remaining whipped cream. Return the mold to the freezer. When ready to serve, garnish mold with slices of citron and a glacéed cherry. Makes 10 servings.

Frosted Lemons

6 large lemons
1 pint Lemon Ice
Angelica

Wash the lemons and cut a lengthwise slice from the side of each. Remove the pulp and the juice and save them for other cooking purposes. (If you are making the Lemon Ice, part of the juice can be used in it.) Fill and mound the lemon shells with Lemon Ice that is frozen very hard and replace the slices that were cut off the sides. Brush the outside of the lemon shells lightly with water. Store them in the freezer until ready to serve. Decorate with angelica. Makes 6 servings.

Mandarin oranges or regular oranges may be prepared in the same way.

Frozen Tourte with Assorted Fruits

1 thin round 9-inch Génoise layer
Sugar Syrup flavored with kirsch
1½ cups heavy cream
1 pint Vanilla Ice Cream, softened
2 to 3 tablespoons kirsch
½ cup diced fresh pineapple

¼ cup diced fresh strawberries
1 pint cherry ice cream, softened
1 pint chocolate ice cream, softened
Chantilly Cream
Glacéed cherries

Place the Génoise layer in a round 9-inch springform pan. Sprinkle with the Sugar Syrup. Whip ½ cup of the cream and fold it into the Vanilla Ice Cream along with the kirsch, pineapple, and strawberries. Spread over the cake layer. Freeze until firm. Whip another ½ cup of the cream and fold it into the cherry ice cream. Freeze until firm. Whip the remaining ½ cup cream and fold it into the chocolate ice cream. Spread over the cherry ice cream layer. Freeze until firm. When ready to serve, transfer the tourte to a serving plate and garnish with rosettes of Chantilly Cream and glacéed cherries. Makes 12 to 16 servings.

FRUIT
DESSERTS

FRUIT AS A DESSERT MAY BE SERVED FRESH and as is, macerated raw in sugar syrup with or without alcohols and other flavorings like rose water, pepper, vanilla bean, or real almond flavoring, or cooked with sugar and syrup and similarly flavored. In French cuisine, when the fruit is cooked by itself or with other fruits the dish is called a *compote*, and when macerated raw, by itself or with a mixture of other fruits it is called a *macedoine*. Both are perfect choices for a party, since they can be made in advance. And even when a warm compote of berries, for example, has to be made at the last minute, it takes only 2 minutes to prepare.

Always choose the ripest and best-quality fruit that is available.

How to Poach or Stew Fruits

Fruit that is to be poached or stewed should not be overripe. The fruit may be left whole, halved, quartered, or sliced. It should be cooked in a medium Sugar Syrup, sometimes with a piece of vanilla bean cooked with the syrup or vanilla extract added after the fruit has finished cooking. Red or white wine is often used to replace all or part of the water. The fruit may be served in the syrup, or it may be transferred with a perforated spoon to a serving dish and the syrup cooled until it is reduced by one-fourth or by half before it is poured over the fruit. Cointreau, crème de menthe, kirsch, or rum is often added to the syrup. Poached or stewed fruits are usually served cold with various flavored creams or ice creams.

Baked Apples

6 tart baking apples
6 teaspoons butter
Sugar
6 tablespoons dry white wine

Hot water
2 tablespoons apricot jam

Wash and core apples, being careful not to break through the blossom end. Starting at the stem end, pare apples about one-third of the way down. Place them in a 10-by-7-by-2-inch baking pan, pared side up. Put 1 teaspoon butter in the cavity of each apple and finish filling the cavity with sugar. Pour 1 tablespoon wine over each. Pour hot water into the pan to a depth of ¼ inch. Cover pan with aluminum foil and bake in a preheated oven (400°F) 25 minutes. Remove foil, and baste with some of the liquid in the pan. Continue baking, uncovered, 15 to 20 minutes. Remove apples to individual serving dishes. Blend apricot jam with the liquid left in the pan. Heat and cook about 1 minute. Spoon over apples. Makes 6 servings.

Apples Bourgeoise

6 medium-sized tart apples
Vanilla Syrup
¾ cup mixed glacéed fruit
French Pastry Cream

Toasted, slivered, blanched almonds,
 or Macaroon Crumbs
Sugar

Peel the apples, cut in half, and remove cores. Cook in Vanilla Syrup until apples are soft but still retain their shape. Cool them in the syrup. Transfer apples, cut side up, to a heatproof serving dish. Fill the apple cavities with glacéed fruit and coat with French Pastry Cream. Sprinkle with almonds or Macaroon Crumbs. Sprinkle with sugar. Place in a preheated oven (450°F) 5 to 7 minutes, or until glazed. Makes 6 servings.

Apples Brissac

6 medium-small apples
Vanilla Syrup
Grand Marnier
1 round Génoise layer

1 (6-ounce) glass currant jelly
1 tablespoon water
12 diamond-shaped pieces angelica
Sabayon Sauce

Peel and core the apples and poach them in Vanilla Syrup until they are tender. Cool them in the syrup. Add Grand Marnier to taste to ¼ cup of the poaching syrup and sprinkle it over the Génoise layer. Place the cake on a serving plate. Melt the jelly with the water, brush it over the apples, and arrange them around the top of the cake. Decorate each apple with 2 pieces angelica. Serve with Sabayon Sauce flavored to taste with Grand Marnier. Makes 6 servings.

Apples Chateaubriand

¾ cup sugar
2 cups water
1 (2-inch) piece vanilla bean
8 medium-sized tart apples

6 (3-inch) rounds bread
Butter
1½ cup red-currant jelly

Combine the sugar, water, and vanilla bean in a 2-quart saucepan. Bring to the boiling point and simmer 5 minutes. Peel and core apples and add, four at a time, to the hot syrup. Cook, uncovered, until apples are tender when pierced with a toothpick but still hold their shape. Cool them in the syrup. Fry the bread rounds in butter over medium heat, turning to brown both sides. Put a round of bread in each of 8 serving dishes and place a well-drained apple on each round. Melt the jelly and spoon it over apples. Makes 8 servings.

Apple Compote

6 large apples
1 tablespoon freshly squeezed
   lemon juice
2½ cups water
¾ cup sugar

2 cups water
Dash salt
1 (2-inch) piece vanilla bean, or
   1 teaspoon vanilla extract

Peel apples, remove cores, and cut apples into quarters. Mix the lemon juice and ½ cup of the water, and dip apples in this mixture to prevent discoloration. Meanwhile, combine sugar, 2 cups water, salt, and vanilla bean (if using) in a 2-quart saucepan and bring to the boiling point. Reduce heat and boil slowly 5 minutes. Add apples, cover, and cook gently until they are tender but still hold their shape, basting occasionally or turning carefully. If the vanilla bean was not used, add the vanilla extract now. Cool in the syrup. Makes 6 servings.

Spiced Apples

Prepare as in preceding recipe but add 2 (2-inch) cinnamon sticks to the sugar and water and cook with the apples. Sprinkle each serving with a dash of grated nutmeg.

Apple Dumplings Normande

6 medium-large cooking apples (Rome
   Beauty, Jonathan, or Northern Spy)
¾ cup sugar
¼ teaspoon salt
1¼ teaspoons ground cinnamon

Triple recipe Plain Pastry Dough
6 teaspoons butter
1 tablespoon milk
Sugar
Chantilly Cream

Wash apples, peel, and core, being sure not to cut through the blossom end. Mix the next 3 ingredients and spoon 2 tablespoons into each of the apple cavities. Roll two-thirds of the pastry into a 15½-inch square, ⅛ inch thick. With a fluted pastry cutter, cut the pastry into 4 squares of equal size. Place an apple in the center of each and top each with 1 teaspoon butter. Bring opposite corners of pastry together over the top, pressing the sides together firmly. Repeat with the remaining dough, cutting 2 squares and using the 2 remaining apples. With a fluted pastry cutter, cut six 1-inch circles from the leftover dough and place one over the center top of each apple, pressing it down with your index finger. Brush the surface of each dumpling with milk and sprinkle lightly with sugar. Bake in a preheated oven (425°F) 35 minutes, or until apples are tender and pastry is brown. Serve warm or cold, with Chantilly Cream. Makes 6 servings.

Apple Fritters

3 large firm tart apples
3 tablespoons sugar
½ teaspoon ground cinnamon

1 tablespoon rum or kirsch
Fritter Batter
Oil for frying

Peel and core apples, and cut into crosswise slices about ¼ inch thick. Combine the sugar and cinnamon and sprinkle 1 tablespoon over the apples. Sprinkle with rum or kirsch and marinate 1 hour. Drain well, pouring the juice into the Fritter Batter. Dip a few apple slices at a time into the batter and deep fry in oil preheated to 375°F until they are golden brown. Drain fritters on paper towels and arrange them in a baking pan. Sprinkle them with the remaining sugar and cinnamon. Place in a preheated oven (450°F) minutes to glaze. Makes 6 to 8 servings. Serve with chilled Sabayon.

Vanilla Sugar may be used instead of the sugar and cinnamon.

Apples Mariette

6 tablespoons Sweet Chestnut Puree
Rum to taste
6 large whole apples, poached as for
  Apples Chateaubriand

Apricot Jam Sauce
Toasted, shredded, blanched almonds

Flavor Sweet Chestnut Puree to taste with rum and spoon it into the cavities of the apples. Cover with Apricot Jam Sauce and sprinkle with almonds. Serve warm or cold. If desired, replace the Chestnut Puree with rum-flavored chopped glaceed chestnuts. Makes 6 servings.

Apricot Jam Sauce

1 cup apricot jam
⅓ cup water
1½ tablespoons sugar

1½ tablespoons brandy, cognac,
  kirsch, maraschino liqueur, or rum

Combine apricot jam, water, and sugar in a small saucepan. Bring to the boiling point. Stir and cook 4 to 5 minutes, or only until thickened. Push through a sieve. Cool and add brandy, cognac, kirsch, maraschino liqueur, or rum. Makes about ¾ cup.

Poached Whole Apples with Chantilly

Small apples should be used for this recipe.

8 cooking apples, 2 inches in diameter
2 tablespoons freshly squeezed
    lemon juice
2½ cups cold water
1 cup sugar

⅛ teaspoon salt
1 (2-inch piece) vanilla bean, or
    1 teaspoon vanilla extract
2 teaspoons sugar
⅓ cup heavy cream

Peel the apples and remove cores, leaving the apples whole. Rinse apples in cold water. Combine 1 tablespoon of the lemon juice with ½ cup cold water and dip the apples into this mixture to prevent them from discoloring. Meanwhile, mix the remaining lemon juice, 2 cups water, the sugar, salt, and the vanilla bean (if using) in a saucepan, bring to the boiling point, and add 2 or 3 apples at a time. Cover and simmer until apples are tender when pierced with a fork. Using a perforated spoon, transfer apples to a serving dish. Repeat until all apples are cooked. If vanilla bean was not used, add vanilla extract to the syrup. Serve the apples in individual dishes, 1 per serving, with a little of the syrup poured over each. Beat 2 teaspoons sugar with the cream until the cream stands in soft peaks and serve on the apples. Makes 8 servings.

Apple Snow

2 cups chilled unsweetened applesauce
1½ teaspoons vanilla extract
1 tablespoon freshly squeezed
    orange juice

Dash salt
3 egg whites
3 tablespoons sugar
Grated nutmeg

Combine the first 3 ingredients and set aside. Add salt to egg whites and beat them until they stand in soft peaks. Gradually beat in sugar. Fold in the applesauce mixture. Pile into individual serving dishes and sprinkle each with nutmeg. Makes 6 servings.

Apricots Bourdaloue

1 recipe Génoise
12 apricot halves, poached in
    Vanilla Syrup
½ cup Apricot Sauce II
Glacéed cherries

Angelica
½ cup heavy cream, whipped
1 cup Frangipane Cream
2 tablespoons Macaroon Crumbs

Bake the Génoise in a 6-cup savarin mold (ring mold). Cool cake in the mold 10 minutes and turn it out onto cooling rack to finish cooling with the top side up. When it is cold, place it on a serving plate. Drain apricot halves well and arrange them around the top of the cake, having them slightly overlapping. Cover with Apricot Sauce. Garnish with glacéed cherries and angelica. Fold the whipped cream into Frangipane Cream and fill the hole in the center of the cake. Sprinkle with Macaroon Crumbs. Makes 6 servings.

Apricot Compote

¾ cup sugar
2 cups water
¹⁄₁₆ teaspoon salt
1 tablespoon freshly squeezed
    lemon juice

1 (2-inch) piece vanilla bean, or
    1 teaspoon vanilla extract
12 fresh apricots

Combine the first 4 ingredients in a 1½-quart saucepan with the vanilla bean (if using). Bring to the boiling point and simmer 5 minutes. Add apricots to the syrup. Cover and cook gently 5 minutes, or until apricots are tender. Remove, peel, and remove pits. Add vanilla extract if vanilla bean was not used. Chill and serve in individual dishes. Makes 4 servings.

Poached Apricots Antoinette

Poach apricots as in Apricot Compote. For each serving, place 2 apricot halves in a serving dish and top them with a scoop of coffee ice cream or Vanilla Ice Cream. Add 1 teaspoon kirsch to 2 tablespoons of the syrup and pour it over the ice cream.

Apricots with Chocolate Ice Cream Negus

12 firm, ripe apricots, poached,
    peeled, and pitted
Vanilla Syrup

Chocolate ice cream
Apricot Sauce
Chantilly Cream

Line the bottoms of 6 individual serving dishes with ice cream and place 2 apricot halves in each. Cover with Apricot Sauce. Put Chantilly Cream on top. Makes 6 servings.

Poached Apricots with Raspberry Ice Cream Sobieski

Raspberry ice cream or ice
6 large apricots, poached, peeled, pitted
1 (6-ounce) glass currant jelly

Chantilly Cream
Anisette

Put ice cream or ice in each of 6 individual serving dishes, filling them one-third full. Place 2 well-drained apricot halves in each dish. Melt the jelly in a little water, sieve, and spoon it over the apricots. Flavor Chantilly Cream with anisette to taste and spoon over the apricots. Makes 6 servings.

Baked Bananas with Almonds

4 large bananas
1 tablespoon freshly squeezed
   lemon juice
6 tablespoons butter

½ cup sliced almonds, blanched
1 tablespoon rum or sherry
¼ cup light brown sugar

Peel the bananas and cut them in half lengthwise. Place them in a shallow baking dish. Brush with the lemon juice. Melt the butter in a skillet. Add the almonds, stir, and cook until they have turned golden brown. Add rum or sherry and pour over bananas. Sprinkle with brown sugar. Bake in a preheated oven (375°F) 15 minutes. Makes 8 servings.

Bananas Copacabana

2 tablespoons rum
2½ cups Vanilla Syrup
3 bananas

Vanilla Ice Cream
Chocolate Sauce
Sliced, toasted almonds

Place the rum and Vanilla Syrup in a 1-quart saucepan. Bring to the boiling point. Peel the bananas, cut them in half crosswise, and add them to the hot syrup. Cover and cook 2 to 3 minutes. Cool bananas in the syrup. Line the bottoms of 6 individual serving dishes with ice cream. Place a drained banana half in each. Cover with Chocolate Sauce. Sprinkle the tops with almonds. Makes 6 servings.

Bananas Bourdaloue

2 cups milk
1 (2-inch) piece vanilla bean, or
   1½ teaspoons vanilla extract
4 tablespoons cornstarch
1 cup granulated sugar
1/16 teaspoon salt
4 large egg yolks, beaten
1 (9-inch) baked Sweet Pastry tart shell

1 cup water
Dash salt
1 teaspoon freshly squeezed lemon juice
6 medium-sized bananas
½ cup Macaroon Crumbs
Confectioners' sugar
2 tablespoons butter, melted
Apricot Sauce

Heat 1¾ cups of the milk, with the vanilla bean (if using). Combine cornstarch, ½ cup granulated sugar, and the salt in a saucepan, add the reserved ¼ cup milk, and mix well. Gradually add the hot milk. Stir and cook until the mixture is very thick. Blend a little of the hot mixture with the egg yolks and gradually stir them into remaining hot mixture. Stir and cook over low heat until mixture is about as thick as mayonnaise. Remove from heat and strain. If vanilla bean was not used, add vanilla extract now. Cool completely. Turn half of the pastry cream into the tart shell, reserving the remaining half to use later. Combine remaining ½ cup granulated sugar, 1 cup water, the salt, and lemon juice in a saucepan and bring to the boiling point. Peel bananas, cut in half crosswise, then cut the halves in half lengthwise. Put the bananas in the hot syrup and cook 2 to 3 minutes. Remove bananas from syrup, drain well, and set aside. Place the drained bananas over the pie filling, covering the cream completely. Spread the remaining cream over the bananas, sprinkle with Macaroon Crumbs and dust with confectioners' sugar, and drizzle with butter. Place in preheated oven (450°F) 3 to 4 minutes to glaze. Serve with Apricot Sauce. Makes 6 servings.

Flambéed Bananas Martinique

¼ cup (1½ stick) butter
½ cup sugar
½ cup freshly squeezed orange juice
1 tablespoon freshly squeezed
    lemon juice

¼ cup apricot jam
6 large firm, ripe bananas
¼ cup dark rum
Toasted, slivered, blanched almonds

Melt the butter in a saucepan. Add the sugar and cook until the mixture begins to turn golden (caramelize), stirring constantly. Add the orange juice, lemon juice, and jam. Stir and cook 1 to 2 minutes. Peel the bananas, cut them in half lengthwise, and place them in the sauce. Cook 3 to 4 minutes. Transfer bananas to a chafing dish or a serving dish. Heat the rum, ignite, and quickly pour it over the bananas. As soon as the flame is out, sprinkle with almonds. Makes 6 servings.

Banana Fritters

3 bananas
1 tablespoon sugar
1 tablespoon freshly squeezed
    lemon juice

2 tablespoons rum or brandy
Sweet Fritter Batter
Oil for frying
Lemon Sauce, Orange Sauce, or Rum Sauce

Peel the bananas and cut them into slices 1 inch thick. Add the next 3 ingredients and marinate 1 hour, turning occasionally. Drain the bananas well and dip the slices into Sweet Fritter Batter. Drop them, a few at a time, into deep fat preheated to 375°F. Fry until golden brown. Drain on paper towels. Serve hot with Lemon Sauce, Orange Sauce, or Rum Sauce. Makes 6 to 8 servings.

Bananas Orientale

2 tablespoons freshly squeezed
    lemon juice
1 slice lemon
Vanilla Syrup
4 bananas

Almond ice cream
Custard Sauce
Rose water
Toasted, slivered almonds

Combine the first 3 ingredients in a 1½-quart saucepan and bring to the boiling point. Peel the bananas and cut them into slices 1 inch thick. Add them to the syrup, cover, and cook 1 to 2 minutes. Cool in the syrup. Put ice cream in 6 individual serving dishes, filling them one-third full. Cover with well-drained bananas. Flavor Custard Sauce to taste with rose water and spoon over the bananas. Sprinkle with almonds. Makes 6 servings.

Cantaloupe Balls and Strawberries with Kirsch

2 small cantaloupes
1½ cups sliced strawberries
3 tablespoons sugar

4 tablespoons kirsch
Fresh mint

Cut the cantaloupes in half. Remove the seeds and cut the flesh into balls with a French melon-baller. Scoop out the meat that remains in the shells and save it to add to fruit cups and salads. Reserve the shells. Combine the cantaloupe balls, strawberries, sugar, and kirsch and macerate 30 minutes. Notch the cantaloupe shells and fill them with the cantaloupe balls and strawberries. Garnish each with a sprig of mint. Makes 4 servings.

Flambéed Cherries Jubilee

1½ pounds fresh, sweet cherries
¼ cup sugar
½ cup Madeira
¼ cup water
1 small piece cinnamon

2 tablespoons red currant jelly
¼ cup kirsch

Wash the cherries and remove stones. Combine the sugar, wine, ¼ cup water, and the cinnamon in a saucepan. Bring to the boiling point, reduce heat, and simmer 5 minutes. Add cherries and cook 5 minutes, or until cherries can be easily pierced with a toothpick. Transfer cherries to a large serving dish. Stir in red currant jelly and boil syrup gently 3 to 4 minutes. Pour over cherries. Just before serving, heat the kirsch, ignite, and quickly pour it over the cherries. Bring to the table flaming. The secret of success in making Flambéed Fresh Cherries is to have both the cherries and the kirsch hot, and to ignite the kirsch as it is being poured over the cherries. Makes 6 servings.

Cherries in Kirsch

2½ pounds fresh, sweet cherries
½ cup sugar
¾ cup water

2 cups dry red wine
¼ cup kirsch
Vanilla Ice Cream (optional)

Wash and pit the cherries. Crack 18 of the pits and tie them up in a cheesecloth bag. Combine the next 3 ingredients, add the bag of pits, bring the mixture to the boiling point, and cook 5 minutes. Add cherries, cover, and simmer 10 minutes. Using a perforated spoon, remove the cherries to a serving dish. Cook the syrup until reduced to 1¾ cups and strain it through a fine sieve. Add the kirsch to the syrup and pour over the cherries. Serve in individual dishes as a dessert. If desired, top with ice cream. Makes 10 servings.

Cherries Victoria

6 small round slices Brioche
¼ cup Cognac
1½ pounds fresh, sweet cherries
¼ cup sugar
¼ cup water
½ cup port

1½ cups fresh strawberries
Sugar
Dash salt
¼ teaspoon vanilla extract
1 teaspoon freshly squeezed lemon juice

Soak the Brioche slices in the Cognac and place a slice in each of 6 custard cups. Pit the cherries and cook them in the sugar, port, and water, as in recipe for Flambéed Cherries. While hot, pour them over the Brioche slices. Wash and hull the strawberries, crush, and sweeten to taste with sugar. Add the salt, vanilla extract, and lemon juice. Pour over the cherries. Makes 6 servings.

Fig Compote

1 quart ripe figs
¾ cup sugar
2 cups water
Dash salt
1 tablespoon freshly squeezed
    lemon juice

1 (2-inch) piece vanilla bean, or
    1½ teaspoon vanilla extract
2 tablespoons kirsch

Wash the figs, cut in half lengthwise, and set aside. Combine the next 4 ingredients in a 2-quart saucepan, with the vanilla bean (if using). Mix well, bring to the boiling point, and simmer, uncovered, 5 minutes. Add figs and cook 5 minutes. Add the kirsch (and the vanilla extract if the vanilla bean was not used) and let the figs cool in the syrup. Makes 8 servings.

Nectarines Bourdaloue

Use the recipe for Apricots Bourdaloue, replacing the apricots with nectarines. Makes 6 servings.

Nectarines Sobieski

Use the recipe for Apricots Sobieski, replacing the apricots with nectarines.

Orange-Coconut Compote

6 medium-sized navel oranges
½ cup sugar

1 cup water
½ cup grated fresh coconut or flaked coconut

Peel and section the oranges. Set aside. Combine the sugar and water in a saucepan, bring to the boiling point, and boil 1 minute. Add orange sections and simmer 1 minute. Cool. Chill in the syrup. Serve in tall sherbet glasses, each garnished with 1 tablespoon coconut. Makes 8 servings.

Peach Compote

In the recipe for Apricot Compote, replace the apricots with peaches. Makes 6 servings.

Peaches Bourdaloue

Use the recipe for Apricots Bourdaloue, replacing the apricots with peaches. Makes 6 servings.

Peaches in Chantilly Cream

1 cup fresh peaches, crushed
1 cup sifted confectioners' sugar
⅛ teaspoon salt

1⅓ cups heavy cream
1 teaspoon vanilla extract
1 tablespoon granulated sugar

Combine the peaches, ¼ cup of the confectioners' sugar, and the salt and set aside. Whip 1 cup of the cream until almost stiff and gradually beat in the remaining confectioners' sugar and the vanilla extract. Fold in the peaches. Turn the mixture into a serving bowl. Add the granulated sugar to the remaining ⅓ cup cream and beat until it stands in stiff peaks. Using a pastry bag, pipe whipped-cream rosettes over the top of the mixture. Makes 6 servings.

Flambéed Peaches

6 large or 9 medium-sized peaches
Boiling water
¾ cup sugar
2 cups water
1 teaspoon freshly squeezed lemon juice

Dash salt
1 (1-inch) piece of vanilla bean, or
    1½ teaspoon vanilla extract
¼ cup kirsch

Dip the peaches in boiling water, then in cold water, and remove the skins. Cut peaches in half, remove pits, crush the pits, and place them, the next 4 ingredients, and the vanilla bean (if using) in a 1½-quart saucepan, bring to the boiling point, and simmer 5 minutes. Add one-third of the peaches at a time and cook them until they are tender when pierced with a toothpick. As the peaches are cooked, transfer them to a serving dish. If vanilla extract is used instead of vanilla bean, add it to the syrup, discard pits, and pour syrup over the peaches. Heat the kirsch, ignite, and pour over the peaches. Bring to the table flaming. Makes 6 servings.

Flambéed Peaches with Strawberries

Poach 6 large or 9 medium-sized peaches as instructed for Flambéed Peaches. Sweeten ½ cup crushed strawberries to taste with sugar. Heat, put in a serving dish, and pour the hot poached peaches over the strawberries. Heat ¼ cup kirsch, ignite, and pour over peaches and crushed strawberries. Bring to the table flaming. Makes 6 servings.

Flambéed Peaches Montreal

12 poached peach halves
12 almond macaroons
⅓ cup Benedictine

Sugar
⅓ cup kirsch

Drain the syrup from poached peaches and pat them dry with paper towels. Soak the macaroons in Benedictine and sprinkle them with sugar. Arrange them in a serving dish large enough to accommodate the peaches, and place a poached peach half on each macaroon. Heat the kirsch, ignite, and pour it over the peaches and macaroons. Bring to the table flaming. Makes 6 servings.

Praline Peaches

12 poached peach halves, with syrup
12 (3-inch) rounds Génoise,
 ½ inch thick

Praline Condé
Sugar
2 tablespoons apricot jam

Drain the peach halves and pat dry with paper towels. Reserve the syrup. Place a peach half on each round of Génoise and spoon Praline Condé on top. Sprinkle with sugar. Place in a preheated oven (425°F) 5 minutes, or until the surface has glazed. Arrange the peaches in a silver dish or an attractive china bowl. Simmer the poaching syrup 5 minutes, add jam, and pour the mixture over the peaches. Makes 6 servings.

Peaches Sobieski

Use the recipe for Apricots Sobieski, replacing the apricots with 6 medium-sized peaches.

Peaches Surprise

6 poached peach halves
Vanilla Ice Cream
Apricot jam

6 rounds Génoise or Sponge Cake
Kirsch or Cointreau
Toasted, sliced almonds

Drain peaches and pat dry with paper towels. Fill cavity of each with a scoop of ice cream, rounding it high enough to make the peach look whole. Coat the ice cream and the sides of the peach with jam. Sprinkle cake rounds with kirsch or Cointreau and top each with a stuffed peach. Scatter almonds over the top. Serve immediately. Makes 6 servings.

Pears Bourdaloue

1 cup milk
1 cup light cream
1 (2-inch) piece vanilla bean, or
    1½ teaspoons vanilla extract
4 tablespoons cornstarch
1 cup sugar
¹⁄₁₆ teapsoon salt
4 large egg yolks, beaten
1 (9-inch) baked Plain Pastry tart
    (pie) shell

1 cup water
Dash salt
1 teaspoon freshly squeezed lemon juice
3 medium-sized firm, ripe pears
½ cup Macaroon Crumbs
Confectioners' sugar
2 tablespoons butter, melted
Apricot Sauce

Heat the milk and ¾ cup of the cream with vanilla bean (if using). Combine cornstarch, ½ cup of the granulated sugar, and ¹⁄₁₆ teaspoon salt in a saucepan, add remaining ¼ cup cream, and mix well. Gradually add the hot milk mixture. Stir and cook until the mixture is very thick. Blend a little of the hot mixture with the egg yolks and gradually stir them into the remaining hot mixture. Stir and cook over low heat until mixture is about as thick as mayonnaise. Remove from heat and strain. If vanilla bean was not used, add vanilla extract now. Cool completely. Turn half of the pastry cream into the tart shell, reserving the remaining half to use later. Combine the remaining ½ cup granulated sugar, the water, a dash of salt, and the lemon juice in a saucepan and bring to the boiling point. Peel pears, cut them in half lengthwise, and remove cores. Put half of the pears in the hot syrup, cover, and cook 8 to 10 minutes, or until pears are tender when pierced with a toothpick. Remove pears from the syrup and set aside to drain. Repeat with the remaining pears. Place all the drained pears over the cream in the tart shell. Cover the pears with the remaining cream. Sprinkle with Macaroon Crumbs, dust with confectioners' sugar, and drizzle with butter. Place in a preheated oven (450°F) 3 to 4 minutes to glaze. Serve with Apricot Sauce. Makes 6 servings.

Pear Tartlets Bourdaloue

Sweet Pie Pastry
1 tablespoon cornstarch
⅓ cup flour
⅛ teaspoon salt
¾ cup sugar
5 egg yolks
1 cup milk

1 cup light cream
1 (2-inch) piece vanilla bean, or
    1½ teaspoons vanilla extract
3 tablespoons butter
1 tablespoon cognac, kirsch, or rum
8 poached pears
1 cup Macaroon Crumbs

Line eight 4-inch tart pans with Sweet Pie Pastry rolled ⅛ inch thick. Bake in a pre-heated oven (450°F) 5 minutes. Remove from the oven and set aside. Combine the next 4 ingredients in the top of a double boiler, or in a 1½-quart saucepan. Beat in the egg yolks and ¼ cup of the milk. Heat the remaining milk, the cream, and the vanilla bean (if using) together, and gradually beat into the sugar and egg mixture. Beat and cook over hot water (not boiling) or over very low heat until the cream is smooth and thick-ened. Strain into the top of a double boiler and place over hot water. If vanilla bean was not used, add vanilla extract now. Beat in butter and cognac, kirsch, or rum. Put 3 table-spoons of the cream into each of the tart shells and place a poached pear on top. Cover the pears with the remaining cream and sprinkle with Macaroon Crumbs. Return tarts to the oven (450°F) and bake 5 minutes. Chill and serve. Makes 8 servings.

Pear Compote

1¼ cups sugar
3 cups water
½ teaspoon salt
¼ cup freshly squeezed lemon juice

1 (2-inch) piece vanilla bean, or
    2 tablespoons vanilla extract
8 medium-sized pears
Fresh mint

Combine the first 4 ingredients and the vanilla bean (if using) in a 1½-quart saucepan. Bring to the boiling point and simmer, uncovered, 5 minutes. Peel, core, and quarter the pears. Add to the syrup, cover, and cook gently 20 to 25 minutes, or until pears are tender when pierced with a fork. If vanilla bean was not used, add vanilla extract now. Remove pears and reduce syrup. Pour over pears and chill. Serve in compote dishes, garnished with mint. Makes 6 servings.

⁓ Flambéed Pears

Follow directions for Flambéed Peaches , replacing the peaches with 6 medium-large firm ripe pears. Makes 6 servings.

⁓ Pears with Creamed Semolina Pudding Floretta

¼ cup farina (semolina)
1 cup sugar
½ teaspoon salt
2 cups milk
1 (2-inch) piece vanilla bean, or
    1½ teaspoons vanilla extract
1 envelope unflavored gelatin
1¼ cups cold water

1 cup heavy cream, whipped
2½ pounds medium-small firm, ripe pears
1 tablespoon freshly squeezed lemon juice
2 cups red Bordeaux
1 small stick cinnamon
¼ cup red currant jelly
10 small circles candied orange peel
Pistachio nuts

Combine the farina, ½ cup of the sugar, the salt, and milk in a 1½-quart saucepan. Add vanilla bean (if using). Bring mixture to the boiling point, reduce heat, and cook 5 to 10 minutes, or until the mixture thickens. Meanwhile, soften gelatin in ¼ cup cold water and blend with the hot farina mixture. If vanilla bean was used, remove it; if not, add vanilla extract now. Chill the mixture in a pan of ice water until it begins to set. Fold in whipped cream and turn the mixture into a lightly oiled 8-inch ring mold. Chill until firm.

Peel the pears, leaving them whole with stems attached. Combine 1 cup cold water and the lemon juice, and drop the pears into the mixture as they are peeled to prevent discoloration. Combine the remaining ½ cup sugar, the wine, and cinnamon in a 1½-quart pan, mix well, and bring to the boiling point. Add the pears and simmer 10 minutes, or until pears are tender (do not cook pears too much). Transfer pears to a bowl. Return syrup to the heat and cook until it spins a short thread (230°F). Add the jelly and mix well. Stir and cook slowly until the sauce coats a spoon. Unmold the farina onto a serving plate. Drain the pears. Dip 4 or 5 pears in the jelly glaze and place them in the center of the mold. Arrange the remaining pears around the outside of the mold. Garnish top of the mold with the circles of candied orange peel and with pistachio nuts. Makes 6 servings.

⁓ Pears in Red Wine

8 medium-sized firm ripe pears
½ cup water
1 tablespoon freshly squeezed
    lemon juice

¾ cup sugar
2 cups dry red wine

Peel, quarter, and core pears and drop them into the water with the lemon juice to prevent discoloration. Combine sugar and wine and cook 5 minutes. Add pears, cover, and cook gently until they are tender when pierced with a fork. Transfer pears to a serving dish. Cook syrup until it has reduced by one-fourth. Pour the syrup over the pears. Chill. Serve cold. Makes 8 to 10 servings.

Poached Pear Meringue Cake Schouvaloff

6 medium-small pears
½ cup sugar
2 cups water
1 teaspoon freshly squeezed lemon juice
¹⁄₁₆ teaspoon salt
1 (2-inch) piece vanilla bean, or
   ½ teaspoon vanilla extract

1 (8-inch) round Sponge Cake
⅓ cup apricot jam
Soft Meringue, made with 3 egg whites
Red currant jelly
Pistachio nuts
2 tablespoons kirsch

Wash and peel the pears, cut them in half crosswise, and remove the cores. Combine the sugar, water, lemon juice, salt, and vanilla bean (if using). Bring to the boiling point and simmer 5 minutes. Add half of the pears. Cover and cook gently 8 to 10 minutes, or until pears are tender when tested with a toothpick. Transfer pears to a bowl. Add remaining pears to the syrup and cook gently until they are tender. Combine all the cooked pears in the syrup, add vanilla extract if vanilla bean was not used, and let pears cool. Place the Sponge Cake on a baking sheet. Spread it with jam and arrange the pears on the jam, with stem ends pointing toward the center. Cover with two-thirds of the Soft Meringue and smooth it over the top. Put the remaining meringue in a pastry bag fitted with a star nozzle and pipe a lattice pattern over the top. Place in a preheated oven (275°F) 20 to 25 minutes, or until the meringue is dry and slightly colored. Cool. Place cake on a serving plate. Drop a bit of jelly into each of the squares of the lattice pattern. Place a pistachio nut on each. Mix kirsch with the syrup in which the pears were poached and spoon some over each serving. Makes 6 servings.

Fresh Pineapple Compote

1 medium-sized fresh pineapple
¾ cup sugar
1½ cups water
1 tablespoon freshly squeezed
   lemon juice

Dash salt
1 (2-inch) piece vanilla bean, or
   1½ teaspoons vanilla extract
2 tablespoons rum or kirsch

Peel the pineapple, slice, cut into wedges, and remove core. Set aside. Combine the next 4 ingredients and the vanilla bean (if using) in a saucepan, bring to the boiling point, and simmer 5 minutes. Add pineapple, cover, and cook 5 minutes, or until pineapple is tender. Using a perforated spoon, remove pineapple from syrup. Cook syrup until reduced by one-fourth, add rum or kirsch and vanilla extract if vanilla bean was not used, and pour over pineapple. Cool in the syrup. Makes 6 servings.

Pineapple Fritters

1 medium-sized fresh pineapple	Sweet Fritter Batter
2 tablespoons sugar	Oil for frying
2 tablespoons rum or cognac	Pineapple-Rum Sauce or Lemon Sauce

Peel the pineapple and cut it into slices ¾ inch thick. Cut the slices into quarters and cut out and discard the cores. Sprinkle the pineapple with sugar and rum. Macerate 1 hour, turning occasionally. Drain pineapple well. Drop the pineapple quarters, a few at a time, into the Sweet Fritter Batter. Deep fry in oil preheated to 375°F until golden brown. Drain on paper towels. Serve fritters with Pineapple-Rum Sauce or Lemon Sauce. Makes 6 to 8 servings.

Pineapple and Strawberry Cup

¼ cup sugar	3 cups fresh pineapple wedges
¾ cup water	1 cup sliced, fresh strawberries
1 teaspoon freshly squeezed lemon juice	
1 (2-inch) piece vanilla bean, or 1 teaspoon vanilla extract	

Combine the first 3 ingredients with the vanilla bean (if using) in a saucepan. Bring to the boiling point and boil, uncovered, 2 minutes. Remove from heat and cool. Remove vanilla bean if used, or add vanilla extract now. Add fruit and chill. Serve in compote dishes. Makes 6 servings.

Plum Compote

In the recipe for Apricot Compote, replace the apricots with 2 pounds of plums. Makes 6 servings.

Raspberry Compote

1 quart raspberries
¾ cup sugar
1 cup water

Wash raspberries and drain well. Set aside. Combine sugar and water in a 1-quart saucepan. Mix well and stir and cook 5 minutes. When it is only warm, pour over raspberries. Cool and chill. Makes 6 servings.

Rhubarb Compote

2 pounds rhubarb
⅓ cup water
Dash salt

1 cup sugar
1 (2-inch) piece vanilla bean, or
    1½ teaspoons vanilla extract

Cut off the leaves and coarse big ends of the rhubarb stalks. Wash and peel the older stalks, but do not peel the young tender ones, since the peel turns pink when cooked. Cut stalks into 1-inch pieces. Add water, salt, sugar, and vanilla bean (if using). Cover and cook over low heat 25 to 30 minutes. Or, if desired, omit water, mix salt with sugar and sprinkle over rhubarb, add vanilla extract, and bake in a covered casserole in a pre-heated oven (375°F) 45 to 50 minutes, or until rhubarb is tender. Do not stir. Makes 6 servings.

Spiced Rhubarb

Add two 2-inch cinnamon sticks and 4 whole cloves to rhubarb and cook in either of the ways described in the recipe for Rhubarb Compote.

Strawberry Compote

In the recipe for Raspberry Compote, replace raspberries with 1 quart fresh strawberries. Add ¼ cup red currant jelly to the syrup in the last 2 minutes of cooking. Strain before pouring over the drained strawberries. Makes 6 servings.

Strawberry Cream

1 quart strawberries
5 tablespoons granulated sugar
2 tablespoons kirsch
1 cup heavy cream, whipped

2 tablespoons confectioners' sugar
½ teaspoon vanilla extract
6 whole hulled strawberries

Wash, hull, and slice the 1 quart strawberries. Sprinkle with the granulated sugar and the kirsch. Combine the whipped cream, confectioners' sugar, and vanilla extract. Fold in sliced strawberries. Turn into a freezer tray and place in the freezer until very cold but not frozen. Remove and serve at once in tall sherbet glasses. Top each glass with a whole hulled strawberry. Makes 6 servings.

Strawberries Romanoff

1 quart strawberries
¼ cup freshly squeezed orange juice
2 tablespoons curaçao

Chantilly Cream

Wash and hull the strawberries. Add the orange juice and curaçao and macerate 1 hour in the refrigerator. Serve with Chantilly Cream. Makes 6 servings.

Compote of Mixed Fruits

¾ cup sugar
2 cups water
Dash salt
freshly squeezed lemon juice
1 (2-inch) piece vanilla bean, or
    1½ teaspoons vanilla extract

2 pears, peeled and quartered
2 peaches, peeled and quartered
2 nectarines or apricots, peeled 1 tablespoon
    and quartered
1 cup fresh pineapple wedges
Sweet cherries

Combine the first 4 ingredients in a saucepan, with the vanilla bean (if using). Bring to the boiling point and simmer, uncovered, 5 minutes. Add the pears, cover, and cook gently 10 minutes. Add the remaining fruit, cover, and cook 5 to 10 minutes, or until fruit is tender. If vanilla bean was not used, add vanilla extract. Cool in the syrup. Add cherries but cook them separately according to the recipe for Cherries in Kirsch, omitting the kirsch. This method prevents the cherries from discoloring the other fruits. Makes 8 servings.

Mixed Fruits in Champagne or Liqueur

Cook ½ cup sugar and 1½ cups water together 5 minutes. Set aside to cool. Prepare a macédoine of fruit (orange sections, apple slices, pear slices, and banana slices) as in preceding recipe and place it in a large crystal bowl. Pour the cold syrup and 1 cup dry champagne or 1 cup of any desired liqueur over the fruit. Place the bowl in a pan of crushed ice and let it stand for 2 hours. Allow ½ cup fruit for each serving.

CAKES
AND
PASTRIES

THE FRENCH WORD *GATEAU*, which we translate as "cake," has a far wider scope of meaning than in America. French cakes are baked from some kind of cake batter and then usually filled and iced. So something like an almond cake here, actually a *pithiviers*, is more like what in America would be called a pie made from puff pastry. The French *gâteau* refers to everything from the Lemania Cake to meringue-layered cakes like the Mascotte Cake, to tortes like the Black Forest Cherry Torte or the Dobos Torta. Even a profiterole tower, called a Croquembouche, is a *gâteau*.

So in this chapter there are cakes of all descriptions, as well as cookies, small cakes and petits fours (including their complementary fondants, icings, and butter creams), choux pastries, puff pastries, crepes and waffles, tarts and tartlets, and tortes.

CAKES

 ## Génoise

Génoise is a very fine-textured and very versatile moist Italian (and then French) butter cake of which the only leavening agent is the air beaten into the eggs, and the richness is due to having lukewarm melted butter folded into the batter near the end of the mixing period. It is light like a Sponge Cake but has a firmer and moister texture and cuts more easily. It is used as the basis of other fine French cakes, petits fours, and many French desserts for which a layer of cake firmer than Sponge Cake is required.

Génoise is more difficult to make than a regular Sponge Cake or a conventional butter cake; therefore it is important that all rules be followed carefully. The ingredients must be at room temperature. The eggs should be beaten together with the sugar in a warm bowl until they have doubled in volume. If the beating is done by hand, the bowl should be placed over (not in) warm water. If an electric mixer is used (which shortens the beating time), the bowl should be warm (not hot) before the ingredients are added. After the eggs have been beaten and the sugar added, the rest of the ingredients should be very gently folded into the batter.

The amount made by this recipe may be baked in a 15½-by-10½-by-1-inch jelly-roll pan, in 2 round or square 9-inch layer-cake pans, or in 2 or 3 round or square 8-inch layer-cake pans, depending on the thickness desired.

After the cake is baked, it must be removed from the pan immediately to prevent it from becoming damp and heavy.

6 large eggs
1 cup fine granulated sugar
1½ teaspoons vanilla extract

1 cup sifted cake flour
¼ cup (½ stick) butter, melted

Choose pans of the size desired, grease the bottoms lightly, line with waxed paper, and grease the paper lightly. Set aside.

Break eggs into the large bowl of an electric mixer, having both bowl and beater warm (not hot). Or, break eggs into a large warmed mixing bowl. If this cake is mixed by hand, place the bowl over warm water. (The water should not be hot, and the bowl should not be placed down in the water.) Beat eggs until foamy. Gradually beat in sugar and beat at high speed on the electric mixer, or beat vigorously by hand until the volume of eggs and sugar has doubled. Scrape sides and bottom of the bowl frequently so that the sugar will be well blended with the eggs. The mixture should stand in stiff peaks when the beater is withdrawn. Beat in the vanilla extract. If the eggs were beaten by hand, remove the bowl from over the warm water. Sift the flour and carefully fold in 2 tablespoons at a time, using a rubber spatula. Cool the melted butter to lukewarm and fold in 1 teaspoon at a time, being careful not to include any of the residue that has settled to the bottom of the pan. Pour the batter into the prepared cake pans. Bake in a preheated (350°F) oven 35 to 40 minutes, or until a cake tester or toothpick inserted in the center of the cake comes out clean. Remove the cake from the pan immediately, strip off the paper from the bottom, and cool the cake on a wire rack. Génoise may be frosted as desired and served as a dessert, or used in the preparation of other desserts, or for frosted petits fours. Makes one 15½-by-10½-inch layer, or two 9-inch layers, or two to three 8-inch layers, depending upon the thickness desired.

Sponge Cake

6 large eggs, separated
1¼ cups sugar
2 teaspoons grated lemon zest
1 tablespoon freshly squeezed
    lemon juice

1 teaspoon vanilla extract
½ teaspoon salt
1½ cups sifted cake-flour
Confectioners' sugar (optional)

Beat the egg yolks over hot water (not in it), until they are very thick and lemon-colored. Gradually beat in the sugar and lemon zest, beating well after each addition. Beat in the lemon juice and vanilla extract. Set aside. Add the salt to the egg whites and beat until they are stiff but not dry. Pile the whites on top of the egg yolk mixture. Sift flour over the whites and carefully fold both into the egg yolk mixture. Turn the batter into an ungreased 10-by-4-inch tube-cake pan that has been rinsed in cold water and well drained. Bake in a preheated oven (325°F) 1 hour, or until the cake has browned and pulls away from the sides of the pan. Invert the cake on a wire rack to cool. Loosen cake from the sides of the pan with a spatula. Turn the cake top side up on the cooling rack and lift off the pan. If desired, dust the top with confectioners' sugar. Or, if desired, cut the cake into layers and put them together with apricot jam, currant jelly, or any desired filling. Makes one 10-inch tube cake. (For Jelly-Roll Sponge Cake Layer, see page 594.)

Almond Puff Pastry or Pithiviers

Puff Pastry	1 egg
½ cup almond paste	2 tablespoons milk
1 cup French Pastry Cream	Confectioners' sugar (optional)

Roll out Puff Pastry ¼ inch thick on a lightly floured board. Cut it into two 9-inch circles, using a 9-inch round layer-cake pan as a guide. Combine almond paste and French Pastry Cream and spread over one of the circles to within ½ inch of the edge of the pastry. Cover with the second circle of Puff Pastry. Moisten the edge of the pastry and seal it by pressing firmly all around with your thumb. Beat the egg and milk together and brush over the top of the pastry. With a sharp knife, make curving lines out from the center and cut a small hole in the center of the pastry. Place the cake on a greased baking sheet lined with heavy brown paper. Chill 30 to 40 minutes. Bake in a preheated oven (450°F) 10 minutes, or until pastry has puffed and has begun to brown. Reduce oven temperature to 350°F and bake 25 minutes. Reduce temperature to 300°F and bake 10 minutes, or until the cake is golden brown. Sprinkle with confectioners' sugar while hot, if desired. Makes one 9-inch cake.

Almond Ring

1 envelope (1 scant tablespoon) active dry yeast	1½ teaspoons salt
¼ cup lukewarm water	About 6 cups sifted all-purpose flour
1 cup sugar	¼ cup (½ stick) butter, melted
¾ cup shortening	⅔ cup chopped blanched almonds
1½ cups milk, scalded	1 egg white
3 egg yolks, beaten	1 tablespoon water
	⅓ cup slivered blanched almonds

Soften the yeast in the lukewarm water with 1 teaspoon of the sugar. Add the shortening to the hot milk, cool it to lukewarm, and add to the yeast, along with the remaining sugar, the egg yolks, salt, and 2 cups of the flour. Beat the batter until it falls in sheets from a spoon. Gradually add the remaining flour, stirring and kneading until the dough can be handled. Knead a few seconds longer. Shape the dough into a ball and place it in a buttered bowl. Butter the top of the dough. Cover and let rise in a warm place (80° to 85°F) until it has doubled in bulk. Punch down dough, shape it into 2 balls, cover, and let it rest 10 minutes. Roll each ball of dough into a 16-by-8-inch rectangle ¼ inch thick. Brush each with butter and sprinkle each with half of the chopped almonds. Starting at the long side, roll up each rectangle jelly-roll fashion. Place on a baking sheet and join the ends to form 2 rings. With scissors, cut 1½-inch slices on a slant almost through to the opposite side of the ring. Combine the egg white and 1 tablespoon water, beat until foamy, and brush over the tops of the rings. Sprinkle with slivered almonds. Cover the rings and let them rise in a warm place until they have doubled in size. Bake in a preheated oven (375°F) 25 to 30 minutes, until browned. Makes 2 rings.

Caraque Cake

5½ squares (5½ ounces) semisweet chocolate
4 large eggs
½ cup sugar

⅔ cup sifted all-purpose flour
¼ cup strong brewed coffee
1 tablespoon crème de menthe
Fondant Cake Icing

Have all ingredients at room temperature. Butter a round 9-inch layer-cake pan, line it with waxed paper, and butter the paper. Set aside. Cut a circle of waxed paper 2 inches in diameter. Melt 1 square of the chocolate and spread it on the waxed paper to make a 3-inch circle. Chill until cake is ready to be frosted.

Break the eggs in a mixing bowl and place it over (not in) a pan of hot water. Gradually beat in the sugar and continue beating until the eggs and sugar have doubled in volume and hold their shape when the beater is withdrawn. (If possible, use an electric mixer, since this requires much beating.) Sift the flour 4 times and carefully fold it into the eggs, using a rubber spatula. Melt 4 squares of the chocolate over hot water, cool about 2 minutes, and fold into the batter, along with the coffee. Pour the batter into the prepared cake pan. Bake in a preheated oven (350°F) 30 minutes, or until a toothpick inserted in the center comes out clean. Cool the cake in the pan 10 minutes. Turn out onto a wire rack to finish cooling. Transfer cake to a serving plate. Add the crème de menthe to semimelted Fondant (For Fondant Cake Icing recipe, see page 570.) Pour the icing over the top of the cake, being careful not to let it run down the sides. Let the icing set. Melt the remaining ½ square of chocolate, mix with the remaining icing, and with a cake-decorator's tube make a design around the edge of the cake. Remove the chocolate circle from the waxed paper and place it in the center of the cake. Makes one round 9-inch cake.

Swiss Carvelle Cake

8 squares (½ pound) unsweetened chocolate
Butter-Cream
2 round 9-inch Génoise layers, completely cooled

1 tablespoon butter
Chocolate decorettes

Add 1 square of the chocolate to the Butter-Cream mixture while it is still hot and stir until chocolate has melted and is well blended with the frosting. Beat 2 to 3 minutes. Chill and beat again 2 to 3 minutes. Spread frosting between the Génoise layers and over the top and sides of the cake. Melt the remaining chocolate with the butter in a small bowl over hot water (not boiling). Mix well. Cover the bottom of a round 9-inch layer-cake pan with waxed paper cut to fit. Pour the chocolate mixture into it. Cool 2 to 3 hours, or until chocolate has hardened. Remove chocolate from the pan and cut into wedges while still on the paper. Remove the wedges from the paper and arrange them over the frosting that is on the top layer, having them slightly overlapping. Sprinkle chocolate decorettes on the frosting around the sides. Makes one 2-layer 9-inch cake.

Chocolate or Chocolatine Cake

3 round 8-inch Génoise layers, completely cooled	Chocolate Butter-Cream
	Toasted, chopped, blanched almonds

Spread Chocolate Butter-Cream between the Génoise layers and over the top and sides. Sprinkle the sides of the cake with almonds. Makes one 3-layer 8-inch cake.

Christmas Log or Bûche de Noël

3 large eggs	¼ teaspoon salt
1 cup granulated sugar	1 teaspoon double-acting baking powder
5 tablespoons water	Confectioners' sugar
1½ teaspoons vanilla extract	Coffee Butter-Cream
1 cup sifted cake flour	3 tablespoons cocoa

Line a greased 15½-by-10½-by-1-inch jelly-roll pan with waxed paper and grease the paper lightly. Beat eggs until they are thick and lemon-colored. Gradually beat in granulated sugar. Add the water and vanilla extract all at one time and beat. Sift together the next 3 ingredients and add to the beaten eggs all at one time. Beat mixture only until it is smooth. Pour the batter into the prepared jelly-roll pan. Bake in a preheated oven (375°F) 15 minutes. Turn out onto a towel sprinkled with confectioners' sugar. Trim crust from the edges. Roll up towel and cake together. Cool. Unroll cake and spread it with Coffee Butter-Cream. Roll up the cake jelly-roll fashion. Add the cocoa to the remaining frosting and spread over the outside of the roll. Run the tines of a fork down the length of the roll to simulate the bark on the log. Make branch stumps on the log with frosting and run the tines of a fork over them. Place the roll on a serving tray and add Christmas decorations. Makes 10 servings.

Frankfurt Crown

½ cup (1 stick) softened butter
¾ cup sugar
1 teaspoon grated lemon zest
4 large eggs
¾ cup sifted all-purpose flour

½ cup sifted cornstarch
2 teaspoons double-acting baking powder
Rum, kirsch, or Grand Marnier
Butter-Cream
Praline Powder and pistachio nuts

Have all ingredients at room temperature. Place the first 3 ingredients in a mixing bowl. Mix until fluffy and well blended. Beat in the eggs one at a time. Sift together flour, cornstarch, and baking powder and gradually add to the first mixture. Turn the batter into a well-greased lightly floured 8½-inch ring mold, or a 9-inch tube-cake pan. Bake in a preheated oven (325°F) 40 minutes, or until a toothpick inserted in the center of the cake comes out clean. Cool in the pan 10 minutes. Turn out of the pan onto a wire rack. When cold, split the cake into 3 or 4 layers and sprinkle each with rum, kirsch, or Grand Marnier. Put the layers together layer-cake fashion with the Butter-Cream. Frost the top and sides of cake with the Butter-Cream. Sprinkle with Praline Powder. Put remaining Butter-Cream into a pastry tube with a rosette nozzle and decorate the top of cake with rosettes. Garnish each rosette with 2 pistachio nuts. This cake is best eaten after it is 1 day old. Makes one 8½- or 9-inch cake.

Hungarian Cake

9 egg whites
1½ cups sifted confectioners' sugar
½ cup fine cracker crumbs
8 squares (½ pound) unsweetened
    chocolate, grated
2 tablespoons flour
1 teaspoon double-acting baking powder
½ cup ground nuts (hazelnuts, almonds,
    walnuts, or pecans)

½ cup sweet white or red wine
2 teaspoons vanilla extract
1 tablespoon freshly squeezed lemon juice
Chocolate Butter-Cream
Shaved chocolate
Confectioners' sugar
Glacéed cherries (optional)

Grease 2 round 9-inch layer-cake pans, or 3 round 8-inch layer-cake pans. Line them with waxed paper cut to fit the pans and grease the paper. Set aside. Beat egg whites until they stand in soft peaks and gradually fold in sifted confectioners' sugar. Combine the next 5 ingredients, mixing them well, and carefully fold them into the egg whites. Fold in the wine, vanilla extract, and lemon juice. Turn the batter into the prepared pans. Bake in a preheated oven (350°F) 40 to 45 minutes, or until a cake tester inserted in the center comes out clean. Cool on a wire rack. Frost the layers with Chocolate Butter Cream. Garnish each with shaved chocolate, sprinkle with confectioners' sugar, and, if desired, put a glacéed cherry in the center. This cake may also be stacked in conventional layer-cake fashion with the top decorated as described. Makes two 9-inch layers or three 8-inch layers.

Kugelhopf

1 envelope (1 scant tablespoon) active dry yeast	2 teaspoons grated lemon zest
¼ cup lukewarm water	4 cups sifted all-purpose flour
½ cup granulated sugar	2 large eggs
1¼ cups milk, scalded	½ cup raisins
¾ cup (1½ sticks) butter	¼ cup chopped blanched almonds
1 teaspoon salt	About 3 dozen whole blanched almonds
1½ teaspoons vanilla extract	Confectioners' sugar

Soften the yeast in the lukewarm water with 1 teaspoon of the granulated sugar. Combine the hot milk with the butter and cool to lukewarm. Add the remaining granulated sugar, the salt, vanilla extract, lemon zest, and yeast mixture. Stir in 2 cups of the flour and beat well. Beat in the eggs, one at a time. Continue beating 5 minutes. (The longer the batter is beaten, the better the cake.) Stir in the raisins and the chopped almonds. (If the raisins are too dry, steam them in a sieve over boiling water for a few minutes.) Gradually add the remaining flour. Mix well. Cover the bowl and let the dough rise in a warm place (80° to 85°F) until it has doubled in size, about 1½ hours.

Butter two 7-inch crown (kugelhopf) pans generously. Place a circle of whole blanched almonds in the bottom of each. Put half of the dough in each pan. Cover and let dough rise in a warm place until it has doubled in bulk. (The dough should have risen enough to almost fill the pans.) Bake in a preheated oven (350°F) 40 to 45 minutes. Cool the cakes in the pans 5 minutes, then turn them out onto wire racks, crown side up. Sprinkle generously with confectioners' sugar. Makes two 7-inch cakes.

Chocolate Kugelhopf

Make the Kugelhopf recipe, omitting the lemon zest, raisins, and almonds, and using 4¼ cups flour. Divide the dough in half. Melt 2 squares (2 ounces) unsweetened chocolate with 3 tablespoons milk and 2 tablespoons sugar in a cup over hot water. Cool slightly and add to one part of the dough. Roll out each part of the dough ¼ inch thick on a lightly floured board, adding a little more flour if dough is too soft to roll. Place the chocolate dough over the white dough and roll it up jelly-roll fashion. Place the roll in a well-buttered 9-inch kugelhopf or tube-cake pan and allow it to rise in a warm place until doubled in bulk. Bake as directed in a preheated oven (350°F) 45 to 50 minutes. Cool and frost with Chocolate Glaze. Makes one 9-inch cake.

Swiss Lémania Cake

½ cup (1 stick) softened butter
1 cup sifted fine granulated sugar
¾ teaspoon baking soda
¼ teaspoon salt
1 teaspoon grated lemon zest
3 large eggs, separated
1¾ cups sifted all-purpose flour

¼ cup sifted cornstarch
2½ tablespoons freshly squeezed
   lemon juice
½ cup milk
Lemon Butter-Cream
Confectioners' sugar
Glacéed cherries

Stir butter until it is fluffy and lemon-colored. Gradually blend in the sugar, baking soda, salt, and lemon zest. Beat until the mixture is smooth and creamy. Beat in the egg yolks, one at a time, beating vigorously after each addition. Sift the flour with the cornstarch. Combine the lemon juice and milk. Add the flour mixture to the butter and egg mixture alternately with the milk and lemon juice. Set aside. Beat the egg whites until they stand in soft peaks, then carefully fold them into the batter. Pour into 2 well-buttered, lightly floured round 8-inch layer-cake pans. Bake in a preheated oven (375°F) 25 to 30 minutes, or until a toothpick inserted in the center comes out clean. Cool in the pans 10 minutes. Turn out onto a wire rack to finish cooling. Put the layers together with Lemon Butter-Cream and decorate the top with alternating rows of sifted confectioners' sugar and glacéed cherries. Or omit the filling and treat each layer as a separate cake, decorating the tops with alternating rows of cherries and sugar. Makes 2 round 8-inch layers.

Lutétia Cake

1 round 9-inch Génoise layer,
   2 inches thick
Walnut Butter-Cream
Apricot Glaze
Chocolate Fondant Cake Icing

Sweet Chestnut Puree
½ cup confectioners' sugar
About 1½ teaspoons water
8 walnut halves
2 blanched almonds, chopped

When the Génoise is cold, split it to make 3 layers of equal thickness. Spread Walnut Butter-Cream between the layers. Spread a thin layer of Apricot Glaze over the top and sides of the cake and frost with Chocolate Fondant Cake Icing. Put Sweet Chestnut Puree in a cake-decorator's tube and pipe any design desired over the top. Combine the confectioners' sugar with enough water to make it of coating consistency. Add 3 to 4 walnut halves at a time to the mixture and mix until walnuts are well glazed. Transfer walnuts to waxed paper and let them set until they are dry. Decorate the walnuts with bits of almonds and a little of the Chocolate Fondant and arrange them over the top of the cake. Makes one round 9-inch cake.

Mascotte Cake

8 large egg yolks
1 cup sifted confectioners' sugar
1 cup finely chopped blanched almonds
1 cup fine white breadcrumbs
2 tablespoons rum

6 large egg whites
½ cup chopped, toasted, blanched almonds
2 cups Butter-Cream
Toasted, sliced, blanched almonds
Praline Powder

Beat the egg yolks until fluffy. Gradually beat in the confectioners' sugar and continue beating until the mixture is lemon-colored. Add the chopped almonds and mix well. Gradually beat in the breadcrumbs and rum. Set aside. Beat egg whites until they stand in soft peaks and fold them into the egg yolk mixture. Butter an 8-inch spring-form pan, dust it lightly with breadcrumbs, and pour in the batter. Bake in a preheated oven (350°F) 40 to 50 minutes, or until the cake springs back when pressed in the center with your index finger. Cool in the pan. Remove it to a pastry board and split it into 3 layers of equal thickness. Stir the chopped toasted almonds into the Butter-Cream. Spread it between the layers and over the top and sides. Sprinkle the frosting with toasted, sliced, blanched almonds. Sprinkle a circle of Praline Powder in the center of the cake. Makes one round 8-inch 3-layer cake.

Mocha Cake

2 square 9-inch Génoise layers, completely cooled
Mocha Butter-Cream
Toasted, chopped, blanched almonds

Put the cake layers together with Mocha Butter-Cream and spread over the top and sides. If desired, make an additional 1 cup frosting and, using a cake-decorator's tube with a rosette nozzle, pipe rosettes over the top of the cake, covering it completely. Cover the sides of the cake with the almonds. Makes one 2-layer 9-inch cake.

Mexican Cake

5 large egg yolks
⅔ cup sugar
¾ cup sifted all-purpose flour
3 tablespoons cocoa
¼ teaspoon salt
4 large egg whites

5 tablespoons butter, melted
½ teaspoons vanilla extract
Chocolate Butter-Cream
Apricot Glaze
Chocolate Fondant Cake Icing
¾ cup Royal Icing

Beat egg yolks until they are light and lemon-colored. Gradually beat in sugar and continue beating until the mixture is thick and pale in color. Sift together the next 3 ingredients and gradually fold into the egg yolk mixture. Beat egg whites until they stand in soft peaks, then fold them into the mixture. Cool the melted butter and gently fold it and the vanilla extract into the batter. (Be careful not to include the sediment that collects in the bottom of the saucepan in which butter was melted.) Turn the batter into a buttered, lightly floured, round 8-inch cake pan. Bake in a preheated oven (350°F) 35 to 40 minutes, or until a toothpick inserted in the center comes out clean. Cool in pan 10 minutes. Remove cake from pan and cool on a wire rack. When the cake is cold, split into 2 or 3 layers as desired. Put the layers together with Chocolate Butter-Cream. Spread the top and sides of the cake with Apricot Glaze. Frost the cake with Chocolate Fondant Cake Icing. Before the fondant has set, put the Royal Icing into a pastry bag and pipe parallel lines across the top of the cake. Draw the point of a knife lightly across the lines at intervals to make an attractive decoration. Makes 8 servings.

 Niçoise Cake

½ recipe Puff Pastry	Curaçao, to taste
¼ pound almonds, blanched	1 teaspoon milk
½ cup sugar	Confectioners' sugar
¼ cup finely chopped candied orange peel	Sliced almonds
	1 preserved orange slice
1 teaspoon grated orange zest	1 glacéed cherry
1 large egg	

Roll half of the Puff Pastry ¼ inch thick and cut it into an 8-inch circle, using a round 8-inch cake pan as a guide. Place the circle on a cookie sheet that has been rinsed with water and well drained. Finely grind the blanched almonds, using the finest blade of a food chopper, or grind them in an electric blender, a few at a time. Add the next 4 ingredients and mix until smooth. Add curaçao. Spread the mixture over the pastry circle to within ½ inch of the edge. Brush the edge with water. Roll the remaining Puff Pastry a little less than ¼ inch thick and cut it into an 8-inch circle. Place it over the almond filling and press the edges together firmly. Chill. Brush the top with milk and sprinkle with confectioners' sugar and sliced almonds. Bake in a preheated oven (350°F) 1 hour, or until pastry is golden brown. Remove from the oven. Cool. Garnish center with the preserved orange slice and the glacéed cherry. Makes one 8-inch cake.

Saint-Honoré Cake

Roll double recipe Plain Pastry Dough (Pâte Brisée) into a circle ¼ inch thick. Cut a 9-inch pastry circle, using a 9-inch cake pan as a guide. Transfer it to an ungreased cookie sheet. Fill a pastry bag with Choux Paste and pipe a rim of the paste 2 inches high around the pastry circle. Beat 1 egg yolk together with 1 tablespoon milk and brush it over the pastry. Bake in a preheated oven (400°F) 30 minutes, or until the bottom of the pastry is brown and the Choux Paste rim is well puffed.

Using the pastry bag, form Choux Paste into 17 small cream puffs on an ungreased baking sheet. Bake in a preheated oven (425°F) 20 to 25 minutes. Turn off the oven heat. Prick puffs with a sharp knife to permit steam to escape and leave them in the oven 15 minutes to dry out. Remove and let cool. Fill puffs with French Pastry Cream or with Chantilly Cream. Dip the top of each in Caramel Syrup and arrange them around the edge of the cake. Fill the center of cake with French Pastry Cream. Fill the spaces between the cream puffs with whipped cream or Chantilly Cream, piped through a pastry tube, and garnish with brandied cherries. Garnish the center with a preserved orange slice cut into quarters, with Chantilly Cream or whipped cream piped between the quarters and a small cream puff in the center. Makes 8 servings.

Swiss Zigomar Cake

10 large eggs, separated	2 cups ground almonds, blanched
2 cups sugar	½ cup apricot brandy or peach brandy
4½ squares (4½ ounces) unsweetened chocolate	½ teaspoon salt
	1 cup sifted fine cracker meal
3 teaspoons ground cinnamon	2 cups Rum Butter-Cream
2 tablespoons freshly squeezed lemon juice	¼ cup chopped pistachio nuts
	½ teaspoon instant coffee
1 teaspoon grated lemon zest	Chocolate Fondant Cake Icing

Beat the egg yolks until they are well mixed. Gradually beat in the sugar. Continue beating until mixture is thick and lemon-colored. Grate 4 squares of the chocolate and add, along with the next 5 ingredients. Mix well. Set aside. Add the salt to the egg whites and beat them until they stand in soft peaks. Fold them into the egg yolk mixture, alternating with the cracker meal. Turn the batter into a buttered 9-inch springform pan. Bake in a preheated oven (350°F) 50 to 60 minutes, or until a toothpick inserted in the center comes out clean. Cool the cake in the pan for 10 minutes, then remove it to a wire rack. When the cake is cold, split it into 3 layers. Reserve ⅔ cup of the Rum Butter-Cream. Melt the remaining ½ square chocolate and add it to the rest of the frosting. Spread over the first layer of cake, reserving the remaining chocolate rum frosting. Cover with the second layer. Spread the reserved white rum frosting on the second layer and sprinkle it with pistachio nuts. Cover with the remaining cake layer. Add the instant coffee to the reserved chocolate-rum frosting and spread it over the top and sides of the cake, reserving a small amount to use as decoration on top of the cake. Chill the cake 1 hour for frosting to set. Cover the top with Chocolate Fondant Cake Icing. Put the Chocolate

Fondant Cake Icing through a cake-decorator's tube and make a design around the edge of the cake. Make a big "Z" in the center of the cake with the rest of the chocolate-rum frosting. Makes one 9-inch 3-layer cake.

TORTES

German Black Forest Cherry Torte

9 large eggs
1 tablespoon water
1 cup sugar
¾ cup fine white breadcrumbs
½ cup ground blanched almonds
⅓ cup cocoa

½ cup sifted all-purpose flour
Cherry Filling
Chantilly Cream
Brandied cherries
Chocolate Curls
Unsweetened chocolate

Separate 8 of the eggs and beat the yolks and the whole egg together with the water. Gradually beat in the sugar. Add the breadcrumbs and almonds. Mix well. Sift the cocoa with the flour, add, and mix well. Beat the 8 egg whites until they stand in soft peaks and fold them into the mixture. Turn into a greased and floured round 9-inch cake pan 2 inches deep. Bake in a preheated oven (350°F) 30 minutes, or until a toothpick inserted in the center of the cake comes out clean. Cool the cake in the pan 5 minutes, then turn out onto a wire rack to finish cooling. When cold, split the cake into thin layers. Put layers together layer-cake fashion, spreading the first layer with cold Cherry Filling and then with a layer of Chantilly Cream, and the second with Chantilly Cream. Spread Chantilly Cream over the top and sides of the cake. Make rosettes over the top with Chantilly Cream put through a cake-decorator's tube fitted with a rosette nozzle. Garnish each rosette with a cherry. Decorate the center and around the edge with Chocolate Curls. Sprinkle sides with shaved unsweetened chocolate. Makes one 9-inch 3-layer cake.

Cherry Filling

2 cups pitted fresh sweet red cherries
2 tablespoons water
¼ cup sugar

1 tablespoon cornstarch
Dash salt
⅛ teaspoon almond extract

Put the cherries and the water in a heavy 1-quart saucepan. Cover and cook over low heat 10 minutes, or until cherry juice has formed in the pan. Mix the sugar, cornstarch, and salt. Increase heat to medium and stir and cook until the juice is clear and has thickened. Add the almond extract and cool. Use as filling for cake or spoon into small baked tart shells. Makes about 1 cup.

Hungarian Dobos Torta

This torte was created by the famous Hungarian pastry chef named Dobos. It consists of several thin layers of cake of sponge type spread with Chocolate Butter-Cream Frosting and a layer of Caramel Glaze over the top.

5 large eggs, separated	½ cup sifted cake flour
½ cup sugar	¼ teaspoon salt
1 tablespoon strained freshly squeezed lemon juice	Chocolate Butter-Cream
1 teaspoon vanilla extract	Caramel Glaze

Line 6 lightly greased round 8-inch layer-cake pans with waxed paper and grease the paper. Set aside. With a wire whisk, beat the egg yolks until they are fluffy. Gradually beat in the sugar. Beat in the lemon juice and vanilla extract and continue beating until the mixture is thick and lemon-colored. Sift the flour over the egg yolk mixture and fold it in very gently. Set aside. Add the salt to the egg whites and beat them until they stand in soft peaks. With a rubber spatula, carefully fold them into the cake mixture. Put an equal amount of the batter into each of the 6 prepared pans, spreading it over the bottoms to cover them uniformly. (If only 2 pans are available, bake 2 layers and repeat the operation until 6 layers have been baked.) Bake the cakes in a preheated oven (350°F) 5 to 8 minutes, or until the cake springs back when the center is pressed lightly with your index finger. Remove the cakes from the pans immediately and strip the paper off the bottoms. Cool on a wire rack. When cakes are cold, spread layers with Chocolate Butter-Cream and put them together with the sixth layer on top. Using a spatula, quickly spread the top with Caramel Glaze. When the glaze has hardened, heat a knife in hot water, wipe it dry, and make wedge-shaped incisions around the top, cutting through the glaze. Or glaze top layer before putting it on cake, cut it into wedges, and arrange them over top of cake between rows of frosting piped on with a cake-decorator's tube. Makes one 6-layer 8-inch torte.

Swiss Kirsch Torte

¹⁄₁₆ teaspoon salt	¼ cup heavy Sugar Syrup flavored with kirsch
5 large egg whites	
½ teaspoon freshly squeezed lemon juice	Kirsch Butter-Cream
1 cup granulated sugar	Toasted, chopped, blanched almonds
1½ teaspoons vanilla extract	Confectioners' sugar
¾ cup grated blanched almonds	Chopped, blanched almonds
1 round 8-inch Génoise layer	1 drop green food coloring

Add the salt to the egg whites and beat them until they stand in soft peaks (not dry). Beat in the lemon juice. Beat in ¾ cup of the granulated sugar, about 1 tablespoon at a time, and continue to beat until the meringue is thick and smooth. Fold in remaining ¼ cup granulated sugar, the vanilla extract, and the grated almonds. Cut a sheet of brown paper to fit a baking sheet. Trace two 8-inch circles, about 1 inch apart on the paper, using an 8-inch round cake pan as a guide. Spread the circles with the meringue, to a thickness of about ⅛ inch. Bake in a preheated oven (350°F) 10 minutes. Remove from the oven and strip off brown paper. Cool meringues on wire racks until crisp. Meanwhile, place the Génoise layer on a wire rack with a baking pan underneath it. Sprinkle the Sugar Syrup over it, spooning any syrup that drips into the pan over the cake. Place 1 cold meringue circle on a serving plate and spread it with a layer of Kirsch Butter-Cream. Cover it with the Génoise layer, spread cake with the frosting, and place the remaining meringue circle on top. Frost the top and sides. Sprinkle the sides with toasted almonds. Sprinkle the top with a thick layer of sifted confectioners' sugar. Color about 2 teaspoons chopped blanched almonds with food coloring and sprinkle them in the center of the cake. This cake should stand in a cool place for at least 6 hours, or overnight, before serving. Makes one 8-inch round cake.

Austrian Sacher Torte

¾ cup sugar
¾ cup (1½ sticks) softened butter
1½ teaspoons vanilla extract
6 eggs, separated

6 squares (6 ounces) semisweet chocolate
2 cups sifted cake flour
Apricot jam
Chocolate Butter-Cream

Gradually blend the sugar with the butter and vanilla extract. Beat in the egg yolks, one at a time. Melt the chocolate over hot water and cool slightly. Beat the egg whites until they stand in soft peaks, then fold in the cooled melted chocolate and add to egg yolk mixture. Fold in the cake flour. Turn the batter into 2 well-buttered, lightly floured, round 9-inch layer-cake pans. Bake in a preheated oven (350°F) 25 to 30 minutes. Remove the tortes from the pans and place them on a rack to cool. Spread apricot jam between the layers and over the top. Coat with Chocolate Butter-Cream. Makes one 9-inch 2-layer torte.

BABAS AND SAVARINS

Baba Au Rhum

1 envelope (1 scant tablespoon)
  active dry yeast
¼ cup lukewarm water
½ cup plus 3 teaspoons sugar
¼ cup lukewarm milk
2 cups sifted all-purpose flour
4 eggs

½ teaspoon salt
⅔ cup butter, melted
¾ cup water or apricot juice
1 teaspoon freshly squeezed lemon juice
¼ cup rum
Fruit, ice cream, or Chantilly Cream

Soften the yeast in the lukewarm water with 1 teaspoon of the sugar. Add 2 teaspoons sugar and the milk. Stir in the flour and the eggs and beat about 2 minutes. Cover the bowl and let the dough rise in a warm place (80° to 85°F) until it has doubled in bulk. Punch down the dough, add the salt and butter, and work these ingredients into the dough. Put the dough into 8 individual buttered baba molds, filling each two-thirds full. Cover and let dough rise until it fills the mold or molds. Bake in a preheated oven (400°F), about 15 minutes, or until a toothpick inserted in the center comes out clean.

While the baba are baking, mix the ½ cup sugar, ¾ cup water or apricot juice, and the lemon juice in a saucepan. Stir and cook until the boiling point is reached. Continue cooking without stirring for 5 minutes. Remove from heat and add rum. Invert the hot baba on a serving plate and pour the rum syrup over it. If desired, just before serving, heat 2 tablespoons rum, ignite, pour over the baba, and bring it to the table flaming. Makes 8 individual babas. Serve with fruit, ice cream, or Chantilly Cream.

Savarin

Make the dough for Baba au Rhum. Let rise in a large and buttered ring mold. Bake for 25-30 minutes. Unmold, puffed side up. Sprinkle with confectioners' sugar. The center may be filled with fruit, such as pitted black cherries, berries, sliced bananas, apricots, or peaches marinated in brandy, kirsch, or rum, piled high, or with ice cream. Or, if desired, sprinkle the top with chopped pistachio nuts and sprinkle chopped, toasted, blanched almonds around the sides at the bottom. Makes one 8½-inch savarin.

Individual Savarins Chantilly

Bake savarin dough in individual savarin molds (small ring molds). Place the savarins on a plate, puffed side up. Prick the tops with a fork and pour warm heavy kirsch-flavored Sugar Syrup over them. Let stand 30 minutes. Coat with Apricot Glaze. Put Chantilly Cream in a pastry bag fitted with a star nozzle, and pipe it into the center of each savarin, piling it high. If desired, soak half of the savarins in heavy Sugar Syrup flavored with dark rum to taste. Allow 1 savarin per serving.

Kirsch Savarins

Place a seedless muscatel raisin in the bottom of each greased, individual savarin mold (small ring mold). Fill the molds with savarin dough. Cover and let rise in a warm place (80° to 85°F) until doubled in bulk. Bake in a preheated oven (400°F) 15 minutes, or until a toothpick inserted in the center comes out clean. Unmold. Place the hot savarins on a plate, puffed side up. Prick them with a fork and pour warm kirsch-flavored Sugar Syrup over them. Let stand 30 minutes. Frost half of the savarins with white Fondant Icing and the remainder with pink Fondant Icing (made by adding 1 to 2 drops red food coloring to white Fondant). Allow 1 savarin per serving.

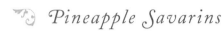 *Pineapple Savarins*

8 fresh pineapple rings	Apricot Sauce
8 individual savarins	8 brandied cherries
French Pastry Cream	Pineapple-Rum Sauce
1 to 2 tablespoons rum	

If fresh pineapple is used, poach the whole rings as directed in the recipe for Fresh Pineapple Compote. Fill the centers of small savarins with French Pastry Cream flavored with rum to taste. Cover each with a drained pineapple ring. Spread with Apricot Sauce. Put a cherry in the center of each pineapple ring. Serve with Pineapple-Rum Sauce. Makes 8 servings.

COOKIES AND SMALL CAKES

Iced Almond Pretzels

1 cup (2 sticks) softened butter	¼ teaspoon almond extract
1 cup sugar	About 2½ cups sifted all-purpose flour
1 teaspoon grated lemon zest	Confectioners' sugar
3 large egg yolks	Fondant Cake Icing, plain or chocolate
1 cup ground almonds	

Stir the butter until it is creamy. Gradually add the sugar and lemon zest, mixing well after each addition. Beat in the egg yolks, one at a time. Add the almonds and almond extract and mix well. Gradually stir in the flour, using only enough to make a soft, stiff dough. Chill until dough can be handled, 2 to 3 hours. Shape the dough into long, thin rolls, the diameter of a pencil. Cut them into 3- to 4-inch lengths and shape them into pretzels or figure 8's. Place the pretzels on a greased baking sheet and bake in a preheated oven (350°F) about 8 minutes, or until lightly browned. Remove the pretzels from the baking sheet, and while they are still warm roll them in sifted confectioners' sugar. Or ice with Fondant Cake Icing, made with plain or Chocolate Fondant. Makes about 3 dozen.

Caraques

1¾ cups (3½ sticks) softened butter
¼ teaspoon salt
1½ teaspoons vanilla extract
¾ cup sugar

6 large egg yolks
3¾ cups sifted all-purpose flour
Ganache Cream
Pistachio Fondant

Mix the butter with the salt and vanilla extract and gradually blend in the sugar. Beat in the egg yolks 2 at a time. Gradually stir in the flour, mixing well after each addition. Shape the dough into a ball. Place on a pastry board, invert a bowl over the dough, and let rest for 1 hour. Divide the dough into 3 equal parts. Place 1 part at a time on a lightly floured board, keeping the remaining dough under the bowl. Roll each part ⅛ inch to ¼ inch thick. Cut into round cookies with a 1½-inch cookie cutter. Place on a lightly buttered baking sheet and bake in a preheated oven (350°F) 10 to 15 minutes, or until cookies are lightly browned. Transfer to a wire rack. Repeat until all dough is used. After all the cookies have been baked and cooled, make them into sandwiches with Ganache Cream as the filling. Let stand until filling is set. Ice the tops with Pistachio Fondant and put a large dollop of Ganache Cream in the center of each. Allow frosting to set, then store in a tightly covered container in a cool place. Makes about 4 dozen.

Ganache Cream

Melt 5 squares (5 ounces) unsweetened chocolate and 3 tablespoons butter in the top of a 1-quart double boiler. Gradually stir in ⅓ cup heavy cream. Cool. When cold, use as a filling for Caraques or petits fours.

Pistachio Fondant

Heat 1 cup Fondant (see page 570) over hot water until semi-melted. Stir in ¼ cup finely ground pistachio nuts. Makes enough frosting for 4 dozen Caraques.

Chocolate Parfaits

Make and bake round cookies, using the recipe for Caraques. When the cookies are cooled, make them into sandwiches, using Chocolate Butter-Cream as the filling. Let stand until filling is set. Frost the tops with Chocolate Glaze and top each with half a peeled blanched almond or sprinkle with finely chopped pistachio nuts. Makes about 4 dozen.

Apricot Cookies

These little cookies will keep for weeks if stored in a cool place in tightly covered containers.

¾ cup finely ground almonds, blanched
½ cup sugar
¼ cup sifted all-purpose flour
3 egg whites

½ teaspoon vanilla extract
¼ teaspoon almond extract
Confectioners' sugar
Apricot jam

Combine the first 3 ingredients and set aside. Beat the egg whites until they stand in soft peaks. Carefully fold in the almond-sugar mixture, along with the vanilla and almond extracts. Using a teaspoon, or a pastry bag fitted with a ½-inch plain nozzle, drop small mounds of the mixture on a buttered and lightly floured baking sheet. Sprinkle confectioners' sugar over each, and bake in a preheated oven (350°F) 8 to 10 minutes. Cool on the baking sheet about 1 minute, and transfer to a wire rack. If the cookies cool before you can remove them from the baking sheet, return them to the oven for about 30 seconds. Put cookies together in pairs with apricot jam spread between them. Makes about 2½ dozen.

French Cookies

1 cup sugar
¼ teaspoon salt
1½ teaspoons vanilla extract
½ teaspoon almond extract

1 cup softened butter
2½ cups sifted all-purpose flour
1 tablespoon water

Gradually add the sugar, salt, vanilla extract, and almond extract to the butter and mix until creamy and fluffy. Add 1½ cups of the flour and then add the water. Stir in the remaining flour and mix well. (This makes a very stiff dough, but do not add more water.) Shape the dough into two rolls 1½ inches in diameter and 10 inches long. Wrap in waxed paper and chill 3 to 4 hours or overnight. With a sharp knife, cut the rolls into slices ¹⁄₁₆ to ⅛ inch thick. Place the slices on lightly buttered baking sheets. Bake in a preheated oven (400°F) 4 to 5 minutes or until cookies begin to brown around the edges. Do not bake too brown. Cool and store in an airtight container. Makes 8 dozen cookies.

Pistachio Meringues

¼ teaspoon salt
5 large egg whites
½ teaspoon freshly squeezed
   lemon juice
1 cup sugar

1½ teaspoons vanilla extract
¾ cup ground pistachio nuts
Cornstarch
Praline Butter-Cream
Pistachio Fondant

Add the salt to the egg whites and beat until foamy. Add the lemon juice. With an electric beater, beat at high speed until the egg whites are stiff enough to hold their shape but not dry. At low speed, beat in ¾ cup of the sugar, 2 tablespoons at a time.

Add the vanilla extract and continue beating until the egg whites stand in stiff peaks and are shiny and moist. Combine the remaining ¼ cup sugar with the pistachio nuts and carefully fold into the egg whites. Mark 1¾-inch circles on brown paper, using a cookie cutter or glass as a guide. Butter the paper lightly and dust lightly with cornstarch. Spread on each circle a layer of meringue ¼ inch thick. Place the paper on baking sheets. Bake in a preheated oven (200°F) 60 minutes. Turn off heat and cool in the oven 30 minutes. When cool, remove to a tray or pastry board. Crumble enough of the meringues to make 1 cup fine meringue crumbs. Set aside. Make sandwiches of the remaining meringues with Praline Butter-Cream as the filling, and use it to frost the tops and sides, spreading it thinly. Sprinkle the tops and sides with the reserved meringue crumbs. Decorate the tops with a dollop of Pistachio Fondant. Place each meringue in a paper case. Store in a tightly covered container in a cool place. Makes about 3 dozen.

Ladyfingers

⅛ teaspoon salt
3 large eggs, separated
2 tablespoons granulated sugar
1 cup sifted confectioners' sugar,
    plus additional

¾ teaspoon vanilla extract
¾ cup sifted all-purpose flour

Add the salt to the egg whites and beat them until soft peaks form. Beat in the granulated sugar and continue beating until the whites are stiff but not dry. Set aside. Beat the egg yolks and then beat in the 1 cup confectioners' sugar and vanilla extract. Continue beating until eggs are thick and lemon-colored. Add the egg yolk mixture to the egg white mixture all at one time and carefully fold it in. Fold in the flour. Drop the batter by rounded teaspoonfuls into greased ladyfinger pans, or put batter in a pastry bag and pipe it into the ladyfinger pans. If ladyfinger pans are not available, pipe the batter into fingers about 2½ inches long on greased cookie sheets. Bake them in a preheated oven (350°F) 12 to 15 minutes, or until lightly browned. Remove from pans or cookie sheets and immediately sprinkle the bottom of each with confectioners' sugar. To keep Ladyfingers moist, store a slice of bread in the storage container. Makes 2½ dozen.

Madeleines

1¼ cups sifted cake flour
½ teaspoon double-acting
    baking powder
¼ teaspoon salt
3 large eggs
1 teaspoon vanilla extract

⅔ cup granulated sugar
2 teaspoons grated lemon zest
¾ cup (1½ sticks) butter, melted and cooled,
    plus small amount additional
Sifted confectioners' sugar

Sift the first 3 ingredients together and set them aside. Beat the eggs in a 2-quart mixing bowl until light and lemon-colored. Add the vanilla extract. Gradually beat in the granulated sugar. Continue beating until the volume has increased to four times the original volume. Gradually fold in the flour mixture and the lemon zest. Stir in the butter. Brush madeleine pans with additional melted butter. Spoon 1 tablespoon of batter into each shell, filling it two-thirds full. Bake in a preheated oven (350°F) 12 minutes, or until a toothpick inserted in the center comes out clean. Remove the cakes from the pans onto wire racks. Dust the tops with confectioners' sugar. Makes 3 dozen.

 ## Mocha Pavés

1 (15½-by-10-inch) Génoise layer, 1 inch thick
Coffee Butter-Cream Filling and Frosting
Mocha Fondant Cake Icing
2 squares (2 ounces) semisweet chocolate

Split the Génoise into 2 thin layers and put them together with Coffee Butter-Cream Filling and Frosting between. Let the cake stand in a cool place until the filling is firm, then cut it into 2-inch squares. Frost the tops and sides with Mocha Fondant Cake Icing. Melt the chocolate and, using a cake-decorator's tube with the smallest nozzle, make designs as desired on the tops of the cake squares. Makes about 3 dozen individual cakes.

Nut Cream Rolls

5 large eggs, separated
½ cup sugar
¼ cup softened butter
1 teaspoon grated lemon zest
¼ teaspoon salt
⅓ cup sifted cake flour

⅓ cup fine white breadcrumbs
½ cup finely chopped toasted nuts
   (almonds, hazelnuts, pecans, or walnuts)
Confectioners' sugar
French Pastry Cream

Beat the egg yolks and ⅓ cup of the sugar together until mixture is thick and lemon-colored. Beat in the butter, lemon zest, and salt. Combine the flour, breadcrumbs, and nuts and stir into the egg mixture. Beat the egg whites until they stand in soft peaks, then beat in the remaining sugar. Fold the egg whites into the egg yolk mixture. Spread the batter in a greased, waxed paper-lined, 15½-by-10½-by-1-inch jelly-roll pan. Bake in a preheated oven (350°F) 18 minutes, or until a toothpick inserted in the center comes out clean. Immediately turn the cake upside down on a towel that has been sprinkled lightly with confectioners' sugar and remove the waxed paper. Roll up the cake, jelly-roll fashion, in the towel, to prevent the cake from sticking together. When the cake is cold, unroll it on a piece of waxed paper. Remove the towel and cut the cake in half crosswise. Spread each half with French Pastry Cream, roll up each half separately, and wrap in waxed paper. Let the rolls stand in a cool place 1 to 2 hours before serving. To serve, cut each roll into 4½-inch lengths. Lay a 1-inch strip of paper across the center of each. Dust the cake on each side of the paper with sifted confectioners' sugar. Remove paper. Makes 8 servings.

Souvaroff

1¾ cups (3½ sticks) softened butter	3 to 4 tablespoons light cream
2 teaspoons vanilla extract	Apricot jam or currant jelly
¾ cup sugar	Confectioners' sugar
5 cups sifted all-purpose flour	Caramel Glaze

Mix the butter and vanilla extract. Gradually blend in the sugar. Stir in the flour one-quarter at a time until all has been added. Add just enough cream to make a dough that can be easily rolled. Shape the dough into a ball, invert a bowl over it, and let rest 1 hour. Divide the dough into 3 equal parts. Roll one part at a time, keeping the rest covered with the bowl. Roll dough about ¼ inch thick. Cut into rounds or ovals with a pastry cutter. Place the rounds on a lightly buttered baking sheet and bake in a preheated oven (400°F) 8 to 10 minutes, or until lightly browned. Transfer the pastries to a wire rack to cool. Repeat until all the dough is used. After all the pastries are baked and cooled, make sandwiches of them, using jam or jelly as the filling. If desired, sprinkle the tops with confectioners' sugar, or spread lightly with Caramel Glaze. Makes 4 to 5 dozen.

Viennese Anise Drops

These delicious little cookies have a cake-like base with a crisp meringue-like top.

1½ cups sifted all-purpose flour	¼ teaspoon anise seeds
¼ teaspoon double-acting baking powder	2 large eggs
⅛ teaspoon salt	1 cup sugar

Sift together the first 3 ingredients. Finely crush the anise seeds, sift into the flour mixture, and mix well. Set aside. Break the eggs into a measuring cup and add enough cold water to make ½ cup liquid. Turn into a mixing bowl, add the sugar, and beat until mixture is very thick. Fold in the flour mixture, sifting in one-fourth at a time. Drop the batter from a teaspoon onto greased cookie sheets, allowing 2 inches between cookies for spreading. Leave the cookies, uncovered, in a cool place (not in the refrigerator) 8 to 10 hours or overnight to dry a little. Bake in a preheated oven (350°F) 5 to 6 minutes. Cool on wire racks. Makes about 4 dozen cookies.

Spritz

1 cup (2 sticks) softened butter	1½ teaspoons vanilla extract
½ cup sugar	About 2½ cups sifted all-purpose flour
1 large egg	

Stir the butter until it is fluffy. Gradually blend in the sugar. Beat in the egg and the vanilla extract. Stir in enough flour to make a dough that may be forced through a pastry bag. Using nozzles of various shapes, pipe the dough onto unbuttered cookie sheets. Bake in a preheated oven (375°F) 7 to 10 minutes, or until cookies are lightly browned. Transfer to wire racks. When cold, decorate as desired with melted semisweet chocolate, frosting, glacéed fruit, or nuts. Makes about 7 dozen.

Viennese Jelly Bars

2¼ cups sifted all-purpose flour	1 large egg
⅔ cup sugar	2 teaspoons vanilla extract
½ teaspoon double-acting baking powder	¾ cup (1½ sticks) softened butter
¼ teaspoon salt	Jelly or apricot jam

Sift together the first 4 ingredients. Add the egg, vanilla extract, and butter. Mix well to form a soft dough. Divide dough into 4 equal parts on a lightly floured board. Shape each part into a roll 12 inches long and 1 inch in diameter. Place 2 rolls on each of 2 ungreased cookie sheets 3 inches apart and 2 inches from the edges of the cookie sheet. With a knife handle, make a depression ½ inch deep lengthwise down the center of each roll. Fill the depression with jelly or jam. Bake in a preheated oven (350°F) 15 to 20 minutes, or until lightly browned around the edges. While strips are still warm, cut them into diagonal bars. Cool on wire racks. Store in airtight containers. Makes 3½ dozen.

PETITS FOURS

The name *petit four*, if we believe the great 19th century chef Antonin Careme, comes from most of them being baked in a slow oven after the major cakes have been cooked. There are basically two kinds: little, fancy, biscuits (cookies), tuiles, wafers, macaroons, shortbreads etc., and iced or frosted *petits fours*, generally Génoise cut into small shapes and dipped in Fondant Icing. Some are confectionary, like glacéed and candied fruits and jellies.

Almond Wafers

¼ teaspoon salt
5 large egg whites
¾ cup sifted confectioners' sugar
⅓ cup sifted all-purpose flour
6 tablespoons butter, melted

2 tablespoons milk
1 teaspoon vanilla extract
4 tablespoons almond paste
½ cup blanched slivered almonds

Combine the first 3 ingredients and beat until the mixture is very light. Stir in the flour, butter, and milk. Add the vanilla extract and almond paste and beat until batter is smooth. Stir in the almonds. Drop the batter from a teaspoon onto lightly buttered cookie sheets, allowing 2 inches between wafers for spreading. Bake in a preheated oven (375°F) 10 minutes, watching closely to prevent burning. Remove from oven and allow wafers to stand on the cookie sheets about 30 seconds, then remove to wire racks to finish cooling. Store in tightly closed jars or tin boxes. Makes about 2 dozen.

Almond Wafer Cornets

Drop Almond Wafer batter from a tablespoon onto a lightly buttered cookie sheet. Bake in a preheated (375°F) oven about 6 minutes. After removing the wafers from the cookie sheet, and while they are still warm, shape them into cones over your index finger. Cool and store. Makes 1 dozen.

Cigarettes

This fragile French cookie, shaped like a cigarette, breaks easily. It is wise to bake a test cookie before dropping all the cookie batter. If the test cookie breaks when it is rolled, add a little more flour (1 to 2 tablespoons). If the cookie is thick and difficult to roll, add 1 to 2 teaspoons more melted and cooled butter.

2 large egg whites
Dash salt
½ cup granulated sugar
About ⅓ cup sifted all-purpose flour

About 3 tablespoons butter,
    melted and cooled
½ teaspoon vanilla extract
Confectioners' sugar

Combine the egg whites and salt and beat until stiff. Beat in the granulated sugar, 1 tablespoon at a time. Sift the flour over the egg whites and carefully fold it into them. Fold in the butter and vanilla extract. Drop the cookie batter by the tablespoonful onto a buttered and lightly floured baking sheet and spread as thin as possible with a spatula. Bake in a preheated oven (450°F) 2 to 3 minutes, or until cookies are golden brown around the edges. Remove cookies from baking sheets and quickly roll them around a pencil to shape them like a cigarette. Serve plain, sprinkled with confectioners' sugar, or fill them with whipped cream or French Pastry Cream, if desired. Makes 2 dozen.

These cookies may also be given cone shapes by wrapping them around the handle of a wooden spoon. The large ends may be dipped in melted semisweet chocolate, Chocolate Glaze, or Chocolate Fondant Cake Icing, if desired.

Chocolate Wafers

1½ cups sifted all-purpose flour
¾ cup cocoa
1¼ teaspoons double-acting
    baking powder
⅛ teaspoon salt

1¼ cups sugar
¾ cup (1½ sticks) softened butter
1 tablespoon rum
1 egg

Sift together the first 4 ingredients and set them aside. Gradually blend the sugar into the butter. Beat in the rum and the egg. Stir in the dry ingredients and mix well. Chill the dough until it is stiff enough to handle. Roll dough ⅛ inch thick on a lightly floured board, and cut out rounds with a 2-inch cookie cutter dipped in flour. Place on ungreased cookie sheets. Or, if desired, shape the dough into ½-inch balls, place on ungreased cookie sheets, and flatten to ⅛ inch thick with a glass covered with a damp cloth. Bake cookies in a preheated oven (400°F) 8 minutes. Makes about 3 dozen cookies.

Brown-Sugar Nuggets

1 cup (2 sticks) softened butter
½ cup light brown sugar
¼ teaspoon salt
2 teaspoons vanilla extract
2¼ cups sifted all-purpose flour

½ cup finely chopped toasted almonds,
    hazelnuts, or pecans
Confectioners' sugar, granulated sugar,
    or semisweet chocolate

Stir the butter until it is fluffy, then blend in the brown sugar, salt, and vanilla extract. Gradually stir in the flour and nuts, mixing well after each addition. Chill the dough 2 hours, or until it is stiff enough to handle. Shape into balls, crescents, or 1-inch nuggets. Place on ungreased cookie sheets. Bake in a preheated oven (350°F) 12 to 15 minutes, or until very lightly browned. Cool on wire racks. Roll in sifted confectioners' sugar or granulated sugar, or frost with melted semisweet chocolate. Makes about 5 dozen.

Délices with Jelly

¾ cup (1½ sticks) softened butter
¾ cup finely ground almonds
    or hazelnuts

½ cup sugar
1½ cups sifted all-purpose flour
Jelly or apricot jam

Combine the butter and nuts. Gradually add the sugar and flour and mix the dough until it is smooth. Chill the dough, if necessary, until it can be rolled. Roll on a lightly floured board to ⅛ inch thick. Cut into round cookies with a scalloped 1½-inch cookie cutter. Cut a ¾-inch hole in the center of half of the cookies. Save the centers, roll out again to ⅛ inch thick, and cut out additional cookies, making holes in half of them, until all the dough has been used. Place the cookies on a lightly greased cookie sheet and bake in a preheated oven (350°F) 7 to 8 minutes, or until they are golden brown. Cool on cooling racks. Spread the solid cookies with jelly or jam, and cover them with those that have holes in them. Makes about 2½ dozen.

Chocolate Délices

Make the recipe for Délices with Jelly. Melt 4 squares (4 ounces) semisweet chocolate over hot water (not boiling). Cool slightly and spread over the solid cookies instead of jelly or jam. Cover with those that have the holes in them. Makes about 2½ dozen.

Langues de Chat

½ cup (1 stick) softened butter
¼ cup sugar
1 teaspoon vanilla extract

2 egg whites
¼ cup sifted all-purpose flour

Stir the butter until it is creamy, then gradually beat in the sugar and vanilla extract. Beat the mixture until it is light and fluffy. Add the egg whites, one at a time, beating well. Sift the flour over the mixture and carefully fold it in. Put the batter in a pastry bag fitted with a small plain round nozzle, and pipe it onto buttered and lightly floured baking sheets in strips about 2 inches long and the diameter of a pencil. Bake in a preheated oven (450°F) 4 to 5 minutes, or until the edges are golden brown. Do not bake too brown. Transfer the cookies to paper towels to cool. Makes about 2 dozen.

Macaroon Butter-Cream Sandwiches

1½ cups peeled almonds
1½ cups fine granulated sugar

2 egg whites
Butter-Cream with any desired flavoring

Blanch the almonds and pat dry with paper towels. Put them through a food chopper twice, using the finest blade; add the sugar while grinding the almonds the second time. Add the egg whites and gradually work the mixture to a smooth paste. Drop from a teaspoon or force through a pastry bag fitted with a fluted nozzle onto baking parchment paper, allowing 2 inches between macaroons. Bake in a preheated oven (325°F) 30 minutes, or until they begin to turn golden. Remove from the paper and cool. Mix Butter-Cream with any desired flavoring—vanilla, kirsch, Cointreau, rum, chocolate, coffee—and spread it between 2 macaroons in sandwich fashion. Store in a cool place in a tightly covered container. Makes about 1½ dozen.

Milanese Cookies

2½ cups sifted all-purpose flour
¾ cup sugar
¼ teaspoon salt
1½ cups (3 sticks) softened butter

3 teaspoons grated lemon zest
2 tablespoons cognac or rum
4 large egg yolks
Semisweet chocolate, melted

Sift together into a mixing bowl the first 3 ingredients. Add all the remaining ingredients except the chocolate and mix well. Chill the dough until it is stiff enough to handle. Shape the dough into 1-inch balls and place them on greased cookie sheets. Flatten the balls to ¼ inch thick with a glass covered with a damp cloth. Bake the cookies in a preheated oven (400°F) 10 to 12 minutes, or until the tops are golden brown. Cool on wire racks. Ice the tops with chocolate. Makes about 4½ dozen cookies.

Palais de Dame

¼ cup dried currants
1 tablespoon rum
¼ cup (½ stick) softened butter
¼ teaspoon salt

6 tablespoons sugar
1 large egg
¾ cup sifted all-purpose flour

Soak the currants in the rum 30 minutes. Stir the butter together with the salt until it is creamy. Gradually blend in the sugar. Beat in the egg. Add the currants and rum and mix well. Gradually stir in the flour. Drop the batter from a teaspoon onto lightly buttered baking sheets, 2½ inches apart. Bake in a preheated oven (350°F) 8 to 20 minutes, or until cookies have browned lightly around the edges. Transfer the cookies to wire racks and when cold store them in a tightly closed container. Makes 2 dozen.

Pineapple Puff Pastry Fondants

Cut Puff Pastry into ovals 1½ inches long and 1 inch wide. Place them on baking sheets, prick them generously with a fork, and bake in a preheated oven (425°F) 5 to 8 minutes, or until golden brown. Transfer the pastries to a wire rack. When they are cold, marinate wedges of candied pineapple in kirsch about 30 minutes, drain, and place a wedge on each pastry oval. Ice with kirsch-flavored Fondant Icing. Decorate, if desired, with glacéed cherries and pistachio nuts, or with a little Chocolate Fondant. The pastry ovals may be stored in tightly covered containers and decorated when needed. Allow 2 per serving.

Tuiles with Almonds

½ cup granulated sugar
2 large egg whites
½ cup sifted all-purpose flour
½ teaspoon almond extract

½ teaspoon vanilla extract
½ cup blanched almonds, finely shredded
¼ cup (½ stick) butter
Confectioners' sugar

Beat the granulated sugar together with the egg whites until the egg whites are frothy. Stir in the next 5 ingredients. Mix well. Drop the batter from a teaspoon in mounds the size of a quarter, onto lightly buttered baking sheets, or pipe through a pastry bag onto lightly buttered baking sheets, leaving 2 inches between cookies to allow room for spreading. Sprinkle tops with confectioners' sugar. Bake the cookies in a preheated oven (350°F) 8 minutes, or until they have browned lightly around the edges. Cool 30 seconds on the baking sheets, then remove, and while the cookies are still hot bend them around a small rolling pin or small glass to give them the shape of a curved roofing tile or *tuile*. Store cookies in a tightly closed container. Makes about 2½ dozen.

ICED PETITS FOURS

Petits fours that are to be iced are usually made of Génoise cut with a sharp knife or cookie cutters into small squares, rectangles, diamonds, triangles, rounds, or hearts. The pieces are coated with Apricot Glaze and covered with Fondant Frosting.

How to Ice Petits Fours

With a sharp knife carefully trim all ragged edges from a Génoise layer. Using the knife or cookie cutters, cut the cake into 1½-inch squares or small rectangles, triangles, diamonds, hearts, or any desired shape. Insert a fork into each piece and dip into Apricot Glaze, covering the bottom and sides. Place the pieces with the uncoated side down 1 inch apart on wire racks placed on cookie sheets. Let stand about 1 hour for the glaze to set. Using a large metal kitchen spoon, pour warm Fondant Frosting over 1 piece at a time, letting the Fondant run over the top and cover the sides smoothly. (The cookie sheet underneath will catch the excess, which should be scraped up, returned to the top of the double boiler, and reheated just until thin enough to pour.) Let the petits fours dry on the racks 1 hour or longer. If any are not sufficiently covered, ice again and let dry. Decorate the tops as desired with glacéed fruit or nuts, or with Confectioners' Sugar Flower and Leaf Icing put through a cake-decorator's tube.

Apricot or Fruit Glaze

1 cup sugar
1 cup boiling water
¾ cup apricot or any fruit jam

Combine the sugar and water in a saucepan. Stir and cook over medium heat until the sugar is dissolved. Bring to the boiling point, uncovered, and boil 10 minutes. Heat the apricot jam in a saucepan until it bubbles around the edge of the pan. Remove from heat and push the jam through a sieve into the syrup. Mix well. Keep warm over hot water until ready to use, or reheat just before using to make the glaze thin enough to pour. Makes enough for 2½ dozen petits fours.

Confectioners' Sugar Flower and Leaf Icing

1 large egg white
2 to 2½ cups sifted confectioners' sugar
Food coloring

Place the egg white in the small bowl of an electric mixer. Gradually beat in 2 cups confectioners' sugar. If frosting is not stiff enough to stand in stiff peaks when the beater is slowly raised, beat in more confectioners' sugar, about 2 tablespoons at a time, until desired stiffness is reached. To color frosting, place 2 tablespoons frosting in each of 4 custard cups and keep covered with a damp cloth to prevent drying. Color one portion green by adding 5 to 6 drops green food coloring; one yellow with 10 drops yellow food coloring; one pink with 4 drops red food coloring; one lavender with 2 drops blue food coloring and 4 drops red. Put a little frosting on the four corners of a piece of waxed paper and place it frosting side down on a cookie sheet. Put green frosting in a cake-decorating tube fitted with a leaf nozzle (no. 65) and pipe leaves onto the paper. Make flowers in the same manner, using a flower nozzle (no. 15) with yellow, pink, or lavender frosting. Let the leaves and flowers dry on the waxed paper, then remove them and arrange them on petits fours. If desired, freeze the leaves and flowers on a tray, wrap the tray for the freezer, and store in freezer until needed. Makes 2½ dozen flowers and leaves.

Fondant For Petits Fours

2¾ cups granulated sugar
¼ teaspoon cream of tartar
Dash salt

1½ cups water
4 to 5 cups sifted confectioners' sugar
½ teaspoon almond extract

Combine the first 4 ingredients in the top of a double boiler. Mix well. Stir and cook over direct low heat until the sugar is dissolved. Increase the heat to medium and cook, without stirring, to 226°F on a candy thermometer. Cool to 110°F, or until the bottom of the pan can rest comfortably in the palm of your hand. With a wooden spoon, beat in confectioners' sugar, using only enough to make a frosting that is still thin enough to pour. Add the almond extract. Let the frosting stand over hot water to keep it at pouring consistency until it is to be used. If it thickens, add a few drops of hot water; if it is too thin, add a little more confectioners' sugar. If colored frosting is desired, add a few drops of food coloring. Makes enough for 2½ dozen petits fours.

Coffee Fondant

In the recipe for Fondant Frosting, replace the water with the same amount of strong brewed coffee, and use 1 teaspoon vanilla extract instead of the almond extract.

Kirsch Fondant

Add 1 tablespoon kirsch, or to taste, to Fondant Frosting.

Chocolate Petits Fours

Génoise
Chocolate Butter-Cream

Finely chopped, toasted, blanched almonds
Melted semisweet chocolate

Split the Génoise into 2 layers, and sandwich the layers together with a thick layer of Chocolate Butter-Cream. Chill until filling is firm. Cut into 1½-inch squares and glaze as previously directed. Frost with a thin layer of Chocolate Butter-Cream. Sprinkle the edges with almonds. Decorate the top of each piece with a large drop of melted semisweet chocolate. Store, tightly covered, in a cool place.

Coffee Butter-Cream Petits Fours

Génoise
Coffee Butter-Cream

Coffee Fondant for Petits Fours
Candy coffee beans

Split the Génoise into 2 layers and sandwich the layers together with Coffee Butter-Cream. Chill until filling is firm. Cut cake into 1½-inch squares, triangles, or rectangles. Glaze and ice as previously directed, using Coffee Fondant. Decorate the top of each piece with a candy coffee bean. Store, tightly closed, in a cool place.

Kirsch Butter-Cream Petits Fours

In the recipe for Coffee Butter-Cream Petits Fours, replace the Coffee Butter-Cream with Kirsch Butter-Cream, and Coffee Fondant with Kirsch Fondant. Decorate with bits of glacéed cherries.

Pistachio Nut Petits Fours

Add ¼ cup finely chopped pistachio nuts to Butter-Cream. Spread between 2 thin Génoise layers and over the top. Chill until the Buttter-Cream is firm. Cut into squares or other shapes. Glaze and ice as previously directed, using Fondant to which 2 to 3 drops light green food coloring have been added.

Rum Petits Fours

Spread Rum Butter-Cream between 2 thin Génoise layers and over the top. Chill until the frosting is firm. Cut into desired shapes. Glaze and ice as previously directed, using Coffee Fondant or Chocolate Glaze. Decorate each with a candy coffee bean.

Mochatine Petits Fours

Génoise
Coffee Butter-Cream

Coarse granulated sugar, or chopped, toasted, blanched almonds

Split the Génoise into 2 layers and sandwich the layers together with Coffee Butter-Cream. Chill until filling is firm. Cut into squares, triangles, or rectangles. Glaze and ice as previously directed, using Coffee Butter-Cream. Sprinkle the edges with coarse granulated sugar or chopped almonds. Decorate the top of each piece with a rosette of the Butter-Cream. Store, tightly covered, in a cool place.

Orange Petits Fours

Génoise
Thick orange marmalade
Orange Butter-Cream

Chocolate Fondant
Candied orange peel

Split the Génoise into 2 layers and sandwich the layers together with marmalade. Spread the top with Orange Butter-Cream. Chill until Cream is firm. Using cookie cutters or a sharp knife, cut into assorted shapes (round, crescent, square, rectangular, etc.). Glaze and ice as previously directed, using Chocolate Fondant. Decorate each with a small piece of candied orange peel.

PASTRIES MADE OF CHOUX PASTE

Small Cream Puffs

Make small cream puffs from Choux Paste. Bake and cool. When cold, fill them with any of the following:

- French Pastry Cream mixed with finely chopped candied fruit macerated in rum, kirsch, or other liqueur. Ice with Fondant Cake Icing flavored the same as the filling. Decorate with glacéed cherries or other candied fruit.
- Almond Pastry Cream flavored with rum. Sprinkle with sifted confectioners' sugar.
- Butter-Cream Filling and Frosting flavored with rum, kirsch, or other liqueur. If desired, add finely chopped candied fruit macerated in the same liqueur as used to flavor the filling. Ice with Fondant Cake Icing. Decorate each with a bit of angelica.
- Chantilly Cream flavored with vanilla extract, rum, kirsch, or other liqueur. Ice with chocolate-, mocha-, coffee-, or vanilla-flavored Fondant Cake Icing.

Allow 2 cream puffs per serving.

Chocolate Eclairs

Choux Paste
French Pastry Cream
Chocolate Fondant Cake Icing

Pipe Choux Paste through a pastry bag fitted with a ½-inch nozzle in 1-by-4-inch strips, 2 inches apart, on a greased baking sheet. Bake in a preheated oven (425°F) 30 to 35 minutes, or until golden brown. Do not underbake. Turn off oven heat. Pierce the éclairs with a knife near the bottom to allow steam to escape. Leave them in the oven 20 minutes to dry out the centers. Cool, split, and fill with French Pastry Cream. Ice with Chocolate Fondant. Makes 2 dozen.

Coffee Eclairs

Make the éclairs as directed in the recipe for Chocolate Eclairs. Fill with Mocha Pastry Cream. Frost with Coffee Fondant Cake Icing. Garnish each with a candy coffee bean. Makes 24.

Iced Small Eclairs

Make small éclairs, about 1½ inches long. Bake and cool. Fill them with Chantilly Cream or French Pastry Cream flavored with vanilla, rum, kirsch, coffee, chocolate, or other desired flavoring. Frost with Fondant Cake Icing. Allow 1 to 2 per serving.

Profiteroles with Chocolate Sauce

½ recipe Choux Paste
1 egg, beaten with 1 tablespoon water

Chantilly Cream
Thick Chocolate Sauce

Put Choux Paste in a pastry bag fitted with a ¾-inch nozzle, and pipe small balls about the size of walnuts onto greased cookie sheets. Or drop the paste from a teaspoon. Brush egg mixture over the tops of the balls. Bake in a preheated oven (425°F) 20 to 25 minutes. Turn off oven heat. Prick puffs with a knife to allow steam to escape and leave them in the oven 15 minutes to allow centers to dry out. Cool. Fill from underneath with Chantilly Cream. Arrange the little cream puffs in champagne glasses, 3 for each serving, and cover them with chilled Thick Chocolate Sauce. Makes 6 to 8 servings.

Profiteroles may also be filled with Vanilla Ice Cream.

Chocolate Custard Sauce

1 cup milk
1 cup light cream
1 (3-inch) piece vanilla bean,
    or 2 teaspoons vanilla extract
⅔ cup sugar

⅛ teaspoon salt
4 large egg yolks
2 squares (2 ounces) unsweetened chocolate

Heat milk and ¾ cup of the cream, with the vanilla bean (if using). Combine the next 2 ingredients in the top of a double boiler, or in a saucepan. Add the egg yolks and mix well. Stir in the remaining ¼ cup cream, then add the hot milk and cream. Stir and cook over hot water or very low heat until the custard coats a metal spoon. Add the chocolate and stir until it is melted. Cool. Strain. If vanilla bean was not used, stir in the vanilla extract. Makes about 2¼ cups.

Réligieuses

6 (3-inch) baked Plain Pastry
    (Pâte Brisée) tartlet shells
18 Small Eclairs, 3 inches long
6 Small Cream Puffs

French Pastry Cream
Whipped cream, sweetened to taste
Caramel Syrup
Mocha Butter-Cream

For each serving you will need 1 baked pastry shell, 3 Éclairs, and 1 cream puff. Fill the shells and Eclairs with French Pastry Cream and the cream puff with whipped cream. Fit the ends of 3 filled Eclairs into each filled tartlet shell, pushing them into the cream and bringing the tops together to form a pyramid. Dip the bottom of each cream puff in Caramel Syrup and place one on top of each pyramid. Put whipped cream in a cake-decorator's tube and pipe it around the eclairs. Frost the top of the pyramid with Mocha Butter-Cream. Makes 6 servings.

Croquembouche

Roll Puff Pastry in a circle ¼ inch thick on a lightly buttered baking sheet. Cut it into an 8-inch circle using a round 8-inch layer-cake pan as a guide. Remove the pastry trimmings. Prick the pastry over the top with a fork. Bake in a preheated oven (425°F) 12 to 15 minutes, or until browned. Make 100 Small Cream Puffs (the size of walnuts) from Choux Paste, bake, and cool. Fill with French Pastry Cream. Mix 2 cups sugar, ⅔ cup water, and ½ teaspoon cream of tartar in a heavy 1½-quart saucepan. Stir and cook until the boiling point is reached. Continue cooking, without stirring, until the syrup has thickened and turned amber. Place the pastry base on a large serving plate. Invert a charlotte mold or other suitably shaped dish on the pastry base to serve as a foundation. Dip the bottoms of the cream puffs, one at a time, in the syrup and place them around the edge of the base, touching one another. Make a second row on top of the first, placing the cream puffs between those on the bottom. Continue in this manner, building a pyramid of the cream puffs. Top it with one cream puff.

SMALL PUFF-PASTRY PASTRIES

Iced Bâtons

Roll Puff Pastry ¼ inch thick in an 8-by-12-inch rectangle. Prick the pastry all over with a fork. Spread thinly with Royal Icing. Using a sharp knife, dipped in water frequently to prevent the icing from sticking, cut the rectangle into 3-by-1-inch strips. Place the strips on a slightly moistened baking sheet and set aside for the icing to dry. Chill thoroughly. Bake in a preheated oven (400°F) 10 to 12 minutes. Allow 2 per serving.

Condés

Roll Puff Pastry ¼ inch thick in an 8-by-12-inch rectangle. Place the pastry on a slightly moistened baking sheet. Prick it all over with a fork. Spread the top with Royal Icing. Sprinkle with chopped blanched almonds. Chill thoroughly. Bake in a preheated oven (400°F) 10 to 12 minutes. Transfer the pastry to a pastry board. Using a very sharp knife, cut it into 4 strips 3 inches wide, then cut the strips crosswise into pieces 1 inch wide. Allow 2 to 3 pieces per serving.

Couques

Roll Puff Pastry ¼ inch thick. Using a 2-inch biscuit cutter with a scalloped edge, cut the pastry into biscuits. Shape them into ovals by rolling them over once on a pastry board sprinkled with sugar. Place them on buttered baking sheets, sugared side up, and bake in a preheated oven (450°F) 8 to 10 minutes, or until the ovals are puffed and browned. Allow 2 to 3 per serving.

Sugared Croissants

Roll Puff Pastry ¼ inch thick into 9-inch circles, using a round 9-inch cake pan as a guide. Cut each circle into 12 wedges. Starting at the widest end of the wedge, roll each loosely to form a cylinder thicker in the center than at the ends. Shape the rolls into crescents, sprinkle them lightly with confectioners' sugar, and place them on an baking sheet. Chill thoroughly. Bake in a preheated oven (400°F) 5 minutes. Reduce oven temperature to 350°F and bake 10 to 15 minutes, or until the crescents have browned. Allow 2 to 3 per serving.

Horseshoes

Puff Pastry
Apricot jam
1 egg

1 tablespoon milk
Sugar

Roll Puff Pastry ¼ inch thick on a lightly floured board in 12-by-6-inch strips. Cut the dough into 3 lengthwise strips 2 inches wide. Pipe or spread a little jam down the center of each strip. Fold the dough over and press the edges together. Cut each strip in half. Press the ends of the dough together to prevent the jam from seeping out while baking. Form the strips into horseshoe shapes, and place them on a cookie sheet lined with 3 layers of brown paper. Chill 2 hours. Brush with the egg beaten together with the milk and sprinkle with sugar. Bake in a preheated oven (450°F) 8 minutes. Reduce oven temperature to 350°F and bake 5 minutes more. Place a cold cookie sheet under the one on which the Horseshoes are baking, reduce temperature to 300°F and bake another 5 minutes, or until browned. Allow 2 Horseshoes per serving.

Puffed Jam Turnovers

Roll Puff Pastry ¼ inch thick and cut into 3-inch rounds with a scalloped round cookie cutter. Place 1 rounded teaspoon jam (any kind) in the center of each round. Dampen the edges of the rounds with water and fold the dough over to make them into half-moon shapes. Press the edges together. Place the turnovers on a lightly mois-tened baking sheet. Beat 1 egg together with 1 tablespoon of milk and brush the tops. Chill thoroughly. Prick the top of each in one or two places with a fork. Bake in a pre-heated oven (425°F) 5 minutes. Reduce oven temperature to 350°F and bake 12 to 15 minutes, or until turnovers have browned. Allow 2 turnovers per serving.

Napoleons

Roll Puff Pastry into a rectangle ¼ inch thick and cut it into strips 1½ inches wide and the length of a baking sheet. Place them on baking sheets lined with 3 or 4 lay-ers of brown paper. Prick pastry all over with a fork and chill 1 to 2 hours. Bake in a preheated oven (450°F) 8 minutes. Reduce oven temperature to 350°F and bake 8 to 10 minutes. Place cold baking sheets under the hot ones in the oven to prevent the bottoms of the Napoleons from becoming too brown and bake 8 to 10 more minutes. Transfer the strips to wire racks. When they are cold, cut them into 3-inch pieces with a very sharp knife or a serrated knife. Make the small strips into several-layered sand-wiches with French Pastry Cream as the filling. Spread the tops with Royal Icing or dust them with sifted confectioners' sugar. Allow 1 Napoleon per serving.

Palmiers

Roll Puff Pastry ¼ inch thick into an 8-by-15-inch rectangle. Sprinkle with sugar. Fold each end of the dough to the center of the rectangle. Sprinkle with sugar. Fold each end of the folded dough to center of the rectangle, making 4 layers of dough on each side of the center. Then fold the two sides of the dough together as in closing a book. Roll the rolling pin down the dough lightly once. With a sharp knife, cut the dough into crosswise slices ½ inch thick. Place the slices about 1 inch apart on a bak-ing sheet. Bake in a preheated oven (425°F) 10 to 12 minutes, or until golden brown. Allow 2 Palmiers per serving.

Sacristains

Roll Puff Pastry ¼ inch thick into a rectangle 12 by 8 inches. Beat 1 egg together with 1 tablespoon milk and brush the surface. Sprinkle with finely chopped almonds and dust with confectioners' sugar. Cut the pastry into crosswise strips ½ to ¾ inch wide. Shape them like corkscrews by taking one end of the strip in each hand and giving it a twist. Place them on baking sheets and bake in a preheated oven (400°F) 10 to 12 minutes, or until they are golden brown. Allow 3 per serving.

Viennese Pastries

Roll Puff Pastry ⅛ inch thick and cut it into 3-by-3-inch squares. Place 1 teaspoon Almond Pastry Cream, French Pastry Cream, or jam in the center of each square. Bring the four corners of the square to the center, having them cover the filling. Beat 1 egg together with tablespoon water and brush the pastries. Sprinkle with chopped almonds and confectioners' sugar. Bake in a preheated oven (400°F) 10 to 12 minutes, or until browned. Allow 2 pastries per serving.

CREPES AND WAFFLES

Dessert Crêpes

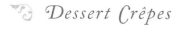

1 cup sifted all-purpose flour	2 cups milk
½ teaspoon salt	1 tablespoon rum or cognac
1 tablespoon granulated sugar	2 tablespoons butter, melted, plus additional
3 large eggs	Confectioners' sugar

Sift together the first 3 ingredients into a mixing bowl. Set aside. Beat the eggs, add the milk and rum or cognac, and stir into the flour mixture. Blend in the 2 tablespoons butter. Let the batter stand 2 hours to develop the required texture. Heat a 6-inch skillet or a French crêpe pan and brush the bottom lightly with melted butter. For each crêpe, pour in 2 tablespoons of the batter. Quickly tilt and rotate the pan to spread the batter uniformly over the bottom. Tip out the excess batter, if any. Cook over medium heat 1 to 2 minutes, or until the underside is brown and bubbles have formed over the top. Turn and cook 30 seconds to 1 minute, or until the other side has browned. When each crêpe is cooked, serve immediately, or stack the crêpes in pancake fashion in a pan lined with a clean towel, and when all are cooked fold the ends of the towel over them. Just before serving, heat the crêpes, without unwrapping, in a preheated oven (350°F) only until they are hot, 10 minutes. Serve sprinkled with confectioners' sugar or with syrup or honey. Or spread them with jelly or marmalade and roll them up, or serve them as Crêpes Suzette. Makes 18 crêpes, or 6 servings.

Crêpes Suzette

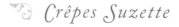

Crêpes Suzette Sauce
Dessert Crêpes
Brandy or Grand Marnier

Have the sauce hot and place the crêpes in it, spooning it over them until they are well covered. Fold them into quarters. Heat the brandy or Grand Marnier in a small saucepan, ignite it, and quickly pour it over the crêpes. Bring the dish to the table flaming. Serve the crêpes with some of the sauce poured over them. The crêpes may be made ahead of time, but the sauce should be made just before it is used. Allow 3 crêpes per serving.

Crêpes Suzette Sauce

1 medium-sized navel orange
4 large lumps sugar
4 tablespoons sweet butter

1 teaspoon freshly squeezed lemon juice
¼ cup Cointreau or curaçao
¼ cup Benedictine or Grand Marnier

Wash the orange well and dry it thoroughly. Rub the lumps of sugar over the skin, then place them on a board and crush them. Transfer the crushed sugar to a heatproof dish or to the inset pan of a chafing dish. Squeeze out the juice from the orange and discard the rind. Add the butter, orange juice, and lemon juice to the sugar and mix well. Cook until the sugar and butter have melted, then add the liqueurs and heat to the boiling point. Makes enough sauce for 6 servings.

Filled Waffles

Make Parisian Waffles. While they are hot, cut each into 4 sections and cool them under a weight so that they will retain their shape. When they are cold, put each 2 sections together, with Praline Butter-Cream between.

Sponge-Cake Waffles

4 large eggs, separated
1 cup sugar
¼ cup cold water
1 teaspoon vanilla extract

2 teaspoons grated orange zest
½ teaspoon grated lemon zest
¼ teaspoon salt
1 cup sifted cake flour

Beat the egg yolks until they are light and lemon-colored. Gradually beat in the sugar. Continue beating until the mixture is thick. Add the next 4 ingredients, and beat well. Add the salt to the egg whites and beat them until they stand in soft peaks. Pile them on the egg yolk mixture, sift the flour over them, and carefully fold them into the mixture. Set the heat control on the waffle iron to low and preheat it 5 minutes, or until the iron is hot. Brush the iron lightly with melted butter. Spoon the batter into the iron (the amount depends on the size of the waffle iron) and bake 2 to 3 minutes, or until the steam subsides. Serve hot or cold with ice cream or

Chantilly Cream, or with sweetened berries, sliced apricots, nectarines, or peaches and Chantilly Cream. Makes 3 or 4 waffles.

Parisian Waffles

1 cup sugar
1 teaspoon vanilla extract
½ cup (1 stick) softened butter

4 large eggs, separated
1½ cups sifted all-purpose flour
⅓ cup milk

Gradually blend the sugar and vanilla extract with the butter. Stir and beat the mixture until it is creamy and lemon-colored. Beat in the egg yolks, one at a time. Add the flour and milk alternately to the mixture. Beat the egg whites until they stand in soft peaks and carefully fold them into the batter. Set the heat control of the waffle iron to low and preheat it 5 minutes, or only until it is hot. Brush the iron lightly with melted butter. Spoon the batter into the hot waffle iron (the amount depends on the size of the waffle iron). Bake 2 to 3 minutes, or until waffles are brown. Cut each waffle into 4 sections. Serve hot or cold with ice cream. Or, if desired, put 2 sections together in shortcake fashion, with sliced ripe peaches, raspberries, or strawberries, sweetened to taste, and whipped cream. Makes 4 or 5 waffles.

Rich Dessert Waffles

1 cup sifted cake flour
1 tablespoon sugar
1 teaspoon double-acting
   baking powder

1 teaspoon salt
2 large eggs, beaten
1 cup heavy cream

Sift the first 4 ingredients together into a mixing bowl. Beat the egg yolks together with the cream and add to the dry ingredients. Mix the batter until it is smooth. Beat the egg whites until they stand in soft peaks and carefully fold them into the batter. Spoon the batter into a preheated waffle iron and bake 3 to 4 minutes, or until the steam subsides. Serve with Lemon Sauce, Orange Sauce, Chocolate Sauce, or any other desired dessert sauce. Makes 3 or 4 waffles.

TARTS AND TARTLETS

WHAT IN AMERICA IS CALLED A PIE is a *tarte* in France (generally without a top) and a *tart* in England. American tarts are small individual pies, which in France are called *tartelettes*. Here the term *tart* has been used for the larger size and tartlet for the smaller. Oval or boat-shaped tartlets are called barquettes.

Apple Sauce Meringue Tart

1 (9-inch) baked Plain Pastry tart shell
Cooked apricot jam
4 cups thick sweetened applesauce
⅓ cup toasted, blanched, shredded
 almonds
1½ tablespoons each finely chopped
 candied pineapple, citron, and
 orange peel (optional)

⅛ teaspoon salt
2 large egg whites
5 tablespoons sugar
Apricot jam

Spread the bottom of the tart shell with apricot jam. Combine the applesauce, almonds, candied fruit (if using), and salt. Turn into the tart shell. Beat the egg whites until they stand in soft peaks, then gradually beat in the sugar, beating well after each addition. Put the meringue in a pastry bag fitted with a star nozzle and pipe the meringue over the top in lattice fashion. Drop about ¼ teaspoon apricot jam into each space left by the lattice. Bake in a preheated oven (325°F) 15 minutes. Cool before serving. Makes one 9-inch tart.

Lattice-Top Apple Tart

Plain Pastry Dough (Pâte Brisée)
 for 2-crust 9-inch tart
3 cups thick unsweetened applesauce
1 teaspoon grated lemon zest
½ teaspoon ground cinnamon
¼ teaspoon ground mace

¼ teaspoon salt
1 cup sugar
3 large egg yolks
½ cup (1 stick) butter, melted and cooled
1 egg white, beaten with 1 tablespoon milk

Line a round 9-inch tart pan with half of the pastry dough. Combine the next 5 ingredients. Mix the sugar, egg yolks, and butter and blend with the applesauce mixture. Turn the mixture into the pastry shell. Roll out the remaining pastry ⅛ inch thick, cut it into strips ½ inch wide, and arrange the strips over the top of the pie in lattice fashion. With your thumb, press the ends of the lattice pastry against the pastry for the under crust, sealing them well. Turn up the edge and flute it with your thumb and index linger, or crimp it with a fork. Brush pastry with egg white. Bake in a preheated oven (425°F) for 15 minutes. Reduce oven temperature to 350°F and bake 25 to 30 minutes, or until the crust has browned. Makes one 9-inch tart.

Cheese Tart with Almond Crust

6 zwieback
½ cup toasted, blanched almonds
¼ cup (½ stick) softened butter
11 ounces cream cheese

2 large eggs
1 teaspoon vanilla extract
1 cup sugar
1 cup sour cream

Put the zwieback and the almonds through a food processor, using the finest blade, or grind a little at a time in an electric blender. Add the butter and mix well. Turn the mixture into a 9-inch pie plate and press it over the bottom and sides, making it of uniform thickness. Have the cream cheese at room temperature and place it in a mixing bowl. Beat in the eggs, one at a time. Add the vanilla extract and ½ cup of the sugar. Beat until mixture is well blended. Spoon into the prepared tart crust. Bake in a preheated oven (350°F) 25 minutes. Reduce oven temperature to 275°F and bake 5 minutes longer. Cool, if desired. Blend the remaining ½ cup sugar with the sour cream and spread it over the hot or cold tart. Serve warm or chilled. Makes one 9-inch tart.

 Apricot Tart

1 (9-inch) Plain Pastry tart shell
½ cup apricot jam
French Pastry Cream
Poached apricot halves

2 tablespoons apple jelly
2 tablespoons water
Confectioners' sugar
Pistachio nuts (optional)

Bake the pastry shell and set it aside to cool. Spread the apricot jam over the pastry. Cover the jam with French Pastry Cream, filling the shell half full. Drain the apricot halves and arrange them decoratively over the filling. Combine the jelly and water and heat until jelly is melted. Brush it over apricots. If desired, sift confectioners' sugar over the top and sprinkle with pistachio nuts. Makes one 9-inch tart.

Orange Tart

1 (9-inch) Sweet Pie Pastry tart shell
3 cups fresh orange segments
⅔ cup sugar
Water, if needed
2 tablespoons cornstarch

¹⁄₁₆ teaspoon salt
½ teaspoon vanilla extract
Apricot jam
Preserved orange slices
Glacéed cherries

Bake the tart shell and set it aside to cool. Combine the orange segments and sugar and let stand 30 minutes for juice to form, then turn them into a sieve and place it over a bowl for about 15 minutes to drain the juice. Measure the juice and add water, if necessary, to make 1 cup. Blend with the cornstarch and salt until mixture is smooth. Stir and cook in a small saucepan 3 to 4 minutes, or until thickened. Add the vanilla extract. Cool. Spread a layer of jam over the tart shell. Add the orange segments and pour the thickened juice over the top. Chill 2 hours. Garnish as desired with preserved orange slices and glacéed cherries. Serve cold. Makes one 9-inch tart.

Strawberry Tart

1 (9-inch) tart shell made from Plain Pastry or Puff Pastry	Confectioners' sugar, sifted
	½ cup heavy cream (optional)
3 pints strawberries	1 tablespoon sugar (optional)
1 cup sugar	Kirsch to taste (optional)

Bake the tart shell and set it aside to cool. Wash, hull, and slice enough strawberries to make 2 cups. Combine with ⅔ cup of the sugar. Cut the remaining strawberries in half, combine with the ⅓ cup sugar, and let strawberries stand about 30 minutes for juice to form. Put the sliced strawberries in a strainer over a bowl for about 15 minutes to drain the juice. Do the same with the halved strawberries in a separate strainer. Reduce the juices until syrupy. Place the sliced strawberries on the pastry shell and cover them with the strawberry halves, red rounded side up. Brush the thickened syrup over the berries. Chill 2 hours. Sprinkle the edge of the crust with sifted confectioners' sugar. If desired, combine cream and 1 tablespoon sugar and whip until it stands in soft peaks, flavor to taste with kirsch, and serve with the tart. Makes one 9-inch tart.

Strawberry Tartlets

Bake six 3-inch Plain Pastry tartlet shells. Prepare the strawberries as directed in the recipe for Strawberry Tart and divide them equally among the 6 tartlet shells. Proceed as directed in the recipe. Serve with kirsch-flavored whipped cream. Makes 6 tartlets.

Milanese Pastry Tart Shells

1½ cups sifted all-purpose flour	½ cup ground toasted nuts (walnuts, pecans, almonds, or hazelnuts)
⅛ teaspoon salt	
¼ cup sifted confectioners' sugar	½ cup butter
½ teaspoon grated lemon zest	About 3 tablespoons water
1 teaspoon grated orange zest	

Sift together the first 3 ingredients. Add the lemon zest, orange zest, and nuts, and mix until well blended. Add the butter and cut it in with a pastry blender or with two knives. Gradually add enough water to hold the pastry together. Chill the dough 1 to 2 hours. Divide dough into 8 equal parts. Roll each part into a circle ⅛ inch thick. Fit the rounds into 8 tart pans 2 inches across the bottom and 3½ inches across the top. Turn the edges of the pastry rounds under and crimp them with the tines of a fork. Prick each with a fork in several places to prevent blistering. Bake in a preheated oven (350°F) 15 to 20 minutes. Store in the tart pans until ready to use. Makes 8 tart shells. This pastry may also be baked in 12 very small tart pans.

Bulgarian Apple Tartlets

8 medium-sized tart apples
1 tablespoon freshly squeezed
    lemon juice
1¾ cups cold water
⅔ cup sugar
⅔ cup dry red wine

¾ cup French Pastry Cream
¼ cup chopped muscat raisins
2 tablespoons chopped, toasted,
    blanched almonds
8 baked Milanese Pastry Tart Shells
¼ cup red currant jelly

Peel and core the apples and immerse them in the lemon juice mixed with ½ cup water to prevent discoloration. Combine the sugar, 1¼ cups water, and ⅓ cup of the wine. Bring to the boiling point. Add apples 4 at a time to the syrup and cook slowly about 10 minutes, or until apples are tender when pierced with a toothpick, turning them in the syrup to cook them uniformly. Repeat with the remaining apples. Remove from heat and add the remaining wine. Cool the apples in the syrup and chill. Drain the apples, reserving the syrup. Combine the next 3 ingredients and spoon the mixture into the cavities of the apples, mounding it over the tops. Place an apple in each tart shell. Cook the syrup until it has reduced by one-fourth. Add the jelly to the syrup. Bring to the boiling point and spoon over the apples. Makes 8 servings.

Apricot Tartlets

Bake small square tartlet shells of Sweet Pie Pastry. Macerate candied apricots in Cointreau 30 minutes, drain well, and place one in each tartlet shell. Cover with Cointreau-flavored Fondant Cake Icing. Decorate each with a small piece of candied apricot and a pistachio nut in each corner. The icing may be omitted and each tart decorated with a glacéed cherry that has been macerated in Cointreau for 30 minutes. Allow 1 tartlet per serving.

Banana Tartlets

3 tablespoons cornstarch
⅔ cup sugar
¼ teaspoon salt
2 cups milk
3 large eggs, lightly beaten
4 bananas

1 teaspoon freshly squeezed lemon juice
6 (4-inch) baked tartlet shells
3 tablespoons currant jelly
⅓ cup heavy cream
2 tablespoons confectioners' sugar

Combine the first 3 ingredients in a saucepan. Add 1¾ cups of the milk and stir and cook over medium-low heat until the mixture has thickened. Mix the remaining ¼ cup milk with the eggs and blend with the first mixture. Stir and cook over low heat until the mixture has the consistency of mayonnaise. Remove the saucepan from the heat and set it in a pan of ice water to chill the mixture. Mash 1 banana together with lemon juice, add it to the chilled custard, and then spoon the custard into the tartlet shells. Slice the remaining bananas ⅛ inch thick and place them over the filling. Melt the jelly over hot water and spread a thin layer over the bananas. Chill. Combine the cream and confectioners' sugar, beat until the cream stands in soft peaks, put it into a pastry bag, and pipe a rosette over each tartlet. Makes 6 tartlets.

Cherry Pastries

Fill cold baked 1½-inch tartlet shells with Kirsch Butter-Cream. Place half a glacéed cherry that has been macerated in kirsch for 30 minutes in the center of each. Ice with Fondant Cake Icing flavored with kirsch. Decorate with two lines of Chocolate Fondant. Allow 2 pastries per serving.

Cherry Tartlets

1 cup sugar	3 cups pitted whole fresh cherries
3 tablespoons cornstarch	¼ teaspoon almond extract
⅛ teaspoon salt	8 baked tartlet or barquette shells
1 cup pitted crushed fresh cherries	Almonds or pistachio nuts (optional)
¼ cup water	Whipped cream (optional)

Combine the sugar, cornstarch, and salt in a saucepan. Add the crushed cherries and the water. Mix well. Stir and cook over medium heat until the juice is clear and thick. Remove from heat, cover, and cool to lukewarm. Add the whole cherries and the almond extract. Mix well. Spoon the mixture into the tartlet or barquette shells. If desired, chop almonds or pistachio nuts and sprinkle around the edges, or serve topped with whipped cream. Makes 8 tartlets.

Linzer Tartlets

1 cup sifted all-purpose flour	½ cup granulated sugar
⅛ teaspoon salt	2 large egg yolks
¼ teaspoon ground cinnamon	Raspberry or currant jam
⅛ teaspoon ground cloves	1 egg white
1 cup (2 sticks) butter	Confectioners' sugar
1½ cups unpeeled almonds, grated	

Sift together the first 4 ingredients. Add the butter and cut it into the flour with a pastry blender or two knives. Add the almonds and mix well. Blend the sugar with the egg yolks and stir into the flour mixture. Knead the dough until all the ingredients are well blended and the dough is smooth. Press two-thirds of the dough into 8 ungreased tartlet pans, about 2 inches in diameter, covering the bottom and sides well. Chill the remaining one-third of the dough. Spread raspberry or currant jam in the tartlet shells. Roll the chilled dough ⅛ inch thick and cut strips ⅜ inch wide and make a cross with 2 strips on the top of each tart. Crimp the edges with a fork or with a pastry cutter. Beat the egg white until foamy and brush it over the tops. Bake in a preheated oven (325°F) 40 minutes, or until pastry has browned. Cool. Before serving, sprinkle with confectioners' sugar, if desired. Makes 8 tartlets. This can also be baked in 8-inch pie plate to make a Linzer Torte.

Hazelnut Barquettes

Bake small boat-shaped Sweet Pie Pastry tartlet shells and set aside to cool. Fill with Hazelnut Butter-Cream. Ice with Fondant Cake Icing. Sprinkle cocoa in a line down the center and garnish with half a hazelnut in each corner. Allow 1 barquette per serving.

Nut Tartlets

Bake small Sweet Pie Pastry tartlet shells. Cool. Add chopped toasted nuts (almonds, hazelnuts, pecans, or pistachios) to Butter-Cream, and fill the tartlet shells. Cover with Fondant Cake Icing. Dip nut halves in caramel and place one on top of each tart. Allow 1 tartlet per serving.

Peach Tartlets

1 cup sugar
1 cup crushed fresh peaches
⅛ teaspoon salt
¼ cup water

3 cups sliced fresh peaches
8 baked tartlet shells
Whipped cream (optional)

Combine the sugar, crushed peaches, salt, and water in a saucepan. Cook over high heat, stirring, 8 minutes. Remove from heat, cover, and cool to lukewarm. Add the sliced peaches and mix well. Spoon into the tartlet shells. Serve topped with whipped cream, if desired. Makes 8 tartlets.

Neapolitan Peach Tartlets

6 (3-inch) Plain Pastry tartlet shells
6 large peach halves, poached

Apricot Sauce
6 almond halves

Bake the tartlet shells and set them aside to cool. Drain the peach halves well and place one in each tart shell, rounded side up. Coat with Apricot Sauce. Garnish each with half an almond. Makes 6 servings.

How to Poach Peaches

Combine ¾ cup sugar, 2 cups water, and a 2-inch piece of vanilla bean in a saucepan. Bring to the boiling point and boil 5 minutes. Add 6 large peaches and cook to 8 to 10 minutes, or until tender when tested with a toothpick. Cool in the syrup. Peel and halve if recipe calls for them.

CONFECTIONERY

IN THIS CHAPTER, CONFECTIONERY MEANS candies, chocolates, truffles, marzipan, glacéed, stuffed, and candied fruits, caramels and pralines, and fondants. Some advice for their preparation is:

- Make them on a clear, dry day when there is little moisture in the air.
- Use a tested recipe and measure all ingredients accurately.
- Use a clean, heavy saucepan to cook sugar.
- Use a clean, long, wooden spoon that will not burn, melt, or heat up.
- When boiling sugar, wash down the crystals on the sides of the pan with a pastry brush dipped in cold water to prevent sugaring and later crystallization.
- Use a candy thermometer for best results with cooking sugar, making sure that it does not touch the bottom of the pan. Read the thermometer at eye level.
- If you don't have a thermometer, learn to recognize the stages of thread: soft ball, firm ball, hard ball, soft crack, hard crack, and caramelization.
- When working candy, use a smooth surface, such as a marble slab or a large platter.
- Do not stir the candy when it is cooling until it has reached 110°F, or pour it out onto a slab.
- Add flavoring ingredients after the candy has cooled sufficiently to allow beating or mixing.

 Fondant

2 cups sugar	1¼ cups water
2 tablespoons light corn syrup	1 teaspoon vanilla extract

Place all ingredients in a heavy-bottomed 1½-quart saucepan. Mix well. Stir and cook until sugar has dissolved. Remove the spoon when the boiling point is reached. Cover and cook 3 minutes. Steam condensing on the sides of the pan will wash down any sugar crystals that may have formed there. Place candy thermometer in the syrup, being sure that the bulb does not touch the bottom or sides of the pan. Cook, uncovered, without stirring, until the thermometer registers 238°F, or until a soft ball forms when a little of the syrup is dropped into cold water. Wash away any sugar crystals from the sides of the pan with a swab or a pastry brush dipped in cold water. Pour the mixture into a large platter that has been rinsed in cold water, but not dried. Place platter on a wire rack to cool to 110°F, or until platter can be held in the palm of your hand without discomfort. (Do not stir or agitate fondant during the cooling period.) With a spatula or paddle, work the fondant back and forth until it is white and creamy. Spoon into a tightly covered jar and store in the refrigerator 24 hours or more to ripen. Fondant will keep several weeks if it is refrigerated. Use for stuffing dates, figs, for making mint patties, nut bars, and chocolate-dipped bonbons.

Chocolate Fondant

To the Fondant recipe add 1½ squares (1½ ounces) unsweetened chocolate along with the sugar and water. Cook as directed in the recipe. Sprinkle 1 teaspoon vanilla extract over the top of the Fondant before starting to beat or work it.

Fondant Mints

Melt 1 cup Fondant slowly over hot water. Add red, green, or yellow food coloring as desired, and peppermint or wintergreen flavoring to taste. Drop Fondant onto waxed paper from the tip of a teaspoon, in patties the size of quarters. As soon as the patties are firm, loosen them with a spatula, since they may break if allowed to stand too long.

Brown-Sugar Fondant

1 cup granulated white sugar	1¼ cups water
1 cup light brown sugar	1 teaspoon vanilla extract

Combine the first 3 ingredients in a heavy-bottomed 1½-quart saucepan. Mix well. Stir and cook over medium heat until sugar is dissolved. Remove the spoon when the boiling point is reached. Cover and cook 3 minutes. Steam condensing on the sides of the pan will wash down any sugar crystals that have formed there. Place a thermometer in the syrup, being sure that the bulb does not touch the bottom or sides of the pan. Cook without stirring until the thermometer reaches 238° to 240°F, or until the syrup forms a soft ball when ½ teaspoonful of the syrup is dropped into cold water. The lower temperature produces a soft fondant while the higher temperature produces a firm one. With a swab or a pastry brush dipped in cold water, wash away any sugar crystals that form on the sides of the pan. Pour the mixture onto a large platter that has been rinsed in cold water but not dried. Place platter on a wire rack to cool to 110°F, or until platter can be held in the palm of your hand without discomfort. Work the fondant back and forth with a spatula or paddle until the fondant is light and creamy. Put fondant in a jar or bowl and cover tightly. Refrigerate 24 hours or more to ripen. Makes about 1 pound.

Brown-Sugar Fondants

Melt 1 cup Brown-Sugar Fondant at a time over hot water (just below the boiling point). If the fondant does not hold its shape, let it stand 10 minutes over hot (not boiling) water. Drop mixture onto waxed paper from the tip of a teaspoon, into patties the size of a quarter. As soon as the patties are firm, loosen them with a spatula.

Dates Stuffed with Brown-Sugar Fondant

Slit dates lengthwise and remove pits. Fill the cavity with Brown-Sugar Fondant. Press dates into shape. Roll in coarse granulated sugar. If desired, knead chopped toasted nuts or glacéed fruit into fondant before stuffing dates with the mixture.

Brown-Sugar Fondant Nut Bars

Knead ¾ cup chopped toasted nuts (almonds, hazelnuts, pecans, pistachios, or walnuts) into 2 cups Brown-Sugar Fondant. Shape into a 6-inch square. Cut into ¾-inch squares.

How to Dip Candies in Chocolate

To make home-dipped chocolates with a professional look, a special coating chocolate is required or one has to "temper" the chocolate, or both.

Melting the chocolate. The following directions for melting chocolate must be carefully observed. Cut chocolate (not less than 1 pound) into fine pieces and put in the top of a small deep double boiler (about 1-quart capacity for 1 pound chocolate). It is important that the pieces of chocolate be fine, because less heat is required to melt them. Pour water into the bottom of the double boiler, filling it one-third full. Heat the water to 130°F. Add a little cold water if the temperature goes higher. Place the upper part of the double boiler, which contains the chocolate, over the warm water. Stir frequently so that the chocolate at the bottom will not be overheated. Use a candy thermometer and make sure that the temperature of the chocolate never exceeds 110F. Test the water in the bottom part of the boiler occasionally. If it goes below 130°F, pour out some of the water and replace it with 130°F water from another vessel. Stir and heat chocolate until it is melted and smooth. (Do not at any time add water to the chocolate.) Place melted chocolate over 85°F water.

Dipping. Place the prepared centers (fondant, nut, or fruit) on a fork one at a time and dip into the melted chocolate. Lift out, scraping the bottom of the fork across the side of the boiler to remove excess chocolate. Place the dipped pieces on a tray covered with waxed paper. When the tray is filled, cool quickly in the refrigerator to prevent spots from forming on the chocolate. After it is chilled, the candy may be stored in a tightly closed container in a cool place. Leftover chocolate may be remelted and used again. One pound of chocolate will cover 70 to 80 centers with one coat.

Centers for dipping in chocolate may be Fondant, Caramels, Nougat, nuts, raisins, and glacéed or preserved fruits. Some suggestions for Fondant centers follow; plain Fondant, Chocolate Fondant, or Brown-Sugar Fondant may be used for any of these.

Almond Fondant Chocolates

To each 1 cup Fondant, add ¼ cup chopped almonds and 8 drops almond extract. Mix well.

Fruit Fondant Chocolates

To each 1 cup Fondant, add ¼ cup finely chopped glacéed fruit. Mix well.

Nut Fondant Chocolates

To each 1 cup Fondant, add ¼ cup chopped toasted pecans, hazelnuts, or walnuts. Mix well.

Peppermint Fondant Chocolates

Flavor Fondant with peppermint extract or oil of peppermint to taste. Mix well.

Brésiliennes

1 cup finely ground blanched almonds
1 tablespoon rum, or to taste
2 teaspoons strong coffee infusion

About 2 cups sifted confectioners' sugar
4 squares (4 ounces) unsweetened or
semisweet chocolate, grated

Combine almonds, 1 tablespoon rum, and the coffee. Stir and mix well. Add the confectioners' sugar, a little at a time, and additional rum and coffee to taste. Shape the mixture into balls, adding more sugar if it is needed to make the balls hold their shape. Roll the balls in grated chocolate. Store in a cool place. Makes about 1 pound.

Caramels

2 cups sugar
¾ cup light corn syrup
¼ cup (½ stick) butter

2 cups heavy cream
2 teaspoons vanilla extract

Combine the first 3 ingredients and 1 cup of the cream in a heavy-bottomed 2-quart saucepan. Mix well. Stir and cook until mixture comes to a full rolling boil. Pour in the remaining cream so slowly that the boiling does not stop. Stir and cook to 250°F on a candy thermometer, or until a hard ball forms when a little of the syrup is dropped into cold water. Remove from heat. Stir in vanilla extract. Pour into a buttered 8-inch square pan. When the candy is cold, turn it out onto a slab and cut it into ¾-inch squares. Makes 2 pounds.

Chocolate Caramels

2 cups sugar
¾ cup light corn syrup
¼ cup (½ stick) butter
3 squares (3 ounces) unsweetened
    chocolate

2 cups light cream
2 teaspoons vanilla extract
⅔ cup chopped nuts (optional)

Combine the first 4 ingredients and 1 cup of the cream in a heavy-bottomed 2-quart saucepan. Stir and cook until mixture has come to a rolling boil. Pour in remaining 1 cup cream so slowly that the boiling does not stop. Stir and cook to 248°F on a candy thermometer, or until a firm ball forms when a little of the mixture is dropped in cold water. Remove from heat. Stir in vanilla extract and nuts (if using). Pour into a buttered 8-inch square pan. When candy is cold, turn it out onto a slab and cut it into ¾-inch squares. Makes 2 pounds.

Caramel Kisses

1½ cups sugar
¼ cup honey
⅛ teaspoon salt

⅓ cup butter
½ cup light cream
¼ pound blanched, toasted, salted almonds

Combine the first 5 ingredients in a heavy-bottomed 2-quart saucepan. Mix well. Stir and cook until the boiling point is reached. Cook, without stirring, over medium heat, to 255°F on a candy thermometer, or until ½ teaspoon of the syrup forms a firm ball when dropped into cold water. Remove syrup from heat and pour at once into a buttered 15-by-12-by-1-inch pan. Cool until candy can be handled. Cut into 1-inch squares. Place a whole almond in the center of each square. Roll the candy around the almond (using the palms of both hands), keeping almond completely covered with the caramel. Wrap each piece in foil or waxed paper. Store in a tightly covered container. Makes 1¼ pounds.

Chocolate Nut Truffles

1 cup grated or very finely chopped
    nuts (almonds, hazelnuts, or pecans)
½ cup sugar
2 squares (2 ounces) semisweet chocolate

½ cup water
1½ teaspoons vanilla extract
Cocoa

Place the first 3 ingredients in a saucepan. Gradually add water, mixing well after each addition. Stir and cook over very low heat until the sugar dissolves and the chocolate melts, then add the vanilla extract. Cool. Shape the mixture into 1-inch balls and roll them in cocoa. Makes 1½ dozen.

 Marzipan

This is an easy method of making Marzipan. Almond paste may be purchased at bakeries or specialty food shops.

2 cups almond paste	Confectioners' sugar
1 large egg white	Granulated sugar

Crumble the almond paste. Add egg white and mix well. Beat in enough confectioners' sugar to make a mixture that is too stiff to beat. Then knead in ½ cup sifted confectioners' sugar. Store the mixture in a tightly covered container in the refrigerator 5 to 6 hours to ripen. Form the paste into desired shapes. If desired, tint paste with food coloring diluted with a few drops of water, or paint with food coloring after shaping. Roll the pieces in colored granulated sugar. Makes about 1 pound.

 Nougat

2 cups sugar	1 cup honey
1 cup water	½ cup chopped, blanched pistachio nuts
4 tablespoons light corn syrup	1 cup chopped, toasted, blanched almonds
4 egg whites	1½ teaspoons vanilla extract

Place the sugar, water, and 2 tablespoons of the corn syrup in a 1½-quart saucepan. Mix well. Stir and cook until the boiling point is reached. Cover and cook 3 minutes to dissolve any sugar crystals that form on the sides of the pan. Remove cover and place a candy thermometer in the syrup. Cook, without stirring, to 290°F, keeping the sugar crystals on the sides of the pan washed down with a swab or a pastry brush dipped in cold water. Beat the egg whites until they stand in soft peaks. Pour the syrup in a fine stream into the egg whites. Using an electric mixer, continue beating until the mixture is thick and the bowl is cool enough to be held in the palm of your hand without discomfort.

Put the honey and the remaining 2 tablespoons corn syrup in a 1-quart saucepan. Cook to 270°F on a candy thermometer (soft-crack stage). Pour in a fine stream into the egg white mixture, beating constantly at medium speed, until the mixture has lost some of its gloss. Transfer it to the top of a large double boiler and place it over boiling water. Stir and cook 25 minutes, or until mixture is no longer sticky when a small amount is cooled on a spoon. Gradually stir in nuts and vanilla extract. Turn mixture into a well-buttered 8-inch square pan. Cool 10 minutes. Press the nougat down firmly with your hands. Cool completely. Cover pan tightly and set it aside 24 hours for nougat to ripen. Turn candy onto a cutting board and cut into 1½-by-1-inch pieces. Wrap pieces in foil or waxed paper and store in a tightly covered container. Makes about 3½ dozen pieces.

Chocolate-Coated Nougat

Cut nougat into ¾-inch squares and dip in melted unsweetened chocolate, as directed in How to Dip Candies in Chocolate.

Marquise Fondant Cherries

Soak glacéed cherries in brandy at least 1 hour. Drain well and coat with kirsch-flavored Fondant Cake Icing. Cool on a marble slab or waxed paper that has been dusted with confectioners' sugar.

Chocolate-Coated Marquise Cherries

Make Marquise Cherries as directed. When they have dried, dip them in melted unsweetened chocolate. Place them on waxed paper. Chill quickly to prevent spotting. If the chocolate coating is not heavy enough, dip into melted chocolate again. Chill and dry as directed in How to Dip Candies in Chocolate.

Pralines

2 cups sugar
½ cup boiling water
⅛ teaspoon baking soda
¹⁄₁₆ teaspoon salt

¼ cup light cream
2 tablespoons butter
1½ teaspoons vanilla extract
⅔ cup pecan halves

Place ¼ cup of the sugar in a small heavy-bottomed saucepan. Stir and cook over medium heat until sugar has melted. Stir in boiling water. Stir and cook 1 to 2 minutes, or until lumps are dissolved. Pour syrup into a 1½-quart saucepan. Add the remaining sugar, the baking soda, salt, and cream. Stir until well mixed. Bring mixture to the boiling point over medium heat, stirring constantly. Continue cooking, without stirring, to 242°F on a candy thermometer, or until a firm ball forms when a ½ teaspoon of the syrup is dropped into cold water. Remove the candy from the heat and cool to 140°F about 15 minutes. Add butter, vanilla extract, and pecans. Stir until well mixed. Drop from a teaspoon onto waxed paper to form thin wafers 1½ to 2 inches in diameter. These harden quickly, so work fast when dropping them. Store in an airtight container. Makes 3 dozen.

Stuffed Dates

Slit dates down one side and remove the pits. Insert into the cavities a roll of almond paste a little larger than the pit. Dust with confectioners' sugar, if desired.

Walnut-Stuffed Dates

Slit large dates down one side and remove the pits. Insert a small piece of Fondant into the cavity of each and place a walnut half over each.

Candied Orange Peel

Peel of 4 medium-sized navel oranges
⅛ teaspoon salt
2⅔ cups sugar

Wash oranges and cut through the peel of the orange with a knife so that it can be removed in quarters. Place it in a 2-quart saucepan with enough cold water to cover. Bring water to the boiling point and cook slowly 10 to 15 minutes, or until peel is tender. Drain, reserving the water.

Using a teaspoon, scrape out the white inner portion of the orange peel. With scissors, cut the peel into narrow strips. Pour the water in which the orange peel was cooked into a measuring cup and add water, if necessary, to make 1 cup. Pour it into a 2-quart saucepan. Add 2 cups of the sugar and the salt. Mix well. Stir and cook until a candy thermometer registers 238°F (soft-ball stage). Add orange peel and cook slowly 20 to 30 minutes, or until peel has absorbed most of the syrup. Turn the peel into a coarse sieve to drain well. Put remaining ⅔ cup sugar in a bowl, add a few pieces of orange peel at a time and mix until each piece is completely covered with sugar. Shake off excess sugar. Arrange in a single layer on waxed paper to dry. Store in a tightly covered container. Makes ½ pound.

Glacéed Cherries

Wash and dry fresh cherries, leaving the stems attached. Chill. Make Glazing Syrup (see page 572) and place the saucepan over hot water. Hold each cherry by its stem and dip in the hot syrup. Drain well and put the cherries on a rack or on waxed paper to dry, spacing them so that they do not touch.

Glacéed Grapes

Cut fresh grapes from the bunch, leaving ½ inch of stem on each. Proceed as with Glacéed Cherries.

Glacéed Strawberries

Use firm ripe strawberries, leaving the green hulls attached. Wash and dry the strawberries and chill them. Dip each up to the hull in hot Glazing Syrup. Proceed as with Glacéed Cherries.

Glacéed Tangerines

Peel the fruit and separate the sections. Chill. Place each section on the tines of a fork and dip into the hot Glazing Syrup. Proceed as with Glacéed Cherries.

Glacéed Chestnuts or Marrons Glacés

Peel 1 pound chestnuts. Put chestnuts in a saucepan with ½ teaspoon salt and enough boiling water to cover them. Cover and simmer 20 minutes, or until they are tender when pierced with a fork. Drain well. Make Glazing Syrup and set it over hot water. Place chestnuts on a fork and dip them one at a time into the syrup. When chestnuts appear clear, lift them out, scraping the bottom of the fork across the side of the pan to remove excess syrup. Place chestnuts on a buttered baking sheet to dry. Makes about 1 pound.

Masked Nuts

Roast shelled perfect halves of pecans and walnuts and whole shelled blanched almonds in a preheated oven (325°F) 5 minutes, or until the nuts are toasted. When cool, dip them in melted semisweet chocolate as directed in How to Dip Candies in Chocolate.

Stuffed Nuts

Put 2 walnut, pecan, or almond halves together with white or tinted almond paste or Fondant. Roll in coarse granulated sugar, if desired.

GLOSSARY
OF
CULINARY
TERMS

A LA in the style of.

APERITIF short alcoholic drink taken before a meal; appetizer or hors d'oeuvre.

APPAREIL French term for a mixture used in the making of a dish. Such mixtures are of various kinds (see pages 76–79).

APRICOT GLAZE reduced, strained apricot jam used to coat cakes, petits fours, pastries, etc. The French term *abricoter* means to apply such a glaze.

ASPIC clear, brilliant jelly made from stock and used for glazing or dressing cold dishes. In French usage, *aspic* applies to cold dishes molded with jelly; the term for jelly is *gelée*.

ASSAIONNEMENT salad dressing.

AU, AUX with, or cooked with.

AU JUS served with the natural juices (meat).

BAIN-MARIE vessel containing warm or hot water into which another utensil containing food is set while food is cooking or being reheated.

BALLOTTINE piece of meat, poultry, etc., boned, stuffed, and rolled up— usually served hot. See also *galantine*.

BARQUETTE small oval or boat-shaped pastry shell. Barquettes may be filled with various mixtures for hot or cold hors d'oeuvre or small entrées, or with fruit, custard, etc., for dessert. See Index for recipes.

BASTE *(arroser)* to moisten with pan drippings, fat, or liquid while cooking.

BEARD, DEBEARD *(ébarber)* to remove the "beard" from oysters or mussels; to remove fins and small fin bones from fish.

BEAT *(fouetter)* to mix by long and vigorous stirring with a spoon, fork, whip, or an electric beater or mixer.

BEURRE butter; see Butters and Butter Sauces, pages 123–127.

BEURRE MANIE butter thickened with flour, used for sauces.

BEURRE NOIR butter cooked to a very dark brown and sometimes mixed with chopped herbs and vinegar; served as a sauce.

BIND *(lier)* thicken with flour, starch, eggs, cream, etc.; mix chopped meat, vegetables, etc., with a sauce.

BISCUIT in American usage, a raised bread baked in small, round shapes; in English usage, a cracker or a sweet wafer or cookie; in French usage, sponge cake.

BISCUIT GLACEE ice cream shaped in molds.

BLANCH *(blanchir)* used to mean to whiten, as for artichokes, cardoons, celery root, and even some meats such as veal, in boiling water with flour and lemon, but now means to precook lightly by putting into boiling water (see *parboil*).

BLANQUETTE white ragoût or stew made with lamb, veal, or poultry.

BLEND *(melanger)* to mix gently.

BOIL *(bouillir)* to cook in boiling water.

BOMBE *(bombe glacée)* combination of ice creams or ices, fruits, creams, etc., made in a mold.

BONE *(deosser)* to remove the bones from meat, poultry, or fish.

BOUCHEES small puff-pastry patty shells.

BOUILLON strong, clear stock or broth.

BOUQUET GARNI herbs—usually parsley, thyme, and bay leaf—tied in a bunch and used for flavoring stews and sauces; the bouquet is removed before the dish is served.

BRAISE *(braiser)* to brown meat or poultry in a little fat, then add a little water or other liquid and finish cooking with low heat.

BROCHETTE small spit or skewer used for broiling cubes of meat, shellfish, or vegetables. Food so cooked may be called *brochettes* or *en brochette*.

BRUNOISE a mixture of vegetables, chopped or finely shredded and cooked in butter or other fats, used in forcemeats, sauces, etc.

CANAPE bread cut in shapes, fried in butter or toasted, and spread with a savory topping; served as an hors d'oeuvre.

CARAMEL browned sugar.

CASSOLETTE individual heatproof dish; food cooked and served in such a dish.

CHAUD-FROID literally "hot-cold"; a white or brown gelatin sauce used to coat cold cooked meat, poultry, or fish (see Index).

CHIFFONADE leafy salad vegetables (especially lettuce and sorrel) cut into fine strips

CHOP COARSELY *(concasser)* cut up a food into pieces larger than fine chop or mince

COAT A SPOON *(napper la cuillère)* method of determining the thickness of sauces, etc., by dipping a spoon into the liquid; the thickness can be judged by the amount that adheres to the spoon.

COCOTTE small individual heatproof dish in which food is cooked and served; food so presented is called *en cocotte*.

COMPOTE fresh or dried fruits cooked in syrup (see Index).

COQUILLE scallop shell; by extension a dish so shaped, or food cooked or served in a natural scallop shell or a shell-shaped container.

CREPE thin French pancake. Crêpes may be filled, rolled, and baked for an entrée; sweet crêpes are served as a dessert with confectioners' sugar or a sauce.

CROISSANT crescent-shaped roll made of puff pastry or yeast pastry.

CROMESQUI mixture dipped in batter and fried in deep fat; similar to a croquette.

CROUSTADE small or large case made of rich pastry or puff pastry, or a hollowed-out toast case, used for serving various creamed mixtures.

CROUTE bread crust, pie crust, or crust. Meat, pâtés, etc., baked in a crust are called *en croûte*.

CROUTON small cubes or other shapes of bread fried in butter or toasted and served in soups or as a garnish.

DAUBE stew cooked in a hermetically sealed casserole to preserve the flavor.

DECANT (wine) to pour gently into another bottle to get rid of the sediment (see page 39).

DEGREASE *(dégraisser)* to skim off fat from the surface of a liquid.

DIABLE, A LA deviled; method of preparing food. Sauce Diable (see Index).

EMINCER to cut meat or vegetables into very fine slices (not to mince).

EMINCE dish made with thinly sliced leftover cooked meat.

DICE *(couper en des)* to cut into small cubes.

FILLET *(filet)* strip of meat or fish without bone.

FILLET OF BEEF tenderloin.

FINES HERBES parsley, chervil, tarragon, thyme, chives.

FLAMBEED *(flambé)* served with brandy or a liqueur poured on and set alight.

FLEURONS decorations made of puff pastry in shapes, used as a garnish and to ornament dessert pastries.

FLORENTINE cooked or served with spinach.

FOIE GRAS livers of duck or geese fattened in a special way (see pages 492–494).

FOLD *(incorporer)* to blend a light mixture gently into a heavier mixture; most often used with beaten egg whites.

FONDU melted; fondue name given to various dishes in which the main ingredient is melted or (for vegetables) cooked to a pulp.

FORCEMEAT *(farce)* meat or fish chopped fine and seasoned, used as a stuffing or garnish or in the making of other dishes (see pages 72–75).

FOUR oven.

FRUITS DE MER seafood.

GALANTINE boned poultry or meat, stuffed, rolled, and cooked in a gelatinous stock (see pages 489–491).

GARNISH *(garniture)* various items of food used to decorate and to enhance the flavor of a dish (see pages 79–88).

GELEE (adj.) frozen; (n.) jelly.

GLACE frozen; iced; glazed; candied.

GLACEED *(glacé)* glazed; candied.

GOURMANDISES rich tidbits, used of pastries and hors d'oeuvres.

GRATIN, AU sprinkled with breadcrumbs and melted butter and browned. Cheese may or may not be added.

GRILL *(griller)* to broil or grill.

HACHER to chop or mince.

HERBS aromatic plants used in cooking, salads, etc. (see pages 42–44).

JELLY *(gelée)* aspic; preserve made of fruit juice and sugar.

JULIENNE cut in fine, short strips.

JUS LIE thickened meat juice.

LARD *(larder)* to thread strips of pork fat into large pieces of meat with a larding needle.

LARDON strip of pork or bacon used for larding.

MACEDOINE mixture of small or cut-up fruits or vegetables.

MADERE, AU with Madeira wine.

MAIGRE meatless; term also used for dishes that can be served during Lent and on fast days.

MAITRE D'HOTEL BUTTER or SAUCE butter sauce with parsley and lemon juice.

MARINADE herbs, spices, or a seasoned liquid, cooked or uncooked, in which food is steeped for varying lengths of time.

MARINATE *(mariner, macérer)* to steep in a marinade.

MARMITE cooking pot of metal or earthenware, with a lid. This utensil has given its name to certain soups.

MASK *(masquer)* to cover or mask with a sauce.

MEDALLION *(médaillon)* round slice.

MEUNIERE, A LA way of preparing fish, in which the fish is rolled in flour, fried in butter, and garnished with lemon juice and chopped parsley.

MINCE *(hacher)* to cut into small pieces.

MODE, A LA in the style of, as Tripe à la Mode de Caen.

NOISETTE hazelnut; small round slice cut from the fillet, rib, or leg of lamb, mutton, or veal.

PAPILLOTE; EN PAPILLOTE baked in oiled or buttered paper or foil; method used for small cuts of meat or for fish and sometimes vegetables.

PARMENTIER name applied to dishes that include potatoes, after Antoine-Auguste Parmentier (1737–1817), who popularized potatoes in France.

PASTRY BASE *(abaisse)* sweet pastry rolled to any desired thickness and used as a base for a dessert preparation. The French term is also applied to a layer of sponge cake similarly used.

PATE pastry, dough.

PATE originally a meat or fish dish enclosed in pastry, served hot or cold; now extended to meat or fish mixtures baked in a mold or loaf pan (see *terrine*) lined with strips of bacon and served cold (see pages 482–485).

PATISSERIE pastries; the art of the pastry cook; pastry shop.

PAUPIETTE slice of meat spread with a filling, rolled, and braised.

PETITS POTS DE CREME rich custards baked in individual custard cups (see pages 589–591).

PETITS FOURS small cookies, iced cakes, pastries, glacéed fruits, etc. (see pages 674–681). The name is said to have originated from the fact that the small cakes were baked in an oven that had been allowed to cool after large cakes had been baked.

PILAF rice cooked in stock with various seasonings; also spelled pilaff, pilau.

POACH *(pocher)* to cook in liquid that has barely been brought to a simmer.

POIVRE pepper; *au poivre*, cooked or heavily seasoned with pepper.

POT-AU-FEU classic French soup, made with meat, poultry, and vegetables. The broth is served separately from the meat and vegetables, making two dishes in one (see Index).

PROFITEROLES small balls of choux paste, baked, and filled either with cheese, puréed meat, and other savory mixtures for hors d'oeuvres or garnish, or with creams or ice cream as a dessert. For dessert, profiteroles may be iced or served with a caramel or chocolate sauce.

PUFF PASTRY, PUFF PASTE *(pâte feuillitée)* delicate, rich pastry made with flour, water, and butter, rolled, folded, and chilled several times.

PUREE *(reduire en purée)* to mash solid foods by putting through a sieve, pounding in a mortar . A puree of anything is food that has been so treated.

QUENELLES dumplings made with various kinds of forcemeat bound with a panada or with eggs, used as a garnish or in soups (see pages 75–76).

QUICHE savory custard tart.

RAGOUT stew.

REDUCE *(réduire)* boil down to a sauce or other liquid in order to thicken the consistency.

RISSOLE pastry filled with forcemeat and fried in deep fat.

ROUX cooked mixture of butter and flour used for thickening sauces (see pages 69–70).

ROYALE molded custard cut into various shapes and used to garnish soups (see Index); also a term applied to various main dishes and desserts.

SABAYON see *zabaglione.*

SALPICON preparation of diced foods bound with a sauce and used to fill pastry cases or made into croquettes, etc.

SAUTE *(sauter)* to cook in a small amount of very hot fat.

SCALLOP *(escalope, scaloppine)* thin slice of meat or fish cut on a bias; the method is most often used with veal.

SCALLOP *(pétoncle)* bivalve mussel with ribbed, rounded shell (see *coquille*).

SIMMER *(mijoter)* to cook below a boil.

SPICES seeds or other parts of aromatic plants used to season food (see pages 44–46).

SUBRICS croquette-type mixtures that are not dipped in egg and breadcrumbs but fried in butter in a shallow frying pan; served as hors d'oeuvre or small entrées.

TART *(tarte),* TARTLET *(tartelette)* pastry crust with fruit, custard, or other filling. In American usage the large version is called a pie, the small individual version a tart, but in French and English usage the large size is a *tarte* (tart) and the small a *tartelette* (tartlet). The terms *tart* and *tartlet* are used in this book.

TARTARE, A LA way of serving chopped raw beef, seasoned with salt and pepper and with a raw egg yolk on top.

TARTAR SAUCE mayonnaise-type sauce made with oil, finely chopped hard-cooked eggs, and chopped chives.

TARTINE slice of bread spread with butter.

TERRINE earthenware dish or mold in which pâté mixtures are cooked; the food cooked in such a dish (see pages 486–489).

TORTE, TOURTE tart, pie, or can be a cake

TOSS *(faire sauter)* to flip food over by tossing the pan.

TOURNEDOS (s. and pl.) small round steak cut from the filet of beef.

TRUSS (brider) to tie up or skewer a fowl for cooking.

VACHERIN dessert made with rings ("crowns") of meringues, mounted one above the other. The center is filled with creams, ice creams, or fruits.

VOL-AU-VENT elaborate large or small puff-pastry shell filled with various creamed mixtures.

ZABAGLIONE (Italian; French *sabayon*) rich wine custard served hot in cups or as a sauce (see Index).

ZEST *(zeste)* peel of citrus fruit.

INDEX

and eggplant macaroni,
199
gnocchi, 207
gnocchi baked with, 59
onion soup with, 280
potato dumplings with,
533
pudding, 194
puffs, 59, 172
rolls, 172–73
sandwiches, 157, 158
savouries, 187–88
soufflé, 194
Swiss-cheese tartlets,
170–71
tart
with almond crust,
690–91
Romanian, 170
Cherries. see also Cherry
chocolate-coated,
marquise, 704
flambéed, 640
glacéed, 705
jubilee, 640
in Kirsch, 640–41
venison steaks with, 478
Victoria, 641
Cherry. see also Cherries
Bavarian cream, 581
filling, 663
pastries, 694
sauce, Bing, 555
tartlets, 694
torte, Black Forest, 663
Chervil, 42
cream sauce, mushrooms
in, 520–21
Chessboard ham mousse,
410
Chestnut(s), 512–13
frou-frou, 612
glacéed, 706
pigeon stuffed with, 458
puree, 476
cassolettes, sultan, 179
with celery root, 513

game with, 179
molded, 579
sweet, 565–66
stuffing, 446
roast goose with,
452–53
Chevrière soup, 279
Chicken, 426–45
Andalusian whole
poached, 428–29
and asparagus salad, 155
barquettes, 138
bouchées à la Reine, 171
breasts of
with asparagus,
434–35
browned, 433
butter-steamed, 434
chaud-froid of, 438
with curry sauce, 434
Florentine, 435
with mushrooms, 434
Sandeman, 436
with savory stuffing,
437
Spanish style, 436
stuffed, 436–37
broth, 259, 283
canneloni, 202
cassolettes Regency, 178
with Chambertin, 430
chaud-froid
breasts of, 438
harlequin, 429
Lambertye, 428
coquilles of, Mornay,
180
curried, 439
curry, Anglo-Indian,
439–40
cutlets Pojarski, 438–39
deviled spring, 430
eggs en cocotte with, 241
forcemeat
for quenelles, 73
timbales, 175
fricassée, 426, 433

fried
Tuscan, 440
Viennese, 432
galantine of, 490
giblet soup, 283
giblets with mushrooms,
444–45
glazed, Muguette, 429
ham and, or egg canapés,
163
and ham aspic Mércèdes,
437–38
Harlequin, 429
how to truss, 426
Kiev, 435
legs
baked, Archduke,
441–42
stuffed Regence, 442
-liver
canapés, 162
canneloni, 202–3
terrine Chagny, 487
livers, 188–89
with bacon, 189
with mushroom toast
Diana, 188
Marengo, 441
mousse, 140
mousseline
forcemeat, 74
with noodles, 192
mousses, 191–92
and mushroom tartlets,
169
and paprika-butter
canapés, 163
pâté, 484
and peach salad, 155
pilaf Asian style,
432–33
poached, 428–29
quenelles
Isabella, 444
in tarragon sauce, 444
ragoût, 442–43
ravioli, 204

Saddle
of hare, 475–76
Diane, 476
of lamb or mutton,
French style, 395
of veal, roast, 385
of venison
grand duchy style,
30–31
with mushrooms, 478
Renoir, 31
roast, 477
Saffron, 46
chaud-froid with, 116
rice with, 210
stuffed eggplant with,
515
Sage, 43
Sainte-Menehould, pigs'
feet, 419
Saint-Germain
beef tongue, 423
epigrammes of lamb, 397
garnish, 87
potage, 274
sole, 324
Saint-Honoré
cake, 661–62
cream, 564
Saint-Mande (garnish), 87
Saint Michel, lamb chops,
396
Salad dressings, 544
Salad(s), 543–52
Alsatian, 156
Andalusian, 545
Argenteuil, 545
artichoke, à la Grecque,
545–46
artichoke and smoked
salmon, 156
asparagus, 156
Beatrice, 546
Beaucaire, 547
beef, 152
beet, 152
cabbage, 152

cauliflower, 153
celery, 153
chicken and asparagus,
155
chicken and peach, 155
chicory and dandelion,
with bacon, 546
composed, 544
crayfish and artichoke,
156
cucumber, 153
dressings, 550–52
egg, 153
egg and tomato, 153
fish, 154, 155
green, 544
hors d'oeuvres, 152–56
lobster, 156
macédoine, 548
Marguerite, 547
Mércèdes, 547–48
mimosa, 548
mixed vegetable, 548
mushroom, 153
mussel, 156
with mayonnaise
Francillon, 360
Niçoise, 544, 549
Parisian, 549–50
potato, 154
poultry, 154
Rachel, 550
rich poultry, 154
roast beef, diable, 155
roast beef and vegetable,
156
shrimp, 156
spinach, Madrid-style,
154
tomato, 155
types of, 544
veal, 155
vegetable
chaud-froid fillets of
sole with, 331
cucumber stuffed
with, 149

mixed, 548
venison, 155
Waldorf, 549
Salmis
of pheasant, 468–69
sauce, 96
Salmon, 315–23, 333, 340
with artichokes and
asparagus, 319
in aspic Vladimir,
336–37
caviar, 134
chilled Moscow, 316–17
cold
d'Orsay, 319–20
with shrimp, 320
steamed, whole, 319
coulibiac of, Russian,
318
cucumbers with, and
herring, 148
cured Norwegian,
136–37
cutlets Pojarsky, 320–21
fillets
Doria, 316
maître d'hôtel, 317
loaf Valois, 322
mousse, 142, 321
mousseline Chantilly,
321–22
with mousseline sauce,
317
and mushroom timbales,
176–77
pâté, 484
poached eggs with, 220
Regency, whole poached,
317–18
Russian coulibiac of,
318
smoked
artichoke and, salad,
156
butter, 126
canapés, 164
sandwiches, 161

Rouennaise, 92
rum, foamy, 560
Russian, 129
sabayon, 561
salmis, 96
Sanford, 130
sherry cranberry, 555
shrimp, 100, 315
 and lobster, 112
Sicilian, 108
smitane, 129
soubise, 100
spaghetti, 206–7
strawberry, 556
suprême, 104–5
 and variations, 104–6
tarragon
 brown, 93
 chicken quenelles in,
  444
 rich, 106
 velouté, 104
tartar, 122
tomato, 90, 116–17
tortue, 94
truffle, 419
Turkish, 129
Valois, 119
vanilla, 561–62
velouté, 101
Venetian, 104
venison, 93
vert, 121
Victoria, 102
vinaigrette, 90, 550–52
Vincent, beef with, 383
white, 90, 98–112
 Béchamel sauce and
  derivatives, 99–100
 velouté and deriva-
  tives, 101–12
 wine, fish velouté, 109
 wine, glazed, 110
 wine, with a fish
  velouté base,
  109–12
ziska, 130

Sauerbraten Berlin style,
 378
Sauerkraut, garnished, 405
Sauge. see Sage
Saumon. see Salmon
Saumure, 71
Sausage, 405–6
 chipolatas, duck with,
  448
 with eggs
  fried, Bercy, 236
  with tomatoes and,
   236
 fried, with cabbage, 405
 kefte, 400
 lamb, Turkish, 400
 lasagne with, 200–201
 mushrooms and,
  200–201
 pork, 405–6
 sandwiches, 160–61
 stuffing, 446
 in white wine, 406
Sautéed
 artichoke bottoms, 498
 brains, 411
 calf's liver, 417–18
 cèpes, 521
 chicken, 430–32
  with Chambertin,
   430
  with curry and mush-
   rooms Stanley, 432
  forestière, 431
  Portuguese style,
   430–31
 guinea fowl à l'Africaine,
  456
 kidneys, 415–16
 lamb chops, 394, 396
 mushrooms, 415–16, 521
 pigeon, 458
 potatoes, Lyonnaise,
  528
 smails, 363
 sweetbreads, 420
 tournedos, 373–74

veal, 385–89, 390
 chops, 385–86
 hearts, 413–14
venison, 478
Sautéing, 51
Savarin(s), 665–67
 Chantilly, 666
 Kirsch, 666–67
 pineapple, 667
Savory, 44
 custards, 192–94
 stuffing, 437
Savouries, 187–91
 brochettes, oyster and
  mushroom, 190
 Camembert, fried, 187
 cheese
  balls, 187
  friar's toast, 187–88
  ham and, hot sand-
   wiches, 189
  tartines marquise, 188
  Welsh rabbit (rarebit),
   188
 chicken livers
  with bacon, 189
  Diana toast, 188
  and mushrooms, 188
 croque-monsieur, 189
 Derby toast, 189
 Dutch toast, 189
 oysters
  angels on horseback,
   191
  fried, 190
  mushroom and,
   brochettes, 190
 Scotch woodcock, 191
 shrimp, fried, breaded,
  190
 Stilton cheese balls, 187
 tartines marquise, 188
 Welsh rabbit (rarebit),
  188
Savoy cabbage, 505
Saxon soufflé pudding,
 620

Notes

Notes

Notes

Notes